(Continued on back endsheets)

Dictionary of Literary Biography® • Volume One Hundred Sixty-Six

British Travel Writers, 1837–1875

Dictionary of Literary Biography® • Volume One Hundred Sixty-Six

British Travel Writers, 1837–1875

Edited by
Barbara Brothers
and
Julia Gergits
Youngstown State University

A Bruccoli Clark Layman Book
Gale Research
Detroit, Washington, D.C., London

The paper used in this publication meets the minimum requirements
of American National Standard for Information Sciences–Permanence
Paper for Printed Library Materials, ANSI Z39.48-1984. ∞ ™

Library of Congress Cataloging-in-Publication Data

British travel writers, 1837–1875 / edited by Barbara Brothers and Julia Gergits.
   p. cm. – (Dictionary of literary biography; v. 166)
"A Bruccoli Clark Layman book."
Includes bibliographical references and index.
ISBN 0–8103–9361–1 (alk. paper)
1. Travelers' writings, English – Bio-bibliography – Dictionaries. 2. British – Travel – Foreign
countries – History – 19th century – Dictionaries. 3. English prose literature – 19th century –
Bio-bibliography – Dictionaries. 4. Great Britain – History – Victoria, 1837–1901 – Biography –
Dictionaries. 5. Authors, English – 19th century – Biography – Dictionaries. 6. Travelers – Great
Britain – Biography – Dictionaries. 7. Travel writing – Bio-bibliography – Dictionaries. I. Brothers,
Barbara, 1937– . II. Gergits, Julia Marie. III. Series.
PR788.T72B74 1996
820.9'355 – dc20
                                       96–16075
                                        CIP

10 9 8 7 6 5 4 3 2 1

To Bernard Benstock
(1930–1994)
Friend, Literary and Travel Mentor

Contents

Plan of the Series

The advisory board, the editors, and the publisher of the *Dictionary of Literary Biography* are joined in endorsing Mark Twain's declaration. The literature of a nation provides an inexhaustible resource of permanent worth. We intend to make literature and its creators better understood and more accessible to students and the reading public, while satisfying the standards of teachers and scholars.

To meet these requirements, *literary biography* has been construed in terms of the author's achievement. The most important thing about a writer is his writing. Accordingly, the entries in *DLB* are career biographies, tracing the development of the author's canon and the evolution of his reputation.

The purpose of *DLB* is not only to provide reliable information in a convenient format but also to place the figures in the larger perspective of literary history and to offer appraisals of their accomplishments by qualified scholars.

The publication plan for *DLB* resulted from two years of preparation. The project was proposed to Bruccoli Clark by Frederick C. Ruffner, president of the Gale Research Company, in November 1975. After specimen entries were prepared and typeset, an advisory board was formed to refine the entry format and develop the series rationale. In meetings held during 1976, the publisher, series editors, and advisory board approved the scheme for a comprehensive biographical dictionary of persons who contributed to North American literature. Editorial work on the first volume began in January 1977, and it was published in 1978. In order to make *DLB* more than a reference tool and to compile volumes that individually have claim to status as literary history, it was decided to organize volumes by topic, period, or genre. Each of these free-standing volumes provides a biographical-bibliographical guide and overview for a particular area of literature. We are convinced that this organization — as opposed to a single alphabet method — constitutes a valuable innovation in the presentation of reference material. The volume plan necessarily requires many decisions for the placement and treatment of authors who might properly be included in two or three volumes. In some instances a major figure will be included in separate volumes, but with different entries emphasizing the aspect of his career appropriate to each volume. Ernest Hemingway, for example, is represented in *American Writers in Paris, 1920–1939* by an entry focusing on his expatriate apprenticeship; he is also in *American Novelists, 1910–1945* with an entry surveying his entire career. Each volume includes a cumulative index of the subject authors and articles. Comprehensive indexes to the entire series are planned.

With volume ten in 1982 it was decided to enlarge the scope of *DLB*. By the end of 1986 twenty-one volumes treating British literature had been published, and volumes for Commonwealth and Modern European literature were in progress. The series has been further augmented by the *DLB Yearbooks* (since 1981) which update published entries and add new entries to keep the *DLB* current with contemporary activity. There have also been *DLB Documentary Series* volumes which provide biographical and critical source materials for figures whose work is judged to have particular interest for students. One of these companion volumes is entirely devoted to Tennessee Williams.

We define literature as the *intellectual commerce of a nation*: not merely as belles lettres but as that ample and complex process by which ideas are generated, shaped, and transmitted. *DLB* entries are not limited to "creative writers" but extend to other figures who in their time and in their way influenced the mind of a people. Thus the series encompasses historians, journalists, publishers, and screenwriters. By this means readers of *DLB* may be aided to perceive literature not as cult scripture in the keeping of intellectual high priests but firmly positioned at the center of a nation's life.

DLB includes the major writers appropriate to each volume and those standing in the ranks immediately behind them. Scholarly and critical counsel has been sought in deciding which minor figures to include and how full their entries should be. Wherever possible, useful references are made to figures who do not warrant separate entries.

Each *DLB* volume has a volume editor responsible for planning the volume, selecting the figures for inclusion, and assigning the entries. Volume editors are also responsible for preparing, where appropriate, appendices surveying the major periodicals and literary and intellectual movements for their volumes, as well as lists of further readings. Work on the series as a whole is coordinated at the Bruccoli Clark Layman editorial center in Columbia, South Carolina, where the editorial staff is responsible for accuracy of the published volumes.

One feature that distinguishes *DLB* is the illustration policy – its concern with the iconography of literature. Just as an author is influenced by his surroundings, so is the reader's understanding of the author enhanced by a knowledge of his environment. Therefore *DLB* volumes include not only drawings, paintings, and photographs of authors, often depicting them at various stages in their careers, but also illustrations of their families and places where they lived. Title pages are regularly reproduced in facsimile along with dust jackets for modern authors. The dust jackets are a special feature of *DLB* because they often document better than anything else the way in which an author's work was perceived in its own time. Specimens of the writers' manuscripts are included when feasible.

Samuel Johnson rightly decreed that "The chief glory of every people arises from its authors." The purpose of the *Dictionary of Literary Biography* is to compile literary history in the surest way available to us – by accurate and comprehensive treatment of the lives and work of those who contributed to it.

The *DLB* Advisory Board

Introduction

Victorians did not invent travel or travel writing, but they passionately loved both. Wandering throughout their own country on foot, horseback, or rail and throughout crowded Continental cities, they spread British social, economic, and political influence wherever they alighted. Eventually investigating jungles, deserts, and mountain ranges, they explored and colonized the globe. Such modern tourist staples as professionally planned tours became big business by the mid nineteenth century and extended the gaze of the English to cover the globe. Thomas Cook, who conducted his first British railway excursion for the Leicester Temperance Society in July 1841, led a small group of travelers on a round-the-world pleasure excursion in 1872–1873. The *who, where, what,* and *how* of travel were all transformed in the nineteenth century, and so, too, was the literature of travel.

Before the nineteenth century British men had traveled – often to fulfill their professional duties in the service of their religious or state rulers or to gain educations or just to see the world. Medieval, Englishmen had traveled to the Holy Land to fight the "infidels" or had joined one of many groups of pilgrims on their way to shrines to seek forgiveness for sins or relief from physical ills. So great had the number of pilgrims become by the fourteenth century that, according to Maxine Feifer, a whole industry of "charitable hospices and mass-produced indulgence handbooks" developed to serve their needs. Geoffrey Chaucer, while known for his pilgrimage tale set in England, traveled abroad as an ambassador negotiating treaties and trade agreements. Chaucer's fictional Wife of Bath and the real Margery Kempe notwithstanding, women were discouraged from participating in pilgrimages, but men from all but the peasant class journeyed not just to Canterbury but to holy sites such as Rome, Venice, the Holy Land, Amiens, and Santiago de Compostela. Through the years, as Feifer remarks, the pious motivation of the pilgrimage became "tinged with more worldly impulses: culture and pleasure – tourism in fact."

By the Elizabethan age, the era of travel for exploration and appropriation, traveling abroad had become an endeavor for the few – something not only inappropriate for women, children, and the old but also unaffordable by most. Feifer adds that whereas all kinds of people had become tourists during "the age of pilgrimage,"

> the Elizabethan tourist was typically an unmarried English male in his early twenties, recently down from Oxford or Cambridge, travelling abroad to see how the world was run and thus prepare himself for membership of the ruling class. Married men ought not go, because their duty was to the family. Old men could not go, because they tired too easily and could not stomach foreign food. Women dared not go, because it jeopardized their chastity.

Nevertheless, while her male counterpart might visit the spa at Baden, the sixteenth-century English maiden or matron traveled to Bath. Male members of the English gentry visited Paris, but women made their way to London – and the situation did not change much during the next two hundred years.

Until the nineteenth century prohibitive costs kept all but the wealthy from traveling, and the potential dangers of world travel kept even them within the well-worn paths of continental Europe. Travel was dirty, tiring, and time-consuming, not to be undertaken without serious commitments of money, time, and energy. Young men traveling to experience life and acquire culture, to explore, or to take up diplomatic posts in foreign lands occasionally traveled lightly. Usually, however, travelers required a huge equipage, because the customary stay was for three years and the traveling group might include distant relatives as well as companions and servants. Feifer describes how "the third Earl of Burlington travelled with an accountant, a portrait painter to copy monuments and statues, and a landscape painter to do the scenery." Items to be transported most often included books, some pieces of furniture such as beds and desks, and massive trunks filled with the wardrobe required for travel, visits to churches and museums, and formal dinner appearances and entertainments at the castles and courts of Europe. In essence such traveling more closely resembled moving to a new location than it did taking up a temporary residence.

In spite of its discomforts the Grand Tour (the first recorded use of the term was in 1670) developed into a tradition for the wealthy with well-defined travel routes. During the eighteenth century the number of British traveling to the Continent grew steadily, interrupted only for short periods by upheavals, particularly the Napoleonic Wars. Edward Gibbon was told in the 1780s that there were "more than forty thousand Englishmen, including servants, on the Continent," and James Buzard comments that the tour was so well established by 1815 that "jokes and complaints about the 'British invasion of Europe' began to make regular appearances in the periodicals."

To guide the many travelers, whose motives for the Grand Tour shifted from the pursuits of culture and education to those of sightseeing and amusement, tour memoirs proliferated, becoming precursors of contemporary guide books such as Marianne Baillie's *First Impressions of a Tour upon the Continent in the Summer of 1818, through Parts of France, Italy, Switzerland, the Borders of Germany and a Part of French Flanders* (1819). These accounts by women travelers took their places beside the eighteenth-century narratives of Joseph Addison, Samuel Johnson, Horace Walpole, Tobias Smollett, and Thomas Nugent.

Many readers of such journey narratives were, of course, armchair travelers. Others, however, carried the books with them as guides to their real journeys. These latter individuals, frequently disdained by travel writers, were characterized as tourists and criticized for being superficial (that is, for needing a book), for moving rapidly from place to place, for acquiring material possessions, for traveling in groups, and for failing to study and contemplate the places they visited. Typical of the reproaches meted out to them are the remarks of Lady Mary Montagu, one of the few early woman travelers, on the British boys in Italy: she felt that "by hoarding together and throwing away their money on worthless objects," they had "gained us the title of Golden Asses." The claim that some who take journeys are travelers, then, while others are mere tourists developed well before the nineteenth century and the evolution of the travel industry. The distinction is part of the literature of travel, and a desire to preserve that distinction sent some men and women of the nineteenth century off the beaten path in search of adventure.

The Travel Industry

During the period from 1837 to 1875 technological progress contributed to the redefinition of travel and the growth of tourism. Instead of walking or relying on horses as means of transport, Victorian travelers or tourists could board trains in nearly all developed countries, and this dramati-

cally reduced the time and cost of travel while increasing its comfort: trains provided fewer stops at questionable inns and less exposure to disagreeable company. By the time Victoria ascended the throne, railroads, which had begun carrying passengers in Britain in 1830, were laying track in Canada, had expanded their services through more than a thousand miles of track in the United States, and within a few decades would be used by Continental travelers going from Zurich to Baden, from Paris to Rouen and Orléans, from Turin to Genoa, and through the Alps from Switzerland to Italy. By 1876 the first Chinese railroad had been completed, and travelers on railways in Britain had increased from 23 million in 1842 to 604 million in 1880.

Yet early Victorians mistrusted railway travel, as they considered it unnatural: the railroad was a means of transport without a soul that would, as William Wordsworth and others argued, sever the bonds between man and nature. Opposition to railway travel derived as much or more from philosophical attitudes and class prejudices as from fear engendered by the dirt and occasional dangers of the journey: manufacturers and industrialists attacked the railway for contributing to the absenteeism and irresponsibility of their workers, and the upper classes objected to having to share their space, even the railway platform, with tourists and excursionists from the lower classes. The nostalgia for a "simpler" and "better" past expressed at the opening of the century echoed again and again as improvements in transport expanded opportunities: new types of people became able to travel, and new destinations for all travelers appeared.

Reaching what had been their exclusive destinations on the Continent, members of the social elite, like many Romantics, decried the devaluation of places that had previously been their provinces alone. They disliked what they perceived of the manners, the lack of imagination, and the noise of some 150,000 visitors who flocked to Europe by the mid 1850s, a number that was to increase greatly in the 1860s as tour operators such as Cook expanded their destinations to include Switzerland and Italy. John Ruskin, who insisted that "travel by train was like being sent somewhere in a parcel," bemoaned both the rapidity of railway transport and the cluttering by the uninformed of such grand places as Saint Mark's Square.

Advancements in ocean travel matched those of the railway. The sailing ships of earlier centuries were graceful and romantic, but they were quite unreliable because they were small, reliant on wind, and vulnerable to storms. Clipper ships were faster but still uncomfortable, and even the large steamers introduced in 1838 to facilitate transatlantic travel were intended more to carry many emigrants in a shorter space of time than to provide the comfort associated with travel for pleasure. Crossing the ocean did, however, become safer and much faster with steam power, despite the risk of explosions from overworked boilers. Travelers could rely on ships to arrive at least on the day they were scheduled to do so: no longer did ships depend entirely on the cooperation of nature. The Peninsular and Oriental (P&O) passenger service was introduced in the late 1830s and by the 1850s made weekly departures from Southampton to Málaga and fortnightly to Alexandria. By 1871 such steamers as the SS *Oceanic* were introduced, with their large public rooms providing luxury transport that inaugurated another new era of travel, one that will be recounted in *British Travel Writing, 1876–1909.*

But not just technology alone changed travel during the nineteenth century. The democratization of travel, frequently deprecated by many travel writers (and writers of fiction, too), was largely facilitated by entrepreneurs such as Cook and George Bradshaw. In 1841 the first issue of *Bradshaw's Monthly Railway Guide* was published, and Edmund Swinglehurst recounts how Cook organized an excursion for 570 travelers to a temperance meeting at Loughborough that same year: "There was a clashing of cast-iron buffers, the thin wail of a whistle, the huffing and puffing of a steam engine, the blare of a brass band, the roar of a crowd of two thousand people, and Mr. Thomas Cook's first excursion train moved slowly out of Leicester station." Excursion fares were necessary to reduce the prohibitive costs of rail travel engendered by the high-fare system. The round-trip tickets Cook introduced made reduced fares available and took care of the confusing connections among the different railways that had to be negotiated in traveling even short distances in Britain. He also issued single round-trip tickets for steamer and rail trips to Scotland and Wales. By the 1850s he was issuing round-trip tickets to seaside resorts, his excursion-day trains leaving at midnight in order to give outings at such places as Brighton, Margate, Bournemouth, and Torquay to workers.

Cook's arrangements for working- and middle-class travel to the London and Paris exhibitions of the 1850s and 1860s included lodging as well as transport. By 1873, when Cook introduced the forerunner of modern-day traveler's checks, his travelers were no longer just the urban proletariat or women, clergy, and other members of the expand-

ing middle class. Arranging for the transport and accommodation of Indian princes traveling to England with their households (sometimes including animals) as well as for trips abroad by Queen Victoria and her retinue, Cook's firm served royalty and the rich and famous from all over the world. His offices circled the globe from Australia to America, Canada to India, and Cape Town to Egypt, and such entrepreneurial innovations as his railway up Mount Vesuvius and a fleet of steamboats on the Nile all made travel accessible — too accessible, in the eyes of some seasoned travelers, who lamented that even Egypt was about to be conquered by railroads and the pleasure seekers of the world. Cookites, as those traveling in groups under the tutelage of a guide came to be called, took in both the religious sites of the Bible and such scenes as those presented by dancing girls, the slave market, and snake charmers; they slept in desert tents, climbed the pyramids, and sailed the Nile. Though frequently ridiculed in fact and fiction, Cook's tours were celebrated in numerous popular songs.

Other developments — such as the weekly half holiday, bank holidays introduced into England and Wales in 1871, an annual holiday for manual workers, and holidays with pay — contributed to changes in that body of people who became travelers and in their reasons for traveling. Although travel books continued to regale the reader with stories of crowded carriage rides; overnight stays in filthy, flea-ridden hotels; and hair-raising horseback rides across mountain passes during thunderstorms, travelers who chose to travel in relative comfort and safety throughout England and the Continent could do so. Travel for pleasure to Paris and for sport to Switzerland became parts of the nineteenth-century travel repertoire for the wealthy in the 1850s, just as English seaside resorts became the destinations of the workers.

In the nineteenth century those who wished to test their mettle and be known as travelers had to seek farther afield than the Continent for their adventures. If hardship and danger posed no obstacles, unbeaten tracks to the East in search of antiquities, treks into the heart of Africa in search of the Nile, and journeys to other parts of the world still "unimproved" or just undergoing "improvement" through colonization and the work of the missionaries were available. As travel literature reveals, some who ventured forth did so as much to distance themselves from tourists as to learn, braving primitive conditions, using antique modes of transportation, and experiencing danger in remote corners of the earth.

While the gradual internationalization of the banking systems enabled travelers to journey farther and at less risk, travelers would continue to find foreign spaces that required coercion, barter, or seduction as a means of survival. In Malaysia, for example, currencies remained in great confusion throughout the nineteenth century. Each region insisted on its own paper or coin money, and travelers had to carry several different forms of cash to purchase necessities. Nor was there a Shepheard's Hotel, such as Cook built in Cairo, available in many parts of the world. In fact, in many places shelter had to be arranged along the way. Even where sleeping places were well established (such as in China or Japan, where trade and travel had been going on for many centuries), Europeans were often not welcome, nor did they find native accommodations appropriate to their needs.

Nineteenth-Century Travelers

Nineteenth-century travelers were a diverse group, including explorers, scientists, wealthy dilettantes, soldiers, missionaries, secretaries, clergymen, and even invalids seeking health in jungles, deserts, and mountains. Whether they traveled in large groups organized with near-military precision, or in solitude, disdaining protection or company, they shared a drive to find and to experience the unknown, as their culture defined it. In their writing they defined the world for their Western readers and participated in shaping economic and political futures for the lands they visited. Their books reveal just how difficult it was — and is — to escape Western influences, particularly if the writers were the ones either intentionally or unintentionally bearing civilization in their wakes.

In part, Victorians traveled because they could: the world had come under their influence; the cliché that "the sun never sets on the British Empire" had real significance. The British Empire had footholds throughout the world — some maintained by commerce, others by military or naval power. The great era of discovery that made Britain the queen of the seas and a major power in the world economy had peaked before the mid nineteenth century. As Mary Louise Pratt writes, the rough outlines of the continents had been mapped, and although colonists had made substantial headway in most continents, much of the interior, the land within those colonial outlines, remained a mystery. The particular contributions of early Victorian travelers were to fill in the map, to bring back whatever might be of use to Europeans, and to convey the culture and religion of the civilized to those thought of as primitives.

The colonizing of the remaining land followed a pattern similar to that of the North American continent, in which waves of Europeans spread across the frontier: traders and trappers first, working with and manipulating the natives; frontier settlers who uprooted the primeval forests and burned prairies; farmers who purchased additional lands as they became available and built towns on familiar European patterns. With each succeeding wave of settlement, native culture was further uprooted. In Africa, South America, Asia, Australia, and New Zealand, European explorers were superseded by settlers in the nineteenth century. From the points of settlement, travelers moved more deeply into the interiors of previously unknown territory and were celebrated for their work and writing by organizations such as the Royal Asiatic Society (founded in 1823), the Royal Geographical Society (founded in 1830), and the Royal Archaeological Institute (founded in 1843).

During this period of British economic, military, and political imperialism, travelers found signs of incipient westernization in nearly every part of the world. Hardly any area, no matter how isolated, was without a British — or at least a European — representative. The discovery of quinine, a preventive for malaria, enabled Europeans to live in jungles and other equatorial environments from which they had been previously blocked. International corporations regularly sent young men into the bush to look after business concerns; missionaries dotted the landscape in mosquito-infested jungles; low-level political representatives worked to coordinate British plans and protect imperial interests.

Clinging to their cultural heritage, these representatives of the empire huddled in European outposts of foreign lands. Marianne North writes of a young man left alone in the jungle who "used to go and sit under a tree and talk English to himself every day for a couple of hours, for fear of forgetting the language." British travel writers, occasionally donning native clothing for convenience or protection, usually regarded any Europeans who truly became part of the alien culture as somehow suspect or mad, certainly vaguely traitorous. When living abroad for whatever purpose, sojourners had to preserve their identities as Europeans or risk ostracism from their countrymen, as did Lady Hester Stanhope, who lived as an eccentric, well-to-do outcast in Syria from 1810 until her death in 1839.

European residents provided travelers with safe points of departure for interior exploration. For example, Isabella Lucy Bird remarks several times in *Unbeaten Tracks in Japan* (1880) that she sought the assistance of British or American missionaries and ambassadors for a hot bath, solid walls, European food, and privacy. European visitors could show their letters of introduction to these widespread representatives of the empire and have some assurance that their importance would be recognized and every effort made to facilitate the traveler's plans, even though such plans were sometimes intrusive or bizarre. Sir Austen Henry Layard, whose original destination was Ceylon, where he was to establish a practice as a barrister through family connections, remained in Turkey and the Middle East through establishing ties with Sir Stratford Canning, the ambassador at the British embassy in Constantinople.

No matter how clearly inexperienced or untrained they were, most travelers included in this volume have given in their books altruistic or practical reasons for leaving their homeland and seeking adventure, although Continental travel was another matter. Many Victorians did not like to acknowledge that they traveled for pleasure rather than for education or acculturation, the primary reasons most often given for travel on the Continent. But enjoying the pleasure of leisurely travel seemed to be a central object, as revealed by such unsubtle titles as those of Countess Marguerite of Blessington's *The Idler in France* (1841) or Frances Elliot's *Diary of an Idle Woman in Italy* (1871).

While some Victorians traveled for pleasure or for contributing to their country's commercial, artistic, and scientific dominance, others began their travels in search of health and, along the way, picked up important information. Still others set out to accompany family or friends who were assuming professional positions abroad; others aimed to proselytize to the vast "unwashed." Missionary Mary Louisa Whately, for example, turned social historian and provided accounts that are particularly noteworthy of Egyptian women. As any reader of nineteenth-century fiction knows, travel was a good way for young men (or women, as it turns out) to earn their fortunes: Laurence Oliphant served as a secretary to Lord Elgin and as an official correspondent to the London *Times,* reported on foreign affairs, and wrote travel books; James Bryce and William Francis Butler served their country while tirelessly maintaining journals that provided bases for erudite travel books. Women traveled abroad while serving as governesses: Anna Leonowens, Anna Jameson, and Emmeline Lott observed and critiqued foreign culture as they served. Whatever rea-

sons such British travelers had for their itinerant pursuits, their experiences along the way made for excellent travel books.

Regardless of their original aims as travelers, nineteenth-century British travel writers provided ethnographic or scientific data of great use to the burgeoning empire. Amateur scholars took notes and interviewed natives; they looked for evidence of cannibalism in the South Seas, recorded rites of passage for young Africans, wrote of harem and Gypsy life, observed the treatment of Coptic Christians in Muslim society, described the peoples of the Canadian wilderness, told the story of sheep farming in New Zealand, reviled slavery in America, and depicted the manners and morals of the residents on the eastern seaboard of North America. Scientific research, though done by amateurs, became a central interest of travel — one mixed with political, economic, or military goals, as Pratt and others have discussed. Many travelers carefully collected seeds and spores; identified and named fish, flora, fauna, and insect species; dug and transported artifacts and antiquities; and measured nearly everything quantifiable — mountain elevations, river water rates, and the heights, weights, and cranial sizes of natives.

The famous David Livingstone, for example, began his travels as a reasonably well schooled missionary. He found converting natives to be far more difficult than he anticipated; in fact, he failed utterly in his attempts. His exploration of the African interior was far more interesting and successful, even if it did eventually lead to his demise. Livingstone's adventures were fully supported by the Royal Geographical Society, which eagerly awaited his return and sent help when he failed to reappear. It was the preeminent organization to which scientific-minded travelers looked for financial support and recognition. Charles Darwin, whom twentieth-century readers know as a Victorian scientist, began as a travel writer. His excruciatingly detailed journals led to his book *Narrative of the Surveying Voyages of His Majesty's Ships Adventure and Beagle* (1839), which recorded the experiences and observations that began his investigations into evolution and, following his years of reflection on them, shaped his theories about the survival of the fittest. He found his calling as he traveled, as did Florence Nightingale.

In effect, Victorian amateurs created careers and professional identities for themselves as they observed. Any reasonably intelligent and courageous person could discover a new species, revolutionize theories about how life evolved, discover the sources of the greatest rivers on earth, or uncover treasures of antiquity in the sands of the desert. It was an exciting time. The career of Richard F. Burton demonstrates just how valuable professional eclecticism was to the empire. Burton was indeed well-trained, though not as the geographer, map maker, and ethnographer known to twentieth-century readers; he was an amazingly talented linguist and a bold, brave man. Disguised as an Arab, he traveled throughout the Mideast and gained entry to Mecca. His facility with languages enabled him to make astute observations about other cultures, observations that he fully intended to be used to facilitate Britain's economic and political ends. Layard was not particularly well educated, yet reading his autobiography or examining in the British Museum the Assyrian finds of this amateur archaeologist, who turned to yet other interests midway through his life, provokes awe in even the most learned twentieth-century specialist.

Women travelers also participated in this social science and scientific research done by amateurs and professionals working in unfamiliar fields. Louisa Meredith described the exotic animals of Australia and championed conservation and animal rights, a burgeoning movement in the nineteenth century. Harriet Martineau and Lucie Duff Gordon commented on the social conditions of Egypt and thereby contributed to the development of anthropological and social science research methods. Bird's first books combine good, rousing adventure stories with ethnographical observations, but her later books, written in the late 1880s and 1890s, are far more scientific (some would say dry) — replete with citations of scholarly sources, careful interviews, supporting data, measurements, maps, photographs, and critical commentary. Women's contributions received grudging recognition when the Royal Geographical Society granted fellowships (though not memberships) to fourteen women, including Bird.

Travel Writing

Travel writing was a natural and profitable outgrowth of the Victorian fascination with learning about the "unknown." In fact, travel literature is an ancient art with antecedents thousands of years old, but it is an ancient art with a sketchy history. While Percy Adams examines some of its beginnings and characteristic features in *Travel Literature and the Evolution of the Novel* (1983) and in a 1988 anthology that suggests classifying travel literature by content (guidebook, land journey, and water voyage) and form (letters, journals, narratives, dia-logues), its development has been described only in fragments.

Other recent critical and historical studies use gender and place as bases for classifying works in the genre. Paul Fussell's *The Norton Book of Travel* (1987) appears at first to provide an overview comparable to those of Norton anthologies of literature, but it is as eclectic as other recent anthologies — *The Oxford Book of Travel Verse* (1989) and *Worst Journeys: The Picador Book of Travel* (1993). Arguably, Homer's *Odyssey* might be deemed travel literature; certainly Herodotus's historical account of his travel is. Yet, though critics of literature question the distinctness of the boundary between fiction and fact, that travel writing is nonfiction may be all that has been safely defined about the genre. Homer's *Odyssey* and Chaucer's *Canterbury Tales,* for all that they reveal about travel and travelers, remain in poetry sections of our libraries and bookstores. A novel such as Ann Bridge's *Illyrian Spring* (1935), which for some fifty years after its publication continued to serve as a guidebook to British touring of the Dalmatian coast, is nevertheless a novel. That travel writing is a sufficiently distinct form of nonfiction prose to merit a rubric but not significant enough to warrant its own section is evident in the *Cambridge Bibliography of English Literature,* which categorizes it together with nature and adventure writing as miscellaneous prose.

Thus, though largely ignored until quite recently, British adventure and discovery tales had been popular for hundreds of years before the Victorian period. So popular was voyage and journey literature before the nineteenth century that numerous fictional tales of discovery and adventure were written, as Adams relates in *Travelers and Travel Liars, 1660–1800* (1962). While John Hawkesworth was reportedly paid £6,000 for his authorized edition of Capt. James Cook's travels (1773), Henry Fielding earned only £1,000 for writing *The History of Tom Jones* (1749). Despite competition from the novel in the nineteenth century, travel writing reached new heights of popularity, making the most successful writers famous and financially secure. Victorians who remained home, unwilling or unable to travel, could travel vicariously by reading any of quite literally hundreds of travel books: John Pemble says that "travel books on Italy alone were appearing at the rate of four a year in the 1840s." Everyone wanted to know about pushing through dense jungles and fighting unreasonable natives to discover the source of the Nile or about riding a horse hundreds of miles, accompanied by a known desperado, through snow-covered mountains in Colorado. Publishers such as John Murray and Richard Bentley sought out and fostered new travelers for their stables of travel writers.

Some historians of travel and tourism state that travel writing did not become a profession until the 1870s, the decade in which writers were actually sent to locations with the specific intention of producing useful and entertaining books. Yet Karl Baedeker and Murray had published guidebooks in 1835 and 1836 on Germany and northern Europe, and numerous earlier books had similarly directed the traveler by providing information about routes, places, lodgings, hazards, and pleasures of travel to specific sites. Mariana Starke's *Travels in Italy* (1802), James Howell's *Instructions for Forreine Travell* (1642), and the thirteenth- and fourteenth-century guides for pilgrims are but a few examples of the guidebooks. Other writers at the beginning of the nineteenth century had earned handsome livings by writing travel accounts; Countess Marguerite of Blessington and Louisa Stuart Costello, the latter considered by many to be the first woman to support herself through her travel writing, described excursions to churches and libraries as well as the inhabitants and histories of the places she visited on the Continent. Writers such as Dickens used their travels, as they used all their experiences, to produce the books through which they earned their livings, or, like Bird, they wrote about their travels as by-products of those experiences but gradually became intentional and conscientious travel writers.

For the Victorian, travel and travel literature were so popular that magazines such as *Bentley's Miscellany* frequently published travel essays, while other publications such as *Blackwoods Magazine,* James Buzard writes, carried essays expressing disgust with the "tribe of travelling bipeds" whose chronicling "spoils all rational travel . . . [and] disgusts all intelligent curiosity." Dickens complained that there was "not a famous Picture or Statue in all Italy, but could be easily buried under a mountain of printed paper devoted to dissertations on it," and Frances Trollope likewise produced travel books and fictions about the excesses of travel, if not of travel writing, in *The Robertses on Their Travels* (1846).

Unlike novels, travel books were considered educational and sensible by most Victorians, for these books were dedicated to teaching readers about the unknown and thus escaped the censure of frivolousness applied to novels, which were most often regarded as written by and for women and were condemned for lacking the seriousness of his-

tory and other factual works. Victorian readers were occasionally titillated by the racy narrative interludes that laced some travel texts, although most of those episodes were innocent enough to be overlooked — except, perhaps, in the case of Richard F. Burton's books, which fundamentally offended British monogamous values. At other times readers were treated to imaginative embellishments necessary to turn the long disquisitions on history, politics, or regional dress into exciting and suspenseful adventures. In fact, in many ways representations of "fact," "objectivity," and "truth" are slippery notions in these texts: a travel writer might (and did) confidently describe the convenient and peculiar hip shelves that African women had evolved for carrying babies or might narrate stories of tribal cannibalism based on third- and fourthhand testimonies. While Victorian travelers relied on "journals" supposedly written on the spot to prove the truth of what they had seen, they sometimes collapsed several journeys into one and relied on the accounts of others for some of their material.

Victorian travel books share many traits with each other. A reader can expect a narrative that details the writer's journey in following a straightforward, linear sequence — even if the actual journey did not at all resemble the final presentation. The narrative presents a blend of humorous, perhaps spicy, anecdotes; detailed description of peoples and places; "scientific" observation and discoveries; philosophizing about the role of the British Empire in world affairs; advice to future travelers through that area; and comparisons between British culture and any others that the writer encounters. These texts often begin abruptly, after an often-overdone preface establishes the writer's "bragging rights" about specific discoveries. In *Through the Dark Continent; or, The Sources of the Nile around the Great Lakes of Equatorial Africa and down the Livingstone River to the Atlantic Ocean* (1878) Sir Henry Morton Stanley, for example, plagues his readers with a long, tendentious preface that defends his having helped the kaiser establish a foothold in Africa and thanks dozens of governments, scientific academies, and universities for their support. The narrative then begins quickly. Readers can also expect a narrator who is curiously neutral, one who observes and lectures with a generic voice that allows readers brief glances at his or her personality but carefully keeps them distanced. Even Edward Lear, the boisterous writer of limericks and well-respected painter of landscapes and birds, keeps his unrestrained personality under control when he writes travel literature.

Travel writers frequently apologize for their supposedly poor writing. They carefully disclaim literary ambitions on the grounds that they are presenting the "truth" as simply as possible. Bird, for example, defends her choice of structure for *Unbeaten Tracks in Japan*:

> It was with some reluctance that I decided that it should consist mainly of letters written on the spot to my sister and a circle of personal friends, for this form of publication involves the sacrifice of artistic arrangement and literary treatment, and necessitates a certain amount of egotism; but, on the other hand, it places the reader in the position of the traveller, and makes him share the vicissitudes of travel, discomfort, difficulty, and tedium, as well as novelty and excitement.

She continues, "I am painfully conscious of the defects of this volume." Victorian travel writers fairly typically insist that they are not gifted writers and that they write only to inform and share interesting incidents. Women writers in particular write apologetic prologues that prepare readers to expect workmanlike writing at best; however, even a brief study of travel writing demonstrates that these writers crafted their texts with care, having read travel books of their forebears and contemporaries and commenting freely on the accuracy or completeness of observations by their competitors.

Travel literature is a self-referential genre, one in which writers rely on the interpretations and analyses of other writers to shape their own – perhaps through agreement, often through disputation. Bird, particularly in her later books, researched geographical areas with great thoroughness and cited her sources for the convenience of her readers. In *The Yangtze Valley and Beyond* (1899) she identifies the *Geographical Journal* and the *Chinese Gazetteer* as her resources; she thanks the various European authorities, often explorers or ambassadors who provide her with interpretations and analyses. As one reads more travel literature, it becomes clear that the writers are conversing with one another, reflecting on and refining the comments and observations of others. They also count on readers to know other travel books: Duff Gordon critiques her cousin, Martineau, for being so concerned with pyramids and so uninterested in people, describes Lady Hester Stanhope in the last years of her life, lauds Edward Lane, and laughs over Emmeline Lott. Duff Gordon expects her readers to know these other works or to be interested enough to seek them out. Florence Nightingale mentions John Gardener Wilkinson's *Modern Egypt and Thebes* (1843) and Martineau's *Eastern Life: Present and Past* (1848). By

the Victorian period travel writing became a genre with conventional features and a history, and women as often as men were its practitioners.

As the motives for travel writing are varied – to guide others in visiting a particular location, to map previously uncharted territory, to elucidate the rich cultural history of a place, to relate the story of some significant antiquarian or scientific discovery for members of a royal society, or to inform the English public about life in one of its territories – so too are the forms it most resembles, among which are the various subcategories of autobiography. Travel writing enables readers to glance at the author's inner workings, to apprehend the nature, concerns, and opinions of authors. Like Victorians, contemporary readers of travel literature appreciate peeks into the lives of not only the notorious and the famous but also the unnamed and the previously unknown.

Victorian Travel Writers

This volume of British travel writers focuses on those Victorians whose works were most popular and/or most influential between 1837 and 1875. Although the editors have tried neither to be purists nor to stretch definitions of what comprises travel writing in order to include works that somehow better fit another classification, most travel books are hybrids – drawing in part from other genres such as autobiography, history, natural history, anthropology, sociology, archaeology, or geography.

This volume considers the lives and works of some of the most legendary Victorian travelers: Livingstone; Burton and his friend-turned-enemy, John Hanning Speke; and Bird and Duff Gordon, two of the most famous women travelers. Most works of these authors are readily available in reprinted full or abridged editions. In addition to studies of those writers who were influential and popular in their times, many whose reputations have suffered since the Victorian years are also included: Costello and Mary Anne Barker; Samuel White Baker and Oliphant. Some women, such as Marianne Postans and Whately, made significant contributions, but although their works were recognized during their lifetimes, no records beyond those in their publications tell us of their own lives. Some major literary figures, such as Dickens, are treated as minor travel writers because they wrote few travel books – and because their careers are so thoroughly discussed in other sources. To indicate some of the richness of travel writing beyond the space limitations of this volume, we have included two bibliographies: one of some works by Victorian writers whom we have not covered among the entries, and the second, a list of secondary books about travelers and travel writing.

– *Barbara Brothers and Julia M. Gergits*

Acknowledgments

This book was produced by Bruccoli Clark Layman, Inc. Karen L. Rood is senior editor for the *Dictionary of Literary Biography* series. Denis Thomas was the in-house editor.

Production coordinator is Samuel W. Bruce. Photography editors are Julie E. Frick and Margaret Meriwether. Photographic copy work was performed by Joseph M. Bruccoli. Layout and graphics supervisor is Emily Ruth Sharpe. Copyediting supervisor is Laurel M. Gladden. Typesetting supervisor is Kathleen M. Flanagan. Systems managers were George F. Dodge and Chris Elmore. Laura Pleicones and L. Kay Webster are editorial associates. The production staff includes Phyllis A. Avant, Ann M. Cheschi, Melody W. Clegg, Patricia Coate, Joyce Fowler, Stephanie C. Hatchell, Kathy Lawler Merlette, Jeff Miller, Pamela D. Norton, Delores Plastow, Lisa A. Stufft, William L. Thomas Jr., and Allison Trussell.

Walter W. Ross and Steven Gross did library research. They were assisted by the following librarians at the Thomas Cooper Library of the University of South Carolina: Linda Holderfield and the interlibrary-loan staff; reference-department head Virginia Weathers; reference librarians Marilee Birchfield, Stefanie Buck, Stefanie DuBose, Rebecca Feind, Karen Joseph, Donna Lehman, Charlene Loope, Anthony McKissick, Jean Rhyne, Kwamine Simpson, and Virginia Weathers; circulation-department head Caroline Taylor; and acquisitions-searching supervisor David Haggard.

The publishers acknowledge the generous assistance of William R. Cagle, director of the Lilly Library, Indiana University, and his staff, who provided many of the illustrations in this volume. Their work represents the highest standards of librarianship and research.

Dictionary of Literary Biography® • Volume One Hundred Sixty-Six

British Travel Writers, 1837–1875

Dictionary of Literary Biography

Samuel White Baker
(8 June 1821 – 30 December 1893)

Barbara Brothers and Julia M. Gergits
Youngstown State University

BOOKS: *The Rifle and the Hound in Ceylon* (London: Longman, Brown, Green, & Longmans, 1853; Philadelphia: Lippincott, 1854);

Eight Years' Wanderings in Ceylon (London: Longman, Brown, Green, & Longmans, 1855; Chicago & New York: Belford, Clarke, 1855); republished as *Eight Years in Ceylon* (London: Longmans, Green, 1874);

The Albert N'yanza, Great Basin of the Nile, and Explorations of the Nile Sources (2 volumes, London: Macmillan, 1866; 1 volume, London: Macmillan, 1866; Philadephia: Lippincott, 1866); abridged as *Baker and Lake Albert,* edited by E. A. Loftus (Edinburgh & New York: Nelson, 1954);

The Nile Tributaries of Abyssinia, and the Sword Hunters of the Hamran Arabs (London: Macmillan, 1867; Philadelphia: Lippincott, 1867); republished and enlarged as *Explorations of the Nile Tributaries of Abyssinia: The Sources, Supply, and Overflow of the Nile; the Country, People, Customs, etc., . . . with a Supplementary Sketch Relative to the Captivity and Release of English Subjects and the Career of the Late Emperor Theodore, by Rev. W. L. Gage* (Hartford, Conn.: Case, 1868);

Cast up by the Sea (London: Macmillan, 1868; New York: Harper, 1869);

Ismailïa: A Narrative of the Expedition to Central Africa for the Suppression of the Slave Trade, Organized by Ismail, Khedive of Egypt (2 volumes, London: Macmillan, 1874; 1 volume, New York: Harper, 1875);

Cyprus as I Saw It in 1879 (London: Macmillan, 1879);

True Tales for my Grandsons (London: Macmillan, 1883; New York: Macmillan, 1884);

Samuel White Baker

The Egyptian Question: Being Letters to the Times and Pall Mall Gazette (London: Macmillan, 1884);

In the Heart of Africa (New York: Funk & Wagnalls, 1884);

Wild Beasts and Their Ways: Reminiscences of Europe, Asia, Africa, and America (London & New York: Macmillan, 1890).

OTHER: Clive P. Wolley, *Big Game Shooting, with Contributions by Sir S. W. Baker [and Others]* (London: Longmans, Green, 1894).

Samuel White Baker fits the stereotype of the Victorian explorer precisely: in fact, he almost certainly contributed to its development. A big-game hunter who was an excellent shot, Baker was independently wealthy from the fruits of the empire, incredibly strong, loyal to a fault, sexist, and occasionally racist. He is described on title pages of late-nineteenth-century editions of his works as "Late Pasha and Major-General of the Ottoman Empire," "Gold Medalist of the Royal Geographical Society and *Grande Médaille d'Or de la Société de Géographie de Paris*," "Author of 'Rifle and Hound in Ceylon,' 'Albert N'yanza, Great Basin of the Nile,' 'Nile Tributaries of Abyssinia,' 'Ismailïa,' " and so forth. This list of accomplishments encapsulates Baker's political, scientific, and popular importance as well as illustrates Victorian priorities. Although he was a staunch individualist, a man who forged his own ways through the world, he worked throughout his life to serve his family and country. Without official support he undertook exploration of the Nile in the hope of extending the discoveries of Richard Francis Burton, John Hanning Speke, and Capt. James Grant. Later, with government sanction, Baker accepted the task of eliminating slavery in large portions of Egypt. His energy and tenacity were nearly boundless.

Baker saw himself as a participant in a grand British movement, a natural outward thrust dictated by the national character. In the preface to *Eight Years' Wanderings in Ceylon* (1855) he explains the British need to explore, discover, and conquer:

> Englishmen ... are naturally endowed with a spirit of adventure. There is in the hearts of all a germ of freedom which longs to break through the barriers that confine us to our own shores. ...

> This innate spirit of action is the mainspring of the power of England. Go where you will, from north to south and from east to west, you meet an Englishman. Sail around the globe, and upon every point of strength the Union Jack gladdens your eye, and you think with wonder of the vast possessions which have been conquered, and the immense tracts of country that have been peopled by the overflow of our little island.

His writing career began with his adventures; as he traveled, he wrote copious journal entries that formed the bases of his extremely popular books. From the publication of his first travel book, *With Rifle and Hound in Ceylon* (1853), he enjoyed popular success. His books sold well, making him and both of his wives (particularly Florence, his second wife) famous.

Baker descended from a long line of adventurers, navy officers, writers, politicians, and plantation owners. His family hearkened from Kent, with the family seat at Sissinghurst, near Maidstone. Able to trace their ancestry to pre-Tudor times, the Bakers were an illustrious if not aristocratic family. His grandfather, Valentine Baker, was a Royal Navy officer who served during the American revolutionary and concurrent Continental wars. He was famous for having defeated a much larger and better equipped French warship. With his wartime profits he helped to forge the British Empire with profitable estates in Jamaica and Mauritius and settled down to become a respectable merchant in Bristol.

Of Valentine Baker's seven sons and two daughters, only two sons apparently made it to adulthood. Samuel, the explorer's father, was sent to Jamaica in 1815 to learn the family business, but unlike his future son, he did not enjoy his rugged training in the wilds of Jamaica. The elder Samuel became a respected merchant, settled in London to better run his business, and married the daughter of Thomas Dobson of Enfield. On 8 June 1821 in Ridgeway Oaks, their home, Samuel White Baker was born, the second of five sons among what would be eight Baker children. When his older brother, Thomas, died in 1832, Baker assumed the weighty position of eldest among this particularly comfortable generation of Bakers, who enjoyed the affluence of well-handled plantations and investments and rode the crest of British imperialism. The Baker sons, in particular, grew up thinking of themselves as leaders and forgers of an ever-widening sphere of British influence.

Because Baker's father was suspicious of ordinary methods of instruction, Baker's education was nontraditional. In Enfield he was first taught by his mother, rather than tutors or governesses, whose services the family could well have afforded. Interested in nature, he filled his pockets with strange, sometimes unfortunate things such as caterpillars and beetles. Once he buried one of his sisters to see if "this would make her grow any faster." He later went to school in Rottingdean, near Brighton. At home on holiday he experimented with gunpowder and received some serious flash burns when he blew out the kitchen windows. Energetic and fearless, he was an inquisitive, occasionally overly experimental child.

At Highnam Court in Gloucester, to which the family moved in 1833, he learned how to hunt and shoot but was apparently ill educated, despite attending a local school. He grew into a strong young man, blond and Saxon in appearance. From 1833 to 1835 he went to Gloucester College, where, he proudly stated, he was never caned because he was too big and strong to be affected by it. He excelled in boxing, fencing, shooting – basically, anything athletic. In 1838 his father sent him to the curate of Tottenham, Rev. P. H. Dunster, for private lessons because he was worried about Samuel's ignorance and lack of discipline. Baker read science and travel literature as well as the usual classics, but he did not have an academic disposition and found long study irksome. His father next sent him to Frankfurt, Germany, where he stayed with Herr Behrens, a banker. Although ostensibly in Frankfurt to study German, Baker practiced much riflery and designed his own gun that he later used for big-game hunting.

Back in London he found working for his father to be too limiting. He married Henrietta Martin, a young woman whom he had known much of his life and whose sister, Elizabeth, married Baker's brother John in Maisemore Church on the same day, 3 August 1843. Although Baker was only twenty-two years old, this first marriage was happy and productive, as Baker explored possibilities in exotic, often dangerous lands while managing his family's plantations in Mauritius and Ceylon and perfecting his hunting ability.

In June 1845 Baker and Henrietta, who was pregnant, left England with their eighteen-month-old son, Charles Martin, for Mauritius to join John and Elizabeth, who had gone ahead to tend the family's plantation of Fairfund. The birth of a second son, John Lindsay Sloane, in June 1845 was followed shortly by the death of Charles Martin, and at the end of 1846 John Lindsay Sloane, the last son, died after having been poisoned by a servant. The Bakers had seven children, of whom only four survived into adulthood.

Displeased with Mauritius, Baker left for Ceylon to try shooting elephants. Although he disliked Colombo, the port city, he generally liked Ceylon: it was more British and rich with coffee plantations. Determined to try a longer stay, he sent for his wife, who apparently took in stride their moves and primitive living conditions; en route in September 1846, Baker's infant daughter Jane died and was buried at sea. In that same year Baker was shipwrecked and became ill with what he called "jungle fever," probably malaria, which bothered him throughout his travels. Following a doctor's orders to try the

Victorian cure of fresh air and altitude, he retired to Newera Eliya, a mountain retreat in Ceylon, to recover.

Baker's first book, *With Rifle and Hound in Ceylon,* which he wrote and published while living there, describes various Ceylon hunting experiences both before and after he took up permanent residence on the island. One included a jungle trip in November–December 1851, the hunting party consisting of his two brothers Valentine and John and the Honorable E. Stuart Wortley and Edward Palliser, all of whom were frequent companions.

Through a combination of narration and diary excerpts (all of Baker's travel books incorporate diary passages), Baker recounts the excitement of the hunt and the daily activities of camp life and sets forth the preparations: their retinue consists of "four personal servants, an excellent cook, four horsekeepers, fifty coolies . . . in all, sixty people," as well as their gear ("two tents . . . four beds . . . complete dinner and breakfast services for four persons, and abundance of table linen") and their provisions ("sherry, madeira, brandy and curaçao, biscuits, tea, sugar, coffee, hams, tongues, sauces, pickles, mustard, sardines *en huile,* tins of soups . . . currant jelly for venison, maccaroni . . . [and] last, but not least, a double supply of soap and candles"). Then follows a list of the guns that each of the four took. Such descriptive precision is characteristic of Baker's presentation.

In Baker's second travel book, *Eight Years' Wanderings in Ceylon,* written from his copious journals and published shortly after his return to London, Baker relates, in addition to his hunting adventures, his experiences in establishing a permanent plantation in Ceylon. Enticed by the fresh air and water and heartened by the abundance of game, Baker had fallen in love with the area on his hunting trips and had determined that it was the ideal place for a British plantation. He writes excitedly in the book, "Why should not the highlands of Ceylon, with an Italian climate, be rescued from their state of barrenness? Why should not the plains be drained, the forests felled, and cultivation take the place of the rank pasturage, and supplies be produced to make Ceylon independent of other countries?"

Thus in 1848 Baker bought a thousand acres of land for twenty shillings an acre and set about the prodigious task of planning for the new settlement. Skilled at organizing and arranging, Baker purchased such necessities as tools, seeds, farm animals of various kinds (including purebred cattle and a thoroughbred horse), furnishings, building materi-

Baker in 1857

als, and farm equipment, and he hired several overseers and servants to accompany them into the wilderness. In *Eight Years' Wanderings* he comments that the extremely high cost of improving the land, which must be cleared and provided with roads, far exceeds the low cost of the land. Wells and cisterns have to be dug, residential and farm buildings constructed, and natives brought to understand their new roles. It is an expensive and dangerous enterprise. In a short time Baker and his brother John overcame recalcitrant natives, diseases afflicting their animals, and crop failures, and before long they were making a profit.

This success, however, was hard won, even for the overachieving Baker. In the beginning the plantation was plagued with accidents, failures, and diseases. Samuel, who had arrived first, managed the building of cottages with the help of eighty men felling trees, clearing ground, and constructing buildings. Trouble arose later with Henry Perkes, a drunken groom. First he ran a carriage and horses over a cliff, and then he drove an elephant to death from exhaustion: Baker noted that Perkes had "literally forced the poor beast up the steep Pass for seven miles, till it fell down and shortly after died."

Baker adds that "Mr. Perkes was becoming an expensive man: a most sagacious and tractable elephant now added to his list of victims; and he had the satisfaction of knowing that he was one of the few men in the world who had ridden an elephant to death." Their potatoes were eaten by grubs; rams died from too much clover and fighting; an epidemic hit the cattle and horses; and finally the bailiff's wife died. Yet after that most severe tragedy, they did very well – so well, in fact, that they embarked on a program of civilizing the wilderness, until "an extremely pretty church had been erected, and a public reading-room established." Baker's wife cared for their three daughters (Edith, Agnes, and Constance), sketched the countryside, and designed furniture, while her sister, John's wife, painted landscape pictures.

After the Bakers got their plantation under control, they turned their attentions to hunting. Sometimes Samuel and his brother John experimented as hunters and campers by minimally outfitting themselves. Leaving most of the usual Victorian paraphernalia of wilderness camping behind, they relied on native huts, their skill in hunting, and little gear. In fact, Baker's description of their gear sounds much like that used by modern backpackers: he often hunts with only a blanket, a pot, materials to ignite a fire, guns, and spices for meat. His narrative includes pictures of his efficient shelters and very tolerable lean-tos that he built with branches and twigs; with his blanket he constructed a handy pup tent that shed water well.

Other hunting expeditions were more ambitious and varied. He regularly hunted with John and two good friends, Lord Wharncliffe (named the Honorable E. Stuart Wortley in *With Rifle and Hound*) and Edward Palliser, a fellow plantation owner, but others occasionally joined them, and the arrangements were frequently as elaborate as those described in *With Rifle and Hound* for the 1851 jungle trip. If we are to judge from *Eight Years' Wanderings,* much of Baker's time was spent in perfecting his hunting skills and experimenting with various methods of stalking, trapping, shooting, knifing, and otherwise killing animals. In the first chapter of *With Rifle and Hound* Baker distinguishes between the "act of killing" and "sport" – in the latter, one's enjoyment "increases in proportion to the wildness of the country." Though he vividly describes place in these first two travel books, place is their setting rather than their subject.

Baker's hunting during his eight years in Ceylon is truly astounding. At one time or another he hunted cheetah, leopard, elephant, boar, and elk, and he trapped civet cats, mongooses (accidentally), and other small mammals. Occasionally defensive about this apparent carnage, he would insist that "the very person who abuses wild sports on the plea of cruelty indulges personally in conventional cruelties which are positive tortures. His appetite is not destroyed by the knowledge that his cook has skinned the eels alive, or that the lobsters were plunged into boiling water to be cooked." Certainly he was right and, to his credit, he tried to find consumers for whatever meat he could not use. Natives most often would follow him or come and happily take the meat from him when he would signal with a gunshot. Refusing to give away the meat, he traded it to the local natives for whatever they had to barter: "Of course I give them splendid bargains," he wrote, "as I barter simply on the principle that no man shall come for nothing."

During general disquisitions on handling guns or raising hunting dogs, Baker often digresses into wonderful hunting stories. For instance, on each of two consecutive days of being hunted by the hounds, elks had killed themselves by jumping off a cliff rather than facing the dogs that would have torn them to shreds. Baker speaks admiringly of the elks' courage, even though they both died horribly, in at least one case taking some dogs over the edge with them. In a cave that Baker's party used as a hunting camp, he showed off his culinary skill by making an impressive stew of elk: "The pot held six gallons, and the *whole elk,* except a few steaks, was cut up and alternately boiled down in sections. . . . A few green chillies, onion in slices fried, and a little lime juice, salt, black pepper and mushroom ketchup, and, – in fact, there is no use thinking of it, as the soup is not to be had again."

Throughout *Eight Years' Wanderings* Baker adds bits of stories, recipes, adventures, and hunting advice, as he does in his later travel books. Hunting allowed him to revel in nature and exercise his strength and stamina, and Baker seems to have been a man who required testing and challenges to be satisfied. When he had these challenges, he sounds completely happy: "There is a peculiar delight which passes all description, in feeling thoroughly well strung, mentally and physically, with a good rifle in your hand, and a trusty gun-bearer behind you with another; thus stalking quietly through a fine country, on the look-out for *'anything'* – no matter what." Often risking his own life or those of his dogs Bertram, Killbuck, Hecate, Bran, Lucifer, Lena, Bluebeard, Ploughboy, and Gaylass, he headed into the jungle alone to test his wit and skill against wild animals. Baker did, however, pay close

attention to the needs and injuries of his dogs, as he sewed up boar-tusk injuries, removed ticks, and even pulled leeches from their noses.

A timelessness prevails in the narratives of Baker's first two travel books: neither are chronological. In *Eight Years' Wanderings,* for example, once his plantation is under way, the narrative displays no progress or change. The discourse simply moves from topic to topic: discussions of hunts, natives, flora and fauna, and politics follow each other without apparent organization or direction. Readers find a seamless existence bounded by changing seasons and weather but not controlled by modern notions of time or narrative progress. These early books are energetic, exuberant descriptions of hunts and scenery interspersed with advice for travel, hunting, and shooting and with brief stories of hunts or adventures. Baker clearly loved his time in Ceylon.

When Baker nearly died from a fever contracted after a particularly harsh hunt in 1854, the family returned to England. He had already begun writing *Eight Years' Wanderings,* and England had changed much during those years. Baker's father had survived the loss of his wife, had remarried, and moved away from the family home; the hard times of the 1840s had given way to the 1850s and the beginning of great political, economic, and social changes. Henrietta, Baker's quietly artistic wife, bore yet another child, Ethel, their seventh child in twelve years. Baker's two books had made him something of a mythical figure, an icon of British heartiness and skill.

When Henrietta became ill, they went to Bagnerers-de-Bigorre in the Pyrenees for her health, and this move allowed Baker to hunt bear. On 29 December 1855 Henrietta died unexpectedly of typhus. Ordinarily the quintessential man of action, Baker was so grief-stricken that he was unable to make decisions or move from the spot, even though he was now responsible for his four children. Luckily his wife's twenty-two-year-old younger sister, Charlotte Martin, took charge, and this ensured their safe return to England. Baker soon arranged for his daughters' care – in fact, he never lived with them again – and then left, trying to join his brothers Valentine and James, who were fighting in the Crimea, but the war ended before he could participate. Not surprising, to assuage his grief he hunted frequently and energetically, first in Sabanja, on the Sea of Marmara, and then in the Balkans.

After Henrietta's death the thirty-five-year-old Baker was plainly bored with England and family life, or at least with the traditional Victorian paterfamilias role. Through the appropriate channels he tried to join Dr. David Livingstone's expedition (supported by government funds) to the Zambezi, but his offer was politely refused. In 1858 he traveled with the wealthy Maharajah Duleep Singh party to Hungary, but their boat was stopped by ice in Widdin, a Turkish town in which many Hungarian refugees had taken shelter. There Baker found Florence Barbara Mary Finnian Von Sass, a seventeen-year-old Hungarian refugee.

Florence's situation was mysterious, although most biographers repeat the story that Baker purchased her. According to this legend, Baker and the maharajah visited a slave market, where they found a beautiful young woman about to be sold after the death or disappearance of her nurse. Because Baker supposedly outbid the pasha for Florence, the party was forced to abandon their boat and race on horseback across the border to Bucharest. However Baker acquired Florence, they lived together as husband and wife from 1858 until 1865, when they returned to England after their trip to explore the sources of the Nile. Under the scrutiny of Victorian high society Baker attempted to explain his actions: he had not been able to marry her immediately because she was Catholic; she could not speak English; and she was so young. Though Baker was straitlaced in his adherence to Victorian moral standards, their union in defiance of social strictures resembled those of other famous Victorian nontraditional couples such as Dante Gabriel Rossetti and Elizabeth Siddal or George Eliot and George Henry Lewes.

To Victorians the legality of Samuel and Florence's marriage was relevant; to twentieth-century readers the reality of the Bakers' long, devoted union is far more compelling. Florence immediately fit into Baker's life: she made every attempt to learn English, although she and Baker often conversed in German; she accompanied him on his explorations, even the most dangerous and strenuous; and she worked hard to conform to the prototype of the "good" Victorian wife when they returned to England. Notable for her blonde hair, pleasing features, brilliant smile, and dark eyes, she remained a striking woman even into her old age. Florence and Baker never had any children, and thus released from maternal responsibilities, Florence was free to accompany Baker and tend to his needs without interruption.

Instead of proceeding to England in 1858 with his seventeen-year-old "bride," Baker sought a post as managing director for a railway from Cernavoda across the Dobruja region of Romania to Küstenja on the Black Sea. Baker told his new colleagues that Florence was his wife, but they did not entirely believe it. His work was successful – he was always good at planning, organizing, and carrying out complex jobs – but when the railroad was completed he was again anxious to find some new endeavor.

Baker decided to follow John Hanning Speke to Africa to aid in the discovery of the sources of the Nile River. Supported by the Royal Geographical Society, Richard Burton and Speke were already on this pursuit to discover the source of the Nile because it served as a symbolic and real image of imperial power. In fact, Burton and Speke were already fighting about the implications of their discoveries. Baker hoped to time his travel to meet Speke and his partner, Capt. James Grant, on their explorations; unlike his peers, however, Baker financed his exploration entirely, with no support from the Royal Geographical Society or his publisher. His expedition would have been impossible without his considerable wealth.

Florence refused to be sent to safety and accompanied Baker on this truly heroic journey in 1861. So difficult and prolonged was this trip that most of the Baker family and the British public assumed that Samuel and Florence were long dead before they reappeared in civilization. Throughout the trip Baker kept extensive journals, which he kept even when it was necessary to manufacture pens from rusty nails and ink from rotting fruit. Two of his most famous books, *The Albert N'yanza, Great Basin of the Nile, and Explorations of the Nile Sources* (1866) and *The Nile Tributaries of Abyssinia, and the Sword Hunters of the Hamran Arabs* (1867), derive from these copious journals. Unlike his earlier travel books, these are chronologically and geographically organized with regular narrative progress and indications of locations and dates. Baker found it important to account for his exploration in greater detail and precision than had been necessary in his Ceylon books, because these exploration narratives document his discoveries. From this mammoth, multiyear trip Baker's place in history derives.

With typical Baker aplomb he decided that it was essential to learn to speak Arabic to carry out his work (Florence also did so), for he recognized that to rely on an interpreter might well lead to disaster. He had to rely on his forcefulness and persuasiveness to get permission to travel in disputed territories and to secure the support and guidance of native people. No interpreter could have been as effective or trustworthy as Baker himself. In addition, he generally distrusted the willingness and ability of

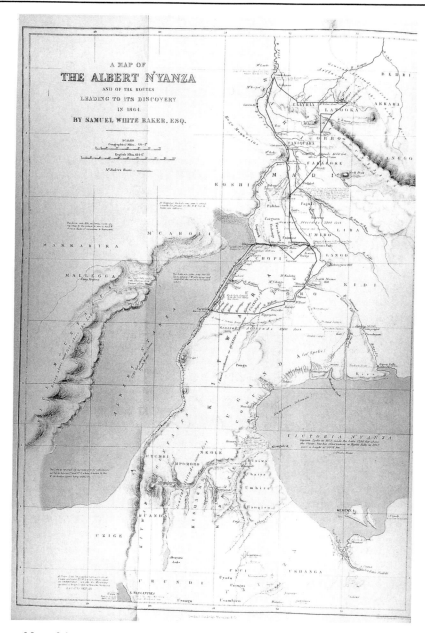

*Map of the route Baker and his wife followed on their search for the source of the
Nile River (courtesy of the Lilly Library, Indiana University)*

natives to translate, and certainly native Egyptians or Abyssinians had little reason to help yet another invader of their lands.

Although written later than *The Albert N'yanza,* his second exploration narrative, *The Nile Tributaries of Abyssinia,* provides an excellent overview of the first leg of the Bakers' trip, the Abyssinian rivers that feed into the Nile. The preface establishes immediately that Baker accomplished his goal: "It has been determined by the joint explorations of Speke, Grant, and myself, that the rainfall of the equatorial districts supplies two vast lakes, the Victoria and the Albert, of sufficient volume to support the Nile throughout its entire course of thirty degrees of latitude." Baker's book moves between actual journal entries and more general narrative and description; it is easy to follow the progress of the expedition.

At the beginning of the trip Baker and Florence sailed up the Nile in well-to-do fashion, in a leased *philae,* a sailing ship. He was not pleased with the landscape and noted that it "appears as though it bore the curse of Heaven; misery, barrenness, and the heat of a furnace are its features," and the "miserable people . . . snatch every sandbank from the retiring stream, and immediately plant their scanty garden with melons, gourds, lentils, &c. this being their only resource for cultivation."

The Bakers arrived at Korosko on 11 May, and on 16 May, mounted on pack camels, they headed into the Nubian Desert. They accomplished the amazing feat of crossing the entire 230 miles in seven days because they were worried about running out of water. By the midpoint of their desert crossing his men were on short rations because they had counted on Baker's supplies. On 22 May they arrived in Abou Hammed, where they bathed and rested, and they resumed their trip on 27 May. They found desert traveling, in addition to quite reasonable dangers from heat exposure or dehydration, to present disquieting and alien experiences. Static electricity sparked through their clothing and blankets and leaped from pieces of metal. Their wooden tools and gunstocks quickly succumbed to the dryness. "All woodwork is warped; ivory knife-handles are split; paper breaks when crunched in the hand, and the very marrow seems to be dried out of the bones by this horrible simoom," Baker wrote.

On 31 May they arrived in Berbera, where they were greeted by Halleem Effendi, a former governor who allowed them to camp on his property near the Nile. Effendi warned them not to seek the source of the Nile because "the White Nile is the country of the negroes; wild ferocious races, who have neither knowledge of God nor respect for the Pasha, and you must travel with a powerful armed force; the climate is deadly; how could you penetrate such a region to search for what is useless, even should you attain it?" Baker wrote that the natives did not understand the relevance of scientific research, nor could they understand why someone would leave his soft, comfortable life to explore a sparsely populated, arid region.

As the entourage traveled, Baker hunted every conceivable kind of animal; as always, he had many adventures along the way. For instance, he decided to stalk an ariel and succeeded, but he became lost — and Florence finally set out with the men to find him. He also hunted a hippopotamus that had killed a man who had been trying to protect his melon patch. When Baker gave the meat to local Arabs, a distasteful melee ensued: "No sooner was the carcase flayed," he recounts, "than the struggle commenced for the meat; the people were a mass of blood, as some stood thigh-deep in the reeking intestines wrestling for the fat, while many hacked at each other's hands for coveted portions that were striven for as a *bonne bouche*." He remarks several times on his servants' habit of eating raw meat, particularly livers and hearts, just after they have gutted the carcasses; however, even the Bakers soon developed a taste for hippopotamus meat – cooked, that is.

Baker's daily adventures were not limited to hunting and fishing. A thunderstorm and heavy rains drove scorpions into camp for succor, and the Bakers' surly translator, Mahomet, was stung as he tried to make a fire. On another occasion the Bakers tried to teach Bacheet, one of their servants, to use a spoon rather than his fingers to fish flies out of the tea. He learned quite well but made one fairly serious faux pas, perhaps demonstrating some wry rebellion: "Bacheet, who was in waiting," Baker writes, "suddenly took a tea-spoon from the table, wiped it carefully with the corner of the table-cloth, and stooping down beneath the bed, most carefully saved from drowning, with the tea-spoon, several flies that were in the last extremity within a vessel by no means adapted for a spoon." Not all the Bakers' moments are colored with such bemusement as this domestic mishap of removing flies from a chamberpot. Occasionally Baker's "carpet would be spread under a shady tree; upon a branch of this his water-skin should be suspended, and the day's work over, [he] can write up his journal and enjoy [his] pipe while coffee is being prepared."

On 24 June Baker was lucky enough to witness an instance of the yearly inundations of the Nile. With no more warning than an ominous thundery sound the river rose so suddenly that some of his men nearly drowned: "an army of water was hastening to the wasted river: there was no drop of rain, no thunder-cloud on the horizon to give hope, all had been dry and sultry; dust and desolation yesterday, to-day a magnificent stream, some 500 yards in width and from fifteen to twenty feet in depth, flowed through the dreary desert!" The dry season had ended, and on 5 July the party headed across the desert again for Cassala, "the capital of the Taka country, on the confines of Abyssinia." Out of the desert and in more lush territory Florence succumbed to fever, a difficulty both Bakers repeatedly experienced on their Nile journeys. In Cassala, a Nubian city, they stayed with Malem Georgis, a Greek merchant, and prepared for the trip out of Egypt and up the Nile tributaries of Abyssinia.

Throughout Baker's Blue Nile river exploration he was plagued by servant problems. At every town he had to acquire a new set of servants, bearers, and camel drivers and to seek help from local officials in impressing enough men and animals into duty. This enforced servitude caused problems at every juncture. The fact that the governor seized the resources Baker needed from owners who refused to part with their animals did not help Baker's popularity. Baker responded to his servant problems with a combination of British aplomb and boldness. After his Tokrooris servants had tried to desert because they were afraid of Basé natives who were following the hunting party, Baker threatened to ask the governor to give each of the servants five hundred lashes for deserting. They remained, becoming especially happy when Baker allowed one of the men to leave for Mecca. Baker provides a fairly typical assessment of natives:

> If natives are driven, they invariably hate their master, and turn sulky; if you give in to them, they lose respect, and will never obey. They are exceedingly subject to sudden impulses, under the influence of which they are utterly unreasonable. As the expedition depends for success entirely upon the union of the party, it is highly necessary to obtain so complete a control over every individual, that the leader shall be regarded with positive reverence, and his authority in all matters accepted as supreme.

Baker argues for the usual Victorian blend of firmness, consistency, and kindness, but he did not scruple to hit his men if he deemed they needed it.

By 12 September the river was falling. Because they had been so long away from civilization, Florence and Baker were reduced to wearing clothing that she devised from skins and some cloth that they had purchased from natives. Barbed bushes penetrated any cloth, no matter how thick, and Florence therefore made gazelle-skin gaiters for Baker so that he could hunt with impunity. She also wore a version of men's clothing so that she could ride astride animals.

When the entourage arrived at Wat el Négur on 3 December, incipient border warfare had made the area extremely uneasy. Mek Nimmur, a local chief, was attacking, robbing, and kidnapping. Baker wanted to travel into Basé and Mek Nimmur's land to explore the Setite, Royn, Angrab, Salaam, Rahad, Dender, and Blue Nile Rivers. When an entire party of Hamran Arabs returned with Sheik Abou Do Roussoul, Sheik Owat's nephew, Baker invited them to join his party for sport. The group left from Geera on 23 December with three Hamran sword hunters — Abou Do, Jali, and Suliman — and a tracker, Taher Noor.

Baker in the outfit that he designed to wear during his travels in Africa

Baker thoroughly enjoyed hunting with the Hamran sword hunters, who proved valiant, brave, even brilliant hunters — the kind of men Baker modeled himself upon. After settling in a relatively safe camp, they went out after lions but found an elephant, which the sword hunters attacked: "No gladiatorial exhibition in the Roman arena," Baker writes, "could have surpassed this fight. The elephant was mad with rage, and nevertheless he seemed to know that the object of the hunters was to get behind him." They killed seven elephants and took only the tusks. Baker always backed up the sword hunters with his loaded rifles, but he preferred to allow them to fight their prey. This enterprise was extremely dangerous: Jali, one of his hunting servants, broke his leg when an elephant stepped on his leg while charging him. Baker even enjoyed the failures of the hunt:

> Although we had failed I never enjoyed a hunt so much either before or since; it was a *magnificent* run and still more magnificent was the idea that a man, with no

weapon but the sword, could attack and generally vanquish every huge animal of creation. I felt inclined to discard all my rifles, and to adopt the sabre, with a first-class horse instead of the common horses of this country, that were totally unfit for such a style of hunting, when carrying nearly fifteen stone.

In February 1862 Baker headed to the Royn River and on 19 March began the trip to Mek Nimmur's territory with the guidance of a hunting party. Mek Nimmur arranged for a guide to the Angrab and Salaam Rivers, and Baker gave Mek Nimmur such expected gifts as "a very beautiful Persian lance-head, of polished steel inlaid with gold . . . purchased at Constantinople" and some weapons. Such presents were necessary on both the Blue and White Nile journeys to secure the cooperation and friendship of those among whom they traveled and upon whom Baker had to rely for supplies and guides. Such presents, of course, added greatly to the necessary size of their party and its conveyances.

By 11 April Baker had completed his exploration of the Salaam and Angrab Rivers and decided to go to Gallabat, the frontier market town of Abyssinia. On 28 April they left for the Rahad River, but serious illness began to kill the animals, and bad conditions plagued them – endless prairies, flies, and burning sun. On 23 May they arrived at the confluence of the Dender and the Blue Nile and headed back to Khartoum; they soon found themselves traveling through a populated area in which they had to buy supplies instead of rely upon Baker's hunting prowess, as they had for most of their journey. Thus ended the first successful leg of Baker's explorations of the Nile, over which he recommends engineering some "control": "The Nile is a powerful horse without harness, but, with a bridle in its mouth, the fertility of Egypt might be increased to a vast extent."

In *The Nile Tributaries of Abyssinia* Baker pays little attention to the geographical research that was the supposed goal of the trip and adds a few asides about riding up into the mountains to ascertain the headwaters. Much of the book relates details of his hunting – the precise manner of stalking game, what kind of gun and bullet to use, and the particular anatomical site where animal must be shot to be killed. Baker frequently identified fish and game by both Latin and popular names, and, though his travel books include professional renderings of his sketches, his descriptions are precise enough to make the drawings unnecessary. Native superstitions and beliefs are also related – for example, the origins of the wandering

evil spirit of the genii is in the desert whirlwinds that can carry sand and dust several thousand feet high – and he lists the tribes he has seen. Baker is a virtual walking encyclopedia: he can describe how to prepare an onion to eat as a substitute for meat, or what conditions influence how long it takes a dead hippo or a dead crocodile to rise to the surface of the water.

Baker's descriptive powers would make any writer envious. Succinct, precise, and vivid, for example, is his description of the Nubian Desert:

> A few hours from Korosko the misery of the scene surpassed description. Glowing like a furnace, the vast extent of yellow sand stretched to the horizon. Rows of broken hills, all of volcanic origin, broke the flat plain. Conical tumuli of volcanic slag here and there rose to the height of several hundred feet, and in the far distance resembled the pyramids of Lower Egypt. . . . Noiselessly the spongy tread of the camels crept along the sand – the only sound was the rattle of some loosely secured baggage of their packs. . . . Passing through this wretched solitude we entered upon a scene of surpassing desolation. Far as the eye could reach were waves like a stormy sea, grey cold-looking waves in the burning heat; but no drop of water; it appeared as though a sudden curse had turned a raging sea to stone.

Nor is it just the landscape that Baker places before the reader as if it had been photographed and enlarged to life size. He describes native appearances and customs, such as the Bedouins' hairdressing, for example, just as graphically:

> The great desire with all tribes, except the Jalyn, is to have a vast quantity of hair arranged in their own peculiar fashion, and not only smeared, but covered with as much fat as can be made to adhere. Thus, should a man wish to get himself up as a great dandy, he would put at least half a pound of butter or other fat upon his head; this would be worked up with his coarse locks by a friend, until it somewhat resembled a cauliflower. He would then arrange his tope or plaid of thick cotton cloth, and throw one end over his left shoulder, while slung from the same shoulder, his circular shield would hang upon his back. . . . Fat is the great desideratum of an Arab; his head . . . should be a mass of grease; he rubs his body with oil or other ointment; his . . . tope is covered with grease, and internally he swallows as much as he can procure.

Baker generally seems less judgmental than typical wealthy Englishmen in his attitudes toward natives and their different customs, although he repeats what twentieth-century readers would regard as racist platitudes about the capacities and appearances (particularly the nudity) of some African tribes. The narrative treats his servants well, and it

Elephant hunting with native swordsmen, an illustration from Baker's The Nile Tributaries of Abyssinia, and the Sword Hunters of the Hamran Arabs

shows his genuine affection and respect for many of the individuals he met, particularly the Hamran sword hunters who joined him.

Baker's sense of humor is evident in the ironic eye he can turn on the differences between some aspects of European and native cultures. During his wait for favorable weather conditions that will allow him to continue his journey, for example, he likens a temporary home that he has purchased for two shillings — a sound roof conveyed on the shoulders of thirty men, and sticks for the walls — to a freehold manor

in park-like grounds, commanding extensive and romantic views of the beautifully-wooded valley of the Atbara, within a minute's walk . . . [and enjoying] perfect immunity from all poor-rates, tithes, taxes, and other public burthens, not more than 2,000 miles from a church, with the advantage of a post-town at the easy distance of seventy leagues. The manor comprised the right of shooting throughout the parishes of Abyssinia and Soudan, plentifully stocked with elephants, lions. . . .

The second leg of Baker's journey, the search for the source of the White Nile, shares much with the first, but it was more complex and dangerous. In the preface to *The Albert N'yanza* Baker promises a tale that will take his reader "through scorching deserts and thirsty sands; through swamp, and jungle, and interminable morass; through difficulties, fatigues, and sickness, until I bring him, faint with the wearying journey, to that high cliff where the great prize shall burst upon his view." The narrative far surpasses this.

Baker, who had first to overcome authorities' refusals to allow him to travel into the interior, left on 18 December for Saint Croix and Gondokoro and arrived at the latter, a former mission station transformed into an ivory clearing house, on 2 February 1863. There slave traders, hoping that Baker's men would attack him, incited his men to rebel. Florence, however, came to his rescue by flourishing a rifle. Baker waited until Speke and Grant arrived, and they graciously gave him maps of what they had discovered. There is every reason to believe that Speke and Grant wished Baker well in his researches.

Travel through the Sudan and central Africa had become very dangerous at this time because of the slave trade. Slave traders befriended some chiefs by attacking their enemies, killing many other chiefs, and enslaving the surviving residents. Hostilities among tribes were heightened, and no one trusted anyone. Because his band of men had been reduced by the mutiny, Baker had to travel in the company of Turkish slave traders whose "cowardice and brutality" sickened him: they not only stole the cattle of natives but mutilated the bodies of their enemies, and this made dealing with the area natives all but impossible. Baker's situation was made even more precarious by the lack of loyalty from his remaining servants, who would have joined a Turkish band of marauding traders in cattle stealing and slave hunting if Baker were to die. "Altogether I am thoroughly sick of this expedition," Baker remarks in his diaries quoted by his narrative, "but I shall plod onwards with dogged obstinacy; God only knows the end. I shall be grateful should the day ever arrive once more to see Old England."

For a time the Bakers – building a house and planting a garden, their usual activities when finding themselves in amenable circumstances for a span of months – arranged their lives somewhat comfortably to await the right time of year and weather conditions to push on to confirm Lake Albert as the source of the Nile. But in spite of Florence's ill health, they were forced to abandon their camp and garden prematurely at the whim of the local Turkish traders, who precipitously decided to leave the area. Baker observed, "It is impossible to remain in this country with my small force alone; the natives have become so bad (since the cattle razzia [stealing raids]) that a considerable armed party is obliged to go to the stream for water. It is remarkably pleasant travelling in the vicinity of the traders; they convert every country into a wasp's nest." He had an insufficient contingency of men and complained that he was "more like a donkey than an explorer, that is saddled and ridden away."

In January 1864, nearly three years after they had resolved to find the source of the Nile and add another accomplishment to those already gained for England by earlier explorers such as James Bruce, Baker and Florence at last reached the Victoria Nile. This, they believed, would lead them to Lake Albert, the reservoir that Baker had presumed to be the source of the Nile. Even a summary of what should be the climax of their journey may illustrate how much Baker's narrative artistry contributes to his effectiveness as a travel writer.

Within days of completing their mission, the Bakers were again betrayed – this time by natives whose treachery would cost them a year and bring them close to death. Day after day at the river bank they were told that Kamrasi, the king of the Unyoro people, would visit them, and helplessly they waited to cross the river. "Time passing fruitlessly while every day is valuable," Baker observed in a diary entry for 27 January. "The rains will, I fear, commence before my work is completed; and the Asua river, if flooded, will cut off my return to Gondokoro." Finally it seemed that Kamrasi would allow them passage through his lands and the food and porters necessary for the journey. Progress, however, was slow, impeded on one hand by district chiefs who insisted on the entourage remaining an extra day and on another by the illnesses of his wife, his men, and himself: "Started at 7:30 A.M. she being carried in a litter; but I also fell ill upon the road, and having been held on my ox by two men for some time, I at length fell in their arms, and was laid under a tree for about five hours."

Again the Bakers were detained by Kamrasi's men; their fevers continued, and their supply of quinine became exhausted. One of their group died of fever, heightening the tension. "It rained in torrents, and our hut became so damp from the absorption of the marsh soil, that my feet sank in the muddy floor. I had fever daily at about 3 P.M. and lay perfectly helpless for five or six hours," Baker reported, and on 16 February he added, "*All my porters have deserted.*"

A man posing as Kamrasi visited them, but instead of providing help he issued daily requests to take Baker's last watch, rifle, sword, or any other items his eyes lighted upon. "This miserable, grasping, lying coward, is nevertheless a king," Baker wrote, "and the success of my expedition depends upon him." Exasperated, Baker expostulated on how both Turks and natives expected him to give and then give some more: "It is the rapacity of the chiefs of the various tribes that render African exploration so difficult. Each tribe wishes to monopolize your entire stock of valuables," which were necessary to procure food, porters, and other assistance that the travelers depended on. As if Kamrasi's treatment had not been insulting enough, the king demanded that Baker leave Florence with him. When Baker threatened to shoot him, Kamrasi realized that he had gone too far and allowed them to proceed with an escort to the lake.

Their difficulties continued, however, as the Bakers found themselves in an even more precarious situation. The escort was unreliable and even somewhat threatening, and Florence suffered sunstroke as they were crossing a river. "I had scarcely completed a fourth of the distance," Baker recounted, "and looked back to see my wife followed close to me, when I was horrified to see her . . . sinking gradually through the weeds, while her face was distorted and perfectly purple. Almost as soon as I

some comic relief into his adventure story: the natives — who frequently complain about their loads, take off into the bush, and thus leave the Bakers stranded — show up, having carried a dead ox a distance of eight miles in order not to be accused of stealing or losing Baker's property. Good news comes as their guide declares that by noon they will be able to wash in the lake, and indeed on 14 March, the party reaches the shore of the lake — from which, "thirsty with heat and fatigue," they drink. The lake was finally circumnavigated in 1875 by Henry Morton Stanley and surveyed in 1901 by Col. C. Delmé-Radcliffe. Baker had indeed found a source of the Nile.

In a fishing village, Vacovia, the Bakers set up a camp in which to recover. There they located two dugouts in which to continue their journey by rigging up sails and hiring some natives who were experienced in maneuvering the canoes. Gradually they moved up the Somerset River and discovered impressive waterfalls, which Baker named Murchison Falls after Sir Roderick Murchison, president of the Royal Geographical Society. Baker describes the beauty of the lake and its surroundings, and he then reminds his reader how important it is to "hurry forward . . . as our return to England depended entirely upon the possibility of reaching Gondokoro before the end of April, otherwise the boats would have departed."

Though it seemed that all must now go smoothly, the Bakers again experienced the treachery of the natives, who would have stolen the oars of the canoes had it not been for Baker's canniness. Inexperienced rowers and a gale nearly overturned the boats, and delayed by weather, Florence and Baker had little time to enjoy the beauty of the wildlife and their surroundings. Both of the Bakers were so ill from fever that they were sometimes unconscious and too weak to stand: "neither my wife nor I," Baker notes, "could walk a quarter of a mile without fainting." The natives housed them in decaying huts whose roofs had such holes that no protection from the rain was afforded, and for two months the tribe made them prisoners on the island of Patooan, where it seemed that they would die of hunger. As soon as they got off the island they had no guide; the vegetation was eight feet high, and it was the rainy season. Baker writes, "Death would have been a release that I would have courted, but I should have liked that one 'English beefsteak and pale ale' before I died!" For months after leaving Patooan the Bakers, their malaria somewhat relieved by the Turkish remedy of a steam bath, were forced to depend on their wits.

In February they started for Gondokoro and the boats that would take them north to Egypt and home, but upon their arrival they found neither boats nor letters, as everyone apparently had given them up for dead. Worse yet, a plague was killing thousands of people, and though they tried to cleanse the boat that they hired, members of Baker's retinue — including an African servant boy whom they had adopted — died of the disease along the way. Nor were their adventures over after they left Khartoum: they were nearly shipwrecked on the river cataracts, and in another instance they had to defend themselves against some Arabs who attacked them because the Bakers had asked to share space under a tree.

In his conclusion Baker comments on the foolishness of attempting to Christianize the "Negroes" by reflecting on an Austrian mission that had failed. First, he states, the social plague of slavery be abolished from the land. He reiterates his belief that, if the European powers are sincere, the land could be cleansed of destructive disease and honest commerce that would bring prosperity to central Africa could become possible. The black man, whose failure to domesticate the elephant (as the Asiatic natives have done) betokens what Baker sees as the African's inferiority, could then become ready to receive the missionaries and progressively civilized. In fact, Baker does not like Africans and says that they are "quite on a level with . . . the brute and not to be compared with the noble character of the dog. There is neither gratitude, pity, love, or self-denial; no idea of duty; no religion; but covetousness, ingratitude, selfishness and cruelty." Yet Baker shouldered the "white man's burden" by insisting that African natives deserved humane treatment.

On 5 March 1865 the Bakers arrived in Khartoum, nearly ten years after Baker had left England following the death of his first wife. Upon their arrival in Cairo Baker received news that he had been awarded the Royal Geographical Society's Victoria Gold Medal "at a time when they were unaware whether I was alive or dead, and when the success of my expedition was unknown." Twenty-four-year-old Florence and the forty-four-year-old Baker were quietly married in Saint James Church in Piccadilly on 4 November 1865. Baker reassumed his role as head of the family, and Florence began her new career as a Victorian matron with four adult stepdaughters. On 13 November, after giving the inaugural address to the Royal Geographical Society, he introduced his gorgeously dressed, strikingly beautiful wife to the assemblage. Thunderous applause greeted her, and their popularity was secured im-

Baker's painting of himself confronting a wounded elephant (from Florence Baker, Morning Star, *1972)*

Gold Medal "at a time when they were unaware whether I was alive or dead, and when the success of my expedition was unknown." Twenty-four-year-old Florence and the forty-four-year-old Baker were quietly married in Saint James Church in Piccadilly on 4 November 1865. Baker reassumed his role as head of the family, and Florence began her new career as a Victorian matron with four adult stepdaughters. On 13 November, after giving the inaugural address to the Royal Geographical Society, he introduced his gorgeously dressed, strikingly beautiful wife to the assemblage. Thunderous applause greeted her, and their popularity was secured immediately. They were invited everywhere, touted by aristocracy who refused to acknowledge that Florence's past was at all questionable. Only the queen, that most rigid of moral guardians, refused to receive her. In August 1866 Baker was knighted for services to the British Empire. Capt. James Grant wrote a heated letter decrying Baker's awards

and fame to nearly every notable person in England, including the newspapers, but nothing challenged Baker's immense popularity.

Baker somehow found time to use his extensive journals to write, first, the book he had begun on his return trip to England, *The Albert N'yanza,* and in the following year Macmillan published his second Nile book, *The Nile Tributaries of Abyssinia.* The books blend an overview of Africa with anecdotes of amusing, exciting, and dangerous incidents. Both were well received, frequently published in new editions, and were sources of further fame and prestige for Baker.

Baker published in the following year his first and only novel, *Cast Up by the Sea* (1868). Set in a small Cornwall fishing village in the year 1784, the novel exhibits Baker's deft description: "The interior of this cottage was a combination of neatness and disorder; fishing-nets were hung from beams in the ceiling, spare corks and leads for nets were

On a brief trip through Egypt with the prince and princess of Wales, Baker was offered the job of stopping the slave trade. He accepted the responsibility, and was made a pasha, with an annual compensation of £10,000. He assembled an armed force of 1,645 men and began his extraordinary mission in April 1869. As usual, he made careful plans, giving directions for the purchase of medicines and drugs and for the manufacture of special bullets for killing hippos. He apparently arranged for all of the £9,000 worth of necessary supplies – from tools and clothing to music boxes – and had two twin-screw steamers and a paddle steamer built for his tours of the Nile. A train retinue of forty-one railway cars was necessary to carry the goods to Cairo, where they were loaded onto eleven hired vessels and a steamer to tow the flotilla to Korosko. His trip quickly became a highly politicized military endeavor. As before, he kept a journal of his proceedings and used it in producing *Ismailïa: A Narrative of the Expedition to Central Africa for the Suppression of the Slave Trade, Organized by Ismail, Khedive of Egypt* (1874), the recounting of his four years as governor general of the Equatorial Nile Basin south of Gondokoro that he wrote in a brief sixty-four-day period.

In the preface written for an 1878 edition of *Ismailïa* Baker sets forth the difficulty of abolishing slave trading from the area, for he describes this institution as "almost necessary to the existence of Egyptian society":

> Every household in Upper Egypt and in the Delta was dependent upon slave service; the fields in the Soudan were cultivated by slaves; the women in the harems of both rich and middle class were attended by slaves; the poorer Arab woman's ambition was to possess a slave; in fact, Egyptian society without slaves would be like a carriage devoid of wheels – it could not proceed.

The evil Baker saw in slavery lay not so much in the owners' treatment of the slaves as in the brutality of their "capture, with attendant lawlessness and murders." The slave trade had left the "rich and well-populated countries ... desolate; the women and children were carried into captivity; villages were burnt, and crops were destroyed or pillaged; the population was driven out; a terrestrial paradise was converted into an infernal region; the natives who were originally friendly were rendered hostile to all strangers." The system had brought ruin to portions of central Africa with a healthy climate and rich soil, areas where people needed only a paternal government to help them develop their rich resources and a legitimate trade that would bring

peace and prosperity. In the present state of affairs Baker's task was, as he put it, the "Herculean task of cleansing the Augean stables." He discovered quickly that despite a ban on slavery and the slave trade, the practices continued nearly unabated throughout the outlying areas. Although the khedive was anxious to please the British and Baker did not doubt his sincerity, the Egyptians and Arabs could ill afford to let it be crushed.

Baker thus seemed set up for failure, for he found that his difficulties included the perfidy of lower-level Arab and Egyptian government officials in addition to the enmity of the Turkish and Arab slave traders who had grown wealthy from the system. Baker observed that Khartoum's governor-general was honest but ineffectual, and the government was rife with corruption. He compared the opposition in Sudan, which "was openly avowed to the reform," to that of the Confederacy in the United States.

Failure to provide materials that Baker had ordered was just one tactic used to defeat his campaign to abolish the slave trade in the territories of the lower White Nile. Upon his arrival in Khartoum Baker discovered that not one of the fifty vessels he had ordered were ready for the journey down the Nile; instead, the governor had ordered a house for Baker for a year. Though Baker with his usual energy and determination set about purchasing the necessary vessels, making them ready for sail, and successfully assembling the steamer that he had transported in pieces across the desert, his departure from Khartoum was delayed by more than a month. That delay was soon compounded by others. Dense islands of vegetation forced his troops to hack their way through what should have been a flowing river. After fifty-one days Baker had to turn back and wait six months for the rainy season, so that the river would rise enough for them to proceed to Gondokoro, their destination, 1,450 miles from Khartoum.

The obstacles to Baker's success included both men and nature. Some who opposed him were among the troops he commanded – 1,645 men including an Egyptian regiment, most of whom turned out to be convicted felons, members of a Sudanese or black regiment, and 200 irregular cavalry. Col. Raouf Bey, for example, not only used delaying tactics but also led a conspiracy of officers to abandon the expedition. He sent back to Khartoum some 1,100 men – not just the sick, as Baker had ordered – and thus reduced the size of the expedition to 502 men. Bey also helped Abou Saood, a principal behind the slave trade, to escape. Baker's re-

A hippopotamus attack on the Bakers' boat at night, an illustration from Baker's Ismailïa

The obstacles to Baker's success included both men and nature. Some who opposed him were among the troops he commanded — 1,645 men including an Egyptian regiment, most of whom turned out to be convicted felons, members of a Sudanese or black regiment, and 200 irregular cavalry. Col. Raouf Bey, for example, not only used delaying tactics but also led a conspiracy of officers to abandon the expedition. He sent back to Khartoum some 1,100 men — not just the sick, as Baker had ordered — and thus reduced the size of the expedition to 502 men. Bey also helped Abou Saood, a principal behind the slave trade, to escape. Baker's remaining troops worked less than diligently when they were assigned such tasks as harvesting the produce necessary to support the expedition. Baker described the Africans themselves as "cunning and treacherous," as they promised to serve as hired porters or to furnish his troops with food — but instead stole from them, deserted their villages and disappeared during the night, harbored deserters, and even conducted guerrilla warfare against Baker's forces.

Though posing as a merchant who held the exclusive government contract for trading through many of the central African regions in which Baker was to suppress the slave trade, Abou Saood was ac-

tually a slave trader. He continued the now-illegal trade, murdered the sheik of Belinian, stole cattle of the natives, conspired with Bey to have the officers abandon the expedition, swindled the government, entered into intrigues with the natives, and incited their hostility to Baker by conducting raids and warring with some tribes against others. Carrying off cattle and slaves to prove that Baker and the government were powerless to protect them, Abou Saood attacked the tribe of Rot Jarma, who had sworn allegiance to the government of Egypt and thus considered himself under the protection of Baker. Another tribe that should have welcomed Baker's men, since it was offered the opportunity "to pasture upon this beautiful land from which they had been driven," were employed by Abou Saood's companies as mercenaries. Abou Saood and such tribes as this preferred the "good old times of plunder and prisoners."

The condition of the White Nile was also an obstacle to Baker's success; in fact, at times Baker regarded the river as the greatest enemy. On his way upstream to Gondokoro (which Baker names Ismailïa in the title he gives to his book) Baker was forced to take a tributary, Bahr Giraffe, because the river became a "frightful stinking morass" that in just one place took a day for seven hundred men to cut through one and a half miles. Baker refers to the river as the "Slough of Despond" and states that the "fabulous Styx must be a sweet rippling brook, compared to this horrible creation." The condition of the river also made communication with Cairo and the khedive almost impossible. Previously it would have presented no difficulty for steamers to communicate monthly between Khartoum and Gondokoro "with the post and all necessary supplies."

But Baker's expedition was cut off and discipline among his men diminished, since they had no fear of government action. The navigability of the White Nile was absolutely essential to the development of the area: it was the only means through which legitimate trade could be established and maintained, because the slow movement of the Bahr Giraffe stream effectively prohibited it from being cleared. Baker observed that the Nile "if once opened, together with the immense power of the stream, would, with a little annual inspection, assure the permanency of the work." He concluded that "a special expedition must be sent from Khartoum to take this important work in hand, as it would be quite useless to annex and attempt to civilize Central Africa, unless a free communication exists with the outer world by which a commercial channel could be opened."

Daily difficulties that Baker had to surmount included the illnesses of his troops from malaria, dysentery, and other climate-related diseases and his loss of men through accidents such as that of one "unfortunate man . . . carried off by a crocodile while sitting on the vessel with his legs hanging over the side." Another soldier died of sunstroke, and fresh water was sometimes difficult to locate. Feeding such a large contingency of people would have been difficult in the best of circumstances, and locating wood as fuel for the steamers was also a problem.

At Tewfikeeyah (the Gondokoro camp) planting a garden was another Herculean task similar to that of clearing the vegetation from the river. "The Egyptian troops were generally sickly and dispirited," Baker writes, "and went to their daily work in a slouching, dogged manner, that showed their passive hatred of the employment [in clearing and cultivating the land]." In addition to the laziness and ineptitude of the soldier-workers, the bullocks of central Africa refused to draw the plows, Baker records: "they determined upon an 'agricultural strike.'" Once the garden was planted such natural enemies of agriculture as guinea fowl, sparrows, insects, and the crimson-headed goose took over. So effective were the efforts of these enemies that the

land had to be resown quite thickly, and when the crops appeared above ground crickets and other insects became new enemies.

Yet Baker worked hard, and had some success, at rough-and-tumble diplomacy. In Masandi he tried to persuade King Kabba Rega of the wisdom of listening to the khedive and accepting the ban on slavery. To demonstrate his determination to establish an official presence, Baker had a residence built – a two-room building, one room of which was his home, with an odd Victorian hodgepodge of carpets, drawings, mirrors, and dust catchers. By 31 May when his entourage had diminished to a few more than one hundred men, Baker was attacked by several thousand natives. He talked them out of fighting, but he built a fort just in case it might happen again. After they were attacked several more times, Baker retaliated by making Rionga the representative of the area instead of Kabba Rega.

Baker's narrative redirects attention from this difficult, maddening venture to the flora and fauna. When the expedition encountered matted vegetation, Baker notes that the plant life that chokes the stream is the *Pistia Stratiotes*: "These surface plants, which resemble floating cabbages with fine thready roots, like a human beard of sixteen inches in length, form dense masses which are very difficult to clear." He also identifies animals by their Latin names and then adds concise descriptions for those readers who have not traveled, hunted, or fished in Africa. Baker describes African musical instruments just as precisely: one native band "consisted of two iron bells, a flageolet and an instrument made of hard wood that was arranged like the musical glasses of Europe. The latter was formed of ten pieces of a metallic sounding-wood suspended above long narrow gourd shells."

As in his earlier travel books, he quotes from his diaries "to convey an exact idea of the Bahr Giraffe" or some other place, event, person, plant, or animal. Not only are the Latin names or the measurements of temperature, latitude, sea level, or information in the appendices specified, but also the descriptions of customs, dwellings, and weapons of the African tribes. Precision is clearly a standard to which Baker adheres even when he telling a story. Once, for instance, "suddenly awakened by a shock, succeeded almost immediately by the cry, 'The ship is sinking!'" Baker finds that a "hippopotamus had charged the steamer from the bottom, and had smashed several floats off her starboard paddle. A few seconds later he charged our diahbeeah, and striking her bottom about ten feet from the bow, he

Florence and Sir Samuel Baker at their Devon estate in the early 1890s

about to attack the vessel. With one blow he capsized and sank the zinc boat with its cargo of flesh. In another instant he seized the dingy in his immense jaws, and the crash of splintered wood betokened the complete destruction of my favourite boat. . . . The movements of the animal were so rapid as he charged and plunged alternately beneath the water in a cloud of foam and wave, that it was impossible to aim correctly at the small but fatal spot upon the head.

Baker does hit it with a "No. 8 Reilly shell" as the animal charges "straight at the diahbeeah," but its wound is not fatal and more exciting details follow before the party can safely retire for the rest of the night. After another incident the contents of a crocodile's stomach, including "five pounds' weight of pebbles," are related with similar specificity: "Mixed with the pebbles was a greenish, slimy matter. . . . In the midst of this were . . . [a] necklace and two armlets. . . . The girl had been digested. This was an old malefactor that was a good riddance."

An expert huntsman, the fifty-two-year-old Baker also portrays himself as Baker the just and Baker the humane in ridding the area of its social and natural evils. When one of his men deserts, Baker has him brought before a firing squad, for the "punishment of death must certainly follow desertion," but at the last moment Baker makes "allow-

ance for his youth and ignorance . . . [and] reduce[s] the punishment to that of flogging, which I trusted would be a warning to him and all others." He points out that he typically allows the natives "to make the first hostile move before I [proceed] to forcible measures." Indeed, he often unnecessarily exposes himself to danger in attempting to settle disputes through negotiation and thereby demonstrate that he and the government are just and resolute in their promises. Fairness rather than force is how he seeks to gain allegiance and compliance with the ban against slavery.

Baker returned to England in September 1873 and wrote *Ismailia,* a book not as wildly popular as his others – perhaps because of its topic, the ills of slavery, and the anxiousness of the English to point fingers. His opinions about the future of Africa are clear in a speech he made in Brighton, where he argued that "Our mission is said to be to civilise Africa; then I say let us call it by the simple word – improve. . . . and the first thing that must be done in endeavouring to improve a savage country is to annex it." For Baker, English rule brings honesty and order.

Generally Baker enjoyed his fame and comfortable life, but in 1879 Baker again tired of England's prosaic landscape, and he and Florence traveled to Cyprus, the closest he could get her to Africa. They arrived in Larnaca on 4 January 1879 and began traveling in a gypsy caravan, in a covered wagon complete with furniture and pulled by oxen, not horses, because of the condition of the roads. They ended their tour of the island with a three-month stay in a monastery (Trooditissa) in the Troodos mountains. Here Baker wrote his book, *Cyprus as I Saw It in 1879* (1879).

With no reference books at his disposal, he claims that this book is not a history. *Cyprus,* however, includes tables listing revenue from imports and exports; charts on rainfall and temperature; quotations from Gen. Luigi Palma di Cesnola, *The Great Centre of the Worship of Venus* (1871); and various intelligence reports. More than just a relating of his experience on the island (as Baker claims it is), the book is an extremely well-written account of the geography and history of Cyprus, another testament to his prodigious learning, memory, and powers of observation. For some time afterward Baker's book – even though it was the least popular of his travel books, perhaps because it was the most traditional – is one that other writers on Cyprus pointed to as the authoritative work. Rather than being an adventure story of

quotations from Gen. Luigi Palma di Cesnola, *The Great Centre of the Worship of Venus* (1871); and various intelligence reports. More than just a relating of his experience on the island (as Baker claims it is), the book is an extremely well-written account of the geography and history of Cyprus, another testament to his prodigious learning, memory, and powers of observation. For some time afterward Baker's book — even though it was the least popular of his travel books, perhaps because it was the most traditional — is one that other writers on Cyprus pointed to as the authoritative work. Rather than being an adventure story of hunting and exploration with the hero (and the heroine, as in the African books) in constant peril, the book is a guidebook that emphasizes information rather than personal and anecdotal narrative.

Then the Bakers headed for India — Allahabad, Delhi, and Calcutta — followed by trips to Hong Kong, Canton, and Shanghai. Beginning in San Francisco, they visited the United States, and Baker hunted in the Rocky Mountains. They did not return from their world tour until 1882. This multiyear voyage was full of entertainment and hunting, with only a little politics and adventure. In fact, the Bakers regularly left England for the winter throughout the rest of Samuel's life.

His remaining days were calm. In 1883 he wrote *True Tales for my Grandsons,* a collection of short stories, and in 1890 *Wild Beasts and Their Ways: Reminiscences of Europe, Asia, Africa, and America* was published. Fond of rich food, Baker developed gout. Except for his hunting he did not exercise, and he refused to change his diet or habits. Florence reportedly told a doctor that they were not animals that required airings. Baker maintained contact with the public by writing copious and frequent letters to the *Times.* On 30 December 1893 he died and was cremated on 5 January 1894. Florence lived until 11 March 1916.

Baker is best remembered today as the explorer of both the White and Blue Nile Rivers, a big-game hunter extraordinaire, and the enforcer of British antislavery policies in Egypt. However, he also deserves to be remembered for his lively, informative travel books, which remain entertaining more than one hundred years later. Unlike many Victorian travel writers, Baker does not mar his books with excessive hostility to natives. Though his attitudes are generally those of the

Victorian Age in which he lived, he shows genuine affection and the highest respect for many non-Europeans, including natives who are fellow hunters and various Arabs, Turks, and African tribesmen he meets. He certainly exercises far more patience with his servants than most of his peers, even to adopting some of them as family members. Although his solution to the natives' "problems" is predictable (that of effecting stronger, closer British ties), he does not participate in cruel or dishonest means of repression. He may at times have seemed incredibly naive or ethnocentric, but Baker truly believed that British rule was best for everyone.

His books tell exciting stories of discoveries, famine, danger, adventure, delicate negotiations, and astonishing endurance. They are not only of historical and cultural significance but also prove that fact can be both stranger and more dramatic than fiction. His travel books combine autobiography, the description of place, and the presentation of other cultures in a seamless web of effective prose.

Biographies:

T. Douglas Murray and Arthur Silva White, *Sir Samuel Baker: A Memoir* (London: Macmillan, 1895);

Dorothy Middleton, *Baker of the Nile* (London: Falcon, 1949);

Michael Brander, *The Perfect Victorian Hero: Samuel White Baker* (Edinburgh: Mainstream, 1982).

References:

Florence Baker, *Morning Star: Florence Baker's Diary of the Expedition to Put Down the Slave Trade in the Nile, 1870–1873,* edited by Anne Baker (London: William Kimber, 1972);

Richard Hall, *Lovers on the Nile: The Incredible African Journeys of Sam and Florence Baker* (New York: Random House, 1980);

Alan Moorhead, *The White Nile* (New York: Harper, 1960).

Papers:

Baker's papers are held by the Sheffield City Libraries and the National Library of Scotland, Central Library in Edinburgh; the East Lothian District Library; the Royal Geographical Society; the British Museum; the Bodleian Library, Oxford; and the Baker family.

Lady Mary Anne Barker

(1831 – 6 March 1911)

Carol Huebscher Rhoades

BOOKS: *Station Life in New Zealand* (London: Macmillan, 1870; New York: Lent, 1872);

Stories About: —— (London & New York: Macmillan, 1871);

A Christmas Cake in Four Quarters (London & New York: Macmillan, 1871);

Spring Comedies (London & New York: Macmillan, 1871);

Travelling About over New and Old Ground (London & New York: Routledge, 1872);

Ribbon Stories (London & New York: Macmillan, 1872);

Station Amusements in New Zealand (London: Hunt, 1873);

Holiday Stories for Boys and Girls (London: Routledge, 1873);

Boys (London: Routledge, 1874);

First Lessons in the Principles of Cooking (London: Macmillan, 1874);

Sybil's Book (London: Macmillan, 1874);

This Troublesome World; or, "Bet of Stow" (London: Hatchards, 1875);

Houses and Housekeeping: A Fireside Gossip upon Home and Its Comforts (London: Hunt, 1876);

A Year's Housekeeping in South Africa (London: Macmillan, 1877); republished as *Life in South Africa* (Philadelphia: Lippincott, 1877);

The Bedroom and Boudoir (London: Macmillan, 1878);

The White Rat, and Some Other Stories (London: Macmillan, 1880);

Letters to Guy (London: Macmillan, 1885);

Harry Treverton, His Tramps and Troubles Told by Himself, as Lady Broome (London: Routledge, 1889);

Colonial Memories (London: Smith, Elder, 1904).

Lady Mary Anne Barker

OTHER: Lady Annie Brassey, *The Last Voyage,* edited by Barker as Mary Anne Broome (London: Longmans, Green, 1889).

SELECTED PERIODICAL PUBLICATIONS –
UNCOLLECTED: "On Exmoor: A Sketch," *Macmillan's Magazine,* 42 (September 1880): 387–390;

"A Distant Shore – Rodriguez," *Macmillan's Magazine,* 46 (May 1882): 67–72.

Lady Mary Anne Barker is best known for her first book, *Station Life in New Zealand* (1870), which is considered the best of the settlers' tales from the years of colonization of the islands and is a classic of early New Zealand literature. During her lifetime Lady Barker was also acclaimed for her children's stories, and she is occasionally classified as a children's, rather than a travel, writer. Many of her children's stories derive from her travel experiences, and those books, even if written ostensibly for children, were aimed also at adult readers in the British leisured classes.

The early and continued popularity of *Station Life in New Zealand* can be attributed to Barker's observant and lighthearted style, through which she vividly portrays the lives of genteel sheep farmers. While she writes in general about the sheep business (Samuel Butler, in his *A First Year in Canterbury Settlement* [1863], gives more-useful details for the hopeful immigrant), her text concentrates on the scenery, the weather (a concern in all her books), the healthy prospects for the immigrant who works hard, and the eminent suitability of New Zealand as the site of a new and better England. Similarly optimistic assessments of other colonies and of the effects of colonization on both the native peoples and the colonizers are the foci in Barker's later travel writings on South Africa, Australia, Mauritius, and Trinidad.

She extolled the benefits of colonization for the British laborers and educated gentlemen who sought to improve their lives with meaningful employment but who had few possibilities for doing so in England. On one level Barker's books were pleasant, amusing reading (as almost every review of her work stresses); more subtly, the books served as a type of imperial propaganda in reinforcing the gentry's notions that the colonies provided alluring sites for solving British unemployment and "undesirable person" problems and that those persons could then become recognized (as they had not been at home) as possessing the "good and civilized" qualities of the British. Each of her travel books is domestically oriented, the colonial home doubling as the most important site of imperial endeavor and as the representation of Home. For Barker, as for many colonial settlement and travel writers, England was the true destination of any traveler away from it: " 'It is exactly like England!' " she remarks in *Travelling About over New and Old Ground* (1872). "That is the highest praise the exile can bestow on any place. We grumble at the dear old nest so long as we are in it, but when we spread our wings and fly away, our thoughts turn back more faithfully even than our tongues."

Born in Jamaica in 1831, Mary Anne Stewart (later Lady Barker and then Lady Broome) was connected throughout her life with the colonies of the British Empire. Her father, Walter George Stewart, was island secretary of Jamaica. Little is known about Barker's early life other than that she was the oldest of Stewart's children and that she traveled five times between school in England and holidays in Jamaica during her childhood. Having received the typically scanty training given most upper- and middle-class girls, she was, as she admitted, poorly educated in England. Yet her books reveal that she could speak and read French and German and that she had a keen interest in literature and writing.

In 1852 she married Capt. George Barker, who later received a knighthood in recognition of his services in the Crimean War and the Indian Mutiny. The couple had two sons — one of whom, Walter George, born on 9 August 1857, later had a career in the army and took the surname Crol-Wyndham after inheriting property from an aunt. Barker lived in England with her sons for most of her married life. She did join her husband in India at the end of 1860, but when he died eight months later she returned to England in 1861. Her only published writing of a personal nature about her time in India appears in the introduction to *Colonial Memories* (1904). In a two-page summary she relates her unsuccessful efforts to learn firsthand about the British involved in the Indian Mutiny and about her journey to Simla and the Himalayas, a journey that she also describes in an impersonal way in *Travelling About over New and Old Ground*.

In 1865 Barker married Frederick Napier Broome, who had also been a child of colonial parents. He was eleven years her junior and in the process of becoming established as a New Zealand sheep farmer. Leaving her sons by Barker in England, she and Broome sailed to New Zealand in mid 1865. The couple lived for a short while in Christchurch while Broome negotiated for the purchase of Steventon, a sheep run named after the vicarage of Jane Austen's father and owned by Austen's nephews, Arthur Charles and Richard C. Knight. Shortly after they had moved to their new home, which they called "Broomielaw," their infant son died. The couple lived at Broomielaw until the end of 1868, when they had to give up the sheep run because a disastrous winter storm the year before had killed more than half their herd.

On their return to England they turned to writing to support themselves. Broome had already enjoyed a reputation as a minor poet, and he continued to write poetry while he worked as a journalist for *Macmillan's Magazine, Cornhill Magazine,* and the *Times.* With encouragement from publisher Alexander Macmillan, Barker also began writing as a means of support.

Station Life in New Zealand derives from letters that Barker wrote to her sister during the three years the Broomes had spent as sheep-farming colonials. Her sojourn thus appears in the traditional epistolary form of travel writing, with the letters identified by place and date and arranged chronologically. No person is ever directly addressed in the letters, and the use of initials for names indicates that the text has been edited for publication.

In earlier periods of New Zealand colonization other women writers such as Isabella Aylmer and Mary Taylor had portrayed a rigorous, difficult life in the country. Through its amused, sometimes ironic tone, however, Barker's book synthesizes two opposing messages. On one hand, she stresses the opportunities in New Zealand for hardworking, progressive settlers who can make the most of the abundant resources the country has. Echoing one theme of earlier colonial literature such as Butler's *First Year in Canterbury Settlement,* Barker discourages the colonial settlement dreams of educated gentlemen who have money but lack fitness or desire for work. On the other hand, her narrative describes, for the most part, the leisured life of people who spend mornings reading and writing and who then divert themselves with horse riding, pig hunting, fishing, and picnics.

Rather than emphasizing the rigors and dangers of colonial life — which were not as severe by the time the Broomes had arrived at any of their various colonial homes — Barker describes problems and difficulties simply as adventures that can be made the substance of good stories. She is not traveling to explore, conquer, or subdue; for Barker, travel is to domesticate. Her good spirits would not allow her to become daunted or to daunt her readers with problems that many colonists not so fortunate in wealth and spirit experienced.

Her writing is notable for its revelations about changes in the focus of mission work so commonly a feature of British imperialism. Barker makes almost no mention of the Maoris in New Zealand, and one has the impression from *Station Life in New Zealand* that the islands were occupied only by the British. While early settlers devoted themselves to mission work among the native peoples and offered Christianizing and "civilizing" as a justification for the increasing British presence in various countries, Barker devoted much of her time in New Zealand to maintaining the British character of her fellow settlers, especially the lonely shepherds. With Broome reading from books of sermons, she established regular Church of England Sunday services and distributed copies of family religious journals such as *Good Words* and *Leisure Hour,* which featured serialized novels, poetry, science, and travel articles in addition to religious stories and essays. Like these periodical stories, Barker's own New Zealand stories are intended not simply to amuse and inform but to reassure readers at home that the colonies are nurturing and, most of all, maintaining the sacred bonds of British domesticity. The close, loving relationship between Barker and Broome becomes a metaphor for the colonial ties to England and the queen.

Barker's reputation as a writer was thus established with the publication of *Station Life in New Zealand,* and later books drew upon her early travel experiences. *Travelling About over New and Old Ground* is a compilation of review-essays on books written by others about travel throughout the world. It is divided into sections on Australasia, North America, South America, Africa, and Asia, and its articles mix Barker's memories of Australia, New Zealand, and India with book-review summary and commentary on selected works of various travelers, explorers, and conquerors. She selects episodes from these books and retells them so that the experiences described, and thus the books themselves, become lively and fresh.

Barker followed up the success of *Station Life in New Zealand* with elaborations on its stories and episodes in *Station Amusements in New Zealand* (1873). Organizing this book topically rather than chronologically, she retells some of the stories originally presented in *Station Life,* but her perspective on the incidents is often more lighthearted in this later book. In terms of the change in perspective between the two books, the most telling incident is that of the storm which destroyed so many of the sheep.

In *Station Life in New Zealand* Barker details how the household is put into desperate straits when a snowstorm rages for several days: food supplies, already low, are strictly rationed, and the two servant girls take to their beds "to die warm." The worst damage of the storm comes with the floods of melting snow that drown the sheep which have survived the snow. This disheartening tale of colonial problems is difficult to recognize in the *Station Amusements in New Zealand* version, which focuses on the delights of wild tobogganing on all the snowdrifts before the flood brings the real disaster. Margaret Butcher, in a discussion with Nelson Wattie, suggests that the refashioned episode "could be

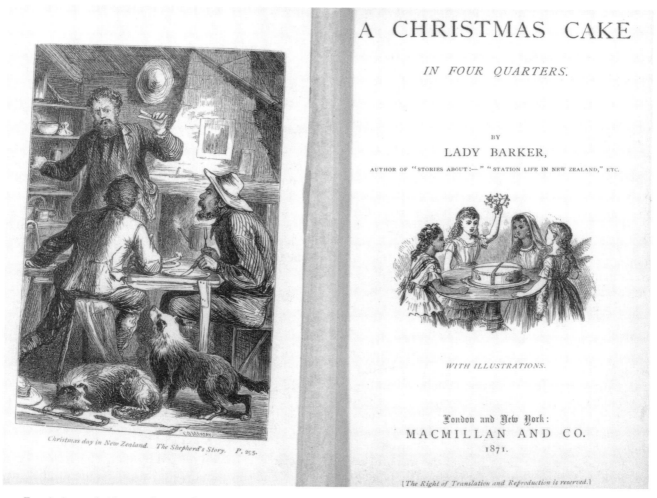

Frontispiece and title page for one of Barker's popular collections of children's stories about New Zealand life (courtesy of the Lilly Library, Indiana University)

read as a metaphor of the colonists' precarious situation, in which case the toboggan so determinedly clung to would represent the colonists' sense of Englishness." The images can be reversed, however, and readers could find the toboggan representing the colonial ingenuity that is driven by the strength and courage of the British.

In *Station Amusements in New Zealand* Barker adopts a more consciously literary style. Frequent direct and indirect literary references to George Eliot, Wilkie Collins, Charles Dickens, and Daniel Defoe pepper the text and thus establish the author as more literate and authoritative – a common tactic, especially among strong-minded women writers of the period. This is not to say that Barker's earlier writing lacks the telling detail, metaphor, or synthesis and organization. The epistolary style, however, conveys an immediacy and truth that the carefully delineated chapters do not. *Station Life in New Zea-*

land has endured because it encapsulates the zest of a life as it was lived. *Station Amusements in New Zealand* is a work of fond recollections that do not as easily convey that spirit. Lovely and memorable moments – such as that of moonlight dancing on the veranda in blue kid and purple velvet slippers – do entice the reader of the later work, however.

The Broomes spent five years in London writing prodigiously and raising their two young sons – Guy had been born about 1870 and Louis about 1874. In addition to reviewing books, particularly novels, for the London *Times,* Barker wrote a series of children's books: *Spring Comedies* (1871), *A Christmas Cake in Four Quarters* (1871), *Stories About: ——* (1871), *Ribbon Stories* (1872), *Holiday Stories for Boys and Girls* (1873), *Boys* (1874), and *Sybil's Book* (1874). These books of stories were all well received, and the writing was described in reviews as "graceful," "delightful," "pleasant," and being of "consummate beauty."

The domestic theme of Barker's travel books found further expression in *First Lessons in the Principles of Cooking* (1874) and *The Bedroom and Boudoir* (1878). Barker's cooking book provided for others the help that she had needed when she had begun station life without any culinary training. The hazards and dilemmas of settlers, who had previously employed servants and could not fend for themselves in the kitchen, are recounted in several amusing recollections. The incidents are yet another part of the not-so-subtle message that permeates the New Zealand and Australian stories: prospective settlers must be self-sufficient and resourceful. *The Bedroom and Boudoir,* part of Macmillan's Art at Home series, guides untrained English brides through the intricacies of choosing paints, wallpapers, flooring, furniture, and other furnishings for the bedrooms to create a healthy and delightful atmosphere for the middle-class home.

Following the publication of *First Lessons in the Principles of Cooking* Barker was appointed superintendent of the National School of Cookery in London. Although the aim of the school was to train lower-class women as servant-cooks, the majority of the students were middle- and upper-class young women. Barker, knowing the value of the skills that the school taught, worked diligently to promote its purposes. During the same period she was also editor of the monthly Church of England family magazine, *Evening Hours.*

While Barker was diversifying her career, Broome obtained the first of a series of government appointments that resulted in colonial residencies that became the subjects of Barker's later travel books. Broome was colonial secretary in Natal from 1875 to 1877, and his wife and sons resided there with him for a year. The exact dates of their time in Natal are difficult to pinpoint. The letters are dated from 16 October 1875 to 25 September 1876, and yet Barker later states that she returned to England in early 1877.

Barker returned to an epistolary style in *A Year's Housekeeping in South Africa* (1877), but in this work the letters are more evidently written for a general audience; again, no individual is directly addressed. She does not enjoy the African countryside: the red dust, the quick changes of temperature, and the sudden rains compound the difficulties of obtaining fresh meats and dairy products. Although she is as determined as ever to make the best of an unpleasant situation and, as she says, to "tell stories against [her]self" so that she may pleas-

antly turn her adventures and domestic life into travel writing, the South African letters present a less amusing tone.

What makes these letters so unpleasant for readers is Barker's portrayal of Africans. It would be easy to attribute her attitude to the times: she reflects colonial attitudes. These notions were not, however, always acceptable to the readers in England. In October 1877 the *Westminster and Foreign Quarterly Review* expressed dismay at her flippant descriptions of blacks as mischief-making and stupid "monkeys." Her political and social naiveté is particularly galling in view of her wide travels and her position as the wife of a government official: "it is not any one's business to laugh at people suffering under the injustice of English officials," the review concluded.

Unfortunately Barker's racist descriptions so permeate her text that the detail with which the landscape and domestic scene are related loses its effect. Her desires to envision a picturesque colony, both for herself and for her reader, distort her perspective. Anxious to see and represent a Kaffir village, for instance, she seeks "a really respectable kraal . . . [with] very good character." It is interesting to note, however, that Barker does try to learn some of the Kaffir language, and while she does not feel any solidarity with the women of the country, she does emphasize the beastliness with which the women are usually treated by their male relatives.

The letters end with paeans on the promise of the empire – literally, in the rousing rendition of nightfall at a volunteer army camp, "with the words of the most beautiful tune in the world ["God Save the Queen"] ringing straight from each man's heart." Metaphorically at the same time: "On the veldt the lilies are pushing up their green sheaths and white or scarlet cups through the yet hard ground, and the black hillslopes are turning a vivid green. . . . Spring is always lovely everywhere, but nowhere is it lovelier than in fair Natal!"

The next twenty years of Barker's life were spent in travel with Broome as he advanced through the government ranks in colonial administration and in trips back to England for health and family reasons. Broome became colonial secretary in Mauritius in 1877 and then lieutenant governor in 1880. From May 1883 to December 1889 he was governor of Western Australia and then served as governor of Barbados (1890) before assuming the governorship of Trinidad in 1891, a post he held until his death in 1896. As a reward for his services he was knighted on 3 July 1884, and Barker became Lady Broome.

Frontispiece for A Year's Housekeeping in South Africa, *published at the end of Barker's two-year residence in Natal*

With *Letters to Guy* (1885) Barker combines her talents as a children's book writer with her travel writing. The book is an edited collection of the letters she wrote to her thirteen-year-old son, Guy, who had been left at school in England when Broome became governor of Western Australia. The letters cover the first year of the Broomes' six-and-one-half-year residence in Western Australia and were published within a year of the time they had been written. Nineteen letters are included in the collection, and, while they are ostensibly addressed to a young boy, their optimistic descriptions of the quickly developing colony also appeal to an older audience. Their tone throughout is amusing and lighthearted, tempered with an occasional admonition to Guy to pay attention to lessons so that he will grow up a well-educated, loyal Englishman. The letters are a kind of geography lesson, useful for both Guy and the wider audience of the book.

The Broomes traveled extensively – more than a thousand miles – during their first year, and the letters detail the modes and difficulties of travel, usually by a large, horse-driven van over rough or barely existent roads, to visit remote towns and stations. Governor Broome and Barker seem always to

have been met by enthusiastic and independent settlers who were working hard to establish the Australian colony while remaining loyal subjects of Queen Victoria. Barker portrays the colony in idealistic terms: it is, like New Zealand, a better England. Unpleasantries such as the burning of Governor Broome in effigy midway through his term and the question of the place of Aborigines within the new society are glossed over or, more often, not discussed at all.

While Barker was often praised for the excellence of her observations, her views are often clouded by her strong belief in the beneficence of British colonial projects. Her representations of the Australian Aborigines typically reveal her insistence on the savage and uncivilized nature of those people, although Alexandra Hasluck praises Barker's "unsentimentalized and unidealized" portrayals of the natives. Barker's views reinforce the rationalizations that the British confiscation of lands was only proper and fitting for a country with such an abundance of resources for "civilized" man's use. Barker's attitude toward the Aborigines is most clearly shown when she has to decide, in letter 16, "which I shall tell you about first, the natives or the pets."

The natives are described first, but in terms that are echoed in the next letter about the pet birds and dogs: the Aborigines are "tame" when they are helpful to the whites, and they are savages and animal-like when they are not. Barker is uncritical of the treatment the Aborigines receive from the whites; indeed, she sees those who have been imprisoned on Rottnest Island as being fortunate, because they are treated kindly and have the possibility of becoming "civilized." As in all of her travel books, Barker's value as a traveling social historian is limited: she excellently describes the lives and perspective of middle- and upper-middle class British colonialists, and she ignores or stereotypes other social groups.

Letters to Guy ends with a paean to the Western Australians, whose progress was championed and aided by Broome during his governorship. The appeal of the book for its original readers owes as much to the confirmation of the ideals of progress and the possibilities of a better England through the colonies as it does to the charm and delight with which Barker endows all her writings.

Despite many years of what must have been interesting travel after *Letters to Guy* was published, Barker wrote few new tales. Another collection of children's stories, *The White Rat, and Some Other Stories,* appeared in 1880, and *Harry Treverton, His Tramps and Troubles Told by Himself* (1889) is attributed to Barker, although she claims only to have edited the book. Barker was devastated by her husband's unexpected death in 1896, as she had been deeply in love with him. Because he was so much younger, no provisions other than an insurance policy for £5,000 had been made for her financial support, and Barker gave this to her son Guy, so that the young man could remain in the army. The government of Western Australia eventually granted Barker a small annual pension of £150, on which she lived for her remaining years in London.

Barker's remaining periodical publications, essays primarily drawn from her previously published travel books, appeared under her name as Lady Broome. Collected under the title *Colonial Memories,* these appeared originally in the *Cornhill Magazine* between January 1899 and May 1904. Barker had often traveled with her large collections of canaries, parrots, and parakeets, and these short reminiscences of her stays on Mauritius and Trinidad expand on her rapt observations of bird and plant life. The essays sum up her prejudices and opinions, her delights and amusements. Her last years were spent at her home in Eaton Terrace, and she died there on 6 March 1911.

It is a testimony to Barker's style that *Station Life in New Zealand* has remained in print more than one hundred years after its first publication. While the early reviews of her book stressed her light and amusing tone, contemporary reviewers admire her strength and adaptability as a woman traveler. The importance of her writing lies in her perspective as a participant in, rather than as an outside observer of, the scenes and life around her. That she was also a careful writer and judicious editor, as she reveals when she discusses her editing of Lady Annie Brassey's extensive journals in the preface she wrote for *The Last Voyage,* is evident in the readability of all her works. Although her reasons for travel and her experiences set her apart from many of the explorer-adventurer women travelers whose works have recently been revived, Barker has earned a place in women's history for the confidence, authority, and good spirits that gird her faith in the Victorian world.

References:

Dorothy Jones, "Ladies in the Bush: Catharine Traill, Mary Barker and Rachel Henning," *SPAN,* no. 21 (October 1985): 96–120;

Nelson Wattie, "An English Lady in the Untamed Mountains: Lady Barker in New Zealand," in *English Literature of the Dominions: Writings on Australia, Canada and New Zealand,* edited by Konrad Gross and Wolfgang Klooss (Würzburg: Königshausen & Neumann, 1981), pp. 97–108.

Isabella Lucy Bird

(15 October 1831 – 7 October 1904)

Julia M. Gergits
Youngstown State University

BOOKS: *The Englishwoman in America,* anonymous (London: Murray, 1856; New York: Arno, 1859);

The Aspects of Religion in the United States of America, anonymous (London: Sampson, Low, 1859; New York: Arno, 1859);

Notes on Old Edinburgh, signed as I. L. B. (Edinburgh: Edmonston & Douglas, 1869);

The Hawaiian Archipelago: Six Months among the Palm Groves, Coral Reefs, & Volcanoes of the Sandwich Islands (London: Murray, 1875; New York: Putnam, 1882);

A Lady's Life in the Rocky Mountains (London: Murray, 1879; New York: Putnam, 1879);

Unbeaten Tracks in Japan: An Account of Travels in the Interior, Including Visits to the Aborigines of Yezo and the Shrines of Nikkô and Isé (2 volumes, London: Murray, 1880; 1 volume, New York: Putnam, [1880?]); republished as *Unbeaten Tracks in Japan: An Account of Travels on Horseback in the Interior, Including Visits to the Aborigines of Yezo and the Shrines of Nikkô and Isé,* 2 volumes (New York: Putnam, 1881); abridged as *Unbeaten Tracks in Japan* (New York: Dutton, [1916]);

The Golden Chersonese and the Way Thither (London: Murray, 1883; New York: Putnam, 1883);

Journeys in Persia and Kurdistan, Including a Summer in the Upper Karun Region and a Visit to the Nestorian Rayahs, 2 volumes (London: Murray, 1891; New York: Putnam, 1891);

Heathen Claims and Christian Duty (New York: Board of Foreign Missions of the Presbyterian Church, [1893?]); republished as *Heathen Claims and Christian Duty, by Mrs. Bishop. Our Omnipotent Leader, by C. H. Spurgeon* (London: Morgan & Scott, 1894; Boston: Printed for American Board, 1898);

Among the Tibetans (London: Religious Tract Society, 1894; New York & Chicago: Revell, 1894);

Korea and Her Neighbors: A Narrative of Travel, with an Account of the Recent Vicissitudes and Present Position of the Country (New York & Chicago:

Revell, 1897; 2 volumes, London: Murray, 1898); republished as *Korea and Her Neighbours: A Narrative of Travel, with an Account of the Vicissitudes and Position of the Country,* 2 volumes (London: Murray, 1905);

Japan and the Faith of Christendom: With Special Reference to the Work Supported by the Guild of St. Paul, in the Diocese of South Tokyo (London: Townshend, 1898);

The Yangtze Valley and Beyond: An Account of Journeys in China, Chiefly in the Province of Sze Chuan and among the Man-Tze of the Somo Territory (Lon-

29

don: Murray, 1899; New York: Putnam, 1900);

Chinese Pictures (London: Cassell, 1900; New York: Bowman, [1900?]);

A Traveller's Testimony (London: C.M.S., 1905).

OTHER: Susan Ballard, trans., *Fairy Tales from Far Japan,* prefatory note by Bird (London: Religious Tract Society, 1898).

Isabella Lucy Bird was the most famous and influential of the Victorian "lady travelers." Traveling supposedly for her health, she climbed mountains and volcanoes and rode horseback astride, not sidesaddle, over hundreds of miles in the dead of winter in Colorado. In her travels she suffered from frostbite, broken ribs and arms, cholera, and burns from close brushes with volcanoes. She survived near drowning in Malaysia and attacks in China that left her with a concussion at the age of sixty-three. Her most famous travel books grew out of her letters to her beloved sister, Hennie, who stayed in England, patiently collecting Isabella's letters. With Hennie's encouragement Bird revised her letters to produce popular travel books that earned her an instant reputation as one of those spinster travelers who escaped the confines of Victorian society to establish a career. Bird was among the first women invited to join the Royal Geographical Society. Her books were more than entertaining stories of travel and adventure; they provided information of substantial use to the empire as it pushed for new markets and sources of raw materials.

Bird's upbringing produced the combination of energy, seriousness, and courage necessary to a solitary lady traveler. Her father, Edward, a dreamer and idealist, was related to the Wilberforce family, an intellectual and impeccable lineage. As a barrister he traveled to Calcutta with his first wife, where he suffered a devastating loss when she and their only child, a son, died of cholera. Upon returning to England, Edward demonstrated his religious earnestness by becoming a minister and marrying a minister's daughter, Dora Lawson. Isabella Lucy Bird was born on 15 October 1831 in the family home in Boroughbridge Hall, Yorkshire. Her sister, Henrietta, was born soon after the family had moved to Tattenhall in Cheshire.

According to Pat Barr, Bird's family was illustrious without being ostentatious. The women in particular were strong-minded and courageous, holding closely to Christian ideals as they traveled throughout the world as missionaries. Bird's aunts (two Marys) were surprisingly successful in their Christian missions in India and Persia. Bird's mother provided additional examples of strong-mindedness and sacrifice by scrimping from her meager allowance to support Sunday school classes.

Perhaps because of the success of these strong, intelligent, and useful women relatives, the two Bird girls were given a more rigorous education than was usual for Victorian women. Their parents taught them to read early and ambitiously. Barr notes that their mother taught them "literature, history, drawing, French and the Scriptures," and their father took charge of Latin and botany. Both Isabella and Henrietta took responsibility for further educating themselves by creating study programs that they followed throughout their lives. Bird taught herself biology (she eventually took classes in microbiology and became proficient with a microscope), botany, emergency medical treatment, and photography. She became a handy map reader and mapmaker, used scientific instruments to measure altitude and temperature, and taught herself a smattering of a great many languages, although she was not a talented linguist. In addition, she refined the art of bullying men into doing what she required.

Bird's adolescence and early womanhood were difficult and painful, for she suffered from a mysterious spinal problem aggravated by a benign tumor on her spinal cord. Headaches, neuralgia, and back problems — a host of physical miseries — scarred her puberty and young adulthood. Her doctors determined that her head was too large for her frame and advised her to avoid holding it up. In 1849 she gained some relief through surgery to remove the tumor, but she continued to suffer from various problems. Her family thought of her as an invalid, apt to die young. As a well-educated middle-class lady, she was supposed to marry and raise a family, yet both of the sisters avoided marriage, Henrietta never marrying and Isabella only late in life doing so (and then soon becoming widowed).

Bird seems to have rebelled, if only subconsciously, against the traditional path set out for women, even for such adventurous women as her aunts. Her illness made her unfit for marriage or missionary work. Biographers have theorized that many if not all of her problems were psychological, caused by her constricted and hopelessly dependent life. When Victorian doctors had no other solutions to irremediable physical ailments, they often recommended travel because "a change of air" was supposed to be healthy. Not surprising, when they were driven to extremities by the apparent hopelessness of her case, Bird's doctors recommended that she take a sea voyage. Her father agreed to support a trip to Canada and the United States and to allow her to stay until she spent her allowance. She managed to make ninety pounds last nearly a year. Thus began a pattern of travel and writing, for during her travels she wrote detailed journal entries and letters that formed the bases of her books.

Those familiar with Bird's *A Lady's Life in the Rocky Mountains* (1879) will be surprised by *The Englishwoman in America* (1856). Bird's later travel writing is professional and sophisticated: in those books she portrays an accomplished and hard-nosed traveler, impatient of ordinary tourists and determined to escape from Europeans. In *The Englishwoman in America,* however, Bird presents a delicate woman traveler, prone to illness and often unsure what to do next. Although there are glimpses of the dynamic traveler she will become, for the most part this persona is a conventional, well-protected Victorian lady traveling for health and edification.

The narrator makes insensitive and racist remarks, provides inaccurate information, and repeats unemended European stereotypes of Americans. With her preconceptions of Native Americans crafted by nineteenth-century fiction, she looks in vain for representatives of what James Fenimore Cooper had depicted as the "noble savage" of *The Last of the Mohicans* (1826) and laments that the "primitive" races she sees will inevitably be eradicated as progress churns on. "The memory of *Uncas* and *Magua* rose before me," she writes, "and I sighed over the degeneracy of the race. These people are mendicant and loquacious." Of African Americans, she remarks that a small baby whom she has held "was so awfully ugly, so much like a black ape, and so little like the young of the human species, that I was obliged to avert my eyes from it, lest in a sudden fit of foolish prejudice and disgust I should let it fall." Luckily for the history of travel literature, Bird learned from her adventures.

The Englishwoman in America seems to be based on her journals, rather than on letters to her sister, Henrietta. Like so many Victorians, Bird dedicated substantial time to documenting each day's events, complete with historical, geographical, and political information as well as personal anecdotes. The book is in many ways predictable, following in the literary footsteps of Frances Trollope (*Domestic Manners of the Americans,* 1832) and Charles Dickens (*American Notes for General Circulation,* 1842). Relying on personal experience and loosely gathered facts, she judges the merits and demerits of Americans, much as Trollope and Dickens did; however, in her

Henrietta Amelia Bird, the sister to whom Isabella Bird directed the letters that became the bases for her early travel books

preface she notes that although she had been prepared to scoff at Americans (by whom she means residents of both Canada and the United States), she has learned to appreciate them: "I went to the States with that amount of prejudice which seems the birthright of every English person," she admits, "but I found that, under the knowledge of the American which can be attained by a traveller mixing in society in every grade, these prejudices gradually melted away."

In *The Englishwoman in America* Bird describes her mode of travel, adventures with "natives" (fellow travelers, usually), and views of several cities in early stages of rampant growth — Chicago, Detroit, Toronto, and Hamilton, for example — as she crosses the prairies of both Canada and the United States. She is more precise than usual about when (1854) and where (Liverpool) she has departed from England; in her later books she omits dates that might particularize her narrative. She travels by paddle steamer — the *Canada,* part of the burgeoning Cunard line — and arrives in Halifax after only minor misadventures caused by a drunken roommate "who combined in herself the disagreeable qualities of both nations."

It is difficult to track Bird's route through Canada and the United States because, after her clear beginning in Halifax, she backtracked and crisscrossed her earlier routes, changing companions and making new friends as she went. Hers was anything but a linear journey, and the reader gets an impression of her wandering with no apparent destination. Because she employed so many methods of transport, the reader also learns as much about nineteenth-century travel as about Canada or the United States. For example, stagecoaches, she explains, are uncomfortable and inimicable to companionship, because the occupants fight for position and tire of one another's company after twelve hours of jostling and rocking over "corduroy" roads — rough paths covered by downed logs that prevent the stage from sinking into a mud morass but create a washboard ride.

Traveling by steamer across the Great Lakes was not much better, for several times her ship was hit by vicious storms on Lake Ontario or Lake Erie. On one crossing to Hamilton, Canada, Bird recounts storms so severe that waves throw the steamer on its side, put out its engine fires, and swamp the lower decks. In the wet dark of her cabin she contemplates death, considering the irony of drowning when she had expected to die of lingering illness. After surviving the trip, she promises not to travel "those fearful lakes" again.

Train travel, particularly in the United States, was the best of all, for passengers could purchase a series of tickets that enabled them to change trains without troubling about their luggage or disembarking to purchase more tickets. Bird remarks that her ticket from the east to Chicago is about three feet long, and at appropriate stops the conductor simply pulls off a piece of her ticket, leaving her with the remainder. English train travelers at the time had to look after their own luggage, and this caused quite a fray when trains stopped and passengers fought for their bags buried in mountains of boxes, trunks, and other bags. Yet Bird praises the friendliness and thoughtfulness of railroad employees and fellow passengers: "We must be well aware that in many parts of England it would be difficult for a lady to travel unattended in a second-class, impossible in a third-class carriage; yet I travelled several thousand miles in America, frequently alone[,] . . . and never met with anything approaching to incivility. . . ."

Bird had many adventures while in Canada and the United States. She saw Niagara Falls, met the leading citizens of both nations, studied human nature, and discovered numerous examples of human foibles, nobility, and generosity. She stayed on a newly cleared farm in the Canadian bush, and just before leaving for New York she contracted cholera. As she writes, her tone softens and she moderates many of the harsh, thoughtless statements made earlier in the book. She decides, for example, that the lower classes in both countries are generous and harmless, even if they are Catholic and Irish or French.

Upon returning home she revised her notes and produced a manuscript given to John Murray, a prestigious and respectable publisher of the most noted travel writers, for his consideration. It became the first of her books published by Murray, who was to remain the publisher of her major works. Published anonymously, this book gave Bird an audience and a vocation that she would cling to, even when her life was full of tragedy and despair. She became a regular contributor to such periodicals as *Good Words, The Leisure Hours,* and *The Family Treasury,* and despite her lifelong disclaimers of authorial aspirations, she became a professional writer.

After a second whirlwind trip to the United States, she wrote *The Aspects of Religion in the United States of America* (1859), a forgettable book only distantly related to travel literature. Her preface recommends the book to those interested in the "truth" about the mishmash of religions in the United States. Writing as a strong Evangelical, intolerant of Catholicism and appalled by anything that seems even slightly irreligious, she praises the United States for its religious revival: "The influence of the Holy Spirit has been felt during the past eighteen months in the United States to an extent unprecedented in any other country or period." While extolling the New England states, she attacks the South for the hypocrisy of its religiosity while it maintains slavery, and she laments the unfortunate incursions of Catholicism in the "west" — Illinois, Wisconsin, and Indiana. At least in part she traveled to the United States to fulfill her father's purposes, collecting information that reaffirms values he had embraced in his own work.

Bird's father died in 1860, throwing her family onto their own resources with a modest annuity for support. To save money the family moved to Castle Terrace, Edinburgh. At twenty-nine years old Bird was an overly serious and scholarly old maid, remembered by acquaintances as bucktoothed, stout, sickly, and short (four feet, eleven inches tall). In Edinburgh she again became an invalid, but she befriended Ella Blackie, wife of John Blackie, professor of Greek at the university in Edinburgh. Despite her recurring illness, she joined the intellectual and philanthropical community, one that encouraged her bluestocking propensities. Until 1866, when their mother died, both sisters lived with and for her. In 1869 Bird published *Notes on Old Edinburgh*, a dramatic and powerful description of slum conditions. Although she lived an active, useful life, Bird gradually tired of proper society, developing an aversion for doorbells, morning visits, late-night suppers, and corsets. Her illnesses recurred, and her doctors again recommended travel.

In 1869 Bird traveled throughout Europe, which afforded her no relief; in 1872, to Australia, which she thoroughly hated; and finally, miraculously, to Hawaii, then known as the Sandwich Islands, which she learned to love. From this unplanned visit to the islands came Bird's first letter-based travel book, *The Hawaiian Archipelago: Six Months among the Palm Groves, Coral Reefs, & Volcanoes of the Sandwich Islands,* published in 1875, after her return to England. Far more successful than her earlier ventures, this book made her famous: according to Barr, the *Spectator* called it "remarkable, fascinating and beautifully written." While on these islands, Bird discovered her identity as a traveler who eschewed social conventions in the interest of travel. It became clear that Bird was compelled to travel in order to live happily, perhaps to live at all.

Paradoxically Bird's spirits were restored in part by a rousing good hurricane that nearly sunk the rickety ship on which she was traveling, steaming away from New Zealand and bound for California. "In the deck-house," she wrote of this reinvigorating experience, "the strainings, sunderings, and groanings were hardly audible, or rather were overpowered by a sound which, in thirteen months' experience of the sea in all weather, I have never heard, and hope never to hear again, unless in a staunch ship, one loud, awful, undying shriek, mingled with a prolonged, relentless hiss." By this time Bird had become a traveler who thrives on such adventure and discomfort as hurricanes, bugs in the flour, mice in her bed, and water flowing in her windows. Anything that forces people to behave naturally rather than "properly" inspired her. She had agreed to stop in the Sandwich Islands with a Mrs. Dexter, her nominal companion, whose son was desperately ill. (Mrs. Dexter in fact disappears quickly from the narrative, except for occasional and brief references.) The Dexters provide merely a pretext for remaining in Hawaii as long as possible: Bird writes that she was "travelling for health," and "the benefit which I derived from the climate tempted me to remain for nearly seven months." In fact, she was nearly tempted to stay forever.

She was immediately smitten with the native Hawaiians: "Such rich brown men and women they were, with wavy, shining black hair, large brown, lustrous eyes, and rows of perfect teeth like ivory. Everyone was smiling." Hawaiians preserved their ebullient and sunny lives, compromising with Western culture yet mocking it. For instance, they laughed heartily at the ridiculous dress of European women; Bird writes that she "was conscious that we foreign women with our stout staffs and grotesque dress looked like caricatures, and the natives, who have a keen sense of the ludicrous, did not conceal that they thought so." Unfortunately the natives were undermined by European diseases and debilitated by leprosy, and Bird predicts that native Hawaiians would become extinct, their culture disappear, and Hawaii pass to the invaders.

Two other important experiences also changed Bird. First, she saw that everyone, even the natives, rode horses for pleasure and business. Everyone, even women, rode astride and not sidesaddle. Bird had ridden when she was a small girl, accompanying her father on his rides, but her back problems had made riding impossible because the awkward sidesaddle had intolerably twisted her spine. Now encouraged by the missionary wives, she grew determined to adapt to the circumstances and ride astride the horse – as a man would: "It was only my strong desire to see the volcano which made me consent to a mode of riding against which I have so strong a prejudice," she wrote in anticipation of one adventure, "but the result of the experiment is that I shall visit Kilauea thus or not at all." Victorians felt riding astride to be improper for women on horseback, who were supposed to wear "suitable" riding garments – full-length gowns made of sturdier fabric and cut more fully in the skirts. Because riding astride was possible only when one wore pants or pantaloons, Bird's determination to do so was also a decision to wear men's clothing, albeit in a much-modified form.

She borrowed the riding outfit of a missionary's wife but later designed her own costume – one having loosely fitting pantaloons with ruffles that covered her boots and an overskirt that she could modestly pull over her legs when white men, the only ones who seemed surprised by her method of riding, approached her. Once while riding in Hawaii she overtook a group of men who looked surprised: "When I saw the politely veiled stare of the white men it occurred to me that probably it was the first time that they had seen a white woman riding cavalier fashion!" Yet once she had made this decision, she thoroughly enjoyed riding throughout the islands and over extremely rough and remote ter-

Isabella Bird with Murphy O'Rourke and Mirza Yusuf at Erzurum, now in Turkish Armenia

rain, sometimes in the company of only one or two native guides. As she gained freedom from social restraints, Bird's back problems miraculously disappeared.

A second important influence on Bird was that of Miss Karpe, an eccentric woman traveler who apparently became Bird's prototype of the ideal traveler. Miss Karpe, an American, invited Bird to accompany her to Hilo Bay to visit volcanoes, and her fortitude and energy surprised Bird: "Miss K.," writes Bird in closing her description of their party of sightseers, seems "the typical American travelling lady, who is encountered everywhere from the Andes to the Pyramids, tireless, with indomitable energy, Spartan endurance, and a genius for attaining everything, and myself, a limp, ragged, shoeless wretch, complete the group. . . ." Miss Karpe was a type much castigated and berated by popular journals and by "serious" travelers as a nuisance: the spinster lady determined to see the world and understand it for herself. Bird's narrative comically contrasts her weakness with Miss Karpe's foresight and energy; however, Bird soon outmatched even Miss Karpe's energy and courage.

Her success at horseback riding and viewing volcanoes made her more joyful, almost giddy. She rode daily, sought new adventures, and wrote to Hennie, "I even wish that you could see me in my Rob Roy riding dress, with leather belt and pouch, a *lei* of orange seeds of the pandamus round my throat, jingling Mexican spurs, blue saddle blanket, and Rob Roy blanket strapped on behind the saddle!" She became disdainful of those who rode less expertly than she did, forgetting that on her first ride up the volcano she had nearly fallen from her horse because of her inexperience. She discusses finer points of horseflesh and Mexican saddles, and she notes that she has surpassed Miss Karpe, who was not a good horsewoman: "I feel able now to ride anywhere and any distance . . . , while Miss Karpe, who began by being much stronger than I was, has never recovered from the volcano rise, and seems quite ill."

With a native guide named Deborah, Bird explored parts of Hawaii known only to natives. She rode up and down perilous gulches, crossed high-running rivers with only a rope to pull her across, and slept in native grass huts. She luxuriated in knowing she was the only white woman within miles, the first time she acknowledged the thrill of escaping European influence. At first afraid, she soon discarded her fears and enjoyed freedom from European strictures of behavior, clothing, and language. She jokes in recounting how five native cats had jumped on her during one night: "Had there been a sixth I think I could not have borne the infliction quietly."

On her travels around Hawaii she stayed with missionaries, investigated leprosy, and climbed Mauna Loa, which singed her eyebrows. The soft air, easy people, and undemanding culture allowed Bird to discover her courage, boldness, and tenacity. According to Barr, she even received a proposal of marriage from a Mr. Wilson, who liked this easygoing, no-nonsense Englishwoman – but she declined. Most important, she recovered a ruddy health that she had never enjoyed in civilization. Whenever she narrates her arrival in a city, Bird recounts her ailments; whenever she is in the wilderness or among natives, she focuses on her adventures. She may well have been ill in the wilderness, but her health does not absorb her attention.

Her letters to Hennie had been so fervent that her sister offered to join Bird in Hawaii. Hennie's letter shook Bird out of her love affair with Hawaii and propelled her to California, as Bird replied:

> I shall be in the Rocky Mountains before you receive my hastily-written reply to your proposal to come out here for a year, but I will add a few reasons against it. . . . [T]he strongest of all is, that if we were to stay here for a year, we should just sit down "between the sun and moon upon the shore," and forget "our island home," and be content to fall "asleep in a half dream," and "return no more!"

Alluding to Alfred Tennyson's 1832 poem "The Lotos-Eaters," Bird suggested the danger of losing moral fortitude by staying in such an easy environment. Although Bird loved her sister deeply, she did not want to travel with Hennie, who would have prevented Bird from risking her life in the wild adventures that she was beginning to seek. Bird left the Sandwich Islands to sail to California, and from there she traveled inland to Estes Park, Colorado.

Bird's 1873 adventures in the Rocky Mountains of Colorado cemented her growing reputation as a lady adventurer and travel writer. Except for a few reviewers who took exception to Bird's "manly" bloomers, her book was well received. (Bird was so incensed at one negative review that she tried to convince John Murray to challenge the writer to a fight.) In *A Lady's Life in the Rocky Mountains,* revised from letters and published after her return to England, Bird chronicles her adventures in

Estes Park, hints at her love for a desperado, and abandons whatever fragments were left of the delicate, sickly English lady traveler. Although many popular Victorian novels, poems, and travel books have faded into oblivion, this book – eccentric, jovial, and perceptive – has remained in print.

Instead of a preparatory introduction to her travels in *A Lady's Life in the Rocky Mountains,* she launches into a description of Lake Tahoe: "I have found a dream of beauty at which one might look all one's life and sigh." The text preserves the immediacy of her letters to Hennie, even though Bird has carefully excised the most personal references. This casual, often clipped narrative may seem disjointed to those unaccustomed to travel literature, but after a short time it is quite comfortable. Readers step into the middle of a discourse instead of being treated as strangers who require background details.

Bird dated her first letter 1 September; it was 1873, and winter was threatening in the high altitudes. She timed her westward travel to avoid the rush of fellow travelers who had discovered the healthy air of the Rocky Mountains. She quickly moved through San Francisco, which she hated, of course, because it was a city. Taking a train through the Sierra Nevada, she observed magnificent landscapes marred by the inroads of men: skimpy towns, degraded Indians, drunkenness, and greed. Her goal being Colorado, not the coastal region, Bird was grateful for the train because it sped her travel inland. The Civil War had ended and, nearing the close of the Indian wars and westward expansion of the American frontier, Bird was searching for examples of untouched nature, hoping to see the Wild West before it disappeared. Uninterested in pioneer life, she wished to witness the lives of the predecessors of pioneers – those of the trappers, hunters, and discoverers who were opening the wilderness for settlers. She observed with regret that "progress" was civilizing the landscape, eradicating the very things that made it precious.

Bird traveled alone and with a few letters of introduction to powerful people; she was already legendary, however. Throughout her travels she wrote for magazines and journals, making her adventures famous even before they appeared in book form. *A Lady's Life in the Rocky Mountains,* for instance, was first published in parts in such periodicals as *Out West* and *Leisure Hour.* Local newspapers reported her plans to ride through much of Colorado, and people began to expect the most amazing feats of horsemanship and exertion from her. She wrote that "the newspapers, with their intolerable personality, have made me and my riding exploits so notorious, that travellers speak courteously to me when they meet me on the prairie, doubtless wishing to see what sort of monster I am!" Her identity as a lady traveler had crystallized.

Stopping in Truckee, high in the California Sierras, she rode out to see Lake Tahoe and contemplate the paradox of the calm beauty of the lake and the horrors of murder and cannibalism that the saga of the Donner party had brought to the area. The lake aroused in her a Romantic passion for the landscape: "Before long," she wrote, "a carnival of colour began which I can only describe as delirious, intoxicating, a hardly bearable joy, a tender anguish, an indescribable yearning, an unearthly music, rich in love and worship."

A Lady's Life in the Rocky Mountains, unlike her previous travel writing, relates more personal anecdotes and fewer generic pieces of information. For instance, while staying in Cheyenne she helped a consumptive man who had a sick wife and baby; in Greeley she helped a distraught, shorthanded landlady. Bird fitted in wherever she was, lending a hand at whatever work might be necessary. She enjoyed being mistaken for a serving or washing woman; an onlooker sympathized with her because she was too small for such hard work. She wrote that she had been tempted to accept an offer of six dollars per week to clean, cook, and bake, but she had declined because she disliked making bread.

Her first experience of the Colorado wilderness was during her stay with the Chalmerses in the foothills north of Denver. The incompetence of a driver on her journey to Estes Park necessitated her staying with this dirty, shiftless family. Bird demonstrated her resourcefulness and burgeoning ability to rough it when she agreed to pay five dollars a week to stay in a partially roofed, three-walled room around which animals sported: "One night a beast (fox or skunk) rushed in at the open end of the cabin, and fled through the window, almost brushing my face, and on another the head and three or four inches of the body of a snake were protruded through a chink of the floor close to me, to my extreme disgust." In this rough camp she lost track of days and resorted to helping the family cook and clean. Despite the natural beauty surrounding her, Bird was struck with the hard, narrow life of pioneers.

Of Chalmers, the head of the house, she says, "He is slightly intelligent, very opinionated, and wishes to be thought well-informed, which he is not." The wife is "lean, clean, toothless, and speaks . . . in a piping, discontented voice, which seems to convey a

personal reproach." The grown children are "piggish" and totally uneducated. This family wore itself out, working from dawn to dusk yet making no headway because they were incapable of planning carefully or completing a single task. The result was day-in, day-out drudgery. Although the Chalmerses tried to help her reach Estes Park, they failed because the senior Chalmers was incompetent. Bird became impatient with the family and left, subsequently staying briefly with a well-educated English couple who were eking out a living on the prairie.

Despite mishaps and misdirections she eventually reached her goal and found it to be everything she had hoped in her trip from civilization (San Francisco) backward to an almost completely primitive existence in Estes Park. Although Griffith Evans, her landlord, ran a rugged resort for hunters and invalids, it was the end of the season, and few tourists remained. She lorded it in her own log cabin, complete with skunk nest and a view of the lake. She enjoyed genial hospitality and excellent meals: "There has been fresh meat each day since I came, delicious bread baked daily, excellent potatoes, tea and coffee, and an abundant supply of milk like cream. I have a clean hay bed with six blankets, and there are neither bugs nor fleas." Through the last days of fall in the valley she helped the ranch hands round up cattle, explored mountain vistas, and made herself an integral part of the social community with her excellent puddings, humor, and willingness to pitch in.

During her Estes Park stay Bird's letters recount her interest in an outlaw, Jim Nugent. Her affection for the gun-toting, Indian-killing alcoholic — Mountain Jim — is expressed in *A Lady's Life* as concern for a fellow man, but circumstances indicate that she cared for him romantically. She describes Nugent as a striking man, simultaneously attractive and repulsive:

> His face was remarkable. He is a man about forty-five [nearly Bird's age], and must have been strikingly handsome. He has large grey-blue eyes, deeply set, with well-marked eyebrows, a handsome aquiline nose, and a very handsome mouth. His face was smooth-shaven except for a dense moustache. . . . Tawny hair, in thin uncared-for curls, fell from under his hunter's cap and over his collar. One eye was entirely gone, and the loss made one side of the face repulsive, while the other might have been modelled in marble. "Desperado" was written in large letters all over him.

Bird identified with this drunken, lost man, if only subconsciously, as she reveals in an anecdote immediately after this description of him: she tells

Bird (right) outside her tent in Bakhtiari territory, western Iran

readers that her landlord mistook her for Nugent "dressed up as a woman!" She trusted him with her life and honor. In spite of protests from two men who disapproved having a woman accompanying them to Long's Peak, she camped out with an entirely male group and climbed the 14,700 feet to the top with his help. Her letters suggest that Nugent asked her to marry him, and although she admitted that she was tempted, she declined because he was so unstable.

Departing from Estes Park, Bird undertook a winter ride of several hundred miles on a horse (perhaps a namesake) called "Birdie." On this strong, calm horse she rode to Denver and south to Colorado Springs to see Pikes Peak. On 28 October she wrote that she had been too tired to write, because she had ridden all day and "The observing faculties are developed, and the reflective lie dormant." All along the way she stayed with local ranchers and in occasional hotels, and she asked for directions and bought food as she went. Nearly al-

ways alone and unprotected, she somehow navigated across miles of snow-covered plains and mountain terrain with only minor mishaps. Even when Comanche Bill, a locally well-known outlaw, approached her on the lonely prairie, she behaved calmly and politely. Preferring to trust her fellow man's instinctive kindness to a lady, she declined to carry a gun:

> I have seen a great deal of the roughest class of men both on sea and land during the last two years, and the more important I think the "mission" of every quiet, refined, self-respecting woman – the more mistaken I think those who would forfeit it by noisy self-assertion, masculinity, or fastness. In all this wild West the influence of woman is second only in its benefits to the influence of religion, and where the last unhappily does not exist the first continually exerts its restraining power.

It became one of her principles that a true lady could travel anywhere, even without escort, because her honesty and modesty would call out the latent gentleman in the most hardened ruffian.

When Bird returned to Denver, she discovered that she had no money. Evans essentially shipwrecked Bird when he used a $100 bill that she entrusted to him: the banks failed, and he could not get her money back nor cash a draft on a British bank. Rather than lament the irremediable, she forced him to board her through much of the winter. She went back to Estes Park to stay in her frozen cabin, where with two hunters and Nugent she worked as hard as any man cleaning, cooking, riding, and tending animals. They shared in the housework, none of them defining any job as "woman's" or "man's" work.

In early December she finally left Estes Park, with Nugent accompanying her as far as Saint Louis, Colorado. Her last words in the book are understated: "A drive of several hours over the plains brought us to Greeley, and a few hours later, in the far blue distance, the Rocky Mountains, and all that they enclose, went down below the prairie sea." Unfortunately, soon after she left Colorado Evans killed Nugent, who he claimed had threatened one of his guests.

Upon returning to Edinburgh Bird resumed her life as a renowned middle-class lady, a life of corsets, morning visits, and late-night suppers. She completed *The Hawaiian Archipelago* for its 1875 publication and enjoyed her increasing fame. The scientific community began to take her work seriously; according to Barr, *Nature,* the respected scientific journal, noticed her book and praised the "accuracy and breadth of her botanical knowledge." To enhance her scientific knowledge and almost certainly to avoid the ennui of behaving as a proper lady, Bird took histology lessons. However, she could not tolerate Victorian society, and her mysterious symptoms recurred. She left for Japan in 1878.

In *Unbeaten Tracks in Japan: An Account of Travels in the Interior, Including Visits to the Aborigines of Yezo and the Shrines of Nikkô and Isé* (1880) Bird challenges European stereotypes of Japan: Victorians thought of the Japanese as an extremely energetic people, likely to adapt the Western idea of progress far sooner than other Asian countries, for they believed the Japanese to be malleable and derivative, eager to abandon their traditions in exchange for technological progress and access to worldwide markets. For this trip Bird avoided European outposts and the "beaten path," preferring to travel through remote rural areas. She hoped to test the truth of European stereotypes and assumptions, because she

suspected that Westerners were blinded by prejudice and avarice.

This book is better written than her earlier ones; Bird was a more mature traveler and writer, with keen-sighted observations. Her first view of Japan was felicitous:

> The air and water were alike motionless, the mist was still and pale, grey clouds lay restfully on a bluish sky, the reflections of the white sails of the fishing-boats scarcely quivered; it was all so pale, wan, and ghostly, that the turbulence of crumpled foam which we left behind us, and our noisy, throbbing progress, seemed a boisterous intrusion upon sleeping Asia.

Europeans disturb the quiet beauty with their "throbbing progress" – in this case, a steamship – and the disturbance signifies the impact of westerners on a delicately organized world, one mistakenly dubbed "sleeping Asia." Yet Bird's first assessment of the Japanese people was not complimentary. In fact, she presents them as hardworking but miniature people: "The first thing that impressed me on landing was that there were no loafers, and that all the small, ugly, kindly-looking, shriveled, bandy-legged, round-shouldered, concave-chested, poor-looking beings in the street had some affairs of their own to mind."

Overwhelmed by the noise of Tokyo and the pressure of European society, she laments, "I long to get away into real Japan." She was undeterred by her friends' warnings that a European woman could not travel alone through the backcountry, that there were no hotels or food, and that fleas infested every inn. Her European friends lived in isolated communities that were, except for some of the flora, indistinguishable from England; Europeans could not imagine traveling without the extensive support granted them by their contrived, protected neighborhoods.

Traveling to Yokohama to stay with missionaries and doctors, she searched for a guide and translator who could take her, otherwise unaccompanied, through Japan. She had trouble finding a servant-translator because of her sex. Her second applicant looked promising, but he "knew really only a few words of English, and his horror at finding that there was 'no master' and that there would be no woman-servant, was so great, that I hardly knew whether he rejected me or I him." Finally she hired Ito, seventeen years old. Her friend, Mr. W., warned her that Ito was probably dishonest and that Europeans, "naturally" honest, had difficult times handling Asian servants. This prospect disturbed Bird, who wrote that she had "never been able to manage anyone in my life, and shall surely have no control over this clever, cunning Japanese youth, who on most points will be able to deceive me as he pleases." After a few squalls in which she gained an upper hand by a combination of patience, sternness, and a few blazes of bad temper, Bird managed Ito handily. Never again did she worry about bad servants, although she suffered occasionally from their dishonesty.

She reduced her traveling gear to the barest necessities. Even by twentieth-century camping standards she packed impressively, carrying only one hundred and ten pounds of equipment:

> My two painted wicker baskets lined with paper and with waterproof covers are convenient for the two sides of the pack horse. I have a folding chair – for in a Japanese house there is nothing but the floor to sit upon, and not even a solid wall to lean against – an air pillow of Karuma travelling, an india-rubber bath, sheets, a blanket, and last, and more important than all else, a canvas stretcher on light poles, which can be put together in two minutes; and being 2 1/2 feet high is supposed to be secure from fleas. The "Food Question" has been solved by a modified rejection of all advice!

She decided to "live off the land" and to purchase what she needed as she went through small villages rather than to pack tinned meats, teas, and spices.

After her friends' dire warnings Bird was understandably nervous once she was alone in Japan. Previously she had traveled where she knew the language and culture, where she had friends and acquaintances. Even when galloping along with only a native guide in Hawaii, she had been a short distance from Europeans, who in fact had controlled nearly all the land in which she had lost herself. In Japan, however, she set off into a culture about which she knew little, with a guide she mistrusted, and with minimal equippage to guarantee comfort.

Despite her misgivings she traveled with official support and within a country familiar with travelers, albeit usually Asian businessmen or officials. She was granted freedom to travel by mysterious papers with many gold seals and red ribbons, papers which had to be presented whenever they were demanded in each town. Her journey was arranged through the Transport Agency, and for the most part she needed only to pay in order to receive the best food in the region (usually not all that good, to judge from her complaints) and whatever horses or conveyances were available. Within a short time Bird became so comfortable that she proclaimed, "I no longer care to meet Europeans – indeed I should go far out of my way to avoid them. I have become quite used to Japanese life. . . ."

She traveled to Nikkô and found it to be paradise. Her accommodations were Japanese, but the owners were accustomed to European guests. In fact, her rooms were so gorgeous that she worried about damaging something: "I almost wish that the rooms were a little less exquisite, for I am in constant dread of spilling the ink, indenting the mats, or tearing the paper windows." She dwelt on how the Japanese made a room beautiful by using the simplest materials: paper and simple wood frames made walls; a single spray of cherry blossoms adorned a table; woven mats provided texture.

Bird was surprised by how dearly Japanese men loved their children: "It is most amusing about six every morning to see twelve or fourteen men sitting on a low wall, each with a child under two years in his arms, fondling and playing with it, and showing off its physique and intelligence." Her tone suggests that she found this interest men would take in their offspring to be peculiar. In Bird's eyes these men were somehow generally less manly than Europeans, despite their hard work and patience.

The Japanese returned the favor by continually mistaking Bird for a man. By this time she was portly, homely, and forty-seven years old. She had adopted an outfit even more idiosyncratic than her controversial Hawaiian riding one had been, apparel she deemed appropriate for Japanese travel: riding bloomers and an overskirt, green glasses, Japanese straw hat and sandals, and a Japanese straw raincoat. Apparently she presented a frightening appearance, as girls ran for shelter when they saw her approaching: "I wear a hat," she wrote, "which is a thing only worn by women in the fields as a protection from the sun and rain, my eyebrows are unshaven, and my teeth are unblackened, so these girls supposed me to be a foreign man." She acknowledged that Europeans were not necessarily the most lovely of people, at least not to other cultures. Of course, within her own culture women were just as strongly marked as Japanese peasants were: with corsets, long dresses, and uncomfortable shoes.

Bird also dressed as a Japanese woman to gain entry to a Shinto shrine: "I went in a Japanese woman's dress, borrowed at the tea-house, with a blue hood over my head, and thus escaped all notice, but I found the restraint of the scanty 'tied forward' *kimono* very tiresome." She experimented with clothing to an extent impossible in England, particularly for a scholarly, middle-aged lady.

Bird (left) preparing to take photographs at Swatow, China

As was customary with Bird, she stopped traveling, if at all possible, on Sundays. Her health seemed worse than it had been in Colorado; her narrative mentions her bad back, sick headaches, and general weakness; however, her schedule remained ambitious. While resting in Kurumatoge on 30 June, she summarized her week's journey, capturing the fleeting, chaotic impressions of a week of whirlwind travel:

> After the hard travelling of six days the rest of Sunday in a quiet place at a high elevation is truly delightful! Mountains and passes, valleys and rice swamps, forests and rice swamps, villages and rice swamps; poverty, industry, dirt, ruinous temples, prostrate Buddhas, strings of straw-shod pack-horses; long, grey, featureless streets, and quiet, staring crowds, are all jumbled up fantastically in my memory.

She finds Japan to be far more impoverished than she has expected, and she apologizes for criticizing Japanese peasantry. The crowds were curious but not offensively or dangerously so, yet the "persons, clothing, and houses are alive with vermin, and if the word 'squalor' can be applied to independent and industrious people, they were squalid." She found it odd that such a hardworking, determined people could be satisfied in living with what she can designate only as filth.

Bird suffered at least three falls from her horse and one near drowning from floods, and her mishaps were grist for subtle, self-deprecating humor, as when her horse bucked as she rode into a town: "As I rode through on my temporary biped the people rushed out from the baths to see me, men and women alike without a particle of clothing." Another time she was torn from her horse by a trailing vine: "I was little the worse for the fall, but on borrowing a looking-glass I see not only scratches and abrasions all over my face, but a livid mark round my throat as if I had been hung!"

Bird made a special trip to visit the aboriginal Ainu, a group of Caucasians who lived on the Japanese islands before the Asians. She liked them and found them beautiful but doomed (she always found primitive people to be doomed), with a "lofty, sad, far-off, gentle, intellectual look. . . ." They allowed her to share their huts and food; they eventually told her a little about their beliefs, but only after they extracted a promise from her that she would not report anything she learned to the Japanese government. She lamented that the Ainu had no religion, at least none in her terms, and she predicted their demise as civilization encroached: "They are . . . as completely irreclaimable as the wildest of nomad tribes, and contact with civilization, where it exists, only debases them." Her Japanese book, apparently like her actual trip to Japan, ends quickly after the section on the Ainu.

On her way home from Japan in late December 1878 Bird stopped for a five-week tour of Malaysia, a peninsula little known to the British. The experience engendered her next book, *The Golden Cheronese and the Way Thither* (1883), which records her brief love affair with the Malaysian wilderness. At age forty-seven she wrote of herself as a hardened, aged, expert traveler — impatient with fragile young ladies, annoyed by cities, and seduced by untouched jungle and tame monkeys. Unlike her previous books, this one begins with a history lesson because she assumed that her readers knew little or nothing about Malaysia. Her lessons are prejudiced by Western assumptions: she says that Malaysia has "no legitimate claim to an ancient history." Its "real" history began with its discovery by the Portuguese, who, according to Bird, defeated the Moors. She provides an overview of flora and fauna, and her descriptions of Malaysians use the best of nineteenth-century theories of racial evolution, including careful comments on foreheads, lip thickness, and skin tone.

The book again derives from her long letters to Hennie. Bird first traveled through Chinese territory, and her initial experience with the Chinese was infelicitous. Landing first in Victoria (Hong Kong), she found the city a "Babel" of "coloured people." "The Chinese," she wrote, "are a noisy people, their language is inharmonious, and the lower-class male voices at least are harsh and coarse." When she traveled to Canton, she added that the Chinese were intolerant of European attempts to colonize their country and fought particularly hard against missionary efforts. Although she enjoyed Victoria, she wearied of its civility, saying that she was "a savage at heart, and weary for the wilds."

At the recommendation of the British chief justice in Victoria, she decided to travel to Malaysia. Equipped with letters to the governor and colonial secretary of the straits settlements, she set out on the SS *Sindh*. Landing briefly in Cambodia and refusing to take a guide, she went exploring and lost herself in the countryside. Stumbling into a house where she hoped to get some water and relief from the heat, she surprised a large extended family: "Remember that the temperature was 92°," she wrote, "so the women may be excused for having nothing more than petticoats or loose trousers on in the privacy of their home, the children for being in a state of nudity, and the man for being clothed in a loin cloth!" They fled from her "like bats" but soon reappeared; they hospitably provided her with milk and left her alone as she rested from the heat.

Finally she set out for Malaysia aboard the *Rainbow* on 20 January 1879. For company she had no fellow Europeans or traveling companions, except for the Portuguese sailors who manned the ship and one Welshman married to a Malay woman. Upon arrival at Malacca she sat for three hours, surrounded "by a crowd of Chinamen and Malays without any possibility of being understood by any of them" and wondering just what to do if the governor had not received notice of her arrival. Luckily help arrived, and she was soon comfortably housed.

Under the protection of the lieutenant governor of Malacca she slept in the old Stadthaus, the tattered and empty former residence of the Dutch governor. It seemed haunted — its forty empty rooms, grand reception hall, and ballroom all decorated with "great arched corridors, and all manner of queer staircases and corners." Of particular interest was the bathing room, essential in the tropics:

> Like most European houses in the Peninsula, it has a staircase which leads from the bedroom to a somewhat grim, brick-floored room below, containing a large high tub, or bath, of Shanghai pottery, in which you must by no means bathe, as it is found by experience that to take the capacious dipper and pour water upon yourself from a height, gives a far more refreshing shock than immersion when the water is at 80° and the air at 83°.

Relief from heat, not cleanliness, seemed to be the primary function of these bathrooms. Although Bird traveled with a rubber bathtub, she does not describe what she did with — or in — it. This description of a cleaning/cooling bath and its proper use is rare.

Though plagued by mosquitoes, Bird enjoyed the tropics, which she found fascinating despite their "indefiniteness, dreaminess, featurelessness, indolence, and silence." In addition to discussing the minerals, rare stones, and colonizers (including Americans and Chinese) of the region, Bird describes the Malaysians who – with their fierce Moslem faith, sequestering of women, and concepts of honor – suggested to her a medieval society untouched by modern nineteenth-century encroachments.

With the help of Captain Shaw she moved into the interior to Sungei Ujong, the only catch being that she had to bring his two daughters along. Despite warnings about "tigers, crocodiles, rogue elephants, and savages," Bird was excited at the prospect of entering the native state. Traveling in the *Moosmee*, a "small, unseaworthy, untrustworthy, unrigged steam-launch," Bird enjoyed the jungle, with its "cobra, python, . . . boa-constrictor, the viper, . . . large and small apes and monkeys, flying foxes, iguanas, lizards, peacocks, [and] frogs." As unseasoned travelers, Shaw's daughters presented problems for Bird. When one girl developed sunstroke, Bird grumbled, "Heretofore I have always travelled 'without encumbrance.' Is it treasonable to feel at this moment that these fair girls are one?" They arrived at the residency with the help of Capt. P. J. Murray, the British resident and a world traveler who trusted the natives and dealt with them honestly. He enabled her to visit the local sites, including a sanitarium and the homes of dignitaries such as Datu Bandar, the rajah second in rank to the reigning prince. She approved of their cool, tasteful homes. Of the rajah's home she wrote, "[O]ne could not say that it reminded one of anything except of the flecked and coloured light which streams through dark, old, stained glass."

Next she traveled to Selangor, a place that, she wrote to Hennie, is not indexed in the encyclopedia. Finally, yearning for solitude and wilderness, she traveled to Perak. This move into the jungle gave Bird an opportunity for a rare moment of political reflection. Unlike her intolerant, even ignorant, opinions expressed in *The Englishwoman in America*, her comments are seasoned and reasonable:

> Public opinion never reaches these equatorial jungles; we are grossly ignorant of their inhabitants and their rights, of the manner in which our interference originated, and how it has been exercised; and unless some fresh disturbance and another "little war" should concentrate our attention for a moment on these distant States, we are likely to remain so, to their great detriment, and not a little, in one aspect of the case at least, to our own.

Western ignorance of the complex political and economic structures, age-old customs, and deeply felt religious beliefs of foreign cultures hurt not only those smaller, less powerful countries, but also the powerful and seemingly invincible Europeans. Bird suggests the value of a reciprocal relationship that she had earlier discounted, particularly when it concerned "primitive" peoples.

On 16 February, having reached her Eden by an uncomfortable ride on an elephant, Bird secured solitude deep in the jungle. Luxuriously tended by a butler and other Malay servants, she reveled in having no other Europeans at hand. She made friends with her roommates, two monkeys and a retriever. Dinner in their company was peaceful and entertaining: "My 'next of kin' were so reasonably silent; they required no conversational efforts; they were most interesting companions. 'Silence is golden', I felt; shall I ever enjoy a dinner party so much again?" Allowed to wander freely, Bird regretted leaving Perak and once again found civilization trying; she reflected, upon her return, that she never felt well "except in the quiet and freedom of the wilds."

Barr writes that Bird's homeward journey from Malaysia was not pleasant. She contracted a fever in Cairo and then developed pleurodynia, "rheumatism of the chest muscles." By her May 1879 arrival at her sister's beloved home, the Tobermory cottage, Bird was quite ill and frail. John Bishop, a longtime friend and physician, helped Hennie to nurse Bird back to health. (Apparently he had proposed to Bird in 1877, but she had refused because she did not think marriage suitable for her.) Bird filled her time preparing books for publication, studying, and giving lectures. She settled into her Victorian-lady routine, grumbling and lapsing into ill health but generally enjoying peace and quiet.

The idyllic life was destroyed when Hennie unfortunately contracted typhoid in April 1880; by early June Hennie had died, and this left Bird deeply depressed, dwelling on loneliness and hopelessness. Still wearing black in mourning the death of her sister, Bird on 8 March 1881 married John Bishop. Her marriage to Bishop has mystified biographers: he was not a traveling man, and she stopped globetrotting while he was alive. According to both Anna Stoddart and Barr, Bird tried to settle into the duties of a typical Victorian wife, interrupted only by her writing, lecturing, and publishing schedules. After living a nomadic life for at least twenty-five years, Bird had abandoned what had defined her. In November 1881, while Bird was at work on *The Golden Chersonese*, her husband contracted erysipelas, a skin disease which led to com-

Bird's photograph of the boat she used during her travels in China

plications. After a long battle with illness, he died 6 March 1886, only two days before their fifth anniversary. Refusing solace, Bird mourned deeply but eventually threw off self-pity and planned a more ambitious trip than ever: she left for Persia and Tibet in January 1889.

Hennie having died, Bird's later books are composed not solely from letters but from extensive journal entries, notes, drawings, photographs, some letters to friends, and secondary sources that she consulted before, during, and after her trips. Her journey to Tibet was the first of her Asian travel books (the second would be the first-published narrative, *Journeys in Persia and Kurdistan* [1891]), and it was the testing ground for her new method of gathering information and writing travel narratives without her beloved sister as primary audience and editor. An unsuccessful venture, *Among the Tibetans* (1894) reads like an exercise or a rough excerpt from a far longer text. It sounds testy, and Bird reverts to her evangelical, narrow-minded views that she had shed years earlier. The fact that the book was published by the Religious Tract Society rather than by John Murray helps to explain the tone and purpose of the text, as Bird returns to the rhetoric of religious imperialism. She disliked both Hindus and Muslims on this trip, finding both to be "feeble" and "cunning," and she portrayed them as animal-like, remnants of a once-grand race that is aging badly and devolving into lower life forms.

Among the Tibetans begins quickly, with Bird discussing her horse, Gyalpo — a large, spirited animal that she says is quite unsuitable to an old woman — and her guide-bodyguard Usman Shah, who beats people as they travel, cheats her ruthlessly, and turns out to be a convicted murderer. While she loves her horse, she distrusts Usman Shah. After some mishaps, even when she enters ancient Tibet and leaves the Muslims behind, she finds Tibetans ugly: they have "high cheekbones, broad, flat noses without visible bridges, small, dark, oblique eyes, with heavy lids and imperceptible eyebrows, wide mouths, full lips, thick, big, projecting ears."

In Leh she met two Moravian missionaries, a Mr. Redslob and Dr. Karl Marx, who acted as interpreters, guides, and guardians. At least part of her purpose in visiting Tibet was to examine missionary hospitals and schools, and while traveling in the East she established mission hospitals in memory of her sister and her husband. Two of her biographers argue that her evangelical turn was sparked by her guilt: her two most beloved people, both of whom were serious Christians and believed in mission work, had died. Bird traveled and indulged herself by assuming their work, which she funded with earnings from travel books. Yet she acknowledges that missionary work did not look particularly successful, for if one counted converts, "the devoted labour of nearly forty years and complete self-sacrifice for the good of Kylang must be pronounced unsuccessful." She argues that success must not be counted, however, nor even hoped for — since the effort itself is important enough.

Despite her age and supposed frailty, she undertook a daunting itinerary through severe mountain territory and nearly died while traveling through this desolate and grand mountain landscape. In crossing a ford she broke a rib and her horse drowned. She recognized her injuries as soon as she realized that she was not dead, but she made light of them to encourage her traveling companions. The book ends abruptly. Bird seems not to have invested much time or effort in *Among the Tibetans,* perhaps because the memories of her recent bereavements and the annoyances of relearning how to be an expert traveler burdened her. Her next journeys were more successful, and the books they inspired are more substantial, erudite, and entertaining — although they may be more weighty than modern readers prefer.

After this first experience as an Asian traveler, in 1890 Bird wandered through the Punjab and began to consider returning to England, but she fortunately met Maj. Herbert Sawyer, a recently widowed thirty-five-year-old on a secret mission for the International Branch of the Quartermaster's Department of the Indian army. He invited her to join him on travels through much of western Persia, including some rough and embattled territory. Without his help Bird could not have visited this area of the world, despite her pluck, stubbornness, and courage. Traveling with a European male companion, particularly one with military and political connections, was the only way she could have fulfilled this part of her plan.

A reasonable question, however, is why Major Sawyer, identified only as "M" in *Journeys in Persia and Kurdistan,* cared to travel with a fifty-nine-year-old woman. Biographers have surmised that an el-derly yet famous lady traveler may have provided an excellent cover story for Major Sawyer, one that allowed him to carry out his mission with far less risk. Whatever the reason, the two became fellow travelers, a pair who stayed together for several months at a time in the remotest territory of Persia. They usually set up two separate but close camps; Bird hired her own servants and translator, and she purchased her own camping gear and food; but they traveled together and stayed at caravansaries and British governing residences together. Bird sacrificed some of her highly valued freedom to gain access to otherwise inaccessible territory.

Journeys in Persia and Kurdistan, published in two volumes, is Bird's finest mature writing. It lacks the sparkle and energy of *The Hawaiian Archipelago* and *A Lady's Life in the Rocky Mountains,* but it provides a compendium of information, anecdotes, and personal, political, and philosophical reflections. The often-distant tone of the book may be explained by its publication history: before Bird could publish the work, it had to be approved by the International Department of the Indian War Office, and Bird therefore excised most personal information about Major Sawyer. The adventures that the volumes describe are impressive. In fact, because of threats to their safety, Bird had carried a loaded revolver, something she had ordinarily refused to do.

As the narrative opens, Bird explains her preparatory purchases and research, but she spends considerable time educating her readers about Persia. She even provides a glossary and recommends for the edification of her readers such other books as George N. Curzon's *Persia and the Persian Question* (1891) and Austen Henry Layard's books on the Bakhtiari region. She believed that British intervention had not been healthy for Persia. "After a journey of nine months through Persia," she wrote, "I am strongly of the opinion that if the Empire is to have a solid and permanent resurrection, it must be through the enterprise of Persians, aided it may be by foreign skill and capital, though the less of the latter that is employed the more hopefully I should regard the Persian future." The British were exploring the region to ascertain how far the Russians had extended their influence. Victorians wanted a presence in the area but needed insurance that it would not cost too much in either money or lives.

The first leg of her overland trip was from Baghdad to Tehran in mid January. The weather could not have been worse. Bird liked extremely cold weather and snow, but that winter in Persia was rainy and cold, producing deep, sticky mud and creating excellent conditions for hypothermia, from which she seemed to suffer several times. Perched on her horse, she endured numbness, headaches, back pain, and drowsiness. Her men lamented that they were going to die and cursed the "English sahibs, who will travel in the winter, wishing our fathers may be burned." Their camping sites were horrendous, the worst she ever experienced. In one caravansary she ordered her men to pitch her tent in the animal yard — among several hundred goats, mules, and horses and on top of "damp manure, two or three feet deep" — because no suitable room was available in the inn. In February, riding through a blizzard with air temperatures of nine degrees, she bemoaned the torture and anguish of the day's journey and added that she had a "chill which crept into my heart, threatening a cessation of work." Regardless of the trauma and danger, she insists, "I really like the journey."

Throughout her journey she contemplates the condition of women under Muslim rule. Except for occasional references to customs that restrict women's lives, Bird usually ignored such customs, but throughout her Persian book she critiques polygamy and laments the enforced ignorance of women under the harem system. During one stop she was exiled to a single room in the home of the Persian governor because she could not join the men, nor could she stay in the harem. She observes of the harem that "There are over thirty women, some of them negresses. Some are Kurds and very handsome, but the faces of the two handsomest, though quite young, have something fiendish in their expression. I have seldom seen a *harem* without its tragedies of jealousy and hate, and every fresh experience makes me believe that the system is as humiliating to men as it is to women." Because of Muslim strictures, Bird could not explore cities without wearing a mask and a black overgarment and being accompanied by an armed escort. Few Persian men believed that Bird could read, write, and keep accounts; even upon seeing her at work, they insisted that it was a trick — such as teaching a horse to count by striking the ground with its hoof.

The second leg of their trip, from Julfa into Bakhtiari territory in Luristan, was in the spring. Although the weather was better, the natives of the region were far less cooperative, and the two camps of the travelers were robbed repeatedly despite their armed guards and appeals to local magistrates. Each time Bird and Sawyer were robbed, local officials replaced missing money or goods through taxing the residents. If a village refused to pay, it faced harsh

recrimination from the national government, which was determined to secure British goodwill.

As early summer arrived, the weather turned hot and dry. To avoid the heat of the day, Sawyer called them to "boot and saddle" between 3:00 and 4:00 A.M. Bird describes sitting in her tent and broiling at temperatures between 100 and 125 degrees and being unable to open the fly because the entire town clamored for medicine to cure various skin or eye ailments. Villagers assumed that she was a hakim, a lady doctor able to work miracles. Her own men begged her to help in dosing and performing minor surgery on the animals when necessary. She reflected that to be mistaken for a doctor was bad enough, but to be taken also for a veterinarian was going too far.

Sawyer left Bird on 9 August in Burujerd, his mission complete, and she seemed glad to have her freedom and solitude returned. With her servants and guides she traveled into Kurdistan and ended in Urmi in October, where the book ends abruptly.

Bird traveled back to Edinburgh for a rest on 13 December and arrived home on Boxing Day, 1891. Her work and writing received further recognition from the scientific community: along with about a dozen other women, she was granted membership in the Royal Geographical Society (RGS). The RGS had not intended to allow membership to women, but when it voted to accept all members of the Royal Scottish Geographical Society, it inherited the women members of that organization. Although Bird enjoyed the serious recognition of her accomplishments, she found the society's reluctance to recognize the accomplishments of women to be degrading and called it "a dastardly injustice to women."

She soon tired of the round of lectures, late-night suppers, social activism, and petty conventionalities; she preferred being a lady adventurer to being known as one. At the age of sixty-three she planned yet another ambitious itinerary: she left for a tour of several years through Asia. In January 1894, determined to explore areas Europeans had ignored and to found yet more medical missions dedicated to her sister and husband, she steamed for Yokohama aboard the *Mongolia*. In *Korea and Her Neighbors: A Narrative of Travel, with an Account of the Recent Vicissitudes and Present Position of the Country* (1897) she records her observations and makes recommendations about how to handle the odd, stubborn Korean nation. Until 1883 Korea was known as the "Hermit nation," but treaties and the Japanese invasion opened its ports. Bird made four visits to Korea between January 1894 and March 1897, and her own photographs provided the illustrations for the book. She had become an accomplished amateur photographer, and the book describes her technical difficulties with great care.

Bird's interest in medical missions continued, and she appealed to readers to be fair in their assessments of that beleaguered profession. In the preface of the book Sir Walter C. Hillier, consul general for Korea, links missionaries to an economic and political mission that reinforces a cynical interpretation of nineteenth-century missionary work: "I am tempted," he writes, "to call attention to another point in connection with this much-abused class of workers that is, I think, often lost sight of, namely of their utility as explorers and pioneers of commerce." Missionaries created markets for British goods and taught natives to be tractable servants, good "coolies" for encroaching Europeans.

At the beginning of *Korea and Her Neighbors* Bird sounds racist, but once her traveling had made her more familiar with the people and the country, she sounds more observant and sympathetic. According to Bird, China's influence had ruined Korean culture by leaving them with no art, only derivative forms based on questionable Chinese prototypes. The upper classes, who read and wrote Chinese, scorned writing in vernacular Korean; boys learned Chinese characters, poetry, art, and music. On the verge of the Russo-Japanese War Korea identified with China; when Japan invaded to "free" Korea from Chinese influence, Korean culture was radically disrupted. Bird complains, "It is into this archaic condition of things, this unspeakable grooviness, this irredeemable, unreformed Orientalism, this parody of China without the robustness of race which helps to hold China together, that the ferment of Western leaven has fallen." Koreans, of course, would dispute such a simplistic analysis of their culture and history.

Korea and Her Neighbors begins objectively, with little sense of Bird's narrative persona. Most of the first quarter of the book is written in the third person, but gradually Bird sees order and even a form of beauty in what had appeared chaotic, and her more natural voice emerges:

> I came to see on later journeys that even on that road there can be a beauty and fascination in the scenery when glorified and idealized by the unrivalled atmosphere of a Korean winter, which it is a delight even to recall, and that the situation of Seoul for a sort of weird picturesqueness compares favorably with that of almost any other capital, but its orientalism, a marked feature of which was its specially self-asserting dirt, is being fast improved off the face of the earth.

Unfortunately what she most approves were Japanese innovations that were "improving" upon native Korean city design and operation. She insists that Seoul has no art, history, interesting buildings, or religion — that, in fact, it has nothing whatsoever to recommend it to an ordinary tourist or even a fairly determined traveler accustomed to rough conditions. Bird's Seoul was a city for business, commerce, and government, not for the entertainment of foreigners — at least not at that time.

Encumbered by only the usual red tape, she was treated reasonably well as she traveled into the countryside. Her official letter of free transport, *Kwang-Ja,* did her no good at all, and she was stopped in every village and questioned closely by officials. Generally she met with curiosity and healthy doses of mistrust and even disdain, but no one impeded her travel. Peasants, unlike those in China, demonstrated no hostility.

Korean inns surprised even the hardy, travel-hardened Bird with their intense filth, noise, and chaos: "The regular inn of the towns and villages," she wrote, "consists chiefly of a filthy courtyard full of holes and heaps, entered from the road by a tumble-down gateway. A gaunt black pig or two tethered by the ear, big yellow dogs routing [*sic,* rooting] in the garbage, and fowls, boys, bulls, ponies, *mapu,* hangers-on, and travellers' loads make up a busy scene." Into these filthy courtyards her men pushed their entourage, sometimes having to fight for space because few innkeepers wanted a European woman under their roofs. Avoiding more-elegant teahouses because they were also dens of prostitution, she put up with fleas, rats, and extremely curious Koreans, and she was driven to note that there was a "seamy side" to Korean travel that made it "entirely unsuitable to the 'globe trotter,' and that even the specialist may do well to count the cost before embarking upon it." She sacrificed privacy, comfort, and quiet to tour the Korean countryside. Somehow Bird surmounted the difficulties of dressing, cleaning, eating, and using a privy with the entire population of a village peering at her through every hole in the wall.

The plight of Korean women interested Bird. In Muslim countries she saw few women except those of the lowest classes. In Korea she visited the women's quarters somewhat unwillingly, as she found them too "gaudy" and tasteless — in part, it seems, because of their European decorations such as Brussels tapestry carpets and French clocks. But as she traveled inland she saw more women, peasants who were bolder and freer. In Korea men had to marry to attain adulthood, to advance from being a nobody to being a somebody. Yet though marriage was important for the man, he did not have to be kind or reasonable to his wife. In fact, women were trained to submit to a marriage contract that completely subordinated them. Young brides were married with their eyes sealed shut; they did not speak during the entire ceremony and celebration: "Silence is regarded as a wife's first duty," Bird observed. "The wife has recognized duties to her husband, but he has few, if any, to her." Lower-class women had more freedom, education, and value within their families than upper-class women did.

Bird anatomized Korean eating habits by noting that Koreans "eat not to satisfy hunger, but to enjoy the sensation of repletion." Although she became a vegetarian during her trip because she could not get fresh chicken, she found the variety of foods eaten by Koreans to be appalling:

> The Korean is omnivorous. . . . Pork, beef, fish, raw, dried, and salted, the intestines of animals, all birds and game, no part being rejected, are eaten. . . . Cooking is not always essential. . . . Wheat, barley, maize, millet, the Irish and sweet potato, oats, peas, beans, rice, radishes, turnips, herbs, and wild leaves and roots innumerable, seaweed, shrimps, pastry made of flour, sugar, and oil, *kimshi*, . . . soups, persimmons, sponge-cakes, cakes of the edible pine nuts and honey, of flour, sugar, and sesamum seeds, onion, garlic, lily bulbs, chestnuts, and very much else are eaten.

This wide selection of delicacies seems attractive to modern readers more accustomed to Korean, Japanese, and Chinese fare, but to a nineteenth-century audience, such things as lily bulbs, raw and cooked fish, or animal intestines seemed disgusting.

Bird found Koreans woefully backward in their farming and industry, although peasants worked hard and carefully. Korean villages did not specialize in a specific industry, but rather produced what they needed: "There are no special industries in any of the river towns, and if they were all to disappear in some catastrophe it would not cause a ripple on the surface of the general commercial apathy of the country." Preferring, apparently, the nineteenth-century specialization spurred by industrialization, Bird saw such economic self-sufficiency as a flaw.

In August 1894 Bird's trip was interrupted by the outbreak of the Sino-Japanese War in Korea. She escaped quickly, with little money and none of her luggage. When she returned in January 1895, she entered into secret conferences with the king and met the queen, soon to be murdered by Japanese operatives. Bird says that the king entrusted

her with important information, and she served as a spy or unofficial ambassador, certainly an odd position for a Victorian lady. Bird explains at great length how the Japanese mismanaged the Koreans by thoughtlessly insisting that the Koreans abandon facets of their culture, including their hairstyles.

Bird noticed signs of warfare throughout the cities and countryside: "Even in my walks over the battlefield, though the grain of another year had ripened upon it, I saw human skulls, spines with ribs, spines with the pelvis attached, arms and hands, hats, belts, and scabbards." Bird's solution to Korea's problems was for the country to be taken in hand by friendly Russia.

The last portion of the book is almost purely historical/political. She describes the government, education, and religions, and she provides no notes of her travels for about one hundred pages. Her trip serves as the barest of structures to her reformative purposes. Earlier in her career Bird's stories dominate the text, and her sense of humor and her romanticism come through clearly. Now, however, facts about the country and her assessments reflecting her political agenda prevail. She continued to travel in China and Japan, where she gathered material for her last book.

That final book, but not her final journey, is *The Yangtze Valley and Beyond: An Account of Journeys in China, Chiefly in the Province of Sze Chuan and among the Man-Tze of the Somo Territory* (1899). Bird had visited portions of China previously, but in January 1896 she decided to explore more deeply and carefully. As she does with *Korea and Its Neighbors,* she begins *The Yangtze Valley and Beyond* with a ponderous amount of geographical, political, economic, and cultural information. For about one-fifth of its length the book sounds much like an objective analysis of China and not a travel book. After that, Bird's usual voice resurfaces.

The British took the economic and military power of China seriously, even if they did not approve of it. Throughout Asia Chinese were in powerful positions as businessmen, bankers, and educators – from the lowest to the highest positions, Chinese representatives thrived. Furthermore, the Chinese had enjoyed longer experience trading with their neighbors. Bird repeats the usual racial stereotypes, both good and bad, of the Chinese – whom she characterizes as "sober, industrious, thrifty, orderly, peaceable, indifferent to personal comfort," yet also "suspicious, cunning, and corrupt." She adds that their worst trait, the most dangerous of all, is that they lack a conscience. However, Bird also found much to praise in China. Unlike her British col-

Isabella Bird in Manchu dress

masses, the individual being lost sight of." With such severe cultural differences, Bird concludes, Europeans must proceed slowly in any negotiations.

Her life was at risk throughout her travel in China, because Chinese peasants hated Europeans and blamed them, perhaps rightly, for many of their troubles. Her servants were no longer simply guides and bearers; they had to protect her from bodily harm, as peasants threw mud and rocks and shouted execrations. Even though she traveled traditionally, either in a small junk or carried aloft in an open litter, the Chinese quickly spotted her as an alien. Several times her appearance incited riots, and she once had to draw her revolver. Another time she was seriously injured by a blow to her head: "The yells of 'Foreign devil,' and 'Foreign dog,' were tremendous. Volleys of stones hailed on the chair, and a big one hit me a severe blow at the back of my ear, knocking me forwards and stunning me." On yet another occasion she was rescued when a more reasonable man convinced the crowd that foreign soldiers "would come and burn their houses and destroy their crops, and worse."

In fact, Bird understood how and why the populace had been incited against Europeans. She blamed the mandarin class, professional bureaucrats who leeched from the people and provided only a poor imitation of governance. She writes, "Into this amount of responsibility, multifarious duties, and overwork, comes the foreigner with his treaty rights, a new and difficult element to deal with, and who may be an arrogant, bullying, and ignorant person." Foreigners made the lives of ordinary Chinese more difficult.

The inns in the Chinese backcountry were worse than those of Korea, to her dismay. Because she insisted on having a private room at each inn, no matter how small or modest, she often found herself set down in a storage or lumber room — frequently adjacent to the pigsty or stable or above the cistern or cesspool. At one memorable inn in Szechwan province conditions were particularly bad, for "The walls were black and slimy with the dirt and damp of many years; the paper with which the rafters had once been covered was hanging from them in tatters, and when the candle was lit beetles, "slaters," cockroaches, and other abominable things crawled on the walls and dropped from the rafters, one pink, fleshy thing dropping upon, and putting out, the candle!" Oddly enough, despite these exceptionally bad arrangements, Bird ate well and slept soundly for more than ten hours.

Bird comments on nearly every aspect of Chinese life, culture, geography, climate, and typical

leagues, she appreciated each city's bustle even if she yearned for the countryside, and she recognized farming, sailing, and trading skill, even though she maligned what she believed to be an unwillingness of China to move into the modern era.

Bird found the Chinese to be insular and resistant to knowledge, as Europeans understood it: she discovered examples of misinformation even among supposedly well-informed men. To her annoyance, she was told that the Chinese had won recent battles with the British (though Bird knew this to be untrue) and that missionaries wanted to work deep within China "to find out the secret of China's greatness and the way to destroy it by magic arts." She repeats a stereotype that became quite fixed in European imaginations — that the Chinese cared nothing for the individual and much for the group, as her explanation for the operation of Chinese charity shows: "Their works of merit are very much on a large scale, for the benefit of human beings in

flora and fauna. She describes – and laments – the practice of binding women's feet, a deforming practice that she compares to British corseting. She details middle- and upper-class education for boys and criticizes its rote memorization; she praises hardworking peasantry and notes that the women are especially good-hearted and pleasant; and she analyzes the unlikely prospects that missionary work will succeed in Christianizing China. She witnessed funerals, weddings, New Year's celebrations, riots, farming, religious practices, and medical treatments. With her old vigor and courage, she pushed her men up mountains and into valleys, across rivers and over plains. Even when she had a concussion and her heart began to trouble her, she persisted in her travels.

Bird's carefully reasoned conclusion is that Europeans should not disrupt the Chinese Empire. In a long concluding section she explains that strongarm or bullying tactics would be damaging to the Chinese. Her observations proved that, contrary to European belief, the ordinary peasant enjoyed substantial freedom in China, for "He is free in all trades and industries: to make money and to keep it: to emigrate and to return with his gains: free to rise from peasant's hut to place and dignity: to become a millionaire, and confer princely gifts upon his province: free in his religion and his amusements: and in his social and commercial life." Any disruption of the system that enabled the Chinese to preserve this lifestyle would be destructive. She writes that European eagerness for trade routes and agreements led to hasty decisions and even poorly thought-out military intervention, and she asks for patience, encouraging her readers with signs that China was reforming itself by using Western ideas to pull out of its "sleep" and accommodate itself to the nineteenth century.

She returned to England in 1897 to a distinctly unsettled lifestyle of giving public lectures; writing, editing, and overseeing publication of her books; laboring for reform; and visiting friends. By 1900 she tired of her life and argued with her doctors, who insisted that she was too unwell to undertake yet another trip. She had a degenerative heart condition and a supposedly bad back, a woman who had broken her arm, ribs, and several minor bones and had survived a concussion and several near drownings in the course of her travels. Yet she set off for Tangier and a horseback ride of one thousand miles across Morocco, a trip that brought out Bird's nearly endless energy and adventurousness.

Upon her return to England, however, she fell into a decline from which she did not recover. After a life full of action and denial of mortality, she succumbed to a combination of bodily ills – a fibrous tumor, thrombosis, and worsening heart disease. On 7 October 1904 she died.

Isabella Lucy Bird Bishop redefined the conception of the "lady traveler." Instead of the genteel, tender lady preserving her china as she rides decorously up the Nile, Bird was a resilient British woman riding, as a man would ride, astride a huge stallion; badgering her servants into obedience; and insisting on being allowed to see, hear, and understand the world for herself. Rather than the effusions of a lady observing pyramids and repeating platitudes about their age and the inevitable decay of civilizations, she often questioned the stereotypes and assumptions that her culture held about contemporary cultures. Bird's travel books are an essential component to the study of Victorian nonfiction prose, imperialism, and travel literature – and to the study of nineteenth-century Canada, Korea, Japan, Hawaii, Tibet, Malaysia, and Colorado.

Biographies:
Anna Stoddart, *The Life of Isabella Bird (Mrs. Bishop)* (London: Murray, 1906; New York: Dutton, 1907);
Pat Barr, *A Curious Life for a Lady: The Life of Isabella Bird* (London: Macmillan/Murray, 1970);
Anne Gatti, *Isabella Bird Bishop* (London: Hamilton, 1988).

Papers:
Bird's papers are held by her London publisher, John Murray.

Marguerite, Countess of Blessington (Margaret Power Farmer Gardiner)

(1 September 1789 – 4 June 1849)

D. C. Woodcox
Truman State University

BOOKS: *The Magic Lantern; or, Sketches of Scenes in the Metropolis,* anonymous (London: Longman, Hurst, Rees, Orme & Brown, 1822);

Sketches and Fragments, anonymous (London: Longman, Hurst, Rees, Orme & Brown, 1822);

Journal of a Tour through the Netherlands to Paris in 1821, anonymous (London: Longman, Hurst, Rees, Orme & Brown, 1822);

English Fashionables Abroad: A Novel, 3 volumes (London: Colburn, 1827);

Rambles in Waltham Forest, signed C. M. H. (London: Cox, 1827);

Ella Stratford; or, The Orphan Child (Philadelphia: Peterson, [1830?]);

The Repealers: A Novel, 3 volumes, volume 2 of which is titled *Grace Cassidy; or, The Repealers: A Novel* (London: Bentley, 1833); republished in 2 volumes as *The Repealers: A Novel* (Philadelphia: Carey, Lea & Blanchard, 1833);

Conversations of Lord Byron . . . with the Countess of Blessington (London: Colburn, 1834; Philadelphia: Carey & Hart, 1836); republished as *Journal of Correspondence and Conversations between Lord Byron and the Countess of Blessington* (Cincinnati, Ohio: Stratton, 1851); revised as *A Journal of the Conversations of Lord Byron with the Countess of Blessington . . . to Which Is Prefixed a Sketch of Lady Blessington by Her Niece, Miss Marguerite Power, and a Memoir by the Editor of This Edition* (New York: Scribners, 1893; London: Bentley, 1894);

Tour in the Netherlands (London: Longman, 1834);

Two Friends: A Novel (3 volumes, London: Saunders & Otley, 1835; 2 volumes, Philadelphia: Carey, Lea & Blanchard, 1835);

The Confessions of an Elderly Gentleman (London: Longman, Rees, Orme, Brown, Green & Longmans, 1836; Philadelphia: Carey, Lea & Blanchard, 1836);

Marguerite, Countess of Blessington, 1834 (engraving by H. T. Ryall)

Gems of Beauty Displayed in a Series of Twelve Highly Finished Engravings from Designs by E. T. Parris, with Fanciful Illustrations, in Verse (London: Longman, Rees, Orme, Brown, Green & Longmans / New York: Appleton, 1836); republished as *Gems of Beauty Displayed in a Series of Twelve Highly Finished Engravings of Spanish Subjects, from Designs by the First Artists, with Fanciful Illustrations, in Verse* (London: Longman, Orme, Brown, Green & Longmans / New York: Appleton, 1839);

The Honey-moon (Philadelphia: Carey & Hart, 1837);

The Victims of Society (3 volumes, London: Saunders & Otley, 1837; 2 volumes, Philadelphia: Carey, Lea & Blanchard, 1837);

The Confessions of an Elderly Lady (London: Longman, Orme, Brown, Green & Longmans, 1838; Cincinnati, Ohio: James, 1838);

The Governess, 2 volumes (London: Longman, Orme, Brown, Green & Longmans, 1839; Philadelphia: Lea & Blanchard, 1839);

Desultory Thoughts and Reflections (London: Longman, Orme, Brown, Green & Longmans, 1839; New York: Wiley & Putnam, 1839);

The Idler in Italy (3 volumes, London: Colburn, 1839; 2 volumes, Philadelphia: Carey & Hart, 1839);

The Belle of a Season (London: Longman, 1840);

The Idler in France, 2 volumes (London: Colburn, 1841; Philadelphia: Carey & Hart, 1841);

The Lottery of Life, 3 volumes (London: Colburn, 1842); republished as *The Lottery of Life: A Novel* (New York: Winchester, 1842);

Meredith (3 volumes, London: Longman, Brown, Green & Longmans, 1843; 1 volume, New York: Winchester, 1843);

Etiquette of Courtship and Marriage (New York: Burgess & Stringer, 1844);

Strathern; or, Life at Home and Abroad: A Story of the Present Day, 4 volumes (London: Colburn, 1845);

The Memoirs of a Femme de Chambre: A Novel, 3 volumes (London: Bentley, 1846);

Marmaduke Herbert; or, The Fatal Error: A Novel, Founded on Fact, 3 volumes (London: Bentley, 1847; New York: Burgess & Stringer, 1847);

A Catalogue of the Costly and Elegant Effects, Comprising All the Magnificent Furniture, . . . the Extensive & Interesting Library of Books, Comprising Upwards of 5,000 Volumes, . . . the Property of the Rt. Honble. the Countess of Blessington . . . Which Will Be Sold by Auction by Mr. Phillips on the Premises, Gore House, on Monday, the 7th of May, 1849, and Twelve Subsequent Days (London, 1849);

The Regal Gallery: Lives and Portraits of Queens of England, 2 volumes (London, 1850);

Country Quarters: A Novel, 3 volumes (London: Shoberl, 1850); republished as *Country Quarters: A Love Story* (Philadelphia: Peterson, [1877]);

One Hundred Valuable Receipts for the Young Lady of the Period, Including the World Famous Directions of How to Become Beautiful Forever (New York: De-Witt, 1878).

Collections: *The Works of Lady Blessington* (Philadelphia: Corey & Hart, 1838);

The Blessington Papers, edited by Alfred Morrison (London: Privately printed, 1895).

OTHER: "Galeria; or, The Deserted Village," in *Chairolas, Prince of Paida,* by Edward George Earle Lytton Bulwer-Lytton (Philadelphia: Carey, Lea & Blanchard, 1836);

Lionel Deerhurst (Barbara Hemphill), *Lionel Deerhurst, or Fashionable Life under the Regency,* edited by Blessington (London: Bentley, 1846).

Margaret Power Farmer Gardiner, countess of Blessington, a noted beauty and salon hostess, was also a diarist, novelist, gossip writer, and travel writer. People appreciated her works for their shrewd observations as well as for the social and personal attraction that the drama of what R. R. Madden called "the most gorgeous Lady Blessington" aroused, and she wrote to finance the fashion and entertainments for which she was famous. She summarized in 1839 what she saw as the ethos of fashionable life that she knew during the late-Regency and early-Victorian years: "'Be prosperous and happy, never require our services, and we will remain your friends.' This is not what society says, but is the principle on which it acts." She could well base this observation on her own experiences.

Born Margaret Power at Knockbrit, County Tipperary, Ireland, on 1 September 1789, she was the fourth of six children of Edmund and Ellen Sheehy Power. Her father was an incautious country "squireen" — hard-drinking, brutal, and incorrigible. Power served as a magistrate, and in this capacity he was hated and persecuted by his neighbors for rounding up insurgents. Attempting to run a newspaper and several businesses that failed, he lived beyond his means. Despite his mounting debts, he did not moderate his lavish tastes, and his improvidence sunk the family further into debt and made his family life miserable. The similarities between the amounts of energy that both father and daughter had and between their inabilities to economize while in debt are striking. The intellectual traits that characterized Blessington's adult life manifested themselves early. Her formal education was limited to what she received from Anne Dwyer, a neighbor and friend of her mother, but Blessington was a reflective and inquisitive child who read much and entertained her family, friends, and neighbors by inventing stories.

To ameliorate his financial situation Power sold his daughter, at the age of fourteen, into marriage with a man from County Kildare, Capt. St.

Leger Farmer of the Forty-seventh Regiment, Royal Artillery. Although warned by Farmer's relatives that the captain suffered bouts of insanity, Power and his wife dismissed such warnings, ignored their daughter's pleas, and forced her into the marriage in March 1804. Farmer's intemperance, roughness, sadism, and violent temper caused her to leave him after three months of marriage: the young girl refused to accompany him in joining his regiment and returned home, where her family reluctantly took her in.

The couple agreed to a separation. When she was eighteen years old Blessington, to secure some tranquility and escape harassment from her family, made a liaison with an English army officer, Capt. Thomas Jenkins, who was stationed nearby. Living in England and traveling with him for ten years, she continued to educate herself by reading widely, and by 1816 she had moved from Hampshire to London with Jenkins. Farmer, meanwhile, had drawn his sword against his colonel, had been forced to sell his commission, and had joined the East India Company. In 1817 Farmer, intoxicated after a drinking party, fell from a window in the King's Bench prison and was killed.

Blessington did not remain a widow long. Four months later, in 1818, she married a widowed Irish peer, Charles John Gardiner, Second Viscount Mountjoy and First Earl of Blessington, and changed her first name to Marguerite. She had met Lord Blessington in London, where the earl had been attracted by her beauty and the social and intellectual skills she had developed. He paid Jenkins £10,000 as "reimbursement" to release her: for the second time in her life she was sold. Lord Blessington, seven years older than his new wife, was wealthy (in 1816 his estates in Ireland had yielded £30,000), good-natured, and fond of extravagant living, a taste that the new Lady Blessington shared. Drawing on her rank, beauty, shrewdness, generosity, and literary tastes, she created in their new home at St. James's Square, London, a brilliant salon of intellect, wit, and fashion — and she enjoyed being at its center. Its clientele was almost entirely male, because most of the wives of those influential men did not consider Lady Blessington respectable.

In 1822 Blessington published anonymously her first literary work, *The Magic Lantern; or, Sketches of Scenes in the Metropolis,* a volume of sketches and essays. A second and third work, *Sketches and Fragments* and *Journal of a Tour through the Netherlands to Paris in 1821,* followed in that same year, and these were her only publications for almost a decade. In

August of that same year Lord and Lady Blessington, the youngest sister of the latter, and a large retinue of servants began an extended tour of the Continent. They lived splendidly wherever they took up residence. By March 1823 they were in Genoa, where, during nine weeks, they became well acquainted with George Gordon, Lord Byron.

Her *Conversations of Lord Byron ... with the Countess of Blessington* (1834) records their relationship. The book is needlessly drawn out but presents a valuable and balanced portrait of the poet. Count Alfred d'Orsay — a charming, selfish dandy and dilettante painter and sculptor who had met the Blessingtons at their salon in London in 1821 — also became a close friend of the family that year. Twelve years Lady Blessington's junior, he traveled and lived with them throughout their stay in Italy. In 1827 d'Orsay married Lady Harriet Anne Frances Gardiner in an arranged marriage in Naples. Harriet, the earl's only child by his first wife, was fifteen years old, and her marriage (for which d'Orsay received a marriage settlement of £40,000) was probably loveless and decidedly unsuccessful. The two separated officially in February 1838.

In May 1829 Lord Blessington died of an apoplectic stroke in Paris, and Lady Blessington was again a widow but with a jointure of about £2,000 a year. When her stepdaughter and d'Orsay separated in 1831, d'Orsay became Blessington's companion. The close association between Blessington and d'Orsay gave rise to scandalous rumors. Perhaps they were lovers; more probably their relationship was platonic. Michael Sadleir suggests that her earlier marriage to Farmer had caused her to suffer an aversion to sex and that d'Orsay was impotent. Certainly he was spoiled and she was indulgent. After a two-year residence in Paris d'Orsay accompanied Lady Blessington to London, where they took up residence in Seamore Place, Park Lane, Mayfair. In 1836 Blessington acquired Gore House in Kensington, where she and d'Orsay lived and entertained extravagantly for the next thirteen years. Despite the scandal of her relationship with d'Orsay, she again established herself as the leading hostess of London's intellectual, fashionable, and political worlds.

The costly standard of their social lives soon strained the income (already tight at the time of Lord Blessington's death) from Blessington's estate. To meet expenses Lady Blessington resumed her literary career with a three-volume roman à clef titled *The Repealers: A Novel,* published in 1833. Almost a dozen other novels followed, most of them hastily composed to meet expenses: *Two Friends: A Novel*

(1835); *The Confessions of an Elderly Gentleman* (1836); *The Honey-moon* (1837); *The Victims of Society* (1837); *The Confessions of an Elderly Lady* (1838); *The Governess* (1839); *The Lottery of Life* (1842); *Meredith* (1843); *Strathern; or, Life at Home and Abroad: A Story of the Present Day* (1845); *The Memoirs of a Femme de Chambre: A Novel* (1846); *Marmaduke Herbert; or, The Fatal Error: A Novel, Founded on Fact* (1847); and *Country Quarters: A Novel* (1850).

Next to her *Conversations of Lord Byron* Lady Blessington's best-known and most popular works were two of her travel books – *The Idler in Italy* (1839), which describes her 1822 Paris sojourn, trip through Switzerland, and five-year residence in Italy; and *The Idler in France* (1841), which recounts her years in Paris from 1828 through 1830. Her two other travel books, *Journal of a Tour through the Netherlands to Paris in 1821* and *Tour in the Netherlands* (1834), have less merit. Another travel sketch appeared in 1834 in The Book of Beauty; or, Regal Gallery, an annual gift-book series that Blessington edited until 1849 for Charles Heath, and it was later used again in *The Lottery of Life*. Madden, Lady Blessington's nineteenth-century biographer, thought that "it is very questionable if any of the works of Lady Blessington, with the exception of the 'Conversations with Lord Byron,' and perhaps the 'Idler in Italy,' will maintain a permanent position in English miscellaneous literature. The interest taken in the writer was the main source of the temporary interest that was felt in her literary performances." *The Idler in Italy* has lost any such permanent position, but interest in *Conversations* and in Lady Blessington remains.

Blessington's journals formed the basis for her travel writings. Several descriptive and narrative passages from the journals appear almost verbatim in both of the *Idler* books; however, she revised and frequently rewrote the contents of the journals. In view of her financial straits, the travel books were intended to sell well, and she deleted the most personal references and developed those episodes she thought would most interest the public. Thus, her travel books probably have more interest for social historians than for biographers. Her ability to be intimate while discreet allowed her to produce something immensely popular. Both *Idler* books are rich in anecdotes, and the travel works interleave description and narratives about meeting the famous. Blessington's travel writings also comment on what is most likely to interest an audience, as she offers glimpses of foreign luxury, art (she favors the sweet and florid), and customs.

Blessington's husband, Charles John Gardiner, First Earl of Blessington, circa 1810–1820 (portrait by J. Holmes; from Lady Blessington at Naples, *edited by Edith Clay, 1979)*

Reviews of her fiction frequently characterize her prose as "graceful" and "sparkling," and the same qualities distinguish her travel books. Her style is eloquent, cultivated, and light. For instance, *The Idler in Italy* offers this impressionistic description of Naples – which, "viewed by moonlight[,] is enchanting."

> The moon pouring out an effulgence of silvery light, from a sky of the deepest azure, through a pure and transparent atmosphere, places all the prominent buildings in strong relief; and whilst it makes every object distinctly visible, it mellows each tint, and blends the innumerable details into one vast harmonious whole, throwing a bewitching and indescribable softness and repose on the scene.

Her descriptions tend toward the picturesque, with their emphasis on feeling, and she offers forthright, keen assessments of social customs – for instance, of the relationships between French mistresses and their servants, of French adeptness at conversation,

French sociality, and French diplomatic tact. She also provides acute perceptions on the experience of buying antiques in Paris and wondering about their histories, as well as on English notions about the Italians juxtaposed to the realities. She weighs and assesses, but her British standards never stray from practicality. She may praise French conversational skills, but there is no doubt where her national loyalties lie.

As an author Blessington also contributed poems, verse tales, and articles to magazines and annuals. In addition to her editing of the annual gift book The Book of Beauty she worked as editor for *The Keepsake* from 1841 until her death, and from 1846 she served as a well-paid gossip writer for the *Daily News.* She did all this work under increasing financial pressure, particularly after 1845 when the Irish potato blight significantly reduced her annual revenues. Blessington had a considerable income from all her writing — at one time more than £2,000 per annum — but her expenses still exceeded her income.

By early 1849 Blessington and d'Orsay had used the last of her inheritance, and she was bankrupt. In April of that year d'Orsay fled to the Continent to avoid arrest by his creditors. Having arranged to sell everything from Gore House at an auction in early May, Blessington followed him to Paris later that month. Within twenty-four hours of moving into her new, modest apartment in Paris that June, she died of apoplexy complicated by heart disease and was buried at Chambourcy, near Saint Germain-en-Laye, close to Paris.

In speaking of her death, d'Orsay cried, "In losing her, I lost everything in this world. She was to me a mother, a dear, dear mother, a true loving mother!" He survived her by three years and was buried next to her. Notwithstanding the vicissitudes of her life and the often unmerited scandal that accompanied her, Blessington wrote in a letter to her novelist friend Edward Bulwer-Lytton that she had "a sort of silent respect" for herself. Walter Savage Landor composed an epitaph in Latin, and Bryan Waller Procter added one in English for her tomb. Cornwall's eulogy records the same feeling of silent respect that Blessington felt about herself:

In her lifetime she was loved and admired for her many graceful writings, her gentle manners, her kind and generous heart. Men famous for art and science in distant lands sought her friendship; and the historians and scholars, the poets and wits and painters, of her own country found an unfailing welcome in her ever-hospitable home. She gave cheerfully to all who were in need, help and sympathy, and useful counsel; and she died lamented by many friends. Those who loved her best in life, and now lament her most, have reared this tributary marble over the place of her rest.

Biographies:

R. R. Madden, *The Literary Life and Correspondence of the Countess of Blessington,* 3 volumes (London: Newby, 1855);

J. F. Molloy, *The Most Gorgeous Lady Blessington* (London: Downey, 1896);

Michael Sadleir, *Blessington-D'Orsay: A Masquerade* (London: Constable, 1933); republished as *The Strange Life of Lady Blessington* (Boston: Little, Brown, 1933; revised and enlarged edition, London: Constable, 1947; New York: Farrar, Straus, 1947).

References:

Willard Connely, *Count D'Orsay, the Dandy of Dandies* (London: Laurie, 1952);

Kathleen Hickok, *Representations of Women: Nineteenth-Century British Women's Poetry* (Westport, Conn.: Greenwood Press, 1984);

Ernest James Lovell, *Lady Blessington's "Conversations of Lord Byron"* (Princeton: Princeton University Press, 1969);

William H. Marshall, *Byron, Shelley, Hunt and "The Liberal"* (Philadelphia: University of Pennsylvania Press, 1960).

Papers:

The University of California, Los Angeles, has Blessington letters and manuscripts in its special collections, and the Harry Ransom Humanities Research Center of the University of Texas at Austin also has letters.

George Borrow

(5 July 1803 – 26 July 1881)

J. Lawrence Mitchell
Texas A&M University

See also the Borrow entries in *DLB 21: Victorian Novelists Before 1885* and *DLB 55: Victorian Prose Writers Before 1867.*

BOOKS: *Tales of the Wild and the Wonderful,* anonymous (London: Hurst, Robinson, 1825);

The Zincali; or, An Account of the Gypsies of Spain, with an Original Collection of Their Songs and Poetry, and a Copious Dictionary of Their Language (2 volumes, London: Murray, 1841; 1 volume, New York: Wiley & Putnam, 1842); republished as *The Zincali; or, An Account of the Gipsies of Spain,* 1 volume (New York: Winchester, 1843);

The Bible in Spain; or, The Journeys, Adventures, and Imprisonments of an Englishman, in an Attempt to Circulate the Scriptures in the Peninsula (3 volumes, London: Murray, 1843; 2 volumes, New York, 1843); republished as *The Bible in Spain; or, The Journeys, Adventures, and Imprisonments of an Englishman, in an Attempt to Circulate the Scriptures on the Peninsula* (New York: Worthington, n.d.);

Lavengro: The Scholar, The Gypsy, The Priest (3 volumes, London: Murray, 1851; 1 volume, New York: Putnam, 1851); republished as *Roving Adventures; or Lavengro, The Scholar – The Gipsy – The Priest* (Cincinnati: Moore & Anderson, 1852); expanded as *Lavengro: The Scholar, The Gypsy, The Priest,* edited by W. I. Knapp (London: Murray, 1900); abridged as *Lavengro* (London: Oxford University Press, [1930]);

The Romany Rye; A Sequel to "Lavengro" (2 volumes, London: Murray, 1857; 1 volume, New York: Harper, 1857);

Wild Wales: Its People, Language, and Scenery, 3 volumes (London: Murray, 1862);

Romano Lavo-Lil: Word-Book of the Romany; or, English Gypsy Language, with Many Pieces in Gypsy, Illustrative of the Way of Speaking and Thinking of the English Gypsies; with Specimens of Their Poetry, and an Account of Certain Gypsyries or Places Inhab-

George Borrow (portrait by H. W. Phillips; National Portrait Gallery, London)

ited by Them, and of Various Things Relating to Gypsy Life in England (London: Murray, 1874);

A Supplementary Chapter to "The Bible in Spain," Inspired by Ford's "Hand-book for Travellers in Spain" (London: Wise, 1913);

An Expedition to the Isle of Man in the Year 1855: A Hitherto Unpublished Diary ([London]: Shorter, 1915);

Celtic Bards, Chiefs, and Kings, edited by Herbert G. Wright (London: Murray, 1928).

OTHER: *Celebrated Trials, and Remarkable Cases of Criminal Jurisprudence, from the Earliest Records to the Year 1825,* 6 volumes, edited by Borrow (London: Knight & Lacey, 1825).

TRANSLATIONS: Friedrich Maximilian von Klinger, *Faustus: His Life, Death and Descent into Hell* (London: Simpkin & Marshall, 1825); republished as *Faustus: His Life, Death, and Doom. A Romance in Prose* (London: Kent, 1864);

Romantic Ballads, Translated from the Danish; and Miscellaneous Pieces (London: Wilkin, 1826; New York: Putnam, 1913);

Targum; or, Metrical Translations from Thirty Languages and Dialects (Saint Petersburg: Schulz & Beneze, 1835);

Alexander Pushkin, *The Talisman, . . . with Other Pieces* (Saint Petersburg: Schulz & Beneze, 1835);

Embéo e Majaró Lucas [The Gypsy Luke] (Madrid: D. Joaquin de la Barrera, 1837);

Elis Wyn, *The Sleeping Bard; or, Visions of the World, Death, and Hell* (London: Murray, 1860);

The Turkish Jester; or, The Pleasantries of Cogia Nasr Eddin Effendi (Ipswich: Webber, 1884);

Johannes Ewald, *The Death of Balder* (London: Jarrold, 1889 [1892]);

Russian Popular Tales, 2 parts (London: Thomson, [1904]);

Adam Gottlob Oehlenschläger, *The Gold Horns*, edited by Edmund Gosse (London: Wise, 1913);

Alf the Freebooter, Little Danneved and Swayne Trost, and Other Ballads (London: Wise, 1913);

Axel Thordson and Fair Calborg: A Ballad (London: Wise, 1913);

The Brother Avenged and Other Ballads (London: Wise, 1913);

Brown William, The Power of the Harp, and Other Ballads (London: Wise, 1913);

Child Maidelvold and Other Ballads (London: Wise, 1913);

The Dalby Bear and Other Ballads (London: Wise, 1913);

Ellen of Villenskov and Other Ballads (London: Wise, 1913);

Emilian the Fool: A Tale (London: Wise, 1913);

Ermeline: A Ballad (London: Wise, 1913);

The Expedition to Birting's Land and Other Ballads (London: Wise, 1913);

Finnish Arts, or Sir Thor and Damsel Thure: A Ballad (London: Wise, 1913);

The Fountain of Maribo and Other Ballads (London: Wise, 1913);

The Giant of Berne and Orm Ungerswayne: A Ballad (London: Wise, 1913);

Grimhild's Vengeance: Three Ballads, edited by Gosse (London: Wise, 1913);

Grimmer and Kamper, The End of Sivard Snarenswayne, and Other Ballads (London: Wise, 1913);

Hafbur and Signe: A Ballad (London: Wise, 1913);

King Diderik and the Fight between the Lion and Dragon, and Other Ballads (London: Wise, 1913);

King Hacon's Death, and Bran and the Black Dog (London: Wise, 1913);

Little Engel: A Ballad, with a Series of Epigrams from the Persian (London: Wise, 1913);

Marsk Stig: A Ballad (London: Wise, 1913);

Marsk Stig's Daughters, and Other Songs and Ballads (London: Wise, 1913);

The Mermaid's Prophecy, and Other Songs and Ballads (London: Wise, 1913);

Mollie Charane, and Other Ballads (London: Wise, 1913);

Niels Ebbesen and Germand Gladenswayne: Two Ballads (London: Wise, 1913);

The Nightingale, The Valkyrie and Raven, and Other Ballads (London: Wise, 1913);

Proud Signild and Other Ballads (London: Wise, 1913);

Queen Berngerd, The Bard and the Dreams, and Other Ballads (London: Wise, 1913);

The Return of the Dead and Other Ballads (London: Wise, 1913);

The Serpent Knight and Other Ballads (London: Wise, 1913);

Signelil: A Tale from the Cornish, and Other Ballads (London: Wise, 1913);

The Song of Deirdra, King Byrge and His Brothers, and Other Ballads (London: Wise, 1913);

The Songs of Ranild (London: Wise, 1913);

The Story of Tim (London: Wise, 1913);

The Story of Yvashka with the Bear's Ear (London: Wise, 1913);

The Tale of Brynild, and King Valdemar and His Sister: Two Ballads (London: Wise, 1913);

Ulf Van Yern and Other Ballads (London: Wise, 1913);

The Verner Raven, The Count of Vendel's Daughter, and Other Ballads (London: Wise, 1913);

Young Swaigder, or the Force of Runes, and Other Ballads (London: Wise, 1913);

The Expedition to Birting's Land and Other Ballads (London: Wise, 1914);

Tord of Halfsborough and Other Ballads (London: Wise, 1914);

Goronwy Owen (Goronwy Ddu o Fôn), *Ode to Lewis Morris [Cywydd i Lewis Morys]*, edited by Clement Shorter (London, [1915]).

Alongside works by Henry Fielding, Tobias Smollett, and Laurence Sterne, four of George Borrow's books — *The Bible in Spain; or, The Journeys, Adventures, and Imprisonments of an Englishman, in an Attempt to Circulate the Scriptures in the Peninsula* (1843);

Lavengro: The Scholar, The Gypsy, The Priest (1851); *The Romany Rye; A Sequel to "Lavengro"* (1857); and *Wild Wales: Its People, Language, and Scenery* (1862) — have been recognized as worthy of inclusion in the World's Classics series on travel and topography. *Lavengro* and its sequel, *The Romany Rye,* are, however, primarily semifictionalized autobiography and are not set beyond the borders of England.

Gypsies and philology, especially gypsy language, or Romany, are recurrent topics in all Borrow's works. He traveled widely and wrote extensively about his travels, but in only one case was a country (Wales) his primary focus, and he sometimes claimed credit for having visited places that he almost certainly never had visited. Of course, like many travel writers he was the hero of all his narratives. Even when his descriptions concern sites as near as Wales, they conjure up strange, invariably compelling vistas reminiscent of romantic landscapes. Yet Borrow was clearly driven to travel by a Faustus-like yearning for knowledge, especially for knowledge of exotic languages. Inevitably he suffered some misadventures during his travels abroad, including a spell of imprisonment in Spain, but his "unlimited capacity for enjoying in its own terms whatever happened to him" permeates his prose.

Borrow's books vividly depict a largely preindustrial world. They also provide idiosyncratic but evocative character sketches of many interesting individuals: John Joseph Gurney, a leading light in the Society of Friends (Quakers); John Thurtell, a boxing promoter and ne'er-do-well who was hanged for murder in 1824; William Taylor, a journalist acquaintance of William Godwin; Robert Southey; Sir Walter Scott; and Ambrose Smith, also known as Jasper Petrulengro, Borrow's gypsy "blood brother." His friendship with Smith stimulated Borrow's nascent interest in gypsy language and lore and eventually led him to investigate gypsy dialects in countries as different as Hungary, Spain, and Wales. Though his philological studies never matched those of the more linguistically sophisticated Charles Leland, they were still influential. When Georges Bizet was composing *Carmen* (1875), he turned to Borrow's *The Zincali; or, An Account of the Gypsies of Spain, with an Original Collection of Their Songs and Poetry, and a Copious Dictionary of Their Language* (1841) and *The Bible in Spain* for information about Spanish gypsies.

Many later writers — from Robert Louis Stevenson and Sir Arthur Conan Doyle to Gerald Brenan, D. H. Lawrence, and Virginia Woolf — found reading Borrow to be influential. In *Essays of Travel* (1905) Stevenson includes Borrow's *The Bible in Spain* upon "the three shelves of eternal books that never weary," alongside volumes by John Bunyan, Scott, William Shakespeare, Molière, Michel Montaigne, Charles Lamb, and Sterne. In *D. H. Lawrence: A Personal Record by E. T.* (1935) Jessie Chambers reports that Lawrence "greatly admired George Borrow" and suggests that Lawrence shaped his idea for conflating autobiography and fiction (as he had done in *Sons and Lovers,* 1913) from reading *Lavengro.*

Readers have formed disparate impressions of Borrow and his work: for biographer Eileen Bigland he is "the Ulysses of the nineteenth century," and for critic W. J. Keith, Borrow is "a rustic Don Quixote." The poet Edward Thomas chose to emphasize the nonrealistic vein in Borrow's work, asserting that Borrow presents "the country of his soul . . . essentially an imaginative country." In time, Borrow's *The Bible in Spain* became one of the standards by which any book on Spain would be measured. V. S. Pritchett notes that "For the Bible sellers, Spain can have changed little since the days of Borrow." Like Geoffrey Chaucer before him, Borrow repudiated the stultifying middle-class values associated with the false gentility that Borrow blamed for the disintegration of what Michael Collie has called "venerable communities" of gypsies, Jews, and Quakers. This concern for the fate of minority groups, with whom Borrow readily identified, also draws the modern reader to his work.

George Henry Borrow was born in East Dereham, Norfolk, on 5 July 1803. His father, Thomas Borrow, originally from Cornwall, was a career soldier, first in the Coldstream Guards (1783–1792) and later in the West Norfolk Militia (1792–1819), one who worked his way through the ranks during thirty-eight years of service and retired with the rank of captain. Borrow's mother, Ann Perfrement, married Thomas in 1793, when she was twenty-one years old. Brian Vesey-Fitzgerald reports romantic but uncorroborated stories about the gypsy blood of Ann Perfrement and about her having been an actress when she met her husband in Norwich. There is some uncertainty about the birth date of their first son, John (sometime between 1797 and 1801), and about his paternity. Borrow's own characteristically indirect statements in *Lavengro* hint at this illegitimacy and focus on the differences between the two brothers — John served in the military and became an artist.

Because his father's military career necessitated frequent moves, young George went to school wherever his father was stationed, from Norwich

May 3 1835 St Petersburg

Sir and dear Sir.

    I write a few hasty lines for the purpose of informing you that I shall not be able to obtain a passport for Siberia, except on the condition that I carry not one single Mantchou Bible thither. The Russian Government is too solicitous to maintain a good understanding with that of China to encourage any project at which the latter could take umbrage. Therefore pray inform me to what place I am to despatch the bibles. I have had some thoughts of embarking the first five parts without delay to England, but I have forborne from an unwillingness to do any thing which I was not commanded to do. By the time I receive your answer every thing will be in readiness, or nearly so, to be forwarded wherever the Committee shall judge expedient. I wish also to receive orders respecting what is to be done with the types. I should be sorry if they were to be abandoned in the same manner as before, for it is possible that at some future time they may prove eminently useful. As for myself, I suppose I must return to England, as my task will be speedily completed. I hope the Society are convinced that I have served them faithfully, and that I have spared no labour to bring out the work, which they did me the honor of confiding to me, correctly and within as short a time as possible. At my return; if the Society think that I can still prove of utility to them, I shall be most happy to devote myself still to their service. I am a person full of faults and weaknesses as I am every day reminded by bitter experience, but I am certain that my zeal and fidelity towards

Letter from Borrow to the Reverend Joseph Jowett, written during Borrow's stay in Saint Petersburg, Russia, where he worked on translating parts of the Bible (British and Foreign Bible Society)

those who put confidence in me are not to be shaken. Should it now become a question what is to be done with these Manchou Bibles which have been printed at a considerable expense I should wish to suggest that Baron Schilling be consulted; in a few weeks he will be in London, which he intends visiting during a summer tour which he is on the point of commencing. He will call at the Society's House, and as he is a Nobleman of great experience and knowledge in all that relates to China, it would not be amiss to interrogate him on such a subject. I again repeat that I am at command. In your last letter, but one, you stated that our noble President had been kind enough to declare that I had but to send in an account of any extraordinary expenses, which I had been put to in the course of the work, to have them defrayed. I return my most grateful thanks for this most considerate intimation which nevertheless I cannot avail myself of, as according to one of the articles of my agreement my salary of £200 was to cover all extra expenses. Petersburg is doubtless the dearest capital in Europe, and expenses meet an individual, especially one situated as I have been, at every turn and corner, but an agreement is not to be broken on that account.

I have the honor to remain
Rev^d and dear Sir
Your obedient humble Servant
George Borrow.

Revd Joseph Jowett.

to Edinburgh and any points between. Throughout life Borrow suffered from some undiagnosed ailment — perhaps manic depression, perhaps epilepsy — that he called "the horrors." Yet his education apparently did not suffer unduly. During his year at Edinburgh High School (1813–1814) he consolidated his knowledge of Latin, and in Clonmel, Ireland, he began studying Greek in school and Irish outside school. He finished his education back in East Anglia, with a stint at Norwich Grammar School from 1816 to 1819. Little is known of his scholastic record, although he certainly continued his Latin and Greek, and he found an exiled priest, Thomas D'Eterville, to teach him French, Italian, and a little Spanish. Having left school before he became sixteen years old, Borrow was articled to the law firm of Simpson and Rackham, although he had no serious intention of practicing law. Indeed, his growing philological interests in Danish, German, Hebrew, Romany, and Welsh must have precluded any but the most cursory acquaintance with Blackstone and legal scholarship during his five-year term.

In 1824 Thomas Borrow died, and George finished his legal apprenticeship. Almost immediately he set off for London — determined, like many another young provincial, to make his living as a writer. At first Borrow was convinced that he could survive as a translator, but British readers did not share his enthusiasm for Danish literature and obscure Welsh poets such as Dafydd ap Gwilym. So he was reduced to doing hackwork such as compiling the multivolume *Celebrated Trials, and Remarkable Cases of Criminal Jurisprudence, from the Earliest Records to the Year 1825* (1825). This work offered an apprenticeship in writing and helped him develop stylistically: he learned to recognize and admire the art of telling a plain story, and his interest in the eccentricities of human character blossomed.

Not until 1840 did Borrow find his way, upon the recommendation of an old friend, to the premises of John Murray of Albemarle Street, London. A conflict soon developed between what Borrow wanted to write about and what his publisher, Murray, felt the public would be receptive to. Thus while Borrow's preoccupation with languages, especially Romany dialects, is everywhere evident in his work and while few place-names or words of any interest appear unetymologized there, Murray and his consultant, Richard Ford, were consistently encouraging Borrow to provide more "personal narrative." Soon after the publication of *The Zincali,* Borrow cheerfully acknowledged, "You were quite right. . . . [F]rom the little that I can learn the public care not

one straw about research — extracts from obsolete books, or Sanscrit." Nevertheless, Borrow was not easily driven from his chosen path: both his early work, *The Zincali; or, An Account of the Gypsies of Spain, with an Original Collection of Their Songs and Poetry, and a Copious Dictionary of Their Language,* and the last one published in his lifetime, *Romano Lavo-Lil: Word-Book of the Romany* (1874), centered on that preeminent correlative passion to his philological interests — gypsy customs.

There is no easy explanation for Borrow's fascination with a community then widely regarded as societal outcasts: it certainly derives in part from his own sense of alienation, perhaps triggered by class insecurity, by his father's apparent preference for his elder brother, by Borrow's ambivalence about his sexuality, and in part from the challenge and attraction of a language unencumbered by any scholarly tradition. In any case, wherever he went on his travels — to Russia, Spain, Hungary, or Wales — he would seek out a gypsy enclave and record what he found there. If others surpassed him in scholarship, Borrow was never surpassed in enthusiasm, and the quality of his literary production, not his scholarship, has kept his work alive.

Borrow's pursuit of philological lore is balanced by his interest in humanity in all its manifestations. The reader who finds his linguistic predilections irritating would no doubt be surprised to learn that Borrow insisted in *The Bible in Spain* that "my favourite, I might say my only study, is man." People, not landscapes or nature, were his forte, particularly those on the margins of society — the hostler, the tinker, the itinerant preacher, the pugilist, the émigré. He writes in the appendix to *The Romany Rye* of "hunting after strange characters" as a comparable pleasure to that of "analysing strange words and names." In fact, the characters to whom he was drawn helped assuage his self-doubts. By seeking them out, identifying with them, and writing about them, Borrow found himself. When he stained his face with walnut juice while a schoolboy, he was both identifying with the gypsies and confirming his father's unfavorable perception of his countenance as "absolutely swarthy, God forgive me! I had almost said like that of a gipsy."

He took this identification a step further when he became blood brother to Ambrose Smith (the model for Jasper Petulengro of *Lavengro*) and later even took to the road as a tinker for a time. In fact, in the appendix to *The Romany Rye* Borrow also boasts of making a kind of assimilation: he writes of "becoming tinker, gypsy, postillion, ostler." If there were any question about his father's status as a gentleman, he could become a romany rye, a gypsy gentleman; if his father had once fought "Big Ben" Brain in Hyde Park, he could fight the "Flaming Tinman" in Mumper's Dingle.

Borrow was not an especially "literary" individual, and he sometimes even revealed an overt hostility to literature – as in his mischievous suggestion in *The Romany Rye* that a volume of William Wordsworth could cure insomnia. Borrow's response to Wordsworth also intimates an odd lack of sympathy for the natural world. Apart from horses and snakes, nature is notably absent from his work, as Vesey-Fitzgerald astutely observes in *Gypsy Borrow* (1953): "You can read all his books, and you will find scarcely a mention of a bird or a butterfly or a flower or a mammal."

Yet one literary figure can properly be called Borrow's literary master – Daniel Defoe. To him Borrow paid tribute, in word and in action. Writing to a friend, Dawson Turner, he envisaged *Lavengro* as "a kind of Biography in the *Robinson Crusoe* style," and early in the book appears a crucial passage wherein the narrator recounts the overwhelming influence that *The Life and Strange and Surprising Adventures of Robinson Crusoe* (1719) had on him as a child, for from this book, he claims, he learned to read. Other evidence of Borrow's fixation on Defoe is readily available: Borrow apparently acquired his knowledge of Dutch by reading *The History and Remarkable Life of Colonel Jack, Commonly Call'd* (1722) in that language. Collie has located a 1790 Dutch translation of that work that has Borrow's marginal annotations to it in the British Library.

The pride that Borrow took in his father's legendary Hyde Park battle of 1790 with "Big Ben" Brain, boxing champion of England from 1791 to 1794, signals his attachment to a sport that both epitomized "manliness" and familiarized him with many eccentric characters from the margins of society, among them the ill-fated John Thurtell. Mousehold Heath, on the edge of Norwich, was a regular camping ground for gypsies and a frequent venue for prizefights. But the first fight that Borrow witnessed was in North Walsham ("Eaton" in *The Zincali*), a dozen or so miles from Norwich, when he was a teenager. Thurtell promoted this fight between Tom Oliver and Ned Painter on 17 July 1820 and may indeed have introduced the boy to what Borrow unconvincingly labels "those disgraceful and brutalizing exhibitions called pugilistic combats."

Borrow grew to be a man of impressive proportions, six feet three inches tall and not at all averse to using his fists. Pugnacity became part of

his character and of his writing style. As Richard Ford admiringly characterized Borrow's *The Bible in Spain* to Murray, "He hits right and left and floors his man wherever he meets him." There is certainly an admirable directness about Borrow's style, even if it sometimes becomes gratuitously combative, as in his tiresome anti-Catholic diatribes that Murray tried to curb or in the attacks made in the appendix of *The Romany Rye* on "gentility-nonsense," "canting-nonsense," and on many of his former friends.

Pugilism is most prominent as a topic in *Lavengro*. There appear the voluble magistrate who loves boxing but "cannot patronise the thing very openly," the invocation of all the greats of the prize ring, and the epic struggle with "The Flaming Tinman" in Mumper's Dingle. Borrow's is a romantic imagination, and his major works consistently reveal him as the wanderer, the romantic hero of his own narratives.

The Zincali was a product of Borrow's first trip to Spain, in 1835 under commission from the British and Foreign Bible Society, which had authorized him to determine the feasibility of distributing a Protestant version of the Bible in a Catholic country. Originally he was to explore prospects in Portugal alone, but his antipathy toward the Portugese led him to press on to Spain. In Badajoz he was pleased to encounter gypsies, for they provided him both with protection against the civil war then raging and with the inspiration to study them. Borrow first began collecting songs and envisaged a work of translation; later he began to think about a comparative "vocabulary" of Romany and did considerable research in the National Library in Madrid.

In April 1839 he went to Seville to collect Andalusian gypsy vocabulary and songs, and there he produced a draft glossary. Much of his work had been done earlier during a five-year period of "moments snatched from more important pursuits, chiefly in ventas and posadas, whilst wandering through the [Spanish] country." However, only after having married the widowed Mary Clarke and settling down at Oulton did Borrow manage to get the manuscript in shape for publication, thanks to the willingness of his wife to transcribe it. Upon the recommendation of Richard Ford, whose authoritative two-volume *A Hand-Book for Travellers in Spain, and Readers at Home* was to appear later, in 1845, *The Zincali* was published on 17 April 1841 by John Murray.

Six hundred of the 750 first-edition copies were sold in the first week, and the book had appeared in three editions by 1843. The public responded more enthusiastically to the personal than

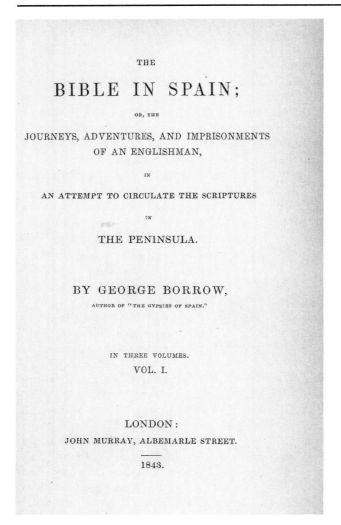

THE

BIBLE IN SPAIN;

OR, THE

JOURNEYS, ADVENTURES, AND IMPRISONMENTS
OF AN ENGLISHMAN,

IN

AN ATTEMPT TO CIRCULATE THE SCRIPTURES

IN

THE PENINSULA.

BY GEORGE BORROW,

AUTHOR OF "THE GYPSIES OF SPAIN."

IN THREE VOLUMES.
VOL. I.

LONDON:
JOHN MURRAY, ALBEMARLE STREET.
———
1843.

Title page for the book in which Borrow describes his experiences during his 1835 trip to Spain (courtesy of the Lilly Library, Indiana University)

to the philological material — that is, to the travelogue embedded within the quasi-scholarly material. As Borrow reported regretfully to Andrew Brandram of the Bible Society in 1841, "The public take very little interest in Sanskrit derivations and in gypsy words." In 1843 the *Edinburgh Review* saw his work as "something betwixt Le Sage and Bunyan" — not an unflattering comparison.

Drawing on Borrow's experiences with the gypsies in England, Russia, Hungary, and Spain, the first volume attempts a general survey of their ethnic history. Embedded in what might otherwise have been a rather dry narrative is a vivid account of well-to-do Moscow gypsies who profited from the popularity of female gypsy choirs and who mistook Borrow for "one of their wandering brethren from the distant lands." Other reports, far more fantastic in nature, derive from books that Borrow had con-

sulted in Madrid. Among them is a report by a seventeenth-century writer, Don Juan de Quiñones, concerning alleged cannibalism in the forest of Las Gamas. Borrow knew the place well and, as one who had shared a meal there with gypsies, testified that supper "did not consist of human flesh but of a puchera, the ingredients of which were beef, bacon, garbanzos, and berdolaga or field-pease."

The second volume contains the collection of songs and poems that Borrow set out to compile, along with a substantial glossary as well as a section on the language of the gypsies and another on a so-called robber language that we dropped in later editions. Here Borrow reveals his familiarity with Richard Head's *The English Rogue Described in the Life of Meriton Latroon* (1665) and its appended vocabulary of cant. Borrow's own glossary has value, but it contains an ill-assorted assembly of words and is unreliable in matters of etymology, although it offers putative cognates from Arabic, Greek, Persian, Russian, and Sanskrit. *The Zincali* is an odd mix of convincing eyewitness evidence and implausible secondary sources, but Borrow at least offers a critical review, and his ability to confirm or refute something on the basis of his own experience lends authority to his first major work.

Whatever the faults of the work, it so whetted the appetite of the public that Murray and Ford encouraged Borrow to write a sequel that would be free of dubious scholarship and that would emphasize Borrow's own experience. To this end Borrow approached the British and Foreign Bible Society for access to letters that he had written to it, and he used these as the basis for a second, far better-known book about Spain — *The Bible in Spain*. Setting to work in August 1841, he promised Murray "a queer book . . . containing all my queer adventures in that queer country."

Once again Ford reviewed the manuscript for Murray and reported positively on it, although he objected to some of the passages having been deliberately left unfinished: "A Novel writer, or even a writer of Travels, may pretend to be ignorant of things in order to keep them back; but they have no right to conceal what they admit they know." He also urged that the author disclose some personal details — about his birth, parentage, and education. He was unaware how obsessively reticent Borrow was about his background, and his request went unheeded.

When published on 10 December 1842 (with an 1843 imprint) in an edition of one thousand copies, this "queer book" was an overnight success and made Borrow's reputation. The popularity of *The*

Bible in Spain can be attributed in part to the implicitly heroic, even quixotic, nature of the narrative: an English gentleman enduring hardships and danger in a war-torn foreign land in order to promulgate the word of God. What could be more appealing to respectable English readers, especially to the evangelical set? Only the London *Times* reviewer, perhaps aware of Borrow's former Norwich associates such as John Thurtell, dared ask whether Borrow was a Christian or not. But in his preface Borrow had astutely presented himself as part missionary, part pilgrim who had claimed, "I am no tourist, no writer of books of travels; but I went there on a somewhat remarkable errand, which necessarily led me into strange situations and positions, involved me in difficulties and perplexities, and brought me into contact with people of all descriptions and grades." Having included so many things quite unconnected with religion or with his mission in Spain is thus excused as necessary to providing a "faithful narrative." *The Bible in Spain* inevitably retraced some of the ground covered in *The Zincali,* but the incidental observations of the earlier book that had focused exclusively on gypsy affairs became a full-fledged travel narrative, unstinting in detail, in the later book.

Initially Borrow is diligent in researching the potential market for the New Testament, as he arranges for its distribution among Lisbon booksellers, hires colporteurs, quizzes local children about their knowledge of Scripture, and leaves religious tracts in hostels and remote spots frequented by banditti. At times he presses his case with more ardor than diplomacy, as when he sits by the well in Evora, for example, and repeats to all passersby his usual inflammatory line — that "the Pope was an arch-deceiver, and the head minister of Satan here on earth." Yet he is not immune to the attractions of Lisbon and its environs: he kisses the tomb of Henry Fielding, admires the "stupendous" aqueduct, and rhapsodizes over the "Portugese Paradise" of Cintra.

His curiosity, "the leading feature of [his] character," leads him in some unexpected directions, too. A visit to the College of English Catholics is hardly what one would expect from such a self-confessed anti-Papist, and his question rhetorically anticipates the reader's puzzlement: "What motive could a Protestant have for intruding upon their privacy?" Echoing Alexander Pope, the answer is quintessentially Borrovian: "I visited this strange old house to converse with its inmates, for my favourite, I might say, my only study, is man." For Borrow, curiosity about humankind always

overcame ideological differences. Yet he was also a man who freely voiced his prejudices, a pattern of behavior deemed overly offensive even in a period far less sensitive to ethnic stereotypes. Thus his characterization of the Jews of Lisbon as "a vile infamous rabble" was omitted in the single-volume issue of the second edition (1843), and the whole passage was toned down so as to distinguish this community from English Sephardic Jews.

During his three weeks in Badajoz, Borrow first encountered "those singular people, the Zincali, Gitanos, or Spanish gypsies" and spent much of his time in their company. With one of them, Antonio Lopez, he set off for Madrid, and his narrative thus incorporated a privileged glimpse of gypsy life from the inside, for Borrow was accepted as a "London Calo" (gypsy). He learned from experience that to speak Romany in a lodging house (posada) could bring trouble; he heard the life story of a crone who had lived in Morocco; and he had some difficulty in fending off the offer of a gypsy *romi* (wife). His narrative is particularly effective at suggesting the strange inflections of gypsy speech, as in that of his gypsy crone, who says of her Moroccan husband: "I went with him, and he was my ro [husband], and we lived among the deserts, and hokkawar'd [cheated] and choried [stole] and told baji [fortunes]; and I said to myself this is good, sure I am among the Errate [gypsies] in a better chim [country] than my own."

Even from the most reticent individuals Borrow's questioning, often direct to the point of impertinence, seems to draw responses. When the mysterious "traveller of the night" who recognizes Borrow as an Englishman is in turn recognized as a Jew, the traveler reveals most of his "secrets" before they reach their destination. Yet how seriously are readers to take the claims of a strangely garbed, itinerant sausage maker (*longanizero*) that he has two wives and a fortune in buried gold and silver and that he practices usury on the side and has Jewish brethren among the highest ranks of the church? William I. Knapp, one of the gentlest of Borrow's critics, reminds readers that "From the moment our pilgrim reached the shores of the Peninsula, he seemed to have resumed his early habit of exaggeration and hyperbole." Other incidents and adventures are better documented: the executions by garroting that Borrow witnessed, the heads of banditti on poles on the road to La Coruña, the Italian peddler nostalgic for the "green English hedgerows," and what Borrow calls with characteristic grandiloquence "the Manchegan prophetess" — a blind girl fluent in Latin.

However, Borrow's aggressive pursuit of New Testament sales, not his consorting with gypsies and thieves, got him arrested after he persisted in attempting to print a Spanish version of the New Testament. He never received written permission, but his distribution of copies was tolerated until he set up shop, hired placard bearers to advertise for him, and became a real nuisance to the authorities. He was arrested and confined to the Carcel de la Corte and thereby precipitated something of an international incident. Borrow's account of it in *The Bible in Spain* represents him as being eager to proselytize among the inmates and to investigate the robber language of Spain. He even had the temerity to refuse to leave until he received an apology! When *The Bible in Spain* was published some years later, Borrow made the most of the incident in the subtitle. Such a mixture of adventure and missionary zeal could hardly fail with the public. But the passage of the Copyright Act of 1842 and the replacement of the standard three-volume with a cheaper one-volume edition (as in Murray's Colonial and Home Library series) ensured even wider dissemination and greater success for *The Bible in Spain*.

Many books through the years have extolled the beauties of Wales, and for Borrow *Wild Wales* was his creative swan song. Some of them, such as Edward Thomas's *Beautiful Wales* (1905) or Rhys Davies's *My Wales* (1937), are works of Welsh or Anglo-Welsh writers singing praises of their homeland. But *Wild Wales,* though the work of an Englishman, reaches into the heart of the country and certainly popularized Wales among the English middle class in late Victorian times. Collie and Fraser justly recognize it as "one of the classics in Welsh travel literature." Yet some inevitably are dissenters. Davies's argument is openly nationalistic: "Borrow's *Wild Wales* has rarely stirred Welshmen to enthusiasm. . . . [I]t seems devoid of true Welsh flavour and remains the book of an alien." Another Welshman, Ernest Rhys, explains the success of the book by transforming Borrow into a Celt, one who "was sensitive to place like so many men who have a Celtic strain in them (he was of Cornish descent) and certainly his 'Wild Wales' with all its grotesque errors and egotism is one of the few books in English that have succeeded in capturing the elusive spirit of Cymru."

Wild Wales was the product of two extended trips to Wales in 1854 and 1857, on which Borrow was accompanied some of the way by his wife and stepdaughter. Through the years he had come to rely on both of them for many of the practical necessities of life, and he pays tribute to his "exceedingly clever wife" in the book: "[I] always allow my wife to buy and sell, carry money to the bank, draw cheques, inspect and pay tradesman's bills, and transact all my real business, while I myself pore over old books, walk about shires, discoursing with gypsies, under hedgerows, or with sober bards – in hedge ale-houses." Borrow's first trip was made to north Wales, with headquarters in Llangollen, encompassing Bangor and Snowdon; the second was to south Wales through Lampeter, Llandovery, Swansea, Neath, and Chepstow. Through a walking tour of some four hundred miles, Borrow diligently took notes on all that he saw and learned, and by this time he had mellowed sufficiently to appreciate the picturesque, sometimes dramatic landscape.

Collie deems the work "a sort of miracle, really, when one looks back at the magical metamorphosis from crude notebook to urbane personal narrative." Perhaps the rediscovery of his own Celtic past, as he visited his Cornish relatives for the first time in 1853, was the catalyst. Yet Murray did not at first see the merits of the work and thought that it lacked "stirring incidents." After some changes had been made, however, he agreed to publish a three-volume edition of one thousand copies. This edition sold quickly, in spite of the unenthusiastic reception it received from reviewers; the single-volume edition issued in 1865 sold far more slowly.

For his title Borrow took the key phrase "Wild Wales" from the prophetic verses attributed to Taliesin in *Destiny of the Britons:* "Their Lord they shall praise / Their language they shall keep / Their land they shall lose / Except Wild Wales." Since his youth he had been fascinated with Wales and its language, which he had first heard from a Welsh hostler in Norwich. That "strange songster," ap Gwilym, was likewise one of the first poets whose work Borrow translated. Borrow sings the poet's praises in peculiarly pertinent terms: "He was . . . in love with nature alone – wild, beautiful, solitary nature – her mountains and cascades, her forests and streams." However, Borrow's celebration of ap Gwilym's world had to mature, as Borrow seems to recognize when his alter ego, Lavengro, announces mysteriously, "It is neither fit nor proper that I cross into Wales at this time, and in this manner."

The book may be a work of maturity, but Borrow has not lost his feistiness. His old prejudices reveal themselves still, if not quite with their former ferocity: he is as anti-Papist and antigentility as ever. Thus, he characterizes a convent as "a place devoted to gorgeous idolatry and obscene lust," and the Pope is once again "the arch thief of the world." To the Liverpool-born girl in Anglesey who prefers

Borrow's grave, Brompton Cemetery

English to Welsh because it is "most genteel" Borrow responds drily, "Gentility will be the ruin of Welsh." He is as curious as ever, supremely confident that it is *his* business to find out other people's. The book presents a picture of a man charging around Wales like a one-man census taker, asking people what their religions are (Calvinistic Methodist, as often as not), whether they speak Welsh (almost all do), whether they have any books in the house (usually a Welsh Bible), what they know about local landmarks or local writers, and so on. Borrow invariably knows more than the person whom he is interrogating: he will correct an error, translate an inscription, etymologize a word. In other words, he remains Borrow. Outside the village of Pentraeth Coch, for instance, he approaches a bridge across a brook. On the bridge stands an aged man:

> "To what place does this water run?" said I in English.
> "I know no Saxon," said he in trembling accents.
> I repeated my question in Welsh.
> "To the sea," he said "which is not far off. . . ."
> "You seem feeble?" said I.
> "I am so," said he, "for am I old."

> "How old are you?" said I.
> "Sixteen after sixty," said the old man with a sigh. . . .
> "Are you poor?" said I.
> "Very," said the old man.
> I gave him a trifle which he accepted with thanks.
> "Why is this sand called the red sand?" said I.
> "I cannot tell you," said the old man.

Sometimes there is simply too much of this dialogue, and one suspects self-parody (of which Borrow was quite capable). Or this may be the strategy of a man who is profoundly uncomfortable with normal conversation and whose only mode of communication is this kind of aggressive interrogation. It is not surprising that this sort of behavior led some contemporary critics to label Borrow egocentric and self-indulgent. In another more interesting incident, Borrow appears in *Wild Wales* as a folklorist. In this role he collects all sorts of extraordinary data about corpse candles, a holy well, second sight, a sea serpent, the legend of the dog, the mysterious *afanc* (a beaver-like creature), and so on. Yet he will occasionally voice pointed criticism. When shown a drowning pit and a whipping post, he reflects laconically that such sights provide "another memorial of the good old baronial times, so dear to romance readers and minds of sensibility."

When Borrow traveled to the Iberian Peninsula, he was entrusted with a specific mission – the dissemination of the Protestant Bible; when he traveled to Wales, his only mission was to see and enjoy "a very nice picturesque country." This difference in aims makes *Wild Wales* an example of the travel book in its purest form. Interwoven into the fabric of the book are the outlines of a sort of literary landscape, for Borrow had an extraordinarily retentive memory and enjoyed showing off his esoteric knowledge of literature in Welsh. Yet it is fair to say that "Borrow the philologist" was more interested in literary associations such as birthplaces, gravestones, and manuscripts than he was in literature. Such concrete literary gleanings gave point to, and even dictated, to some degree, Borrow's wanderings around Wales. Wherever he went Borrow ferreted out local lore about writers whom he deemed worthy of attention, added to it from his own storehouse, and then shared it with his readers.

Outside Llangollen he meets the grandson of Jonathan Hughes, the poet, and sees his eisteddfod prize and antique, three-cornered armchair; by the River Dee an old man's way of speaking reminds him of Morgan in Tobias Smollett's *The Adventures of Roderick Random* (1748); a *niwl* (mist) in the mountains reminds him of a similar one in which ap Gwilym once lost his way; and he locates and sits in the chair of Huw Morris, the Nightingale of Ceiriog. Other names tumble from his pages: Merlin; Evan Evans, friend of Thomas Gray; Owen Pugh; Edmund Price; Goronwy Owen; Lewis Morris; Robert Williams; Red Rhys of Snowdon; and Twm o'r Nant, sometimes dubbed "the Welsh Shakespeare."

In *Wild Wales* Borrow is unusually appreciative of the countryside. Perhaps he felt a growing sense that the world he knew was threatened by the Industrial Revolution; perhaps it was just the changing perception that comes with age. In any case, Borrow responds enthusiastically to "prospects" and picturesque scenes, especially to anything "wild," wherever he goes. Outside Corwen he finds "a beautiful but wild country of mountain and wood;" outside Pentre Voelas is "a wild hilly region . . . [where] there were dingles and hollows in abundance, and fantastic-looking hills." At times his eagerness for scenery costs him, as when he takes a recommended shortcut and gets hopelessly lost for two hours: "all these fine prospects were a poor compensation for what I underwent: I

was scorched by the sun . . . and my feet were bleeding from the sharp points of the rocks which cut through my boots like razors."

There are remarkably few encounters with evidence of the Industrial Revolution. Borrow meets people who have worked in England and who know such northern industrial cities as Bolton and Manchester, and he admires "mighty Telford's" iron bridge across the Menai Straits. But he despises railroads and has to be told that "the huge black buildings" that he saw early in this trip are collieries. He visited Wales in part to escape the busy and increasingly industrialized world so evident in England. In these circumstances, the slightly nostalgic tone of the book is to be expected.

Borrow was a man at odds with the world, a man who, through his extraordinary efforts and accomplishments, caught the attention of the public with a series of compellingly obsessive books. In Borrow's lifetime his fame was hard earned and short-lived, but after his death his reputation grew steadily among late Victorians and into the twentieth century, until some of his works became institutionalized as school set texts. But interest has faded in gypsy lore, fanciful etymologizing, and other philological ruminations, and Borrow – in all his guises as scholar, gypsy, and priest of the open road – has been largely forgotten, and his books are rarely read either by the general public or by college students.

Letters:

T. H. Darlow, ed., *Letters of George Borrow to the British and Foreign Bible Society* (London, New York & Toronto: Hodder & Stoughton, 1911);

Angus M. Fraser, ed., *A Journey to Eastern Europe in 1844* (Edinburgh: Tragara, 1981);

Fraser, ed., *Letters to John Hasfeld 1835–1839* (Edinburgh: Tragara, 1982).

Bibliographies:

T. J. Wise, *A Bibliography of the Writings in Prose and Verse of George Henry Borrow* (London: Privately printed, 1914);

Michael Collie and Angus M. Fraser, *George Borrow: A Bibliographical Study* (Winchester: St. Paul's Bibliographies, 1984).

Biographies:

William I. Knapp, *Life, Writings, and Correspondence of George Borrow*, 2 volumes (London: Murray, 1899);

Clement K. Shorter, *George Borrow and His Circle* (Boston & New York: Houghton Mifflin, 1913; London: Hodder & Stoughton, 1914);

Herbert Jenkins, *The Life of George Borrow* (London: Murray, 1914);

Eileen Bigland, *In the Steps of George Borrow* (London: Rich & Cowan, 1951);

Brian Vesey-Fitzgerald, *Gypsy Borrow* (London: Dobson, 1953);

René Fréchet, *George Borrow (1803–1881): Vagabond – Polyglotte – Agent Biblique – Ecrivain* (Paris: Didier, 1956);

Michael Collie, *George Borrow, Eccentric* (Cambridge: Cambridge University Press, 1982);

David Williams, *A World of His Own: The Double Life of George Borrow* (Oxford: Oxford University Press, 1982).

References:

W. J. Keith, "George Borrow," in his *The Rural Tradition: A Study of the Non-Fiction Prose Writers of the English Countryside* (Toronto: University of Toronto Press, 1974), pp. 105–125;

Edward Thomas, "George Borrow," in his *A Literary Pilgrim in England* (London: Methuen, 1917), pp. 244–253.

Papers:

Important Borrow manuscripts are in the following locations: the British Library; the Harry Ransom Humanities Research Center, University of Texas at Austin; the Hispanic Society of America (New York); the Henry E. Huntington Library, San Marino, California; the New York Public Library; and York University, Toronto.

Lady Annie (Allnutt) Brassey

(7 October 1839 – 14 September 1887)

Scott A. Leonard
Youngstown State University

BOOKS: *A Cruise in the "Eothen"* (London: Printed for private circulation, 1873);

Natural History of a Voyage in the "Sunbeam" (London: Longmans, 1878);

Around the World in the Yacht "Sunbeam" (New York: Holt, 1878); republished as *A Voyage in the Sunbeam, Our Home on the Ocean for Eleven Months* (London: Longmans, Green, 1878); abridged as *A Voyage in the "Sunbeam"* (London: Longmans, Green, 1881);

Sunshine and Storm in the East; or, Cruises to Cyprus and Constantinople (London: Longmans, Green, 1880; New York: Holt, 1880);

Tahiti: A Series of Photographs Taken by Colonel Stuart-Wortley, with Letterpress by Lady Brassey (London: Sampson Low, 1882);

In the Trades, the Tropics, & the Roaring Forties (London: Longmans, Green, 1885; New York: Holt, 1885);

Lady Brassey's Three Voyages in the "Sunbeam" (London: Longmans, Green, 1887);

The Last Voyage, edited by Lady Mary Ann Broome (London & New York: Longmans, Green, 1889).

SELECTED PERIODICAL PUBLICATION –
UNCOLLECTED: "Mr. Gladstone in Norway," *Contemporary Review*, 48 (October 1885): 480–503.

Annie Brassey

To her professed astonishment Lady Annie Brassey's first widely published and most famous book, *Around the World in the Yacht "Sunbeam"* (1878), propelled her to instant and international celebrity. It sold so quickly that its sixth edition appeared within a year of its initial printing, and by 1881 it had so endeared itself to British readers that Longmans, Green published an edition "adapted for school and class reading" that stayed in print for a decade; the narrative remained in print for thirty years in both French and English. *Sunshine and Storm in the East; or, Cruises to Cyprus and Constantinople*

(1880) and *In the Trades, the Tropics, & the Roaring Forties* (1885), Lady Brassey's two later "Sunbeam" books, also fared well. Each remained in print in both French and English well into the 1890s, and the latter was even translated into German during the 1880s.

Brassey relates an anecdote in *Trades* that suggests the extent of her literary eminence. During an unannounced stopover in the Bahamas in 1883 she found that many of the inhabitants either owned or had read borrowed copies of *Around the World in the Yacht "Sunbeam,"* and such was her fame that a steady pilgrimage of curious fans asked permission to visit the famous vessel. Even on the last day of their Bahamian stay, amid their final preparations for the long passage to the Azores, Brassey reports that her guests "continued to arrive in a continuous stream for more than an hour."

In the years between 1873 and 1887 Brassey's travel writings evolved from letters home into eagerly anticipated, urbane travelogues enjoyed throughout the world. Her career as a travel writer began with the practice of writing "long journal letters home to [her] father to be afterwards circulated among other relatives and more intimate friends." *A Cruise in the "Eothen"* (1873), a comparatively short book of 149 pages that was published for private circulation, was her initial foray into travel writing. Only after her family and friends had urged her to publish the diary of her round-the-world voyage did Brassey reluctantly begin to think of herself as a travel writer. That runaway success of *Around the World in the Yacht "Sunbeam"* encouraged her to make accounts of the family's voyages more widely available.

Sunshine and Storm in the East, which described and contrasted the family's 1874 and 1878 excursions to Constantinople, followed. Both *Sunshine and Storm* and *Around the World* demonstrate the epistolary origin of her travel writing through their chatty, familiar tones and tendencies to assume that readers would know her and her family so well that only pet names and oblique references need be used. Despite the provoking omissions that result from this familiarity, the overall effect of Brassey's style is quite appealing. She seems to chirp and chat with friends and acquaintances over tea, rather than to drone over slides of the family vacation. Indeed, her friend and literary advisor Lady Mary Ann Broome identifies this "extraordinarily intimate and friendly feeling between herself and her readers" as the quality most responsible for creating her worldwide audience. Brassey's cheery banter is the more remarkable when one considers that, like Charles Darwin, she endured chronic seasickness; in addition, especially after 1880 Brassey suffered from recurrent bouts of neuralgia and a malaria-like fever.

Despite her international fame and the relatively wide circulation of her travel writings during the late nineteenth century, very little has been written about Lady Annie Brassey. Even obituary notices are brief. Such a dearth of biographical data results both from Brassey's self-effacing books and from the reticence of her family and friends to violate the charmed circle of her privacy. Lady Broome, who had been entrusted

with Brassey's final journals and the rough draft of *The Last Voyage* (1889), remarks that the "brief jottings" recording the "simple sufferings and helpless weakness" marking Brassey's final illness were "too private and sacred for publication." What little biographical information exists about her must be gleaned from oblique references in her books and from the preface to *The Last Voyage,* in which her husband, Lord Thomas Brassey, eulogizes her.

Lord Brassey's "memoir" of his wife records that she was christened Anna Allnutt. Apparently an only child, she was left motherless while yet an infant and thereafter lived with her father and grandfather in Clapham. There, according to Lord Brassey, "she acquired that love of the country, the farm, and the garden which she retained so keenly to the last. [There] she learned to ride; and [there] with little guidance from teachers, she had access to a large library, and picked up in a desultory way an extensive knowledge of the best English, French, German, and Italian literature."

After residing a few years in Clapham, the family moved to a Charles Street address in London and hired a governess, Miss Newton, to educate young Anna in a more organized fashion. How Anna Allnutt was able to gain a reading knowledge of four languages in "a few years" is not specified in Lord Brassey's memoir. Nor is it recorded what piqued her special interest in botany, "the science which she found so useful later, in describing the profuse and varied vegetation of the tropics." Nevertheless, her travel books confirm these scant facts about her education.

Annie Allnutt married Thomas Brassey 9 October 1860, a time during which, as Lord Brassey frankly admits, "no definite career had opened out" for him. Uncertainty about livelihood did not, however, mean that the young couple was destitute, for Brassey's family had lived for nearly six centuries at Bulkeley. At the time of their marriage, the Brasseys still held land in Bulkeley, although they had moved the ancestral home to Buerton by 1663. Brassey's father (also named Thomas) had vastly enriched the estate as he advanced himself from positions first as an apprentice, then a land surveyor (1821), and then a railroad contractor who oversaw, by the 1850s, projects in France, Italy, Canada, the Crimea, Australia, Argentina, India, Moldavia, and Austria.

The younger Thomas was eventually able, with the help of his bride, to launch a career in politics in 1861. Earning a reputation for "nerve,

AROUND THE WORLD IN
THE YACHT 'SUNBEAM'

*OUR HOME ON THE OCEAN FOR
ELEVEN MONTHS*

BY

MRS. BRASSEY

*With Illustrations. Chiefly after Drawings by the
Hon. A. Y. Bingham*

NEW YORK
HENRY HOLT AND COMPANY
1878

Frontispiece and title page for Brassey's third travel book (courtesy of the Lilly Library, Indiana University)

high spirit, and ability among supporters of the Liberal party," Annie Brassey worked hard in her husband's campaigns. Lord Brassey, while asserting that her efforts were motivated by love for him, also suggests that she believed in the Liberal cause: "she had too much intelligence not to form a judgment of her own on public issues. Her sympathies were instinctively on the side of the people, in opposition to the old-fashioned Toryism." Indeed, her books frequently digress to reflect on political matters in a way that bespeaks a complex mélange of intellectual conviction, social liberalism, economic conservatism, racialized nationalism, and old-fashioned noblesse oblige, as Lady Brassey's remarks on the possibility of native rule in India illustrate in *The Last Voyage:*

> Under native rule, roads, sanitation, education, everything which belongs to the higher civilization, is ne-

glected, while money is lavishly spent on elephants, equipages, menageries, jewelry, palaces, and barbaric splendors of every kind. It is a great abuse, much needing correction, that the native states, though they have received from the British complete guarantees against foreign invasion and internal rebellion, maintain armed men, for the vanity of military display, to the number of 315,000.

> It would have lightened our burdens greatly if the internal government of India could have been left under native princes. Such an alternative, unfortunately, was not open to us. The native rulers would have proved for the most part incapable of the task. They would have been led on by internecine warfare to mutual destruction. The trade with England depends on the peace which we have been instrumental in preserving.

Between her marriage in 1860 and her family's voyage in 1872 to North America, the Brasseys had three children: Thomas Allnutt ("Tab"), Mabelle Annie, and Muriel Agnes ("Muñie"). Their fourth child, Marie Adelaide, seems to have been born sometime between the 1872 voyage to North America and the family's 1876–1877 circumnavigation, for one reads in *Around the World in the Yacht "Sunbeam"* of Lady Brassey's deep concern about the health of an infant when, somewhere between Honolulu and Japan on 8 January 1877, she writes that "All the early part of the morning we were in the greatest anxiety about baby; she could hardly draw her breath, and lay in her cot, or on her nurse's lap, almost insensible, and quite blue in the face, in spite of the application of mustard, hot water and every remedy we could think of. The influenza with her has taken the form of bronchitis and pleurisy."

While the reader can be fairly confident that "baby" is Marie Adelaide and thus infer that she was born earlier than the events recounted in *Around the World in the Yacht "Sunbeam,"* the passage also illustrates Brassey's tendency to assume her readers' familiarity with her personal affairs. This characteristic feature of her style furthermore makes it difficult to construct an accurate biography. There are, for example, references to a "baby" throughout *"Eothen,"* apparent references to Marie's older sister Muriel; but on at least one occasion the "baby" mentioned in *"Eothen"* is actually Félise, the family pug, for Lady Brassey confesses to disguising the dog in "the long baby outfit" in order to smuggle her onto trains and boats, where pets were forbidden.

As a member of Parliament and civil lord of the Admiralty, Thomas Brassey traveled widely to gather intelligence on new methods of manufacture, labor-management relations, work and wages, and the readiness of colonial forces to maintain the law and order necessary to ensure English commerce. The British government commissioned first the *Eothen* and later the *Sunbeam* to facilitate his travels, journeys that provided his wife the occasion for and substance of the books that made her so famous. He also published books and papers describing both the family's voyages and his views on matters of state such as work and wages, manufacturing methods, and labor unions. Like his wife's books, Lord Brassey's writings have long been out of print. Nevertheless, his works received critical notice in the *Times* (London) and other literary journals. In all, Lord Brassey's civic obligations necessitated at least eight long cruises between 1869 and 1885.

Annie Brassey's first book, *A Cruise in the "Eothen,"* records events between 28 August and 29 November 1872. Boarding the *Hibernia,* a large pas-

senger steamer bound for North America with a cargo of emigrants, Brassey, her servants, and her children left for Quebec, where her husband was to meet them in the *Eothen.* Brassey's basic plans for travel, as well as her literary methods, are discernible in this first book. The entries are diary-like, frequently brief and impressionistic, but occasionally offering extended reflections on a variety of topics. In each of her travel books the Brasseys visit their expatriate peers, visit notable sights, and (frequently together) inspect factories and military installations in order to fulfill Lord Brassey's mission. In these narratives Lady Brassey focuses her observations on such domestic concerns as table setting, food quality, architecture and decoration, gardening, costuming, the relative refinement of equipage, and the manners of both European and native inhabitants of a land. She characteristically also assigns the world's populations to their "proper" spheres in respect to the British "social scale," and she maps those territories of the world administered by European cultural practices and those territories not so administered.

A Cruise in the "Eothen" thus begins with an observation that distinguishes between the top and bottom of the nineteenth-century European social scale:

> The train [to Liverpool, and thence to the ship that is to carry them to Canada] was crowded with poor emigrants, bound for America, and when we arrived it was just the dawn of a cold grey morning, and very miserable the poor creatures looked, sitting on their boxes, surrounded with children and bundles, till they were all carted away together to the docks. . . . We walked into the North-Western Hotel, which forms part of the station, and where we were tolerably comfortable.

After she has arrived in North America and met her waiting husband, Lady Brassey begins assessing the degree to which the New World has come under the administration of European social customs: "the FIRST thing that struck us, was the wooden houses, plank roads, and plank footways; the SECOND, the colonial means of conveyance — a calash, which is a vehicle something between a Maltese go-cart and a calèsh." This remark demonstrates Brassey's bent for comparing the cultural attainments of the people she visits with the sophisticated forms of Europe and her acute sensitivity to the trappings and perquisites of wealth and privilege.

The torrent of images and events that rush through Brassey's account of their itinerary sweep the reader along at dizzying speed. But she is not merely an energetic tourist; she is endowed with a consuming curiosity and a powerful desire to see the world, the entire world, through her own eyes. As she concludes the Canadian leg of their journey, Brassey writes, "we took with much regret, our last look of [Niagara] Falls, hoping earnestly it might be only farewell for a time. I don't think I ever felt so sorry to leave any place before. There is a sort of fascination about them which makes one feel almost ready to cry with regret at leaving." From Niagara the Brasseys traveled by train back to Toronto, resettled themselves aboard the *Eothen,* and made their way to Boston via the Saint Lawrence Seaway, Prince Edward Island, and Nova Scotia.

The Brasseys found Boston charming, primarily because it reminded them so much of home. Brassey writes that "one is everywhere constantly reminded of old England; for there is the same language heard, the same physical aspect, dress, manner, and style of building." They visited Harvard, which they compared to Oxford; toured a shoe factory in Lowell; attended the opera and theater during the evenings; and marveled at the many excellent and inexpensive bookstores, as well as the public library that contained "a large and valuable collection of books in every language, which may be either lent to the readers to take home, or may be read in the spacious rooms provided for that purpose." Brassey's observations on Boston conclude by noticing that the resemblance between England and Boston ends "when one sees at every turn huge drays and wagons with Negro drivers." Her general discomfort and repugnance at the constant close contact with "pickaninnies," "Negroes," "niggers," and "darkies" lie close to the surface of all her observations, though the degree to which she is affected does not become explicit until near the end of *"Eothen."* There, during a lunch at Delmonico's, she expresses relief at being "waited on by French waiters, which was a most pleasant change after all the Negroes and coloured people who have attended on us lately."

Puzzling as it may seem to modern readers, Brassey's wide travels and constant exposure to people of color never altered the bizarre mixture of curiosity, condescending noblesse oblige, and disgust with which she regarded non-European inhabitants of the world. Voicing the anxiety that her long-anticipated visit to the Caribbean would not live up to her expectations as completely as she would like, the narrator of *In the Trades, the Tropics, & the Roaring Forties* consoles herself with the thought that "at all events we shall see niggers, in

whom (their babies especially) I always delight. I think the latter are something like kittens – far preferable in their babyhood."

Indeed, the tension between Brassey's preconceptions of how the places that she visits look and how they *should* look constitutes one of the chief organizing principles of her books. Especially in the early works, she repeatedly laments that such places as Canada, Constantinople, and China are not as exotic as she has supposed them to be. In *"Eothen,"* for example, Brassey observes that "the Indians themselves, from the effects of intermarrying, the introduction of civilization, and modern clothing, are almost indistinguishable from the French population, though some of them retain, particularly when old, a peculiar cast of features." In *Sunshine and Storm in the East* Brassey describes her surprise at the incongruity of finding European clothes and shops in the otherwise "picturesque" bazaars and expresses disappointment that Constantinople's smoky skies "had a much more Manchesterian aspect than [she] liked to see."

Around the World in the Yacht "Sunbeam" recounts the Brasseys' circumnavigation of the globe. Departing Chatham on 1 July 1876 the Brasseys steamed downriver, visiting friends and taking on provisions along the way, until on 6 July the *Sunbeam* headed to sea, making for Madeira, Tenerife, and Cape Verde before undertaking the blue-water passage to Rio de Janeiro. As the *Sunbeam* slowly worked its way around the coast of South America from Rio to Valparaiso, Chile, the Brasseys took numerous trips inland by horse, oxcart, and train to see rain forests, mountains, deserts, the Pampas, colonial outposts, mines, plantations, and the legendary free and easy life of the gauchos. From Valparaiso they sailed to Tahiti and then to the Sandwich (now the Hawaiian) Islands.

The pace of the narrative picks up after the Hawaiian Islands, even though the second half of the voyage requires almost twice as many pages. On 3 January 1877 the *Sunbeam* left Hawaii for the Orient and a truly daunting itinerary in Japan, China, Singapore, and Ceylon. Rising by 4:00 A.M. to record her impressions of the previous days' activities, Brassey usually breakfasted and left the *Sunbeam* by 8:30 A.M., toured all day, and returned just in time for the 6:30 P.M. bell calling her to dress for dinner – usually off-ship when they were in port. Many nights their dinner visits would end well after midnight; nevertheless, Lady Brassey would be up and writing at her usual early hour the next day.

Leaving Ceylon on 5 April, the *Sunbeam* made its next landfall off the coast of Somalia, turned north, and put into port off Aden. From there the family cruised up the Red Sea, through the Suez Canal, into the Mediterranean, and finally returned to Chatham on 26 May 1877. On this final leg of the journey the Brasseys made time to visit Cairo and take the children to the pyramids, pay their respects to the duke of Edinburgh at Malta, and visit the British installation at Gibraltar.

In *Around the World in the Yacht "Sunbeam,"* as elsewhere, Brassey's crisply drawn word pictures convey the colors, smells, textures, and sights of the places she visits. Readers enjoyed the vicarious thrill of "seeing" a world still largely untamed and teeming with primeval wonders. But however great her power of painting a landscape, Brassey is at her best when describing the natives. Whether she is comparing the colors and textures of the loose, comfortable garments worn by Tahitian and Hawaiian women, or distinguishing skin colors of various indigenous peoples of Tierra del Fuego, Brassey's keen eye for detail makes these occasions vivid. A particularly amusing moment occurs in Japan when Brassey, with Victorian delicacy, describes the skin art on the men hired to convey her party on a country tour:

> We had not long left the town before our [rickshaw pullers] began to undress each other; for their clothes were so tight that it required no inconsiderable effort to remove them. Some of them were beautifully tattooed. My wheeler had the root of a tree depicted on one foot, from which sprang the trunk and branches, spreading gradually, until on his back and chest they bore fruit and flowers, among which birds were perched. On his other leg was a large stork, supposed, I imagine, to be standing under the shadow of the same tree.

In addition to its brilliant visuality, the great appeal of *Around the World in the Yacht "Sunbeam"* may be attributed to the sheer audacity of the adventure it describes. The *Sunbeam* was one of the first yachts to combine steam and sail power, and this allowed the Brasseys to maintain their course even when the wind was calm or contrary — although it also meant that the boiler could burst or the coal in the hold could catch fire. In fact, the boat did catch fire twice on this journey, once during the middle of the night when only the pilot and an insomniac maid saved the ship from complete disaster.

But few of the Brasseys' adventures were accidental; the family actively sought excitement wherever they visited. On another occasion, they took a Christmas Eve hike inside Mauna Loa's crater to get a closer view of the "lake of fire." Their return trek was accomplished after sundown and, with the darkness, Lady Brassey calmly notes that they could see the reddish glow of molten rock one or two feet beneath their feet as they walked. Not only was the journey intensely hot, but there was so little oxygen there that, before she could make it back to the rim, Lady Brassey lost consciousness and had to be carried the rest of the way.

While accounts of high-seas misadventure and inland derring-do make Brassey's books thrilling reading, they serve another purpose as well. By balancing descriptions of the wild and untamed non-European world with anecdotes demonstrating the reassuring orderliness and vitality of European civilization, Brassey can, in effect, domesticate the unfamiliar. With the regularity of a stylistic tic, she juxtaposes the most exotic scenes with those of the most cultured propriety. For example, following her description of an encounter with "quite naked but very happy" Tierra del Fuegan aboriginals "shouting and jabbering away in the most inarticulate language imaginable," she records that the ship's carpenter "had prepared a board, on which the name of the yacht and the date had been painted, to be fixed on shore, as a record of our visit." The sign is a gesture that regulates uncultivated nature and uncivilized humanity by orienting them, metonymically at least, to Europe. The point is reiterated a few weeks later on the passage from Tierra del Fuego to Valparaiso, as Lady Brassey writes:

> In the afternoon a large shoal of whales came round the yacht. I was below when they first made their appearance, and when I came on deck they were spouting up great jets of water in all directions, suggestive of the fountains at the Crystal Palace. We were lying so still that they did not seem to be in the least afraid of us, and came quite close, swimming alongside, round us, across our bows, and even diving under our keel. There was a shoal of small fish about, and the whales, most of which were about fifty or sixty feet in length, constantly opened their huge pink whale-bone fringed mouths so wide that we could see right down their capacious throats. The children were especially delighted with this performance, and baby has learned quite a new trick. When asked, "what do the whales do?" she opens her mouth as wide as she can, stretches out her arms to their fullest extent, then blows and finishes up with a look around for applause.

Like the commemorative English sign on the tree, the vast and ungovernable power of the whales that the Brasseys encounter is domesticated by making a

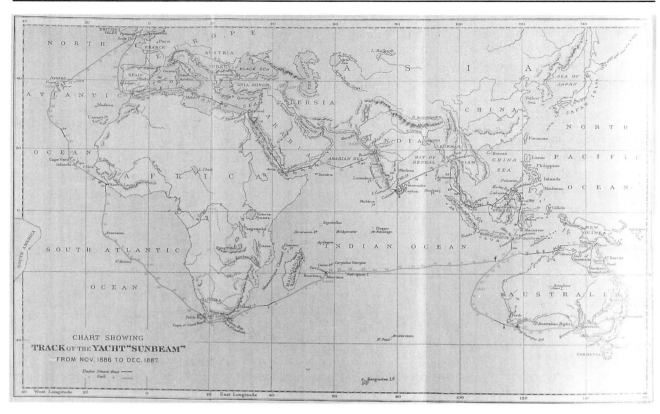

Map of Brassey's 1886–1887 voyage on the Sunbeam

child's game of their behavior and recounting the adventure as a cute baby story.

The nineteenth-century European impulse to regulate and administer "uncivilized" peoples and the indifferent power of nature included even time. In *Sunshine and Storm in the East,* for example, when Brassey is in Constantinople for the first time, she remarks that "Turkish time is puzzling, for it changes every day. What is with us twelve o'clock of the night – that is, the close of one day and the beginning of the next – is with the Turks the moment of sunset. Consequently there is a daily alteration of a few minutes, and this makes it extremely difficult to keep your watch right, and not to be too late or too early for everything."

In another account of the passage from Valparaiso to Tahiti in *Around the World in the Yacht "Sunbeam"* Lady Brassey remarks languidly that "with perfect weather, plenty of books to read, and writing to do, no possibility of interruptions, one can map out one's day and dispose of one's time exactly as one pleases, until the half-past six o'clock dressing-bell – which always seems to come long before it is wanted – recalls one to the duties and necessities of life." Even when the

Brasseys are afloat in the steamy tropics, their uneasiness with a construction of temporality that fluctuates a little every day demonstrates the degree to which European customs ultimately created a self-policing consciousness and an inability to achieve psychic equilibrium without regular, repeated performances of customs and rituals such as formally dressing for dinner every day at 6:30 P.M.

Brassey's next book, *Sunshine and Storm in the East; or, Cruises to Cyprus and Constantinople,* recounts two voyages to Constantinople – the first in 1874, the second in 1878. Both sojourns entailed the social calls, inspections, collecting, and adventures found in *A Cruise in the "Eothen"* and *Around the World in the Yacht "Sunbeam,"* but Brassey focuses attention on the change in Constantinople "from all that was bright and glittering to all that was dull and miserable and wretched." The narrative describing the first trip spends chapters on the opulence and decadence of Sultan Abdul Aziz. At pains to evoke the exoticness of Constantinople and its ruler, Brassey repeats all available hearsay about intrigues among the sultan, his harem, the grand vizier, and the pashas. Much narrative space is also devoted to describing the bustling activity of the "picturesque" bazaars. Despite Brassey's distaste for Oriental ostentation and her censure of the sultan's reputed capriciousness and cruel displays of power, she and her retinue go to great lengths just to catch a glimpse of his royal caravan making its way to daily prayer. After several unsuccessful attempts to see the sultan and his entourage, Brassey finally decides to rent both a carriage and a caïque in order to be able to follow the sultan, whether he goes to the mosque by land or by sea.

Brassey's second visit to Constantinople was, indeed, quite different from the first. The Turkish war with the Russians had sent a flood of refugees into Constantinople. The many wives of the sultan who had entertained Brassey so grandly four years previously had, by the second visit, impoverished themselves by selling their luxuries in order to feed the starving masses streaming from the front. While extolling the charity of her friends in the sultan's house and still remaining enchanted with the exotic beauties of the mosques, bazaars, and Roman antiquities, Brassey presents her strongest impressions of the miserable weather and filthy crowds of starving men, women, and children:

> It was impossible to sleep, and I lay and looked out of the window in the moonlight, and pictured to myself all the scenes of misery that had taken place at the [train] station close by. Men, women, and children . . . sit there for days in long lines extending nearly a mile on either side of the station, waiting for a passage by one of the few passing trains, clinging frantically to steps and buffers when carriages and cattle-trucks were full, only to be dragged away and left behind, or thrown off and killed at the first curve or sudden jerk. Carts went round every morning to carry a little coarse food, and to bring away the dead. One morning, after a severe frost and heavy snow, six carloads of little children were carried away from among the crowds of refugees.

The Brasseys' return voyage was plagued by severe storms. They had scarcely rounded the Golden Horn and left old Stamboul in their wake when the weather turned very bad – five gales in eleven days – and forced them to drop anchor at Gallipoli, Syra, Milós, and Malta. While Brassey did make short excursions ashore at these stops, her husband wanted the crew ready to sail at the first sign of a break in the weather. Such was Lord Brassey's urgency that, even though the passengers had been promised a day's sightseeing at Milo, he gave an order to set sail upon seeing a promising rise in the barometer – and so hasty was their departure that the provisions they had just ordered were left piled on the dock.

In the Trades, the Tropics, & the Roaring Forties recounts the Brasseys' penultimate voyage, from 27 September 1883 to 30 December 1883, which took them from Dartmouth to Venezuela via Madeira and Trinidad and back home, after stops at Jamaica, the Bahamas, Bermuda, and the Azores. For this journey the family met Lord Brassey and the *Sunbeam* at Madeira, where they stayed from 30 September until 11 October. While it is clear from passing references that Lady Brassey's health was deteriorating, the number of overland excursions, visits, inspections, and additions to her collection did not abate.

In addition to the usual attractions of Brassey's writing, this narrative is also interesting for its undercurrent of marital stress. Indeed, Brassey represents the tokens of her dutifulness to her "Tom" with increasing frequency in each book after *Around the World in the Yacht "Sunbeam."* There Brassey's disappointment at being obliged to miss visiting Milo, for instance, is couched in hints that her ability to see Tom's decision as "reasonable" has been dearly bought. But with *In the Trades* Brassey's irritation is more apparent. At one point she sighs that her lifelong dream of a leisurely cruise in the tropics "is not to be thought of. We must not, however, grumble."

Yet Brassey does grumble about both the itinerary and her husband's high-handedness. Lord Brassey decides, even as they are leaving Madeira, that it is a dangerous time of year to make for their original landfall in Barbados and sets a new course for Tobago. Then, after counting the hours until she can see Tobago, Brassey describes her "horror" at waking one morning to find that island well astern after her husband has suddenly, and without announcing it, decided to forego their stop there after all. Though she shows "proper" wifely submission by remarking mildly that she was "somewhat consoled by the thought that there is not a great deal to be seen at Tobago," she nevertheless devotes several pages to an encyclopedic description of what she might have seen had the party been allowed to disembark there. Thinking about these events, Brassey irritably laments that "it is rather provoking after coming so far, to be so pressed for time (as we always are, and always shall be . . . as long as Tom is in office) that we are unable to visit the various islands we pass so close to, each and all of which possess some special interest." Such remarks obviously do not suggest that the Brasseys were at war with one another; nevertheless, the scant record hints that they had been months apart before their rendezvous in Madeira, and they had

Frontispiece and title page for Brassey's last travel book, completed by her husband following her death at sea in the South Pacific

made their onshore excursions separately, as often as not, at ports of call thereafter.

The Last Voyage chronicles the final chapter in Brassey's eventful life in a way that does her credit. The prefatory material suggests that Lady Broome assembled the final manuscript of *Voyage* by stitching together Lady Brassey's sometimes terse notes, Lord Brassey's own interpolations, and excerpts from what had become known in the family as the "*Sunbeam* papers" (Lord Brassey's records of the voyages). While the narrative captures some of Brassey's characteristic charm and good cheer, it is not surprising that much of what makes the other books such a pleasure to read is muted or missing from *The Last Voyage.*

The first part of the text, apparently written during a particularly bad period of her final illness,

is quite sketchy, but upon reaching Shikarpur and the emir's residence, Brassey rallied for a time and the entries become much fuller. Despite great physical discomfort she was able to maintain her usual breakneck pace for several months. The Brasseys' visits to Goa, Ceylon, Burma, Singapore, Borneo, New Guinea, and Australia were every bit as eventful as those of other voyages had been. To the last she made increasingly arduous excursions from the boat to go sightseeing and asked to be carried ashore where, seated in a chair fixed to two long poles, she frequently went on extended tours and inspections.

The Brasseys traveled separately to India, but after their reunion they resumed their accustomed shipboard routine, which was broken only once when, on the first day from Bombay, one of their party abruptly committed suicide by jumping overboard. Having briefly visited Singapore, the Brasseys went on to Borneo, where Lady Brassey and her daughters took a trip up the Segama River to explore some caves and catch glimpses of the headhunters still living in the jungle. From Borneo the *Sunbeam* traveled south, stopping briefly at Makassar. Less than one hundred miles from the spot where her body would eventually be slipped overboard to its final resting place, Brassey presciently wrote on 23 April, "I dread this voyage somehow, and begin even to dislike sailing."

By the beginning of May 1887 Brassey's health was in final decline. Though she normally avoided making references to herself, she began with increasing frequency to write of her constant neuralgia and fatigue and, after catching a cold in Melbourne, noted with asperity that she could not seem to get over her bronchitis. At one point she remarked that "not having a secretary to help me, I find [writing] really hard; for my arm is often so bad that I can hardly use it."

On 10 May the *Sunbeam* was safely harbored in King George Sound, from which port the party traveled by train and horse to see the surrounding forests before making for Adelaide. Despite what must have been considerable discomfort, Brassey attended a hunt in the Adelaide bush and spoke at a meeting of the St. John's Ambulance Society. At Adelaide, too, she and her husband parted company, Lord Brassey sailing the yacht from Adelaide to Melbourne and Lady Brassey taking a train across country. Neither was feeling particularly well by their 11 June reunion, but both managed to visit the gold mines. Thus, through a combination of train and boat travel she managed to see most of Australia. Despite her gradual decline, she attended evening entertainments; spoke with acknowledged difficulty at several "ambulance meetings"; toured the Newcastle coal mine, the Mount Morgan gold mines, and the Springsure opal mines; and played the gracious hostess aboard the *Sunbeam.* Her entries stop abruptly on 29 August with an account of her attempt to induce a doctor to replace her in delivering an "ambulance lecture" to the inhabitants of Thursday Island.

According to the ship's log (part of the appendices accompanying *The Last Voyage*), Brassey died 14 September 1887 at 11:00 A.M. and was "committed to the deep at sunset, latitude 15.50 South, longitude 110.38 East." Lord Brassey's narrative opens where his wife's ceases, though he confesses to having "compressed [it] within the closest limits." These final pages skirt the obvious pain of having to bury his wife at sea: they list, instead, the remaining ports of call and occasionally describe their commercial interest to the empire. With nautical precision and a personal reserve that admits no extraneous discussion, Lord Brassey concludes *The Last Voyage* with the words, "the *Sunbeam* entered Portsmouth Harbour at noon on December 14."

Lady Annie Brassey's works have significance for several reasons. They are well-written and packed with details that make the latter nineteenth century more visible to later readers. Such readers will find compelling Brassey's richly detailed word pictures of the people, places, and ecosystems that the British Empire touched and forever altered. Her travel writings also clearly articulate England's belief in its natural right to administer world affairs and its unperturbed acceptance of a "natural" social hierarchy. Teachers of nineteenth-century British literature may find Brassey's books useful as a demonstration of one woman's uncomplicated embrace of England's imperial aspirations and her genial acceptance of nineteenth-century views of the "Anglo-Saxon race" and the naturalness of class distinctions and gender roles.

Annie Brassey was quite simply a British Lady, a woman whose duties and activities were well established long before she assumed them. As befitted her station, she had "broad sympathies," and it was thus quite in character for her to encourage missionaries in their work among the natives of South America, Tahiti, Hawaii, and Australia; to bemoan the reputation for poor quality that Manchester cotton and brass manufacture had earned among even the "niggers" of Madagascar; to visit prisons and hospitals in every English colony; to catalogue flora, fauna, and domestic arrangements encountered when visiting the outposts of British civilization; and to promote generally the "duties and necessities" of civility wherever she found herself.

Brassey did not kick against the goad. Nothing in her writings suggests subversion of the patriarchal, imperialist, orientalizing paradigm. With the possible exception of some minor marital rancor, she seems thoroughly to have been at peace with her assigned role, to have worked diligently to exemplify rather than transcend the expectations of a woman of her class and advantages. In vain does one seek an inkling of rebellion, a whisper that she secretly resents the constraints within which she was expected to live. It is therefore ironically fitting that her husband's words in the preface of *The Last Voyage* both describe and in important ways define her: she was "happy at a ball, happy on her horse, happy on the grouse-moor, devoted to her father, a favourite with all her relatives, and very, very sweet to me." She was, he concludes, full of "gladness of heart, thankfulness for every pleasure [and] . . . happy . . . to make the best of what Providence [had] ordered." Certainly today's cultural critics and students of nineteenth-century England will find much raw historical data to enrich their understanding of this watershed era in human history. They will be well rewarded for their efforts to find and read the travel books of Lady Annie Brassey.

References:

Bryce McMurdo Wright, *Description of the Collection of Gold Ornaments from the "Huacus" or Graves of Some Aboriginal Races of the Northwestern Provinces of South America Belonging to Lady Brassey* (London: Whittingham, 1885);

Wright, *"Sunbeam" Treasures: A Description of the Natural History and Other Objects Lent by Lady Brassey to the International Fisheries Exhibition* (London: Clowes, 1883).

James Bryce

(10 May 1838 – 22 January 1922)

Mike Rubingh
Miami University

BOOKS: *The Holy Roman Empire* (Oxford: Shrimpton / London: Macmillan, 1864; revised edition, London: Macmillan, 1871; revised and enlarged edition, London: Macmillan, 1873; New York: Macmillan, 1877; revised and enlarged again, London & New York: Macmillan, 1904);

The Academical Study of the Civil Law (London & New York: Macmillan, 1871);

The Judicature Act of 1873 in Its Relation to the History of the Judicial System of England (London: Clowes, 1874);

Transcaucasia and Ararat: Being Notes of a Vacation Tour in the Autumn of 1876 (London: Macmillan, 1877; revised and enlarged edition, London & New York: Macmillan, 1896);

Speeches of James Bryce and Horace Davey on the Second Reading of the Infant's Bill Delivered in the House of Commons, Wednesday, March 26, 1884 (London: Buck, 1884);

The Government of Ireland Bill: Speech Delivered in the House of Commons on the Motion for the Second Reading of the Bill for the Future Government of Ireland on 17th May, 1886 (London: National Press Agency, [1886]);

Handbook of Home Rule: Being Articles on the Irish Question (London: Kegan Paul, Trench, 1887);

Mr. Gladstone and the Nationalities of the United Kingdom (London: Quaritch, 1887);

The Predictions of Hamilton and de Tocqueville (Baltimore: Publication Agency of the Johns Hopkins University, 1887);

The American Commonwealth (3 volumes, London & New York: Macmillan, 1888; revised edition, 2 volumes, London & New York: Macmillan, 1889; revised and enlarged edition, London & New York: Macmillan, 1893–1895); abridged and republished as *The American Commonwealth: Abridged Edition for the Use of Colleges and High Schools, Being an Introduction to the Study of Government and Institutions of the United States,* 1 volume (New York & London: Macmillan, 1896;

James Bryce (Gale International Portrait Gallery)

revised edition, New York & London: Macmillan, 1906);

Legal Studies in the University of Oxford: A Valedictory Lecture Delivered before the University, June 10, 1893 (London & New York: Macmillan, 1893);

Impressions of South Africa (London: Macmillan, 1897; New York: Century, 1897; revised and enlarged edition, London: Macmillan, 1899; New York: Macmillan, 1900);

William Ewart Gladstone: His Characteristics as Man and Statesman (New York: Century, 1898);

Studies in History and Jurisprudence, 2 volumes (London: Clarendon Press, 1901; New York: Oxford University Press, 1901);

Mr. Bryce on the Boer Rights of Belligerency under the Law of Nations (London: South African Conciliation Committee, 1901);

The Importance of Geography in Education (New York: Stanford, 1902);

The Relations of the Advanced and the Backward Races of Mankind (Oxford: Clarendon Press, 1902);

Studies in Contemporary Biography (New York & London: Macmillan, 1903);

Viscount James Bryce Letter to Thomas R. Bacon (London, 1904);

Recollections of Gladstone (Boston: Mason, 1905);

Address by the Right Honorable James Bryce on the Aims and Programme of the Sociological Society (London: Sociological Society, 1905);

The Methods and Conditions of Legislation: An Address Delivered in Carnegie Hall at the Thirty-first Annual Meeting of the New York State Bar Association, Held at the City of New York on the 24th and 25th of January, 1908 (New York, 1908);

The Hindrances to Good Citizenship (New Haven: Yale University Press, 1909);

The Government of British Cities (New York, 1911);

South America: Observations and Impressions (London & New York: Macmillan, 1912; abridged edition, New York: Macmillan, 1912; corrected and revised edition, New York: Macmillan, 1914);

Presidential Address [International Congress of Historical Studies, April 3, 1913] (Oxford: Hart, 1913);

The Ancient Roman Empire and the British Empire in India; The Diffusion of Roman and English Law throughout the World: Two Historical Studies (London & New York: Oxford University Press, 1913);

University and Historical Addresses Delivered during a Residence in the United States as Ambassador of Great Britain (London & New York: Macmillan, 1913);

The Menace of Great Cities (New York: National Housing Association, 1913);

Neutral Nations and the War (London & New York: Macmillan, 1914);

Evidence and Documents Laid before the Committee on Alleged German Outrages: Being an Appendix to the Report of the Committee Appointed by His Britannic Majesty's Government and Presided over by the Right Hon. Viscount Bryce (New York: Macmillan, [1915?]);

Race Sentiment as a Factor in History: A Lecture Delivered before the University of London on February 22, 1915 (London: Hodder & Stoughton, 1915);

The Attitude of Great Britain in the Present War (London: Macmillan, 1916);

Some Historical Reflections on War, Past and Present; Being Portions of Two Annual Presidential Addresses Delivered to the British Academy, June 1915 and July 1916 (London: Oxford University Press, 1916);

The Last Phase in Belgium: Statement . . . on the Belgian Deportations (London: Speaight, 1916);

War and Human Progress (New York: American Association for International Conciliation, 1916);

The Next Thirty Years: Thoughts on the Work That Awaits Students of the Human Sciences; Presidential Address Delivered at the Annual Meeting of the British Academy, July 19, 1917 (London: Oxford University Press, 1917);

Proposals for the Prevention of Future Wars (London: Allen & Unwin, 1917);

The Worth of Ancient Literature to the Modern World (New York: General Education Board, 1917);

Essays and Addresses in War Time (London & New York: Macmillan, 1918);

For the Right: Essays and Addresses (New York & London: Putnam, 1918);

Letter from Viscount Bryce to the Prime Minister (London: His Majesty's Stationery Office, 1918);

Modern Democracies, 2 volumes (London & New York: Macmillan, 1921);

The Study of American History (Cambridge: Cambridge University Press, 1921; New York: Macmillan, 1922);

International Relations: Eight Lectures Delivered in the United States in August, 1921 (New York: Macmillan, 1922);

Lord Reay, 1839–1921 (London: Oxford University Press, 1922);

Memories of Travel, edited by Lady Bryce (London & New York: Macmillan, 1923);

World History [Annual Raleigh Lecture on History, 1919] (London: Oxford University Press, 1924);

The Double Journey (London: John Lane, 1925).

OTHER: *Two Centuries of Irish History, 1691–1870,* edited, with an introduction, by Bryce (London: Kegan Paul, Trench, 1888);

Leonard Woolsey Bacon, *A History of American Christianity,* preface by Bryce (New York: Scribners, 1899; London: Clarke, 1899);

Leslie Stephen, *Essays on Freethinking and Plainspeaking,* introductions by Bryce and Herbert Paul (New York & London: Putnam, 1905);

Abraham Lincoln, *Speeches and Letters of Abraham Lincoln, 1832–1865,* edited by Merwin Roe, with introduction by Bryce (New York: Dutton, 1907; London: Dent, [1919]);

William Archibald Dunning, The British Empire and the United States: A Review of Their Relations during the Century of Peace Following the Treaty of Ghent, introduction by Bryce (New York: Scribners, 1914);

Arnold Joseph Toynbee, *Armenian Atrocities: The Murder of a Nation, with a Speech Delivered by Lord Bryce in the House of Lords* (London & New York: Hodder & Stoughton, 1915);

W. M. Flinders Petrie and others, *The Book of History: A History of All Nations from the Earliest Times to the Present,* introduction by Bryce (New York: Grolier Society / London: Educational Book, [1915?–1921]);

Louise Creighton, W. R. Sorley, and others, *The International Crisis: The Theory of the State; Lectures Delivered in February and March 1916, . . . under the Scheme for Imperial Studies in the University of London at Bedford College for Women,* opening address by Bryce (London & New York: Oxford University Press, 1916).

SELECTED PERIODICAL PUBLICATIONS–
UNCOLLECTED: "Stray Notes on Mountain Climbing in Iceland," *Alpine Journal* (1874): 50–53;

"Impressions of Iceland," *Cornhill Magazine,* 29 (1874): 553–570;

"Constantinople," *Harpers,* 56 (1878): 7–70;

"The Migrations of the Races of Men Considered Historically," *Scottish Geographical Magazine,* 8 (August 1892): 400–421;

"The Historical Causes of the Present War in South Africa," *North American Review* (1899): 737–759;

"The Nation's Capital," *National Geographic Magazine* (June 1913): 717–750;

"Impressions of Palestine," *National Geographic Magazine,* 27 (1915): 293–317;

"Western Siberia and the Altai Mountains," *National Geographic Magazine,* 39 (May 1921): 469–507;

"The Scenery of North America," *National Geographic Magazine* (April 1922).

Like his friends Leslie Stephen and Theodore Roosevelt, James Bryce combined an active physical life of hiking and climbing with an active intellectual life as historian of ideas and political theorist. He had the peculiarly Victorian gift of combining devotion to nature with an equally strong devotion to ideas. *Active* is perhaps too tame a word to describe the man who was a professor at Oxford, member of Parliament, president of the Alpine Society, chief secretary for Ireland, British ambassador to the United States, mediator in United States–Canada relations, significant voice in the development of the League of Nations, and traveler to practically every part of the world.

Bryce organized his travels in conjunction with official business or during brief summer breaks, so his writings are rarely localized, day-to-day descriptions of places and people. They thus lack the color and human interest of the works of Sir Richard Burton or Charles Darwin. Bryce frequently labeled his writings "impressions," but that word is deceptive in characterizing works such as his five-hundred-page *Impressions of South Africa* (1897), most of which details the intricate historical roots of the Anglo-Boer crisis, or his six-hundred-page *South America: Observations and Impressions* (1912), which offers nearly one hundred pages of reflections on racial issues on that continent. His works are anything but impressionistic. He traveled to educate himself, and like many Victorian travelers, he wrote to educate others. Although his most well-known and distinctive work, *The American Commonwealth* (1888), is not a travel narrative per se, it was the result of his listening to Americans of all professions and social classes during his travels across the country. It was a best-seller in both Britain and America, was taught in American schools, and prompted William Howard Taft to comment, at Bryce's death, that he "knew us better than we knew ourselves."

As Christopher Mulvey notes, Bryce's grasp of the principles of the American experiment in democracy made his estimation of the United States unique among English travelers. Bryce recognized the promise of development in America far better than did Matthew Arnold, Anthony Trollope, and other British travel writers too quick to criticize or dismiss the promising if sometimes awkward adolescent nation. *The American Commonwealth* was widely republished and is ranked by many as second only to Tocqueville's masterpiece *Democracy in America.* Bryce is an especially crucial figure for those studying English perceptions of America and Americans.

Bryce's *Transcaucasia and Ararat: Being Notes of a Vacation Tour in the Autumn of 1876* (1877), *Impressions of South Africa, South America: Observations and Impressions,* and *Memories of Travel* (1923) are his major contributions to travel writing. Their distinction is perhaps best captured metaphorically through one of Bryce's passions — that of climbing mountains, and in particular his single-handed ascent of seventeen-thousand-foot Mount Ararat. Bryce writes as if from a mountaintop: his writings provide an excellent sense of landscape and a rich historical context as they inevitably reveal their author as a Victorian

"Great and Little Ararat from the North-East," frontispiece to the 1896 revised and enlarged edition of Bryce's
Transcaucasia and Ararat

colonialist given to generalizing about races and speculating on how to "improve" the less advantaged races. Bryce's imperial eyes are evident throughout his writings, but his love of democracy, his Scotch-Presbyterian sense of justice and fairness, and his concern for oppressed peoples such as the Irish and Armenians constantly break through.

James Bryce III was born on 10 May 1838 to James Bryce II and Margaret Young Bryce in Belfast, and he spent the first eight years of his life in Ireland, his parents' birthplace. His grandfather was a strong-willed secessionist Presbyterian preacher, and his uncle John was a progressive educator in northern Ireland. Bryce's character should be read against that typical of this Scottish Covenanter heritage: obstinate, religious, intellectual, and ambitious. Bryce's father taught mathematics and geography in Glasgow and inspired in his son an early love of geology. Bryce's mother was a strong figure and a voracious reader. The family moved to Glasgow in 1846, where Bryce distinguished himself at Glasgow High School and later at Glasgow University. While attending the latter, Bryce rose at 6:30 A.M., walked three miles to his eight o'clock class and three miles back, and then retraced those three miles for a twelve o'clock class and three miles back. Such everyday twelve-mile journeys in his

youth prepared Bryce for his later hiking and climbing exploits. The Bryces spent summer vacations on the coasts of Scotland, Ireland, and Wales, and James nurtured his love of travel and the outdoors on these trips.

He went to Oxford in 1857 and was immediately the focus of a religious controversy. As a Presbyterian, he refused to sign the Thirty-Nine Articles, an Anglican admissions requirement at Trinity College, but he was urged to take the entrance tests anyway. Bryce's papers were judged "brilliant" by the examiners, and when he took first place the vice president waived the requirement. This victory gained early fame for Bryce with reformers such as Matthew Arnold, Lewis Campbell, Benjamin Jowett, Arthur Hugh Clough, James Anthony Froude, and Goldwin Smith at the other Oxford colleges.

Bryce collected a string of awards at Oxford, met Alfred Tennyson on the Isle of Wight, and joined the Old Mortality Club – a group including John Nichol, Thomas Hill Green, A. C. Swinburne, and Bryce's close friend A. V. Dicey – which read and discussed papers on literature, philosophy, and science. Sharing the sympathies that this group held for the risorgimento, Bryce attempted to join Giuseppe Garibaldi's army but was stopped by the threat of the Trinity dean to terminate Bryce's scholarship. In 1862 he visited Germany and, inspired by his visit, wrote an essay on the Holy Roman Empire that won the Arnold Prize. In 1864 the university press published his revised essay as *The Holy Roman Empire,* a first book that garnered praise from many scholars who were amazed at the age of its author. Bryce decided to go into law, and he continued studying and teaching during years in which he met William Gladstone, Lord John Acton, and Dean Stanley, eminent British liberals who encouraged Bryce's liberal views and whom he later praised in *Studies in Contemporary Biography* (1903). In 1870 he accepted from Gladstone the Regius Chair of Civil Law at Oxford, but he resolved to travel to the United States before he took up that appointment.

In the United States Bryce and Dicey saw New York City for the first time and met Thomas Wentworth Higginson, Julia Ward Howe, Henry Wadsworth Longfellow, Oliver Wendell Holmes, James Russell Lowell, Adam Sedgwick, and painter John La Farge. Bryce even met the aging Ralph Waldo Emerson on the train and accompanied the scholar and his son on a hike up Mount Washington. Bryce and Dicey also met Andrew White, president of three-year-old Cornell University, and Charles Eliot, president of Harvard University, before returning to England. Bryce returned with a strong sense of the life and promise of America, and he was attracted by an American character that he found open and relaxed in contrast to the formality and stuffiness of the British. In *Cornhill Magazine* (December 1872) he wrote far more approvingly on the relations between the sexes in America than had such other Victorian travelers as Frances Trollope and Charles Dickens. Yet he had also observed the voter manipulation of Tammany Hall politics and had been dismayed to see such close connections between democratic principles and corruption. All these experiences set the stage for Bryce's later ambassadorship and travels in the United States. By his death he had made journeys to the United States eight times.

As a fellow of Oriel College Bryce traveled to Switzerland and Germany in 1862 and 1863, countries to which he returned in later years. Noting in letters his antipathy to aspects of Catholicism, he first toured Italy in 1864. Yet he returned there, also, several times later in life, as the Dolomites became a favorite spot. In 1866 the twenty-eight-year-old Bryce and Leslie Stephen went touring and climbing in the Carpathian Mountains of Transylvania. Stephen soon wrote essays about the Alps that Bryce came to regard as models for writing

about mountain climbing, and the two returned to the Carpathians in 1878, a year before Bryce was elected to membership in the Alpine Club. Stephen found Bryce a "thoroughly competent mountaineer" who steadily kept up with him. Three decades later, when Bryce's conquests included peaks such as the Shreckhorn, Monte Rosa, the Pelmo, Marmolada in the Dolomites, Hekla, the Romsdal, and Ararat, Stephen recommended him for president of the Alpine Club, a position Bryce held from 1899 to 1901.

Bryce describes several journeys with Stephen in two essays, "The Mountains of Poland" and "The Mountains of Hungary" (1878). In the first Bryce recommends approaching the range of peaks called the Tatry by way of Kraków, which he finds far superior in embodying the spirit of Poland than "upstart" Warsaw. They visited two landmarks, the Hill of Kosciuszko and the nearby salt mines, before departing the city. They climbed many peaks, including Swinnica (7,574 feet), the highest of them, but they found the clouds and rain oppressive. They talked politics with two Poles, who accused them of being supporters of William Gladstone and being prejudiced against Prime Minister Benjamin Disraeli, Lord Beaconsfield. Bryce respected the conservative earl of Beaconsfield's political savviness and ambition, but in *Studies in Contemporary Biography* Bryce later depicted him as a cunning outsider who reached the highest echelons of British politics by flattery and stealth. Bryce and Stephen concluded the Polish segment of their journey atop the steep Polnischer Kamm, straddling the border of Poland and Hungary.

The first pages of the second segment, "The Mountains of Hungary," critique the tendency of mapmakers to delineate an imaginary chain of Carpathian Mountains bordering Hungary and Poland: Bryce calls this continuous chain a mapmaker's fiction. He laments the obstinacy of the dwarf pine, or Krummholz, the "hateful little tree" that can obstruct a peak. Resting at a village, Bryce is impressed by Magyar cheerfulness, gypsy folk songs, and march music, and neither Bryce nor Stephen mentions Gladstone when the people toast the English and Disraeli for supporting the Turks against the Russians.

In 1872, the year Iceland was granted a constitution by Denmark, Bryce and companions Courtenay Ibert and Aeneas Mackay found a steamer arriving and leaving at opportune times and therefore diverted to Iceland a trip that they had planned to Norway. Unfortunately their arrangements for returning failed, and the three decided to cross

Bryce in the 1890s (photograph by Miss M. V. Bryce)

Iceland's central rock and snow desert in order to catch a mail steamer at another port, a journey that the natives of Iceland claimed had not been attempted in fifteen years. It was a rough but successful trip, and the hardships made for a memorable three weeks. Bryce labeled Iceland a landscape best described by negatives, but he also acknowledged a certain grandeur in the Manichaean contrasts between volcanic rock and snow, geyser and glacier.

Expecting gloom and sullenness in the people, he was delighted to find cheer and talkativeness, as the solitude and hostility of the environment encouraged sociability. While he found the people poor and the houses miserable, he was surprised at the levels of literacy and education among the people in these conditions. He found it possible to communicate haltingly in Latin with many of them, and he tells a humorous story of an Icelander who attempted to barter for their horses in that language. He noted surprisingly good libraries in houses no better than hovels, and he listened to many myths and sagas – such as his favorite, *Njál's Saga* – that comprise significant parts of Icelandic culture.

Bryce left Iceland wondering why the modern Icelander is so different from his heroic precursors in the sagas; he decided that the glories of Iceland belong to the past.

Bryce ran for office in 1874 as Liberal candidate for the borough of Wick. He lost a close election, a disaster for the Liberals. In August he traveled to Norway and climbed the Romsdal, and in September he was called on business to Portugal, where he returned the following year on a tour of southern Spain as well. He observed the Moorish and Jewish peoples, was impressed by the Ramadan season and the Sook (marketplace), and visited Tangiers. Bryce's orientalism overcame his usual historical tendencies on this trip; he romanticized the scenery and the people in a letter to his sister and summed up his tour as "Arabian-night-like."

In August and September 1876 Bryce and friend Mackay traveled through Russia, Armenia, and Turkey, and his account of this journey is preserved in *Transcaucasia and Ararat: Being Notes of a Vacation Tour in the Autumn of 1876,* his most engaging and significant work of travel writing. The book begins in Nijni (Gorki) after the two men have already been through Saint Petersburg and Moscow. Bryce is quick to debunk reports about the exoticism of the Nijni Fair; he notes the popularity of Western goods and, as he is wont to do in all his travel writings, is quick to praise the virtues of free trade. Traveling by steamship down the Volga River, Bryce found such travel delightful. At Saratov where the Volga meets the Don, Bryce and Mackay changed plans and boarded a train instead of a steamship to Rostov. In Russia Bryce also found rail travel pleasing – "the most enjoyable in the world, except [in] America, if one is not in too much of a hurry." Having passed through Rostov two days later, they approached their first goal, the Caucasus Mountains.

The Caucasus Mountains lie like a huge wall between the eastern shores of the Black Sea and the western shores of the Caspian. Because the highest peaks rise nearly eighteen thousand feet and the lowest are nearly all above eight thousand feet, navigable passes are rare, the most trafficked being that at Darial. Bryce was fascinated with these mountains; he noted that both the ancient Greeks and Orientals – for example, Herodotus, Strabo, Ptolemy, Pompey, and Justinian – saw the Caucasus as the boundary of geographical knowledge, if not of the world itself. In the Arabian Nights stories, Mount Kaf is the edge of the world. In Greek myths the Caucasus is the region of the Pillars of Hercules; of the destination of the *Argo,* Colchis; of the Amazons, the griffins, and the one-eyed Arimaspians. Prometheus also was chained to Mount Kazbek there. The lack of navigable passes, moreover, preserved the mysteriousness of the Caucasus into the nineteenth century. This myth and mystery associated with a terrain attracted Bryce, as he was also later attracted to Mount Ararat. Bryce also wanted to see the sites of the recent Crimean War and the object of the exploits of English climbers such as his friend Douglas William Freshfield, later to be the author of *The Exploration of the Caucasus* (1896).

In Poland and Hungary the native peoples had celebrated England and its prime minister, as Bryce and Stephen quietly dissented; in Russia Bryce and Stephen found their political situation reversed. People saw them as representatives (albeit dissenting ones) of an English homeland pursuing a hard-line policy toward Russia, the chief colonial rival of Britain in the "great game" in the East. In Vladikavkaz they joined two Russian ladies and, after "a preliminary skirmish about English sympathy with Turkish cruelties," headed over the Darial Pass through the beautiful Georgian high country to Tbilisi, the capital of Transcaucasia. Unfortunately September was vacation time in the city, and Bryce and Mackay found few of the writers and scientists whom they had hoped to meet. After a short break they set out in a comfortable wheeled cart for the city of Yerevan, capital of Armenia, and their second major goal — the double mountain visible from the southern edge of that city.

Bryce had planned the ascent of Mount Ararat long before his trip and had researched the history and lore associated with it. His narrative presents the results of his research, beginning with the biblical references to Ararat in Genesis, 2 Kings, and Jeremiah; continuing through those in Josephus, the church fathers, and Sir John Mandeville; and concluding with those of nineteenth-century mountaineers such as Robert Parker Parrott (1829), Aftonomof (1834), and Abich (1845), the first few to climb the peak and officially record their efforts. The fame of Mount Ararat as the presumed resting place for Noah's ark makes it sacred to Judaism, Christianity, and in a lesser degree Islam. Bryce encountered the widespread superstition that Ararat could not be climbed: when he mentioned his plans to members of an Armenian monastery, the archimandrite immediately told Bryce that such an ascent was impossible.

Bryce, Mackay, and their seven Kurd and two Cossack porter-guides made good time to a height of twelve thousand feet, but then problems appeared. Mackay felt his lack of adequate training and had to stop; neither the Kurds nor the Cossacks knew the route at thirteen thousand feet, and the former group, ill-equipped for climbing, stopped to wait. The Cossacks accompanied Bryce slightly farther but, also badly equipped for climbing and perhaps respecting the sacredness of the mountain, then left him to go on alone. The clouds and Bryce's isolation increased the possibility that he might become lost, and the last few thousand feet were a race against time, for Bryce needed three hours to descend with any daylight remaining. At 2:25 P.M., thirty minutes before the deadline he had allowed himself, Bryce reached a level expanse of snow and glimpsed through the surrounding clouds the Araxes plain at a dizzying distance below. He savored the triumph briefly before turning back, miraculously avoiding disorientation on his descent, finding the Cossacks in the dusk at 6:00 P.M., and reaching the others when it was so dark that he could barely recognize Mackay a few yards away. With the meager provisions they had left — "a lump of bread, a scrap of meat, two eggs, and a thimbleful of cold tea" — the group celebrated Bryce's conquest.

After such a highlight Bryce and Mackay were eager to begin their sea journey home but were trapped by wind and waves in the swampy Black Sea port of Poti, a place Bryce decided "best left to its frogs." They finally departed via steamship and followed the southern shore of the Black Sea, stopping at the Turkish ports of Batumi, Trabzon, Giresun, and Samsun before reaching Constantinople. Although Bryce was opposed to female suffrage in England and the United States, his narrative fulminates at what he found there under the rule of the Turkish sultan and in the horrible ways that Islamic men treat women. The journey completed, Bryce concluded with two chapters discussing the politics of the region, an addition that illuminated the continuing "Eastern Question," an international political concern and subject of serious parliamentary debate soon after Bryce had returned. War broke out in 1877 between Russia and Turkey, and the feelings of Bryce and England were torn between apprehension at Russian colonial expansion and dismay at Turkish atrocities. Given his extensive knowledge of the East, he was regarded as an authority in Eastern international politics.

Although Bryce regarded Russia as a chief colonial rival of Britain, he adamantly supported the Armenian Christians of Russia. The Armenians were hated and stereotyped as usurers by their neighbors. They had long been harassed by the

Turks, who saw them as protected European favorites. In an impassioned eighty-page chapter, "Twenty Years of the Armenian Question," that was added to an 1896 fourth edition of *Transcaucasia and Ararat* Bryce denounces Turkish genocide of the Armenians living in Turkey. Yet he also blames his British countrymen, whose fears of Russian colonialism had nurtured political support for Turkey that had helped to provoke what Bryce called "a remorseless tyrant and a fanatical populace." Bryce felt that England was obliged to act promptly in defending the Armenians against Turkish jealousies.

Bryce continually raised the plight of the Armenians to leaders in both Britain and America. He became the voice of the Armenian nation in Britain, but he lamented that what he could do was both too little and too late. Thousands had already been massacred. These international political developments, the religious conflict, and the genocide probably increased sales of Bryce's book. The 1877 first edition of *Transcaucasia and Ararat* was well received by readers eager to put themselves in the footsteps of a British traveler to the East; the book was reprinted in a second edition within two months and in a third edition within a year.

Bryce's Liberal opposition to English sympathies for Turkey, his expertise during the Eastern Questions Conference of 1879, and his enduring friendship with William Gladstone and other Liberals immediately carried Bryce, largely through his criticism of the Disraeli administration for its complicity in the Turkish atrocities, back into political life when Gladstone returned as prime minister in 1880. Bryce was elected to Parliament as representative of a poor section of East London, the Tower Hamlets, whose large German population Bryce had charmed by addressing them in their own language. Bryce divided his early years in office between parliamentary duties and travel in America, his first eight years culminating in his masterwork *The American Commonwealth,* a book surprisingly popular for a scholarly work. It is unfortunate that Bryce did not also compose these travels separately in a personal narrative for an even wider audience.

In 1886 Bryce became undersecretary for foreign affairs, a position that led to much travel. Two years later he traveled to Egypt and India in a journey that biographer H. A. L. Fisher covers in "Impressions of Egypt and India," a selection of Bryce's letters. Bryce found it easy to immerse himself in antiquity while touring Egypt, but he found it difficult to do this in India, where he talked politics much as he did at home. He found the restless concern of Indians for their future to be exciting but

also disturbing, for he did not see in India the outlets for this Western-induced restlessness that he had seen in America. Bryce was aware of the dangers of development without the necessary foundation of accompanying Western freedoms and restraints, but Bryce's concerns may also betoken the English fear of another Indian Rebellion of 1857. Following his delight in America's prospects, Bryce seems far less sanguine about India, and many of his comments seem nostalgic for a past India.

In 1889 Bryce married Marion Ashton of Lancashire, and they honeymooned in the Alps and Italy, where he interviewed Lajos Kossuth, the Hungarian patriot and statesman. Bryce's wife joined him on many of his later travels, including a marathon journey across Canada in 1890. In 1898 they set up a permanent country residence at Hindleap, Sussex. In 1906 Gladstone asked him to fill the unenviable position of chief secretary for Ireland, a role which Bryce, as an Ulster Scot who had spent his earliest years in Ireland, found difficult. Although he began admirable academic reforms in Ireland, he was glad to resign his post and take up the ambassadorship to the United States in 1907.

Bryce's second major work of travel writing, *Impressions of South Africa,* is thorough both in its descriptions of native landscape and biology and in its understanding of the complex, intertwined histories of Briton, Boer, and native peoples in the expanses of southern Africa, but its encyclopedic style occasionally makes reading it less satisfying. The book sold well, being reprinted within a month of its first appearance, and was reprinted in second and third editions in the next two years. It provides a remarkably detailed historical portrait that reveals many of the causes of the 1899 Boer War that it anticipated. Although Bryce's letters from shorter trips occasionally reveal an orientalist desire for the exotic, such longer books as this one reveal his desire to understand regional histories and political currents and to make this knowledge enrich his accounts.

Bryce and Marion stayed with Cecil Rhodes, prime minister of Cape Colony and a former fellow Oriel man at Oxford University. Being accompanied by his wife did not temper Bryce's rigorous traveling ambitions. They traveled twelve hundred miles in a mule wagon, climbed Table Mountain above Cape Town and the eleven-thousand-foot Machacle in Basutoland, entered the gold mines of the Witwatersrand, and talked to the miners. They stopped at many settlements in journeying through the Cape, Bechuanaland (Botswana), Matabeleland, Mashonaland, Manicaland, the Portugese territories, Natal, Transvaal, the Orange Free State, and

Basutoland, and Bryce recorded every change in the landscape of the regions and in the political orientation of the people. The pages in which Bryce discusses native cultural distinctions such as Kaffir religion or Basuto architecture are a welcome relief from the central story of colonial political conflict.

Bryce's motive in writing this book was his outrage at the Jameson Raid on the Dutch Transvaal in late 1895, just after he and his wife had returned from South Africa. They had been well treated by Dr. Jameson during their trip, and they were shocked to discover that he had later headed such an aggression. Bryce had observed tensions between the inland Boer farmers and the threatening British powers, but he had left with the impression that the will to coexist was strong among the Briton and Boer inhabitants and only a foolish move could lead to a crisis. Bryce was horrified with the British action and its sordid goal of wresting the Transvaal mines from the hands of President Paul Kruger, and he began the book in protest, a book intended to illuminate the South African situation for his fellow Britons. Bryce was followed by Sir Henry Campbell-Bannerman, John Morley, and David Lloyd George in strong Liberal opposition to Sir Austen Chamberlain, and though he conceded that, once begun, the war should be fought to an end, his criticisms of farm burning and concentration camps and his sympathy with the Boer farmers aroused much antagonism in England.

While Bryce frequently took the minority position on political issues, he was less radical on racial matters, as some of his blunt comments about South African tribes reveal. Bryce considered the average Kaffir "a lazy fellow" given to the pleasures of hunting and fighting while his wife or slave did the real work. He saw employment in the mines as a way of teaching natives discipline and improvement. In his Romanes Lectures of 1902, *The Relations of the Advanced and the Backward Races of Mankind,* Bryce delineates four possible results of interracial relations between a stronger and a weaker race: destruction, absorption, commingling, and separatist juxtaposition. He gives examples of each of these and notes that religion frequently levels racial difference, but he concludes that contact between advanced and backward races inevitably lowers the former and that a promising future for mankind demands that certain "advanced" races remain unsullied to guide the rest.

Bryce does not treat issues of race relations with consistency in his books. Sometimes he criticizes harshly the hypocrisy of southern Christian whites in the United States, as he argues that race

An imagined encounter between Ambassador Bryce and President Theodore Roosevelt, drawn by American cartoonist John Tinney McCutcheon

and blood should not be grounds for establishing different political rights, but as author of the voluminous *Modern Democracies* (1921) Bryce demands that voting rights be restricted according to one's property ownership and education. In all fairness, one should recognize that Bryce had seen the manipulation of Irish voters by Tammany Hall political machinery in the United States and had judged that problem to be more serious than it actually was. His *Race Sentiment as a Factor in History: A Lecture Delivered before the University of London on February 22, 1915* (1915) is less offensive and may atone for some of his earlier blindness. In it Bryce argues that race has been too exaggerated in national identity, especially in the nineteenth and twentieth centuries, and he criticizes the ethnic nationalisms that precipitated World War I.

In his boyhood Bryce had enjoyed such reading as William Hickling Prescott's *History of the Conquest of Peru* (1847) and Baron Friedrich Heinrich Alexander von Humboldt's *Aspects of Nature in Different Lands and Different Climates* (1849), and in 1910 he took a leave and embarked on a South American trip, a dream inspired by that youthful reading. Starting in Panama, Bryce and his wife made a large circle through Peru, Bolivia, Chile, Argentina, Uruguay, and Brazil, and this experience was the basis for Bryce's *South America: Observations and Impressions,* which he wrote in about a year — an amazing feat for a man almost seventy-four years old. The book lacks the adventure of *Transcaucasia and Ararat* and the political relevance of *Impressions of South Africa,* but in other ways it is superior to them. It is more enjoyable reading, and it has an expansiveness of scale and descriptive beauty that surpasses those earlier works.

One would not, for example, expect the construction site of the Panama Canal to occasion sublime feeling in a traveler, but for Bryce it evokes all the excitement and ambition of connecting two oceans. He also grows poetic at the southern end of the continent, as he describes the bleak beauty of the Strait of Magellan. In Peru he and his wife visited Lima, Arequipa, and Cuzco, and Bryce preferred this last, the Sacred City of the Sun, for its historical importance as capital of the once-expansive Incan empire. Bryce criticizes the Spanish conquest, especially for its religious justifications, and he speculates that the craftsmanship of the Peruvian Catholic churches is attributable more to native Peruvian than to Spanish artistry. Yet he frequently seems fatalistic about the Peruvian and other South American natives. He argues that the deliberate Spanish annihilation of the holy Incan line abolished the pride of that race and left the people without initiative.

Impressed by natural resources, he is blunt in condemning what he sees as Indian "squalor" and "laziness," and he makes little attempt to value environmental or cultural difference. He is ambivalent about the 1810–1826 independence movements across South America, surprisingly so in view of his praise for democracy in most other settings. He occasionally claims that South American character and cultures are not ready for democracy and that political instabilities in the histories of its many nations are evidence of this. On the other hand, his chapter on "The Relation of Races in South America" contrasts his 1902 advocacy of racial purity with a rather un-Victorian defense of mixed races. His pessimism can be seen as a common European first judgment of the peoples of South America. Bryce defended his book against those whom he imagined would find it unduly optimistic. While not always successful, his book certainly tries to move beyond the typical European judgment of South Americans:

The natural propensity of a West European or North American traveller to judge Spanish Americans by his own standards needs to be corrected not only by making allowance for differences of intellect and character, but also by a comprehension of the history of these peoples and of their difficulties, many of them due to causes outside their own control, which have encompassed and entangled them ever since their ancestors first set foot in the Western world. Whoever compares these difficulties as they stand to-day with those of a century ago will find grounds not only for more lenient judgments than most Europeans have passed, but also for brighter hopes[.]

Any fair assessment of Bryce's views of the people and future of South America must consider his reflections on politics and race in the last third of his book. A mix of strong negatives and strong positives, his position is deeply ambivalent.

Bryce's delight in scenic beauty is not so mixed, and this occupies much of the book. He explored the native ruins around Lake Titicaca, sailed for two days on the giant lake, and was intrigued by the native rafts called balsas. His book condemns Peruvian art as inferior to Egyptian and Mycenaean work but finds Peruvian buildings and stonework equal to those of Egypt and superior to those of North America. Impressed by the chasm-hidden city of La Paz, the highest capital city in the world at an elevation of some twelve thousand feet, he rode an electric cable car into the gorge and met the vice president of Bolivia. Between stops at Antofagasta and Santiago in Chile he climbed the Andes to view the Transandine Tunnel on the border of Chile and Argentina. Bryce's love of scenic natural grandeur appears in little tension with his admiration for grand works of human engineering. Montevideo and Buenos Aires are highlights of Uruguay and Argentina respectively, and the Bryces' trip is capped with stays in São Paulo and Rio de Janeiro.

Published in September 1912, *South America: Observations and Impressions* was reprinted in each of the following months through January 1913, and revised editions came out in 1914 and 1916. Bryce's shorter essays on his later travels to Australia and the South Pacific in 1912, to the Altai Mountains of eastern Russia in 1913, and to Palestine in 1914 complete his volume of collected travel writings, *Memories of Travel,* edited by his wife and published after his death.

Commentators agree that while Bryce's speeches in Parliament were occasionally pedantic, given to digressions and to the unpardonable sin of attempting to present both sides of an issue, Bryce was nonetheless a masterful diplomat. Indeed, Bryce's willingness to learn the many sides of an issue led him to succeed as a mediator between parties, although it kept him from the heights of political power. When Roger Casement returned to England in 1912 with reports of the Putumayo rubber atrocities in Peru, Bryce was recently returned from his own South American journey and brought Casement directly to U.S. president William Howard Taft. In so doing, Bryce facilitated publication of Casement's investigations in America, pressured the British parties involved, and eased what might have been exploded by the media into a tense situation between England and the United States.

Bryce was amply rewarded for his diplomatic and scholarly skills in his day. He received thirty-four honorary degrees from nine countries, most from the United States, and he belonged to many societies both in England and on the Continent. In 1914 he was nominated viscount. In earlier years he had carried on a friendly correspondence with Matthew Arnold despite the political differences between the two men. He knew American presidents Theodore Roosevelt, William Howard Taft, and Woodrow Wilson, and Bryce's death was mourned by many Americans as well as British subjects. A widely circulated American cartoon depicted Uncle Sam laying a wreath before Bryce's picture. His friend William James said in humorous tribute that to James Bryce, "all facts were born equal." Henry Fairfield Osborn includes Bryce with Alfred Russel Wallace, Charles Darwin, T. H. Huxley, John Burroughs, and John Muir in his *Impressions of Great Naturalists* (1925). The triple-peaked Mount Bryce in the Canadian Rockies is named after him, and the James Bryce Memorial Lectures series began in his honor.

Bryce's writings, though not to be read quickly or for pleasure, received much early success. His connections to a widespread network of British and American intellectuals undoubtedly helped spread his name, and his ability to merge accessible travel writings with analyses of contemporary political conflicts certainly gained wider audiences for his works. The typical pattern in each of his three major travel works, in which a long descriptive narrative precedes a shorter section of reflection and forecasts, satisfied the Victorian desire for edification along with pleasure.

Bryce is an eminent Victorian whose star has sunk greatly in a century of specialization. His reputation since the middle of the twentieth century is

Drawing of Bryce by William Rothenstein, 1915 (courtesy of the Lilly Library, Indiana University)

limited to a small group of historians and political scientists working in the period: Mitau, Rassekh, Stearns, Coghlan, Rio, Fanning, and Tulloch are some who have explored his ideas, and their focus is predominantly on *The American Commonwealth*. His travel writing is apt to seem awkward to the modern reader for precisely the reasons that attracted the Victorian reader: it conveys a general sense of British superiority; it intends to educate; and it educates so at length.

While a danger of travel writing is that of dwelling on the odd, the novel, the impressionistic, and the anecdotal — at the cost of historical and political understanding — Bryce's writings too often err in the other direction. They would benefit from more personal narratives, more dialogue. Too often his breadth of historical and cultural knowledge reduces people and places to mere types. Bryce's journeys undoubtedly suffered with complications and ambiguities, logistical and emotional conflicts, but few of these emerge in his writings. Bryce had friends and acquaintances from all nations, but his travel writing does not adequately capture that much-loved, living, interacting James Bryce. Like his ascent of Ararat, Bryce's travel writing frequently abandons human interaction for the snow and ice of objectivity.

Letters:

Allan B. Lefcowitz and Barbara F. Lefcowitz, eds., "James Bryce's First Visit to America: The New England Sections of His 1870 Journal and Related Correspondence," *New England Quarterly,* 2 (1977): 314–331.

Bibliography:

Burton C. Bernard, *James Bryce and St. Louis: A Bibliographic Introduction to the Writings of James Bryce* (St. Louis, Mo.: Bernard, 1988).

Biographies:

Edmund Ions, *James Bryce and American Democracy, 1870–1922* (London, Melbourne & Toronto: Macmillan, 1968);

H. A. L. Fisher, *James Bryce,* 2 volumes (New York: Macmillan, 1977).

References:

Allan B. Lefcowitz and Laurence W. Mazzeno, "Matthew Arnold and James Bryce," *Arnoldian,* 10, no. 1 (1982): 29–41;

Christopher Mulvey, *Anglo-American Landscapes: A Study of Nineteenth-Century Anglo-American Travel Literature* (London: Cambridge University Press, 1983);

Transatlantic Manners: Social Patterns in Nineteenth-Century Anglo-American Travel Literature (Cambridge: Cambridge University Press, 1990).

Papers:

Most of Bryce's papers are stored at the Bodleian Library, Oxford University. His letters to Americans are in various libraries, especially Harvard University, Johns Hopkins University, Cornell University, Princeton University, and the Library of Congress.

Isabel Arundell Burton

(20 March 1831 – 22 March 1896)

John R. Pfeiffer
Central Michigan University

BOOKS: *The Inner Life of Syria, Palestine, and the Holy Land: From My Private Journal,* 2 volumes (London: King, 1875);

Arabia, Egypt, India: A Narrative of Travel (London & Belfast: Mullan, 1879);

The Life of Captain Sir Richd. F. Burton, 2 volumes (London: Chapman & Hall, 1893; New York: Appleton, 1893);

The Romance of Isabel Lady Burton: The Story of Her Life, Told in Part by Herself and in Part by W. H. Wilkins, 2 volumes (London: Hutchinson, 1897; New York: Dodd, Mead, 1897);

The Passion Play at Ober-Ammergau, edited by W. H. Wilkins (London: Hutchinson, 1900).

OTHER: Richard F. Burton, *Explorations of the Highlands of Brazil, with a Full Account of the Gold and Diamond Mines; also, Canoeing down 1500 Miles of the Great River São Francisco, from Sabará to the Sea,* 2 volumes, edited by Isabel Burton (London: Tinsley, 1869);

Richard F. Burton, *The Gold-Mines of Midian and the Mined Midianite Cities: A Fortnight's Tour in North-Western Arabia,* edited by Isabel Burton (London: Kegan Paul, 1878);

The Kasîdeh — Couplets — of Hajî Aboû El-Yezdî: A Lay of the Higher Law, translated and edited by F. B. [Frank Baker (Richard F. Burton)], preface by Isabel Burton (London: Quaritch, 1880);

José Martiniano de Alencar, *Iraçéma, the Honeylips: A Legend of Brazil,* translated by Burton (London: Bickers, 1886);

Joao Manuel Pereira da Silva, *Manuel de Moraes: A Chronicle of the Seventeenth Century,* translated by Burton and Richard F. Burton (London: Bickers, 1886);

Lady Burton's Edition of Her Husband's Arabian Nights, 6 volumes, edited by Burton (London: Waterlow, 1886–1887);

Luiz de Camões, *Os Lusiadas [The Lusiads],* translated by Richard F. Burton, edited by Isabel Burton (London: Quaritch, 1890);

Isabel Arundell Burton

Richard F. Burton, *Personal Narrative of a Pilgrimage to Al-Madinah & Meccah,* 2 volumes, edited by Isabel Burton (London: Tylston & Edwards, 1893);

Richard F. Burton, *A Mission to Gelele, King of Dahome, with Notices of the So-Called "Amazons," the Grand Customs, the Yearly Customs, the Human Sacrifices, the Present State of the Slave Trade and the Negro's Place in Nature,* 2 volumes, edited by Isabel Burton (London: Tylston & Edwards, 1893);

Richard F. Burton, *Vikram and the Vampire; or, Tales of Hindu Devilry,* edited by Isabel Burton (London: Tylston & Edwards, 1893);

Caius Valerius Catullus, *The Carmina of Caius Valerius Catullus,* translated by Richard F. Burton and Leonard C. Smithers, with prefatory letter by Isabel Burton (London: Printed for the translators, 1894);

George W. Harris, *"The" Practical Guide to Algiers,* preface by Burton (London: Philips, 1894);

Richard F. Burton, *First Footsteps in East Africa; or, An Explanation of Harar,* 2 volumes, edited by Isabel Burton (London: Tylston & Edwards, 1894).

SELECTED PERIODICAL PUBLICATIONS – UNCOLLECTED: "An Apology for Captain Burton: Letter from Isabel Burton in the *London Academy,*" *New York Times,* 21 March 1886, p. 6;

"Lady Burton's Sacrifice," *New York Times,* 5 July 1891, p. 11;

"Sir Richard Burton: An Explanation and a Defense," *New Review,* 7 (November 1892): 562–578.

Isabel Burton's achievement and reputation as a travel writer rest upon five published works. *The Romance of Isabel Lady Burton* (1897), an autobiographical work, provides a calendar of her life and travels. It frames her narrative of the *The Life of Captain Sir Richd. F. Burton* (1893), which recounts the life, explorations, and writings of her famous husband and also supplies the context for her own travelogues – *The Inner Life of Syria, Palestine, and the Holy Land* (1875), *Arabia, Egypt, India* (1879), and *The Passion Play at Ober-Ammergau* (1900).

Burton reveals little about her early years. In *The Romance* we learn that she was born in London to Eliza Gerard, sister of the First Baron Robert Gerard, and Henry Raymond Arundell, of the old and proud Roman Catholic Arundell family of Wardour. She remained a Catholic, and her religion is a subtext in her writing. As the eldest of the eleven children of the second marriage of her widower father, she was educated at the convent of the Canonesses of the Holy Sepulchre at Boulogne, near Chelmsford.

In her childhood and youth she exhibited the health, energy, athleticism, boldness, and exotic imagination that manifested themselves throughout her life. She ran with her siblings in the fields, climbed trees, ice skated, and rode horses. In her late teens Benjamin Disraeli's *Tancred* (1847) was

the catalyst of her fascination with "gypsies, Bedawin Arabs, and everything Eastern and mystic; and especially a *wild* and *lawless* life." She reported that a gypsy fortune-teller, Hagar Burton, foretold that her life would be "all wandering, change, and adventure" and that she would be married to one with whom she would share "one soul in two bodies in life or death, never long apart . . . [from] your husband."

Those familiar with Richard Francis Burton scholarship are often prejudiced against Isabel Burton. Biographers have spent one hundred years questioning her handling of her husband's legacy. Such scholars have been infuriated because she burned her husband's private journals and some of his unpublished manuscripts. Yet her talent was extraordinary, and her books continue to be important.

As an Englishwoman Burton assumed that she was from a nation superior in moral culture as well as in technological/military strength, but she tried to learn the languages of the countries she visited and wrote about. Exploration was an endeavor most commonly undertaken by men; therefore Burton's accounts of her travels, written consciously for women readers, were especially valuable. She seems also to have appreciated what anthropologists have called the problem of the "intrusion of the observer": she realized that people are often not themselves when their audience is a privileged stranger – and a woman besides. Therefore Burton occasionally disguised herself as a boy or a native woman in Syria to gain both protection from harassment and an opportunity to see people behave naturally.

Her *The Life of Captain Sir Richd. F. Burton* assembles extracts from published materials, letters, journals, and poems, and from these it weaves carefully tailored representations of the personalities of the couple, a warmly sentimental account of their relationship, and samples of accounts by both of them of their lives and travels. Isabel met Richard in Boulogne, France, in August 1850, and during their eleven-year courtship Richard would leave for months or years to go exploring. In 1857, while her fiancé was searching for the source of the Nile River with John Hanning Speke, Isabel joined the honeymoon party of her sister Blanche and Blanche's husband, Hugh Pigott, in a tour of Europe. She visited Paris, Lyons, Marseilles, Nice, Genoa, Pisa, Leghorn, Venice, Dieppe, and Geneva, and she kept journal records, later used in writing *The Romance,* of what was then by far the most extensive travel of her life.

After their marriage on 22 January 1861 the two fenced, swam, rode, read, wrote, drank, smoked, gambled, hunted, and traveled. As Richard Burton's wife, Isabel became a more serious journal keeper and traveler than she had been, and she also became his amanuensis and editor. The travel works by Richard that would become classics had already been written — *Personal Narrative of a Pligrimage to Al-Madinah & Meccah* (1855–1856), *First Footsteps in East Africa* (1856), and *The Lake Regions of Central Africa* (1860) — and she used them as models.

Almost immediately after their marriage Richard was posted to the consulship of West African Fernando Po, and Isabel traveled part of the way there with him. They dallied in Spain, Portugal, and the island of Madeira, and in her biography of Richard she describes the filth, cheating, and thievery in the inns — as well as their readings of an aneroid barometer and thermometer to determine the altitudes of the Spanish mountains. Richard refused to let Isabel travel to or live with him in Fernando Po because of the dangerous climate in that low-lying, malarial place.

Having been born into gentility, Burton was able to use her influence to get Richard relieved from Po and reassigned as consul in Santos, Brazil. This created an opportunity for her to learn Luso-Portuguese, the colonial language of Brazil. She delighted in describing landscape and scenery, and in 1886 her translation of José Martiniano de Alencar's *Iraçéma, the Honeylips* (originally published in 1865) included an emotionally charged description of the Brazilian jungle.

Richard did not do well in Brazil. In this unprestigious post he drank excessively and neglected his duties. Using her influence again, however, Isabel got him reassigned as consul in Damascus — an appointment where Isabel wrote that they spent the happiest time in their lives. Her best book, *The Inner Life of Syria, Palestine, and the Holy Land,* is devoted to this Damascus period, from December 1869 to October 1871. As the subtitle of the book acknowledges, she wrote this work from her private journal; its aim was to "convey an idea of the life which an Englishwoman may make for herself in the East." She announced that although she would describe the "inner life of the Harim [*sic,* harem]," she would write a book that was "suitable for English girls . . . [and] which may appear on every table *sans . . . reproche.* . . . A minute detail of some parts of the domestic life of *all* classes of Harims . . . would not be suitable for English girls," she concluded, and she therefore decided not to describe certain (presumably erotic) aspects of dance and mime. She also re-

Burton in 1861 (wedding gift portrait by Louis Desanges; Council of the London Borough of Richmond upon Thames)

spected the privacy of her Arabian hosts: "I have been received with open arms," she wrote; "I have been admitted to prayer in the mosque tribune. . . . I cannot put them under a microscope to make my book entertaining."

The Inner Life recounts their sea voyage from England, where Richard rejoined Burton to prepare for their move to Beirut, and displays her considerable knowledge of the geography and history of mideastern places. They took a house some seventeen miles outside Damascus, and from this perspective Isabel's word-pictures of the city and surrounding country exhibit her skill in describing landscape: "[U]pon the plain [is] the city of Damascus," she writes,

> . . . my beautiful white City with her swelling domes and tapering minarets, her glittering golden crescents set in green of every shade, sparkling with her fountains and streams. . . . The river valley spreads its green carpet almost thirty miles around the city, and is dotted with tiny white villages. All around . . . are the reeking sands of the sunburnt Desert.

Burton in her room at her Trieste residence, 1890

Her snapshot descriptions of the pageant of the "Hajj," the most important religious event in the culture of the region (the annual pilgrimage to Mecca), have acuity and energy. She describes the "Bazars"; health and medical lore; horses and their training and treatment; camels; visiting customs; cafés; and Arab music, singing, and dancing. A Victorian and religious propriety constrain her account of the dancing:

> You must understand that Arab dancing is more curious than pretty, but it is strange to you and wild. . . . I must explain to you that there are some things we may see, and some that we may not see. . . . [The dancers] are to be fully clad, and are not to exceed in Raki [literally, an Arabian cognac; metaphorically, "ardor"]. . . . You see, in point of dress they are far more decent than our own ballet girls, and that even the Lord Chamberlain [English censor of public performances] could not object to them. . . . One thing which perhaps you will not understand is that [their] dancing means something, whereas ours is only intended for exercise, or to give people a chance of talking.

More chapters in *The Inner Life* are devoted to the Turkish government, the Great Mosque, the grand houses of wealthy Arabs, the cemeteries, the post office, ecclesiastical and banking customs, and laws and legal practices. She describes a desert trip to explore archeological interests of Palmyra, and she goes on to describe churches, schools, a Moslem wedding, and such procedures as those for resolving village disputes and for treating sickness – this last, a realm in which she had considerable knowledge and skill. She reports conflicts between Moslems, Christians, and Jews, and she describes quite analytically the Sufi practice and its coda, a quasi-religious discipline as esoteric as Zen Buddhism. Fifty pages narrate a utopian vision of a Christianized, unified world in which she and Richard play central roles.

The Burtons' tomb at Mortlake, England

Burton goes on to tell how she nursed a hyena and panther as pets, and her account typifies the considerable attention she gives to the treatment of animals whenever she describes a culture. Eventually she participated in sponsoring a chapter of the Society for the Prevention of Cruelty to Animals in Trieste. A good shot who claimed that she could hit an orange at seventy yards, she carried a revolver, a bowie knife, and a little rifle on desert treks. Snakes that she found on safari in the spring-fed pools where she bathed were to her only minor annoyances. Her description of nature – of the skies and the desert – is a motif throughout her account.

She contrasts the status of European and mideastern women, but what she does not describe is interesting, because what she omits are details to which women conventionally attend. She mentions baking local bread, for instance, but she does not give the recipe. Her narrative gives little attention to children; some information concerns childbirth, but furniture and housekeeping practices are not much described. Nor does Burton give much detail about the materials or designs of clothing. She also tells little about how water is husbanded, a striking omission in a desert culture where water is important.

Late in 1872 Burton's influence again secured what would be Richard's fourth and final consulate in Trieste. This poorly paid post was mostly a sinecure, but with Trieste as their headquarters they spent the last years of Richard's life revisiting south central and eastern Europe, Asia, Arabia, Egypt, and India. Spurred especially by the great popularity of *The Inner Life,* which had appeared in at least five editions, Burton wrote and published two more books from these travels.

The first – *Arabia, Egypt, India* – chiefly describes in twenty chapters and two appendices Burton's first trip to India. It also briefly recounts their travel through France, Italy, Egypt, and Arabia and offers a description of their quarters at Trieste. Her treatment of India emphasizes its beautiful landscape, stifling climates, indigenous cultures, and political ferment as its colonial peoples began to feel a growing desire for self-determination and independence that it would not attain until the twentieth century.

There the Burtons spent time at Hyderabad, Bombay, and Goa. Because of her devout Catholicism, Burton's account of historic Goa – a Roman Catholic, Portuguese colony – forgives the Portuguese colonial scourge. Her appendices, co-authored with Dr. T. Gerson da Cunha and Father Miguel Vicente d'Abreu, trace the history of English and Portuguese relations in India up to that time and provide a historical table of the viceroys, archbishops, and religious establishments of Goa.

Her description in *The Romance* of what was to be their most permanent home in Trieste characterizes it as a place where travelers lived. It was full of strange possessions – unusual books, clothing, weapons, scientific instruments, and drugs (both medicinal and recreational). Beginning in 1880 each of their trips was logged in Burton's journals and eventually described in *The Life of Captain Sir Richd. F. Burton* or in *The Romance*.

A major stop in 1880 was at Oberammergau in southern Germany, about fifty miles southwest of Munich. Every ten years this was the site of an eight-hour performance of the Passion play commemorating the trial, torture, and crucifixion of Christ, and both Burtons wrote accounts of the performance that they saw in August. Claiming financial exigency, however, a London publisher produced only what Isabel called Richard's "cynical" review of the production, and her reverent book – *The Passion Play at Ober-Ammergau* – had to wait until 1900, after her death. Her assessment included advice for travelers to the play, about which she wrote, "I thought the performance as near dramatic and artistic perfection as human acting could be, and that it could be done nowhere else than here."

Her accounts of the last decade of their lives are remarkable for what they tell of how to travel when one is ill. The Burtons were increasingly afflicted – he with gout and bronchial and heart problems; she with lingering aftereffects from a fall down the stairs of a Paris hotel and from early symptoms of the ovarian cancer that would cause her death.

As a travel writer Burton was most stylistically proficient in her first work, *The Inner Life of Syria, Palestine, and the Holy Land,* and her later books show little development. She composed them chiefly from journal entries that she augmented with letters, poetry, and extracts from articles and narratives – all spliced together in a discourse lacking an elegance about which she seems only rarely to have been concerned. In her preface to *The Life of Captain Sir Richd. F. Burton* she excuses

herself as being without "leisure to think of style or polish." *The Inner Life of Syria, Palestine, and the Holy Land* is the best edited of her books, with fewer lapses of grammar and infelicities of diction than in *Arabia, Egypt, India* and *The Life of Captain Sir Richd. F. Burton*. She was clearly energized by writing and publishing. Despite poor health and increasing demands of other affairs and writing projects in her last years, she began to edit a memorial edition of Richard's oeuvre; she completed seven of what might have totaled forty volumes.

She had extraordinary intellectual resources. She was fluent in French, Portuguese, Italian, and Spanish, and she had some knowledge of German, Arabic, and Yiddish. The library of the Burtons at Trieste included about eight thousand titles when Richard died, and some of the world's best maps and atlases were housed there. The Burtons not only read the work of but knew personally Henry T. Buckle, one of the most influential historians of the age. Isabel was also aware of the English literary tradition – she had read or mentioned in her own works such artists as Richard Brinsley Sheridan; Tobias Smollett; Percy Bysshe Shelley; George Gordon, Lord Byron; Wilkie Collins; A. C. Swinburne; Robert Browning; the actor Sir Henry Irving; William Winwood Reade; Thomas Carlyle; William Shakespeare; John Milton; Charles Darwin; Dante Gabriel Rossetti; Thomas Hughes, author of *Tom Brown's Schooldays* (1857); John Ruskin; Edmund Spenser; and John Stuart Mill. She mentions also actress Sarah Bernhardt, composer Richard Wagner, Jean-Jacques Rousseau, François Rabelais, and the Grimm brothers.

Her own poetry is interesting. Her sonnet celebrating Richard's six-volume translation of the *Arabian Nights* employs a Petrarchan structure and rhyme scheme more challenging than the Elizabethan:

TO RICHARD FRANCIS BURTON

"The Thousand Nights and a Night"

Adown the welkin slant the snows and pile
On sill and balcony; their feathery feet
Trip o'er the landscape, and pursuing sleet,
Earth's brow beglooming, robs the lift of smile:
Lies in her mourning-shroud our Northern Isle,
And bitter winds in battle o'er her meet;
Her world is death-like, when, behold! we greet
Light-gleams from morning-land cold grief to guile:

A light of golden mine and orient pearl,
Vistas of fairy-land, where Beauty reigns
And Valiance revels; cloudless moon, fierce sun,
The wold, the palm-tree; cities; hosts; a whirl
Of life in tents and palaces and fanes:
The light that streams from "Thousand Nights and One."

Here, as in her prose, she could not resist describing scenery, architecture, and people — with the flourish of a traveler's point of view.

Biography:

Jean Burton, *Sir Richard Burton's Wife* (New York: Knopf, 1941).

References:

B. J. Kirkpatrick, *A Catalogue of the Library of Sir Richard Burton, K.C.M.G., Held by the Royal Anthropological Institute* (London: Royal Anthropological Institute, 1978);

Eliza Lynn Linton, "The Partisans of the Wild Women," *Nineteenth Century,* 31 (March 1892): 455–464;

Joanna Richardson, "Sir Richard and Lady Burton," *History Today,* 25 (May 1975): 323–331.

Papers:

Isabel Burton materials are likely to be found in almost every collection listed in the chapter on "Burton Manuscripts" in *Sir Richard F. Burton: A Biobibliographical Study,* by James A. Casada (Boston: G. K. Hall, 1990). The principal repositories include the collections of the East Sheen District Library, Sheen Lane Centre, East Sheen, London; and the Orleans House Gallery, Riverside, Twickenham, Middlesex.

Sir Richard Francis Burton

(19 March 1821 – 20 October 1890)

John R. Pfeiffer
Central Michigan University

See also the Burton entry in *DLB 55: Victorian Prose Writers Before 1867.*

BOOKS: *Goa, and the Blue Mountains; or, Six Months of Sick Leave* (London: Bentley, 1851);

Scinde; or, The Unhappy Valley, 2 volumes (London: Bentley, 1851);

Sindh, and the Races that Inhabit the Valley of the Indus; with Notices of the Topography and History of the Province (London: Allen, 1851);

Falconry in the Valley of the Indus (London: Van Voorst, 1852);

A Complete System of Bayonet Exercise (London: Clowes, 1853);

Personal Narrative of a Pilgrimage to El-Medinah and Meccah (3 volumes, London: Longman, Brown, Green & Longmans, 1855–1856; 1 volume, New York: Putnam, 1856); republished as *Personal Narrative of a Pilgrimage to Al-Madinah & Meccah,* 2 volumes, edited by Isabel Burton (London: Tylston & Edwards, 1893); republished as *A Pilgrimage to Meccah and Medinah,* 1 volume, edited by Hugh J. Schonfield (London: Joseph, [1937]);

First Footsteps in East Africa; or, An Exploration of Harar (London: Longman, Brown, Green & Longman, 1856); 2 volumes, edited by Isabel Burton (London: Tylston & Edwards, 1894); 1 volume (New York: Dutton, [1910]);

The Lake Regions of Central Africa: A Picture of Exploration (2 volumes, London: Longman, Green, Longman & Roberts, 1860; 1 volume, New York: Harper, 1860);

The Lake Regions of Central Equatorial Africa, with Notes of the Lunar Mountains and the Sources of the White Nile; Being the Results of an Expedition Undertaken under the Patronage of Her Majesty's Government and the Royal Geographical Society of London, in the Years 1857–1859 (London: Clowes, 1860);

The City of the Saints, and Across the Rocky Mountains to California (London: Longman, Green, Longman & Roberts, 1861; New York: Harper,

Richard Francis Burton

1862); republished as *The Look of the West, 1860: Across the Plains to California* (Lincoln: University of Nebraska Press, 1963);

Abeokuta and the Camaroons Mountains: An Exploration, 2 volumes (London: Tinsley, 1863);

Wanderings in West Africa from Liverpool to Fernando Po, as F. R. G. S., 2 volumes (London: Tinsley, 1863);

A Mission to Gelele, King of Dahome: With Notices of the So-called "Amazons," the Grand Customs, the Yearly Customs, the Human Sacrifices, the Present State of the Slave Trade, and the Negro's Place in Nature, 2 volumes (London: Tinsley, 1864);

The Nile Basin: Part I. Showing Tanganyika to Be Ptolemy's Western Lake Reservoir. A Memoir Read before the Royal Geographical Society, November 14, 1864. Part II. Captain Speke's Discovery of the Source of the Nile: A Review, part 1 by Burton, part 2 by James MacQueen (London: Tinsley, 1864);

The Guide-Book: A Pictorial Pilgrimage to Mecca and Medina (London: Clowes, 1865);

Stone Talk: Being Some of the Marvellous Sayings of a Petral Portion of Fleet Street, London, to One Doctor Polyglott, Ph.D., as Frank Baker (London: Hardwicke, 1865);

Explorations of the Highlands of the Brazil; with a Full Account of the Gold and Diamond Mines. Also, Canoeing Down 1500 Miles of the Great River São Francisco, from Sabará to the Sea, 2 volumes (London: Tinsley, 1869);

Letters from the Battle-Fields of Paraguay (London: Tinsley, 1870);

Proverbia Communa Syriaca (London: Trubner, 1871);

Unexplored Syria: Visits to the Libanus, the Tulúl el Safá, the Anti-Libanus, the Northern Libanus, and the 'Aláh, 2 volumes, by Burton and Charles F. Tyrwhitt-Drake (London: Tinsley, 1872);

Zanzibar: City, Island, and Coast, 2 volumes (London: Tinsley, 1872);

Ultima Thule; or, A Summer in Iceland, 2 volumes (London & Edinburgh: Nimmo, 1875);

Etruscan Bologna: A Study (London: Smith, Elder, 1876);

A New System of Sword Exercise for Infantry (London: Clowes, 1876);

Two Trips to Gorilla Land and the Cataracts of the Congo, 2 volumes (London: Sampson Low, Marston, Low & Searle, 1876);

Scind Revisited: With Notices of the Anglo-Indian Army; Railroads; Past, Present, and Future, Etc., 2 volumes (London: Bentley, 1877);

The Gold-Mines of Midian and the Ruined Midianite Cities: A Fortnight's Tour in North-Western Arabia (London: Kegan Paul, 1878);

The Land of Midian (Revisited), 2 volumes (London: Kegan Paul, 1879);

The Ogham-runes and el-Mushajjarj: A Study (London: Royal Society of Literature, 1879);

The Kasîdah — Couplets — of Hajî Aboû El-Yezdî: A Lay of the Higher Law, Translated and Annotated by His Friend and Pupil F. B. (London: Privately printed, 1880; Portland, Maine: Mosher, 1896);

Correspondence with His Excellency Riaz Pasha upon the Mines of Midian (Alexandria, Egypt: Alexandria Stationers & Booksellers, 1880);

Report on Two Expeditions to Midian (Alexandria, Egypt, 1880);

Report upon the Minerals of Midian (Alexandria, Egypt: Stationers & Booksellers, 1880);

The Partition of Turkey (Trieste, 1881);

How to Deal with the Slave Scandal in Egypt ([Trieste], 1881);

Camoens: His Life and His Lusiads. A Commentary, 2 volumes (London: Quaritch, 1881);

The Thermae of Monfalcone (aqua dei et vitae) (London: Cox, 1881);

A Glance at the "Passion Play" (London: Harrison, 1881);

Lord Beaconsfield: A Sketch (N.p., [1882?]);

To the Gold Coast for Gold: A Personal Narrative, 2 volumes, by Burton and Verney Lovett Cameron (London: Chatto & Windus, 1883);

The Book of the Sword (London: Chatto & Windus, 1884);

The Jew, The Gypsy, and El Islam, edited by W. H. Wilkins (London: Hutchinson, 1898; Chicago & New York: Stone, 1898);

Wanderings in Three Continents, edited by Wilkins (London: Hutchinson, 1901; New York: Dodd, Mead, 1901);

The Sentiment of the Sword: A Country-house Dialogue, edited by A. Forbe Sieveking (London: The Field, 1911);

Selected Papers on Anthropology, Travel & Exploration, edited by Norman M. Penzer (London: Philpot, 1924; New York: McBride, 1924);

Love, War and Fancy: The Customs and Manners of the East, from Writings on the Arabian Nights, edited by Kenneth Walker (London: Kimber, 1964; New York: Ballantine, 1964);

Anthropological Notes on the Sotadic Zone of Sexual Inversion throughout the World, Including Some Observations on Social and Sexual Relations of the Muhammedan Empire (New York: Falstaff, n.d.);

Three Months at Abbazia (N.p., n.d.).

Collection: *The Memorial Edition of the Works of Captain Sir R. F. Burton,* 7 volumes, edited by Isabel Burton (London: Tylston & Edwards, 1893–1894).

OTHER: Randolph B. Marcy, *The Prairie Traveller: A Handbook for Overland Expeditions, with Illustrations and Itineraries of the Principal Routes between the Mississippi and the Pacific, and a Map,* edited, with a preface, by Burton (London: Trübner, 1863);

Wit and Wisdom from West Africa; or, A Book of Proverbial Philosophy, Idioms, Enigmas, and Laconisms, compiled by Burton (London: Tinsley, 1865);

Vikram and the Vampire; or, Tales of Hindu Devilry, translated by Burton (London: Longmans, Green, 1870; New York: Appleton, n.d.);

Francisco José Maria de Lacerda e Almeida, *The Lands of Cazembe: Lacerda's Journey to Cazembe in 1798,* translated and annotated by Burton, with two translations of other works by other translators (London: Royal Geographical Society, 1873);

Vātsyāyana, called Mallanāga, *Kama Shastra; or, The Hindoo Art of Love (Ars Amoris Indica),* translated by Burton as B. F. R and by F. F. Arbuthnot as A. F. F. (N.p.: Privately printed, 1873); republished as *Ananga-Ranga (Stage of the Bodiless One); or, The Hindu Art of Love (Ars Amoris Indica)* (Cosmopoli: Printed for the Hindoo Kama Shastra Society, 1885);

Johann von Staden, *The Captivity of Hans Stade, of Hesse, in A.D. 1547–1555, among the Wild Tribes of Eastern Brazil,* annotated by Burton (London: Hakluyt Society, 1874);

Luiz Vaz de Camões, *Os Lusiadas (The Lusiads),* 2 volumes, translated by Burton (London: Quaritch, 1880);

Vātsyāyana, *The Kama Sutra of Vatsyayana,* translated by Burton (London & Benares: Printed for the Hindoo Kama Shastra Society, 1883); republished as *The Kama Sutra: The Classic Hindu Treatise on Love and Social Conduct* (New York: Dutton, 1962);

Camões, *The Lyricks,* 2 volumes, translated by Burton (London: Quaritch, 1884);

A Plain and Literal Translation of the Arabian Nights' Entertainments, Now Entitled the Book of the Thousand Nights and a Night, 10 volumes, translated, with introduction and afterword, by Burton (Benares: Printed for the Hindoo Kama Shastra Society, 1885);

Supplemental Nights to the Book of The Thousand Nights and a Night, 6 volumes, translated by Burton (Benares: Printed for the Kama Shastra Society, 1886–1888);

J. M. Pereira da Silva, *Manuel de Moraes: A Chronicle of the Seventeenth Century,* translated by Burton and Isabel Burton, bound with Isabel's translation of *Iraçema, the Honeylips: A Chronicle of the Seventeenth Century,* by José Martiniano de Alencar (London: Bickers, 1886);

Sheikh Nefzawi, *The Perfumed Garden of the Cheikh Nefzaoui: A Manual of Arabian Erotology,* translated by Burton (Cosmopoli: Printed for the Kama Shastra Society of London and Benares, 1886; New York: Golden Hind Press, 1933);

The Behâristân (Abode of Spring) (Benares: Printed by the Kama Shastra Society, 1887);

Sa'di, *The Gulistân; or, Rose Garden of Sa'di,* translated by Burton (Benares: Printed by the Kama Shastra Society for Private Subscribers Only, 1888);

Priapeia; or, The Sportive Epigrams of Divers Poets on Priapus: The Latin Text Now for the First Time Englished in Verse and Prose, translated by Burton, as Outidanos, and by Leonard Smithers, as Neaniskos (Cosmopoli: Printed by the Translators for Private Subscribers Only, 1890);

Arthur Leared, *Marocco and the Moors: Being an Account of Travels, with a General Description of the Country and Its People,* second edition, revised and edited, with an introduction, by Burton (London: Low, Marston, Searle, & Rivington / New York: Scribner & Welford, 1891);

Giovanni Battista Basile, *Il Pentamerone; or, the Tale of Tales,* 2 volumes, translated by Burton (London: Henry, 1893; New York: Boni & Liveright, 1927);

Caius Valerius Catullus, *The Carmina of Caius Valerius Catullus, Now First Completely Englished into Verse and Prose,* translated by Burton and Smithers (London: Printed for the translators, 1894);

Tales from the Gulistân, translated by Burton (N.p., 1928);

José Basílio da Gama, *The Uruguay (A Historical Romance of South America),* translated, with a preface, by Burton (Berkeley: University of California Press, 1982).

SELECTED PERIODICAL PUBLICATIONS – UNCOLLECTED: "Notes and Remarks on Dr. Dorn's Chrestomathy of the Pushtu or Afghan Language" and "A Grammar of the Jataki or Belohcki Dialect," *Royal Asiatic Society Journal (Bombay Branch),* 3 (January 1849): 58–69, 84–125;

"Notes Relative to the Population of Sind; and the Customs, Language, and Literature of the People," *Bombay Government Records,* new series, 17, part 2 (1855): 613–657.

Sir Richard Francis Burton was the preeminent nineteenth-century British travel writer, a brilliant linguist and translator, an extraordinary explorer, a pioneer anthropologist, a poet, a civil engineer, a field cartographer, a soldier, one of Europe's best swordsmen, a diplomat, and a geologist. He published more than thirty books describing his travels and explorations as well as many articles, all

"The Cathedral of Goa," illustration from Burton's first book, Goa, and the Blue Mountains *(courtesy of the Lilly Library, Indiana University)*

reflecting his extensive knowledge of the places and cultures he visited. In his accounts of his travels from India to Brazil Burton analyzed climate, labor and slavery, manufacturing, commerce, economics, history, literature, and folklore.

Two impressive achievements established his stature as a travel writer and explorer: he was the first European to give a detailed, accurate description of the sacred Islamic city of Mecca, and his expeditions to central Africa in search of the source of the Nile River led to its discovery by his associate, John Hanning Speke. Burton is also notable for his translations of *The Kama Sutra of Vatsyayana* (1883) and *A Plain and Literal Translation of the Arabian Nights' Entertainments* (1885). An athlete of great physical strength and endurance, Burton was phenomenally industrious, but he lacked good business sense and made no money from investments in any of the countries he explored. Indeed, he had financial problems all his life. His personality made him one of the most controversial public figures of his age.

Richard Francis Burton was born on 19 March 1821 at Barnham House, Hertfordshire, England, the firstborn of Martha Baker Burton and Joseph Netterville Burton. He was baptized at Elstree. His maternal grandfather, Richard Baker of Barnham House, had wealth, some of it intended for his grandson, but never, to Burton's lifelong dis-

appointment, to materialize. His father was of English and Irish descent, with some possible French ancestry or "gypsiness" that later fascinated Burton's wife, Isabel Arundell. Burton's father rose to the rank of lieutenant colonel in the British army, and this indicates that his family, too, enjoyed some prosperity. Burton was closest to his sister, Maria Catherine Eliza, whose daughter Georgiana would later write a biography of Burton to refute the one written by his wife. He was also close to his brother, Edward, his companion until Burton was expelled from Oxford.

Shortly after Burton's birth his father moved the family to Tours, France, where they lived until 1830. They then moved back to Brighton, England, to enroll the two Burton brothers in Richmond Preparatory School. After an epidemic of measles sent the boys home, they resumed life abroad, living for the next ten years in Orléans and Blois, France, and then in Italy – in Lyon, Livorno, Pisa, Siena, Rome, and Naples. The brothers were furnished with tutors to prepare them for the university and the world. In these years Burton learned the languages and cultures, the athletic games, and the vices of much of southern Europe. He learned Bernais, a mix of French, Spanish, and Provençal; Italian in northern Italy; some Greek in Marseilles; Italian in Naples; Spanish; and some German and Portuguese.

Sent to Trinity College, Oxford, in 1840 to study for the ministry, Burton met Thomas Arnold, Benjamin Jowett, and John Henry Newman, the last of whom especially impressed Burton. These young men made Burton respect the intellectual potential of the university, a respect evident in the often elaborate scholarliness of his books. When he interpolated colloquial Greek diction into his Greek examination, Burton lost his bid for a fellowship to an inferior applicant. This discouragement was a watershed in Burton's life. He turned to the study of Arabic (his autobiography says that he also investigated Chinese) during his last months at Oxford, while he behaved in a manner calculated to incur rustication — the less dishonorable form of expulsion. He miscalculated and was formally expelled in 1842 at the age of twenty-one.

Through his father's aid in purchasing a commission for him, Burton thereafter landed in Bombay, India, on 28 October 1842 as an ensign in the army mustered under the British East India Company. His official duties were those of a surveyor, army intelligence gatherer, and regimental interpreter. He studied the local languages, including Armenian, Hindustani, Gujarati, Sindhi, Persian, Pashto, Punjabi, Sanskrit, Telugu, and Turkish, and he continued to study Arabic. Burton's preferred way to acquire a language was to study until he reached a nearly native command of it and then to "go native" by eating the food, wearing the clothes, and living among the people, sometimes disguised as one of them.

Burton caught cholera in the epidemic that swept Sind (now part of Pakistan) in 1846 and later suffered from ophthalmia (conjunctivitis), so he was granted two years of sick leave beginning early in 1847. He spent the first part of his leave in Goa on the coast of India, south of Bombay. Using notes from these months (all his major works on India were written several years after these visits), he wrote his first travel book, *Goa, and the Blue Mountains; or, Six Months of Sick Leave* (1851). Burton's voice is both authoritative and attentive to the reader, inviting leisureliness and trust. He is intensely self-conscious about reporting what he thinks will please. His account of this land and culture is often depressing but also vibrant with what would become his typical combination of irony and precise exposition. Chapter 1, "The Voyage," begins,

> What a glad moment it is, to be sure, when the sick and seedy, the tired and testy invalid [Burton] from pestiferous Scinde or pestilential Guzerat, "leaves all behind

him" and scrambles over the sides of his Pattimar... [–] a very long boat . . . composed of innumerable bits of wood tied together with coir, or cocoanut [*sic*] rope, fitted up with a dark and musty little cabin, and supplied with two or three long poles intended as masts, which lean forward as if about to sink under the weight of the huge lateen sail. . . . Everyone that has ever sailed in a pattimar can oblige you with a long list of pleasures peculiar to it. . . . [B]y day your eyes are blinded with glare and heat, . . . [and] by night mosquitos, a trifle smaller than jack snipes, assault your defenseless limbs.

Burton was moved by the beauty of weather, landscape, and nature in the places he reached. Seeing the city of Panjim, or New Goa, from the sea, he wrote, "The air was soft and fragrant, at the same time sufficiently cool to be comfortable. A thin mist rested upon the lower grounds and hovered half way up the hills, leaving their palm-clad summits clear to catch the silvery light of dawn. Most beautiful was the hazy tone of colour all around contrasted with the painfully vivid tints, and the sharp outlines of an Indian view seen a few hours after sunrise." Burton also supplies an understated description of the Blue Mountain region:

> The rock upon which we tread falls with an almost perpendicular drop of four thousand feet into the plains. . . . A bluish mist clothes the distant hills of Malabar, dimly seen upon the horizon in front. Behind, on the far side of the mighty chasm, the white bungalows of Coonoor glitter through the green trees, or disappear behind the veil of fleecy vapour which floats along the sunny mountain tops. However hypercritically disposed, you can find no fault with this view; it has beauty, variety, and sublimity to recommend it.

Goa presents autobiographical material, describes modes of travel, recounts the history of the Portuguese political state and of the Inquisition in India, and describes the various racial groups and cultures, often with emphasis on anatomy and physical appearance. Burton does not restrain his antipathy for what he sees as mongrelized people, such as the Goan races. Moreover, he introduces a hypothesis to which he later returns in his books on Africa, the belief that converting indigenous peoples from Hinduism or Islam to Christianity was insidious. Burton also comments on the animals, agriculture, and climate, and he describes what is made in the country that could be bought and sold abroad. He notes topography and geology, and even in this early work he has an eye for the mining of gold and precious gems, a major subject in later books. Chapters 4 and 5 of *Goa* contain the tale of a pretty young nun, a Latin professor in a local convent,

50   § 5. TENT FURNITURE.

materials, under the influence of the rain, will certainly tear up the pegs.

The ground is often such that the tent-pegs will not "hold;" if it be sandy, scrape the surface sand away before driving them in, and put a flat stone under the foot of the pole as a step for it to rest on, or it will work a deep hole, and, sinking down, will leave the tent slack and unsteady. If the sand is very deep, it is an excellent plan to bury sticks or bushes, two or three feet deep, and to tie the tent corners to the middle of them, instead of to pegs. Bags of sand, or of shingle, may also be buried.

Bushing a tent means the burying of bushes in the soil so far as to leave only their cut ends above the ground to which a corresponding number of the ropes of the tent are tied. Heavy saddle-bags are often of use to fasten the tent to, and in rocky ground heavy piles of stones may be made to answer the same purpose.

Natives are apt to creep up, and, putting their hands under the tent, to steal things: a hedge of bushes is some protection against them.

A tent should never be pitched in a slovenly way; it is so far more roomy, secure, and pretty, when tightly stretched out, that no pains should be spared in drilling the men to do it well. I like to use a piece of string, marked with knots, by which I can measure the exact places in which the tent-pegs should be struck; the eye is a very deceitful guide in estimating squareness. It is wonderful how men will bungle over a tent when they are not properly drilled to pitch it. (*See* p. 244.)

§ 5. TENT FURNITURE.—A portable bedstead, with musquito curtains, is a very great luxury, raising the sleeper above the damp soil, and the attacks of most creatures that creep on it; in tours where a few luxuries can be carried, it is a very

§ 5. TENT FURNITURE.   51

proper article of baggage. Hammocks and cots have but few advocates, as it is rare to find places adapted for swinging them; they are quite out of place in a small tent.

Chairs and tables.—It is advisable to take very *low* strong and *roomy* camp-stools, with tables to correspond in height,

as a chamber is much less choked up when the seats are low, or when people sit, as in the East, on the ground. The seats should not be more than 1 foot high, though as wide and deep as an ordinary footstool. Habit very soon reconciles travellers to this; but without a seat at all, a man can never write, draw, nor calculate as well as if he has one. A good stool is of this sort, with a full-sized leather or canvas seat, or one made of strips of dressed hide. The table should be a couple of boards, not less than 2 feet long, by 9 inches broad, hinged lengthwise together, and resting on a stand, on the same principle as the above chair. It would be well to have it made of common mahogany, for deal warps and cracks excessively. There is no difficulty in carrying furniture like the above on a pack-horse.

For want of a chair, it is very convenient to dig a hole or a trench in the ground, and to sit on one side of it, with the feet resting on its bottom; the opposite side of the trench serves as a table.

To tie clothes, or anything, up to a smooth tent pole, see *Clovehitch*, p. 134.

D 2

Pages from Burton's annotated copy of Francis Galton's The Art of Travel *(1855) (Henry E. Huntington Library and Art Gallery)*

who appears to have acquiesced in Burton's failed attempt to kidnap/rescue her from the institution. Biographers believe that the tale is veiled autobiography and that, Burton's attempt having been discovered, the would-be rescuer fled the area. Goa was important as the home of the classic Portuguese writer Luiz Vaz de Camões, whose *Os Lusiadas* Burton later translated and published in 1880. *Goa* was received respectfully but was not a financial success, had no further editions, and won no satisfying acclaim.

Burton's second and third travel books are each about the Sind province pacified by Gen. Robert Napier in northwestern India in the early 1840s. Each reveals a further development in Burton's command of what is to become an extraordinary species of travel writing, written both for a general reading public and for investors, diplomats, scientists, and demographers. *Scinde; or, The Unhappy Valley* (1851) begins, as does *Goa,* with a view from the

water, a view of Karachi, the port city of Sind that he visits. In *Scinde* Burton criticizes civilized Europe by comparing it to the culture he visits. For example, he calls the ways that European mothers treat their children inferior to the extraordinary nurture that Indian mothers provide their children. In anticipation of his writing in *Letters from the Battle-Fields of Paraguay* (1870) he describes the horrors of the Sind war, as he combines war journalism and the travel-adventure narrative. As his account moves inland from Karachi, Burton reports the misery of urban civilization and pleads for better housing for the British soldiers in India. He predicts the bloody uprising against the culturally insensitive British colonial presence that occurred a few years after he had left India in order to explore Arabia and Africa. His discourse also exhibits his notoriously (or marvelously) arcane vocabulary in such diction as *olid, chunamed floor, antigropiloses, graveolent,* and *cacodemon.* He adopts an editorial *we* that becomes gently cynical, precisely informed, sympathetic to the common soldier, and wittily learned about local folklore. The dust, heat, humidity, and antiquity of the early-nineteenth-century Indian colony pervade his account. *Scinde* is a model of the smorgasbord of contents of Burton's later books, meandering and desultory in following a natural force of curiosity through the main places of the country from Karachi, through Hyderabad, and to the northern frontier of Sind. He ends by suggesting his own boredom: "How affecting (to oneself) – how romantic, and how ennuyeux."

The next book, *Sindh, and the Races that Inhabit the Valley of the Indus; with Notices of the Topography and History of the Province* (1851), is a work that many Burton scholars regard as his second best, although it appeared in only three editions. It grew from four papers Burton had written earlier: "Notes and Remarks on Dr. Dorn's Chrestomathy of the Pushtu or Affghan [*sic*] Language," "A Grammar of the Játakí or the Belohckí Dialect," "Brief Notes Relative to the Division of Time, and Articles of Cultivation in Sind; to Which are Appended Remarks on the Modes of Intoxication in That Province," and "Notes Relative to the Population of Sind; and the Customs, Language, and Literature of the People."

In *Sindh* Burton's travel writing becomes a species of mercantile espionage and disciplined anthropology. Hoping that those he met would attribute his odd accent to his being half Arab and half Iranian, Burton had traveled in oriental disguise. The thirteen chapters that compose the "Contents" of Sindh clearly outline not only the main topics of this book but also those to which Burton would repeatedly return in his travel works. He starts with the geographical location, climate, "appearance," military and commercial condition, topography, and history of Sindh; goes on to describe the main rivers, canals, and system of taxation; recounts Sindhi legends and discusses the languages and dialects; identifies celebrated Sindhi authors, their works, and the folktales of the region; characterizes the educational system (through its colleges and medical schools); and describes its social conditions, uses of drugs, and occult practices. He also examines the popular sects, religious rites, and "saints"; identifies the foreign tribes settled in Sind; presents the social customs of men (exercises and games such as wrestling, horse racing, chess, backgammon, Parcheesi, dice, and cards) as well as of women (their habits, intrigues, dress, dancing, and prostitution, this last of which Burton mentions only in connection with women); and discusses the current state of Hinduism.

In *Sindh* his love of describing and analyzing a linguistic universe is fully manifest. For Burton language is the key to understanding a human culture. He believed that a student of another culture should start with its words, then distill the grammar that reflects the complexity of the relationships of those objects and ideas named by the words. At the same time Burton's practical and even cynical sense is revealed: he wants to encourage the use of Sindhi instead of "solecistic Persian" as the official language, because "nothing can be so well adapted practically to facilitate fraud and injustice as the employment of two languages, one of them understood only by the educated classes." Moreover, older and popular vernacular folktales should be collected and preserved: "We are not likely to derive much amusement or improvement from the literary effusions of a semi-barbarous race, but as a means of power they are valuable weapons in our hands." Not a philanthropic liberal, Burton advises that understanding the ethnology of people allows one to control them with propaganda rather than with expensive police and military force.

Burton soon wrote a somewhat happier book about India, his urbane and learned *Falconry in the Valley of the Indus* (1852). At first little noticed, *Falconry* became a classic on the subject. Set in Sind in the mid 1840s, the book is autobiographical, not only about the narrator's experiences with falconry but also about his career at Oxford – his "firsts" in the language examinations on Hindustani and Gujurati, his going in disguise into Hyderabad, and his different uses of the names of places, such as Scinde and Sind. In *Falconry* the gloomy sense of the Sindhi region and culture (that of Portuguese India) conveyed in Burton's earlier books lifts somewhat, and the account paints the Indus River valley as luxuriant and fecund. Burton denigrates hunting with weapons, which ruffles the feathers of many potential readers:

> There is an eternal sameness in the operation of shooting, which must make it, – one would suppose, – very uninteresting to any but those endowed with an undue development of Destructiveness. It is a strange sight to see a man toiling at one amusement from early autumn to early spring, knocking over his birds almost unerringly, with fifty appliances to rob them of all chance of escape. . . . Our ancestors took up the gun and allowed the "nobles of the air" to be shot down as vermin. We can be wiser than they, and [with falconry] enjoy both amusements combined.

His preference for hunting with birds rather than weapons formed part of the basis of the antagonism between Burton and John Hanning Speke, his later companion in the search for the source of the Nile, for Speke, when traveling, shot wild game for his collection in England. Burton was a bigot and an elitist, both instinctively and by proud personal code, but he also had sympathy, especially for the innocently vulnerable.

In May 1849, still sick with cholera and ophthalmia, Burton left India and returned to England. From late spring 1849 to the fall of 1852 he recuperated, wrote his early Indian books, met and courted Isabel Arundell, and resolved to travel to Mecca disguised as an Arab, an undertaking that would become his most celebrated exploratory adventure. The story was that no white man had entered that sacred city and lived. In fact a few others had, but none had written a precise account, especially of the Great Mosque. Burton succeeded, and in 1855 he published in three volumes the most well-known of his travel books, *Personal Narrative of a Pilgrimage to El-Medinah and Meccah* (1855–1856). Burton's narrative persona significantly changed from that of the congenial, somewhat detached, dourly teasing guide of the Indian books to that of a central character. Burton's narrator becomes a focused man of energy, knowledge, analytical complexity, physical toughness, and iron nerve. *Personal Narrative* is a classic of travel writing as autobiography.

The book takes its readers from Egypt, where Burton practiced his disguise as an Afghan-Arab (one that he had to maintain to preserve his life), to Suez and then on a very uncomfortable journey by ship down the Red Sea to Jeddah, where he disembarks with the retainers that he has acquired and begins his journey overland, first to Medina and then to Mecca. Burton's *Personal Narrative* records his travel by sailboat and then by foot across the desert. Most remarkable in his recounting of events is his report of his severely infected foot, which was extremely painful and did not heal quickly: part of the time he could not walk. Even so, he pressed on, made observations, took secret notes, and made new friends; eventually his foot healed, and he reached his dangerous goal. Day after laborious day Burton's travel, in great discomfort, is a subtext not only of *Personal Narrative* but of all his east and central African exploration books. His account succeeds, moreover, in conveying to late-twentieth-century readers how interminable a distance can be when it is traveled by walking. In spite of real and understated hardships, he succeeded in reaching Mecca and described the Great Mosque accurately and completely, as no European before him had done.

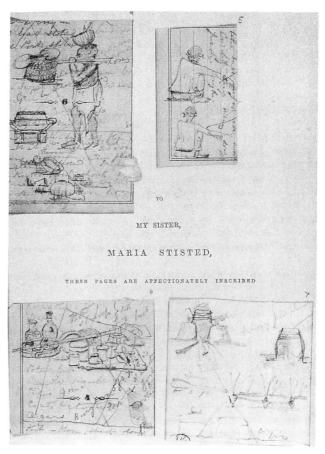

Sketches made by Burton and later pasted into his copy of The Lake Regions of Central Africa *(Henry E. Huntington Library and Art Gallery)*

Personal Narrative launched Burton's reputation as an explorer. It gave him prestige with the Royal Geographical Society, which subsequently awarded him funds for his trips to Africa. The book has appeared in nearly twenty editions, including translations into French, German, Spanish, Indian, and Arabic. It has never been out of print.

Immediately after his return from Mecca in 1853, Burton was eager for a second daring expedition. In late 1854 and early 1855 he traveled through Somalia and reached Harar, a city reputed to be hostile – in fact, "forbidden" – to Europeans. This adventure is described in the first of his three east African books, *First Footsteps in East Africa; or, An Exploration of Harar* (1856). The book reads like an adventure novel, describing three months and ten days of travel from Zayla to Harar and back to Berbera. The account of the trip through Somalia is fleshed out with Burton's anthropological and linguistic description of the peoples. Accompanied by his famous guide "End of Time," Burton was disguised again, this time as a Moslem merchant.

In its time Burton's book gave the best general description of northern Somali society. *First Footsteps* also includes Burton's version of his first meeting and travel with John Hanning Speke, who joined his party on 3 April 1854 in Berbera. It describes the 1855 attempt to reach the Nile by way of Harar, a venture aborted by an ambush from Somali tribesmen that left Burton with a spear wound through his cheek and jaw and Speke with eleven spear wounds on the back of his hand, his right shoulder, and both legs. Yet, no matter how sensationally distracting his adventures, Burton was always a scholar-linguist: Appendix III provides a "Grammatical Outline and Vocabulary of the Harori Language." In the belief that description of mutilation surgery performed on preadolescent girls was not fit for print, most early editions of *First Footsteps* omit the notorious fourth appendix on "Excision and Infibulation" in Nubia.

Burton's second African book, *The Lake Regions of Central Africa: A Picture of Exploration* (1860), is magisterial and controversial. Written mostly in Bologna after his return from Africa in 1859, it presents the story of his expedition involving more than three hundred people from the island of Zanzibar to east Africa and the Mrima country, then westward into central Africa through five regions, and ultimately to the "Sea of Ujiji," also called Lake Tanganyika, the second largest lake in Africa. Burton has been credited by western historians as the European discoverer of this lake.

Included are Burton's accounts of his relation with Speke and, more piquantly interesting, with the African native guide, Seedy Mubarak Bombay, who served Burton, the team of Speke and Capt. James Augustus Grant, and Henry Stanley in the extraordinary series of expeditions that opened not only the connections of the Nile to Lake Victoria but also the Zaire (Congo) River from Tanganyika to the Atlantic. Burton describes threats to himself and Speke during negotiations with tribal chiefs and their interminable days, sicknesses, and infections so prostrating that he and Speke had to be carried. Burton observed with some contempt that these peoples had few traditions, no annals, and no ruins, and such comments suggest that Burton's understanding of the resources of oral language cultures was curiously limited. He understood some of the constraints of oral storytelling procedures, but he seems not to have understood what later-twentieth-century anthropologists and folklorists have now established — that oral cultures, such as those of native American and African tribal peoples, developed effective mnemonic protocols in stories and *thulas*

that enabled them to have a highly defined and continuing cultural history in the form of oral annals. That they left few "ruins" hardly proves cultural inferiority and may mean only that their civilizations were ecologically far less disruptive than self-styled "higher" civilizations.

The Lake Regions describes Burton's initial glimpse of Lake Tanganyika in an excellent sample of Burton's verbal depiction of landscape, fittingly of the place with which he is most associated:

> Tanganyika Lake . . . [lies] in the lap of the mountains, basking in the gorgeous tropical sunshine. Below and beyond are short breaking wavelets. Further in front stretch the waters, an expanse of the lightest and softest blue, in breadth varying from thirty to thirty-five miles, and sprinkled by the crisp eastwind with tiny crescents of snowy foam. The background in front is a high and broken wall of steel-coloured mountain, here flecked and capped with pearly mist, there standing sharply penciled against the azure air; its yawning chasms, marked by a deeper plum-colour, fall towards dwarf hills of mound-like proportions, which apparently dip their feet in the wave.

Burton's contrast of the natural beauty of the lake and its mountains with the pestiferous dwellings of the people who live on its shores is stark:

> The huts are full of animal life — snakes, scorpions, ants of various kinds, whose armies sometimes turn the occupants out of doors; the rafters are hollowed out by xylophagous insects; the walls are riddled by mason-bees, hideous spiders veil the corners with thick webs, the chirp of the cricket is heard both within and out of doors, cockroaches destroy the provisions, and large brown mosquitoes and flies, ticks and bugs, assault the inhabitants.

That Burton regarded business speculators among his readers is certain. In the first appendix of the book he is as attentive as a shopkeeper to the whole inventory of textile cloth, by kind and color, that will be in demand in the opening of interior Africa. He cites prices exactly and describes special articles of clothing, hardware, grains, and spices. He adds an account of the ivory trade in central Africa and the various qualities of ivory found around Tanganyika, and he notes that the ivory trade is as complicated as the market in sugar in British colonies or cotton in America. Ever aware of the connection between commodities and labor, Burton notes that the principal Tanganyikan city of Ujiji is the mid-nineteenth-century slave market of these regions. He gives a thumbnail analysis of the local economics of the trade, as he explains that slaves sell in Zanzibar for fourteen to fifteen dollars

"The Prophet's Block," in Salt Lake City, Utah, illustration from Burton's The City of the Saints and Across the Rocky Mountains to California *(courtesy of the Lilly Library, Indiana University)*

apiece, at a profit of nearly 500 percent, "which means the slave trade will not easily be supressed."

Noteworthy in the book is Burton's presentation of his ultimately irrelevant refutation of Speke's geography of the Mountains of the Moon and of Speke's claims to have discovered the source of the Nile. Although Speke's claim that Lake Victoria was the source of the river proved to be true, Burton's counterargument appears in the preface to *The Lake Regions,* which dismisses Speke's claims by representing him as incompetent. Even after Speke's death Burton more stridently repeated this attack in *The Nile Basin* (1864), a work that reveals Burton's continuing anger with his former partner. Because illness had prevented Burton from sharing in the actual discovery with Speke, Speke had agreed to announce the discovery together with Burton when they returned to England. Still recovering, Burton rested in Zanzibar while Speke reached England ahead of him. There Speke broke his promise by claiming all the credit for himself, and Burton's failure to discover Lake Victoria haunted him for the rest of his life.

The east African book *Zanzibar: City, Island, and Coast* was not published until 1872, although Burton had completed the manuscript and arranged for it to be sent by foreign office pouch to Norton Shaw in London in 1858. The delivery of the manuscript was probably subverted by an erstwhile language exam competitor, Capt. Christopher Rigby, who had replaced Burton's friend, the deceased Colonel Hamerton, at the Zanzibar foreign office post. The manuscript, among the most important of Burton's African studies, was inexplicably returned to him eight years later.

The book contains far more than a description of the island state of Zanzibar. It chronicles Burton and Speke's expedition to the central African lakes and their fabulous search for the source of the Nile. The narrative voice is that of the much more mature Burton. In the fourteen years since his Zanzibar-based African explorations, he had been in America, west Africa, South America, and Iceland and had written many articles and at least ten books. Even though he had not discovered the source of the Nile, Burton became increasingly respected as his role in African exploration became understood. The publication of *Zanzibar*, following the two other East Africa volumes and the four from his expeditions in West Africa, marked him as the world's best-informed person on Africa.

Zanzibar provides powerful scientific, geographical, commercial, and sociological information. Eight chapters focus on such aspects of the island as government, history, ethnology of "foreigners," ethnology of Arabs, and ethnology of the Wasawahili and the slave races. Among them is a six-section chapter on geography and physiology, geology, meteorology, climate, nosology (classification of diseases), fauna, flora, and industry of Zanzibar. More appears in the third chapter: "How the Nile Question Stood in the Year of Grace 1856" includes valuable lists of books on Zanzibar languages and the Nile River. Chapter 12 is portentously titled "Captain Speke," in which Burton sketches a biography of Speke and a relatively objective account of his status and accomplishments; Burton is at best ambivalent, however, in his assessment of Speke's competence as a navigator in making the astronomical observations essential to his claim that he had "located" a likely source of the Nile.

Zanzibar expresses Burton's resignation at not having the glory of discovering the source of the Nile. "In wayfaring, as in warfare," he writes, "opportunity is everything: better an ounce of fortune's favours than a ton of genius or merit." The book also describes the achievement that ultimately consoled him:

> For three months and a half our heart-wearing work was cheered only by two stimulants, the traveller's delight in seeing new scenes unfold themselves before his eyes and the sense of doing something lastingly useful to geographers.... We were also opening for Europeans a new road into the heart of Africa, a region boundless in commercial resources, and bounded in commercial development only by the stereotypical barbarism of its inhabitants; and we hoped that those who might follow us would be able to turn many of the obstacles through which we were compelled to cut a way.

Yet Burton's commercial and imperial motives only rarely overcame his desire to encourage preservation of indigenous culture. He almost always advocated keeping native nomenclature for cities, towns, rivers, lakes, and regions: "Nothing can be so absurd as to impose English names on any part, but especially upon places in the remote interior parts of Africa." But he seemed to violate this principle by later trying to name mountains in the Cameroons "Victoria" and "Isabel," an attempt that

proved unsuccessful when the names were not later recognized by British or provincial authorities.

Burton's life changed radically after his return from central Africa to England in 1859. Speke had been talked into claiming credit for independently discovering the source of the Nile, and with funding from the Royal Geographical Society he returned to central Africa with Captain Grant in early 1860 to confirm his claim. In England Burton proposed marriage to Isabel Arundell, with whom he had remained in fitful contact and courtship for nearly ten years. She desired the marriage but demurred because of her mother's opposition. In April 1860, with no answer from Isabel and without saying goodbye to her, Burton sailed for America.

Burton traveled for nine months with Lt. John Steinhauser (from Aden times) through every state of what he called the "Anglo-American Republic" as well as the Far West. He spent three weeks in Salt Lake City, Utah, from August to September 1860 and then was in California until 15 November 1860 before he returned by way of Panama to England. The book he wrote from these travels, *The City of the Saints, and Across the Rocky Mountains to California* (1861), is engaging as well as surprising in its observations on such a controversial matter as Mormon polygamy.

In Salt Lake City he interviewed Brigham Young, successor to Joseph Smith, the founder of the Mormons. Burton's impressions of Young are most interesting: he found in the man a sense of great sanity and disciplined power. This was high praise from an observer used to meeting Arab sheiks and African chiefs who wielded absolute power over their subjects. Some of the African chiefs that Burton had encountered in west Africa had been much degraded by the power they had used in rites of mutilation, murder, and cannibalism. Burton viewed polygamy objectively. He found the Mormon practice civilized, stable, and emotionally nourishing, but he believed that it prevented the sort of intimacy that can occur in a monogamous relationship. He found it similar to Arabian harem culture. Burton did not defend polygamy so much as refuse to find it worse than monogamous British marriage, but Isabel was later upset to think that he might prefer polygamy.

Burton's accounts of the Mormons and the American West have affinities with those of Mark Twain, who visited and wrote about the Mormons in 1861, the year after Burton's tour. Both accounts engage the reader with wit and humor, but Burton, unlike Twain, who often sacrificed facts for comic effect, tried to combine fact and comic mood. On the trip from Zion (Salt Lake City) to San Francisco, Burton's party narrowly averted encounters with Indians and outlaws who preyed on travelers. Describing such episodes, Burton characteristically tries to sound indigenous and witty. However, he calls scalping "the red nightcap," which does not ring true of American patois and the idiom used to narrate the history and legend of the American frontier. Burton, who clearly possessed a genius for language, dialect, and complicated cultural disguise, did not always catch the right nuance.

Burton's word pictures of the landscape of the American West infuse *The City of the Saints.* He found the American prairie awe-inspiring, but as monotonously interminable as Indian and African jungles. The prairie colors were like the Arabian desert to him, but he could also see with new eyes the panorama of air and land as he approached the Great Salt Lake:

> The atmosphere was touched with a dreamy haze, and a little bank of rose-coloured clouds, edged with flames of purple and gold, floated in the upper air, whilst the mellow radiance of an American autumn diffused its mild, soft lustre over the face of the earth. The sun was sending a flood of heavenly light behind the bold, jagged outline of Antelope Island. At its feet, and then bounding the far horizon, lay, like a band of burnished silver, the Great Salt Lake.

Burton's *The City of the Saints,* which inspired E. N. Jencks's *A Plea for Polygamy* (1929), was widely read, translated into Italian, and reprinted into the late twentieth century in many editions, at least one of which omits the Mormon materials – *The Look of the West, 1860: Across the Plains to California* (1963).

From San Francisco Burton returned to England and married Isabel on 22 January 1861. His request for a half-pay status from the Bombay army was denied ultimately because of his outspoken criticism of certain superiors in India, and he needed a job. Within the year his friends and wife arranged for Burton to be assigned a consulship on Fernando Po, an uncomfortable, equatorial west African island on which the British navy had established a base to suppress the slave trade. Leaving Isabel behind (although she did sail part of the way with him) because tropical diseases were notorious for killing Europeans, Burton began his exploration of west Africa on the voyage to his new post. His discoveries and travels during the next four years are recorded in six books, four of which Glenn S. Burne has characterized as "studies in disenchantment." Writing nearly twenty-five hundred

pages, Burton worked on four of them in the years from 1861 to 1863.

Most of *Wanderings in West Africa from Liverpool to Fernando Po* was serialized in *Fraser's Magazine* in 1863. The same year the only edition of the book appeared. It begins with a review of most of the existing writing on west Africa, some of which Burton discounts because the accounts were by women, and then comments upon his travel-writing method – to describe the new places at once, while the contrasts between the new and familiar are most startling and fresh. In general it describes Burton's first trip from England on 24 August 1861 down the west coast of Africa to his consular seat at Fernando Po.

Among mainland African coastal places that he describes are those he determined to be the three greatest centers of the export slave trade: Gambia and Senegal, Ashanti and Dahomey, and Yoruba and Benin (in addition to the whole coast around the mouth of the Congo River). Once again Burton provides a practical analysis of the economics of slaving, and he includes a chapter on "Gold in Africa," a never-flagging interest. His words on reaching Fernando Po register his ambivalence at this juncture of his life: "Arriving in these outer places is the very abomination of desolation. I drop for a time my pen, in the distant memory of [my] having felt uncommonly suicidal through that first night on Fernando Po."

Shortly after Burton reached Fernando Po, he was off to the African mainland. He called his short initial stay on the island (from 2 October to 9 October 1861) "a long, long, a very long week." He explored Abeokuta and the Cameroons mountains, an experience recorded in *Abeokuta and the Camaroons Mountains: An Exploration* (1863). Burton's intentions in writing *Abeokuta* were to explain how England might secure a commercial advantage on the seaboard of the Yoruban region, for which Abeokuta was the principal city, and to report a proposal for a convict labor station there. Burton's unusually laconic chapter titles reflect his mood, as in chapter 5, "The Usual Sketch – Geographical and Historical," and chapter 8, "The de Omnibus and Cotton Chapter." Burton's humor includes poking fun at the missionaries. In part one of the book he reports travels to Lagos, his experiences at Abeokuta, a historical account of the greater Yoruban region, and the current and prospective economic and mercantile status of the country beyond its ongoing traffic in slaves. On the Yoruban language, in spite of his acumen as a literary critic, Burton expresses odd reservations:

Burton in 1863 (portrait by Ernest Edwards; Collection of Mrs. Christopher Wood)

The Yoruban tongue has no poetry, like the Hausa, nor are words set to tunes as amongst the musical Fulas, except a few artless attempts like the corn-songs of the American negroes. But the African development of the language-power fills it with riddles and childish puzzles; moreover, it is rich in proverbs, the infant literature of the world.

Burton's characterization of proverbs as "infant literature" is provocative. On the one hand, he calls them "artless," seeming to ignore their complexity and elegance. On the other hand, his pains to collect proverbs in some of the languages he learned and the places he visited (India, Africa, and South America) argue that he appreciated distinctions between oral and written discourse. Burton's pursuit of proverbs was actually an excavation of the languages in their most sophisticated, mature, and polished transformations. Proverbs are pieces of poetry so perfect that they become lore-bearing mantras that enable oral peoples to preserve not only their wisdom but also their practical knowledge. To understand proverbial and poetic discourse in a language is to have the nearly magisterial command that Burton sought and often achieved.

Some of Burton's biographers note that his wife feared that Burton might be dallying sexually with females among the peoples that he encountered, for in his writing, especially in *Abeokuta,* he did not condemn the practice of tribal leaders who

hospitably offered their women for the comfort of visitors. Whether the facts justified Isabel's fear is not known. In any case *Abeokuta* is the first book dedicated to Isabel, and it records at least two mountains and one group of islands immediately off Fernando Po that he named "Isabel."

In February 1862 Burton again left Fernando Po for mainland Africa, this time to go up the Gaboon River to learn about the sensational gorilla and a native people known as the Fang, reputed to be ferocious cannibals. Burton's trips up the Gaboon and the Congo Rivers in 1862 and 1863 are described in *Two Trips to Gorilla Land and the Cataracts of the Congo* (1876). The book reveals Burton in various moods, from curiosity about gorillas to voyeuristic interest in the cannibalistic behavior of the Fang. Fawn M. Brodie says that Burton hoped to catch a young gorilla and that he saw at least one, although Burton denies that he saw one on this occasion. Even so, he did learn enough about gorilla behavior to contradict or question reports of their aggressiveness and of their disposition to rape humans. Burton, ignorant of what we now know to be their prudent shyness, hypothesized that the creatures were cowardly. The Fang people he found to be cannibals indeed, given to practices of torture and cannibalism as punishment for crimes and as features of religious rites and festivals. He reported that the number of victims was great but not actually as great as alleged. His descriptions of the practices of cannibalism and torture reflect his willingness to deal with the bizarre and the grotesque in all their manifestations.

In the second part of the book, "The Cataracts of the Congo," Burton describes his travels one hundred miles up the Congo River to the Yellala Rapids, two hundred miles short of Stanley Pool, which Henry Stanley did not reach and name until March 1877. Looking for a water route for commerce with the interior, Burton was too early in 1863 to meet Stanley coming downriver. Of particular importance is Burton's interest in the peoples that he met on the lower Congo. His account of their relative innocence is especially poignant in view of such later literary representations of these natives as that of Joseph Conrad in *Heart of Darkness* (1902), set in exactly the places that Burton describes.

More terrible than the cannibalistic behavior he reports in *Two Trips* is what he saw on his mission for the British government immediately after his return from the Congo cataracts. His account appeared as *A Mission to Gelele, King of Dahome: With Notices of the So-called "Amazons," the Grand Customs, the*

Yearly Customs, the Human Sacrifices, the Present State of the Slave Trade, and the Negro's Place in Nature (1864). This book describes Burton's visit to Agbome, the capital of Dahomey, to record "its mixture of horror and meanness," and Burton adds, "in this pitiless picture of its mingled puerility and brutality, of ferocity and politeness, I trust that none can charge me with exaggeration." Burton was sent to entreat King Gelele to stop the torture and cannibalism that were parts of the rituals of the country's seasons and political events, to stop Dahomey's participation in the slave trade, and to secure the release of native Christian prisoners. Burton wanted to see the Amazon army, the torture, and the murders. He did so and made his depositions to King Gelele, but his visit had no apparent results. His narrative is packed with what can strike a fastidious reader as gratuituously gruesome details:

> In the turret and the barn ["victim shed"] were twenty victims. All were seated on cage stools, and were bound to the posts which passed between their legs; the ankles, the shins under the knees, and the wrists being lashed outside with connected ties. Necklaces of rope, passing behind the back, and fastened to the upper arms, were also made tight to the posts. The confinement was not cruel: each victim had an attendant squatting behind him, to keep off the flies; all were fed four times a day, and were loosed at night for sleep.

Burton's mood in *A Mission to Gelele* is full of conflict. He is fascinated, embarrassed, and appalled at what he sees as by-products of European colonial pressures: Jesuit missionaries, for example, inflict corporal punishment on converted natives. His description of nature in this book seems to reflect his consternation, for it is ironic, disquieted, and associated with the feminine: "Presently the storm came down, raving like a jealous wife." A few lines later, "Baleful gleams of red thready lightning flashed like the glances of fury in weeping eyes, and deafening peals of thunder crashed overhead, not with the steady rumble of a European tempest, but sharp, sudden, and incisive as claps of feminine objurgation between fits of sobbing. These lively scenes . . . passed off in lady-like sulks."

A Mission to Gelele is notable and notorious for two of its subjects. In chapter nineteen of its second volume, "Of the Negro's Place in Nature," Burton candidly declares his racism: "There is hardly a traveller, however unobservant, who has not remarked the peculiar and precocious intelligence of the African's childhood, his 'turning stupid' as the general phrase is, about the age of puberty, and the rapid declension of his mental powers in old age, —

a process reminding us of the simiad [*sic,* simian]." Burton also gives considerable space to describing the reputedly fabulous Amazon troops of Gelele, and he notes that these "wives" of the king were ugly, exceptionally cruel, had male officers, and were at least equal in effectiveness to male troops.

In a fifth African book, *Wit and Wisdom from West Africa; or, A Book of Proverbial Philosophy, Idioms, Enigmas, and Laconisms* (1865), Burton published 2,268 oral proverbs that he, as well as French and English missionaries, had collected. In contrast to many of his other statements about blacks, in this work Burton praises their cultures, saying that "for brevity and elegance . . . [the proverbs] may claim an equal rank with those of any other nation in ancient or modern times," and he records these for the first time in written form. The proverbs are from Wolof, Kanuri, Oji, Ga Yoruba, Efun, Isubu, Dualla, Efik, and Fang, the languages of Yoruba, Ashanti, and Dahomey. Burton had at least a rudimentary command of most of these.

Because Burton's west African posting in the early 1860s had separated him from Isabel and his stipend for the Fernando Po consulship was small, they applied for another and received it. The new post did not pay better, but Isabel could accompany Burton and set up their first home as a married couple in São Paulo and Santos, Brazil. Burton occupied this post from 1864 to 1869 and described his explorations and investigations of Brazil and its adjoining countries, especially Paraguay, in two travel books. The first of these, *Explorations of the Highlands of the Brazil; with a Full Account of the Gold and Diamond Mines. Also, Canoeing Down 1500 Miles of the Great River São Francisco, from Sabará to the Sea* (1869), Burton called a description of "a holiday excursion" that he and Isabel "made to the Gold Mines of Central Minas Geraes via Petropolis, Barbaçena, and the Prairies and Highlands of the Brazil." This joint excursion began on 12 June 1867 and continued until August when, leaving Isabel behind, he embarked on the fifteen-hundred-mile voyage down the Rio São Francisco. In his investigation of the gold mines Burton continued his search for a way to make the vast profits that others had made from their exploration of new lands, but despite leaving nearly two thousand pages of published discussion on the topic of gold, he never succeeded. Burton investigated diamond mines as well on this journey and includes chapters on the mining and processing of diamonds.

This content is prefaced by a "Preliminary Essay" and a "Note" that are astonishing in scope. They describe books and other written records of

Brazil, along with lists of scientists, explorers, and commercial agents from many European nations who had come to Brazil to map and colonize it. Burton identifies writers from Brazil, the Netherlands, France, the United States, and England. The list is impressively lengthy, if not exhaustive. That he was able in such a remote location to acquire and read such books is a stunning achievement in research.

In *Explorations of the Highlands* following his account of gold- and diamond-mining operations Burton attends to the issues of slavery in Brazil, the labor supply, and the region's landscape: "In 1852, when the importation of slaves became a nullity, the country was dismayed, and not without reason, by the prospect of a deficient labour-market." He remains cynical about attempts to suppress the slave trade:

> We still devote fifteen vessels of war, 1500 men, and nearly a million of money per annum, to support a Coffin or Sentimental Squadron, which has ever proved itself powerless to prevent negro-export, whenever and wherever black hands were in due demand, and whose main effect upon West Africa has been to pamper "Sã Leone," that Hamitic Sodom and Gomorrah, to fill a few pockets, to act as a political machine for throwing dust into the public eyes, and greatly to increase the miseries of the slave and the misfortunes of his continent.

By this time in his life Burton was extremely knowledgeable and eloquent about the culture, sociology, and economics of labor and slavery. He analyzes the Brazilian working conditions for Europeans, indigenous South Americans, and blacks, and he finds South American employers to be some of the most enlightened that he has encountered in the world. Also by this time Burton had seen much of South Asia, Africa, Europe, and North America (although not yet Iceland), and so it is noteworthy that he announces in *Explorations of the Highlands* that he prefers the scenic beauty of Brazil to that of all the other countries he has explored:

> There was the usual beautiful Brazilian perspective, tier after tier of mountain, hill, hillock, rise, and wavy horizon, whose arc was dotted with the forms familiar to Rio de Janeiro – sugar loaves, hunchback, topsails, and parrots'-beaks. The clothing of the earth was "Capoeira," or second-growth forest, so old that in parts it appeared almost virginal; the colours were black-green, light-green, brown-green, blue-green, blue and azure in regular succession, whilst the cloud-patches gathering before the sun mottled the landscape with a marbling of shade – travelers from the temperates prefer this mixture of grey to the perfect glory of the day-god.

Isabel carried the manuscript for this book back to England for publication, and she added to it her own preface to report her disagreement with Burton's negative representation of the Catholic Church and his support of polygamy. The book went through three early issues and Spanish and Portuguese translations. Another work that Isabel carried back from Brazil for publication was *Vikram and the Vampire; or Tales of Hindu Devilry* (1870), which augments Burton's travel writing about India and publishes folk stories that Burton had translated from a large eighteenth-century collection in Hindu. Glenn S. Burne tells us that the eleven tales chosen are not about vampires or devils, the subjects principally involving relations between the sexes. It did not sell well in Burton's time, but several editions exist.

After Isabel left Brazil Burton undertook reconnaissance of the war between Paraguay and the allied Brazil, Argentina, and Uruguay. His *Letters from the Battle-Fields of Paraguay* is good war journalism. The book recounts Burton's two visits to "the seat of war," the first from 15 August to 5 September 1868 and the second from 4 April to 18 April 1869. It includes sections on Paraguay in general, a historical sketch, and twenty-seven letters to "Z," each titled to reflect the places, events, and subjects that it describes. The letters follow his day-to-day observations, reporting everything from a bad climate to a typical day at Corrients, a lady going to church with her retinue of women servant-slaves, pretty faces of the "upper ten [percent of society]" women, and his "sundry" visits to the front.

In one letter Burton notes the cruelty caused by Paraguayan general Lopez's desperation and details the paranoid system by which soldiers were prevented from deserting the Paraguayan army: they "never went out of camp . . . in a lesser number than four; and each answered for the other three with his life." Caught asleep on duty, a soldier was shot, and "the two men that stood on parade to his right and left received each twenty-five 'palos' – lashes with a bull's hide. The . . . corporal of the section was degraded to the ranks for two months, and ran the gauntlet till some forty blows were dealt to him 'en circulo.'" Not exempted were "the mothers or wives of the bravest officers, who were compelled by the fate of war to yield themselves prisoners, were forced publicly to disown their sons and husbands as traitors to the country; and failing to do so they were imprisoned, exiled, or flogged to death."

He sketches the campaign of the war in three major phases: the unsuccessful attack on Buenos

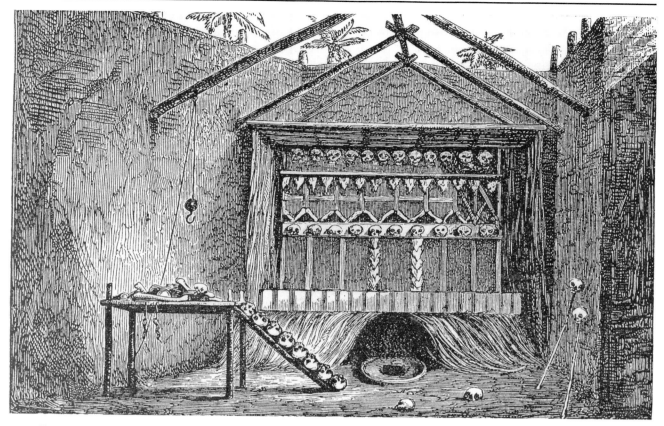

Frontispiece for Burton's Wanderings in West Africa, from Liverpool to Fernando Po *(courtesy of the Lilly Library, Indiana University)*

Aires by President Lopez of Paraguay, his subsequent defensive struggle at the borders of Paraguay, and his guerilla campaign. Although Burton left the region and ended his book before the conflict was concluded, he analyzed Lopez's campaign as futile. *Letters from the Battle-Fields* brought Europeans by far the most, and the most objectively reported, information that had been published on this painful war. Burton characterized it as a "Crimean[-like] campaign" that "abounds in instances of splendid futile devotion. It is a fatal war waged by hundreds against thousands; a battle of Brown Bess and poor old flint muskets against the Spenser and Enfield rifles." Some scholars believe that the book has not been sufficiently appreciated.

In hopes of getting a better assignment than Santos in Brazil, Burton resigned in 1868 before going to the Paraguay battles. In 1870 the Foreign Office decided to appoint him to the consulship that he had long desired at Damascus. This most prestigious of posts in his career resulted, ironically, in the indifferent *Unexplored Syria: Visits to the Libanus, the Tulúl el Safá, the Anti-Libanus, the Northern Libanus,*

and the 'Aláh (1872). It contains a chapter by Isabel Burton (whose own book *The Inner Life of Syria, Palestine, and the Holy Land: From My Private Journal* [1875] became far more popular than her husband's); two chapters by Charles F. Tyrwhitt Drake, an archeologist who had become a close friend of the Burtons; and appendices by W. S. W. Vaux and other contributors. Noteworthy is Burton's dedication of the work to Isabel's father, Henry Raymond Arundell. Its preface illustrates Burton's passionate admiration of Arabs and their culture: "There is literally no limit that can be laid down to the mother-wit, to the ambition, and to the intellectual capabilities of its sons; they are the most gifted race that I have, as yet, ever seen."

Unexplored Syria describes Burton's explorations with Drake and Isabel during his twenty-three months as English consul at Damascus, his explorations of places "ten miles away from the high roads." Burton notes that "maps show a virgin white patch," for "where there are enormously important ruins to be studied, contrary to most people's belief there is nothing there of interest. In

113

fact the traveler . . . knows that an unexplored spot means one either too difficult or too dangerous for the multitude to undertake."

Isabel adds her description of their mapping the Baalbek Plain in northern Syria, as they try to determine the apex of the Libanus Mountain range. She also recounts an unsuccessful effort to excavate and preserve the site of the smaller temple of Baalbek, called the temple of Jupiter, or of the sun. Typically Burton's book provides appendices that reflect his interest in folk material (a list of 187 Syrian proverbs) and his deep learning in theological as well as civil law. Burton summarizes his sense of Syrian culture, Syrian landscape, and his travel-writing process as follows:

> Of history, again, of picturesque legend, of theology and mythology, of art and literature, as of archeology, of palaeography, of numismatology, and a dozen other -ologies and -ographies, there is absolutely no visible end. And if the present of the New World be bald and tame, that of the Syrian Old World is, to those who know it well, perhaps a little too fiery and exciting, paling with its fierce tints and angry flush the fair vision which a country has a right to contemplate in the days to be.

Burton lost his Damascus post after only a year and a half because of angry encounters with a Copt and some Greek Orthodox churchmen. Complaints against him by the Rashid Pasha and Burton's untimely support of Muslim converts to Christianity resulted in his recall by the Foreign Office. In some ways even more depressing than his betrayal by Speke, Burton's recall from Damascus was the lowest point in his life.

Ultima Thule; or, A Summer in Iceland (1875) was written the year after Burton had lost the Damascus post and had accepted an offer to investigate the sulphur resources of the Arctic island nation. He was promised an additional £2,000 if the deposits were profitable. Burton seems not to have collected the bonus, and his book enjoyed only one edition. It is an encyclopedia of facts and statistics in a typical Burton travel account. It includes nine "Sections" and five "Chapters" that describe the meaning and etymology of "Thule," the physical and political geography of Iceland, the educations and professions of its inhabitants, zoological features of the land, and schemes of taxation.

Ultima Thule deserves more respect than it has usually received. Nowhere among Burton's works is his erudition more methodically exhibited than in this work. His study of the geology and culture of Iceland is predictably dense with information, but

Burton students rarely comment on the illumination of the language and literature of Iceland that his off-hand erudition as a philologist, linguist, and man of letters brings to this book.

In it Burton includes a representation of Norse literature that employs the kenning (*Kenningar* [circumlocution]), a staple of Norse poetics, only to disparage it. He seems not to realize that the kenning is more than a humbly "primitive" narrative device. Still, it is to Burton's credit that he saw the linguistic and poetic parameters of a kenning. Burton reveals that his magisterial linguistic knowledge was real when he describes the connections between Persian and Icelandic. Icelandic, he proposes, is the source of all Teutonic languages, but he also notes the oriental features that the language seems to exhibit. His grasp of the structure of a culture from its development from its origins to its modernity, or collapse, is astonishing not only for the power of his analysis but also for the apparent effortlessness with which he articulates it.

In 1872 the Foreign Office offered him the consulship of Trieste, a post that Burton accepted and held until he died. Isabel wrote that they spent some of the happiest years of their marriage there. From 1872 Burton traveled in Europe and again to India, Arabia, North Africa, and West Africa. A trip to Italy provided experiences recounted in *Etruscan Bologna: A Study* (1876), a work that Burton scholars have found to be a "lifeless" book. Burton addresses the continuing mystery of the Etruscan language, but he does not solve it. His purpose is to introduce the findings of *Etruskische Forschungen* (Etruscan Investigations) and to discuss attempts to understand the ancient Etruscan language. The book was reviewed as "shallow" in England, but it apparently impressed Heinrich Schliemann, the discoverer of the lost city of Troy, and others who subsequently sought out Burton in his Trieste office. Also written at this time was *Scind Revisited: With Notices of the Anglo-Indian Army; Railroads; Past, Present, and Future, Etc.* (1877), an encore work describing Burton's return to India with Isabel in 1876.

The revisit to Arabia in 1878 and 1879 is recorded in the last two books that Burton would write on Arabian places. The first, *The Gold-Mines of Midian and the Ruined Midianite Cities: A Fortnight's Tour in North-Western Arabia* (1878), describes a sixteen-day trip in March and April 1877 to look for gold in what is now northwestern Saudi Arabia. Burton called it a continuation of his *Personal Narrative of a Pilgrimage to El-Medinah and Meccah* that explained in detail the changes that had taken place during the more than twenty-five years that had intervened.

Lecture III

1

In my first two Lectures, I had the high honour of telling you the story of [Sultan] Pilgrimage to Meccah. This evening I venture to propose my "First Footsteps in Eastern Africa" — a journey which led directly to the discovery of the Nile Sources — as far as they are now discovered.

Before plunging into the hot depths of the Dark Continent, we will briefly survey its principal features.

Africa according to geography books is 4330 nautical miles from Cape Agulhas, East of the Cape of Good Hope, to Cape Blanco, near Bigerta, its Northern most extremity. Its breadth is 4000 between C. Guardafui on the Indian Ocean and C. Verde on the Atlantic. From the irregularity of its figure " — which is painfully regular — " its area has only 12 millions of Square miles " (Mrs Somerville Chapt. 7)

Thus far the popular writer, to whom data and facts are only wanting. But in truth the area and the population of Africa are equally unknown. Of the outline we have long formed accurate ideas. The Northern half is an irregular square forming about the Equator a base for a triangle pointing South. We still await an explanation of the reason why, but this is the normal form of great Peninsulas; for instance, Corea, Siam, Greenland, the Indian (Dekhan)

First page of the manuscript for one of Burton's travel lectures, written and delivered in Brazil in the mid 1860s (Henry E. Huntington Library and Art Gallery)

The trip went from Alexandria to Cairo, Suez, El Muwayláh, and north to the Wady Aynúnah and to Wady Moraák in the Jebel El-Zahd, with an explanation of the history of the geographical boundaries of Midian. This first-ever account of the Midian reflects the no-longer-disguised Burton as a workmanlike professional explorer-demographer-economist-geologist. As Burton says in the preface to his subsequent work, *The Land of Midian (Revisited)* (1879), he has sketched,

> with the able assistance of learned friends, its history and geography; its ethnology and archeology; its zoology and malacology; and its botany and geology.... The drift was to prepare those who take an interest in Arabia generally, and especially in wild mysterious Midian, for the present work, which, one foresaw, would be a tale of discovery and adventure.

Burton adds that the primary purpose of the expedition was "mineralogical" – indeed, a search for "auriferous and argentiferous" deposits, but also for iron, coal, quartz, lead, tungsten, gypsum, and copper. Yet he also reports what he learns of the ancient peoples of Midian. *The Gold-Mines of Midian* concludes that the Wadies Taryam, Sharmá, and Aynúnah were worked for precious metals until the seventh century A.D. and can be made to yield gold again with modern mining methods. Burton believed that in modern times gold was washed in secret in the area and that Turkish officials dissembled in their insistence that agriculture, not gold, is the "red sulphur" and the "philosopher's stone" of the world.

Burton also collected botanical specimens throughout the region and explained that "The Affinities of the Midianite vegetation generally are with those of the Sahará and of Northern Africa, especially of the desert-growths of Upper Egypt and Nubia." He revealed his interest in archeology and his love of landscape when, traveling the coast of Midian, he stopped at Makná, the capital of Midian, and investigated its ruins. He describes coastal landscapes that he had seen from his ship:

> The first aspect of Midian is majestic, and right well suited to the heroic Bedawi race that once owned the land. Beyond the golden cushions which, embroidered with emerald green, line the shore, rise flat-topped sandbanks and peaky hillocks of arenaceous stone.... Inland they become fort-hills similarly metalled, but painted purple-brown by the intervening atmosphere. The picture's towering background ... is a wall, apparently continuous, ranging between 6000 and 9000 feet above the sea-level.

Burton returned to Egypt and reported his belief in the presence of gold to Ismail I. Khediv, who gave Burton his congratulations and promise of support for a more ambitious exploration. Burton returned to Trieste in April 1877.

The Land of Midian (Revisited) continues *The Gold-Mines of Midian* and records Burton's return to the area between 19 December 1877 and 20 April 1878. The book was written principally as a report to Khedive Ismail on the possibility of mining gold. Burton was to have 5 percent of the produce of the mines, an oral agreement that was not kept when Ismail died. The book is one of Burton's best-ordered, day-by-day accounts of travels, one that provides information of mercantile, industrial, and economic value. Burton again describes beautiful coastal landscape, but the picturesqueness of the landscape and a practical analysis of the region are related, because both have commercial importance. Burton is greatly interested in harbor conditions; tides; depths of channels; locations of bays, islets, shoals, and reefs; frequencies of *zilzilah,* or sea-quakes; and the making of charts and logs for ships that would trade in the new market. *The Land of Midian* provides almost no mention of people except to notice the lack of opportunity to study the Hutaym and the Baliyy. As geography, however, the book is splendid – more important, says Brodie, than Burton's report in his *Personal Narrative of a Pilgrimage to El-Medinah and Meccah.*

In August 1880 Burton and Isabel traveled to Oberammergau, Germany, to attend the passion play produced there every tenth year. Each wrote of the experience and intended to publish their accounts together. Harrison, the publisher, decided to publish only Burton's work, *A Glance at the "Passion Play"* (1881), and Isabel's was not published until after her death, in 1900. Isabel was a devout Roman Catholic, and her description is pious and respectful – in contrast to Richard Burton's, which presents their trip from Munich to Oberammergau with digressions on the people, history, architecture, politics, and reputation of the play in Europe and includes the history of its profits from 1720. Burton conveys that the production did not engage his feelings, but he gives the play an aesthetically judicious analysis and looks for its accuracy in depicting the Jewish-Roman-Christian historical cultures and places. He adds critiques of the melodramatic clichés and improbabilities that he finds in the play: "The Jewish rabble is good, but the costumes are not Jewish enough," he says of the scene in which the Jewish crowd calls for the execution of Jesus. Of Pilate's role, Burton writes this dour analysis:

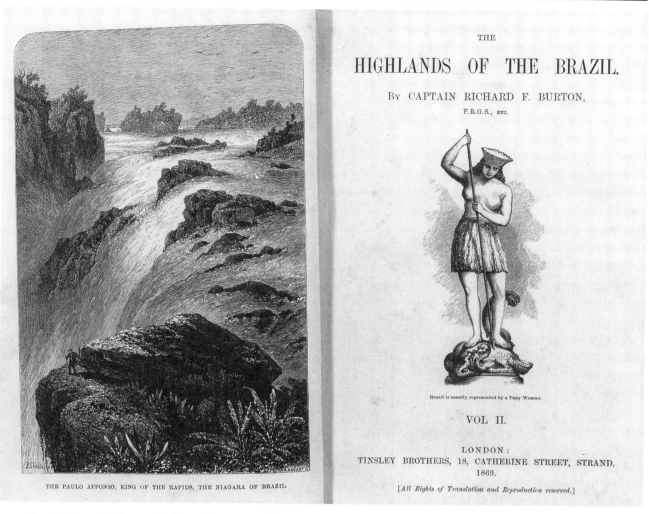

THE

HIGHLANDS OF THE BRAZIL.

By CAPTAIN RICHARD F. BURTON,
F.R.G.S., ETC.

Brazil is usually represented by a Tupy Woman.

VOL II.

LONDON:
TINSLEY BROTHERS, 18, CATHERINE STREET, STRAND.
1869.

[*All Rights of Translation and Reproduction reserved.*]

THE PAULO AFFONSO, KING OF THE RAPIDS, THE NIAGARA OF BRAZIL.

Frontispiece and title page for Burton's narrative of travels in Brazil between 1865 and 1869 (courtesy of the Lilly Library, Indiana University)

I cannot but think that the poor "Pagan" did exactly what would have been done by an Anglo-Indian officer of the last generation in a violent religious quarrel amongst the mild Hindus, with their atrocious accusations against one another. Utterly unable to appreciate the merits and demerits of the case, he would have said, "There'll be an awful row if I interfere. Old Charley (the commander-in-chief) doesn't like me, and I don't want to lose my appointment. After all what matter? Let the nigs do as they please!" He would not have allowed torture nor the violent taking of life; but with that exception, caused by our change of manners, his proceeding would have been that of the feeble and unfortunate sixth Procurator.

He insists that the Christian passion play is not analogous to the Moslem pilgrimage to Mecca, the passion play being mummery while the pilgrimage to Mecca was, he felt, truly nourishing to the pilgrim. He finds the production to be too tame, too

unrealistic, and too inaccurate in historical detail. He sardonically remarks that, contrary to contemporary speculation, the passion plays will not be abolished, and he concludes by wishing good luck to the "passion" village and a "bountiful harvest of marks in 1890!"

Burton's late book on west Africa, *To the Gold Coast for Gold: A Personal Narrative* (1883), was written with Verney Lovett Cameron, and much of it was adapted from *Wanderings in West Africa from Liverpool to Fernando Po* and *Two Trips to Gorilla Land*. Brodie calls the work "a shoddy mockery of his earlier African books," but one extract from it rationalizes Burton's considerable renown as an explorer and travel writer:

The glory of an explorer, I need hardly say, results not so much from the extent or the marvels of his explorations, as from the consequences to which they lead. Judged by this test, my little list of discoveries has not been unfavoured of fortune. Where two purblind fever-stricken men plodded painfully through fetid swamp and fiery thorn-bush over the Zanzibar-Tanganyika track, mission-houses and schools may now be numbered by the dozen. Missionaries bring consuls, and consuls bring commerce and colonisation. On the Gold Coast of Western Africa, whence came the good old "guinea," not a washing cradle, not a pound of quicksilver was to be found in 1862; in 1882 five mining companies are at work; and in 1892 there will be as many score.

Burton died in 1890 of complications from a combination of gout, circulation problems, and heart disease. One last work generated by his travels was not published with explicit titling of its contents until 1930: *Anthropological Notes on the Sotadic Zone of Sexual Inversion throughout the World, Including Some Observations on Social and Sexual Relations of the Muhammedan Empire.* Its core proposition is taken from the "Terminal Essay" in volume ten of Burton's *A Plain and Literal Translation of the Arabian Nights' Entertainments, Now Entitled the Book of the Thousand Nights and a Night with Introductory Explanatory Notes on the Manners and Customs of Moslem Men and a Terminal Essay upon the History of the Nights* (1885). In it Burton proposes that homosexual practices are more or less "popular and endemic" through a geographical band that includes the northern shores of the Mediterranean Sea and the coast of northern Africa, Asia Minor, Indochina, China, Japan, the South Sea islands, and the equatorial regions of the New World. He determines that cultures to the north and south of these regions find the practices physically difficult and disgusting, and he theorizes that sexual inversion is principally a function of climate, geography, and perhaps race. Burton was writing what some readers and reviewers in his time called pornography. It is, however, less likely to offend twentieth-century readers.

Some of Burton's biographers suggest that he went too far in explaining the dark sides of indigenous cultures. Others argue that the roots of culture are invisible without such details as those of sexual practices and the use of mind-altering drugs, and they add that Burton's allegedly dark curiosity and his candor foreshadow an enlightened twentieth-century study of humanity. In any event Burton's travel writing is a major achievement, because it voluminously details historically important exploration. That it does not rank in quality as great literature is an ironic function of what in some ways is its strength — its voluminousness, or almost kleptoma-

nic obsession for including information. It is often repetitious and in frequent need of revision. On the other hand, the qualities that elevate several of his works to nearly classical stature are his magnificent erudition, his wit, and his passion.

Ultimately many people read Burton. In the late twentieth century as many as a dozen of his books remain in print or have been reissued, including some previously neglected works. His importance to posterity is marked by a steady flow of writing about him, including at least nine biographies, during the century following his death in 1890. This reflects the recognition and appreciation that he earnestly desired but did not receive during his life.

Bibliographies:

Norman M. Penzer, *An Annotated Bibliography of Sir Richard Francis Burton, K.C.M.G.* (London: Philpot, 1923);

B. J. Kirkpatrick, *A Catalog of the Library of Sir Richard Francis Burton, K.C.M.G., Held by the Royal Anthropological Institute* (London: Royal Anthropological Institute, 1978);

James A. Casada, *Sir Richard F. Burton, A Bio-bibliographical Study* (Boston: G. K. Hall, 1990);

Burke E. Casari, "Additions to Burton's Bibliography," in *In Search of Sir Richard Burton: Papers From a Huntington Library Symposium,* edited by Alan H. Jutzi (San Marino, Cal.: Huntington Library, 1993), pp. 71–83.

Biographies:

Francis Hitchman, *Richard F. Burton,* 2 volumes (London: Sampson Low, Marston, Searle & Rivington, 1887);

Isabel Burton, *The Life of Captain Sir Richd. F. Burton,* 2 volumes (London: Chapman & Hall, 1893);

Georgiana Sisted, *The True Life of Capt. Sir Richard F. Burton* (London: Nichols, 1906);

Thomas Wright, *The Life of Sir Richard Burton,* 2 volumes (London: Everett, 1906);

Walter Phelps Dodge, *The Real Sir Richard Burton* (London: Unwin, 1907);

Byron Farwell, *Burton* (London: Longmans, 1963; New York: Holt, Rinehart & Winston, 1963);

Fawn M. Brodie, *The Devil Drives: A Life of Sir Richard Burton* (London: Eyre & Spottiswoode, 1967; New York: Norton, 1967);

Michael Hastings, *Sir Richard Burton* (New York: Coward, McCann & Goeghegan, 1978);

Edward Rice, *Captain Sir Richard Francis Burton: The Secret Agent Who Made the Pilgrimage to Mecca, Discovered the Kama Sutra, and Brought the Ara-*

bian Nights to the West (New York: Scribners, 1990).

References:

Thomas J. Assad, *Three Victorian Travellers: Burton, Blunt, Doughty* (London: Routledge, 1964);

Jonathan Bishop, "The Identities of Sir Richard Burton: The Explorer as Actor," *Victorian Studies,* 1 (December 1957): 119–135;

M. E. Bradford, "Sir Richard Francis Burton and the Literature of Travel," *Sewanee Review,* 72 (October–December 1964): 720–724;

Fawn M. Brodie, Introduction to Burton's *City of the Saints* (New York: Knopf, 1963);

Glenn S. Burne, *Richard F. Burton* (Boston: Twayne, 1985);

Alan H. Jutzi, ed., *In Search of Sir Richard Burton: Papers from a Huntington Library Symposium* (San Marino, Cal.: Huntington Library, 1993);

Stanley Lane-Poole, Introduction to Burton's *Personal Narrative of a Pilgrimage to El-Medinah and Meccah* (London: Bell, 1898);

Alan Moorehead, Introduction to Burton's *The Lake Regions of Central Africa* (New York: Horizon, 1961);

Moorehead, *The White Nile* (New York: Harper, 1961);

C. W. Newbury, Introduction to Burton's *A Mission to Gelele* (London: Routledge, 1966);

Norman M. Penzer, Introduction to Burton's *Selected Papers on Anthropology, Travel and Exploration* (London: Philpot, 1924);

Kenneth Walker, Introduction to Burton's *Love, War and Fancy: The Customs and Manners of the East, from Writings on the Arabian Nights* (London: Kimber, 1964);

Gordon Waterfield, Introduction to Burton's *First Footsteps in East Africa* (London: Routledge, 1966).

Papers:

Locations of Burton manuscripts and letters are most fully described in James A. Casada's biobibliography of Burton cited above. Principal collections are at the Huntington Library; the East Sheen District Library in London; the Orleans House Gallery in Middlesex; the Royal Geographical Society in London; the Public Record Office in Surrey; the India Office Records in London; the National Library of Scotland; the Syracuse University Library; the National Archives of Zanzibar; the Royal Asiatic Society in London; the Bodleian Library at Oxford; the Royal Commonwealth Society in London; the Beinecke Rare Book and Manuscript Library at Yale University; the Royal Archives at Windsor Castle; the University of Edinburgh Library; the Houghton Library at Harvard University; and the Library of the Boston Atheneum. Other papers are among such collections as the Quentin Keynes Collection, London; the Francis Galton Papers at University College, London; and the Houghton Papers at Trinity College Library, Cambridge.

William Francis Butler

(31 October 1838 – 7 June 1910)

Dana E. Aspinall
University of Montevallo

BOOKS: *A Narrative of the Historical Events Connected with the Sixty-Ninth Regiment* (London: Mitchell, 1870);

The Great Lone Land: A Narrative of Travel and Adventure in the North-West of America (London: Sampson Low, Marston, Low & Searle, 1872); republished as *The Great Lone Land: A Tale of Travel and Adventure in the North-West of America* (London: Burns & Oates, 1910);

The Wild North Land: Being the Story of a Winter Journey, with Dogs, across Northern North America (London: Sampson Low, Marston, Low & Searle, 1873); republished as *The Wild North Land: Being the Story of a Winter Journey, with Dog, across Northern North America* (New York: New Amsterdam Book, 1903); republished as *The Wild Northland: Being the Story of a Winter Journey, with Dog, across Northern North America* (New York: Barnes, 1904);

Akim-Foo: The History of a Failure (London: Sampson Low, Marston, Low & Searle, 1875);

Far Out: Rovings Retold (London: Isbister, 1880);

The Invasion of England: Told Twenty Years After, anonymous (London: Sampson Low, 1882);

Red Cloud, the Solitary Sioux: A Story of the Great Prairie (London: Sampson Low, Marston, Searle & Rivington, 1882; Boston: Roberts, 1882); republished as *The Hero of Pine Ridge: A Story of the Great Prairie* (Chicago & New York: Donohue, [1885?]); republished as *Red Cloud: A Tale of the Great Prairie* (London: Burns, Oates & Washbourne, 1911);

The Campaign of the Cataracts: Being a Personal Narrative of the Great Nile Expedition of 1884-5 (London: Sampson Low, Marston, Searle & Rivington, 1887);

Charles George Gordon (London & New York: Macmillan, 1889);

Sir Charles Napier (London & New York: Macmillan, 1890);

The Life of Sir George Pomeroy-Colley, 1835–1881; Including Services in Kaffraria, in China, in Ashanti,

William Francis Butler

in India and in Natal (London: John Murray, 1899);

Studies in Irish History, 1649–1775: Being a Course of Lectures Delivered before the Irish Literary Society of London (Dublin: Brown & Nolan / London: Macmillan, 1903);

From Naboth's Vineyard: Being Impressions Formed during a Fourth Visit to South Africa Undertaken at the Request of the Tribune Newspaper (London: Bell, 1907);

The Light of the West, with Some Other Wayside Thoughts, 1865–1908 (Dublin: Gill, 1909; London: Methuen, 1910);

Sir William Butler: An Autobiography, edited by Eileen Butler (London: Constable, 1911; New York: Scribners, 1911).

OTHER: "Oliver Cromwell in Ireland," in *Studies in Irish History, 1649–1775,* edited by R. Barry O'Brien (Dublin: Brown & Nolan, 1903), pp. 1–65;

"The Channel Tunnel and National Defence," in *Channel Tunnel Reports* (London: Channel Tunnel, 1907).

William Francis Butler, who wrote extensively about his travels through British colonial possessions during his military career, warrants attention for his detailed, often compassionate depictions of the lands he visited and peoples he encountered. Following the youthful militaristic passion expressed in his early writings, the more mature Butler presented in his later works a concern about the negative environmental and cultural effects that English colonization visited upon those vast, uninhabited lands and indigenous peoples. His childhood experiences as an Irish Catholic and his experiences with the cultures of Native Americans in North America and of the Dutch colonials and Africans in South Africa during times of intense Anglo-American and European expansion gave Butler a sense of the injustices caused by imperialistic settlement in the late nineteenth century.

His growing anger at insidious British colonial policies, however, never completely replaced his fervent chastising of that government for its failure to maintain those politically and economically strategic possessions. Known for his quick observation, resourcefulness, and often overbearing character, Butler possessed a sensitivity for the polemics of British imperialism that exceeded mere military colonialism. Field Marshall Garnet Wolseley, one of Butler's few lifelong acquaintances, described Butler during his sojourn in Khartoum as "the only wise man out here and anything that has gone wrong has been occasioned because I did not consult him more, take him more into my confidence and follow his advice." Butler's empathy for the conquered people he administered and his enjoyment of war created a lifelong conflict manifest in all his writing.

Butler was born on 31 October 1838 at Suirville, County Tipperary, Ireland, the seventh child of Richard and Ellen Butler of Suirville. Raised in a devout Roman Catholic family, William Butler was acutely aware of penal laws imposed by a notoriously tyrannical English government on Irish Cath-

olics during the early and mid nineteenth century. In 1847 he was enrolled in a Jesuit school at Tullabeg, County Offaly, and from there he entered Dr. James Quinn's school in Dublin. After his years in school Butler entered military service, commissioned as an ensign in the Sixty-ninth Foot Regiment on 17 September 1858.

He was then sent to serve in a regiment stationed at Tonghoo in Burma. By the spring of 1862 Butler's regiment had moved to Madras, and on 17 November 1863 he was promoted to lieutenant. In 1865, with his regiment stationed in southern England at Aldershot, Butler began work on his first published work, *A Narrative of the Historical Events Connected with the Sixty-Ninth Regiment* (1870). Dedicated to "the officers, non-commissioned officers, and private soldiers of the 69th, past, present, and to come," the book reveals a fierce loyalty to his first regiment and a stubborn adherence to military means of international dominance.

Although formally a history of this regiment from its inception in 1756 to the Maharatha campaign of 1819, Butler's first work reads much like the travel narratives that later established his writing reputation. *A Narrative* follows the movements of the troops during war but interrupts its descriptions of strategic maneuvers to create pastoral images of the landscapes encountered by the regiment. Central to the focus of the book are the responsibilities of the regiment during the Napoleonic War of 1815; however, Butler's ardent, lifelong admiration for Napoleon infuses into his narrative a praise for the French emperor that often eclipses that for the troops addressed in the book's dedication. Of the war of 1793, in which the Sixty-ninth Regiment had served, Butler recounts one engagement in which "the siege operations were soon directed by one whose genius no bravery could resist: on the heights overlooking the forts, city, and fleet, there was a young Corsican Captain of Artillary [sic], only twenty-four years of age, who now, stepping suddenly for the first time from the shade of obscurity, commenced his marvelous career of conquest, empire, and defeat." Providing an erudite appraisal of Napoleon's military strengths and weaknesses, Butler takes pains to include the life and development of his most influential role model.

In addition to presenting digressions on the landscapes and people, *A Narrative* assesses the historical significance of the lands involved. For example, his synopsis of the history and importance of the Belgian village of Quatre Bras to Napoleonic expansion inspired the painting *Quatre Bras* (1875), done by Elizabeth Thompson, a painter of nineteenth-century battle scenes and Butler's future wife. Butler's efforts in researching and constructing *A Narrative* encouraged in 1863 the dedication of a monument to its men who had died in an 1806 battle at Vellore, southeast India.

In 1866 Butler moved his regiment to the Channel Islands, where he met and established an acquaintance with Victor Hugo. Hugo disparagingly recalled Butler as an enfant terrible because of his incessant militaristic appetite. Now in his late twenties and with his affinity for Napoleon still strong, Butler immersed himself in military life and wholeheartedly espoused British expansionism and colonial dominance. Soon after leaving the Channel Islands, his regiment embarked on an exercise in Canada, where Fenian raids troubled the sparsely settled traders and pioneers.

In 1868 Butler succeeded Lt. Redvers Buller as a lookout officer on the Canadian frontier, where he traveled fifteen hundred miles a month in making his rounds to military outposts and tracking down deserters. Disillusioned at his apparent inability to rise in the army ranks and living in a time he described as one of "universal peace over the wide world," Butler returned to England with his regiment and broodingly awaited any available opportunity for advancement. In 1870 he learned that Colonel Wolseley, a prominent frontier soldier, was organizing an expedition to the Red River.

Quickly transmitting to Wolseley a telegraph message that simply said, "Please remember me," Butler embarked by ship to Boston and then traveled to the shores of Lake Superior to meet the gathering troops. He was sent independently on a special mission to the Red River settlement, mostly to investigate an uprising of French and Native American fur traders led by Louis Riel. The insurrection proved to be nothing more than an impromptu pillage and temporary occupation of an outpost belonging to the Hudson's Bay Company. Although Butler's book publicly acknowledges some mismanagement of the transfer of power and castigates the British government for such a lapse, the narrative devotes minimal space to the events that led him to the Red River territory. Butler served admirably, facing down Riel during an interview while awaiting the arrival of Wolseley's detachment.

After completing his duties on 24 October, Butler, via the auspices of Donald Smith, governor of the Hudson's Bay Company, began assessing the need for military expansion in Saskatchewan, the military strength of its indigenous population, and the trade routes of the province. An exploration such as this had become necessary because the Canadian government had recently acquired power from the once-autonomous Hudson's Bay Company, a transfer of power also associated with the uprising of Riel. Through winter snow Butler traveled twenty-seven hundred miles and finally arrived at Fort Garry, at the foot of the Rocky Mountains. His journey through both Saskatchewan and the Red River region later became the basis of *The Great Lone Land: A Narrative of Travel and Adventure in the North-West of America* (1872). The book proved remarkably popular, appearing in its fourth edition by 1873. Butler's report to the lieutenant governor of Manitoba served as an appendix to the work, and this report, revered as one of the most important documents in Canadian history, became the rationale for the incorporation of the Northwest Mounted Police.

The Great Lone Land introduces the reader to the allegiances that divided Butler throughout his life. Although conscious of his duties as a travel writer, Butler cannot immerse himself in his duties as proxy guide. Among his accounts of the climate, geography, and people of northwest Canada lies his mournful awareness of the outbreak of war in Europe and the tragic plight of the French government forced to withstand German aggression and the loss of Alsace-Lorraine during Chancellor Otto von Bismarck's expansionist war. Neither can he forgive his own government for the seeming neglect with which it chooses to reward his devoted service. "What was to be done?" Butler asks in reflecting on his difficulties in being promoted; "What course lay open? Serve on; let the dull routine of barrack-life grow duller; go from Canada to the Cape, from the Cape to the Mauritius, from Mauritius to Madras, from Madras goodness knows where, and trust to delirium tremens, yellow fever, or cholera morbus for promotion and advancement." *The Great Lone Land* also conveys Butler's belief in the sanctity of the Irish nation despite the influence of its British overlords: Ireland "is not only a manufacturing nation, but she manufactures nations." As he intimates throughout his meandering digression on Ireland, one of the nations that Ireland has helped elevate to imperial status is England.

Before Butler disembarks from his ship he reveals yet another idiosyncratic feature of his writing: an insistence on the cultural, moral, and social superiority of the Anglo-Irish to Americans. He comments extensively on American culture, and none of these comments casts a favorable light on the youthful nation of onetime rebels. His smug superiority quickly becomes jealous indignation, however, when Butler considers the unprecedented expan-

*Letter from Butler to A. E. Turner (courtesy of the
Lilly Library, Indiana University)*

sion of American borders because of Canadian – and ultimately British – ineptitude. He admonishes the British that the United States

> grew with giant's growth, looking far into the future . . . , cutting his cloth with perspective ideas of what his limbs would attain to in after-time, digging his canals and grading his railroads, with one eye on the Atlantic and the other on the Pacific, spreading himself, monopolizing, annexing, outmaneuvering and flanking those colonial bodies who sat in solemn state in Downing Street and wrote windy proclamations and despatches anent boundary-lines, of which they knew next to nothing.

Butler saw in American militaristic and economic expansion what he admired in Napoleon. He blamed England for its savage intolerance of Irish political and religious autonomy; yet he berated England for its irresolution in the same instances elsewhere.

Butler's anger subsides somewhat when he ponders the immensity of the United States – the single states that are larger than the United Kingdom, the expanse of railroad track already stretching from sea to sea, and especially the united effort of all Europeans to increase their affluence on American soil: "Assuredly the world has never witnessed any experiment of so gigantic a nature as this immense fusion of the Caucasian race now going on before our eyes in North America." Conversely, nothing causes such a retreat from the spirit of liberality evoked by Europe's communing creeds as when his eyes fasten on the indigenous peoples of North America.

Butler's grasp of the capitalist realities implicit in westward expansion, in the greed for money, land, and power that coaxes European masses toward the plains of the United States and Canada, leads him regretfully to signal the imminent extermination of people who have lived there for thousands of years in harmony with the environment. His ruminations about their plight almost always lead him to despair when he considers their demise. Butler's disgust with Britain's cultural elitism reflects his similar sentiment toward England's treatment of Ireland. It also reveals his understanding of the ideological clash created by the European presence, a clash that assures the elimination of the Native American from future generations of Americans:

> Free trade may be an admirable institution for some nations – making them, amongst other things, very much more liable to national destruction; but by no means follows that it should be adapted equally well to the savage Indian. Unfortunately for the universality of British institutions, free trade has invariably been found to improve the red man from the face of the earth. . . .

> The free trader is as a man who takes his shooting for the term of a year or two and wishes to destroy all he can.

This strangely modern mood permeates Butler's writings on the North American continent and influenced his later ruminations on its people. This includes *Red Cloud, the Solitary Sioux: A Story of the Great Prairie* (1882), Butler's only attempt to write fiction. The book is written for children and mixes a fictionalized account of Native American customs and culture with vivid scenes of travel, hunting, fishing, and fighting on the Canadian prairies. It also attempts to relate the biography of Red Cloud, the illustrious and long-lived chief of the Oglala Sioux who forced a surrender of American troops in the Black Hills of South Dakota.

The Great Lone Land describes chiefly the cosmetic uniqueness of Canada's northwest and the remoteness of the area. Especially interesting are his discussions of canoe making; fur trading; mosquitoes; the history of the Hudson's Bay Company; the French Indian voyageurs who trade and live in the wilderness; the myriad rivers and lakes that dot the Canadian territory; missionaries; Native American tribes and legends; dogsleds; bison; and ways in which trading posts, scattered throughout Canada even until the late nineteenth century, were set up to control, manipulate, and bedazzle comparably unsophisticated Native Americans.

In April 1872 Butler received an unattached company, something he had striven for years to obtain. He returned to Canada, where he wrote *The Wild North Land: Being the Story of a Winter Journey, with Dogs, across Northern North America* in 1873. This book, which was popular, covers Butler's travels by foot across northern Canada to the Arctic Ocean in winter. During his travels Butler again comments romantically on the land: "Lonely, silent, and impassive; heedless of man, season, or time, the weight of the Infinite seems to brood over it." Often in vapid poetic ramblings on the vast uninhabited stretches of Canadian wilderness, Butler continues both to voice his urge to conquer and to lament the results of such domination on the conquered people and their ways of life.

Butler displays the stereotypical attitude of most nineteenth-century Europeans toward Native Americans: they once fitted the mythical role of noble savages before the approach of the white Europeans, but "There is so much of simplicity and cunning, so much of close reasoning and child-like suspicion; so much natural quickness, sense of humour, credulousness, power of observation, faith and

WORKING UP THE WINNIPEG.

Illustration from Butler's The Great Lone Land *(courtesy of the Lilly Library, Indiana University)*

fun and selflessness, mixed up together in the Red man's mental composition" that their interactions with the technologically and spiritually superior Europeans are resulting in a miscegeny of ideas and practices detrimental to both races. Butler repeatedly comments on the types of Europeans whose task is to "civilize" the wilds of Canada and America, and he notes the moral inferiority of these people in comparison with the indigenous Americans. While emphasizing his desires for order and for successful expansion of British interests, his book maliciously caricatures the people who actually chart and establish settlements in the unknown lands:

> A raid made by nine troopers of this corps, against an Indian tent occupied by some dozen women and children, appears to have been the most noteworthy event in the history of Hatch's Battalion. Having surrounded the wigwam in the night, these cowards shot the miserable inmates, then scalping and mutilating their bodies they returned to their comrades, bearing the gory scalplocks as trophies of their prowess.

As in *The Great Lone Land,* Butler's need to castigate the British for their ineffectual control over their colonial possessions supplants his lamentations over either the loss of natural bounty or the hopeless plight of the native peoples. *The Wild North Land* is replete with criticisms of England's seeming inability not only to expand its territorial domain but to hold on to what it has. Regardless of his sincerity in lamenting the mistreatment of Native Americans, Butler's concern remains that of "civilization" of this land – in all its most egregious Victorian connotations.

Butler wrote this book from the notes he had taken each night after a long day's travel (averaging thirty miles per day), usually by dogsled, through the wilderness of Canada. Most nights he had slept in a bed in some remote outpost along the way. In addition to describing vividly his sleeping arrangements and the people he meets in these settlements, he enriches his narrative with brief but detailed descriptions of the hardships of nineteenth-century exploration. Except for Cerf-vola, his faithful dog, Butler traveled alone through the Northwest Territories and the Yukon, along the Mackenzie River to the Arctic Ocean. He skillfully relates the loneliness, cold, and oblivion of such travel, and he evokes a sense of awe in the stark beauty of a windless and moonless night, with the temperature at negative 20 degrees Fahrenheit and the aurora borealis playfully stretching across the northern sky. Such inspired illustrations of the extreme north do much to allay a modern reader's antipathy for his imperialistic ideology.

By August 1873 Butler was back in the more comfortable confines of Ottawa, where he learned that his friend and colleague Wolseley was leading an expedition to Ashanti, in the central region of Ghana. He eagerly followed, wiring ahead of his approach. On his arrival he received instructions to follow Wolseley to West Africa, and he reached Cape Coast Castle in October.

From this time Butler's life and writings narrowed into almost purely militaristic and political endeavors. His laments over British destruction of technologically inferior cultures and his reflections on the approaching winds and snow of November in the Canadian wilderness become strident denunciations of British policy in Africa. From Cape Coast Castle, Butler was sent to Accra and then inland to western Akim; his mission was to strengthen the loyal Akim fighting men and to prepare to intercept the Ashanti army as it retreated across the Prah River. Although the Akims, numbering about fourteen hundred, later deserted en masse twenty miles from the destined point of interception, Butler received praise from Wolseley for having diverted the bulk of the Ashanti army from the forces of Wolseley, who engaged and defeated the remaining Ashanti.

Butler's efforts in western Africa resulted in a near-fatal fever, and, after first being promoted to major and decorated, he returned briefly to England to recover. While in England he completed *Akim-Foo: The History of a Failure* (1875), a military explanation of his maneuvers. This work, reminiscent of his earlier *Narrative of the Historical Events,* follows the style of a travel narrative. Intended as an account of his subsidiary operations connected with Wolseley's march to Kumasi in 1873–1874, *Akim-Foo* more firmly than any of his previous works maligns England for attempting too quickly "to upraise an African Empire as an appendage to the British Crown." Nearly all of Butler's digressions become either political or military complaints about Britain's mismanagement of its expansion; he even finds fault with the original proposition to join forces with the Akims in an attempt to establish dominance in West Africa.

Although not nearly as romanticized or extended as his characterization of the Canadian wilderness, the image of the jungle that Butler creates for his readers emphasizes its huge climactic differences:

Morning. – A dense white steam fills the forest; the eye cannot follow the great grey tree-trunks more than half way to their summits; there is the ceaseless drip of raindrops on the broad-leaved undergrowth, and a clammy cold clings to the air; there is, the natives say, "a bad smoke" out to day, and yet long before mid-forenoon this smoke has vanished, and the fiery sun has come out – the clammy chill has changed to suffocating damp heat.

Butler responds less favorably to his African environment than to his Canadian. Possibly his long illness, disgust with English incompetence, and more perilous situation (Butler had begun his journey through the mostly uncharted jungle with only three servants) provoked such less exuberant monodies.

And although Butler urges his readers to pity the indigenous peoples of Africa who are displaced and manipulated by British intercession, his emotions seem choked by the general corruption and malice of the invading body: "wherever trade has sought the savage, be it in remote America or innermost Africa, it has come to him in the guise of the cheat and the liar." Butler's only light moments in *Akim-Foo* occur either when he joins in the complicity of English colonization or when he senses an opportunity to ridicule his adopted English culture. As he enters the disputed areas he must help secure, he meets and negotiates with several kings and tribal chiefs, including Coffee Ahencora and Quabina Fuah. While in the company of Coffee, Butler's most sustained acquaintance, Butler falls sick. Weary from the heat and in need of medical attention, he decides to proceed to the Prah. Before he can leave, Coffee's mother, herself a victim of several unidentified maladies, begs relief from Butler:

"These are very precious," I said. "Their fame is spread far over the earth: the characters engraved on this box are 'fetish' symbols of great power – all pains and ailments are said to vanish before the use of these small globules." The old queen stretched out her hand, her eyes and the eyes of all her ladies beamed with excitement. I placed in her hand the coveted treasures. "What are they called?" she inquired. – "Cockles Antibilious Pills," I replied, with a face of profound gravity. Again spoke the interpreter, "The queen wishes to know when she is to take this great medicine?" – "When she lies down to sleep," I replied. – "And will she be quite well when she wakes again?" asked the interpreter. – "Perfectly," was my reply.

When Butler digresses on another African, the young Fanti known as Dawson, his ridicule is redirected and becomes more personal:

> [W]hile his Wesleyan masters had done so much to improve this little Fanti, they had not been able to rise superior, in their zeal for the conversion of the heathen, to those feelings of rancorous bigotry which prevail against some other fellow Christians at home. . . . "Master," said this small boy to me one day, "are there not Christians in England who are like the fetish people here in the bush?" – "What do you mean, small boy?" – "Are there not some Christian people in England who have pieces of sticks and stones for their gods? The ministers always told us at the school that there were plenty such people in England. They said they were called Catholics."

After his recovery and the completion of *Akim-Foo* Butler received a special service commission in Natal, South Africa. He accompanied Wolseley, who had recently assumed temporary governorship of the province. Butler's position there was as protector of Indian immigrants, with a seat in the colonial council and assembly. Butler remained in South Africa – either in Natal, the Orange Free State, Kimberley, or Basutoland – until October 1875, when he returned to England and became deputy assistant quartermaster general. In 1877, he married Elizabeth Thompson, a noted history painter and minor travel writer.

In 1879 Butler again arrived in South Africa, this time as a soldier preparing for the Zulu War. He saw no fighting for his first year but still rose to the rank of brevet lieutenant colonel on 21 April 1880. From 1 July 1880 until the end of August 1884 he served as chief staff officer at Devonport. There he completed *Far Out: Rovings Retold* (1880), a reprinting of various magazine articles covering his travels to Canada, South Africa, and Cyprus. *Far Out* again reveals his growing hostility toward English expansionist policy – not for the fact of expansion itself, but for its meandering and wasteful deployment. John Ruskin, a man quite similar in ideological makeup to Butler, commented on Butler's work that both the book and Butler's politics were "very singularly also of one mind with me . . . on matters regarding the Queen's safety and the nation's honour."

For three months in 1882 Butler followed Wolseley to Egypt, where he fought at Tel-el-Kebir and received the Bronze Star Medal for his bravery. In returning to Devonport on 18 November 1882 he was made aide-de-camp to Queen Victoria, with the rank of colonel. In 1884 when the relief of Gen.

Charles George Gordon in the Nile region of Egypt pressed upon the British government, Wolseley consulted Butler about possible action. Butler quickly volunteered for service in ascending the Nile by boat. Having established an acquaintance with Gordon some years before and admiring him greatly (especially for Gordon's militaristic bent), Butler briefly experienced again the excitement of his youthful militarism. His admiration for Gordon spilled into his lust for war on the Nile, and he later described the relief expedition in *The Campaign of the Cataracts: Being a Personal Narrative of the Great Nile Expedition of 1884–5* (1887) as the first war during the Victorian era in which the object was entirely noble and worthy. Butler prepared and guided four hundred boats up the cataracts of the Nile and persuaded the commanding general to turn the position of his troops to a flank attack. The victory at Kirbekan on 10 February 1885 resulted largely from Butler's advice, and he was left behind in command of a small force. Upon his return to England Butler received two clasps as decoration.

Despite his reacquired enthusiasm for colonial expansion, Butler still made clear to readers what he felt primarily underlay so many colonial "little wars" in defense of English possessions. In attempting to answer his own question about whether this mission up the Nile could be completed in the short time (three months) allowed for it, Butler answered in the *Athenaeum* in 1887, "Yes, on one condition – that from the moment 'off' is spoken, all the country's pegs by which the science of government pins down the effort of the individual atom be for a time removed, or loosened, so that a line can be run straight through the densely crowded streets of the great city of 'Departmental Administration.'"

The Campaign of the Cataracts briefly recaptures much of his love of exploring new lands, and the text devotes ample time to describing the intricate details of preparing a mission to so remote an area. It traces his journey up the Nile, including the frequent backtracking to speed up lagging boats or to overcome the difficulties of a cataract. Butler also historicizes his mission by comparing it to those of the earliest Christian converts who sought to disseminate the Word of God.

By September 1884 he rose to the rank of brigadier general, defending posts in the Egyptian frontier after the retreat of British troops from the Sudan. When the heat of the desert incapacitated him in June 1886, he returned to England. Ruminating on his career during his free time, Butler still felt neglected by the British military. His warnings to the chiefs of staff on several proposed engagements in both Egypt and South Africa provoked resentment from his superiors. Although he was later appointed Knight Commander of the Order of Bath in 1885, Butler's often pointed criticisms of both the English military and government in matters pertaining to colonial protection and administration resulted in his being unemployed for the following two years.

He spent this period in Brittany and Ireland, and in Ireland Butler wrote *The Campaign of the Cataracts*. While he was idle Butler met and established a friendship with Charles Stewart Parnell, the outspoken and often violent proponent of Irish home rule. Through Parnell's influence Butler rechanneled much of his earlier concern for the indigenous peoples of North America, and he echoed many of Parnell's sentiments in later-published essays such as "Oliver Cromwell in Ireland" (1903).

Butler returned to Egypt in 1890 to command the garrison of Alexandria. During this assignment, mostly an administrative exile brought on by his relentless criticism of the strategic planners in the war office, Butler traveled with his wife, Elizabeth. After two years Butler became major general on 7 December 1892, and he later received a reward for distinguished service in 1894.

In October 1898 Butler received command of the troops in South Africa. Here Butler's sentiments, nurtured first by his own upbringing as an Irish Catholic and combined with both his firsthand observation of Anglo-Canadian treatment of Native Americans and Parnell's philosophies concerning Irish home rule, again exploded in unrepressed animosity toward British colonial rule. Sympathizing completely with the various factions chafing under English hegemony, Butler vocally opposed what he believed to be a purposive embittering of the relations between the races in the Transvaal region. Butler refused to forward to the queen a petition from the "outlanders" (both Dutch and African settlers) asking for British intervention. He incorporated many views into *From Naboth's Vineyard: Being Impressions Formed during a Fourth Visit to South Africa Undertaken at the Request of the Tribune Newspaper* (1907), a collection of letters forwarded to the London *Tribune* during his tenure in South Africa. Butler's political belief that British troubles in South Africa came from "interference" was aroused, and he strongly opposed the colonization of Natal because of the impending disruption of the black and Dutch South Africans who farmed the land.

Butler's open refusal to add dignity to a purely military provocation caused his dismissal from the civil administration of South Africa in 1899. He viewed the entire Transvaal situation as "a plot to force war" on the already violated peoples emigrating from the north or on the Boers who had come before, and he resigned his commission in South Africa on 4 July 1899. Butler returned to England and was assigned to the command of the western district.

On 9 October 1900 Butler achieved the rank of lieutenant general. He served his last years in the military mostly as an adviser and as chair of various departments and committees. These final years were spent balanced between diplomatic endeavors, educational concerns, and the interests of the Gaelic League. He remained in military service for most of his life, until he retired on 31 October 1905. After retiring he was appointed to the Irish Privy Council in 1909 and was later made a governor of the Royal Hibernian Military School, a member of the senate of the National University of Ireland, and a commissioner of the Irish Board of National Education. He died on 7 June 1910 at Bansha Castle, County Tipperary, where he had lived following his retirement. Butler was buried with military honors at Killardrigh, his family's resting place. He was survived by his wife and their five children.

Butler's life is interesting in its accumulation of conflicting attitudes toward military dominance of England's colonies and toward policies of subjecting peoples technologically incapable of defending themselves. The stridently individualistic Butler struggled with these attitudes throughout his life and attempted to solve them through his travel narratives and reports to his superiors. His clear, melodic style still holds much of its freshness and immediacy long after the areas he helped subdue achieved an autonomy that he frequently wished for, in both the conquered lands and his native Ireland.

References:

John Ruskin, "Our Fathers Have Told Us" (1884), in *The Complete Works of John Ruskin,* volume 33, edited by E. T. Cook and Alexander Wedderburn (London: George Allen, 1908), pp. 1–188;

Sir Garnet Wolseley, *In Relief of Gordon: Lord Wolseley's Campaign Journal of the Khartoum Relief Expedition, 1884–1885,* edited by Adrian Preston (London: Hutchinson, 1967).

Louisa Stuart Costello

(1799 – 24 April 1870)

Teresa A. Lyle
Miami University

BOOKS: *The Maid of the Cyprus Isle, and Other Poems* (London: Sherwood, Neely & Jones, 1815);

Redwald; A Tale of Mona, and Other Poems (Brentford: Norbury, 1819);

Songs of a Stranger (London: Taylor & Hessey, 1825);

Specimens of the Early Poetry of France from the Time of the Troubadours and Trouvères to the Reign of Henri Quatre (London: Pickering, 1835);

A Summer amongst the Bocages and the Vines, 2 volumes (London: Bentley, 1840);

The Queen's Poisoner; or, France in the Sixteenth Century: A Romance, 3 volumes (London: Bentley, 1841); republished as *Catherine de Medicis; or, The Queen-Mother: A Romance* (London: Bentley, 1848);

A Pilgrimage to Auvergne, from Picardy to Le Velay, 2 volumes (London: Bentley, 1842);

Gabrielle; or, Pictures of a Reign: A Historical Novel, 3 volumes (London: Newby, 1843);

Memoirs of Eminent Englishwomen, 4 volumes (London: Bentley, 1844);

Béarn and the Pyrenees: A Legendary Tour to the Country of Henry Quatre (London: Bentley, n.d.); republished as *Béarn and the Pyrenees: A Legendary Tour of the Country of Henry Quatre,* 2 volumes (London: Bentley, 1844);

The Falls, Lakes, and Mountains, of North Wales (London: Longman, Brown, Green & Longmans, 1845);

Venice and the Venetians; with a Glance at the Vaudois and the Tyrol (London: Darling, 1845);

A Tour to and from Venice, by the Vaudois and the Tyrol (London: Ollivier, 1846);

Jacques Coeur, the French Argonaut, and His Times (London: Bentley, 1847);

Clara Fane; or, The Contrasts of a Life, 3 volumes (London: Bentley, 1848);

Memoirs of Mary, the Young Duchess of Burgundy, and Her Contemporaries (London: Bentley, 1853);

Memoirs of Anne, Duchess of Brittany, Twice Queen of France (London: Cash, 1855);

The Lay of the Stork (London: Cash, 1856).

OTHER: *The Rose Garden of Persia,* edited and translated by Costello (London: Longman, Brown, Green & Longmans, 1845; Boston: Page, 1899);

Flowers from the Persian Poets, translated by Costello, edited by Nathan Haskell Dole and Belle M. Walker (New York: Crowell, [1901]).

SELECTED PERIODICAL PUBLICATIONS –
UNCOLLECTED: "Sketches of Legendary Cities: Chester," *Bentley's Miscellany,* 16 (October 1844): 350–362;

"Sketches of Legendary Cities: Shrewsbury," *Bentley's Miscellany,* 16 (December 1844): 576–590;

"Sketches of Legendary Cities: Bath," *Bentley's Miscellany,* 17 (February 1845): 168–181;

"Sketches of Legendary Cities: Monmouth," *Bentley's Miscellany,* 17 (March 1845): 265–276;

"Sketches of Legendary Cities: Ross, Tintern Abbey, Chepstow," *Bentley's Miscellany,* 17 (April 1845): 345–356;

"Sketches of Legendary Cities: Hereford," *Bentley's Miscellany,* 17 (June 1845): 605–615;

"Sketches of Legendary Cities: Colchester," *Bentley's Miscellany,* 18 (July 1845): 62–73;

"Sketches of Legendary Cities: Derby," *Bentley's Miscellany,* 18 (October 1845): 341–352;

"Sketches of Legendary Cities: Lewes," *Bentley's Miscellany,* 19 (June 1846): 582–596;

"Summer Sketches in Switzerland," *Bentley's Miscellany,* 20 (July 1846): 46–55;

"Sketches of Legendary Cities: The City of Bristol, *Bentley's Miscellany,* 20 (August 1846): 170–180;

"Sketches of Legendary Cities: The Cities of Gloucester and Cirencester, Past and Present," *Bentley's Miscellany,* 20 (October 1846): 390–400;

"Summer Sketches in Switzerland," *Bentley's Miscellany,* 20 (November 1846): 447–454;

"Summer Sketches in Switzerland," *Bentley's Miscellany,* 20 (December 1846): 566–573;

"Summer Sketches in Switzerland," *Bentley's Miscellany,* 23 (February 1848): 150–158;

"Summer Sketches in Switzerland," *Bentley's Miscellany,* 23 (March 1848): 258–265.

Novelist, painter, and inveterate traveler, Louisa Stuart Costello was an enormously popular writer in the 1830s and 1840s. She not only wrote five travel narratives but also edited and collected many volumes of poetry and memoirs. Moreover, she worked as a reviewer and critic for the *Athenaeum* and regularly contributed short travel essays to *Bentley's Miscellany,* a popular Victorian periodical. Although her work has been largely neglected, Costello's narratives are colored with class, race, and gender considerations as well as a strong nationalist bias, and such competing impulses produce a narrative tension that makes her work relevant to readers interested in colonialism, postcolonialism, and travel literature.

Costello joined the ranks of many other British women who during the nineteenth century created their own grand tour experience. Equipped with published travel books and guides, these women discovered the Continent for themselves. Many wrote travel accounts but undermined their works by highlighting their deficiencies in relation to extant travel literature. While such humility topoi have been long recognized as conventions that women used to negotiate their presence in hostile literary environments, Costello refused to use such self-denigration and unabashedly offered her work as a major contribution to the growing travel literature on Europe. Her accounts consider such topics normally associated with women's travel writing as costumes, manners, and culinary habits, but she also details church architecture, library holdings, and road construction — subjects typically prominent in travel narratives written by men. Thus, Costello's work challenges gender boundaries established in nineteenth-century travel writing.

Born in Sussex in 1799, Costello lived with both parents until her father's death in 1814. Afterward, she and her mother moved to Paris, where Costello supported them and her brother, Dudley, by painting miniatures. Dudley became a foreign correspondent for the *Daily News* and also wrote many travel books. He provided some of the illustrations for Costello's travel works. Sometime before 1825 Costello moved to London, and, through her painting and increasing sales of her publications, she made enough money to continue supporting Dudley and to undertake many trips to the Continent.

Costello began her long literary career with three books of poetry, including *Songs of a Stranger* (1825), and a decade later she published *Specimens of the Early Poetry of France from the Time of the Troubadours and Trouvères to the Reign of Henri Quatre* (1835), a widely read book that firmly established the author's literary reputation. Her first travel narrative, *A Summer amongst the Bocages and the Vines* (1840), begins with her trip by steamboat to Normandy, and in this two-volume work Costello establishes a pattern for her later travel accounts. Here the reader finds the author's meticulous attention to historical detail and her penchant for discussing literary figures who appear prominently in later narratives. She provides not only a lengthy discussion of Richard the Lion-Hearted but also considerations of more recent figures such as Napoleon. In this work and others she repeatedly refers to the effects of the Napoleonic Wars on the Continent. For example, she describes her excursions to churches and libraries, where she notes that many libraries had been stripped of their entire holdings during the wars.

Her depictions of the inhabitants are historically informative; if one can endure Costello's middle-class condescension toward the peasantry, her portrayals of the rural landscapes are complemented by a unique view of the working-class lives of the French masses. Offering a sampling of the country's cultural heritage, *A Summer amongst the Bocages and the Vines* includes many ballads and poems written by local authors. This work was so popular that a second edition appeared as early as 1841.

Costello dedicated her next travel book, a two-volume work called *A Pilgrimage to Auvergne, from Picardy to Le Velay* (1842), to Lady Augusta Gordon. In it Costello immediately establishes her credibility as a travel writer by referring to her earlier work, assuming a reading audience familiar with her past travel accounts. This work documents her journey from England to France in the spring of 1841. She refers to Auvergne as the "Switzerland of France," and she especially encourages poets and painters to visit.

Unlike her earlier work, this account begins with information about the region that she has gathered from its chroniclers, and she also comments on the more recent revolutionary activities in the area. This work contains many anecdotes of her interactions with the French, such as her experience riding with a postal carrier to a nearby town. Throughout these first two works the reader gets a flavor, albeit a middle-class one, of the French villages and country life.

In *Béarn and the Pyrenees: A Legendary Tour of the Country of Henry Quatre* (1844), the success of her previous travel books makes Costello seem particularly self-assured, and she assumes her "cockle hat and staff" in likening herself to Sinbad searching for a romantic adventure or perhaps comparing herself to a pilgrim. This work is based on the author's third ramble in France, which lasted from August 1843 until the end of spring 1844.

Despite an enthusiastic opening, by the end of the volume Costello has presented a negative portrait of this French region. She again comments on the unfortunate effects of the Napoleonic Wars, but her criticism is not limited to ongoing construction work. She describes boring people and bad weather, and she disdains the prisoners and peasants she finds everywhere. After two volumes of condescending depictions of the people and customs of Béarn, Costello paradoxically encourages travelers to visit, for she notes that the region has produced thinkers such as Michel de Montaigne and Charles Louis de Secondat, baron de la Brède et de Montesquieu. Moreover, she cautions, if one enters Bordeaux without expectations, there are rewards for the journey.

Costello's description of a French peasant provides one especially illuminating moment: the peasant is "tall, and well made," with a "fine nose" and "oval" cheeks; "the expression of her smile was the most simple and innocent imaginable, and [a] total absence of anything like thought or intellect, make her face a perfect reflection of that of one of her own lambs." This offhanded remark remains the rule, rather than the exception, throughout the book. Costello generally surveys each physical feature as she paternalistically scrutinizes the behavior of the natives.

Another revealing moment occurs when Costello and her female companion visit the poet-barber Jasmin. Costello retells in prose one of his ballads and in fact includes many of his poems in her book, yet she unfavorably depicts both Jasmin and his wife as buffoons in their anticipation of a coming royal visit that has no basis in fact.

Her fourth travel book, *The Falls, Lakes, and Mountains, of North Wales* (1845), describes a journey beginning in Chester and ending in Shrewsbury and is much shorter than her other travel accounts. It also differs from them in attending almost exclusively to the landscape and countryside rather than to the architecture of the region. In fact, this volume contains more sketches of the landscape than all her

Frontispiece to Costello's Specimens of the Early Poetry of France from the Time of the Troubadours and Trouvères to the Reign of Henri Quatre

other works combined. *The Falls, Lakes, and Mountains, of North Wales* offers many lithographs and engravings that beautifully re-create the environs of North Wales, and Costello provides a map and table of distances she traveled.

This book made a journey through northern Wales accessible for Welshmen who had neither the time nor means to visit the Continent, and Costello's repeated references to magic, demons, and murder make the countryside seem mysterious and attractive to adventurous readers. While her other books have also referred to superstition, she identifies Wales as the quintessential land of mystery and intrigue. Her admiration for this region is so great that she declares that North Wales has in miniature everything that the European countries have. This work reads almost like a travel brochure, intended to boost tourism to Wales. Yet it still resembles Costello's earlier travel works in its emphasis on historical figures. For instance, the author

"*Ragatz in the Valley of the Rhine,*" *illustration from Costello's* Tour to and from Venice, by the Vaudois and the Tyrol

painstakingly details how Edward I had conquered North Wales in the thirteenth century. The background about his family and reign that she provides makes entertaining reading of the complex royal history.

A year before her mother's death Costello published her last travel account, *Venice and the Venetians; with a Glance at the Vaudois and the Tyrol* (1845), and, owing to its popularity, it was republished the following year with a new title, *A Tour to and from Venice, by the Vaudois and the Tyrol* (1846). Here Costello recounts her grand tour experience beginning in Turin and ending in Venice, "the most bewitching of all places in the world of fancy or reality."

Touring of Italy had been suspended during the war with France, and after tours were again possible, travel books about Italy flooded the presses. Italy promised romance, and Costello joined Mary Shelley, Elizabeth Barrett Browning, and others in writing accounts of the crowded streets, quaint cafés, and gondola voyages. Unlike some female writers, however, Costello shows no anxiety in describing her experience of the grand tour. Although she mentions previous accounts, she claims an equally important place for her own, and she even recommends her account both to those who have already known the beauty of Venice and to those who have not.

Her portraits of the people and environments of Milan and the other cities along the route to Venice sometimes reiterate her earlier themes: disgusting natives, bad weather, unpleasant accommodations. Somewhat uncharacteristically, however, Costello notices the attractive men in Milan: "the men who paused to gaze at us as we passed were good-looking and healthy." While women travel writers generally avoid eroticized descriptions of the country, Costello uses sexual metaphors to characterize the landscape and people — particularly in the Vaudois Valley, where she comments on the "supineness and carelessness about the people."

In addition to providing portraits of the valleys and landscapes, Costello delights in gallery visits, and she finds in each sculpture or painting a reference to history or literature — to figures such as Dante, Petrarch, and Shakespeare. She is equally drawn to the literary significances of towns along the tour. For example, on her excursion to Verona, the setting of Shakespeare's *Romeo and Juliet* (circa 1595), she digresses on several literary themes before the real Veronan atmosphere returns her consciousness to the present, and its "slovenly, shabby, ugly people" elicit a strong negative response: "its lower orders . . . are wild and coarse . . . not uncivil but savage, with none of the native grace and gentleness which had so pleased me hitherto."

Costello finds a different milieu in Venice: it is the "reality of all my day-dreams" and the "realization of a poet's dream." Much to her amazement, she finds the Venetians dressed well: "I have seldom seen ladies more elaborately dressed than here. . . . [B]eautiful children in muslin and ribbons were flitting about like cherubs." It is not surprising that a city with the rich cultural heritage of Venice is Costello's favorite place in Europe.

In addition to these five full-length travel narratives Costello published two travel series – "Sketches of Legendary Cities" and "Summer Sketches in Switzerland" – in *Bentley's Miscellany* between 1844 and 1848. These short essays are characteristic of Costello's longer work, as they reiterate the same themes and prejudices.

Louisa Stuart Costello's literary career spanned fifty years. Although she translated European poetry and edited the memoirs of notable women in history, her most prolific work remained in the realm of travel and historical narrative. Her texts have been neglected during the twentieth century, but in her own time Costello was popular enough to attract the attention of French king Louis Philippe, who presented her with a piece of jewelry in admiration of her work. She also received a pension from the influential Burdett family and was awarded an annuity beginning in 1852. These examples evidence the powerful contacts that Costello had cultivated through her writing.

Like other female travel writers, Costello traveled to study history, to gain knowledge, and to make money from publishing her accounts. However, she should be considered an important anomaly in women's travel writing: she never appealed to other authorities to valorize her own voice or experiences, nor did she write in the journal or epistolary genres typically labeled feminine. Moreover, only passing remarks suggest that she traveled with female companions. Costello never provided any information about her cotravelers, and a hasty reader would think she had embarked alone on her journeys. Indeed, Louisa Stuart Costello was a pioneer – a leader who challenged the notion that women could not support themselves and had nothing to say or do about their own experiences.

Bibliography:

R. S. Pine-Coffin, *Bibliography of British and American Travel in Italy to 1860* (Firenze: Olschki, 1974).

Reference:

Shirley Foster, *Across New Worlds: Nineteenth-Century Women Travellers and Their Writings* (New York: Harvester/Wheatsheaf, 1990).

Robert Curzon

(16 March 1810 – 2 August 1873)

David C. Judkins
University of Houston

BOOKS: *The Lay of the Purple Falcon: A Metrical Romance,* as Robert, the Rhymer, with Episcopus C – Reginaldus [Richard Heber] (London: Nicol, 1847);

Catalogue of Materials for Writing: Early Writings on Tablets and Stones, Rolled and Other Manuscripts, and Oriental Manuscript Books (London: Nicol, 1849);

A Visit to Monasteries in the Levant (New York: Putnam / London: Murray, 1849); republished as *Visits to Monasteries of the Levant* (London: Murray, 1849); republished as *Monasteries of the East: Embracing Visits to Monasteries in the Levant* (New York: Barnes, 1854);

Armenia: A Year at Erzeroom, and on the Frontiers of Russia, Turkey, and Persia (London: Murray, 1854; New York: Harper, 1854);

History of Printing in China and Europe ([London?, 1860?]).

SELECTED PERIODICAL PUBLICATIONS – UNCOLLECTED: "A Short Account of Some of the Most Celebrated Libraries of Italy," *Philobiblon Society Miscellanies,* 1 (1854);

"The Book of the Prophet Moses and the History of the Prophet Moses," *Philobiblon Society Miscellanies,* 2 (1855–1856);

"History of Printing in China and Europe," *Philobiblon Society Miscellanies,* 6 (1861);

"The Lord Mayor's Visit to Oxford, July 1826," *Philobiblon Society Miscellanies,* 9 (1865–1866).

Although Robert Curzon is remembered today for the vivid, often humorous accounts of his journeys in the Middle East during the 1830s and early 1840s, he saw himself as a devoted collector and preserver of ancient books and manuscripts. His first travel book, *A Visit to Monasteries in the Levant* (1849), was reprinted several times in England and America during the nineteenth century and twice in the twentieth. Less well known but equally charming is *Armenia: A Year at Erzeroom, and on the*

Frontiers of Russia, Turkey, and Persia (1854), which described the year that Curzon had spent along the border of Turkey and Persia in 1842.

Most of Curzon's surviving correspondence and much of his published writing are devoted to his collecting of manuscripts, and had it not been for this fascination, he would have lacked any reason to visit the ancient monasteries of the Middle East that had changed little throughout the centuries. He apparently did not set out seeking adventures, but he did not avoid them, as he pressed on to discover more dusty libraries with undisturbed ancient texts. His recollections of those adventures and the charm and grace with which they are related capture the reader's interest and allow Robert Curzon to live on – not in the books he collected, but in those he wrote.

Curzon was born in London on 16 March 1810. His father was the son of Viscount Curzon, and his mother was the Baroness de la Zouche. He was educated at Charterhouse and entered Christ College, Oxford, in 1829, where he met his lifelong friend and correspondent, Walter Sneyd. Curzon left Oxford in 1831 without a degree and was sent to Parliament, where he represented his family constituency of Clitheroe. His career in Parliament was short-lived, however, because his borough was disenfranchised with the passage of the Reform Bill of 1832, which Curzon opposed.

In that same year he and Sneyd went to Rome, where they spent several weeks looking for manuscripts and rummaging through old bookshops before Sneyd returned to England. Curzon, twenty-three years old, moved on to Egypt; on 31 July 1833 he arrived in Alexandria, where he began the first of his notable expeditions described in *A Visit.* In 1837 he returned for a second expedition, this time going westward to the Natron Lakes in the Libyan Desert. He then retraced his steps, traveled up the eastern shore of the Mediterranean, and finally reached Constantinople. From there he journeyed to Mount Athos in Greece to explore the monasteries on that slender peninsula.

Probably because of school and family connections as well as his linguistic skills, Curzon was appointed as an attaché to the British embassy in Constantinople in 1841, and in early 1842 he journeyed to Erzurum in Armenia to help resolve border disputes. Later in the year as the talks dragged on, Curzon became very ill and spent nearly a month unconscious with a condition later diagnosed as brain fever. He returned to England to his beloved home, Parham, where he catalogued his manuscripts and reflected on his travels. Except for relatively brief expeditions scouting for books and manuscripts on the Continent, Curzon's extended travels were over.

The first book that Curzon wrote (in collaboration with Richard Heber) was *The Lay of the Purple Falcon* (1847). It has nothing to do with travel, does not include Curzon's name on the title page, and was privately printed and set in a nearly unreadable Gothic type. It is a curious narrative poem reflecting the early-Victorian infatuation with medieval lore. Two years later Curzon published his *Catalogue of Materials for Writing: Early Writings on Tablets and Stones, Rolled and Other Manuscripts, and Oriental Manuscript Books* (1849), also privately printed in folio with twelve plates. In the same year *A Visit to Monasteries in the Levant* appeared in England and the United States. It was well received, with a second edition coming out in England that same year.

A Visit is structured as a series of vignettes recounting incidents in Curzon's wanderings. His ironic, sometimes self-deprecating style, his care with details, and his selfless wonder at new discoveries have endeared him to readers since the work was published. The modern reader may be particularly impressed by his openness to strange customs or outdated ceremonies, his lack of rigidity, and his whimsical skepticism.

Planned for easy and entertaining reading, *A Visit* unfolds at a leisurely pace, moving from episode to episode and largely conflating Curzon's two expeditions into one reflection on his experiences in the Middle East. The narrative is fairly loose and provides readers with little sense that the narrator is growing into a seasoned, more sophisticated traveler. This absence of change in the persona may also be owing to the fact that Curzon seems never to have regarded himself as a writer and even speaks of his "dislike for quill driving." In any case, from his first sights in Alexandria to his final anxieties about pirates as he returns from Mount Athos to Constantinople, Curzon's narrative persona is very much a

neophyte: young, impressionable, and most often unsure about what to expect.

In his introductory chapter to *A Visit* Curzon details several reasons he went to Egypt. He wanted to see, describe, and sketch the remote monasteries that few Europeans had visited. He found the architecture and art interesting and was fascinated with the landscape of the monasteries and the monks who inhabited them. Curzon also seemed to be undertaking a kind of medieval pilgrimage: "In these monasteries resided the early fathers of the church, and within the precincts of their time-hallowed walls were composed those writings which have since been looked up to as the rules of Christian life." Though not obtrusive, a strong strand of Christian faith informs his writing. Not mentioned in the introduction is his interest in manuscripts, but elsewhere he describes himself as "a devout lover of old books — a sort of biblical knight errant."

Upon arriving in Alexandria, Curzon is fascinated by the strange people and sights he sees from his hotel window, but he is also disturbed by the stories he hears that describe extreme cruelty by pashas or beys toward their servants and subjects. He writes of a groom who has a hot horseshoe nailed to his foot because the pasha's horse has thrown a shoe. When a woman accuses a member of a ruler's household of stealing a cup of milk from her, the ruler orders the accused to be disemboweled to see if, in fact, milk is to be found in his stomach. Perhaps such grisly but casual events make the remote, isolated life of a monk seem more attractive, for Curzon seems to turn with a sigh of relief to those highly idiosyncratic figures.

The first monasteries Curzon describes are at the Natron Lakes, indentations in the Desert of Nitra. After spending a night fighting off fleas, he is led by a blind monk to the library,

> where we found several Coptic manuscripts. Most of these were lying on the floor, all on paper, except three or four. One of these was a superb manuscript of the Gospels, with commentaries by the early fathers of the church; two others were doing duty as coverings to a couple of large open pots or jars, which had contained preserves, long since evaporated. I was allowed to purchase these vellum manuscripts, as they were considered to be useless by the monks, principally, I believe, because there were no more preserves in the jars.

Curzon is adept at re-creating a scene, at evoking the look and feel of places that his readers would never see. He contrasts the "parched and dreary" aspect of the desert to its "vastness and openness." He finds within its "silence and loneliness" a "fresh

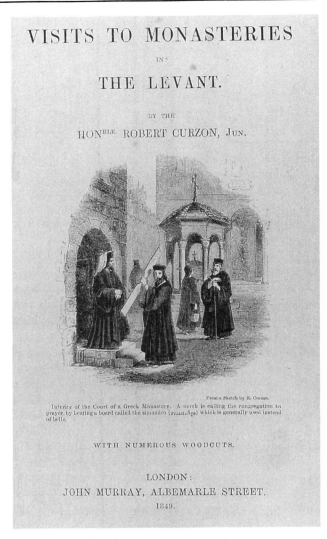

Frontispiece and title page for Curzon's first travel book, with a woodcut (right) based on a sketch by Curzon

breeze . . . more elastic and pure than where vegetation produces exhalations which in all hot climates are more or less heavy and deleterious." He is interested in everything, anxious to investigate, willing to search for the logic and purpose of happenings and customs that lesser travelers would dismiss as barbaric or heathen. Even when he cannot accept or sympathize with the behavior of the monks, he nevertheless does not sound superior when he describes their lives: "It was such men as these who lived on the tops of columns, and took up their abodes in tombs, and thought it was a sign of holiness to look like a wild beast – that it was wicked to be clean, and superfluous to be useful in this world: and who did evil to themselves that good might come. Poor fellows! they meant well, and knew no better; and what more can be said for the endeavours of the best of men?"

Curzon's journey is not as quiet and uneventful as are the lives of the monks whom he visits. On the contrary, whether he is being lifted up by a pulley to an inaccessible cliff dwelling, avoiding a stampede of worshipers at the Church of the Holy Sepulchre on Good Friday, or being waylaid by bandits in Albania, the narrator not only recognizes that he is in extreme danger but recounts such incidents in suspenseful and vivid narratives.

Curzon finally reaches the ultimate home of monasteries – Mount Athos, a narrow, fingerlike peninsula jutting into the Aegean Sea. Here he visits more than twenty ancient monasteries and is fortunate to acquire several manuscripts. Some are released only after hours of bargaining; others are freely given as gifts; and still others are purchased at the price quickly determined. But in some instances the monks are unwilling to part with their books, even though these tomes litter the floor and are covered with years of accumulated dust. Giving only brief descriptions of the monasteries and relatively short accounts of his dealings with the monks, the narrator seems anxious to conclude his story. Clearly the "quill driving" is becoming increasingly tedious; as soon as Curzon is safely back in Constantinople, the book ends without any summary conclusion.

In fact the two journeys were very successful. His mission having been undertaken at the right time, when travel to such remote sites was relatively safe, Curzon accumulated more than one hundred manuscripts. The monasteries were still largely intact, but the monks were no longer using the ancient texts. Curzon found manuscripts in "libraries" where the doors had not been opened for years and where those in charge were unable to read the documents. The well-narrated anecdotes, Curzon's narrow escapes from injury (perhaps even death), and his gentle humor often directed more at himself than at those he meets combine to make the book a success whose popularity continued into the twentieth century.

In 1850 Curzon married Emily Wilmot-Horton. It is not clear if the popularity of *A Visit* had anything to do with his decision to marry. Curzon complained to Sneyd that his father, Viscount Curzon, treated him as a child even after he had returned from Armenia. Perhaps the recognition that came with the publication of *A Visit* led to this change in his life. It does appear that Emily had something to do with his next book, *Armenia,* for in another letter to Sneyd, Curzon states that she advised him to write it. Because *Armenia* was published just two years before the outbreak of the Crimean War, it is safe to assume that Curzon or his publisher hoped that it would be as popular as *A Visit* had become. It was not. But it is better than its present neglect indicates. It was reprinted twice during the year it was first published, but it then slipped into quiet obscurity.

Curzon was on official business during his journey to Erzurum. No longer did he have to call upon friendships or his British identity to get around. This time he was a diplomat for the British Crown. He was, however, unable to travel in a carriage, for the road from the Black Sea to Erzurum was nothing more than a rude path suitable only for a traveler on horseback, and sometimes not even suitable for that mode of transportation.

When he reached the ancient city of Erzurum, strategically located on caravan routes leading from Transcaucasia in the winter of 1842, Curzon was as-

tonished at what he saw. "I have never seen or heard of anything the least like it," he wrote. "As the whole view, whichever way one looked, was wrapped in interminable snow, . . . the snow covered city did not resemble any other town, but appeared more like a great rabbit warren; many of the houses being wholly or partly subterranean, the doors looked like burrows." Apart from this first impression Curzon found the city more curious than interesting. Architecturally there was little to remark. He reports that daily life soon became uneventful and routine, largely because of the extraordinarily cold weather and the heavy snow that inhibited outside activity. The diplomatic duties that had brought him to this remote city also moved at a lethargic pace. The Turks were not interested in arriving at a border resolution and a peace treaty, because the regular border raids tended to weaken the Persians more than the Turks.

Despite this general lassitude and the fact that, as Curzon says in a letter, "One day passes much like another at Erzeroom," he recalled much to make his account interesting – as in his narrative of one incident involving a violation of human rights. Although the affair had nothing to do with his mission and although Curzon did not represent himself as an enlightened westerner come to protect the oppressed Christians, he quietly and diplomatically sought to help a Christian Armenian whom two Turkish soldiers had accused of theft. Circumstances pointed to the soldiers as being the thieves, but when the Armenian did not confess, he was tortured: his front teeth were pulled out; reeds were forced under his fingernails; and other tortures were inflicted on him.

Responding to a plea from the wife of the Armenian, Curzon intervened and was assured by the viceroy, Kiamili Pasha, that the man had not been tortured. After negotiations led to the release of the accused man, Curzon met with him and observed his recent torture scars and missing front teeth. Curzon concludes his narrative by observing that "much injustice may probably be carried on by the inferior officers of the government which never gets to the ears of the Pasha, small officials being notoriously more tyrannical than greater men." He then reflects on the tradition of such gratuitous violence and its effect on modern Turkey:

> [A]ccording to the fashion of the good old times when Turkey, like the United States of America, was a land of liberty, where every free and independent citizen had the right to beat his own nigger, . . . the Sultan had the

privilege of destroying fourteen lives per day of his faithful subjects, who might have committed no crime; after that number, some reason was expected to be shown for further use of the sword . . . on that day. Now the case is altered: fewer crimes are committed in Turkey than in London, and the Turkish pashas endeavor to stop such practices as are considered discreditable on the part of the inferior officers.

Curzon's dry, ironic reflections on these "good old times" undeniably appeal to most readers, a response he also invites when he visits the ruins of a horrible dungeon that "in the good old times was in constant use." At the same time, he is aware that Europe is not a seat of benevolence and open-mindedness. Regardless of their color, religion, or nationality, humans have an equal capacity for brutality – an evil that Curzon abhors and attempts to prevent.

Near the end of his visit Curzon became seriously ill and was unconscious for twenty-seven days. When he revived, an earthquake was apparently just commencing. Although earthquakes were common in the area, this one was particularly devastating, and Curzon concludes his description by noting, "It is difficult to express in words the strange, awful sensation produced by the seeming impossible contradiction of a dead stillness in the midst of the crash of falling buildings, the sullen, low bellowing, which perhaps sounded from beneath the ground, and the tremendous uproar that arose on all sides during the earthquake." After he had regained consciousness, he was moved to Trabzon, where he could fully recover. Too ill to ride a horse, Curzon lay on a litter lashed between two mules for a seventeen-day journey, during which he and the unfortunate animals carrying him were often at great risk crossing high mountain passes on narrow ledges sometimes no more than eighteen inches wide. His nighttime stops were often barely habitable hovels, where he found minimal shelter from the snow and cold. Nevertheless, he "arrived [at Trabzon] in better health and strength than when [he] started."

Curzon concludes his book with an anecdotal history of the area and a discussion of the significance of Russia, whose power and influence had grown alarmingly during the last eighty years. He warns his readers that "the Christian Emperor of Russia is at this moment exciting the minds of his subjects to make war upon the infidel; and his armies march under the impression that they undertake a new crusade. Yet this crusade is carried on in direct contradiction to truth, justice, honor, and every principle of the Christian religion." In 1854 this sentiment was no doubt shared by many of his fellow English-

men, who were becoming increasingly alarmed by Russian actions. Although the book was thus timely and initially a good seller, it has never been reprinted since 1854.

For the remainder of the decade Curzon turned from participating in current events to preparing bibliographical articles for publication in the *Philobiblon Society Miscellanies*. He was also working on a comprehensive history of handwriting, but he never finished this. Writing to Sneyd and encouraging him to join the ranks of the married, Curzon also became very devoted to his wife, by whom he had a son and a daughter. Emily died, however, in 1866, and when Curzon's mother died four years later, he succeeded her as baron de la Zouche.

It was an unhappy turn of events. His father had allowed the family fortune to slip through his hands, and Curzon, who had seemed to find more joy in the past than in the present, found that even more the case. Writing to Sneyd, he observed, "I am in a false position; my expenses are too great for my fortune, and I feel humbled and mortified because I cannot do what is expected of me." Perhaps the enforced humility was too much for him: three years later at the age of sixty-three he died after a short illness.

Robert Curzon left to his son an extraordinary library of manuscripts that eventually went to the British Museum and became a major addition to its Oriental Manuscript collection. At a time when British men and women were seeking increasingly exotic destinations to satisfy their curiosities, Curzon with apparently minimal planning had followed his own interests in ancient texts. Driven by little more than curiosity and vague rumors, he had endured unusual privations and dangers that are most easily tolerated by the young and energetic. Years later he had recalled these adventures with an amusing, understated style that captures the interest and imagination of readers today as much as it has since the first appearance of his narratives.

References:

Seton Dearden, Introduction, in Curzon's *Visits to Monasteries in the Levant* (London: Baker / Ithaca, N.Y.: Cornell University Press, 1955), pp. 7–15;

Meridel Holland, "Robert Curzon: Collector," *John Ryland's Library Bulletin,* 65 (Spring 1983): 123–157;

A. N. L. Munby, "Robert Curzon," in *Connoisseurs and Medieval Miniatures, 1750–1850* (Oxford: Clarendon Press, 1972), pp. 82–106.

Charles Darwin

(12 February 1809 – 19 April 1882)

Patricia O'Neill
Hamilton College

See also the Darwin entry in *DLB 57: Victorian Prose Writers After 1867.*

BOOKS: *Letters on Geology* (Cambridge: Privately printed, 1835);

Journal of Researches into the Geology and Natural History of the Various Countries Visited by H.M.S. Beagle, under the Command of Captain Fitzroy, R.N., from 1832 to 1836 (London: Colburn, 1839), volume 3 of *Narrative of the Surveying Voyages of His Majesty's Ships Adventure and Beagle,* edited by Robert Fitzroy (London: Colborn, 1839); also published as *Journal of Charles Darwin, M.A., Naturalist to the Beagle (1832–1836)* (London: Colburn, 1839; revised and enlarged edition, London: John Murray, 1845); republished as *Journal of Researches into the Natural History and Geology of the Countries Visited during the Voyage of H.M.S. Beagle round the World, under the Command of Capt. Fitzroy, R.N.* (2 volumes, New York: Harper, 1846; 1 volume, London: John Murray, 1852); republished as *A Naturalist's Voyage round the World in H.M.S. "Beagle"* (London, 1884); republished as *Journal of Researches into the Natural History and Geology of the Countries Visited during the Voyage of H.M.S. "Beagle" round the World, under the Command of Capt. Fitzroy, R.N.* (London, New York & Melbourne: Ward, Lock, 1889); republished as *The Voyage of a Naturalist round the World in H.M.S. "Beagle"* (London: Routledge / New York: Dutton, [1905]); republished as *Journal of Researches into the Geology & Natural History of the Various Countries Visited during the Voyage of H.M.S. Beagle round the World* (London: Dent / New York: Dutton, [1906]); republished as *The Voyage of the Beagle* (New York: Collier, [1909]; London: Dent / New York: Dutton, [1936]); republished as *A Naturalist's Voyage round the World in H.M.S. "Beagle"* (London: Oxford University Press, 1930);

Charles Darwin in 1869 (photographed by Julia Margaret Cameron; National Portrait Gallery, London)

The Structure and Distribution of Coral Reefs: Being the First Part of the Geology of the Voyage of the Beagle (London: Smith, Elder, 1842; New York: Appleton, 1896; revised edition, London: Smith, Elder, 1874);

Geological Observations on the Volcanic Islands, Visited during the Voyage of H.M.S. Beagle, Together with Some Brief Notices on the Geology of Australia and the Cape of Good Hope: Being the Second Part of the Geology of the Voyage of the Beagle, under the Command of Capt. Fitzroy . . . During the Years 1832 to 1836 (London: Smith, Elder, 1844); republished with *Geological Observations on South America* (London: Smith, Elder, 1874; New York: Appleton, 1896);

Geological Observations on South America: Being the Third Part of the Geology of the Voyage of the Beagle (London: Smith, Elder, 1846); republished with *Geological Observations on the Volcanic Islands* (London: Smith, Elder, 1876; New York: Appleton, 1896);

A Monograph on the Fossil Lepadidoe; *or, Pedunculated* Cirripedes *of Great Britain* (London: Paleontographical Society, 1851);

A Monograph on the Sub-class Cirripedia, *with Figures of All the Species,* 2 volumes (London: Ray Society, 1851–1854);

A Monograph on the Fossil Balandidoe *and* Verrucidoe *of Great Britain* (London: Paleontographical Society, 1854);

On the Origin of Species by Means of Natural Selection, or, the Preservation of Favoured Races in the Struggle for Life (London: John Murray, 1859; New York: Appleton, 1860; six revisions, London: John Murray, 1861–1876; 2 volumes, London: John Murray, 1888; 1 volume, New York: Appleton, 1890; 2 volumes, New York: Appleton, 1896); republished as *The Origin of Species* (New York: Collier, [1909]);

On the Various Contrivances by Which British and Foreign Orchids Are Fertilised by Insects, and on the Good Effects of Intercrossing (London: John Murray, 1862; revised, 1877); republished as *The Various Contrivances by Which Orchids Are Fertilised by Insects* (New York: Appleton, 1877; revised, 1903);

On the Movements and Habits of Climbing Plants (London, 1865; revised edition, London: John Murray, 1875; New York: Appleton, 1876);

The Variation of Animals and Plants under Domestication (2 volumes, London: John Murray, 1868; New York: Orange Judd, 1868; revised edition, London: John Murray, 1875; New York: Appleton, 1890);

The Descent of Man, and Selection in Relation to Sex (2 volumes, London: John Murray, 1871; New York: Appleton, 1871; revised and augmented edition, 1 volume, London: John Murray, 1874; New York: Burt, [1874]; 2 volumes, New York: Hill, 1904);

The Expression of the Emotions in Man and Animals (London: John Murray, 1872; New York: Appleton, 1873); revised and abridged by C. M. Beadnell (London: Watts, 1934);

Insectivorous Plants (London: John Murray, 1875; New York: Appleton, 1883); revised by Francis Darwin (London: John Murray, 1883);

The Effects of Cross and Self Fertilisation in the Vegetable Kingdom (London: John Murray, 1876; New York: Appleton, 1877);

The Different Forms of Flowers on Plants of the Same Species (London: Murray, 1877; New York: Appleton, 1877);

The Power of Movement in Plants, by Darwin, with the assistance of Francis Darwin (London: John Murray, 1880; New York: Appleton, 1881);

The Formation of Vegetable Mould, through the Action of Worms, with Observations on Their Habits (London: John Murray, 1881; New York: Appleton, 1882);

The Life and Letters of Charles Darwin, Including an Autobiographical Chapter, edited by Francis Darwin (3 volumes, London: John Murray, 1887; 2 volumes, New York: Appleton, 1888); abridged as *Charles Darwin: His Life Told in an Autobiographical Chapter, and in a Selected Series of His Published Letters* (London: John Murray, 1892; New York: Appleton, 1892); revised and augmented as *The Autobiography of Charles Darwin, 1809–1882: With Original Omissions Restored,* edited by Nora Barlow (Cambridge: Cambridge University Press, 1933; New York: Harcourt, Brace, 1959);

The Foundations of the Origin of Species: Two Essays Written in 1842 and 1844, edited by Francis Darwin (Cambridge: Cambridge University Press, 1909);

Charles Darwin's Diary of the Voyage of the H.M.S. "Beagle," edited by Barlow (Cambridge: Cambridge University Press, 1933);

Charles Darwin and the Voyage of the Beagle, edited by Barlow (London: Pilot, 1945; New York: Philosophical Library, [1946]);

Charles Darwin's Notebooks, 1836–1844 (Cambridge: Cambridge University Press, 1987);

Charles Darwin's Beagle *Diary,* edited by Richard Darwin Keynes (Cambridge: Cambridge University Press, 1988).

OTHER: *The Zoology of the Voyage of H.M.S. Beagle, under the Command of Captain Fitzroy, R.N., during the Years 1832 to 1836,* 5 volumes, edited, with introductions, by Darwin (London: Smith, Elder, 1839–1843);

"Geology," in *A Manual of Scientific Enquiry: Prepared for the Use of Her Majesty's Navy, and Adapted for Travellers in General,* edited by Sir John

Frederick William Herschel (London, 1849), pp. 156–195;

Anton Kerner von Marilaun, *Flowers and Their Unbidden Guests,* with a prefatory letter by Darwin (London: Kegan Paul, 1878);

Ernst Kraus, *Erasmus Darwin,* with a preliminary notice by Darwin (London: John Murray, 1879);

Kraus, *Erasmus Darwin und seine Stellung in der Geschichte der Descendenz-Theorie, Mit seinem Lebens- und Charakterbilde von C. Darwin,* preface by Darwin (Leipzig, 1880);

August Weismann, *Studies in the Theory of Descent,* 3 volumes, with a prefatory notice by Darwin (London: Sampson Low, 1880–1882);

Hermann Mueller, *The Fertilisation of Flowers,* with a preface by Darwin (London: Macmillan, 1883);

"A Posthumous Essay on Instinct," in *Mental Evolution in Animals,* by George John Romanes (London: Kegan Paul, 1883);

Kraus, *The Life of Erasmus Darwin . . . Being an Introduction to an Essay on His Scientific Works,* preface by Darwin (London: John Murray, 1887).

Charles Darwin's most famous work, *On the Origin of Species by Means of Natural Selection, or, the Preservation of Favoured Races in the Struggle for Life* (1859), established the scientific basis for understanding the evolution of organic life. Yet as Darwin claimed in his autobiography, the determining event of his career was his journey as naturalist aboard the H.M.S. *Beagle.* The record of his travels appeared first as the third volume of *Narrative of the Surveying Voyages of His Majesty's Ships Adventure and Beagle* (1839). Darwin's *Journal of Researches into the Geology and Natural History of the Various Countries Visited by H.M.S. Beagle* was republished separately that same year, revised in 1845, and subsequently published in more than 159 editions in English. It has also been translated into twenty-two languages.

Darwin's voyage provided him with data for three other treatises on geological phenomena, and in both its form and content his *Journal of Researches* represents one of the best examples of scientific travel writing in the nineteenth century. Yet the popularity of his travelogue derives from its literary style and from Darwin's personal responses to his experiences of exotic places and peoples. As the first of his commercially published works, it offers a fascinating view of his early attitudes and personality. Both a young, somewhat romantic adventurer and an accomplished observer and theorist, Darwin added glamour to the profession of science while insisting, like his mentors, that one's sense of wonder

at the beauty of nature could be enhanced by understanding the underlying causes and relationships of the various organisms in the landscape.

Born on 12 February 1809, Darwin was the son of a prosperous doctor, and had three older sisters, one older brother, and one younger sister. Darwin's mother died when he was eight years old, and he did not distinguish himself in much besides beetle collecting and snipe hunting until he transferred from Edinburgh University to Cambridge University in 1828. Having rejected the idea of following his father into the medical profession, Darwin agreed to take a degree and become a clergyman. This was a respectable position for a second son and required no extraordinary qualifications. At Cambridge Darwin was thrilled by John Stevens Henslow's lectures on botany, and he soon became Henslow's special student. Henslow, a practicing clergyman as well as a Cambridge don, encouraged Darwin to think of himself as a naturalist.

Under Henslow's mentoring Darwin read Alexander von Humboldt's well-known travelogue, *Personal Narrative of Travels to the Equinoctial Regions of the New Continent during the Years 1799–1804* (1814–1829) and John Herschel's *A Preliminary Discourse on the Study of Natural Philosophy* (1831). Humboldt was one of the most famous men in Europe, and his eloquent accounts of South America — and especially his appreciation of underlying meanings of the landscape — inspired Darwin with a desire to see such places for himself. From Herschel, Darwin learned to appreciate the technical methods of scientific investigation. The works of these writers together galvanized Darwin's ambitions to contribute to natural science. His initial plan, to make an expedition to the Canary Islands with Henslow, failed when Henslow's family responsibilities intervened, but Darwin hoped to find another colleague.

In 1831 Henslow arranged for Darwin to accompany the Reverend Adam Sedgwick, a distinguished professor of geology at Cambridge, on an expedition to Wales. Darwin's trip constituted a crash course on the methods of recognizing and interpreting fossils and rock formations. On his return from Wales he received a letter from Henslow informing him that Capt. Robert Fitzroy needed a gentleman naturalist to accompany him on a two-year survey of the South American coast. Henslow recommended that Darwin take the position, and several tense days ensued while Darwin sought to overcome his father's objections. Robert Darwin believed that the voyage would deter Darwin from taking vows and settling down to the life of a clergyman. The support of his uncle and Darwin's own

778 · · · *778*

1836
Sept.

¶ In conclusion. — it appears to me that nothing can be more improving to a young naturalist, than a journey in distant countries. It both sharpens and partly also allays that want and craving, which as Sir J. Herschell remarks, a man experiences, although every corporeal sense is fully satisfied. The excitement from the novelty of objects, and the chance of success stimulates him on to activity. Moreover as a number of isolated facts soon become uninteresting, the habit of comparison leads to generalization. On the other hand, as the traveller stays but a short space of time in each place, his description must generally consist of mere sketches, instead of detailed observation. Hence arises, (as I have found to my cost) a constant tendency to fill up the wide gaps of knowledge by inaccurate & superficial hypotheses. But I have too deeply enjoyed the voyage, not to recommend to any naturalist to take all chances, and to start on travels by land if possible, if otherwise on a long voyage. he may feel assured, he will meet with no difficulties or dangers (excepting in rare cases), nearly so bad as he before hand imagined. — In a moral point of view, the effect ought to be, to teach him good humoured patience, unselfishness, the habit of acting for himself, and of making the best of every thing, or content

(margin:) — Discourse on the study of Natural Philosophy, p. 3. —

Penultimate page of Darwin's Beagle *diary entries (Darwin Museum, Down House, Kent)*

142

enthusiasm for the project, however, finally persuaded Dr. Darwin, and the young man left to meet the captain of the *Beagle*.

In his autobiography Darwin explains his precarious relationship with Fitzroy. Although he admired Fitzroy's sense of duty and his generosity, Darwin also noted the bad temper of the captain. Despite some misgivings on both sides, Fitzroy agreed to take Darwin, and, for the most part, the two young men shared a small cabin amicably for what turned out to be a journey of almost five years.

The mission of the *Beagle* was similar to that of many such voyages by seafaring nations in the nineteenth century. Britain competed with France, Spain, Portugal, and the United States for trade and natural resources from undeveloped countries. Like Humboldt, who had secured financing for his expeditions by offering to report on the mineral resources of the countries he visited, Fitzroy depended on his ability to chart the South American coast, an operation necessary to advance British military and commercial interests. The crew of the *Beagle* were expected to act as representatives of the government. Darwin therefore reported on his political adventures, commenting, for example, on the personality and military activities of the Argentine dictator Gen. Juan Manuel de Rosas, the conditions of the natives in various parts of the continent, the faults of the government of Buenos Aires, and the history of the Falkland Islands. For the most part Darwin reveals a patriotic appreciation of English institutions and values. While acknowledging the immense potential of the Río de la Plata region, Darwin bemoaned the ill effects of its tyrants and revolutions: "A republic cannot succeed," he concluded, "till it contains a certain body of men imbued with principles of justice and honor."

One of the more-fortunate accidents of the voyage was Darwin's susceptibility to seasickness, a vulnerability he struggled against throughout the trip. Hating the disequilibrium of the ship, he planned as many excursions as possible across land: throughout the five-year journey he spent only about eighteen months at sea. Because of this situation he was able to travel inland to less-explored areas, and the contrasting environments of the Brazilian jungles, the plains of Patagonia, and the mountains of the Cordillera gave Darwin extensive firsthand experience of the diversity of nature. By the end of the voyage he had collected 1,529 species and preserved them in spirits. He had labeled 3,907 skins, bones, and other dried specimens. These specimens alone constituted an immense contribution to scientific knowledge about these regions.

Darwin's letters to his family and to Henslow had also become exercises in writing about his observations and speculations. Henslow acted as Darwin's liaison in receiving the fossils and other specimens that Darwin sent him, in distributing them to qualified researchers, and in reading from Darwin's letters to the Cambridge Philosophical Society. A display of Darwin's collection of megatherium fossils also appeared at the prestigious meeting of the British Association for the Advancement of Science. While Darwin was still halfway around the world, his reputation was growing within the scientific community. Letters of encouragement from his sisters and from Henslow gave Darwin added confidence in his abilities, and he worked eagerly on revising his notes as the *Beagle* slowly moved eastward from Australia to the Cape of Good Hope and then crisscrossed the Atlantic Ocean on its way home. By the time he returned to England his diary contained 770 pages of notes; his notebooks on geology covered 1,383 large pages, and those on zoology, 368 pages.

Fitzroy was so impressed with Darwin's diary entries that he requested that Darwin include them in his proposed book on the voyage. In consulting with his family, Darwin offered to write his account as the third volume. *Journal of Researches* rearranges his actual trip as if it were a journal of a trip from England to South America and around the Strait of Magellan as far as Lima and the Galápagos Islands, across the Pacific Ocean to the South Sea Islands and Australia, through the atolls of the Indian Ocean, around the Cape of Good Hope to Saint Helena, and then home. By combining information from several visits he had made to the same places and by focusing on his expeditions inland, Darwin makes himself the main character of a progressive journey. His rhetorical questions and exclamation points emphasize his feelings and thoughts about what he sees and learns; they give immediacy to his descriptions and tantalize readers with the larger implications of his observations.

Darwin's organization of his *Journal of Researches* also adds drama to the narrative of his mission as a scientific traveler. Interweaving his narrative with the observations of earlier travelers and contemporary authorities (many of whom he read after his voyage), Darwin situates himself within the collective enterprise of science. With Humboldt as his model Darwin reports his aesthetic as well as scientific appreciation of the atmosphere around Rio de Janeiro, the sublimity of the ancient forests of

Capt. Robert Fitzroy of the H. M. S. Beagle *(Greenwich Hospital and Royal Naval College, Greenwich)*

shores of the islands, Darwin describes the dramatic struggle between the ocean and the coral:

> It is impossible to behold these waves without feeling a conviction that an island, though built of the hardest rock, let it be porphyry, granite, or quartz, would ultimately yield and be demolished by such irresistible forces. Yet these low, insignificant coral islets stand and are victorious: for here another power, as antagonistic to the former, takes part in the contest. The organic forces separate the atoms of carbonate of lime one by one from the foaming breakers, and unite them into a symmetrical structure. Let the hurricane tear up its thousand huge fragments; yet what will this tell against the accumulated labour of myriads of architects at work night and day, month after month. Thus do we see the soft and gelatinous body of a polypus, through the agency of vital laws, conquering the great mechanical power of the waves of an ocean, which neither art of man, nor the inanimate works of nature could successfully resist.

Darwin's language invites sympathy and interest. Moving from a visual first impression of a scene to the record of its structural composition, the narrative alternately emphasizes the personal sensations of a romantic artist and the impersonal conceptions of a systematic thinker, tracing facts to laws that go beyond any individual's experience of nature.

In addition to his concern with natural phenomena, Darwin also reported on the social relations of the peoples he encountered. His subjective comments on the beauty of South American women or on the wildness of the natives of Tierra del Fuego conform to the conventions of travel writing in the period, and like other travelers, Darwin relates the manners and morals of a people to their economic conditions. Yet he goes further than many writers in his attempts to account for differences in various peoples, just as he ventures to account for the rock formations and distribution of species in different regions. The Patagonians are compared to noble Romans in their resistance to the Spanish; the slaves in Brazil draw Darwin's pity; and the Fuegians evoke his profoundest speculations on the nature of humankind. If the congeniality of the Tahitians and the degradation of the Maori lead Darwin to formulate a hierarchy of civilization, he also recognizes the complexity of natural and historical forces in shaping any society. After the voyage Darwin reflected on his experiences and agreed with Harriet Martineau and others about the culturally conditioned nature of moral values. In his later books, especially *The Descent of Man, and Selection in Relation to Sex* (1871), Darwin drew on his observations of the Fuegians and other peoples to discuss

Tierra del Fuego, and the delightful prospects of Tahiti. The result synthesizes his experiences and his findings so that the work appeals to both general and scientific audiences. Although Darwin complains of difficulty in describing the abundant varieties of plant and animal species and the many landscapes they inhabit, Humboldt's example provides a clear direction for his narrative. Repeatedly Darwin begins with the sensation of a "chaos" of rocks or scenery. Then he unravels the complex history of interactions among contending forces and species that have shaped the present structures of organisms. The pictorial quality of his descriptions and the conversational tone of his writing allow readers to follow him through otherwise complex discussions of natural phenomena.

One of his finest moments in the *Journal of Researches* comes in his description of the formation of the lagoon islands in the Indian Ocean. Darwin's theory of coral reefs, outlined here and published later as part of a larger scientific treatise, was his first attempt to solve a problem by using deductive methods. More important for his nonspecialist audience is the manner in which Darwin allows readers to see and feel the grandeur of these organisms. Beginning with his personal response to the outer

the stages of man's development from conditions of semihumanity to the observable conditions of "savage" and civilized societies.

On the question of slavery Darwin took a more radical stand than many of his contemporaries. Darwin's autobiography recounts his arguments with Fitzroy, who believed that slaves benefited from being under the protection of their masters. Back in England, Darwin was also dismayed at the indifference to the issue of slavery adopted by such distinguished scientists as Charles Lyell. In the second edition of his travelogue, which he dedicated to Lyell, Darwin added a section condemning Brazil for its treatment of slaves and pointing out the hypocrisy of those English and Americans who claim liberty for themselves while condoning the enslavement of others.

Published eighteen months after his return, the *Journal of Researches* remained Darwin's favorite among his books. Despite its scientific orientation, the book was well received by the general public. In his autobiography Darwin notes that it had been translated into French and German, and its second edition had enjoyed sales of ten thousand copies in England alone. Reviews of the first edition of Darwin's book suggest several reasons for its popularity among contemporaries. First, both Fitzroy's and Darwin's narratives demonstrate the humanitarian aims and peaceful consequences of English navigation around the world. Fitzroy's rescue and education of three Fuegians and the consequences of their return to their homeland as well as Darwin's remarks on the wide difference between savage and civilized man gave a moral, heroic tone to their journey. Second, Darwin's "bold generalizations" about the geology of the South American continent and the zoology of extinct forms impressed reviewers. According to the *Quarterly Review,* there were also "ample materials for deep thinking: we have vivid descriptions that fill the mind's eye with brighter pictures than painter can present, and the charm arising from the freshness of heart which is thrown over these virgin pages of a strong intellectual man and an acute and deep observer." While reviewers emphasized Darwin's contributions to science, they also appreciated his comments on the human inhabitants of his ports of call, especially his descriptions of the South American aborigines.

Darwin's scientific colleagues also appreciated *Journal of Researches.* Humboldt flattered Darwin with praise, and younger naturalists were influenced by its approach. Reading proofs of Darwin's manuscript while engaged on his own expeditions,

Joseph Dalton Hooker became one of Darwin's most important admirers and later supported him in the battles over his theory of evolution by natural selection. As early as 1854 Hooker dedicated his *Himalayan Journals* to Darwin. Alfred Russel Wallace, a contributor to the theory of natural selection, also carried a copy of *Journal of Researches* with him on his first scientific expedition in 1848. Perhaps the most telling measure of Darwin's influence on subsequent scientific travelers is the fact that many animals and plants have been given scientific names in his honor.

With the exception of a short trip to Scotland, Darwin never traveled beyond England again. In the same year that he published *Journal of Researches* he married Emma Wedgwood, his first cousin, with whom he had seven children who survived into adulthood. Darwin's chronic ill health, which required him to leave the stressful life of London, did not keep him from continuing his research and writing. From his home in Down, Darwin corresponded with scientists around the world and enjoyed visits from the leading men of science of his day.

Like Darwin's early reviewers, most critics of the *Journal of Researches* have seen its importance to the history of ideas and scientific development. His descriptions of nature and of the people and societies he encountered have also interested cultural and literary historians. Like other travelogues of the period, Darwin's narrative provides important illustrations of the effects of empire on the imagination of the traveler. In addition, it has epitomized the transition from a romantic view of nature to a scientific and Victorian conception of the complexity of organic development.

Letters:

For Private Distribution: The Following Pages Contain Extracts from Letters Addressed to Professor Henslow . . . They Are Printed for Distribution among the Members of the Cambridge Philosophical Society in Consequence of the Interest Which Has Been Excited by Some of the Geological Notices They Contain (Cambridge: Privately printed, 1835); republished as *Extracts from Letters Addressed to Professor Henslow, Read at a Meeting of the Cambridge Philosophical Society 16 November, 1835* ([Cambridge: Cambridge Philosophical Society], 1960);

More Letters of Charles Darwin: A Record of His Work in a Series of Hitherto Unpublished Letters, edited by Francis Darwin and A. C. Seward (London: John Murray, 1903; New York: Appleton, 1903);

The Correspondence of Charles Darwin, 8 volumes, edited by Frederick Burkhardt and Sydney Smith (Cambridge: Cambridge University Press, 1985–1993).

Biographies:

John Bowlby, *Charles Darwin: A New Life* (New York: Norton, 1990; London: Hutchinson, 1990);

Adrian Desmond and James Moore, *Darwin* (London: M. Joseph, 1991; New York: Viking Penguin, 1991).

References:

Gillian Beer, "Four Bodies on the *Beagle:* Touch, Sight, and Writing in a Darwin Letter," in *Textuality and Sexuality: Reading Theories and Practices,* edited by Judith Still and Michael Worton (Manchester & New York: Manchester University Press, 1993), pp. 116–132;

Stanley Edgar Hyman, *The Tangled Bank: Darwin, Marx, Frazer and Freud as Imaginative Writers* (New York: Atheneum, 1962);

James Krasner, "'A Chaos of Delight': Perception and Illusion in Darwin's Scientific Writing," *Representations,* 31 (Fall 1990): 118–141;

James Paradis, "Darwin and Landscape," in *Victorian Science and Victorian Values: Literary Perspectives,* edited by Paradis and Thomas Postlewait (New Brunswick: Rutgers University Press, 1985), pp. 85–110;

John Tallmadge, "From Chronical to Quest: The Shaping of Darwin's 'Voyage of the Beagle,'" *Victorian Studies,* 23 (Spring 1980): 325–345.

Papers:

Darwin's notebooks, letters, and other memorabilia are located at Down House in Kent, under the authority of the Royal College of Surgeons, and at University Library, Cambridge.

Charles Dickens
(7 February 1812 – 9 June 1870)

F. S. Schwarzbach
Kent State University

See also the Dickens entries in *DLB 21: Victorian Novelists Before 1885; DLB 55: Victorian Prose Writers Before 1867; DLB 70: British Mystery Writers, 1860–1919;* and *DLB 159: British Short Fiction Writers, 1800–1880.*

BOOKS: *Sketches by Boz, Illustrative of Every-Day Life and Every-Day People* (first series, 2 volumes, London: Macrone, 1836; second series, London: Macrone, 1837; Philadelphia: Carey, Lea & Blanchard, 1837);

The Village Coquettes: A Comic Opera in Two Acts, as Boz (London: Bentley, 1836);

The Posthumous Papers of the Pickwick Club, 20 monthly parts (London: Chapman & Hall, 1836–1837; Philadelphia: Carey, Lea & Blanchard, 1836–1837);

The Strange Gentleman: A Comic Burletta, in Two Acts, as Boz (London: Chapman & Hall, 1837);

The Life and Adventures of Nicholas Nickleby, 20 monthly parts (London: Chapman & Hall, 1838–1839; Philadelphia: Lea & Blanchard, 1839);

Sketches of Young Gentlemen, Dedicated to the Young Ladies (London: Chapman & Hall, 1838);

Memoirs of Joseph Grimaldi, Edited by "Boz," 2 volumes (London: Bentley, 1838; Philadelphia: Carey, Lea & Blanchard, 1838);

Oliver Twist; or, The Parish Boy's Progress (3 volumes, London: Bentley, 1838; 1 volume, New York: Colyer, 1839);

Sketches of Young Couples: With an Urgent Remonstrance to the Gentlemen of England (Being Bachelors or Widowers), on the Present Alarming Crisis (London: Chapman & Hall, 1840);

Master Humphrey's Clock, 88 weekly parts (London: Chapman & Hall, 1840–1841) – includes *The Old Curiosity Shop,* republished as *The Old Curiosity Shop* (2 volumes, London: Chapman & Hall, 1841; 1 volume, Philadelphia: Lea & Blanchard, 1841), and *Barnaby Rudge: A Tale of the Riots of 'Eighty* (London: Chapman &

Charles Dickens, photographed by Matthew Brady in New York, 1867 (National Archives, Brady Collection, No. B-2216)

Hall, 1841; Philadelphia: Lea & Blanchard, 1841);

American Notes for General Circulation (2 volumes, London: Chapman & Hall, 1842; 1 volume, New York: Harper, 1842);

The Life and Adventures of Martin Chuzzlewit (20 monthly parts, London: Chapman & Hall, 1842–1844; 1 volume, New York: Harper, 1844);

A Christmas Carol, in Prose: Being a Ghost Story of Christmas (London: Chapman & Hall, 1843; Philadelphia: Carey & Hart, 1844);

The Chimes: A Goblin Story of Some Bells That Rang an Old Year Out and a New Year In (London: Chapman & Hall, 1845 [i.e., 1844]; Philadelphia: Lea & Blanchard, 1845);

The Cricket on the Hearth: A Fairy Tale of Home (London: Bradley & Evans, 1846 [i.e., 1845]; New York: Harper, 1846);

Pictures from Italy (London: Bradbury & Evans, 1846); republished as *Travelling Letters Written on the Road* (New York: Wiley & Putnam, 1846);

The Battle of Life: A Love Story (London: Bradbury & Evans, 1846; New York: Harper, 1847);

Dealings with the Firm of Dombey and Son, Wholesale, Retail, and for Exportation (20 monthly parts, London: Bradbury & Evans, 1846–1848; American publication in 19 monthly parts, parts 1–17, New York: Wiley & Putnam, 1846–1847; parts 18–19, New York: Wiley, 1848);

The Haunted Man and the Ghost's Bargain: A Fancy for Christmas-time (London: Bradbury & Evans, 1848; New York: Harper, 1849);

The Personal History of David Copperfield (20 monthly parts, London: Bradbury & Evans, 1849–1850; Philadelphia: Lea & Blanchard, 1851);

A Child's History of England (3 volumes, London: Bradbury & Evans, 1852–1854; 2 volumes, New York: Harper, 1853–1854);

Bleak House (20 monthly parts, London: Bradbury & Evans, 1852–1853; 1 volume, New York: Harper, 1853);

Hard Times: For These Times (London: Bradbury & Evans, 1854; New York: McElrath, 1854);

Little Dorrit (20 monthly parts, London: Bradbury & Evans, 1855–1857; 1 volume, Philadelphia: Peterson, 1857);

The Wreck of the Golden Mary, by Dickens and Wilkie Collins (London: Bradbury & Evans, 1856);

The Two Apprentices: With a History of Their Lazy Tour, by Dickens and Collins (Philadelphia: Peterson, 1857);

A Tale of Two Cities (London: Chapman & Hall, 1859; Philadelphia: Peterson, 1859);

Great Expectations (3 volumes, London: Chapman & Hall, 1861; 1 volume, Philadelphia: Peterson, 1861);

The Uncommercial Traveller (London: Chapman & Hall, 1861; New York: Sheldon, 1865);

Our Mutual Friend (20 monthly parts, London: Chapman & Hall, 1864–1865; 1 volume, New York: Harper, 1865);

Reprinted Pieces (New York: Hearst's International Library, 1867);

The Uncommercial Traveller and Additional Christmas Stories, Diamond Edition (Boston: Ticknor & Fields, 1867);

Hunted Down: A Story, with Some Account of Thomas Griffiths Wainwright, The Poisoner (London: Hotten, 1870; Philadelphia: Peterson, 1870);

The Mystery of Edwin Drood (6 monthly parts, London: Chapman & Hall, 1870; 1 volume, Boston: Fields, Osgood, 1870);

A Child's Dream of a Star (Boston: Fields, Osgood, 1871);

Is She His Wife?, or, Something Singular: A Comic Burletta in One Act (Boston: Osgood, 1877);

The Lazy Tour of Two Idle Apprentices. No Thoroughfare. The Perils of Certain English Prisoners, by Dickens, Collins, and Charles Fechter (London: Chapman & Hall, 1934);

The Life of Our Lord (New York: Simon & Schuster, 1934);

The Speeches of Charles Dickens, edited by K. J. Fielding (Oxford: Clarendon Press, 1960);

The Frozen Deep, by Dickens and Collins, in *Under the Management of Mr. Charles Dickens,* edited by Robert Louis Brannan (Ithaca, N.Y.: Cornell University Press, 1966);

Uncollected Writings from Household Words, 1850–1859, 2 volumes, edited by Harry Stone (Bloomington: Indiana University Press, 1968; London: John Lane, 1969);

Charles Dickens: The Public Readings, edited by Philip Collins (Oxford: Clarendon Press, 1975);

No Thoroughfare: A Drama in Five Acts, by Dickens, Wilkie Collins, and Fechter (New York: DeWitt, n.d.).

Editions and Collections: *Cheap Edition of the Works of Mr. Charles Dickens* (12 volumes, London: Chapman & Hall, 1847–1852; 3 volumes, London: Bradbury & Evans, 1858);

Christmas Books (London: Chapman & Hall, 1852);

Christmas Stories from the Household Words (London: Chapman & Hall, 1859);

The Charles Dickens Edition, 21 volumes (London: Chapman & Hall, 1867–1875);

The Nine Christmas Numbers of All the Year Round (London: Office of *All the Year Round* and Chapman & Hall, 1868);

The Plays and Poems of Charles Dickens, 2 volumes, edited by Richard Herne Shepherd (London: W. H. Allen, 1882);

The Works of Charles Dickens, 21 volumes (London: Macmillan, 1892–1925);

The Works of Charles Dickens, Gadshill Edition, 36 volumes (London: Chapman & Hall / New York: Scribners, 1897–1908);

The Nonesuch Edition, 23 volumes, edited by Arthur Waugh and others (London: Nonesuch Press, 1937–1938);

The New Oxford Illustrated Dickens, 21 volumes (Oxford: Oxford University Press, 1947–1958);
The Clarendon Dickens, 7 volumes published, edited by Kathleen Tillotson and others (Oxford: Clarendon Press, 1966–).

In October 1844 Charles Dickens was in Genoa working on his second Christmas book, *The Chimes: A Goblin Story of Some Bells That Rang an Old Year Out and a New Year In* (1845). Hoping that a long foreign residence would refresh his powers of description and invention, he had come to Italy that July, but after only three months he was again ready for a change. He hatched a plan to dash off to England late in the fall after completing *The Chimes,* and on 6 November that is exactly what he did.

Dickens began the journey in a small, crowded coach that could manage only four miles an hour on the muddy roads to Piacenza, and he continued in various conveyances to Parma, Modena, Bologna, Ferrara, Venice, Verona, Mantua, Milan, and thence to Switzerland. From Strasbourg he went on to Paris, enduring a fifty-hour marathon ride through seas of mud. After a night in Paris he took another coach to Boulogne, then made a channel crossing, and finally went on to London by train. He spent eight days there and then began the same journey in reverse, contending at times with even worse weather. He varied the final stage by crossing to Genoa by sea from Marseilles, in weather so vile that Dickens – normally a good sailor – was ill for virtually the whole journey. He wrote a friend that he was so sick "that I should have made my will if I had had anything to leave, but I had only the basin and I couldn't leave that for the moment."

This account of one of Dickens's many long journeys demonstrates that he was nothing if not a heroic traveler, and surely one must be that before one can be a great travel writer. Obviously Dickens is known primarily for his fourteen novels, but he had many other careers: he was, variously, parliamentary reporter, journalist, editor, actor, public reader of his own fiction, and travel writer. And in many ways the gifts that served him well as a novelist served him equally well in his travel pieces. He had an abundant talent for description, a knack for viewing the familiar and the unfamiliar alike with an innocent eye, and a matchless gift for discerning human interest, pathos, and humor in ordinary experience. Most of all, he could transform all that he experienced into strikingly original language – as in that quotation from the letter recounting his queasi-

ness during his journey, a passage that could never be mistaken as having been written by anyone else.

Dickens traveled as much as he did in part because of his chronic restlessness, but just as he was driven periodically to roam he was driven also to seek permanence in his life. Thus, the rhythm of his life was one of settled periods broken by frenetic journeying. Even when his need to experience something new did not drive him abroad, it led him to such expedients as nightlong, thirty-mile walks, excursions to criminal haunts in London, and even (according to his youngest son) walking the city streets in disguise.

It is tempting to trace these double strands of Dickens's adult life to his childhood. His father, John Dickens, was an ambitious clerk in the Navy Pay Office; Dickens's mother was the daughter of a senior clerk in the same department. The Dickenses therefore moved often as John Dickens moved up the civil service career ladder – and then even more often as he declined into bankruptcy and imprisonment for debt in London's Marshalsea Prison. At about the same time, young Charles, at the age of ten and with his schooling apparently at an end forever, was sent to work at Warren's Blacking Factory, where he remained for several months. This time as a working-class drudge was one of the great formative, and shamefully secret, experiences of his life. It was as if his parents had cast him from a secure, middle-class life into poverty, isolation, and degradation. Dickens overcame this sordid (as he saw it) past to become one of the quintessential self-made men of Victorian England. But he seemed always racked by self-doubt probably rooted in his childhood humiliation, and perhaps as a consequence he drove himself to climb ever higher peaks of achievement.

The outlines of Dickens's early career are impressive: he became a law clerk in 1827; by 1829 he was a freelance legal reporter; and by 1831 he was a parliamentary reporter with a reputation as the finest shorthand writer of them all. Having flirted with a life on the stage, by 1833 he was writing short stories and sketches of London life. Those sketches, appearing in popular journals such as *Bell's Weekly Magazine* and *The Morning Chronicle,* were the sources of his first literary reputation. He was sought out by Joseph Macrone, who collected these pieces in *Sketches by Boz* early in 1836 and published them with illustrations by the already-famous George Cruikshank.

Not long afterward Dickens was approached by two booksellers who were trying to become publishers; they asked him to write the copy for what

AMERICAN NOTES

FOR

GENERAL CIRCULATION.

———◆———

BY CHARLES DICKENS.

IN TWO VOLUMES.

VOL. I.

LONDON:
CHAPMAN AND HALL, 186, STRAND.
MDCCCXLII.

Title page for the book in which Dickens described his first overseas travel experiences (courtesy of the Lilly Library, Indiana University)

Dickens recalled as a "monthly something" that would accompany comic sporting plates drawn by another well-known artist, Robert Seymour. This was the genesis of *The Posthumous Papers of the Pickwick Club* (1836–1837), and the rest of Dickens's success story was assured. Within a year he was the most famous writer in England, his literary career well and truly launched.

These early sketches are closely related both to early Victorian travel writing and to the fiction that Dickens began to write soon afterward. The verbal sketch was in the nineteenth century an extremely popular genre, an attempt to fix in words a fleeting image of complex and ever-changing urban life. Victorian urban sketches often borrow the common devices of travel literature – those of exploring a terra incognita, encountering strange "natives,"

and experiencing personal danger – in treating the urban environment as if it were radically unfamiliar to the reader. One might term this the estrangement of the familiar, but the sketch also enacts the familiarization of estrangement by celebrating the dynamic, ineluctable metamorphoses of place and character that so distinguish modern urban life, where the only constant is change. Dickens's early sketches perfectly capture this double sense of permanent impermanence, whether their subject is shop fronts, boots in an old clothes stall, or London cabs.

The same heightened attention to ordinary London life is very much a part of *The Posthumous Papers of the Pickwick Club*. The early parts of the novel feature accounts of journeys to provincial cities and rural locations near London. Indeed, the early chapters consciously parody accounts of "scientific" journeys of exploration, but the narrative becomes that of a novel in its sixth number with the appearance of Sam Weller, an irreverent Cockney who soon becomes Mr. Pickwick's manservant, inseparable companion, and urban guide. As Walter Bagehot later observed, Dickens described London "like a special correspondent for posterity," and *Pickwick* is filled with descriptive details about London street life, neighborhoods, and characters.

Perhaps this is not travel writing in the ordinary sense of the term, but many of Dickens's first readers surely found in his writing about the city the same excitement that they might encounter in reading about the wilds of America or the jungles of Africa. Their response was partly delight in this appropriation of new territory for fiction, as his focus moved from upper-class subjects to the world of the prosperous, urban middle classes, but it was more than that as well. The rapid pace of urbanization, the physical growth of the city, the tremendous inequalities of income between the middle and the lower classes, and the dynamic social change typical of modern urban life together were making many parts of London seem "foreign" even to its own inhabitants. To quote an early reviewer, "Life in London, as revealed in the pages of Boz, opens a new world to the thousands bred and born in the same city," a world no less strange to them because they had lived and worked in it all their lives.

If Dickens wrote about London as if it were a foreign place, what was most foreign about it was the life of its poorer inhabitants. This was the focus of his second novel, *Oliver Twist; or, The Parish Boy's Progress* (1838). Here one sees foul, overcrowded London streets; the thieves' den where Fagin holds court; the home life of the burglar Bill Sikes and his companion, Nancy, a common prostitute; and much more of similar nature. In part Dickens was capitalizing on an 1830s craze for "Newgate" crime novels – those so named for London's most notorious criminal prison – but his own interest in the lives of the ordinary poor remained throughout his fiction. Here too one can see the intersection and cross-fertilization of the genres of travel writing, the urban sketch, and the emerging middle-class novel: in Dickens's fiction it is often difficult (and probably a pointless exercise) to try to discern where one genre ends and another begins.

Dickens also wrote several more typical travel books. The first was *American Notes for General Circulation* (1842), the result of his visit to the new republic from January to June 1842. Late in 1841 Dickens had planned a holiday from novel writing, both to prevent himself from burning out at having written too much too rapidly in the two or three years before and also to find new material for future works. Why he settled on America as his destination – almost a foolhardy choice given the likelihood of midwinter storms on the north Atlantic Ocean – is not clear, but once he had made up his mind to go, nothing could stop him. The trip began with a gale-tossed crossing on the new Cunard steamer, *Brittania*. Once landed in Boston, Dickens and his wife (the children had been left in England) traveled by rail, barge, boat, and carriage to Hartford, New York City, Washington, D.C., Richmond, and Baltimore. From there they turned west through Ohio and Illinois to Saint Louis, and then back east again via Canada before returning from New York to London.

Dickens's letters from America constitute his freshest, most immediate response to his experiences. As a radical in politics, he had been prepared to see America as a political utopia removed from the ancient and corrupt institutions of Europe. Yet what his correspondence narrates is a tale of progressive disillusionment captured in a remark in a letter of 22 March 1842 to William Macready: "This is not the Republic of my imagination."

What went wrong? Though critics and biographers have advanced many theories, several explanations might be made. First, Dickens found himself profoundly irritated by some common American habits, in particular that of spitting, but also by the national passion for personal journalism that subjected him (and worse, his wife) to front-page scrutiny. Second, the press turned from lionizing him to criticizing him as his stay wore on, perhaps because of his inopportunely timed complaints about the failure of America to recognize international copyright laws. Third, he began to see that his New World utopia had significant political and social problems – notably in slavery, but also in its high level of political violence – problems fully comparable to those of the Old World. And fourth, since every outward journey becomes an inward journey of self-discovery as well, Dickens learned much about himself, and what he learned in part was that his Englishness cut more deeply than he had yet been aware.

Within only four months of his return he published *American Notes for General Circulation*, which uses some of the material he had put into his letters. Dickens had written some of them with the intention of doing this, but his reflections also represent an attempt to craft a coherent overview and interpretation of American society. One should remember that America then was to Europe what Russia was to the West in the 1920s – a vision of the future of mankind. In his essay "English Writers on America" in *The Sketch Book of Geoffrey Crayon, Gent.* (1824), Washington Irving had reminded visitors that in America "one of the greatest political experiments in the history of the world is now performing" – nothing less than a trial of democracy itself. As one might have predicted, the opinions of English travelers divided on America as they divided on their adherence to democratic ideals. Thus, the young republic and the young author should have had much to share in their politics, and Americans' hopes were high as they awaited his book.

While *American Notes* does include sometimes laudatory descriptions of well-known American institutions (such as the Lowell cotton mills, the eastern penitentiary, and a Shaker community) and well-known places (such as the streets of New York City, a prairie, the Mississippi River, and Niagara Falls), its tremendous disappointment with American society is most evident throughout. Even the title, with its punning reference to forged banknotes, betrays Dickens's negative judgment. Only Boston, with its more settled community and more "English" values, seemed at all congenial to him.

Apparently in condemning America Dickens was aligning himself with the Tory visitors who had so irked Irving. The American press, much of which had begun to vilify Dickens even before his visit had ended, almost unanimously attacked *American Notes* as vindictive, superficial, petty, and full of elementary errors. Dickens must have been surprised, however, that the British reviews largely agreed. Perhaps partly to answer his critics, Dickens returned to American material in his next novel, *The Life and Adventures of Martin Chuzzlewit* (1842–1844).

In this novel the third textual reworking of the raw stuff from his American experience is noticeably more satiric: every American vice and crude habit is amplified and exaggerated to the extent that at times it seems as if the entire nation were awash in a sea of tobacco-stained spittle. At the same time, the satire reflects Dickens's realization that he had learned in America not only that the young republic's utopian vision of itself far outstripped reality but also that the human nature beneath that vision was radically flawed.

To be sure, the novel returns Dickens's fictional English travelers to England with a flurry of nationalist nostalgia that recalls his own happy return some months before. But the later sections of *Martin Chuzzlewit* reveal that the worst features of American society — its greed, its urge to level all men to the lowest common denominator, its disrespect for law when it conflicts with self-interest, and its relentless self-puffery — all have slightly more polished but equally horrific equivalents in the England of Mr. Pecksniff, Jonas Chuzzlewit, and Montague Tigg. As a result of his American travels, Dickens was demonstrably sadder but infinitely wiser about human nature and its slim prospects for regeneration, in the United States or in England. What Dickens learned about human nature and society in the course of his American travels and writing about them was crucial to what many critics have seen as the "dark," sharply critical social vision of his mature novels.

Dickens's fictional America is almost all frontier: ignoring the cities of the East (where in fact he had spent most of his time), *Martin Chuzzlewit* focuses on what Dickens saw as the savage, pestilential Mississippi valley. It is as if he were finding in the primordial and threatening landscape of the West, untouched by agricultural improvement, a confirmation that human nature unimproved by civilization is not noble but bestial. There could hardly be a greater contrast to this than the Italian landscape that emerges from his next travel book, *Pictures from Italy* (1846), written in the year after he completed *Martin Chuzzlewit*.

In the first pages of the volume (based largely on letters written in Italy) Dickens makes clear that this work will not cover the same ground as *American Notes,* as he will offer no studies of institutions, no remarks on government, no broad generaliza-

tions about men and manners. Rather, he will focus on his own impressions and imaginative responses to what he saw and experienced as a private traveler. The volume was charmingly illustrated by Samuel Palmer, whose drawings have a similarly impressionistic quality. Dickens's book about Italy was to be much the sort of conventional travelogue that many of his readers had expected him to write about America.

There are, as one would expect, many rather fanciful passages that readers would recognize as Dickensian, full of such "signature" stylistic tricks as repetition, onomatopoeia, personification, imaginative flights of fancy, and caricatures of various persons encountered along the way. There is also much detail about deplorable roads, rickety coaches, ramshackle steamers, icy mountain passes, and other hazards of travel.

Yet certain deeper themes recur: the contrasts of ancient splendor and contemporary squalor; the mostly pernicious effects of Roman Catholicism; the nearly universal physical decay and the correspondingly nearly universal moral decay; official corruption and inefficiency at every level; and economic stagnation. Though Dickens certainly felt affectionate regard for the Italian people, as his sojourn in Italy passed and as he traveled more widely Italy came to represent one side of a coin, the other side of which was America. If America had demonstrated the unfortunate consequences of trying to reinvent a society without reference to the past, Italy might serve as a counterexample of a degenerating human nature and social fabric in the extreme old age of a once-great culture.

Walking through the old, half-deserted towns of northern Italy, Dickens describes falling into a doze when it seems

> That there is nothing, anywhere, to be done, or needing to be done. That there is no more human progress, motion, effort, or advancement, of any kind beyond this. That the whole scheme stopped here centuries ago, and laid down to rest until the Day of Judgment.

America had ignored the past and "progressed" to a state of savage dystopia; Italy had so far decayed from a glorious past that it had "regressed" to torpid but no less horrifying savagery. *Pictures from Italy* hence implicitly foreshadows the uncertainties about contemporary society that Dickens's later novels, beginning with *Dealings with the Firm of Dombey and Son, Wholesale, Retail, and for Exportation* (1846–1848), feature so prominently.

Dombey and Son also features much travel, especially by rail. Though England's rail network was largely in place by the late 1830s, Dickens's earlier novels are set firmly in the age of coaches: young Martin Chuzzlewit travels by rail in America, but by stage in England. As if to announce its emphasis on the present moment, *Dombey and Son* focuses on the dramatic impact that the London railways have had and provides a marvelously evocative account of Mr. Dombey's first journey by rail. The novel also uses Dickens's own extensive experience with Continental travel, for example, in setting a crucial scene between James Carker and Edith Dombey at a French inn. (Dickens also displays his trick of too literally translating colloquial speech in a foreign tongue in order to simulate its idiomatic flavor – as in, "There was the supper! It should be eaten on the instant.")

Indeed, accounts of travel figure in many of Dickens's novels from this time onward. In *Little Dorrit* (1855–1857), for example, foreign locations appear prominently throughout the narrative. The novel opens with a portrait of Marseilles on a hot August day and then introduces two sets of characters, foreign and English, whose fates will intertwine, although they do not yet know it. The protagonist, Arthur Clennam, has just completed a long residence in China, and the reader sees London very much through his eyes upon Clennam's return. Later, after Mr. Dorrit acquires a fortune after years of imprisonment for debt, he decamps for Italy; the fantastic unreality of their settling place in Venice, which Dickens had played upon in *Pictures from Italy,* becomes a powerful metaphor for the unreality of the new lives of the Dorrits. Thus, the foreign locale functions as far more than an exotic backdrop: the Dorrits' Italian journey becomes a symbolic reinforcement of the psychological conditions of those embarked on it.

During the same years he was writing that novel Dickens collaborated on two interesting projects with his young protégé, Wilkie Collins: a play, *The Frozen Deep,* and a comic narrative titled "The Lazy Tour of Two Idle Apprentices" for the magazine that Dickens was editing, *Household Words.* The play was written in 1856 by Collins, but it probably developed from one of Dickens's ideas and was heavily revised by him. He then produced and starred in an amateur production of it in January 1857, followed by a more professional one a few months later as a benefit for the family of his recently deceased friend, Douglas Jerrold. Loosely inspired by Sir John Franklin's failed 1845 expedition to discover a northwest passage around North

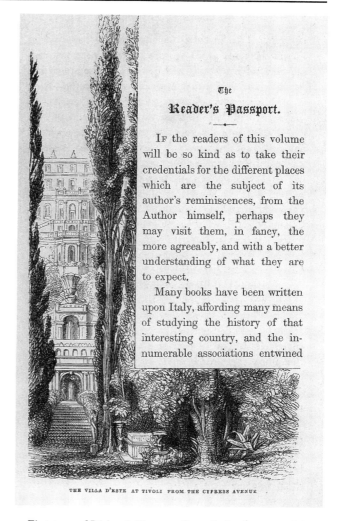

First page of Dickens's Pictures from Italy *(courtesy of the Lilly Library, Indiana University)*

America, the main interest of the *The Frozen Deep* turns on the apparent murder by Wardour of his younger rival in love. In the climax a dying Wardour staggers on stage as he reveals that he has saved his wounded colleague, but at the cost of his own life. Heightening the psychological drama of Wardour's temptation and salvation, the alien Arctic setting is purposefully symbolic of Wardour's heart.

"The Lazy Tour" recounts a trip to northern England by Dickens and Collins in August 1857 and was published in five installments in October as *The Two Apprentices: With a History of Their Lazy Tour.* Using the pseudonyms Frances Goodchild and Thomas Idle (after the characters who appear as the apprentices in William Hogarth's *Industry and Idleness),* Dickens and Collins wander from place to place, take in some traditional sights and events (the

Lake District and races at Doncaster), and make much of the differences in their characters. Dickens-Goodchild goes about everything – even leisure – with furious energy, while Collins-Idle wants only to lie back and do nothing at all. Early in the journey, for example, Dickens drags his companion up the side of a mountain, where they are dangerously lost all night in rain and fog; Collins sprains his ankle, and almost like Wardour, Dickens half carries his young friend to safety.

Dickens began editing *Household Words* in 1849, and as he traveled he wrote occasional travel essays for it, works later collected in *Reprinted Pieces* (1867). Dickens left the magazine in 1859 after a dispute with the publishers and immediately founded a successor, *All the Year Round*. The new magazine began with a serialization of *A Tale of Two Cities* (1859), in which Dickens's French travels again helped him set the scene for much of the action, although the interest of the novel is primarily historical.

More significant is the series of essays that appeared under the general title "The Uncommercial Traveller" in *All the Year Round* for about a year beginning in January 1860. A short preface to the series announced that the author "travel[s] for the great house of Human Interest Brothers, and ha[s] a rather large connection in the fancy goods way." In other words, this was to be a series in which Dickens would write about "many little things, and some great things, which, because they interest me, I think may interest others." The first seventeen essays were quickly collected as a book, published under that same general title as the series, in 1861.

What interested Dickens first was a recent shipwreck and then a series of visits to various institutions and neighborhoods in London's East End. The series changes in tone with the seventh essay, which appeared in April and recounted highlights of a Continental journey. Starting out on the coach to Dover, Dickens encounters a small boy who announces, as they pass a certain grand house, that his father has told the boy that if he works hard he may one day own it. The house is Gad's Hill Place, purchased by Dickens in 1856 and recently renovated as his principal residence, and the boy's story is a memory from his own childhood. *The Uncommercial Traveller* essays after this seem to meander both geographically and chronologically backward to Dickens's boyhood in Chatham and Rochester, and they unleash a flood of memories along the way. The principal theme concerns change – how Chatham has changed, how the narrator has changed, and how both are somewhat the worse for wear.

Here, in fact, appears a central concern of Dickens's next novel, *Great Expectations* (1861), which apparently developed from an idea for an *Uncommercial Traveller* essay that captured Dickens's imagination and became a full-scale narrative.

Dickens revived the persona of "The Uncommercial Traveller" for two further series in 1863 and in 1868, the latter collected posthumously. Though the settings are both domestic and foreign, the foreign are more prominent. "The Calais Night-Mail" and "Some Recollections of Mortality" draw on his many journeys and residences in France. The 1868 series is notable for an essay, "Aboard Ship," that deals with Dickens's voyage home from his second visit to America from November 1867 to April 1868, a visit about which he wrote virtually nothing else for publication. The finest of the essays in this 1868 series, "A Small Star in the East," recounts a visit to the East End in the winter of 1868 and the stoic resignation of the poor to the horrible pains they suffer during their lack of employment in the cold weather. The piece ends with a visit to the new East London Children's Hospital and tells of the wonderful work of the devoted physician and nurse who, as husband and wife, manage it.

Dickens's last novel, *The Mystery of Edwin Drood* (1870), was to appear in twelve monthly parts, but only half was finished at his death in June that same year. It draws in several ways upon Dickens's travel experiences and travel writings. The book is set mainly in the quiet ecclesiastical town of Cloisterham, a thinly disguised version of Rochester that Dickens describes almost as if he were writing a travel guide, but other locations are conjured up almost in passing. The narrative opens in an opium den in London's East End, in the midst of cathedral organist John Jasper's drug-induced dream of a Cloisterham invaded by Turkish warriors. The novel constantly evokes an England come into its world empire: young Edwin Drood is about to be posted to an engineering project in Egypt; the Landless twins, Neville and Helena, have just returned from Ceylon; Jasper's opium is the fruit of forced trade with China; and Tartar, who appears to be destined for marriage to the heroine, Rosa Bud, is a retired but still young naval officer.

With the second half of the novel missing, one can only speculate about how Dickens would have solved the mystery. One of the more daring speculations is that of Edmund Wilson, who argued that Jasper was a devotee of the Indian sect of Thugs, who worshiped their deity by assassinating innocent victims – thus, Jasper has murdered his own

John Jasper in a London opium den, a scene from Dickens's last novel, as sketched by Charles Collins, Dickens's son-in-law (Tage la Cour and Harald Mogensen, The Murder Book, *1971)*

nephew, Drood. But Dickens left few clues about the ending, and the fragment of the novel was, of course, the last fiction he published.

The Mystery of Edwin Drood can nevertheless serve as an occasion to consider the significance of travel writing in Dickens's career as a whole. In his early work he often borrowed freely from travel writing, much as he borrowed from other popular genres. Yet one of the marks that distinguishes a great writer is the ability to use the prevailing features of another form in a creative, even a subversive, manner and thereby breathe new life into the tired, overworn conventions of the day. So it is with Dickens in all he wrote, including travel writing.

Perhaps nowhere in his travel prose is this more striking than when he wrote of his native England, and especially of London, as if it were a foreign place unknown to his readers. Throughout his career, however, his increasingly skillful use of travel and his descriptions of place serve not merely as a setting for the action of his fiction, but as yet another method of reinforcing and reconsidering his major themes and emphases. Toward the end of his life, as The Mystery of Edwin Drood powerfully demonstrates, he was more and more drawn to psychological drama and the inner rather than outer struggles of his characters. The principal interest of

this last novel is not with society as a whole, as in much of his earlier work, but with the mind of one tortured man. The exotic material in The Mystery of Edwin Drood is there not so much to tell us about foreign places as it is to reveal the psyche of John Jasper. This offers tantalizing clues to ways in which Dickens, had he lived, might have developed his interest in psychology.

After Dickens suffered his final stroke, the last coherent words he spoke were that he would go to London. It is fitting indeed that his last thoughts were again of traveling to the city that had played such an important role in his life and art.

Letters:

The Letters of Charles Dickens, edited by Walter Dexter (London: Nonesuch Press, 1938);

The Pilgrim Edition of the Letters of Charles Dickens, 7 volumes to date, edited by Madeline House, Graham Story, and others (Oxford: Clarendon Press, 1965–).

Bibliographies:

J. C. Eckel, *The First Editions of the Writings of Charles Dickens: A Bibliography* (New York: Inman, 1932);

Joseph Gold, *The Stature of Dickens: A Centenary Bibliography* (Toronto: University of Toronto Press, 1971).

Biographies:

John Forster, *The Life of Charles Dickens,* edited by J. W. T. Ley (London: Cecil Palmer, 1928);

Edgar Johnson, *Charles Dickens: His Tragedy and Triumph* (New York: Simon & Schuster, 1952);

Michael Allen, *Charles Dickens' Childhood* (London: Macmillan, 1988);

Fred Kaplan, *Dickens: A Biography* (New York: Morrow, 1988);

Peter Ackroyd, *Dickens* (London: Sinclair-Stevenson, 1990).

References:

Nicolas Bentley, Michael Slater, and Nina Burgis, *The Dickens Index* (London: Oxford University Press, 1988);

John Butt and Kathleen Tillotson, *Dickens at Work* (London: Methuen, 1957);

John Carey, *The Violent Effigy* (London: Faber & Faber, 1973);

G. K. Chesterton, *Charles Dickens: A Critical Study* (London: Methuen, 1906);

Philip Collins, ed., *Dickens: The Critical Heritage* (London: Routledge & Kegan Paul, 1971);

Steven Connor, *Charles Dickens* (Oxford: Blackwell, 1985);

Peter Conrad, *Imagining America* (New York: Oxford University Press, 1980);

Michael Cotsell, "*The Pickwick Papers* and Travel: A Critical Diversion," *Dickens Quarterly,* 3 (September 1986): 5–16;

K. J. Fielding, *Charles Dickens: A Critical Introduction* (London: Longmans, Green, 1965);

George Gissing, *Charles Dickens: A Critical Study* (London: Blackie, 1898);

F. R. Leavis and Q. D. Leavis, *Dickens the Novelist* (London: Chatto & Windus, 1970);

Steven Marcus, *Dickens: From Pickwick to Dombey* (New York: Basic Books, 1965);

Jerome Meckier, *Innocent Abroad: Charles Dickens's American Engagements* (Lexington: University of Kentucky Press, 1990);

J. Hillis Miller, *Charles Dickens: The World of His Novels* (Cambridge, Mass.: Harvard University Press, 1958);

David Paroissien, Introduction to Dickens's *Pictures from Italy* (New York: Coward, McCann & Geoghegan, 1974);

Michael Slater, *Dickens and Women* (London: Dent, 1983);

Slater, ed., *Dickens on America and the Americans* (Austin: University of Texas Press, 1978);

Alexander Welsh, *The City of Dickens* (Oxford: Clarendon Press, 1971);

Angus Wilson, *The World of Charles Dickens* (London: Secker & Warburg, 1970).

Papers:

The largest collection of Charles Dickens's papers, including the manuscripts and corrected proofs of most of his novels, is in the Forster Collection of the Victoria and Albert Museum. A smaller collection, including part of the manuscript of *The Posthumous Papers of the Pickwick Club,* is in the British Library. Other small but important caches are in the Pierpont Morgan and New York Public Libraries. Most of his letters are widely scattered; many are held by private individuals.

Lucie Duff Gordon

(24 June 1821 – 14 July 1869)

Faiza Shereen
University of Dayton

BOOK: *Letters from Egypt, 1863–65,* edited by Sarah Austin (London: Macmillan, 1865); revised as *Lady Duff Gordon's Letters from Egypt* (New York: McClure, Phillips, 1865); enlarged as *Last Letters from Egypt, to Which Are Added Letters from the Cape,* edited by Janet Ross (London: Macmillan, 1875; revised, London: Johnson, 1902; New York: McClure, Phillips, 1902); revised and enlarged again as *Letters from Egypt, 1862–1869,* edited by Gordon Waterfield (London: Routledge & Kegan Paul, 1969; New York: Praeger, 1969).

OTHER: Barthold Niebuhr, *Stories of the Gods and Heroes of Greece,* translated by Duff Gordon as Sarah Austin (London: Parker, 1843);

Wilhelm Meinhold, *Mary Schweidler, the Amber Witch: The Most Interesting Trial for Witchcraft Ever Known,* translated by Duff Gordon (London: Murray, 1844; New York: Cassell, 1888);

Clemens Lamping and François Antoine Alby, *The French in Algiers,* translated by Duff Gordon (London: Murray, 1845: New York: Wiley & Putnam, 1845);

Paul Johann Anselm, Ritter von Feuerbach, *Narratives of Remarkable Criminal Trials,* translated by Duff Gordon (London: Murray, 1846);

Leopold von Ranke, *Memoirs of the House of Brandenburg and History of Prussia, during the Seventeenth and Eighteenth Centuries,* 3 volumes, translated by Duff Gordon and Sir Alexander Gordon (London: Murray, 1849);

Armand François Léon de Wailly, *Stella and Vanessa: A Romance,* 2 volumes, translated by Duff Gordon (London: Parker, 1850);

Countess Sophie d'Arbouville, *The Village Doctor,* translated by Duff Gordon (London: Chapman & Hall, 1853);

von Ranke, *Ferdinand I and Maximilian II of Austria: An Essay on the Political and Religious State of Germany, Immediately after the Reformation,* translated by Duff Gordon and Sir Alexander Gordon

Lucie Duff Gordon (portrait by Henry Phillips; from Gordon Waterfield, Lucie Duff Gordon in England, South Africa and Egypt, *1937)*

(London: Longman, Brown, Green & Longmans, 1853; New York: AMS, 1975);

Count Helmuth Carl Bernhard von Moltke, *The Russians in Bulgaria and Rumelia in 1828 and 1829,* translated by Duff Gordon (London: Murray, 1854);

Heinrich Carl Ludolf von Sybel, *The History and Literature of the Crusades,* translated and edited by Duff Gordon (London: Chapman & Hall, 1861);

"Letters from the Cape," in *Vacation Tourists and Notes of Travel in 1862–63,* edited by Sir Francis Galton (London & Cambridge: Macmillan, 1864), pp. 119–222; republished in *Last Letters from Egypt, to Which Are Added Letters from the Cape,* edited by Janet Ross (London: Macmillan, 1875; revised, London: Johnson, 1902; New York: McClure, Phillips, 1902); published separately as *Letters from the Cape,* edited by John Purves (London: Milford, 1921); republished as *Letters from the Cape, 1861–62,* edited by Hector J. Anderson (Cape Town: Miller, 1925).

As a contemporary of the great Victorians who lived and wrote during the golden age of European orientalism, Lady Lucie Duff Gordon occupied a unique position among her contemporaries. She was an independent thinker whose scorn of conventionality was equaled only by her love of honesty. Her writing career falls into two phases: in the first, from 1844 to 1861, she published ten translations, mostly of German historical works and essays. In the second, from 1861 until her death in 1869, she lived abroad when her consumptive debilities forced her to leave England. From South Africa and Egypt she then wrote letters home that rendered her experience of the two cultures with a brilliance and sympathy that led her family to publish them.

Her first two works, "Letters from the Cape" (1864, republished as a volume only in 1921) and *Letters from Egypt, 1863–65* (1865), were very popular, "reaching a far wider public than her careful translations, because she wrote as she talked and she talked eloquently," explained Gordon Waterfield, her great-grandson and biographer. Her early letters from Clapham, where she had attended school in her teens, reveal her strength of character and originality, qualities that her later, mature letters from the Cape and from Egypt continue to reflect. Intellectual liveliness, keen and disinterested judgment, and a humanity unqualified by conventional bias or prejudice are the qualities most often noted in any description of this unusual Victorian woman. Alexander William Kinglake, whose accounts of his travels in the Middle East fascinated Duff Gordon and made him a welcome guest in her home, described her in superlative terms:

> The classical form of her features, the noble poise of her head and neck, her stately height, her uncoloured yet pure complexion, caused some of the beholders to call her beauty statuesque, and others to call it majestic, some pronouncing it even to be imperious. But she was so intellectual, so keen, so autocratic, sometimes even so impassioned in speech, that nobody, feeling her powers, could well go on feebly comparing her to a mere queen or Empress.

Born in Queen's Square, Westminster, England, on 24 June 1821, Lucie Duff Gordon was the only child of John and Sarah Austin. Of her father, author of *The Province of Jurisprudence Determined* (1832), Lord Brougham said, "If [John] Austin had had health, neither [John Singleton Copley] Lyndhurst nor I would have been Lord Chancellor." Admired and respected for his knowledge and conversation by such contemporaries as Jeremy Bentham, James Mill, and Thomas Carlyle, Austin was a melancholic intellectual whose poor health and habits of perfectionism impeded what might have been a more productive law career. Based on Austin's lectures delivered at the University of London between 1828 and 1831 during his brief, unsuccessful career as professor of jurisprudence, *The Province of Jurisprudence Determined* reflects both his virtues and his shortcomings: many considered it an important contribution in its field for its thoughtfulness and comprehensiveness, but Lord William Melbourne found it "the dullest book" he had ever read.

Austin was twenty-four years old when he met and fell in love with Sarah Taylor, the beautiful and vivacious daughter of John and Susannah Taylor. The engagement of these two extremely different people surprised many, but they were worthy of each other and their attachment was strong and enduring. "Two people more unlike it would have been difficult to find," wrote Janet Ross, Lady Duff Gordon's daughter: "Mr. Austin, habitually grave and despondent; his wife, brilliantly handsome, fond of society, in which she shone, and with almost superabundance of energy and animal spirits." Lucie Austin was born two years after the marriage and from early childhood showed that she had inherited her parents' intellectual keenness. John Austin's uncompromising honesty and constant pursuit of knowledge were complemented by the brilliance and vivacity with which she engaged the world around her and by her generosity and sympathy toward those less lucky than herself.

The Austins' house in Queen's Square was next to that of Mill, and its windows looked into the garden of Bentham, both of whom were intimate friends of James Austin. Such a setting provided Duff Gordon with her earliest education in the intellectual climate of ardent nineteenth-century utilitarian philosophy. Sarah Austin, a gracious hostess, created in her home the ambiance that attracted many writers and radical thinkers, and in the company of these people Duff Gordon, an only child, learned to entertain herself. Her best friend and playfellow was "Bun Don" (Brother John), as she called John Stuart Mill. When she was not with him or in the Benthams' garden, she was playing with mice or other animals. Her mother described the young girl with some concern for the strong tinge of originality in her character:

> She has an insatiable love of reading. Her original way of thinking will save her, I hope, from a trivial or vulgar taste. John Mill is ever my dearest child and friend and he really doats [sic] on Lucie, and can do anything with her. She is a monstrous great girl, but, though she has admirable qualities, I am not satisfied with her. She is too wild, undisciplined and independent; and though she knows a great deal, it is in a strange, wild way. She reads every thing; composes German verses, has imagined and put together a fairy world, dress, language, music, everything and talks to them in the garden; but she is sadly negligent in her own appearance.

What may have appeared as rather eccentric behavior in Duff Gordon in fact resulted from her rejection of conventional decorum, especially if that meant compromising her principles of honesty and human decency. The traveler and naturalist Marianne North, with whose family Duff Gordon spent her holidays when the Austins were abroad, was impressed by her "fearlessness and contempt for what people thought of her." At that time Duff Gordon had a tame snake for a pet that she carried up her sleeve or twisted in her braided hair. "Surely," wrote Marianne North, "[she] must have been more than a woman to tame a snake!"

Duff Gordon's courage, her capacity for original thought, and her independence from anything predetermined are perhaps best illustrated by her decision, at the age of sixteen, to be baptized into the Church of England although her parents were utilitarians. If Duff Gordon had inherited her absolute honesty and seriousness of purpose from her father, she inherited her vivacity, resoluteness, responsibility, and generosity from her mother. Indeed, Duff Gordon represented the third generation of a family of remarkable women. In 1888 Janet Ross, Duff Gordon's daughter, published *Three Generations of English Women: Memoirs and Correspondence of Mrs. John Taylor, Mrs. Sarah Austin, and Lady Duff Gordon*. The volume reveals similarities among the temperaments of the three women and reveals how each of the three was influenced by the rich personality and experience of her mother.

Susannah Taylor, Duff Gordon's grandmother, entertained in her home many of the most cultivated men and women of her day. Admired and valued as a friend by all who knew her, she discussed politics and literature with many eminent thinkers of the time, and she raised her children to value learning and respect those different from themselves. With the passion for learning and brilliant intellect that Susannah Taylor had, Sarah Austin spoke French, German, and Italian and was "an excellent Latin scholar. . . . Her mind was perfectly balanced and fortified by serious, hard study; and to everything she did she brought an attention and a maturity of judgment which few men possess in so large a measure."

Duff Gordon's own education "was of the most random character," her daughter wrote; "she had little regular instruction, and accomplishments were never attempted." Growing up in the Austin home, which nurtured her avidity for reading and provided rich experiences through frequent and long sojourns abroad, Duff Gordon acquired an unusual education that enhanced her imaginative and original approach to life. She first traveled to Germany with her parents in 1826 and returned "transformed into a little German maiden" who had learned to speak German as a native. When Duff Gordon was thirteen years old, the Austins in 1833 went to live in Boulogne because of financial problems. There Sarah Austin was known as "La Belle Anglaise" and became popular for her courage and kindness. Eventually when John Austin was appointed as a commissioner to the island of Malta, Duff Gordon was sent to boarding school at Clapham.

Upon the return of her parents from Malta in 1838, Duff Gordon began to appear in society. At her first ball she met Sir Alexander Duff Gordon; they fell in love and were married on 16 May 1840. At first Lady Gordon opposed her son's aim of marrying a young lady with no dowry, and his father was concerned because the young man had little money. "Alexander has nothing," wrote Mrs. Austin, "but a small salary, his handsome person, excellent and sweet character, and his title (a great misfortune)." Like her mother and grandmother before her, Duff Gordon was destined for a life of modest means, one in which her industriousness and scorn for appearances and material luxury became valuable assets. The Duff Gordons set up house in Queen's Square, not far from where the Austins had lived when Duff Gordon's mother had been a child. History seemed to repeat itself, because Duff Gordon – like her mother and her grandmother – proved to be an admirable hostess, drawing some of the best writers and thinkers into her circle. Among her guests were Alfred Tennyson, who used to read his poetry; Charles Dickens; William Makepeace Thackeray; Thomas Babington Macaulay; and Mark Lemon, the editor of *Punch*.

Lucie Austin as portrayed by a school friend (from Lucie Duff Gordon in England, South Africa and Egypt*)*

During this time Duff Gordon began to earn money by writing, by translating German texts, as her mother did. Her first translation, that of Barthold Niebuhr's *Stories of the Gods and Heroes of Greece,* was published under her mother's married name in 1843. The following year her translation of Wilhelm Meinhold's *Maria Schweidler die Bernstein-hexe* (*Mary Schweidler, the Amber Witch: The Most Interesting Trial for Witchcraft Ever Known*) was published by John Murray and went through three editions in the first year. The translation was highly praised, and J. W. Mackail wrote in his preface to the 1927 World's Classics edition that used this translation that "It is of its kind a masterpiece, and the translator was one of the most remarkable women of the time."

The French in Algiers (1845) was published the following year. It included her translation of two pieces: Clemens Lamping's German narrative, "The Soldier of the Foreign Legion," and François Antoine Alby's French work, "The Prisoners of Abd-el-Kader." Lamping's text narrates the experiences of a young lieutenant in the Oldenburg services who resigns his commission and travels – first to Spain and then to Algiers, where he enters the

foreign legion as a volunteer. The narrative is both of travel and adventure, in which the finally disillusioned hero learns from his experience. Alby's piece relates his experiences as a French naval lieutenant held captive for several months by the Arabs. Both narratives are distanced from the reader's experience by narrative techniques of interfacing. Lamping returns from his voyages after two years, is restored in the service of Oldenburg, and relates his adventures to his friends as he sits by his fireside in the traditional storytelling manner of the returned traveler. Alby distances the story by intruding with the classic apology of the unskilled narrator, assuring his readers that his book would never have been published "but at the request of his friends."

In 1846 Duff Gordon's next major translation, *Narratives of Remarkable Criminal Trials* by Paul Johann Anselm, Ritter von Feuerbach, was published. The book dealt with law reform, and Duff Gordon did research in *Law Magazine; or, Quarterly Review of Jurisprudence* and the liberal quarterlies. She also consulted with her father, no doubt, who had concerned himself with such issues all his life. The translation was favorably reviewed, and the *Law Magazine* wrote, "The present collection of criminal cases form, as far as we are aware, the most interesting specimen existing in our language." Duff Gordon continued to translate histories and essays from German. She collaborated with her husband in translating Leopold von Ranke's *Memoirs of the House of Brandenburg and History of Prussia, during the Seventeenth and Eighteenth Centuries* – "nine books of Prussian history" in imitation of Herodotus, as its German title indicated.

The entire period from 1842 to 1850 was eventful. Duff Gordon's first child, Janet, was born in 1842, and in 1846 Alexander nearly died of cholera. Lord Lansdown loaned the Duff Gordons his villa at Richmond, where Alexander recovered and Duff Gordon continued to entertain. The revolution of 1848 caused the Austins, who had been living in Paris, to return to England, and when King Louis Philippe lost his throne François Guizot, the prime minister and a close friend of the Austins, was forced to seek refuge with the Duff Gordons. The Austins' horror at mob violence in Paris led them to modify their radicalism. Duff Gordon, however, continued to have faith in the people and blamed the injustice of laws for upheavals among the working classes. When the Chartists marched on London, forty men from the workshops came to the Duff Gordons' house to protect their "Lady," who described the event vividly in one of her letters. In 1849 she gave birth to a son, Maurice, and when she soon afterward became ill, the family moved from London to Esher.

Also during the mid 1840s a new addition to the Duff Gordon household had come, a black Nubian boy about twelve years old: Hassan el Bakket, known as "Hatty," had been taken as a slave by an Italian refugee. He was going blind when his master turned him out, and the boy sought refuge with Duff Gordon. After she cared for him and had him cured, he became devoted to her. Although he was offered a good position by the oculist who had treated him, he could not bear to leave Duff Gordon and remained in her service till his death in 1850. "He associated himself entirely with the family," Duff Gordon's daughter recalled. He had become Janet's "beloved playfellow," and both Duff Gordon and Alexander were devoted to him. In her memoirs Ross wrote, "I distinctly recollect Mr. Hilliard, the American author, being shocked at seeing me in Hatty's arms, and my rage when he asked my mother how she could let a negro touch her child. Whereupon she called us to her, and kissed me first and Hatty afterwards."

After the Duff Gordons left London on their way to Esher, they stayed briefly with the Austins in Weybridge, and Duff Gordon's health began to deteriorate. In a letter to C. J. Bayley she described the effects of her consumption with resignation: "I fear you would think me very much altered since my illness; I have lost much of my hair, all my complexion and all my flesh and look thin and old and my hair is growing grey. This I consider hard on a woman just over her thirtieth birthday." Yet even ill health did not quell her vitality. She continued to lead an active life, to write and entertain at her house, The Gordon Arms.

In 1857 the Duff Gordons had to move again because of financial difficulties. For several months they lived in Paris, where they led an inevitably busy life, receiving in their Rue Chaillot house such friends as Alfred-Victor de Vigny, Auguste Comte, Victor Cousin, and Barthelmy St. Hilaire. Back in England in 1858 Duff Gordon gave birth to a third child, Urania, and in the following year her father died. By that time her consumption was worse, having no doubt been aggravated by the strain of nights she had spent at his bedside and the sense of loss that she had suffered.

During the three more years spent in Esher before she was forced to go abroad for her health, George Meredith became the Duff Gordons' neighbor. He admired Duff Gordon and was attracted by Janet, who was now seventeen and very beautiful. "The hospitable house at Esher gave its warm wel-

come," he wrote, "not merely to men and women of distinction; the humble undistinguished were made joyous guests there." Meredith's fascination with Duff Gordon led him to use her as the model for Lady Jocelyn and Janet for Rose, Lady Jocelyn's daughter, in his novel *Evan Harrington* (1861), but Lady Duff Gordon had detractors as well as admirers. "In the circles named 'upper' there was mention of women unsexing themselves," Meredith explained. "She preferred the society of men on the plain ground that they discussed matters of weight and are – the pick of them – of open speech, more liberal, more genial, better comrades."

In July 1861 Duff Gordon sailed for South Africa, where she hoped that the warm climate would help her recover and allow her to return to England, but this was the beginning of an exile that was to last for eight years, until her death in Egypt in 1869. It is also the period of her most interesting and powerful literary work, because in her letters from the Cape and, more particularly, from Egypt, she achieved her potential as a writer.

"To those who think voyages and travels tiresome," she wrote in her letters, "my delight in the new birds and beasts and people must seem very stupid. I can't help it if it does, and am not ashamed to confess that I feel the old sort of enchanted wonder with which I used to read [Captain James] Cook's voyages and the like as a child." In the subject matter of travel Duff Gordon had found the space to embody her thought and values, and in the genre of the letter a vehicle that suited her voice and temperament. The lively narrative of her letters is enchanting. They also candidly and sensitively present a reality so often disguised in accounts of travels, so altered by the heaviness of mental baggage and conventional biases, that what passes for the truth is no more than a perception of the exotic and the alien – seductive and reprehensible at the same time.

Her independence and refusal to be guided by conventions meant that she could assume a fresh view; her genuine interest in humanity meant that she could accept a reality different from her own without being threatened. Rather than being a center protecting its privileged position of power, her narrative voice functions as a moral agent, immune to the hypnosis of old voices. "I have been really amazed at several instances of English fanaticism this year," she writes in one of her letters from Egypt in 1865. "Why do people come to a Mussulman country with such bitter hatred 'in their stomachs' as I have seen three or four times? . . . Why do the English talk of the beautiful sentiment of the Bible and pretend to feel it so much, and when they come and see the same life before them, they ridicule it?" she asked. Sympathy for the oppressed wrenches a cry of indignation from her: "What chokes me is to hear Englishmen talk of the stick being 'the only way to manage Arabs,' as if there could be any doubt that it is the easiest way to manage anybody, where it can be used with impunity."

She judges with a critical mind and is repelled by bigotry. Her perception of a common humanity, of all the richness of cultural differences, leads her to deny any judgment based on the assumption of privileged doctrine: "I know the cruel old platitudes about governing the orientals by fear which the English pick up like mocking birds from the Turks. I know all about 'the sticks' and 'vigour' and all that — but — 'I sit among the people' and I know that, too, that Mahammed feels just as John Smith or Tom Brown would feel in his place."

Duff Gordon's epistolary account of her experiences in distant and exotic countries differs sharply from accounts of foreign cultures such as the two she had translated in *The French in Algiers,* accounts intended to be about a world kept clearly beyond boundaries and not to be traversed. By contrast, her letters narrate events with an immediacy and accessibility to the reader — partly through her use of the epistolary genre, a vehicle of communication employed in dated installments recording events as they occur, and partly through Duff Gordon's voice, which is engaged in the world she describes. Not merely a spectator, she conducts an ongoing dialogue with the reader, who is of course more internalized than an anonymous reading public.

Another reason for the success with which Duff Gordon brings her characters to life and for the sharpness and immediacy with which she creates the contexts of her stories is that she writes of the Dutch and the Malays, the Egyptians and the Nubians, exactly as she does of her own family and friends in England. People, no matter how different their customs and codes, have in her view the same complex needs and desires, so that her attempt to understand them is genuine and communication is not impossible. Duff Gordon does not objectify others. In one of her letters from Egypt she comments on Harriet Martineau's book *Eastern Life Present and Past* (1848), which she had just received:

It is true as far as it goes, but there is the usual defect — the people are not real people, only part of the scenery to her, as to most Europeans. The descriptions are ex-

cellent, but she evidently knew and cared nothing about the people, and had the feeling of most English people here, that the difference in manners is a sort of impassable gulf, the truth being that their feeling and passions are just like our own.

It is curious that the old books of travel that I have read mention the natives of strange countries in a far more natural tone, and with far more attempt to discriminate character, than modern ones. . . . Have we grown so very civilized since a hundred years that outlandish people seem like mere puppets, and not like real human beings?

A hundred years before Edward W. Said, Chinua Achebe, and Frantz Fanon, Duff Gordon was observing and recording some of the most pernicious aspects of European orientalism — and questioning some of the most dearly held views of her time.

Duff Gordon arrived in Cape Town in September 1861. The tone of her first letters home was not enthusiastic. "This is a dreary place for strangers," she wrote. Homesick for her little girl, Urania, and not improving as she had hoped she would, Duff Gordon looked forward to returning to England. Eventually she met some of the local Malays and made friends. As she visited the mosques of these freed slaves and joined in their celebrations and social gatherings, she was always observing the distinctive qualities of their culture, their interactions and relationships. She noted the differences in child rearing. "The intelligent-looking quiet children, who seem amused and happy," she wrote, "never make a noise or have the fidgets. I cannot make out why they are so well behaved. It favours Alick's theory of the expediency of utter spoiling, for one never hears any educational process going on." Duff Gordon was popular among the Malays, who appreciated her directness and courtesy. Unlike other Europeans, she showed respect for them by not laughing at them or talking nonsense. "The English," she observed of her countrymen, "when they mean to be good-natured, are generally offensively familiar, and talk 'nonsense talk.' " Their habit of trying to imitate the speech patterns of the Malays resulted in what appeared (rightly so) to be patronizing familiarity.

Often Duff Gordon's reports are straightforward and journalistic. Gaining in vividness and density of images, passages such as the following demonstrate her direct, simple style and reluctance to qualify her observations when her experiences have not justified such qualification.

The Dutch round Capetown . . . [are] sulky and dispirited; they regret the slave days, and can't bear to pay wages. They have sold all their fine houses in town to merchants etc. and let their handsome country places go to pieces and the land lie fallow, rather than hire the men they used to own. They hate the Malays, who were their slaves and whose "insolent prosperity" annoys them, and they don't like the vulgar, bustling English. The English complain that the Dutch won't die, "and that they are the curse of the colony" (a statement for which they can never give a reason). But they, too, curse the emancipation, long to flog the niggers, and hate the Malays, who work hard and don't drink. . . . The Africanders (Dutch and negro mixed in various proportions) are more or less lazy, dirty and dressy, and the beautiful girls wear pork-pie hats, and look very winning and rather fierce.

In July 1862 Duff Gordon sailed back to England, but her time with her family was short. Because doctors advised her to go to southern France and to a warmer climate in the winter, she went to Eaux Bonnes, where she was not happy. In the fall of that year she embarked on a voyage to Egypt, which henceforth became her home and where she wrote the letters that testify to her vitality, courage, and kindness. In these letters Duff Gordon produced some of her best pieces of writing.

No mind is a clean slate, and if Duff Gordon did not experience Egypt and the Egyptians with total objectivity, what she came with were those qualities of mind and heart that had characterized her demeanor throughout her life. In recounting the life of the travel writer Lady Duff Gordon, one cannot ignore stories of the teenager who kept a snake for a pet or the schoolgirl who decided to be baptized in the Church of England; or of the hostess who captivated such men as Lord Melbourne, Charles Dickens, and George Meredith; or of the mistress who responded to the racism of her American guest by kissing her black servant, Hatty. The traits exhibited in these actions characterize Duff Gordon's travel writing.

In Egypt Duff Gordon lived intimately with the people, particularly in the south, where she settled in Luxor (Thebes) and acquired the name of *Noor-ala-Noor,* "Light of light." She did not care much for the big northern cities of Alexandria and Cairo, where Westernization was advancing quickly during the reign of Ismail Pasha. In the south, Upper Egypt, and especially in Luxor, where the climate was dry and warm and the people unaffected and sincere, Duff Gordon was content:

Every act of life here is exactly like the early parts of the Bible and it seems totally new when one reads it here. Old Jacob's speech to Pharaoh really made me laugh (don't be shocked), because it is so exactly what a fellah says to a Pasha: "Few and evil have been the days," etc.

Duff Gordon's daughter Janet (portrait by Henry Phillips; from Lucie Duff Gordon in England, South Africa and Egypt*)*

(Jacob being a most prosperous man); but it is manners to say all that, and I feel quite kindly to Jacob, whom I used to think ungrateful and discontented; and when I go to Sidi Omar's farm, does he not say, "Take now fine meal and bake cakes quickly," and wants to kill a kid? *Fateereh* [a kind of flaky pie] with plenty of butter is what the "three men" who came to Abraham ate; and the way that Abraham's chief mameluke [a white or east Asian slave], acting as Vakeel, manages Isaac's marriage with Rebekah! All the vulgarized associations with Puritanism and abominable little "Scripture tales and pictures" peel off here, and the inimitably truthful representations of life and character – not a flattering one certainly – comes out, and it feels like Homer.

Duff Gordon's sojourn in Egypt covered a time of rapid change and momentous events. The excavation of the Suez Canal, which cost the lives of so many fellahin and the revolt of Ahmed Arabi, were two major events that Duff Gordon discusses in her letters. Her observations were shrewd and her judgments prophetic. She foresaw the disastrous economic effects of Ismail Pasha's policy for the country – a policy that led eventually to bankruptcy – and criticized him. Many of her letters, however, never reached their destination, because government spies saw to it that they got lost. "I could tell you a little of the value of Counsular information!" she wrote to her husband, "but what is the use? Europe is enchanted with the 'enlightened' Pasha who has ruined the poor country."

Duff Gordon's descriptions of everything around her expose the double standard used by the European colonial. She sees it in the minor gestures, the seemingly insignificant incident, and the casual comment that she includes in her narrative. Most of all she criticizes the ignorance of native culture — and the disinterest that causes it — among the Europeans. Upon arriving in Egypt Duff Gordon is struck by the beauty of Islamic architecture, and she laments the lack of interest in it among her traveling contemporaries: "The Arab architecture is even more lovely than our Gothic," she claims, and she goes on to describe the "noble taste" and "majestic" beauty of the mosque of Sultan Hassan. "No one has said a tenth part enough of the beauty of Arab architecture," she concludes.

Misrepresentation results from ignorance, and Duff Gordon is quick to notice where prejudice rather than knowledge informs an observation. Commenting on Harriet Martineau's book, Duff Gordon remarks, "Miss Martineau's bigotry against the Copts and Greeks is droll enough, compared to her very proper reverences for 'Him who sleeps in Philae,' and her attacks upon hareems outrageous; she implies that they are brothels." Duff Gordon counters this image elsewhere in her letters with correct and informed accounts of harems.

In a letter from Cairo to her mother she describes the impression that she and an Egyptian friend shared upon seeing what must have been a typical orientalist picture:

Sheikh Yussuf laughed so heartily over a print in an illustrated paper, from a picture of Hilton's, of Rebekah at the well, with the old *Vakeel* of Sidi Ibraheem (Abraham's chief servant) *kneeling* before the girl he was sent to fetch like an old fool without his turban, and Rebekah and the other girls in queer fancy dresses, and the camels with snouts like pigs. "If the painter could not go to Es-Sham (Syria) to see how the beduin really look," said Sheikh Yussuf, "why did he not paint a well in England with girls like English peasants? At least it would have looked natural to English people, and the *Vakeel* would not seem so like a madman if he had taken off a hat." I cordially agreed with Yussuf's criticism. Fancy pictures of Eastern things are hopelessly absurd, and fancy poem too. I have got hold of a stray copy of Victor Hugo's "Orientales," and I think I never laughed more in my life.

In the same letter she contemplates the difficulty of communication between Europeans and Arabs. She finds that the Egyptians are not conscious of "the great gulf" that divides Europeans from them. "We do not attempt to explain our ideas to them, but I cannot discover any such reticence in them. . . . I find they appeal to my sympathy in trouble quite comfortably, and talk of religion and other feelings apparently as freely as to each other. In many respects they are more unprejudiced than we are, and very intelligent, and very good in many ways."

On 8 August 1867 Sarah Austin died, and Duff Gordon was to survive her mother by only two years. Duff Gordon died peacefully in Cairo and was buried there on 14 July 1869, although following her request to be "among my own people," arrangements had been made and a tomb prepared for her at Thebes. In an article published in *Macmillan's* in September of that year her friend Caroline Norton wrote of her,

From [the] early and intense loneliness [of Duff Gordon's childhood] probably sprung much of that independence and concentration of thought which marked the progressive stages of her rapidly maturing intellect. A great thinker, a great reader, very original in her conclusions, very eager in impressing her opinions, her mind was not like those of many other women, filled with echoes of other folks' sayings. . . . From the aspect of nature, and the study of human nature such as she found it, she drew her unassisted lessons of knowledge. As life advanced, as the field of her experience widened, many of these conclusions became modified; and commerce with her kind taught her the wide indulgence and sympathy she afterwards showed for all who suffered or struggled in the up-hill labour of life.

Biography:

Gordon Waterfield, *Lucie Duff Gordon in England, South Africa and Egypt* (London: Murray, 1937; New York: Dutton, 1937).

References:

Caroline Norton, "Lady Duff Gordon on Her Works," *Macmillan's Magazine,* 20 (September 1869): 457–462;

Janet Ross, *Three Generations of English Women: Memoirs and Correspondence of Mrs. John Taylor, Mrs. Sarah Austin, and Lady Duff Gordon* (London: Murray, 1888).

Frances Minto (Dickinson) Elliot

(6 March 1820 – 26 October 1898)

Samuel J. Rogal
Illinois Valley Community College

BOOKS: *Diary of an Idle Woman in Italy* (2 volumes, London: Chapman & Hall, 1871; 2 volumes in 1, New York: Brentano's, 187-?; revised edition, London: Chapman & Hall, 1872);

Pictures of Old Rome (London: Chapman & Hall, 1872);

Old Court Life in France (2 volumes, London: Chapman & Hall, 1873; 2 volumes in 1, New York: Brentano's, 1873; New York: Scribner, Welford, 1873); republished as *Romance of Old Court-Life in France* (New York: Appleton, 1873);

The Italians, 3 volumes (London: White, 1875); republished as *The Italians: A Novel,* 1 volume (New York: Appleton, 1875);

The Diary of an Idle Woman in Sicily, 2 volumes (London: Bentley, 1881);

Diary of an Idle Woman in Spain, 2 volumes (London: White, 1884; New York: Croscup & Sterling, 1897);

The Red Cardinal: A Romance, 2 volumes (London: White, 1884; New York: Munro, 1885);

The Ill-Tempered Cousin: A Novel, 3 volumes (London: White, 1885);

The Story of Sophia: A Novel (Leipzig: Tauchnitz, 1891);

Diary of an Idle Woman in Constantinople (London: Murray, 1892; New York: Appleton, 1893);

Old Court Life in Spain (2 volumes, London: Chapman & Hall, 1893; 2 volumes in 1, New York: Brentano's, [1893?]);

Roman Gossip (London: Murray, 1894).

Although the travel narratives, histories, and romances of Frances Minto (Dickinson) Elliot proved fairly popular throughout the late nineteenth century, neither she nor her work has yet received, as the writer of her London *Times* obituary frankly admitted, "a permanent place in the literature of the time." Indeed, the student of nineteenth-century travel literature or romance fiction will be hard-pressed to find even the briefest references to her name or her works in standard literary histories. Nonetheless, a bibliographic survey of her works reveals reprints sufficient to suggest that she had a substantial readership in North America and Europe, as well as in Britain. Leipzig publisher Christian Bernhard von Tauchnitz, who took advantage of the lack of international copyright agreements, quickly added her titles to his cheaply priced Collection of British and American Authors, a series that continued in print until 1939. As late as 1927, fifty-four years after its initial publication, Putnam's published its New York reprint of Elliot's *Old Court Life in France* (1873).

Born on 6 March 1820, the only daughter of Charles Dickinson of Queen Charlton Manor, Somerset, and later of Farley Hill Court, Reading, Frances married John Edward Geils of Dumbrick (near Glasgow), with whom she bore four daughters. Geils died sometime before 1863, for in November of that year she married the Very Reverend Gilbert Elliot, twenty years her senior. He had served as rector of Holy Trinity Church, Marylebone, London, from late November 1846 until his appointment to the deanery of Bristol on 1 May 1850. Through his father, Dean, Elliot was related to the earls of Minto, perhaps the source for Frances Elliot's middle name on the title pages of her published volumes. Her dedication in *Old Court Life in France* reads, "To My Niece, / The Countess of Minto, / This Work / Is Inscribed."

Perhaps residing abroad almost as much as in England, Frances Elliot spent considerable time in Italy, France, and Spain. In *Roman Gossip* (1894) she announces that "My own recollections of Rome carry me back to about 1852," and while

165

residing in that city, she published tales, sketches, and art criticism under the pseudonyms Florentia and Florentine. She also occupied at least two houses in England during her literary career: the home of her parents at Farley Hill Court, Reading, in the late 1860s and early 1870s, and 7 George Street, Hanover Square, London, in the late 1880s and early 1890s. She spent the last three years of her life in Rome and died on 26 October 1898, seven years after the death of her second husband, at the Palazzo Chigi, Siena, in west-central Italy. According to the writer of her obituary, "Mrs. Elliot was well known both in the Italian and English society of Rome."

The importance of knowing the exact number of Elliot's friends or even their identities diminishes in relation to that of knowing her travel and historical narratives. The value of her work arises from her ability to focus with clarity and specificity upon what and whom she sees. Her literary abilities are as effective inside the confines of buildings and rooms as they are outdoors, when she is traveling through and describing large, broad areas. For example, in the second chapter of *Roman Gossip* she gazes hard at Pope Leo XIII, then at least sixty-nine years old:

> As he stands before you, you see a tall attenuated figure in white, with the appearance of being much weaker than he really is (for he enjoys wonderful health for his age). The expression of the long, thin face is pale and ascetic, with bright beady eyes, and a characteristic set smile (which may be called false or diplomatic) plays about his lips, giving a rigid *contour* to the chin and jaw. Something in this bald commonplace countenance produces a disagreeable impression.

Her sharp reaction to her subject flashes vigorously from the page, and simultaneously conveys her perceptions of the appearance of the Pope and what she believes to be tokens of the principal political nature of his personality.

In addition to her ability to perceive what lay beneath the skin or behind the eyes of a person, Elliot was able to weave her human subjects into the contexts to which they belonged. Early in *Roman Gossip* Elliot has characterized papal counselor and Cardinal Secretary of State Giacomo Antonelli as "avaricious and self-seeking to the last degree, and in politics equally cunning and unprincipled," and when she later proceeds to one of the Vatican apartments overlooking the piazza of St. Peter's for an audience with him, she describes how she "passed up the great marble staircase of the *Scala Santa* — and a very long one it is; at least a hundred steps,

encountering at intervals Swiss guards in their quaint uniform and hard ill-favoured faces — up as if to heaven, only with no angels by the way."

Her earlier characterization has prepared her reader for this sarcasm, yet as she and her companion ascend to the seat of the cardinal's power the denouement of the chapter comes with some surprise. Her plan for this chapter devoted to Antonelli develops from a rhetorical scheme in which Elliot has initially placed him at the highest level of papal political influence and then, at the end, sends him crashing onto the hardest of mortal surfaces: "On the 6th of November, 1876, Cardinal Antonelli died, a victim to frequent attacks of gout. No one regretted him." As a travel writer, Elliot did not content herself with mere descriptions of what she saw. She formed definite opinions about people and places, and she proved more than willing to convey these to her readers.

Although she reacted strongly to her subjects, she did not sacrifice close attention to detail. For instance, once she sets foot inside Antonelli's heaven, she observes: "There were no doors to his rooms, only rich portieres, and a bevy of *camerieri,* valets, messengers, and major-domos stood in the anteroom, as became a minister of state. At the end of a long suite of moderately well-furnished *salons,* with immense windows letting in floods of sun, we found him standing beside a writing table, overlaid with letters, news papers, and documents. . . ." Elliot has the eye of a motion picture director as she "zooms" toward her subject — from her interior overview of the apartment, to the writing table, to the cardinal; from the all-encompassing sun flooding the room, to close-up examinations of the papers on the table, the cardinal's clothing, or his eyes and teeth. Elliot proved worthy of her craft, for she wrote smoothly and comfortably; above all, she learned to explore fully the depth and the dimension of a subject.

Elliot employed similar rhetorical techniques to describe large physical structures or broad spatial areas. Again, as with people, she placed what she saw in a specific, suggestive context or environment so that her reader might understand and appreciate its geographical and historical significance. Chapter 17 of *Old Court Life in France,* for example, opens with a description of the renaissance château and palace at Chenonceau in a rural and isolated district of the Touraine. The building appears from a distance "as beautiful as ever — a picturesque mass of pointed turrets, glistening spires, perpendicular roofs, lofty pavilions, and pillared arches . . . built over the river Cher, at once its defence and its attraction." The view from afar yields little beyond

"A Gate of the Louvre, after St. Bartholomew's Day" (after a painting by Debat Ponson), frontispiece to an early edition of Elliot's
Old Court Life in France

general impression, but as the traveler proceeds, the vision sharpens.

Elliot guides her reader's imagination toward the moat of the château, a moat fed by the river and spanned by a drawbridge. On the southern side rises "a stately bridge of five arches . . . where the high roofs and pointed turrets of the main building are seen to great advantage, rising out of scattered woods of oak and ash, which are divided into leafy avenues leading into fair water-meadows beside the Cher." The drawbridge, covered in the sixteenth century during the time of Catherine de Médici, "forms a spacious wing of two stories, the first floor fitted as a banqueting hall, the walls broken by four embayed windows, opening on either side and looking up and down the stream." At the moat and drawbridge the reader should stand ready to cross and enter the château proper; however, Elliot has not finished with the outside of her rural French renaissance world.

As she blends the forces of sensation and emotion into the description of the natural environment of this château at Chenonceau, Elliot stands before the structure and allows its sights, sounds, and fragrances to be hurled down upon her: "A fresh-breathing air comes from the river and the forest, a scent of moss and flowers extremely delicious. The cooing of the cushat doves, the cry of the cuckoo, the flutter of the breeze among the trees." Working with the abstract sounds and scents of nature, Elliot develops for the reader a meaningful transition between past and present. Furthermore, a passage such as the one cited above, in combination with the description of the château, serves as a background for the drama of old court life at Chenonceau. For Elliot, history exists as an active dialogue to be discovered in and compiled from memoirs. The writer of history consults those memoirs; interprets human character traits, human peculiarities, and the animations of nature; and carefully conceives how to

167

transfer the experience borne by a reading of the memoirs to the imaginations of readers.

Elliot perceived travel literature as a form that seeks to make the present meaningful by infusing the significance of history into those scenes. To that end she developed the Idle Woman series of diaries — *Diary of an Idle Woman in Italy* (1871), *The Diary of an Idle Woman in Sicily* (1881), *Diary of an Idle Woman in Spain* (1884), and *Diary of an Idle Woman in Constantinople* (1892). All four volumes convey to readers a tension between the romance, the splendor of the ancient world, and the harsh realities of people struggling to establish some security on the uncertain shores of modernity. For each volume she consulted histories and handbooks and filtered details from them into her own observations and reactions. Writers of those sources, she found, had made little or no attempt to relate past to present, to establish emotional transitions between the old and the new. She had to see for herself (as she did in *Diary of An Idle Woman in Constantinople*) that "Through this court passed all the glory of the [Ottoman] empire — ambassadors on their way to the Hall of the Divan, through files of guards and eunuchs, the galleries round being decorated with scarlet cloth and innumerable small flags, such as are still seen in mosques and shops."

In *Old Court Life in Spain* (1893) Elliot demonstrates further how the travelers' emotions at a particular locale significantly affect both the sound and the sense of their historical accounts of that area. Her opening paragraph of the volume breaks out, "How great is Spain! How mighty! From the rugged mountains of the Asturias, their base washed by stormy waves, and the giddy heights of the Pyrenean precipices — an eternal barrier between rival peoples — to the balmy plains of the South, where summer ever reigns! A world within itself, with a world's variety!" From there she moves directly to her thesis — that the history of Spain is as varied as the land.

The interesting feature of that historical variety, when filtered through Elliot's mind and art, concerns her ability to bridge the gap between the time *of* which she wrote and the time *in* which she wrote. The mind and eyes of the historical narrator commingle with those of her travel narrator. For example, in chapter 36 of *Old Court Life in Spain* Elliot describes the fiesta of the Corpus Domini at Seville in its early fourteenth-century historical context, although that scene could easily have occurred in 1893, when she published those volumes. "The time is early summer," she opens; "the sky an unbroken sphere of blue, as deep and smooth as a turquoise,

canopying the blanched domes and pinnacles of the cathedral and illuminating with ineffable splendour the elegant galleries of the Giralda tower." Elliot serves not only as a historical narrator in conveying the facts of history but also as a travel narrator who places herself in the scene and thus provides her narrative with a point of view. "No shade anywhere," she observes, "on *plaza, patio,* or river bank; nothing but a blazing sun, making golden motes; the thinly leaved palms scarcely leaving a reflection on the hot earth."

Continuing with her portrayal of the fiesta of the Corpus Domini and its processions of monks, penitent, choristers, and chanting canons, she shifts her role to that of a contemporary travel writer by inserting a paragraph beginning with "Now all who have seen a religious procession in Spain will understand the splendour of it." The splendor of the past transcends the ages and emerges as the splendor of the present through Elliot's concrete, active language, as the reader envisions the "medieval magnificence of the robes, wrought with plaques of solid gold and encrusted with priceless jewels" and "the brilliant glow of sacred banners, the sheen of steel caps and armour." The reader steps back in awe from "the glitter of the gigantic dolls (or *pasos*), larger than life, dressed in the most gorgeous robes, representing the Saviour, the Virgin, and saints and martyrs." That same splendor rises above the purely visual in "the sound of trumpets, drums and cymbals as they advance in a blaze of tapers and torches, carried on platforms of wood."

Yet Elliot's accurate presentation of historical details arose from sources far more substantive than her enthusiasm or imagination. She dedicated *Old Court Life in Spain* to Mrs. Humphry (Mary Augusta) Ward, "To Whose Researches / I Am So Much Indebted." Ward had been conducting research in the libraries at Oxford University since 1865 to satisfy her curiosity and interests in old Spain. Her article on the "Poema del Cid" had appeared in *Macmillan's Magazine* in 1872, and she had served as a research assistant to the noted historian John Richard Green for his projected history of early Spain. She had also written articles on early Spanish kings and bishops for the *Dictionary of Christian Biography on Gothic Ecclesiastical History* (1877–1887), a work Elliot cited as one of her fourteen authorities for *Old Court Life in Spain*. In *Old Court Life in France* Elliot had listed forty sources that she had consulted in writing the volumes, twenty-three of them memoirs of influential sixteenth- and seventeenth-century courtiers. One problem with her Italian, French, and Spanish diaries of history and travel concerns her failure to associate persons and events with specific dates, a void no doubt intended to facilitate her narrative transitions from past to present.

Ultimately Elliot's real strength as a traveler and writer of travel literature lies in her desire to understand both past and present. She traced the contrast between the romance of the ancient worlds and the harsh realities of their late nineteenth century. She captured, accurately and concisely, the essence of her role as a writer in her preface to *Diary of an Idle Woman in Constantinople,* where she reflected, "So little remains of the past in this much destroyed city; and of that so little that . . . the actual present is deprived of any link with what has gone before." Through her writing Elliot sought to illuminate her readers and provide a service to the traveler. Given those purposes, no one could have expected or demanded more from her.

References:

Elizabeth A. Bohls, *Women Travel Writers and the Language of Aesthetics* (Cambridge & New York: Cambridge University Press, 1995);

Catherine Barnes Stevenson, *Victorian Women Travel Writers in Africa* (Boston: Twayne, 1982).

Elizabeth Anne (McCaul) Finn

(14 March 1825 – 15 January 1921)

Laura Nilges-Matias
Loyola University of Chicago

BOOKS: *Home in the Holy Land: A Tale Illustrating Customs and Incidents in Modern Jerusalem* (London & Edinburgh: Nisbet, 1866); republished as *A Home in the Holy Land: A Tale Illustrating Customs and Incidents in Modern Jerusalem* (New York: Crowell, 1882);

A Third Year in Jerusalem: A Tale Illustrating Customs and Incidents of Modern Jerusalem; or, A Sequel to "Home in the Holy Land" (London: Nisbet, 1869);

Sunrise over Jerusalem, with Other Pen and Pencil Sketches (London: Day, 1873);

Jeroboam, the Arch Rebel (London: Privately printed, 1900);

The Duty of Christians towards the Children of Israel (London: Society for the Relief of Persecuted Jews, 1907);

Emmaus Identified (London: Privately printed, 1907);

Palestine Peasantry: Notes on their Clans, Warfare, Religion and Laws (London & Edinburgh: Marshall, 1923);

Church Work with Intermediates (Philadelphia & Boston: Judson, [1926]);

Reminiscences of Mrs. Finn, Member of the Royal Asiatic Society (London: Marshall, Morgan & Scott, 1929).

OTHER: Johann Caspar Lavater, *Original Maxims for the Young,* translated by Finn (London, 1838);

Thomas Platerus the Elder, *The Autobiography of Thomas Platter, a Schoolmaster of the Sixteenth Century,* translated by Finn (London, 1839);

James Finn, *Stirring Times; or, Records from Jerusalem Consular Chronicles of 1853 to 1856,* 2 volumes, edited by Finn (London: Kegan Paul, 1878);

"Incidents of Life in Summer Encampments near Jerusalem," in *In a Good Cause: A Collection of Stories, Poems, and Illustrations,* compiled by Margaret Susan Tyssen Amherst (London: Wells, 1885; New York, 1885);

Elizabeth Anne Finn

Songs, Shouts, Stunts, compiled by Finn (Philadelphia & Boston: Judson, [1927]);

James Finn, *A View from Jerusalem,* edited by Finn and Arnold Blumberg (Cranbury, N.J.: Associated University Presses, 1980).

Elizabeth Anne (McCaul) Finn witnessed and vividly portrayed the daily life of Jerusalem against the background of large historic events such as the Crimean War and the establishment of the major

European consulates in Palestine. An evangelical Christian and millenarian Zionist schooled in ancient languages and theological controversies, she was the wife of James Finn, British consul to Jerusalem from 1846 to 1863. During her residence in Jerusalem and upon her return to England, she wrote and published a fictional account of the experiences of English Christian missionaries to the Mideast derived from firsthand observations of Jerusalem's culture, as well as an annotated collection of lithographs based on her sketches of the biblical landscape that she understood in depth. After her husband's death she edited and wrote substantial annotations to his memoirs, *Stirring Times; or, Records from Jerusalem Consular Chronicles of 1853 to 1856* (1878), an analysis of conditions in Palestine during the Crimean War. At the end of her life she dictated her own memoirs, *Reminiscences of Mrs. Finn, Member of the Royal Asiatic Society* (1929). Although her views are marked by an air of cultural and religious superiority, they reveal an extensive and sympathetic knowledge of the languages, histories, and religious beliefs of Jerusalem's Christians, Arabs, and Jews. Her life illustrates the dedication to a larger cause that was typical of many middle-class Victorians.

Yet Finn's works and the record of her life have passed into obscurity. Two features appear to have contributed to her effacement from the pages of historical and literary scholarship: the influence of powerful and scholarly male figures in her life and possibly a reluctance to engage publicly in the egotism of travel writing. In addition, the religiosity of her fictional works may pose difficulties for modern audiences. Some readers may find the value of her work to be mainly historical, but those who appreciate descriptive Victorian writing may discover in it certain aesthetic rewards.

The eldest daughter of a large Irish family, Finn was born 14 March 1825 at the Palace Zamiosky in Warsaw, Poland, where her father, the Hebrew scholar Alexander McCaul, was working as a missionary to Polish and Russian Jews. Finn's memoirs describe her father as having "devoted his life to what he considered to be the highest good of the Jewish people, and through them of the whole world." Because a journey to Palestine was impossible, he had traveled as an emissary of the London Jews' Society to work as a missionary among the Polish and Russian Jews. After his first visit to Poland he temporarily returned home to Ireland in 1823 to become ordained; there he married Finn's mother, whom she identifies only as "Miss Crosthwaite of Virgemont, Dublin." Her mother appears to have provided her with a model for her

own unusual duties as a wife in a strange land; Finn states that she "must have been of unusually strong character to make up her mind to go so far away (for in those days Poland was considered to be quite in the wilds), but she never regretted the step she had taken."

During her earliest years Finn traveled extensively with her family and finally settled in England with them in 1831. Although she was instructed entirely at home, her education was impressive. She began studying Hebrew at the age of three under the tutelage of a Jewish rabbi, and she eventually learned English, Greek, Latin, German, Yiddish, and some French and Italian. By her early teenage years she had published, as the anonymous "daughter of a clergyman," a translation of German maxims, *Original Maxims for the Young* (1838). She married James Finn early in 1846 and almost immediately set out for Jerusalem with him.

The depth of her interest in Jerusalem is everywhere apparent in her work. At the close of her memoirs she assesses with satisfaction the changes that had taken place there since the 1830s, when her father and members of his circle had begun to take an interest in the city and its inhabitants. The British had appointed a consul and established a bishopric, a church, a hospital and a school. Finn was proudest of the protection offered by the British Foreign Office to Jews of any nationality — and of her husband's role in providing it. "It was Mr. Finn's pleasure as well as duty," she wrote, "to carry out these benevolent instructions to the utmost power during all the years of his residence." Her praise appears to have been anything but objective, however. Arnold Blumberg, editor of the manuscript copy for *A View from Jerusalem* (1980) that Finn had edited from her husband's consular diary, calls him a "flawed genius," a righteous zealot who "managed to alienate almost everyone with whom he came into prolonged contact." Both of the Finns appear to have been motivated in part by Christian millenarianism and a tendency to view the impoverished Jews of Jerusalem as potential converts.

Whatever her motives were, Finn appears to have done much good. She worked actively to improve the lives of the Jewish inhabitants, and she saw it as her duty to better their economic conditions by establishing a school in which they could be taught valuable skills and by organizing relief efforts during a famine.

Her first travel work, *Home in the Holy Land: A Tale Illustrating Customs and Incidents in Modern Jerusalem* (1866), was begun during her residence in the

1856   April

had been repeated — And he required a delay to inquire into books & if possible to consult the Mufti (who was at the time on pilgrimage to Nebi Moosa) before pronouncing sentence —

He found it necessary to consult as to this point — if there should appear to his mind a reasonable doubt of the accidental nature of the occurrence — whether Mr Lydis declaration could be received without an oath in justification of his ~~innocent~~ absence of malicious intent —

In consequence of earnest entreaty, the Cadi promised to decide speedily — if possible tomorrow — and would endeavour to give his judgment on Wednesday (the 23rd —)

Interview with Shaikh Fadd'l el Faikh of Jebel Ajloon — and letter given to the Consulate of Damascus —

Examination of papers respecting the timber purchase case of Mshullam in 1843 —

Interview with one of Mahmood Yeki's family —

Diary entries by Elizabeth Anne Finn and her husband, James (Towson State University Media Services, Towson, Maryland)

The Mosque of Omar in 1857; photograph by James Graham, who was one of the earliest photographers in Jerusalem and nurtured Finn's interest in preserving the history of the region through photographs

Mideast and was published upon her return to England. This book and its sequel, *A Third Year in Jerusalem: A Tale Illustrating Customs and Incidents of Modern Jerusalem* (1869), are fictions in which an imaginary female character narrates the events of a story. They are, however, travel works in that they extensively describe the land based on Finn's observations and in their intentions, in part, to provide information about this foreign milieu to their English audience. Billie Melman finds the two works typical of the writings of a group of nineteenth-century women travelers to the Orient. "Women," she writes, "tend to relate their own experiences of travel to that of others and to develop a number of stratagems and ploys to avoid individualist narrative." Thus, certain women travelers (including Finn) who wrote about their experiences in the Orient tended to construct *bildung* narratives from their direct experiences.

One way that Finn avoids the appearance of the narrative egotism that this situation invites is by depicting her main character as a dutiful friend, daughter, sister, and finally wife to scholarly and artistic men. Possibly employed to disguise the range of the author's own knowledge, this technique al-

lows her to relate, within the fictional construct, what appear to be observations made by male characters rather than by her female narrator.

The story begins with the arrival of the narrator, Emily Russell, and her father, a Christian scholar of Hebrew, in Palestine. The two are later joined by Walter, Emily's brother, who has planned to come to Jerusalem to paint biblical characters "amid the scenes in which the incidents actually occurred." The early chapters provide vivid descriptions of the coastline from Galilee to Judaea, and the arrival of father and daughter at Jaffa. The narrator's interest in biblical lore is quickly apparent, as she points out the "aptness" of names of places mentioned in scripture: Joppa, or Jaffa, she notes, means "the beautiful." She obviously regards her father as more learned than she; immediately after the two have their first glimpse of Palestinian Arabs, she uncritically relates her father's comment that the Arabs "have suffered ages of oppression," but display an "Oriental indolence of manner."

During the course of the narrative, as Emily and her brother become established in the city following the illness and death of their father, they meet an English clergyman, Mr. Andersen.

Unidentified child with one of the consulate security men who always accompanied Finn on her travels

Through the main character's conversations with him, Finn reveals the racist attitudes of conventional British evangelicals toward the non-Christian inhabitants of Jerusalem. As Mr. Andersen watches a Christian church being built, he comments on the Arab workmen:

> They still need constant watching, but when they found that their pay depended upon their work, they improved rapidly. At first . . . they had no idea of steady earnings. However, by the time the regular architect came from England, the worst was over, and one or two masons from Malta have taught them to work; for really the Arabs are very quick of perception. They can learn if they like; and when once the stimulus of money has been applied, they understand its meaning, and do very well. I have no doubt that they will make excellent workmen.

In the final chapters of the book the remains of the late Mr. Russell are removed to Mount Zion, and the completion of Walter's painting acquires a spiritual significance that he explains: "Naomi, who had passed through trials and sorrows during her lifetime . . . had left the shadows of evening behind her, and had now attained the evening of her days, where rest and the sunshine of prosperity awaited her." The slanting afternoon sun in the painting is linked symbolically with the reinterment of Mr.

Russell's body, laid to rest "amid the slanting shadows of evening among the olive-trees." The particular quality of the light is a biblical symbol that links the painting and its completion with the final rest of Mr. Russell's body; both events suggest the end of prolonged trials, a millenarian theme emphasized in a footnote in which Finn quotes Zech. 14:7, "at even-time it shall be light," and comments that this "is a promise given to the nation of Israel for their comfort in this cloudy and dark day of their long dispersion."

In *A Third Year in Jerusalem* Miss Russell lives in Jerusalem and runs a school for the gainful employment of Jews. At the end of the story she marries and remains in Jerusalem, and Walter returns with his new bride to England. Feminine charitable work, exemplified by Miss Russell's school, is important in *A Third Year in Jerusalem*. In her *Reminiscences* Finn relates her long acquaintance and working relationship with a remarkable English woman, Caroline Cooper. At Finn's urging, Cooper traveled to Jerusalem in 1848 to conduct charitable activities among the Jews; she ran a needlework school for Jewish women until her death in 1859. Melman points out that Miss Cooper is fictionalized as Miss Brandon in *A Third Year in Jerusalem*. This evangelical missionary believed, as did Finn, in promoting gainful economic activity among the poor rather than in mere proselytizing, and Finn's portrait of her "captures the spirit," Melman writes, "of women's work for women in the mid-nineteenth century and the meanings for middle-class philanthropists and missionaries, of a 'positive' activity and life abroad."

As an amateur biblical scholar and naturalist, Finn took an ardent interest in the Palestinian landscape; its written or sketched portrayal is an important aspect of her work. Frequently she engages in the Victorian practice of word painting – the vivid, verbal construction of a natural scene. In the closing pages of *A Third Year in Jerusalem,* for example, Emily wakes on her wedding day and describes the scene beyond her window:

> I watched the light from the east reflected upon the many houses of Zion, and earliest of all on the east wall of our church, which, by reason of the fresh whiteness of its newly-quarried stones, caught the first gleam of dawning day. . . .
>
> The golden stars were setting silently in the deep blue sky. . . . The deep blue became azure, the golden stars paled to silver.

Another of her descriptive techniques is to note the continuing resemblance between the flora, fauna, and topography of contemporary Palestine and the portrayal of these in the Bible. For example, in her *Reminiscences* she writes of a particularly beautiful ground dove, "with burnished feathers like those of a pheasant," that reminds her of a passage from Jeremiah: "We mourn sore like doves."

This emphasis on landscape is related to Finn's interest in the visual arts. In her memoirs she notes having met an English clergyman engaged in making Talbottypes – prototypical photographs – of the Palestinian landscape. Interested in this new procedure, she afterward sent to England for the proper "apparatus." She also briefly mentions that in 1855 the British painter William Holman Hunt was living in Jerusalem while he painted biblical landscapes. While she says nothing about whether she and Hunt actually met, it appears that they probably did, for in the introduction to her collection of lithographs, *Sunrise over Jerusalem, with Other Pen and Pencil Sketches* (1873), Hunt provides a rather lukewarm "recommendation" of the pictures: "While they do not pretend to be art pictures, the subjects are chosen with great taste," he wrote; they provide "excellent topographical studies of the localities," and serve as worthwhile illustrations. In the preface to the collection Finn seems to concur with Hunt's judgment. She writes that the purpose

of the pictures is to add to existing knowledge of the Holy Land observations made by a long-term resident, one familiar with its seasons and customs. Each of the sixteen prints is accompanied by a comment on the vantage point from which it was taken, its historical and biblical significance, and meticulous notes on the way the light changes in each scene during the course of the day.

Finn's *Reminiscences* provide the fullest record of her foreign residence. In it she describes her childhood travels in Europe; her education, marriage, and journey with her husband; and the daily lives and interactions of Christians, Muslims, and Jews in Jerusalem. She notes the history, trades, and languages of the Jewish Sephardim and Ashkenazim as well as those of the Greek and Latin Christian communities, and she comments frequently on Arab culture. She devotes much space to charitable and evangelical work that she and other English subjects conduct.

The book offers insights into British attitudes toward this foreign milieu. Finn portrays the area as a semicivilized oasis in the midst of Eastern chaos. Her account of the consulate's annual celebration of the queen's birthday gives a glimpse of the ways these transplanted foreigners affirmed, in a strange land, their own culture: "At the end of our evening on that day we always wound up by singing the National Anthem, all standing."

In November 1849 Finn and her husband established the Jerusalem Literary Society, the object of which was the study of antiquities and natural history; it drew "favourable notice" from the archbishop of Canterbury, she writes, and eventually led to the formation of the Palestine Exploration Fund. In 1855 the Finns, with several other consuls and European dignitaries, were allowed by the Turkish pasha to enter the Dome of the Rock and see the foundation of Solomon's temple. This was a reward by the Turkish sultan for the aid of "Christian troops," as she calls them, during the Crimean War.

In her introductory notes to her husband's memoirs Finn comments on the role of Jerusalem in the Crimean War, which was in part a struggle between Eastern and Western Christianity for control of the holy places of that city:

> The terms Eastern and Western churches convey but little living reality to the mind, until one has beheld the thronging multitudes surge around the grand central point to which all the branches of those Eastern and Western churches gravitate; till one has beheld on the spot the ceaseless strife, the never-ending antagonism

and rivalry between the two great divisions of the Roman World christianized. . . .

Now as heretofore, disguise the object as they may, they are striving for a prize that has not been destined by Divine Providence for either; and this prize is no less than a virtual dominion over the Christian World.

Finn remained active long into her old age. In a few pages added to the conclusion of her *Reminiscences,* Finn's daughter writes that in 1875 Finn received as a guest the Patriarch of the Ancient Syrian Church and acted as translator during his theological discussions with English clergymen. She worked for the Palestine Exploration Fund and for a relief committee to aid Russian Jews during the terror of the 1880s, and she provided expertise on Eastern Christianity at a conference of English bishops.

Although the death of British consul James Finn in 1872 was noted in an extensive obituary in the London *Times,* Elizabeth Anne (McCaul) Finn

received no such honor; her death and funeral in 1921 were recorded in a few lines. According to her daughter, however, Finn's funeral at Wimbledon was attended by many friends, including an admiral and "two Jewish Ministers." Among more than two hundred letters of condolence that the family received was one from the archbishop of Canterbury, who wrote that Finn had "done some remarkable work for the bringing together of Eastern and Western Christianity." While her travel works can hardly be said to have achieved anything so grand, they provided Finn's contemporaries with vivid pictures, in image and text, of the everyday lives of people in a region of the world that was of increasing interest and importance to the West.

Reference:

Billie Melman, *Women's Orients, English Women and the Middle East, 1718–1918* (Ann Arbor: University of Michigan Press, 1992).

Sir Francis Galton

(16 February 1822 – 17 January 1911)

Timothy M. Clark
Ohio State University

BOOKS: *The Telotype: A Printing Electric Telegraph* (London: Weale, 1850);

The Narrative of an Explorer in Tropical South Africa (London: John Murray, 1853); republished as *Narrative of an Explorer in Tropical South Africa: Being an Account of a Visit to Damaraland in 1851* (London & New York: Ward, Lock, 1889);

The Art of Travel; or, Shifts and Contrivances Available in Wild Countries (London: Murray, 1855; revised and enlarged edition, London: Murray, 1856, 1860, 1867, 1872); republished as *Francis Galton's Art of Travel* (Newton Abbot, Devon, England: David & Charles, 1971);

Ways and Means of Campaigning (N.p.: Privately printed, 1855);

Arts of Campaigning: An Inaugural Lecture Delivered at Aldershot (London: Murray, 1855);

Arts of Travelling and Campaigning (London: T. Brettell, 1856);

Catalogue of Models Illustrative of the Arts of Camp Life (London: Brettell, 1858);

English Weather Data, February 9, 1861, 9 A.M. (N.p.: Privately printed, 1861);

Circular Letter to Meteorological Observers, Synchronous Weather Charts (N.p.: Privately printed, 1861);

Weather Map of the British Isles for Tuesday, September 3, 1861, 9 A.M. (N.p.: Privately printed, 1861);

Meteorological Instructions for the Use of Inexperienced Observers Resident Abroad (N.p.: Meteorological Society, 1862);

Meteorographica, or Methods of Mapping the Weather (London & Cambridge: Macmillan, 1863);

The Knapsack Guide for Travellers in Switzerland (London: Murray, 1864);

Hereditary Genius: An Inquiry into Its Laws and Consequences (London: Macmillan, 1869; New York: Appleton, 1870; revised edition, New York: Appleton, 1871);

Francis Galton

English Men of Science: Their Nature and Nurture (London: Macmillan, 1874; New York: Appleton, 1875);

The Prayer-Gauge Debate, by Prof. Tyndall, Francis Galton, and Others, against Dr. Littledale, President McCosh, the Duke of Argyll, Canon Liddon, and "The Spectator," edited by John O. Means (Boston: Congregational Publishing, 1876);

Address to the Anthropological Department of the British Association (London: Clowes, 1877);

Psychometric Experiments (London: Clowes, 1879);

Generic Images (London: Clowes, [1879]);

Inquiries into Human Faculty and Its Development (London & New York: Macmillan, 1883; revised edition, London: J. M. Dent, New York: E. P. Dutton, 1908); modern reprint (London: The Eugenics Society, 1957);

Final Report of the Anthropometric Committee (London: Spottiswoode, 1883);

Outfit for an Anthropometric Laboratory (N.p.: Privately printed, 1883);

Anthropometric Laboratory (London: Clowes, 1884);

Record of Family Faculties (London: Macmillan, 1884);

Pedigree Moths: On a Proposed Series of Experiments in Breeding Moths (London: Harrison, 1887);

A Descriptive List of Anthropometric Apparatus (Cambridge: Cambridge Scientific Instrument, 1887);

Natural Inheritance (London & New York: Macmillan, 1889);

Tests and Certificates of the Kew Observatory (N.p.: Kew Committee of the Royal Society, 1890);

The Patterns in Thumb, and Finger Marks (London: Kegan Paul, French, Trübner, 1891);

Finger Prints (London & New York: Macmillan, 1892; reprinted, New York: Da Capo Press, 1956);

Decipherment of Blurred Finger Prints (London & New York: Macmillan, 1893);

Physical Index to 100 Persons Based on Their Measures and Finger Prints (N.p.: Privately printed, 1894);

Finger Print Directories (London & New York: Macmillan, 1895);

Private Circular of Committee for Measurement of Plants and Animals (N.p.: Royal Society, 1896);

Index to Achievements of Near Kinsfolk of Some of the Fellows of the Royal Society (London & Bungay: Clay, [1904]);

Noteworthy Families (Modern Science): An Index to Kinships in near Degrees between Persons Whose Achievements Are Honourable, and Have Been Publicly Recorded, with Edgar Schuster (London: Murray, 1906);

Sociological Papers, by Galton, Patrick Geddes, M. E. Sadler, and E. Westernarck (London: Macmillan, 1906);

Probability: The Foundation of Eugenics (Oxford: Clarendon, 1907);

Memories of My Life (London: Methuen, 1908; New York: Dutton, 1909);

Essays in Eugenics (London: Eugenics Education Society, 1909).

OTHER: *Vacation Tourists and Notes of Travel in 1860,* edited by Galton (Cambridge & London: Macmillan, 1861);

"Visit to North Spain at the time of the eclipse," in *Vacation Tourists and Notes of Travel in 1860,* edited by Galton (London: Macmillan, 1861): 422–454;

Vacation Tourists and Notes of Travel in 1861, edited, with a preface, by Galton (Cambridge & London: Macmillan, 1862);

Vacation Tourists and Notes of Travel in 1862–3, edited, with a preface, by Galton (Cambridge & London: Macmillan, 1864);

Hints to Travellers, edited by Galton, G. Beck, and R. Collinson (London: Royal Geographical Society, 1865); fourth edition, edited by Galton (London: Royal Geographical Society, 1878);

Life History Album, edited by Galton (London: Macmillan, 1884); rearranged edition, edited by Galton (London: Macmillan, 1902);

"Notes on Modern Geography," in *Cambridge Essays contributed by Members of the University,* edited by J. W. Parker (London: Parker, 1885): 79–109;

William Edward Oswell, *William Cotton Oswell, Hunter and Explorer: The Story of His Life,* introduction by Galton (London: Heinemann, 1900);

William Palin Elderton and Ethel Mary Elderton, *Primer of Statistics,* preface by Galton (London: Black, 1909).

SELECTED PERIODICAL PUBLICATIONS – UNCOLLECTED: "Recent expedition into the interior of South-Western Africa," *Journal of the Royal Geographical Society,* 22 (1852): 140–163;

"List of astronomical instruments, etc." In "Hints to travellers," *Journal of the Royal Geographical Society,* 24 (1854): 1–13;

"The exploration of arid countries," *Proceedings of the Royal Geographical Society,* 2 (1858): 60–77;

"Sun signals for the use of travellers (hand heliostat)," *Proceedings of the Royal Geographical Society,* 4 (1859): 14–19;

"Zanzibar," *The Mission Field,* 6 (1861): 121–130;

"Recent discoveries in Australia," *Cornhill Magazine,* 5 (1862): 354–364;

"Report on African explorations," *Proceedings of the Royal Geographical Society,* 6 (1862): 175–178;

"Explorations in Eastern Africa," *The Reader,* 1 (1863): 19, 42–43;

"The Sources of the Nile," *The Reader,* 1 (1863): 615;

"The Climate of Lake Nyanza. Deduced from the Observations of Captains Speke and Grant," *Proceedings of the Royal Geographical Society,* 7 (1863): 225–227;

"Letters of Henry Stanley from Equatorial Africa to the *Daily Telegraph,*" *Edinburgh Review,* 147 (January 1878): 166–191.

Sir Francis Galton is best known for his scientific work, especially in meteorology and heredity, two fields in which his work is considered foundational. He is probably best remembered as the founder of the school of eugenics, the goal of which was to improve humanity by selectively breeding the "best" among the people and restricting the offspring of the "worst." His name first became familiar, however, when he explored Africa as a young man; he later wrote about his adventures and wrote a general guide to travel. These works, while seldom considered today, brought Galton the respect of his contemporaries in the Royal Geographical Society.

Born 16 February 1822 Galton was the youngest child in a family of four daughters and three sons born to Samuel Tertius Galton, a banker, and Frances Anne Violetta, the daughter by a second marriage of Erasmus Darwin, the famed medical practitioner and speculative scientist. Galton was a brilliant child, proficient in Latin and Greek when he was eight years old. Science, however, was his greatest interest, and by the age of fourteen, when he was sent to King Edward's School in Birmingham, he had grown tired of Latin and Greek and had begun to wish for what he felt was a more practical education. He says in his autobiography, *Memories of My Life* (1908), "I had craved for what was denied, namely, an abundance of good English reading, well-taught mathematics, and solid science. Grammar and the dry rudiments of Latin and Greek were abhorrent to me, for there seemed so little sense in them."

Galton spent two years at King Edward's School before he began a medical apprenticeship in Birmingham, a position in which he was given great responsibilities, including those of setting broken bones and aiding in surgery. In 1839 he moved to London in order to obtain better theoretical instruction at King's College. In early 1840, as he was returning to London after visiting his family for Christmas, Galton met a Captain Sayers, who had traveled in Africa and recounted his adventures on the continent for Galton. Biographer D. W. Forrest finds that when Galton decided to begin exploring a decade later, his choice of Africa as his object "may have been determined by this chance meeting."

This passion to travel first struck Galton in the spring of 1840, and he persuaded his father to finance a summer trip to Germany for the ostensible purpose of studying under Baron Justus von Liebig, a famous chemist. Apparently Galton's desire to travel greatly outweighed his desire to learn organic chemistry, however, for after a mere five days he complained that he was not learning what he wanted to learn, and he left for Vienna. From there he visited Constantinople, Athens, Venice, and Milan. When he returned to England, he enrolled in Trinity College, Cambridge, to study mathematics to further his preparation as a physician. An illness left him with no hope of graduating with honors, and in 1844 he took a "poll" degree, one awarded to those whose work merited passing but no honors.

In October 1844 his father died, and Galton's inheritance left him wealthy enough to abandon his medical studies, with which he had become disillusioned. In October 1845 he left London for the Middle East, ostensibly to sail the Nile River, but his travels ranged more broadly than that. On the Steamer to Alexandria he met two Cambridge friends, and the three were later introduced to Arnand Bey, a well-known St. Simonian exile in the service of Mehemet Ali, then ruler of Egypt. Arnand Bey suggested that they travel by camel across the Bishari Desert to Khartoum, a feat not generally attempted by the average tourist. Galton and his party spent seven days battling the extremes of heat and cold in the desert before they arrived safely in Khartoum and resumed their journey down the Nile. After spending a week in Cairo, the party separated, and Galton proceeded to the Holy Land. Staying first in Damascus and then in Salahieh, he spent several weeks there before traveling again by camel to Jerusalem, where he attempted to float down the Jordan River but failed. He then planned to circumnavigate the Dead Sea, but he had to give up this scheme and return to England when he learned that his sister needed his assistance in some legal matters. He arrived in London in November of 1846.

Although Galton never published a travel narrative about this trip, in 1885 he did prepare a manuscript of these early adventures. These experiences would no doubt prove valuable to the young

Woodcut from Galton's first advice book for travelers, The Art of Travel; or, Shifts and Contrivances Available in Wild Countries *(courtesy of the Lilly Library, Indiana University)*

man, however, for as Forrest remarks, Galton had acquired skills useful in his subsequent journey to South Africa: he had learned "how to organise a camp, how to handle unfamiliar animals, how to maintain direction by sun and stars, and how to cope with extreme temperatures."

After his return to England, however, Galton spent the next four years in relative ease, as he settled into the role of an English country gentleman. He spent most of this time improving his shooting and hunting skills and entertaining himself by walking and riding with his friends. Becoming concerned about his future (particularly about his lack of goals), he grew intrigued with the idea of testing his hunting skills in Africa, but he wished for more than the typical hunting trip. He wanted to engage in serious exploration as well. In consultation with the Royal Geographical Society he planned a journey from Cape Town to Lake Ngami and then up the river that was believed to flow from the lake. This journey was to establish Galton's reputation as an explorer and travel writer, for it provided the experience that he would incorporate in his first travel narrative, *The Narrative of an Explorer in Tropical South Africa* (1853).

This work is typical of the travel narratives of the time: it presents an engaging tale of his experiences in the jungle, with emphasis on the superiority and heroism of the explorer. Galton is more interested in presenting an exciting story than in describing the flora and fauna of the land, and he does not attempt detailed anthropological study. He presents the journal of a traveler rather than the observations of a scientist.

Considered as one of the many journeys described in travel narratives of the time, Galton's trip is not extraordinary. It did, however, present him with some interesting experiences. He ran into a problem almost immediately when one tribal leader's attacks on several settlements along Galton's proposed route made the prospect of continuing dangerous. Galton sent a letter to this leader, Jonker, to express the goodwill of the English government and attempt to reach a settlement of peace and safe passage. Jonker replied with a vague letter that made no promises, and this prompted Galton to respond with a more strongly worded letter expressing his intent to travel through the area and his willingness to use force if he were impeded. Receiving no reply to his letter and fearing that the entire expedition might be in jeopardy, Galton decided to go to Jonker's headquarters.

Galton's narrative of this incident provides a typical presentation of an imperial British demeanor. He describes himself as dressed in hunting jacket and cap, and he says that he rode his ox at a trot straight toward Jonker's hut. When he reached it, he pushed the animal's head as far into the tent as possible and surprised the chief, who had been relaxing with an evening pipe. Galton reports that the leader was completely overwhelmed by this aggressive entry by one dressed in such finery. Galton berated him in English and then finally made his demands through an interpreter. Jonker would not look him in the face and humbly assented to Galton's demand that the chief assemble a meeting of tribal leaders to establish peace in the region. In the course of these meetings Galton then convinced the chiefs to allow him to draw up a system of laws to help control the rampant murder and cattle theft in the region. While this code produced peace in the area for a year, Jonker resumed his violent domination of the region after Galton, and the fear of violent consequences that he had threatened, had left.

Galton appears to have had little respect for the indigenous people. He disparages the intelligence of his Damaran guides: "When they wish to express four, they take to their fingers, which are to them as formidable instruments of calculation as a sliding-rule is to an English schoolboy. They puzzle very much after five; because no spare hand remains to grasp and secure the fingers that are required for 'units.'" He does acknowledge that, though they lack skill with numbers, they are skilled in matters related to their livelihoods, for "they seldom lose oxen: the way in which they discover the loss of one, is not by the number of the herd being diminished, but by the absence of a face they know." Galton also sees signs of their depravity in their language, which he says "is not strong in the cardinal virtues; the language possessing no word at all for gratitude; but on looking hastily over my dictionary I find fifteen that express different forms of villainous deceit." He deprecates the people in the most cursory terms: "There is hardly a particle of romance, or affection, or poetry, in their character or creed; but they are a greedy, heartless, silly set of savages."

Lacking water and supplies, Galton was forced to stop short of Lake Ngami and was thus willing to turn back without reaching his goal. He returned to Cape Town and from there took a schooner back to England, where he arrived in April 1852, two years to the day after he had left.

While not containing the mass of scientific data one might expect from the man who was to become one of the most eminent Victorian scientists, Galton's book was nonetheless quite exciting reading. One of Galton's favorite reactions to his work was that of his cousin, Charles Darwin, who wrote to Galton,

> I last night finished your volume with such lively interest, that I cannot resist the temptation of expressing my admiration at your expedition, and at the capital account you have published of it. . . . What labours and dangers you have gone through: I can hardly fancy how you can have survived them. . . . I . . . employ myself in Zoology; but the objects of my study are very small fry, and to a man accustomed to rhinoceroses and lions, would appear infinitely insignificant.

Not only was the book enjoyable to read, but the Royal Geographical Society deemed Galton's efforts worthy enough to earn one of their two annual gold medals. In his autobiography Galton records that this was awarded to him

> for having at his own cost and in furtherance of the expressed desire of the Society, fitted out an expedition to explore the centre of South Africa, and for having so successfully conducted it through the countries of the Namaquas, the Damaras, and the Ovampo (a journey of about 1700 miles), as to enable this Society to publish a valuable memoir and map in the last volume of the Jour-

Galton and his wife, Louisa, at the time of their marriage

nal, relating to a country hitherto unknown; the astronomical observations determining the latitude and longitude of places have been most accurately made by himself.

This recognition established Galton as a distinguished member of the Royal Geographical Society, and he was elected to its council in 1854. He was also elected to the Athenaeum Club on the grounds of scientific distinction, awarded a Silver Medal by the French Geographical Society, and named a Fellow of the Royal Society in 1856.

Aside from one short trip to Egypt, Galton never again traveled outside western Europe. He did, however, produce a book designed to provide travelers with the type of practical information and advice that he had lacked on his journey into Africa. He collected information for the book not only from his own experiences but also from studying such works as Pinkerton's *General Collection of Voyages and Travels* (1808–14), a seventeen-volume collection of narratives from every continent, as well as more up-to-date materials to which Galton had access as secretary of the Royal Geographical Society.

His book *The Art of Travel; or, Shifts and Contrivances Available in Wild Countries* (1855) begins with an exhortation: "If you have health, a great craving for adventure, at least a moderate fortune, and can set your heart on a definite object, which old travellers do not think impracticable, then – travel by all means." The work discusses the very first steps of a journey, ends with a discussion of a "Conclusion of the Journey," and addresses every conceivable circumstance that might intervene. It contains little of the type of research that Galton was later to pioneer (in such fields as anthropology, for instance), but it is replete with practical advice for the traveler. He presents, for example, methods of preventing medical problems:

> To prevent the feet from blistering, it is a good plan to soap the inside of the stocking before setting out, making a thick lather all over it. A raw egg broken into a boot, before putting it on, greatly softens the leather. . . . After some hours on the road, when the feet are beginning to be chafed, take off the shoes, and change the stockings; putting what was the right stocking on the left foot, and the left stocking on the right foot.

Some of the advice is technical, and Galton sometimes goes to interesting extremes in his passion for statistics and diagrams. For example, part of his formula for regaining a lost path is so complicated as to be unintelligible to the average reader:

> Let P be the point where the traveller finds himself at fault, and let P D be a distance within which the path certainly lies; then the circle, E D F, somewhere cuts the path, and the traveller starting from P must first go to D, and then make the entire circuit, D E H F D, before he has exhausted his search. This distance of P D + D E H F D = P D + 6 P D nearly, = 7 P D altogether, which gives the length of road that the man must be prepared to travel over who can answer no other than the question A. Of course, P D may cut the path, but I am speaking of the *extreme* distance which the lost man may have to travel.

This explanation is accompanied by a diagram, which, if it does anything, further confuses the issue.

Galton also informs his readers on a topic about which many were concerned, the management of "savages." His discussion of this reveals an ambivalence toward native peoples:

> A frank, joking, but determined manner, joined with an air of showing more confidence in the good faith of the natives than you really feel, is the best. . . . [T]hey thoroughly appreciate common sense, truth, and uprightness; and are not half such fools as strangers usually account them. If a savage does mischief, look on him as you would on a kicking mule, or a wild animal, whose

nature is to be unruly and vicious, and keep your temper quite unruffled.

Galton clearly considers natives to be inferior to Europeans – indeed, to him they are apparently as much animals as humans – yet despite his denigrating remarks he proclaims them to be "not half such fools" as white explorers usually believe them to be.

Galton not only offers this practical advice but also instructs travelers about the appropriate mental attitude throughout the journey: "Interest yourself chiefly in the progress of your journey, and do not look forward to its end with eagerness. It is better to think of a return to civilisation, not as an end to hardship and a haven from ill, but as a close to an adventurous and pleasant life." And further,

> unless a traveller makes himself at home and comfortable in the bush, he will never be quite contented with his lot; but will fall into the bad habit of looking forwards to the end of his journey, and to his return to civilisation, instead of complacently interesting himself in its continuance. This is a frame of mind in which few great journeys have been successfully accomplished; and an explorer who cannot divest himself of it, may suspect he has mistaken his vocation.

The essential theme of the book is that the traveler should "enjoy his journey rather than strive anxiously for a goal; travel is an experience rather than a quest."

The work was published in five editions through 1872, and each one added more information; and while nothing was added after 1872, three further editions were published. As the book was enlarged, it changed from being something of a sportsman's guide to being more of a professional explorer's manual. While it has little more than historical interest today, in its time it was a useful handbook for travelers, a resource that Forrest claims "has not been effectively superseded," and it quickly became required reading for young men traveling not only to Africa but also to the Americas and elsewhere.

Throughout the rest of his life Galton concerned himself primarily with scientific inquiry. He made considerable contributions to the field of meteorology and produced basic studies in fingerprinting. Indeed, discoveries he made in this latter field are bases for methods used in criminal departments all over the world. This work was published in *Finger Prints* (1892), *Decipherment of Blurred Finger Prints* (1893), and *Finger Print Directories* (1895).

He is, of course, best known for his work in the study of heredity, but his important and brilliant work in this field has been overshadowed by twentieth-century repugnance for his concept of "eugenics." While modern readers are repelled by the bigotry implicit in this theory, Galton's work should not be dismissed; in his opinions about race and the best means for improving humanity he was surely a product of his time. His most important studies in heredity are those of *Hereditary Genius: An Inquiry into Its Laws and Consequences* (1869), *English Men of Science: Their Nature and Nurture* (1874), *Inquiries into Human Faculty and Its Development* (1883), *Natural Inheritance* (1889), and *Noteworthy Families (Modern Science): An Index to Kinships in near Degrees between Persons Whose Achievements Are Honourable, and Have Been Publicly Recorded* (1906).

Galton's work as a scientist has almost completely overshadowed his earlier work as an explorer and travel writer, so that he is seldom consid-ered in discussions of British travelers. He is clearly not among the most important explorers. Yet he did make contributions that were significant to his contemporaries, and his work in Africa brought him recognition that garnered more ready acceptance for his subsequent work.

Biographies:

Karl Pearson, *The Life, Letters and Labours of Francis Galton,* 3 volumes (Cambridge: Cambridge University Press, 1914–1930);

D. W. Forrest, *Francis Galton: The Life and Work of a Victorian Genius* (London: Elek, 1974).

Reference:

Dorothy Middleton, Introduction to *Francis Galton's Art of Travel,* by Galton (Newton Abbot, Devon, England: Charles, 1971), pp. 5–17.

Anna Jameson

(19 May 1794 – 17 March 1860)

Deborah L. Phelps

Sam Houston State University

See also the Jameson entry in *DLB 99: Canadian Writers Before 1890.*

BOOKS: *A First or Mother's Dictionary for Children* (London: Darton, 1810–1830);

Cadijah; or, The Black Palace: A Tragedy (London, 1825);

A Lady's Diary, anonymous (London: Thomas, 1826); republished as *Diary of an Ennuyée* (London: Colburn, 1826; Philadelphia: Littell, 1826);

The Loves of the Poets, 2 volumes, anonymous (London: Colburn, 1829); republished as *Memoirs of the Loves of the Poets* (London: Colburn & Bentley, 1831; Boston: Russell, Odiorne, 1833); republished as *The Romance of Biography; or, Memoirs of Women Loved and Celebrated by Poets, from the Days of the Troubadours to the Present Age: A Series of Anecdotes Intended to Illustrate the Influence Which Female Beauty and Virtue Have Exercised over the Characters and Writings of Men of Genius* (London: Saunders & Otley, 1837);

Memoirs of Celebrated Female Sovereigns, 2 volumes (London: Colburn & Bentley, 1831; New York: Harper, 1832; enlarged and corrected, London: Saunders & Otley, 1834); republished anonymously as *Heroines of History,* edited by Mary E. Hewitt (New York: Cornish, Lamport, 1852); republished as *Lives of Celebrated Female Sovereigns and Illustrious Women,* by Jameson, edited by Hewitt (Philadelphia: Porter & Coates, [1870]);

Characteristics of Women, Moral, Poetical, and Historical, 2 volumes (London: Saunders & Otley, 1832; New York: Saunders & Otley, 1832; enlarged edition, London: Saunders & Otley, 1833; enlarged again, London: Saunders & Otley, 1836; New York: Saunders & Otley, 1837); republished as *Shakespeare's Female Characters: An Appendix to Shakespeare's Dramatic Works* (Bielefeld, Germany: Velhagen & Klasing, 1840); republished as *The Heroines of Shake-*

Anna Jameson (watercolor portrait; Metropolitan Toronto Library, J. Ross Robertson Collection)

speare (New York: Wiley, 1846); republished as *Shakespeare's Heroines* (London: Bell, 1879; Philadelphia: Altemus, [1899]);

The Beauties of the Court of King Charles the Second (London: Colburn, 1833; Philadelphia: Carey & Hart, 1834); republished as *Court Beauties of the Reign of King Charles the Second* (London: Hotten, 1872);

Visits and Sketches at Home and Abroad, with Tales and Miscellanies Now First Collected, and a New Edition of the Diary of an Ennuyée (4 volumes, London: Saunders & Otley, 1834; 2 volumes, New York: Harper, 1834); republished as *Visits and Sketches at Home and Abroad, with Tales and Miscellanies Now First Collected,* 3 volumes (London: Saunders & Otley, 1935); republished as *Visits*

184

and Sketches at Home and Abroad, 2 volumes (London: Saunders & Otley, 1939);

Sketches of Germany: Art, Literature, Character (Frankfurt am Main: Jugel, 1837); enlarged and republished as *Sketches of Art, Literature, and Character* (Boston: Ticknor & Fields, 1857);

Winter Studies and Summer Rambles in Canada (3 volumes, London: Saunders & Otley, 1838; 2 volumes, New York: Wiley & Putnam, 1839); abridged as *Sketches in Canada, and Rambles among the Red Men,* 2 parts (London: Longman, Brown, Green & Longmans, 1852);

Sketches of Italy (Frankfurt am Main: Jugel, 1841);

A Handbook to the Public Galleries of Art in and near London, 2 parts (London: Murray, 1842);

Companion to the Most Celebrated Private Galleries of Art in London (London: Saunders & Otley, 1844);

Memoirs of the Early Italian Painters, and of the Progress of Painting in Italy: From Cimabue to Bassano, 2 volumes (London: Knight, 1845; Boston: Ticknor & Fields, 1859); revised and in part rewritten as *Memoirs of the Early Italian Painters,* by Estelle M. Hurll (Boston: Houghton Mifflin, [1895]);

The Relative Position of Mothers and Governesses (London: Spottiswoode & Shaw, [1846?]);

Memoirs and Essays Illustrative of Art, Literature, and Social Morals (London: Bentley, 1846; New York: Wiley & Putnam, 1846);

Sacred and Legendary Art, 2 volumes (London: Longman, Brown, Green & Longmans, 1848; Boston: Houghton Mifflin, 1857);

Some Thoughts on Art: Addressed to the Uninitiated, 2 parts in 1 volume (New York: Nesbitt, 1849);

Essays upon Art, and Notices of the Collection of the Works of the Old Masters (New York: Nesbitt, 1849); republished as *Republications of Essays upon Art, and Recent Notices of the Works of the Old Masters, at the Lyceum Gallery . . . June 16th, 1849* (New York: Nesbitt, 1849);

Legends of the Monastic Orders, as Represented in the Fine Arts: Forming the Second Series of Sacred and Legendary Art (London: Longman, Brown, Green & Longmans, 1850; corrected and enlarged edition, London: Longman, Brown, Green & Longmans, 1852; Boston: Ticknor & Fields, 1865);

Legends of the Madonna, as Represented in the Fine Arts: Forming the Third Series of Sacred and Legendary Art (London: Longman, Brown, Green, & Longmans, 1852; corrected and enlarged edition, Boston: Ticknor & Fields, 1853; London: Longman, Brown, Green & Longmans, 1857);

A Commonplace Book of Thoughts, Memories, and Fancies, Original and Selected (London: Longman, 1854; New York: Appleton, 1855);

A Hand-Book to the Courts of Modern Sculpture (London: Crystal Palace Library/Bradbury & Evans, 1854);

Sisters of Charity, Catholic and Protestant, Abroad and at Home (London: Longman, Brown, Green & Longmans, 1855; enlarged edition, 1855); enlarged again as *Sisters of Charity, Catholic and Protestant, and the Communion of Labor* (Boston: Ticknor & Fields, 1857);

The Communion of Labour: A Second Lecture on the Social Employments of Women (London: Longman Brown, Green, Longmans & Roberts, 1856);

Studies, Stories, and Memoirs (Boston: Ticknor & Fields, 1859);

The History of Our Lord as Exemplified in Works of Art, 2 volumes, by Jameson and Elizabeth Rigby, Lady Eastlake (London: Longman, Green, Longman, Roberts & Green, 1864; New York: Longmans, 1890);

The False One, and The Legend of St. Christopher (Rochester, N.Y.: Fitch, 1879);

Description and Analysis of the Great Picture by P. Delaroche in the Amphitheatre of the School of Fine Arts at Paris (London, n.d.).

Editions and Collections: *Mrs. Jameson's Works,* 10 volumes (Boston: Ticknor & Fields, 1866);

Jameson's Works, 10 volumes (Boston: Houghton Mifflin, [1885]); republished as *Works by Mrs. Jameson,* 10 volumes (Boston & New York: Houghton Mifflin, [1899–1911?]);

The Writings on Art of Anna Jameson, edited by Estelle M. Hurll, 5 volumes (Boston: Houghton Mifflin, 1896);

Early Canadian Sketches, edited by G. H. Needler (Toronto: Burns & MacEachern, 1958).

OTHER: Friedrich August Moritz Retzsch, *Fantasien (Fancies),* preface by Jameson (London: Saunders & Otley, 1834);

W. G. Coesvelt, *Collection of Pictures of W. G. Coesvelt,* introduction by Jameson (London: Carpenter, 1836);

Gustav Friedrich Waagen, *Peter Paul Rubens: His Life and Genius,* edited by Jameson (London: Saunders & Otley, 1840);

Amelia, Princess of Saxony, *Social Life in Germany, Illustrated in the Acted Dramas of Her Royal Highness the Princess Amelia of Saxony,* translated, with an introduction and notes, by Jameson (London: Saunders & Otley, 1840);

Wilhelm Heinrich Ludwig Gruner, *The Decorations of the Garden-Pavilion in the Grounds of Buckingham Palace,* introduction by Jameson (London: Murray, 1846);

Count Anthony Hamilton, *Memoirs of Count Grammont,* with notes and biographical sketches by Jameson and Sir Walter Scott (Philadelphia: Gebbie, 1888);

"The Duchess of Cleveland," in *The Story of Nell Gwyn,* by Peter Cunningham (London: Gibbings, 1892), pp. 265–305;

"The Duchess of Portsmouth," in *The Story of Nell Gwyn,* by Cunningham (London: Gibbings, 1892), pp. 209–263.

Anna Jameson's reputation as a learned author of lively, often controversial works on various subjects was well established among her Victorian readers and her circle of influential friends, which included such prominent women writers as Elizabeth Barrett Browning, Harriet Martineau, and Elizabeth Cleghorn Gaskell, as well as Lady Byron (Annabella Milbanke) and the renowned Shakespearean actress Fanny Kemble. Jameson published twenty-nine books on subjects ranging from art and literary criticism to treatises on the social position of women. Significant among her works are her travel writings, particularly those concerning her European journeys and her brief residence and travels in Canada. Jameson's works, especially her travel writings, are of interest to late-twentieth-century audiences because they privilege a voice and perspective that were rare for her time. To readers well versed in feminist theory and politics, Jameson's writings appear surprisingly modern.

Jameson was born Anna Brownell Murphy in Dublin, Ireland. In 1798 she and her four younger sisters immigrated to England with her father, Denis Brownell Murphy, noted for his miniature paintings, and her English-born mother. She was educated at home in London and carefully oversaw the education of her sisters. At age sixteen she began a career as a governess, a common position for an educated woman of her class and financial circumstances, but especially suitable for Jameson, who desired the personal development afforded by work that allowed her to travel. She was employed first by the marquess of Winchester and then, in 1819, by the Rowles family, who took her on their tours throughout Europe. In 1822 she returned to London to work for the Littleton family until her marriage to Robert Sympson Jameson in 1825.

Jameson's work encompasses several genres from *A First or Mother's Dictionary for Children* (1810–

1830) to biography and criticism. Her first travel book masqueraded as a diary, with the title *A Lady's Diary* (1826). In later travel books, particularly those concerning Canada, Jameson discards her anonymous editor's mask and presents her own unvarnished opinions about the local scene. Her literary criticism is unsophisticated but contains cogent discussions of character and literary style. Her most popular and enduring work of criticism, *Characteristics of Women, Moral, Poetical, and Historical* (1832), evaluates Shakespeare's heroines by classifying them into four main character types – "Characters of Intellect," "Characters of Passion and Imagination," "Characters of the Affections," and "Historical Characters." *Characteristics of Women* was popular more for its feminist analyses than for its pedestrian insights into Shakespearean drama. In her later years Jameson's extensive writings on art – particularly Christian art, as in her classic *Sacred and Legendary Art* (1848) and *Legends of the Madonna* (1852) – evidence her travels to European galleries and her continuing interest in her own education. She also published biographies of poets, painters, and female royalty.

Another important part of her life and work was her interest in the Woman Question, and her famous lectures and pamphlets *Sisters of Charity* (1855) and *The Communion of Labour* (1856) promoted Jameson's feminist views on the significance of overlooking women or failing to use them in nondomestic capacities. These works passionately argue that women should be freed from the bonds of low-paying, demeaning employment (such as that of the governess) and praise reformers such as Florence Nightingale, communities of religious women, and activists who were blazing a trail for female emancipation through their advocacy of university educations for women.

Jameson wrote her first books during her tenure as a governess. Her experiences on the Continent with the Rowles family are evident in her first well-known work, *A Lady's Diary,* which was later published with the help of her husband. The *Diary* is a fictionalized account of her travels through Europe, and its heroine, a romantic young woman in rather fragile physical health, displays a love of adventure and strong-willed opinions on foreign culture and personalities that captured the enthusiasm of English readers. Modeled on Germaine de Staël's popular *Corinne* (1807) and George Gordon, Lord Byron's *Childe Harold's Pilgrimage* (1818), the diary provided a juvenile adventure tale for girls, an ingenious (though more mannered) counterpart to picaresque novels such as Henry Fielding's *The History*

Robert Sympson Jameson, the author's husband (portrait by
J. W. L. Forster; Law Society of Upper Canada)

of the Adventures of Joseph Andrews, and of His Friend
Mr. Abraham Adams (1742) and *The History of Tom*
Jones (1749), written primarily for male audiences.
Unlike the traveling male hero involved in the co-
medic petty crime and sexual escapades of the picaresque tradition, the heroine of Jameson's *Diary*
amuses herself by getting to know the cultural holdings and local mores of French and Italian cities.

Though ill and brokenhearted, the heroine is
vigorous in her opinions; she expresses disgust with
the languidly beautiful countryside around Saint-
Germain, France. There the "sickening sunshine"
reminds her of her lost romance, her delight in the
"vast garden" that stretches between Milan and
Padua, and her appreciation of the sublimity of sea
and sky in Venice. Above all, Jameson's heroine
revels in the un-Englishness of the Continental
landscape, which she finds alternately disturbing
and cheering but always distractingly foreign: "Had
I never visited Italy," she writes, "I think I should
never have understood the word *picturesque*. . . .
[N]othing else in England *can* deserve the epithet."
When she encounters familiar English things on her
travels, she curtly dismisses them: "We have visited
the pretty English burial-ground, and the tomb of
[Tobias] Smollett, which in the true English style is

cut and scratched all over with the names of fools,"
she says and then moves on, reserving her descriptive energies for the natural beauties of the country.

Like most nineteenth-century British travel
writers and expatriates, Jameson's heroine does not
"go native." She is always cognizant of being an outsider, and this facilitates her acuity. Though she is
aware of being an outsider, however, the heroine
does not keep herself from experiencing the foreign-
ness of the culture. Unlike Jameson's friend and frequent correspondent Elizabeth Barrett Browning,
who spent much of her professional life in Italy yet
never bothered to learn the language, make friends
with native Italians, or tolerate the cuisine, her heroine appreciates life abroad *because* it is foreign. Her
emotional responses to the places and people she encounters are always foregrounded in vignettes of
local mores and rituals, and the heroine's knowledge of French and (to a lesser extent) Italian further enriches the text.

She is therefore reluctant to leave Italy and
travel home. In France she mourns the contrast between the wet, cold, grimy welcome of industrial
Lyons and the warmth and "genial softness of our
Italian evenings." The entries of *A Lady's Diary*
abruptly end here, and a Jamesonian footnote in-

"Winter Journey to Niagara," an 1837 ink drawing by Jameson (Royal Ontario Museum)

forms the reader that the heroine has died, presumably of romantic despair, and is buried near Autun, France. *A Lady's Diary* made Jameson well known, and subsequent editions of *The Loves of the Poets* (1829), *Memoirs of Celebrated Female Sovereigns* (1831), and especially *Characteristics of Women* established her career, particularly among female readers in England, the Continent, and the United States.

Jameson's marriage had been unhappy from the beginning, and in 1829 she separated from Robert, who left London to take a judgeship in Dominica. Jameson went to Germany, where she indulged her penchants for travel and self-education through tours of the galleries and opera houses. From this trip to the Continent came Jameson's second travel book, *Visits and Sketches at Home and Abroad, with Tales and Miscellanies Now First Collected* (1834), which was first published along with a new edition of her successful first travel book. Although *Visits and Sketches* maintains the diary format of *A Lady's Diary*, it lacks the persona of the fictional heroine and centers more on foreign personalities and art than on landscape. In this work, as with her later *Sketches of Germany: Art, Literature, Character* (1837),

Jameson sought to educate the ethnocentric English about German culture. In Germany she became acquainted with a circle of German artists and intellectuals and began a close friendship with Ottilie von Goethe, daughter-in-law of poet Johann Wolfgang von Goethe.

While Jameson was steadily building her writing career, Robert Jameson had been appointed attorney general of Upper Canada in 1833. Although the couple had separated in 1829, he had always supported his wife's work and had even assisted in getting her first books published in England. Now established in his prominent governmental position and assuming that he would make his life in Canada, Robert asked his wife to join him in Toronto.

Pressured by the financial concerns of assisting her family, Jameson lived in Canada during parts of 1836 and 1837, but her stay was not a happy one. She had become accustomed to her independent life as a successful author and as a seasoned traveler to some of the world's most cosmopolitan cities when she suddenly resumed her domestic duties in an isolated and frigid land with a man whom she found incompatible. Most distressing was what Jameson saw as the insular circle of Toronto society, one that expected her to fulfill the traditional role of socially conscious partner to a respected public figure. Recognizing that Robert was comfortable as a big fish in a provincial small pond and chafing at the pretensions that passed for culture in Toronto, Jameson left Canada after only nine months.

However, her Canadian sojourn did provide some pleasures. Although Toronto was unsatisfactory as a place of residence, Jameson found the indigenous cultures of Upper Canada fascinating, and she thoroughly enjoyed a tour through western and southern Ontario. These experiences resulted in her third major travel book, *Winter Studies and Summer Rambles in Canada* (1838). The winter studies of the first part of the book record Jameson's unhappy months in Toronto during the winter of 1837. Her unflattering descriptions of the harsh weather, unattractive landscape, and elitism of Toronto dismayed its residents following publication of the book. An abridged edition in 1852 excised many of the more-negative remarks.

The summer rambles part of the book more generously depicts Canada and its people. After the long winter Jameson had left Toronto to explore the southwestern regions of the province and cross the northern border of the United States. Her summer travels resume the picaresque of *A Lady's Diary,* but they present Jameson as a more vigorous, risk-taking heroine. Jameson recounts meetings with pioneer settlers (and takes special interest, as always, in the lives of the women) and paints a positive portrait of the North American natives. Jameson became acquainted with the Chippewa through the ministrations of American explorer Henry Rowe Schoolcraft, and, in true picaresque fashion, she was adopted into the tribe.

The brighter tone of the summer rambles clearly contrasts to the bleakness of the winter studies. Jameson found the wilds of Upper Canada, like the Renaissance cities of Italy and Germany, provided a culture that she could explore and learn from, unlike that of the quasi-British outpost of Toronto. The necessary self-sufficiency and proud independence of the pioneers and the rich traditions of the native tribal communities impressed the former governess as much as the glories of the Continent. The sharp perspective of *Winter Studies and Summer Rambles in Canada* disturbed some Canadians, but the book was popular enough throughout England and the United States for Canada to claim Jameson as a major Canadian writer.

The last twenty years of Jameson's life were largely dedicated to her continuing interest in cataloguing art, but she also published several collections of miscellaneous writings. These consist of reprinted essays of earlier works, creative efforts that she had completed but not yet published, and assorted memoirs. Even in these grab-bag efforts she has much to say about foreign cultures. One of these, *Studies, Stories, and Memoirs* (1859), is a collection of anecdotes from Jameson's life and travels published to capitalize on and satisfy public demand for her work.

The studies portion, written as a journal while Jameson was living in Canada, discusses the poet Goethe's opinions on Friedrich Schiller; George Gordon, Lord Byron; and the position of women. An essay on the painter Titian, written in Venice in 1845, analyzes his superiority as a master of color, second only to Raphael in Jameson's opinion. The stories part reprints her early children's drama, "Much Coin, Much Care," among short works of fiction. In the memoirs part Jameson includes a eulogy for American painter Washington Allston, whom she had come to know during visits to New England. The work of Allston most strongly influenced Jameson's critical opinion of American art: America, though young, would never have art of any worth until it stopped importing foreign influences and created its own tradition. This philosophy accords with her observations of foreign cultures in her travel books, and it makes her dissection of Toronto in *Winter Studies and Summer Rambles in Canada* less the sour grapes of a disgruntled outsider than the dismay of a woman of sensibility toward Toronto's ill-fitting mask of European sophistication. America, she hints, should not worry about competing with more-established cultures but work to develop its own artistic identity.

Crucial to Jameson's literary legacy, and a subject she pursued to the end of her life, was the betterment of women's lives, largely through additional equal employment and educational opportunities. Her best-known works on this subject, *Sisters of Charity, Catholic and Protestant, Abroad and at Home* and *The Communion of Labour: A Second Lecture on the Social Employment of Women,* celebrate women who struggle to break away from homebound "women's work" of enforced idleness or unpaid domestic duties, as Jameson recognizes those women who worked to reform the condition of women in England and abroad and provided models of autonomy and sisterly solidarity for all Victorian women. To the end of her life Jameson worked for social reform with young feminist educators such as Emily

Faithfull and Barbara Bodichon and helped to found the *English Woman's Journal.*

Anna Jameson is significant as a woman who empowered herself through writing and travel at a time when the domestic sphere was the woman's culturally defined place. When one considers that she published more than twenty-five original works, supported herself and financially assisted her family, and traveled the world alone — all without the help of an inherited income or, for most of her adult life, a husband (who had omitted her from his will, as she discovered upon his death) — her achievements seem especially remarkable. Although she has been customarily mentioned in footnotes to works devoted to better-known female figures of the period, Jameson's critical reputation is enjoying a deserved boost. To a generation of scholars trained in feminist theory, Anna Jameson's life and work appear refreshingly modern. As a travel writer and a woman, she provides a perspective on places and people that readers are used to seeing mainly through the eyes of men.

Letters:

Anna Jameson, Letters and Friendships (1816–1860), edited by Mrs. Steuart Erskine (London: Unwin, 1915; New York: Dutton, 1916);

Letters of Anna Jameson to Ottilie von Goethe, edited by G. H. Needler (London & New York: Oxford University Press, 1939).

Biographies:

Geraldine Macpherson, *Memoirs of the Life of Anna Jameson* (London: Longmans, Green, 1878);

Clara Thomas, *Love and Work Enough: The Life of Anna Jameson* (Toronto: University of Toronto Press, 1968; London: Macdonald, 1968).

References:

Marian Fowler, *The Embroidered Tent: Five Gentlewomen in Early Canada* (Toronto: Anansi, 1982);

Pauline Nestor, *Female Friendships and Communities* (Oxford: Clarendon Press, 1985).

Papers:

Anna Jameson's correspondence is collected in 410 letters to and from Ottilie von Goethe at the Goethe and Schiller Archives, Weimar, Germany. Seventy-eight letters to and from Elizabeth Barrett Browning are held by the Wellesley College Library, Wellesley, Massachusetts; thirty letters to and from Jameson are at the Yale University Library. Twenty-six letters from Jameson to various people are held in the Houghton Library at Harvard University.

Alexander William Kinglake

(5 August 1809 – 1 January 1891)

Joan Corwin

See also the Kinglake entry in *DLB 55: Victorian Prose Writers Before 1867.*

BOOKS: *Eothen; or, Traces of Travel Brought Home from the East,* anonymous (London: Ollivier, 1844; New York: Colyer, 1845); republished as *Traces of Travel Brought Home from the East* (Auburn & Geneva, N.Y.: Derby, 1845); republished as *Kinglake's Eothen* (London: Frowde, 1906);

The Invasion of the Crimea: Its Origin, and an Account of Its Progress down to the Death of Lord Raglan (8 volumes, Edinburgh & London: Blackwood, 1863–1887; 6 volumes, New York: Harper, 1863–1888).

OTHER: "In a Garden of Damascus," in *Enchantment of Gardens* (London, 1924; Boston & New York: Houghton Mifflin, 1926), pp. 163–166.

SELECTED PERIODICAL PUBLICATIONS – UNCOLLECTED: "The Rights of Women," *Quarterly Review,* 75 (December 1844): 94–125;

"The French Lake," *Quarterly Review,* 75 (March 1845): 532–569;

"The Life of Madame de Lafayette," *Blackwood's Magazine,* 112 (September 1872): 361–368.

Alexander William Kinglake, circa 1863 (portrait by Harriet M. Haviland; National Portrait Gallery, London)

In 1843 publisher John Murray made what he was later to call his greatest error of professional judgment: he rejected the manuscript of a travel book by a London barrister named Alexander William Kinglake. *Eothen; or, Traces of Travel Brought Home from the East* was published the following year and almost immediately went into three editions. It had undergone more than thirty printings by the end of the century and has appeared in as many twentieth-century editions. Today the book is still in demand and is available in paperback editions. *Eothen* is not only one of the most popular travel books ever written, but also one of the most influential on travel writing as a literary form. It transformed the travelogue from a tediously detailed narrative annotated with statistical data into a personal and impressionistic account of the travel experience. It was Kinglake's only travel book — his only book at all, in fact, besides the eight-volume *Invasion of the Crimea: Its Origin, and an Account of Its Progress down to the Death of Lord Raglan* (1863–1887) that later became his life's work. Yet it made Kinglake's name as a writer, and because of it he remains an important figure in the evolution of travel writing as a genre.

The small, shy, rather precious gentleman who produced this book began his life in a comfortable, conventional middle-class world. The eldest boy of six surviving children, Alexander William, called "Alec" by his family, was born to a prosperous attorney and banker, William Kinglake, and his wife, Mary Woodforde Kinglake of Castle Cary and Taunton. The Kinglakes first set up house in Mary Street, Taunton, and Alec was born at this home, the Lawn, on 5 August 1809.

Kinglake's mother was a significant influence in his early life, as he reports in *Eothen,* for she taught him "to find a home in his saddle, and love old Homer, and all that Homer sung [*sic*]," rather than to spend his time learning the hymns of Isaac Watts or "collects for the day." He had an abiding love for the Homeric epics, which he read in the Alexander Pope translations: "I pored over the Odyssey as over a story-book, hoping and fearing for the hero whom yet I partly scorned. But the Iliad – line by line, I clasped it to my brain with reverence as well as with love."

Kinglake received all the educational opportunities that his family's income and status allowed. At the age of twelve he was sent to a private grammar school at Ottery St. Mary in Devon, where the headmaster was the Reverend George Coleridge (brother of poet Samuel Taylor Coleridge), to be coached for public school. For Kinglake this removal from the loving tutelage of his mother to the grueling drills and discipline of Coleridge's school was not a happy one, but after completing his training the boy went to Eton. There he made some of his dearest friends, and from the spring of 1823 until he entered Cambridge in 1828 he enjoyed some of the happiest days of his life. Some of those whom he cherished into adulthood were John Savile (later Lord Pollington and Earl of Mexborough), who appears in *Eothen* as his traveling companion Methley, and Eliot Warburton, the friend whose interest in the Levant spurred Kinglake to write *Eothen.*

Kinglake's circle of acquaintance at Cambridge included several talented young poets of his generation, among them Alfred Tennyson and his friend Arthur Henry Hallam, Richard Monckton Milnes, J. M. Kemble, W. H. Brookfield, and W. H. Thompson. There he also met William Makepeace Thackeray, with whom he exchanged visits throughout his life. Although Kinglake never attempted poetry, he tried his skill at oration, joining the union and speaking in debates at the Red Lion Inn. He had a quiet voice, almost inaudible at times, and he was reluctant to speak extemporaneously – both of

which characteristics were viewed as weaknesses by some who considered him a poor speaker. But when he had prepared a speech and when he was heard, the effect was usually inspiring: he had a felicity of expression that he exercised among his friends. As Lady Isabella Augusta Persse Gregory wrote in a memoir for *Blackwood's Magazine* (December 1895), "His words seemed to crystallise into epigram as they touched the air." But the many laborious revisions to his writings show that, unless he believed himself to be prepared in every detail, he did not feel comfortable presenting himself verbally before the public.

Kinglake took his B.A. degree in January 1832, and his professional future was never in doubt: his father had marked him for the law. Reserved, self-contained, and formal in appearance, Kinglake outwardly suited this respectable and conservative calling, but inwardly he longed for a military life. His shortsightedness and the high cost of preferment under the old purchase system in the army, a cost that his father was probably unwilling to pay, prevented such a career. As a result, he suffered in frustration with a code of honor and bravery, an inner call to a life of action.

To prepare for his bar examination, Kinglake moved to London and became a pupil of Bryan Waller Procter, better known as the poet Barry Cornwall. Procter and his wife Anne became great friends of Kinglake. Though quiet and chivalrous, Kinglake could be cynical, and he enjoyed Anne Procter's sharp tongue – for which he was to dub her "Our Lady of Bitterness" in *Eothen.* By a stroke of good fortune Kinglake's Eton friend Eliot Warburton was also reading for the bar with Procter. The Procters were extremely popular among the prominent literary figures of the day, and at their home Kinglake enjoyed the visits of Thomas Carlyle, Charles Dickens, Thackeray, Milnes, and Abraham Hayward, a respected critic and reviewer who was to become one of his closest friends in later years.

During his tuition with Procter, Kinglake's friend John Savile, now Lord Pollington, returned from a trip to Russia. Pollington's highly colored report of his experiences kindled Kinglake's enthusiasm for such an adventure, and Kinglake proposed that they journey together across the Turkish Ottoman dominions, which extended from the Balkans to Egypt.

Eothen, the title of which Kinglake translates as meaning "from the East," is an account of his fifteen months during 1834 and 1835 in the Ottoman territories of the Near East. What was unique about the

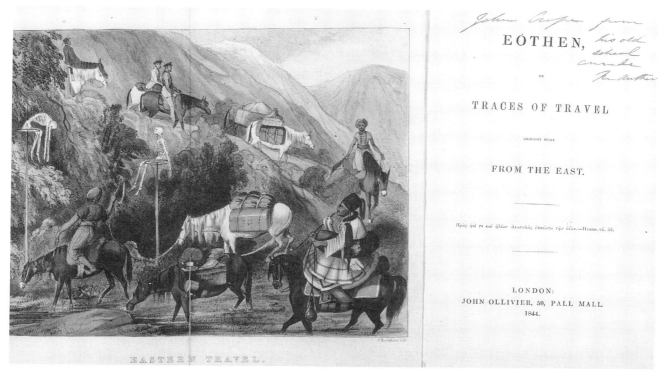

Foldout frontispiece and title page for Kinglake's only travel book (courtesy of the Lilly Library, Indiana University)

book on its publication and what made it a landmark in the evolution of the travel narrative is that Kinglake openly abandoned the traditional style and subject matter of the travel books that preceded his as he produced what has been called the first impressionistic travel book.

Kinglake actually joined Pollington in Hamburg, but *Eothen* opens in Semlin, on what was the Austrian Empire side of the Save (now Sava) River, which flows into the Danube at that site. Across the river lay Belgrade on the Ottoman side, the starting point of their travels in the East, where Kinglake was thrilled to see for the first time "real, substantial, and incontrovertible turbans." The two friends crossed the wilderness to Constantinople, Pollington becoming prostrate with illness along the way and having to be carted in a lady's recreation wagon, and they proceeded south along the Turkish coast to visit the supposed site of Troy and the city of Smyrna. There Pollington was called home, and Kinglake continued the journey with his multilingual dragoman, Mysseri, who later became the owner of a successful hotel in Constantinople. Kinglake traveled to Cyprus and Beirut, through the hills and biblical places of Galilee and south along the Jordan to Jerusalem and Gaza, from which he made the taxing desert journeys to and

from Cairo. On his return north through the Levant he visited the fanatic Moslem village of Nablus and the lush gardens of Damascus. Descending finally from the Pass of the Lebanon, he departed for Satalieh (now Antalya) in Turkey.

At the start of their adventure the two men were accompanied by Mysseri and by Pollington's servant, Steele; other attendants also either began the journey with them or joined the entourage at different times. Most notable among these were the headstrong fanatic Christian Dmethri and a young Nazarene who proved to be an inept guide. Kinglake also met several interesting settled easterners and Europeans, the most memorable of them being his mother's childhood friend Lady Hester Stanhope, who had set herself up in an abandoned convent in the Lebanon range, a day's journey from Beirut, as a kind of queen of the desert. These servants and residents become vivid characters in *Eothen*, where they serve a variety of literary functions, including dramatic interest and humor.

The sights and events Kinglake describes in *Eothen* are extremely diverse. In Semlin he had his first audience with an Eastern potentate, an experience that he transforms in his book into a burlesque dialogue between an egotistical English traveler and a Turkish pasha overcome by the might of a country run by steam and engine ("whirr! whirr! all by wheels! – whiz! whiz! all by steam!"). In plague-ridden Constantinople Kinglake enjoyed a mild flirtation with a veiled beauty who played a trick on him by touching him and crying out "Yumour-djak!" (Plague!). He sailed to Cyprus with a courageous and independent crew of Greek mariners. He tried to bathe in the Dead Sea and was intrigued by his buoyancy in its salt waters. When he and his entourage found themselves on the wrong side of the Jordan River, where they were in danger of Bedouin attack and were forced to make an awkward crossing, his attendants begged him to kill the Nazarene guide who had advised them; he refused. His advice was sought by a Christian family who insisted on the return of a young woman who had forsworn her religion to marry a Mohammedan and by a community of Jews who were periodically persecuted and despoiled by their Moslem neighbors. En route to Satalieh via boat at the end of his journey, he befriended a Russian who with him defied quarantine orders not to touch shore, an incident that he comically describes as the "Surprise of Satalieh." These are a few of the many incidents Kinglake records, and they reveal how lively and entertaining the exotic nature and the variety of his material make the book.

One of the most important themes in *Eothen* concerns Kinglake's motive for travel: the desire to escape the demands of his social and professional life. In the twelfth chapter of the book he describes himself as "one who is aching from very weariness of that poor, dear, middle-aged, deserving, accomplished, pedantic, and pains-taking governess, Europe." Elsewhere he calls the first night in Eastern parts "a glorious time in your life" and a "delightful escape." For Kinglake travel meant release into lands where the rules of Western society did not apply and where he could indulge his adventurous and romantic nature.

One aspect of this release, and another of his themes, is the enjoyment of life's pleasures: Kinglake goes abroad to feast his senses on the East. He sympathizes completely with the Damascene monks, who insist that nothing is more worth visiting than their wine cellars. "Dear old fellows!" he says of these gentle and unpretentious friars, "in the midst of that solemn land, their Christian laughter rang loudly and merrily" – implying that their indulgence in their excellent wine is responsible for the light in their eyes and the spring in their step.

But what gratifies his senses most keenly is female beauty. The women of Constantinople, Smyrna, Cyprus, and Bethlehem all attract his praise. In fact, the beauty of women appears to be one of the "sights" he has traveled expressly to see, and its pursuit even leads him to attend a slave market. Kinglake's appreciation of such beauty led his contemporaries to consider *Eothen* "racy," particularly in a passage where he praises the "romping girls of Bethlehem," whom he finds flirtatious and alluring.

Female beauty in fact is responsible for an unusual moment of spiritual ecstasy. Referred to by some as a "Nothingarian," Kinglake was not a religious man. He considered the Anglican Church only "the most harmless going," and he maintained that above every church door should be inscribed the words "Important if true." So it is surprising at first to find him moved, at the Sanctuary of the Blessed Virgin, by "a faith in loveliness transcending mortal shapes." In his ecstasy he kisses the rock on which the Virgin's altar stands. But it is as a beautiful woman that the Virgin appeals to Kinglake's imagination and inspires him, and throughout the passage he is ironic as well as fervent. The zeal dissipates quickly, leaving him "hopelessly sane" again.

Religion cannot help but come to the attention of a traveler in the Holy Land, and the spiritual figures as another theme in *Eothen*. Kinglake generally finds the Eastern religions to be based on mere superstition and to provide opportunities for humbugs and frauds to deceive believers. His criticism, however, is not confined to any one religion: it is universal. For instance, when a Christian family asks him to intercede with the authorities and have their daughter returned from the mosque in which she has found sanctuary, he sides with the Moslems in Nablus: he has overheard her kinsman insisting that on her return she be beaten to death. Along with hypocrisy, self-delusion and deceit, it is such cruelty that he condemns, and he finds all these evils in the holy city of Jerusalem. In the chapter ironically titled "Terra Santa" he thus unleashes his biting wit on that city, which he describes as a place where religion has grown commercial and the pilgrims appear to be "*transacting* the great business of Salvation." He has some sympathy for the pilgrims but condemns the Latin and Greek churches, whose mercenary management of the shrines results every year in a bloody battle at the event of the Easter Saturday miracle of the heavenly fire.

One self-styled mystic whom he satirizes, though with some affection and gentleness, is Lady Hester Stanhope, who as a young woman had served as hostess for her uncle, the former prime minister William Pitt. Lady Hester's power over local desert Bedouins seems to have stemmed from her imposing bearing and confidence. Kinglake's ultimate evaluation of his mother's friend is that "Lady Hestor's unholy claim to supremacy in the spiritual kingdom was, no doubt, the suggestion of fierce and inordinate pride most perilously akin to madness."

In contrast to his contempt for religious charlatans, the simple piety and sense of duty exhibited by the Damascene monks who minister to plague victims evoke Kinglake's admiration. Each day one of their number attends the sick and returns to an isolated bell tower for the night. In the morning he rings the bell; on the day when the bell does not ring, his brothers assume that he is dead and another is chosen by lot to take his place.

Such honorable, uncomplaining stoicism is a standard by which Kinglake measures those whom he meets on his journey, particularly those confronted by the plague. Plague is a recurrent theme, an almost omnipresent danger wherever he travels, and Kinglake's judgment of character is based on how people respond to its threat.

The crossing from Semlin to Belgrade exposes Kinglake to his first encounter with quarantine and plague hysteria. When he is met on the western side of the Save by an Austrian official whose duty is to conduct travelers across the river, the man, who has been "compromised" – that is, exposed to contagion from his contact with plague-ridden Belgrade – refuses to shake hands until he is sure that Kinglake understands the nature of the danger and the length of the quarantine.

The plague appears most strongly in Cairo, where most of the resident Europeans arouse Kinglake's scorn in their efforts to avoid contact with their fellow human beings. They descend to such base contrivances as having their food pulled up to their windows in baskets. Kinglake's own banker receives his letter with tongs through iron bars.

In contrast to the Cairene Europeans, Arab residents behave with dignified resignation in the face of the disease, and Kinglake is particularly impressed by the warm fellow-feeling exhibited by a Turkish resident. This man – instead of recoiling from Kinglake, who by now has been severely "compromised" – offers his hand: "In that touch," Kinglake recalls, "there was true hospitality." Most admirable of all is the English doctor, the only European physician who has not fled the city but has remained to attend the pasha. The man laughingly seizes and shakes Kinglake's hand, and this inspires Kinglake to write later, "I felt grateful indeed, and

swelled with fresh pride of race, because that my countryman could carry himself so nobly."

"Pride of race" is another important theme in *Eothen,* for although Kinglake is initially rebellious in undertaking the journey and his tone is mischievous and irreverent throughout the book, he remains at heart a conservative Englishman of a clearly defined type. He is attached to England and grows nostalgic about his homeland throughout his adventures. Early in their travels he and Methley joke about their school days at Eton rather than commenting on the sights that surround them; the Sea of Galilee reminds Kinglake of the Lake Country, and in the glaring white heat of the desert sun, he thinks he hears the sound of the bells of a country church at home. Even during the adventure of his first desert crossing he is grateful for the end of each day and appreciates, after many hours' ride on camelback, the familiar comforts with which he has furnished his tent and made it seem "a very home that had sprung up for me in the midst of these solitudes."

This conventional side of Kinglake has its ugly aspects. He complains, for instance, that he can deal with Eastern peoples only through threats and bullying, and he exposes a vicious anti-Semitism when he discusses the Jews he encounters. Ultimately Kinglake remains detached from the peoples among whom he travels.

In fact, *Eothen* is very much about the contrast between the two worlds of East and West – the one exotic, sensual, and dangerous; the other familiar, rational, and progressive. At the start, as Kinglake and Methley prepare to leave Western Semlin, he introduces the theme of the separate and opposite worlds – "wheel-going Europe" on the one side of the Save and the "Splendour and Havoc of the East" on the other.

On his release from Western society Kinglake develops a cocky self-assurance. He enjoys an independence and isolation from Western society that are most complete during his crossing of the Sinai desert. The two such desert crossings in *Eothen* have become classics. Many feel that the passage in the chapter entitled "The Desert," which describes the physical and psychological stresses of monotonous desert travel, has never been equaled in vividness and atmosphere. During his second desert crossing Kinglake becomes impatient with his slow entourage and spurs his dromedary on, with the result that he finds himself alone, and possibly lost, in the desert. This episode incorporates some wishfulfillment, as even his increasing thirst adds a thrill to the experience and leads him to act with a showy

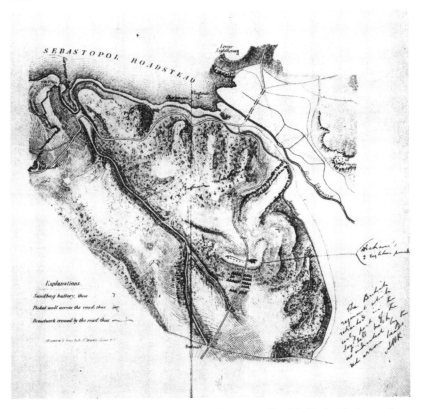

Map of Sebastopol, with Kinglake's annotations recording his firsthand observations on the Crimean War (Layard Papers, The British Library)

disregard for danger when, spotting two bedouin travelers, he rides swiftly to them and, under their startled eyes, drinks from their water flask: "this was enough to make the Bedouins stare a little." Although his tone is full of bravado here, the situation soon becomes dangerous, and Kinglake is finally brought down to earth, literally and figuratively, when he topples from his dromedary and is forced to seek aid from some desperate-looking Algerian refugees. When he reaches Suez at last, he has a renewed appreciation for the comforts of civilized life.

Kinglake's lesson about the adventurous life in this chapter prepares his readers for his decision at the end of *Eothen* to return to England. In the penultimate chapter of the book Kinglake finds himself at the summit of the Lebanon mountain range, meditating on the difference between East and West, "the birthless Past, and the Future that has no end." In the end, he says, "I descended, and went towards the West."

Unlike Richard F. Burton or T. E. Lawrence, Kinglake never adopted Arab dress but wore his coat and waistcoat even in the grueling heat and discomfort of the desert, bearing himself always, he would say, like an English gentleman. This fact, his continuous recurrence to thoughts of home, his "pride of race," and his sense of gentleman's honor should convince the reader that his escape from "governess Europe" and the dull life of a London lawyer was only a temporary junket and was never intended to become a permanent exile.

The writing of *Eothen* reflects Kinglake's motive for traveling in the first place: the journey and the book are both efforts to escape convention. The best analysis of Kinglake's intent appears in his own lively preface, where he confesses that he aims to depart from the conventions of form and content current in travel writing. Most important of all is the matter of what places and events Kinglake chooses to describe, for in these respects he diverges most clearly from what he calls a "regular book of travels" by "dwelling precisely upon those matters which happened to interest me, and upon none other." On the one hand, he pretends to allow that this makes the book "quite superficial in its character." On the other hand, he insists on the book's value as a document of his experience and claims that it conveys his true impressions, rather than those which "*ought to have been* produced upon any 'well constituted mind.'" He willingly acknowledges, "As I have felt so I have written."

Kinglake is aware of how this practice shifts the focus of the book from the countries in which he travels to the traveler himself. As a result of his subjective and impressionistic approach to travel writing, Kinglake neglects many of the traditional sights of the Levant. And even when he feels compelled to describe a famous monument, the results are idiosyncratic, such as in the extremely short, impressionistic chapters on the Pyramids and the Sphinx. In contrast, the everyday lives of the people whom he encounters yield the most detailed passages.

Not only the selection of material, but the style and tone of *Eothen* reflect Kinglake's rejection of travel-writing conventions. The book did not appear until almost a decade after the journey it describes, and Kinglake explains in his preface that he had twice attempted to write the account but had some trouble imagining his audience. Only when Warburton asked him for advice on an upcoming Eastern tour was Kinglake able to write the book — in the form of a letter to his friend. The casual nature of a personal letter freed him from the burden of tradition and allowed him to write as he liked, in the conversational style of which he was a master. This informal style, resulting from the presumed audience of Warburton, is fluid and familiar, with a bantering tone: its hallmark is its wit. *Eothen* is a funny book, and the sense of humor it reveals explains why Kinglake was so popular among his set in London.

What this egocentric form and glib style create in Kinglake's narrator is a vivid persona, exuberant in spirits but self-possessed and detached in attitude — that of a young man, his ego bolstered by a background of impeccable breeding and a classical education, entering on a great adventure. Yet the casual style and the egoistic persona are misleading. They are parts of a meticulous literary production that underwent eleven revisions before its publication. While giving the appearance of spontaneity, the style of *Eothen* is actually the product of Kinglake's habitually exacting care. Through such care, for instance, he is able to manipulate the youth and the romantic aspirations of his persona by directing the humor against himself at times.

John Murray's reason for rejecting the manuscript of *Eothen* lay in its irreverence, in what he called the author's "wicked spirit of jesting at everything." When other publishers had returned the manuscript, Kinglake resorted to his friend John Ollivier, who agreed to publish the book if Kinglake paid Ollivier fifty pounds to ensure against loss.

Published anonymously, *Eothen* was an immediate success and the identity of its author a matter of much interest to its admirers. The editor of the *Edinburgh Review* wrote to Abraham Hayward to ask, "Who is Eothen? I know he is a lawyer and highly respectable; but I should like to know a little more of his personal history; he is very clever but very peculiar."

In spite of Murray's qualms most reviews were favorable; a few journals and newspapers, however, did share Murray's apprehensions and disapproved of its tone. Even Kinglake's dear friend Eliot Warburton, in a largely laudatory review that appeared in the December 1844 *Quarterly Review,* gently condemned his friend's "reckless disregard for popular opinion." Referring to Kinglake's ironic handling of his experiences in Jerusalem, Warburton wrote, "It is with reluctance that we feel called upon thus to notice and protest against the spirit in which he has spoken of matters that should have claimed his forbearance."

Such objections, however, had little effect on the literary influence of *Eothen.* The book quickly inspired several excellent travel narratives in a similar mode. Warburton's own *The Crescent and the Cross* (1845) appeared less than a year after the publication of *Eothen* and was followed by Thackeray's *Notes of a Journey from Cornhill to Grand Cairo* (1846), in which Thackeray attempts to achieve the easy grace of *Eothen,* a book that he much admired. Another friend, Robert Curzon, had traveled before Kinglake to the East but waited until 1849 to publish his *A Visit to the Monasteries of the Levant.* The characteristics these books share with *Eothen* include the new, relaxed style, the lack of ponderous data and description, and the selection of incidents and sights that inspire the individual traveler. These features had a lasting effect on travel writing and continue to exert such influence. In an introduction to the 1982 Oxford University Press edition of *Eothen,* Jan Morris suggests that the influence of the book may be traced from Curzon's *Visit to the Monasteries* through Robert Byron's 1937 *The Road to Oxiana,* which borrows much from *Eothen,* to Paul Theroux's *The Great Railway Bazaar* (1975).

Although reactions from offended readers were in the minority, Kinglake was reluctant to appear again in print, worrying that such a move would be "seriously injurious" to his career in a profession known for its reserve and respectability. He did respond, however, when Murray invited him to write for the *Quarterly Review,* and one result was an article titled "The Rights of Women," which appeared in the same issue as Warburton's review

"Soldiers cruelly loaded" on the march in Algeria; drawing by Kinglake in his Algerian diary (Harford Collection, Cambridge University Library)

of *Eothen.* The article was a review of Richard Monckton Milnes's *Palm Leaves* (1844) and of five recent books by women: *The Englishwoman in Egypt* (1844) by Sophia Poole; the twelfth edition of *The Women of England* (1844) and *The Wives of England* (1843) by Sarah (Stickney) Ellis; and *Characteristics of Women* (1832) and *The Romance of Biography; or, Memoirs of Women Loved and Celebrated by Poets* (1837) by Anna (Brownell) Jameson. Milnes's *Palm Leaves* contains poems on life in the Near East and romanticizes the Eastern institution of the harem. Though Kinglake's review is playfully ironic in tone, it takes Milnes to task by ridiculing his credulity, questioning his facts, and deploring the demeaning nature of the harem. In fact, Kinglake includes a quotation from Lady Mary Wortley Montagu to suggest that far from promoting chastity, the harem allows liaisons to go undetected. The article also spells out Kinglake's view of women, a curious combination of condescension and true admiration.

Another review by Kinglake, "The French Lake," appeared in the March 1845 *Quarterly Review.* It examines Warburton's *The Crescent and the Cross,* an account of the journey for which he had sought Kinglake's advice. Although Kinglake finds his friend's book "vastly superior to the common run of narratives," he disapproves of Warburton's suggestion that the English should occupy Egypt, an idea that he compares to Louis Napoleon's unsuccessful foreign policy in the Near East.

Kinglake worked on unremarkably as a London barrister. Although he was a quiet man who avoided large social gatherings, he led an active life visiting his close and vibrant circle of friends, whom he sometimes entertained at the Trafalgar Tavern in Greenwich. His predilection for the company of articulate women was lifelong, though he never married. Among those whom he saw frequently were the poet Caroline Norton, who was the subject of a famous divorce case, and Lady Lucie Duff Gordon, who was to write a series of remarkable letters in Egypt during her unsuccessful convalescence from tuberculosis.

Fascinated by military affairs and still restless a year after the publication of *Eothen,* Kinglake traveled to Algiers, the Barbary state then at war with France. The record of this journey — in a brief, unrefined journal never meant for publication but published as an appendix to Gerald de Gaury's 1972 biography of Kinglake — comprises his only travel writing besides *Eothen.* The highlight of this trip was Kinglake's acquaintance with the French colonel Maréchal Saint-Arnaud. Kinglake was impressed by him at the time but came to despise him later, when he learned of the officer's role in the French atrocities committed in Algiers and of his devious behavior before and after his appointment as minister of war to Napoleon III.

Kinglake never saw action in Algiers, but when events later came to a head in the Crimea and Britain declared war on Russia, he went abroad to witness the fighting. At the Battle of Alma he rode alongside the great commander Lord Raglan, whom he grew to admire tremendously. Eventually at the plea of Lord Raglan's widow, who was distressed by the ill fame her husband had received as a result of the Crimean losses, Kinglake undertook the task of writing his eight-volume history, *The Invasion of the Crimea: Its Origin, and an Account of Its Progress down to the Death of Lord Raglan.* The work took Kinglake more than thirty years to complete. The first volume was a general success and received great acclaim, particularly for its style, but it also caused much controversy because Kinglake chose to champion Lord Raglan and blame others for the Crimean disaster. When it was denounced in the London *Times* and the *Edinburgh Review,* Kinglake's friend Abraham Hayward answered these critics successfully in a privately published pamphlet, *Mr. Kinglake and the Quarterlys* (1863).

While laboring over the first volume of his history, Kinglake decided to run for Parliament. He had failed to find a seat in 1852, but in 1857 he was elected for Bridgewater in Somerset. Although his weak voice and shy manner made him an ineffectual speaker in Parliament, he might have had some influence over the years, but in 1868 a defeated candidate brought an allegation of bribery against Kinglake's election. Though he was absolved of complicity, his agent was found guilty; the borough was disenfranchised, and Kinglake was barred from Parliament. He was bitter and disappointed over this turn of events and referred to himself thereafter as a "political corpse."

Following his parliamentary career Kinglake devoted his attention chiefly to his history. He did, however, find time to publish (anonymously) one last article — his response to the translation by Louis de Lasteyrie of the memoir *Life of Madame de Lafayette,* written by her daughter, who describes the execution of victims of the Reign of Terror. Kinglake's article, which appeared in the September 1872 *Blackwood's Magazine,* denounced the misplaced piety and nationalism that he felt led the condemned to submit meekly to the guillotine.

Although several of Kinglake's contemporaries have left portraits of him, he remains an elusive figure — partly because of his reserve, partly because of the intense opposites that marked his character: shyness and fierce pride, gentleness and martial dreams, a precise dandyism and a dramatic chivalry, a meticulous style and a youthful exuberance. Warburton wrote of him that, although "pessimistic and cynical to the rest of the world," he was always gentle and kind to his friends. In later life Kinglake included among his closest friends Lady Duff Gordon's daughter Janet Ross, the political activist Olga Novikoff, and the Irish playwright Lady Augusta Gregory, who left a moving memoir of the old-fashioned, gallant little man in his last years. He became deaf in his old age and suffered from gout, which eventually forced him to give up visiting his clubs, the Travellers' and the Athenaeum, where he had spent almost every afternoon and evening for

years. He died of throat cancer on New Year's Day, 1891.

As a writer, Alexander William Kinglake has always enjoyed many admirers, including many great travel writers. According to D. G. Hogarth, in his 1910 introduction to *Eothen,* no less an explorer than Richard F. Burton called it "that book of books." The structure and style of the book have influenced writing about travel in all parts of the globe, not just the Near East, and it is unlikely that any travel book following *Eothen* has been able to avoid some influence, direct or indirect.

Biographies:
William Tuckwell, *A. W. Kinglake – A Biographical and Literary Study* (London: Bell, 1902);
Gerald de Gaury, *Travelling Gent: The Life of Alexander Kinglake (1809–1891)* (London & Boston: Routledge & Kegan Paul, 1972).

References:
James Bryce, Introduction to Kinglake's *Eothen* (New York: Century, 1900), pp. ix–xvii;
Charisse Gendron, "*Eothen* Again," *Victorian Newsletter,* 68 (Fall 1985): 11–14;
Lady Augusta Gregory, "'Eothen' and the Athenaeum Club," *Blackwood's Magazine,* 158 (December 1895): 797–804;
D. G. Hogarth, Introduction to Kinglake's *Eothen* (Oxford: Clarendon Press, 1910; New York: Frowde, 1910);
Iran Banu Hassani Jewett, *Alexander William Kinglake* (Boston: Twayne, 1981);
Jan Morris, Introduction to Kinglake's *Eothen* (Oxford & New York: Oxford University Press, 1982), pp. iii–xvi;
V. S. Pritchett, Introduction to Kinglake's *Eothen* (Lincoln: University of Nebraska Press, 1970), pp. vii–xv;
Peter Quennell, "The Author of 'Eothen,'" in his *The Singular Preference* (Port Washington, N.Y. & London: Kennikat Press, 1953), pp. 118–124;
Jonathan Raban, Introduction to Kinglake's *Eothen* (London: Century, 1982), pp. v–viii.

Sir Austen Henry Layard

(5 March 1817 – 5 July 1894)

Barbara Brothers and Julia Gergits
Youngstown State University

and

Margaret Boe Birns
New York University

BOOKS: *Nineveh and Its Remains: With an Account of a Visit to the Chaldean Christians of Kurdistan, and the Yezidis, or Devil-worshippers; and an Enquiry into the Manners and Arts of the Ancient Assyrians* (2 volumes, London: Murray, 1849; New York: Putnam, 1849; 1 volume, New York: Putnam, 1851); abridged as *A Popular Account of Discoveries at Nineveh* (London: Murray, 1851; New York: Harper, 1852); abridged as *Nineveh and Its Remains: A Narrative of an Expedition to Assyria during the Years 1845, 1846 & 1847* (London: Murray, 1867);

The Monuments of Nineveh: From Drawings Made on the Spot, 2 volumes (London: Murray, 1849);

Inscriptions in the Cuneiform Character, from Assyrian Monuments, Discovered by A. H. Layard (London: Harrison, 1851);

Discoveries in the Ruins of Nineveh and Babylon; with Travels in Armenia, Kurdistan and the Desert: Being the Result of a Second Expedition Undertaken for the Trustees of the British Museum (London: Murray, 1853; New York: Putnam, 1853); abridged as *Discoveries among the Ruins of Nineveh and Babylon; with Travels in Armenia, Kurdistan, and the Desert: Being the Result of a Second Expedition Undertaken for the Trustees of the British Museum* (New York: Harper, 1853); abridged as *Nineveh & Babylon: A Narrative of a Second Expedition to Assyria, during the Years 1849, 1850, & 1851* (London: Murray, 1867);

A Second Series of the Monuments of Nineveh; Including Bas-reliefs from the Palace of Sennacherib and Bronzes from the Ruins of Nimroud: From Drawings Made on the Spot, during a Second Expedition to Assyria (London: Murray, 1853);

The Nineveh Court in the Crystal Palace (London: Crystal Palace Library, 1854);

Sir Austen Henry Layard in his study at Ca Capello (portrait by Ludwig Passini; National Portrait Gallery, London)

The Turkish Question: Speeches Delivered in the House of Commons on Aug. 16, 1853, and Feb. 17, 1854 (London: Murray, 1854);

The Prospects and Conduct of the War: Speech Delivered in the House of Commons on Dec. 12, 1854 (London, 1854);

The Martyrdom of Saint Sebastian Painted in Fresco by Pietro Perugino, in the Chapel of the Saint, at Panicale (London: Arundel Society, 1856);

The Madonna and Saints Painted in Fresco by Ottaviano Nelli, in the Church of S. Maria Nuova at Gubbio (London: Arundel Society, 1857);

The Frescoes by Bern: Pinturicchio, in the Collegiate Church of S. Maria Maggiore, at Spello (London: Arundel Society, 1858);

Giovanni Sanzio and Fresco at Cagli (London: Arundel Society, 1859);

Domenico Ghirlandaio and His Fresco of the Death of S. Francis (London: Arundel Society, 1860);

The Condition of Turkey and Her Dependencies: Speech Delivered in the House of Commons on Friday, May 29, 1863 (London: Murray, 1863);

The Danish Question: Speech Delivered in the House of Commons, July 7, 1864 (London, 1864);

Suggestions for a National Gallery (London, 1868);

The Brancacci Chapel and Masolino, Masaccio, and Filippino Lippi (London: Arundel Society, 1868);

Paper on Mosaic Decoration, Read at a Meeting of the Royal Institute of British Architects (London: Metchim, 1869);

The Right Hon. A. H. Layard and the Anti-slavery Society: Being a Copy of the Letter Addressed by Mr. Layard to M. Laboulaye, as Published among the Slave-trade Papers Recently Laid before Parliament, Together with Remarks on Certain Mis-statements Contained Therein (London: Stock, 1877);

Early Adventures in Persia, Susiana, and Babylonia, Including a Residence among the Bakhtiyari and Other Wild Tribes before the Discovery of Nineveh (London: Murray, 1887; New York: Longmans, Green, 1887);

The Massacre of St. Bartholomew, and the Revocation of the Edict of Nantes, Illustrated from State Papers in the Archives of Venice (London: Spottiswoode, 1888);

Sir A. Henry Layard, G.C.B., D.C.L.: Autobiography and Letters from His Childhood until His Appointment as H. M. Ambassador at Madrid, 2 volumes, edited by William N. Bruce (London: Murray, 1903; New York: Scribners, 1903).

OTHER: Roberto Tapparelli D'Azeglio, *The Court of Rome and the Gospel*, translated, with a preface, by Layard (London: Murray, 1859);

Franz Theodor Kugler, *The Italian Schools of Painting; Based on the Handbook of Kugler*, edited by Charles L. Eastlake, fifth edition, revised and in part rewritten by Layard (London: Murray, 1886);

Kugler, *Handbook of Painting: The Italian Schools, Based on the Handbook of Kugler*, sixth edition, revised and in part rewritten by Layard (London: Murray, 1891);

Michele Suriano and Marc' Antonio Barbaro, *Despatches of Michele Suriano and Marc' Antonio Barbaro, Venetian Ambassadors at the Court of France, 1560–1563*, edited by Layard (Lymington: King, 1891);

Giovanni Morelli, *Italian Painters: Critical Studies of Their Works*, 2 volumes, introduction by Layard (London: Murray, 1892);

"Picture Galleries," edited by Layard, in *A Handbook of Rome and Its Environs, Forming Part II. of the Handbook for Travellers in Central Italy*, generally edited by Rev. H. W. Pullen (London: Murray, 1894).

Austen Henry Layard was perhaps the leading British archaeologist of the nineteenth century. His excavations at Calah (Nimrud) and elsewhere provided crucial evidence of both the antiquity and the cultural achievement of ancient Mesopotamian, particularly Assyrian, civilization. As befitted a Victorian gentleman, however, Layard was not a professional archaeologist, nor did he restrict his intellectual activities to archaeology. He wore many hats in his public career — as a diplomat, a politician, an art connoisseur, and a man of letters. Through two memorable travelogues of his excavations at the Assyrian capital of Nineveh he presents his archaeological activities to readers in narrated forms. Lending a new depth to his readers' awareness of their collective past, Layard's writings chronicle the exhilarating discovery of a layer of civilization that antedates biblical and classical ones. His works also raise questions of cultural imperialism and epistemology central to modern critical debates.

Layard was the son of Marianne Austen and Peter John Layard, who from his earliest adult years had been enrolled in the colonial civil service and spent most of his time in Ceylon (present-day Sri Lanka). When Layard senior returned from Ceylon to England in 1814, he married Marianne Austen, a banker's daughter he had known since childhood. He moved his family to France shortly before Austen's birth in Paris on 5 March 1817.

When Austen Henry was three years old, the Layards moved to Florence, Italy, and Henry grew up among the artistic treasures of that city in the time when their central value to European culture was being avidly explored by artists and intellectuals. By adolescence Layard spoke fluent French and Italian, and the intellectual potential of this bright,

Layard in Constantinople (portrait by M. K. Kellogg; from Gordon Waterfield, Layard of Nineveh, *1963)*

gregarious child was evident to all who encountered him. He had episodes of formal schooling, but his mind and spirit were too undisciplined and reckless for the rigid European school systems of his day. His father, attempting to steer him toward a "useful," worldly pursuit, convinced his son to take advantage of the fact that Benjamin Austen, a wealthy uncle, was willing to act as the young man's patron. Layard entered the legal profession in 1835 under his uncle's sponsorship.

Soon another uncle, Charles Layard, suggested an option for the young man. Charles Layard, like Peter, had served in the Ceylon civil service and had enjoyed a career of greater duration and prestige. Charles Layard thought it might be suitable for his nephew to practice law in Ceylon. Layard took advantage of the opportunity with alacrity, and on 10 July 1839 he set off on the long and arduous overland journey later described in detail in *Nineveh and Its Remains* (1849).

Yet before his departure he had engaged a traveling companion, Edward Mitford – a relative of William Mitford, historian of Greece, and a member of the renowned Mitford family. Layard prepared carefully for the harrowing and time-

consuming trip east, one that was more than just a voyage: it was a work of art. The itinerary was so deliberately planned that it seemed inevitable that a book would be generated as a product of the voyage. Indeed, Smith, Elder publishers advanced £200 to Layard and Mitford for the journal that they were to keep of the trip.

Passing from western Europe through the Balkans and the imperial capital of Constantinople, Layard and Mitford went south at Aleppo to Jerusalem and Petra and returned by way of Amman and Damascus. In April 1840 they entered the region of Mesopotamia at Mosul. Layard instantly found himself captivated by the solitary grandeur of the desert terrain. At the transportation nerve center and trading depot of Mosul, Layard first sighted the ancient Mesopotamian monuments whose excavation would bestow greatness upon him, a sighting recorded in this memorable passage from *Nineveh and Its Remains:*

> Were the traveller to cross the Euphrates to seek for such ruins in Mesopotamia and Chaldea as he had left behind him in Asia Minor and Syria, his search will be in vain. . . . He is now at a loss to give any form to the rude heaps upon which he is gazing. Those of whose works they are the remains, unlike the Roman and the Greek, have left no visible traces of their civilization, or of their arts: their influence has long since passed away. The more he conjectures, the more vague the results appear. The scene around is worthy of the ruin he is contemplating; desolation meets desolation: a feeling of awe succeeds to wonder; for there is nothing to relieve the mind, to lead to hope, or to tell of what has gone by.

This passage contains a rationale not only for Layard's archaeology but for his travel writing: his narrative becomes a medium through which the ruins could tell their story. Ruins, for Layard, have their own personalities and voices.

After remaining a fortnight in Mosul to explore the mounds of Nineveh, Layard and Mitford left for Baghdad and stayed at Hammam Ali. There Layard first sighted Nimrud, and they then continued down the Tigris by raft. But after two months in Baghdad, Layard and Mitford, the latter of whom disliked and mistrusted the Persians, parted company. Mitford left for the east, and Layard obtained consent to explore the territory of the Bakhtiyari tribe in Luristan.

Only in his mellow old age did Layard finally publish the account of his year (from August 1840 to July 1841) among the Bakhtiyari, *Early Adventures in Persia, Susiana, and Babylonia* (1887). His delay is understandable. The book lacks the historical and intellectual interest of his two major Nineveh books, since he filled his extended holiday in Luristan with adventurous roving, lion hunting, and diplomatic skulduggery. Publishing that account would have destroyed the public image that Layard had built for himself as an accredited British emissary and representative, a reputation that gained him the respectability and recognition necessary to pursue his archaeological ambitions. In this early period Layard became a friend and advocate of the chieftain of the Bakhtiyaris, Mohammed Taki Khan, whose usefulness to the British colonial authorities was thus established.

In late 1845, after serving since mid 1842 under Sir Stratford Canning, the British ambassador to Turkey, Layard began excavating at Nimrud. Immediately he began to unearth a treasure trove of Assyrian regal monuments and cuneiform inscriptions, finds hailed by Sir Henry Creswicke Rawlinson and others as the visible remains of Nineveh, the great Assyrian capital. In fact what Layard had unearthed was the city of Calah, which had temporarily served as the Assyrian capital under the bloodthirsty reign of Ashurnasirpal II in the ninth century B.C., but for years this misidentification remained unchallenged. In *Discoveries in the Ruins of Nineveh & Babylon* (1853) Layard correctly identifies Kuyunjik as the true Nineveh, but he does not clarify that this site is different from Nimrud, the Nineveh in his first travel book's title.

Educated Europeans had known for decades that excavations in Mesopotamia might yield dramatic fruit, but it took Layard to bring this about. From its first reportage, Layard's excavation was a sensation. Reports filled the headlines of British newspapers, and the first consignment of bas-reliefs had been placed in the British Museum before Layard returned to London in December 1847, after an eight-year absence. In fact, he was granted a D.C.L. at Oxford in 1848 before John Murray published *Nineveh and Its Remains* and *The Monuments of Nineveh* in 1849. Having spent his year in England writing the books, nursing a liver ailment, and visiting with relatives and government officials, Layard left England in December 1848 to return to Constantinople, ostensibly to perform as an aide to Sir Stratford Canning but primarily to complete his work of excavating the ruins.

Gordon Waterfield quotes a contemporary of Layard in reporting that *Nineveh and Its Remains,* a scholarly work of nearly nine hundred pages, earned Layard a "'perfect fever of attention' so that the book could not come fast enough from the press to meet the ever-increasing demand and people re-

ferred to Layard as 'the most extraordinary man of the day.' " The book diligently recounted the progress and results of the Nimrud excavations, but its tremendous appeal to the British reading public resonated more deeply. Layard's account of his journeys and research was conversational, engaging, and written with a flair that resounded over and above his subject matter. The book is a combination of travelogue, art appreciation, and history that includes even what would today be called action-adventure elements. The emphasis is as much upon the process by which Layard came to Nineveh as upon the actual narrative of the expedition. *Nineveh and Its Remains* is thus in the tradition of earlier Near Eastern travelogues such as those by the Danish Karsten Niebuhr, the Frenchman Constantin François de Chasseboeuf Volney, the American John Lloyd Stephens, and the Englishmen Alexander William Kinglake and Claudius Rich.

An interesting deployment of this narrative technique is in the way Layard represents the native Arabs. Layard disdained the antiquarian prejudice by which the Mesopotamian past would be lauded in contradistinction to a squalid and degraded Arab present requiring British imperial intervention to restore ancient glory. Layard's kindness to his Arab workers extended to the Arab population of Iraq as a whole in his book. He is respectful and informed about their Muslim faith, although he exhibits a special solicitude for the Nestorian Christian minority of Iraq. Layard's narrative is as sociological as it is historical, as filled with empirical observation as with reliquary musings.

But the concerns of Layard's Victorian audience were elsewhere. For them Nineveh was less a site for discovery and derring-do than a biblical city. In the Bible the Assyrian Empire was the near-demonic enslaver of the Israelites, and Nineveh was its stony and wicked capital whose fall was celebrated so exultantly by the Hebrew prophet Nahum. For nineteenth-century English readers, still immersed in a "living" biblical culture, Assyria was a potent symbol of evil. The drama of Layard's expedition narratives inferentially concerns their ability to elucidate the Bible, though that is not an overt concern in *Nineveh and Its Remains*. What makes Layard's expedition so interesting to British readers is the pious curiosity of the age. His historical research made ancient Near Eastern history not just spiritual but factual; his narrative of his excavations establishes or corroborates the historical truth of much said about Assyria in the Bible and in that way is even more literal than the original. His archaeological curiosity was, therefore, compatible with piety.

These two traits – the interrelation of past and present, and the investigative direction of the narrative – are the dominant features of *Nineveh and Its Remains*. While the book begins with an account of his first journey to the East by tracing the genesis of his interest in Mesopotamian remains, once the primary locale is reached, Layard does not simply settle in and provide an account of his excavations. Rather, he liberally intermeshes his archaeological excavations with descriptions of the terrain and the present-day inhabitants of the region. This makes the book relevant as travel literature, as can be seen in this description of a Kurdish village northeast of Mosul:

A pass of some elevation had to be crossed before we could reach the village of Mia, our quarters for the night. Near its summit we found a barren plain, on which several Kurdish horsemen who had joined us, engaged with my own party in the Jerid. The mimic fight soon caused general excitement, and old habits getting the better of my dignity, I soon joined the melee. A severe kick in the leg from a horse soon put an end to my maneuvers, and the party was detained until I was sufficiently recovered from the effects of the blow to continue the journey. It was sunset consequently before we reached Mia. There are two villages of this name: the upper inhabited by Mohammedans, and the lower, by Nestorian Christians. A Kurd met us as we were entering the former, with a message from Abd-Ul-Summit Bey, to the effect that, having guests, he could not receive us there, but had provided a house in the Christian village, where he would join us after his dinner. I rode on to the lower Mia, and found a party of Kurds belaboring the inhabitants, and collecting old carpets and household furniture. . . . We found a spacious and cleanly roof; and with the assistance of the people of the house, who were ready enough to assist when they learnt we were Christians, established ourselves for the night.

The mixture of local observation, dry wit, and straightforward reportage in this passage is characteristic of the travel passages in *Nineveh and Its Remains*. The book, though, does not remain exclusively on this track; one of its striking features is its commingling of genres, seldom to be found in twentieth-century books on similar subjects.

The Monuments of Nineveh was comprised of sketches Layard made of the ruins he had excavated. The romantic mystique of the visual ruin enabled this book to bolster the impression made by his earlier verbal narrative, and from that time Assyrian art and symbolism in the western visual imagination have had a place that they have never relinquished. Because of the drawings, the iconography of the Nineveh excavations became popular

coin, as can be seen in the commercial manufacture of a "Nineveh jug" by the British firm of Ridgway and Abingdon.

If Layard's first book on Nineveh centered on words and his second on icons, then his third was concerned with icons used as words. *Inscriptions in the Cuneiform Character, from Assyrian Monuments, Discovered by A. H. Layard* (1851) was, unlike the previous books, not on his intellectual native ground. Layard was an aesthete and an adventurer, not a scholar or an epigrapher. Rawlinson, the pioneer of British Near Eastern archaeology, had done far more work to decipher the cuneiform inscriptions in which ancient Mesopotamian writing was transcribed than Layard had, and Rawlinson would have been a more natural candidate for such a book. Layard's name, however, was already linked with expertise on the subject – a status that Rawlinson somewhat inevitably resented, for Layard's first two books on Nineveh had enjoyed such an enthusiastic reception in London that he had become famous as the "Layard of Nineveh." Although in writing his cuneiform book Layard was on unfamiliar technical ground, for the most part he acquitted himself quite well. His particular speculations on word meanings and, especially, phonology were often inaccurate, but many of his theoretical assumptions tallied with the course later taken by scholarship on the subject.

William N. Bruce, editor of Layard's autobiography, explains that although Layard's second trip to Mesopotamia (1848–1851) was successful, Layard had suffered considerably during the expedition. Bruce writes that "private troubles and anxieties, combined with frequent attacks of fever, rendered this period far less enjoyable than the former one had been, and when he took his departure in April 1851, he had made up his mind not to go back." Layard's period of archaeology and adventure was concluded: turning to politics, he gained a seat in Parliament as member from Aylesbury for the Liberal Party. Mining his journals and articles for data, he continued, however, to write about his expeditions and discoveries.

The most prominent result of Layard's second expedition was *Discoveries in the Ruins of Nineveh and Babylon* (1853), a very different book from *Nineveh and Its Remains*. There is no swashbuckling, no background of picaresque incident; the emphasis is not on Layard as protagonist but on the consequence and magnitude of the expedition and on its results. Layard is as much the founding head of Assyriology as the young expeditioner discovering long-buried treasures. The title of the book, reflecting the wider geographical range of his second expedition (he had done some work in the southern part of Mesopotamia as well), also denotes his desire to give a comprehensive view of what was known about those two long-buried cities. Even more than in the earlier work, the biblical echoes are pronounced: Nineveh is the capital of sadistic villainy, and Babylon is the world metropolis of astronomy and splendor to which the Jews had been exiled and in which they were reborn. This book was Layard's most significant in terms of its influence on literature: allusions in poetry such as John Masefield's "Cargoes" ("Quinquireme of Nineveh from distant Ophir") or Rudyard Kipling's comparison of the British empire to Nineveh and Tyre in "Recessional" surely owe a debt to Layard's writing.

In *Nineveh & Babylon* Layard privileges scholarly objectivity over authorial self-scrutiny, but the book still possesses considerable narrative momentum. The reader's interest is heightened by Layard's sense of a chase or hunt for these buried antiquities, and, intensified by the potential biblical reverberations about what new impact a major discovery will bring, a mystery always hovers. Layard's narrative skill is something he shares with British novelists such as Charles Dickens, a friend after Layard's return to London and entry into politics. Layard structures his archaeological dig into a unified plot, and such mysterious elements as the unearthing of parentage, childhood, or financial provenance in Dickens's novels are analogous to the excavations of the past in Layard's texts. Like Dickens, Layard engages his reader by focusing on the theme of a secret that will be brought to light and that will contribute to the growth of reason and understanding through its discovery.

Layard skillfully rescues his presentation from the dullness of dry exposition by maintaining this air of mystery. His use of poetic, grandiloquent rhetoric aids him in this effort: "The great tide of civilization has long since ebbed," he reflects, "leaving these scattered wrecks on the solitary shore. Are these waters to flow again, bearing back the seeds of knowledge that they have wafted to the West?" Despite such excursions into melodrama, Layard executes his announced mission – to retrieve Mesopotamian silences for British knowledge – in a restrained and informative manner. *Nineveh & Babylon* is unquestionably Layard's most solid achievement in terms of scholarship, but it marks an end far more than it does a beginning.

Although Layard reached his peak of scholarly responsibility in the cuneiform book and in *Nineveh & Babylon,* by the time the latter was pub-

Layard copying bas-reliefs at Kuyunjik excavations (sketched by S. C. Malan; The British Museum)

lished and the artifacts found on the expedition were safely ensconced in the British Museum, he had turned decisively from archaeology as a career. Part of this was happenstance: political events transpired in such a way that the British Foreign Office required Layard's Near Eastern expertise, and thus his attention was drawn from his scholarly researches. In another way Layard's archaeological and travel interests became attenuated as his youth waned. By the time he was thirty-five the thrill and daring of such adventures among the ruins had palled for Layard. It was as if these were times of intense, romantic youth that had to be put behind him as he entered a more responsible adulthood and vocation. Led by Layard's Arab assistant, Lormuzd Rassam, archaeological work in Mesopotamia, of course, continued – but Layard never visited the region again. It was the province of adventurous youth, to be renounced for the duties of public service.

In December 1851, even as he rode the crest of his Nineveh fame, Layard was named undersecretary of state for foreign affairs, a post he resigned by February 1852. As had been the case of his diplomacy among the Bakhtiyaris a decade before, circumstances intervened at precisely the strategic moment for Layard. The Ottoman Empire had long been recognized for being in a state of decomposition and had thus earned the title "the Sick Man of Europe." Indeed, the British presence in Iraq was intended both to prevent and, potentially, to profit from this decomposition. An expert on things Turkish was badly required at the center of power, and even though Layard was a bit too pro-Turkish for British tastes, he was asked by Lord Stratford de Redcliffe to return to Constantinople to assist the government. But he remained in Constantinople for only a few months before returning to London.

Soon after Russia made unacceptable diplomatic demands on Turkey in 1853, however, Britain intervened — and thus began the Crimean War. Layard was named undersecretary of state in the Colonial Office in 1855. In July 1861 he was once again promoted to undersecretary of state in the Foreign Office, where he remained until 1865, when he became a member of Parliament in the House of Commons for Southwark, as his position as a career politician and government official expanded. However, Layard's sympathy for the Turks made him politically vulnerable. His parliamentary superiors had always found him obstreperous, and Layard, who had by now been knighted for his governmental service, was disposed of by being named as the new minister of Spain in 1869.

Earlier in the year, before Layard was offered the Madrid mission in October 1869, he had married Enid Guest. It had been thought unlikely that Layard, now a bachelor of fifty-two, would ever marry, but he found the younger woman charming and graceful. Having been born in 1843, Lady Layard was precisely half the age of her husband, and she was the daughter of Lady Charlotte Guest, the translator of the late-medieval Celtic legend collection, *The Mabinogion.* Layard had been close to the Guest family for decades. Sir John Guest, Lady Layard's uncle, had been one of the major financial backers of Layard's expeditions and bought many of the remains he unearthed. Lady Layard's family background proved a natural complement to her husband's enthusiasms and interests.

Although the Iberian Peninsula had not been one of Layard's areas of expertise, he performed his mission well during some of Spain's most tumultuous years of the nineteenth century — years marked by a military coup, an abdication, and two different dynasties. In his own view Layard saved Spain from entering into two separate wars against France and the United States. As a reward for his outstanding service, in 1877 he was made ambassador to the Sublime Porte at Constantinople, the job for which he was more precisely suited. Once again Russia was heavily pressuring the Turks, and the British government felt that a diplomat of Layard's acumen and prestige was badly needed, especially as a liaison with the newly enthroned and potentially reformist sultan, Abdul Hamid II. Layard's presence strengthened Turkish resolve in their maneuverings with Russia, but unfortunately he again was more partisan toward the Turks than British policy desired. This led him to make promises to the sultanate that were not fulfilled, and Layard was thus placed in a difficult and tenuous position.

The line between Layard's role as representative of British political power and his longtime interest in cross-cultural research and communication is apparent at this juncture of his career. For millennia empires in the area had arisen and fallen — the Assyrian, many centuries later the Ottoman, and finally, shoring up the Ottoman in order to replace it, the British. Yet in this case the pressures of contemporary politics did not permit Layard to shape the Near East as he would have it.

Upon completion of his Turkish service in 1880 (official notice of the end of his ambassadorship to Constantinople was actually received in March 1881), Layard had hoped to receive the ambassadorship to Rome. When this was not offered, he and Lady Layard elected to retire to Venice, where he would spend the rest of his life. Layard had always remembered his youth in Florence and had continued to cherish Italy. This interest in Italy had been sustained through his correspondence, begun during his years with the Foreign Office, with Giovanni Morelli, an art cataloguer and restorer. Layard shared Morelli's admiration for the less renowned artists of the Italian Renaissance. He later became an extensive collector of this art, and this interest provided him with his final role as a genial aesthete and elder statesman. He and Lady Layard settled in a large house known as Ca Capello on the Grand Canal. Layard found himself once again revered now that he was safely removed from the shadow of political controversy. Lady Layard situated herself at the center of a social circle that was to encompass both European royalty and figures from the aesthetic movement of the 1890s.

In the midst of this active social life Layard continued to write. Paramount in his production during these years was a revision of the English adaptation of a well-known handbook on Renaissance art by the German scholar Franz Theodor Kugler. The original version of this had been done by the late Sir Charles Eastlake, secretary of the National Gallery, with whose widow the Layards struck up a friendship. *The Italian Schools of Painting; Based on the Handbook of Kugler* (1886) became a standard work, although lacking the aesthetic percipience of Walter Pater or John Ruskin, the sophistication of art history studies developing at the time in Germany.

Of more lasting interest is Layard's last remaining travel production, the long-delayed memoir of his youth among the Bakhtiyari, *Early Adventures in Persia, Susiana, and Babylonia, Including a Residence among the Bakhtiyari and Other Wild Tribes before the Discovery of Nineveh.* This book, based largely on diaries and memoirs composed at the time of the event, is less exotic than *Nineveh and Its Remains,* and it is the only one of Layard's travel works in which the search for antique remains is not one of its principal concerns. Indeed, the narrative mainly centers on Layard's complicated relationship with the local chieftain, Mohammed Taki Khan, a friendship that began, according to Layard, when he saved the life of the chieftain's son by strategically administering European medicine. The son, Hussein Kuli, was later taken hostage by the Persians, an incident that first involved Layard in the diplomatic byplay that led to his acquaintance with Sir Stratford Canning. The Bakhtiyaris, as is true of all the Near Easterners mentioned by Layard, are pictured fondly if unsentimentally, as in this description of the meeting of Mohammed Taki Khan and a rival chieftain:

> Accompanied by his two little sons, and by a large retinue of horsemen mounted upon the finest Arab horses, he went to meet the Matamet. The road by which the Eunuch entered the plain was lined by several thousand men, armed with matchlocks, which they discharged incessantly, whilst clouds of Bakhtiari and Arab horsemen engaged in mimic fight – pursuing each other, bringing up their horses on their haunches at full speed, firing their guns or pistols as they turned back in their saddles, and performing various other feats for which their ancestors in Parthian times were renowned.

The focus in *Early Adventures* is less on places than on people; the book is more psychological than descriptive; and its emphasis on a common humanity makes it less orientalist in its assumptions than his earlier books had been. The ease and amiability of the narrative contrast with the statelier, more verbose tone of Layard's archaeological writings.

Caricature of Layard by S. E. M. (courtesy of the Lilly Library, Indiana University)

The book, however, is often too narrowly anecdotal and frequently fails to achieve the wide historical sweep of the Nineveh books. Even though *Early Adventures* is the Layard book that most closely approximates pure travel writing, most readers have judged the travel material in the Nineveh books to be more captivating – although that earlier work is interwoven with historical and archaeological passages. *Early Adventures* did not generate the public flurry of Layard's Nineveh books; however, it did attract wide notice both in England and the United States. It also resurrected awareness of those parts of Layard's career that, though his political and diplomatic activities occluded them by the later nineteenth century, received a dominant share of scholarly notice in the twentieth century.

Layard continued to be active both socially and intellectually well past his seventieth birthday. In 1892, feeling himself weakening physically, he returned to England. He died in London on 5 July 1894, having lived a variegated Victorian life. Later generations remember his most lasting achievement: through joining the appeal of exotic archaeology with the excitement and organization of a travel narrative, he made the past live.

Biographies:
Gordon Waterfield, *Layard of Nineveh* (London: Murray, 1963);
F. M. Fales and B. J. Hickey, *Austen Henry Layard: Tra l'oriente e venezia* (Rome: Bretschneider, 1987).

References:
E. A. W. Budge, *Guide to the Babylonian and Assyrian Antiquities* (London: British Museum, 1922);
Budge, *The Rise and Progress of Assyriology* (London: Routledge, 1928);
Nora Benjamin Kubie, *Road to Nineveh: The Adventures and Excavations of Sir Austen Henry Layard* (Garden City, N.Y.: Doubleday, 1964);

Seton Lloyd, *Foundations in the Dust: The Story of Mesopotamian Exploration* (London: Thames & Hudson, 1980);
Max E. L. Mallowan, *Nimrud and Its Remains* (New York: Dodd, Mead, 1966);
Hormuz Rassam, *Asshur and the Land of Nimrod* (New York: Harper, 1887);
George Roux, *Ancient Iraq* (Harmondsworth, U.K.: Penguin, 1963);
R. W. Thompson and R. Campbell Hutchinson, *A Century of Exploration at Nineveh* (London: Luzac, 1929).

Papers:
Forty volumes of Layard papers are in the Manuscript Room of the British Museum. The Layard and Guest families possess many letters. In addition to Layard's own publications, Enid Guest kept a diary that consisted of thirteen volumes.

Edward Lear

(12 May 1812 – 29 January 1888)

Claire England
University of Toronto

See also the Lear entries in *DLB 32: Victorian Poets Before 1850* and *DLB 163: British Children's Writers, 1800–1880*.

BOOKS: *Illustrations of the Family of Psittacidae, or Parrots* (London: Privately printed, 1832; facsimile, New York: Johnson, 1978);

Views in Rome and Its Environs: Drawn from Nature and on Stone (London: McLean, 1841);

Gleanings from the Menagerie and Aviary at Knowsley Hall, edited by John Edward Gray (Knowsley: Privately printed, 1846);

Illustrated Excursions in Italy, 2 volumes (London: McLean, 1846);

A Book of Nonsense, as Derry Down Derry (London: McLean, 1846); second edition, with changed illustrations (N.p.: McLean, 1846); enlarged edition, as Lear (London: Routledge, Warne & Routledge, 1861; Philadelphia: Hazard, 1863);

Journals of a Landscape Painter in Albania, &c. (London: Bentley, 1851); republished as *Edward Lear in Greece: Journals of a Landscape Painter in Greece and Albania* (London: Kimber, 1965); republished as *Journals of a Landscape Painter in Greece & Albania* (London: Century, 1988);

Journals of a Landscape Painter in Southern Calabria, Etc. (London: Bentley, 1852); republished as *Edward Lear in Southern Italy* (London: Kimber, 1964);

Views in the Seven Ionian Islands (London: Privately printed, 1863; facsimile, Lees, Oldham: Broadbent, 1979);

Journal of a Landscape Painter in Corsica (London: Bush, 1870); republished as *Edward Lear in Corsica: The Journal of a Landscape Painter* (London: Kimber, 1966);

Nonsense Songs, Stories, Botany and Alphabets (London: Bush, 1870; Boston: Osgood, 1871);

More Nonsense, Pictures, Rhymes, Botany, Etc. (London: Bush, 1872);

Edward Lear, 1857 (portrait by William Holman Hunt; Walker Art Gallery, Liverpool)

Tortoises, Terrapins and Turtles Drawn from Life, by Lear and James de Carle Sowerby (London: Sotheran, Baer, 1872);

Laughable Lyrics: A Fourth Book of Nonsense Poems, Songs, Botany, Music, Etc. (London: Bush, 1877);

Queery Leary Nonsense: A Lear Nonsense Book, edited by Constance, Lady Strachey (London: Mills & Boon, 1911);

The Lear Coloured Bird Book for Children (London: Mills & Boon, 1912);

Lear in Sicily May–July 1847, edited by Granville Proby (London: Duckworth, 1938);

The Complete Nonsense of Edward Lear, edited by Holbrook Jackson (London: Faber & Faber, 1947; New York: Dover, 1951);

Edward Lear's Journals: A Selection, edited by Herbert Van Thal (London: Barker, 1952; New York: Coward-McCann, 1952);

Indian Journal: Watercolours and Extracts from the Diary of Edward Lear (1873–1875), edited by Ray Murphy (London: Jarrolds, 1953; New York: Coward-McCann, 1955);

Teapots and Quails, and Other New Nonsenses, edited by Angus Davidson and Philip Hofer (London: Murray, 1953);

Lear's Corfu: An Anthology Drawn from the Painter's Letters and Prefaced by Lawrence Durrell (Corfu: Corfu Travel, 1965);

Edward Lear: The Cretan Journal, edited by Rowena Fowler (Athens & Dedham: Harvey, 1984);

Edward Lear in the Levant: Travels in Albania, Greece and Turkey in Europe, 1848–1849, edited by Susan Hyman (London: Murray, 1988);

Impossible Picturesqueness: Edward Lear's Indian Watercolors 1873–1875, edited by Vidya Dehejia (New York: Columbia University Press, 1989).

OTHER: "A Leaf from the Journals of a Landscape Painter: Journey to Petra with an Introduction by F. L." (Franklin Lushington), *Macmillan's Magazine,* 75 (April 1897): 410–430.

In a small cemetery in San Remo, Italy, Edward Lear's gravestone reads simply: "LAND-SCAPE PAINTER IN MANY LANDS"; and, indeed, this description epitomizes Lear's view of himself. Others remember him principally for his nonsense poetry, occasionally for his paintings, and only rarely for his travel writing. A commonly accepted assessment of Lear suggests that he was a minor artist who found recognition in unexpected areas while seeking fame in a medium above his talents. Yet Lear's references to himself as a landscape or topographical artist were "neither an affectation of false modesty nor in any sense unfair," as a contemporary and close friend wrote in *Macmillan's Magazine* a decade or so after Lear's death. The friend credited Lear with many gifts of genius, including industry, determination, and the careful preparation that he put into his work and travel. Through much of his career, art and travel were integrated in Lear's life – his trips inspired both his landscape painting and all his writing, including, of course, his travel books.

Lear was born on 12 May 1812 at the family's house, Bowman's Lodge, in Holloway, which was near Highgate, a London suburb of prosperous families. Edward was the twentieth and youngest surviving of twenty-one children born to Jeremiah and Ann Skerrett Lear. From an established success in the family's fruit and sugar-refining business, Jeremiah turned in midlife to stockbroking and had a downturn in his finances. The specific circumstances and extent of Jeremiah's debt and bankruptcy are not known, although it is clear that the effect on the family was serious. The house was rented, and some children left home. The oldest daughter, twenty-one-year-old Ann, was expected not to marry but to take over maternal and household duties in place of a mother who devoted herself to her husband and the family's financial crisis. Young Edward, too, was wholly given over to his sister Ann. After a time, the Lears resolved their money troubles, regained Bowman's Lodge, and lived there in reduced style for several years.

In her biography, *Edward Lear: The Life of a Wanderer* (1968), Vivien Noakes says that Lear was a "rather ugly, short-sighted, affectionate little boy," bewildered, hurt, and made unhappy by events in his young life. He was four at the time of the upheaval and already showing signs of poor health, suffering from bronchitis and asthma. In these early years, he had his first bouts with epilepsy. Epilepsy was not well understood, and there was no clinical treatment. A belief, held by Lear himself, related epilepsy to masturbation. Shamefully, he hid the disease and became, as he grew older, ever more inclined to a solitary and lonely life marked by recurring bouts of depression.

Lear was not well schooled in the formal sense; his childhood education mostly came from Ann, who read to him and oversaw his learning. She drew well and encouraged his talent in drawing. For some time, between the ages of eleven and nineteen, he went to school and stayed with a sister in Sussex. During these and later years, he did discover his talent for poetry and for making other people laugh. Lear often ridiculed himself, perhaps to deflect ridicule, and later, in his nonsense sketches, he portrayed himself as a bespectacled flyabout man on skinny legs. While in Sussex he met people in the art world and decided that he wanted to be an artist in the grand style of the Royal Academy. To achieve this ambition, he would require formal training in art, but there was no money. His aging parents made little provision for their family and none for Edward, who was Ann's responsibility.

Ann had a small inherited income, and she and Edward took rooms in a modest part of London. Edward did any graphic work available and began to teach drawing. In 1832, by subscription, he privately published his *Illustrations of the Family of Psittacidae, or Parrots,* based on parrots in the gardens of the Zoological Society of London. This book was the first English work of its kind to illustrate a single species and the first of its size to be produced from lithography. Although a young man, Lear had immediately established his reputation for ornithological drawing. He and Ann moved to better quarters, and their roles reversed permanently. At age twenty he had become the earner.

Ornithologist John Gould employed Lear, and, with Gould, Lear made his first trip to Europe to see the zoo in Amsterdam and visit Bern and Berlin. Lear also began work for Lord Stanley, later thirteenth earl of Derby. Stanley's private menagerie at Knowsley Hall near Liverpool was an extraordinary example of the penchant that the wealthy had for collecting curious and exotic animals to adorn their country estates. For Stanley, the collection was more than a hobby; his animals and birds were objects of scientific curiosity. Stanley employed Lear because careful drawings would substantially aid the identification of specimens and facilitate their scientific classification.

During this period of his life, Lear went on walking tours in Ireland, the Lake District, and south England, and stayed, off and on, at Knowsley Hall. There, as he entertained the family's children, he composed most of the verse that led to his first book of nonsense. In Lord Stanley's employment Lear met and mingled with a society normally closed to a person of his background. These people would later buy his paintings and help him.

Gradually, his eyesight became inadequate to the detail of his art; his bronchitis frequently appeared; and he often felt himself in poor health. Above all, he wanted to fulfill his landscape painting ambition in a better climate, where he could travel and experience the cultural appeal of the Mediterranean. The Derby family provided him that opportunity, giving him money and letters of introduction, and setting his feet on the road to Rome.

In 1837 Lear left for Rome, and, with the exception of one long stay and several shorter visits home, he remained abroad for the rest of his life. Lear found traveling to his taste and was often on the move sketching and staying for a season or so in Europe and around the Mediterranean, through Malta, Corfu, Greece, the Near East, and Egypt.

Early in his travels, he journeyed alone or with a friend. Some biographers, writing about the nature of some of his friendships, have suggested that Lear was spiritually or emotionally homosexual, letting that suggestion contribute to an explanation of his temperament and conduct. Lear never married, although he seriously considered it on one occasion in his middle age. Had he done so, he might have had a less peripatetic existence and therefore fewer unusual travel experiences to record. As it was, he traveled to many out-of-the-way places, through difficult terrain, in uncomfortable and sometimes dangerous circumstances. In his sixties he went to Ceylon (now Sri Lanka) and India, and still had the energy for visits to Corfu, Switzerland, England, and the towns of his adopted Italy.

On his travels he sketched with pen and ink, sometimes putting on a quick color wash. As with his earlier scientific drawing, he liked to see his subject with his own eyes. He would make notes and purchase photographs in order to be reminded of details. Later he would transform his sketches and notes into finished watercolors, oils, or the illustrations for his journals. His individual pieces have survived better than his book illustrations, which often need modern photo-reproduction techniques to enhance their quality.

It was predictable that Lear should decide to produce a travel book of pictures. Lear was a painter and, by extension, an author of the picturesque. The two are related, for his painter's viewpoint informed his writing. He wanted to "topographise all his journeyings." At that time, topographical artists, like scientific illustrators, were on a low rung of the art ladder. Their function was to record, as objectively and accurately as possible, scenes of natural and architectural interest. This drawing did not allow for abstraction and effect, while landscape art, in the grand manner of Lear's ambition, went beyond technique to a more creative presentation.

As commonly used, *picturesque* means having pictorial quality or being suitable for a picture, and Lear uses the word in this manner in his journals. But he was also a painter of the picturesque school, in which the artistic term has an added dimension. The preferred picturesque landscape was one with a striking image, contrasts, and a variety of contour. A foreground with figures or trees would draw the viewer into a picture, and some element (road, valley, or narrowing natural landscape) would focus attention on a central, but distant, point. An irregularity of focus usually interrupts the view and interests the viewer. A common asymmetrical intrusion was architectural: partially concealed Gothic ruin, an

"The landscape painter catches a severe cold . . . ," a self-portrait by Lear; from Angus Davidson, Edward Lear: Landscape Painter and Nonsense Poet (1812–1888), *1940*

old castle on a hill, an ancient temple to one side. By the mid 1800s sculpted landscape and even architecture were created on the asymmetrical model adopted from these paintings.

The genre held the imagination of the European and Anglo-American elite, as well as being a popular art. Romanticized landscapes in picture books and in prose works, such as novels or tour descriptions, met the demand for this type of scenery. Lear's portrayal in words and paintings was conventional. His choice of subjects and his style, particularly in painting, was attractive but not significantly different from the hosts of others who produced much the same views and descriptions. However, Lear's contribution to the genres of picturesque painting and travel writing should not be discounted. His picture books and personal travel diaries did accomplish the objectives of such writing, namely, to bring the far places closer to home and to entertain and educate the reader.

Lear's first travel book was a set of pictures, *Views in Rome and Its Environs* (1841). Noakes calls it "a superb book of fresh, carefully observed drawings rhythmically composed and confidently handled." She adds, however, that "Lear's lack of formal training sometimes lets him down. The perspective is often very odd and the figures generally

bad." She concludes that it is "difficult to believe that they are done by the same person who drew the bold and completely successful nonsense figures." Caricature or the immediacy of impression conveyed in a few pen strokes reflects a different skill than painting a fully realized portrait or landscape. Conscious of real or imagined inadequacies and intending to acquire that long-awaited formal training, Lear enrolled in his late thirties in the Royal Academy in London, but his style was set. He left the academy, perhaps with some lingering sense of disappointment at not having attained an artistic excellence either to his, or the academy's, standard.

The same publisher who brought out his first book, *Views,* subsequently brought out *A Book of Nonsense* (1846) and the next travel book — two volumes of expensive lithographs, the *Illustrated Excursions in Italy* (1846). All the Italian books were successful and contained some pictures of seldom visited places. From acquaintance with these books, young Queen Victoria invited him for twelve drawing lessons to Osborne. Commentary on Lear usually points out that 1846 was a remarkable year for him: he taught the queen, and he had four books published (a book of nonsense, a travel book, a volume of landscape drawings, and a book on natural history). The subject matter of each book characteristically represented a facet of the varied abilities that he exhibited in his long career, and, also characteristically, he made little profit from his efforts.

His first travel book with text as its substantive content was *Journals of a Landscape Painter in Albania, &c.* (1851), covering two trips in the late 1840s in what is now northern Greece, Macedonia, and Albania. The book set a pattern that he followed in later journals: a chronology with a map of his travels and twenty or so illustrations scattered throughout the text. However carefully chosen at the time, illustrations in the original texts of his journals have not survived well. His prose is more lively than the illustrations, although there are often long passages extolling picturesque and natural beauty. Of Albanian scenery, he wrote that the

striking character of its landscape was the display of objects, in themselves beautiful and interesting – rarely to be met with in combination . . . the simple and exquisite mountain forms of Greece . . . the charm of architecture . . . magnificent foliage . . . recalling the greenness of our own island – forest oak and beech, and dark tracts of pine . . . majestic cliff-girt shores, castle-crowned heights, gloomy fortresses and with this a variety of costume and pictorial incident such as bewilders and delights an artist at each step.

Lear speaks of the difficulty of Mediterranean travel; indeed, whatever an educated traveler of his time might have known of classical place-names, there were nineteenth-century variants and confusions. So, too, present-day readers may have difficulty in tracing Lear's geography and might instead simply enjoy the journal entries for their glimpses of humanity and touches of humor. Lear the artist did not like townscapes; while he appreciated architecture as an element of the picturesque, he was more interested in the beauties of nature. People were also not his favorite subjects for art, but they are often featured in his journals and are recognizable as characters that can still be encountered. Situations he records are the enduring stuff of travelers' funny, and not-so-funny, stories.

On his Albanian travels he was entertained at the house of a merchant, and he made a drawing of the man, who was wearing his native dress. The merchant's younger brother appeared (both men were about forty years old) and requested to be sketched also:

> I, for want of paper, was obliged to make a small though accurate portrait of him on the same page as that on which I had drawn the eldest brother, on a larger scale. "Oh" said the young brother, in a fury of indignation "why have you done this? It is true, I am the youngest, but I am not smaller than my brother; and why should you make me so diminutive? What right have you to remind me of my inferior position? Why do you come into our house to act so insultingly?" I was so amazed by this afflicting view of my innocent mistake, that I could hardly apologize when the elder brother took up the tale. "I, too" said he "am vexed and hurt. I thought you meant well; but if you think that you win my esteem by a compliment paid me at the expense of the affection of my brother, you are greatly mistaken. " What could I say? Was there ever such a lesson to unthinking artists in foreign lands? I had made two enemies by one sketch, and was obliged to take a formal addio.

Susan Hyman's *Edward Lear in the Levant,* published in 1988, is based on this journal with selected texts, photographs, commentary, and additional illustrations. The result, a kind of coffee-table version, is a pleasant introduction to a Lear travel journal.

After his Albanian journals were a success, Lear happily wrote that he had received "heaps and loads of compliments and congratulations." Alfred Tennyson, with whom Lear had a long association, wrote a poem, *To E. L. on his Travels in Greece,* in which Tennyson says, "I read and felt that I was there." In the poem Tennyson mentions that evocative name, Athos, but Lear did not visit Athos until some later travels, and Lear's experience of the physical reality dims the connotation of mystical Greece intended in Tennyson's poetic image.

Lear's next book, *Journals of a Landscape Painter in Southern Calabria, Etc.* (1852) is also about the Mediterranean area. It is like his Albanian journal, composed of a text with a package of twenty illustrations. *Calabria* covers his travels in 1847 from Naples south through Sicily and is typical Lear in that his interest in scenery is dominant. In one long sentence or a string of phrases, Lear creates a complete and scenic picture:

> Calabria! No sooner is the word uttered than a new world arises before the mind's eye, torrents, fastnesses, all the prodigality of mountain scenery, caves, brigands, and pointed hats, costumes and character, horrors and magnificence without end. . . . Far far above along the pass [at Canalo] to the western coast, you could discover diminutive figures threading the winding line among those fearful crags and fragments! or deep in the ravine, where torrents falling over perpendicular rocks echoed and foamed around, might be perceived parties of women spreading out linen to dry or . . . goats clustered on some bright pinnacle and sparkling in the yellow sunlight.

Such scenes, text matched with picture, can be traced in Lear's individual paintings or in his book illustrations. A reader of the journals can imagine the phrases to be notes for a picture, a composition recorded verbally before being rendered pictorially. Indeed, that is how Lear worked, and the description can be easily visualized as the subject for an Arcadian or picturesque painting.

"Wishing to confine these journals strictly to consideration of the landscape," Lear decides to say nothing of the political turbulence in Italy, which culminated in the rising of 1848. He merely remarks that these events might result in an understandable suspicion and lack of hospitality toward travelers. He describes one such situation when the people with whom he found a friendly lodging became sullen because they wanted news of the political situation and would not believe that he did not have it to give. In addition to a soured atmosphere, the people were rather odd and the place was dirty, filled with ten dogs and an unpleasant, huge tame sheep. After supper and some angry discussion, Lear, feeling very alone (as he was on this particular trip), could only wrap himself in his traveling blanket and lie on his bed, "whose exterior was not indicative of cleanliness or rest." Awakened in the night by a noise near his bed, he thought he was to encounter some Calabrian romance:

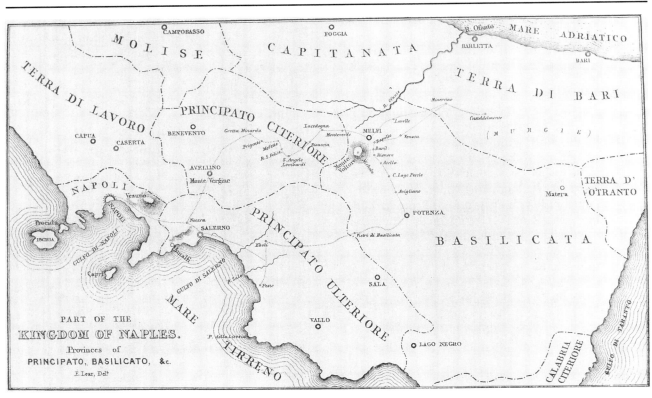

Map drawn and lithographed by Lear for his Journals of a Landscape Painter in Southern Calabria, Etc.

Feeling certain that I was not alone, I reached for the never to be omitted traveller's night companion – a phosphorus box when . . . my bed was suddenly lifted by some incomprehensible agency below, puffing and sobs mixed with a tiny tinkling sound. I jumped off the bed, and with a stick thrust hastily and hardly below the bed, to push the intruder, ghostly or bodily, on to fair fighting ground – Baaa – aa. . . . It was the large dirty tame sheep! So I forthwith opened a door into the next room, and bolted out the domestic tormentor.

About ten years later, during a period of unhappiness about his life and work, Lear privately published his *Views in the Seven Ionian Islands* (1863). It was in the same style as his Italian excursions: twenty lithographic plates each with a short descriptive text. At the time, his pictures were not selling. The book, however, was well received, and he hoped that *Views* would maintain his reputation as a topographical draftsman of Mediterranean scenery.

Although he kept diaries of all his trips, it was nearly twenty years after the first Mediterranean journals before Lear published another journal. This third and last book, similar to the other journals, was *Journal of a Landscape Painter in Corsica* (1870). It records a journey made two years earlier in 1868. Again the standard twenty pictures appear, and a little more color has been added to the flat

sepia of earlier travel-journal illustrations. To save money, as recommended by a publisher who then refused the book, the engravings were taken from woodblocks. The effect is rather poor, so, once more, the text retains more vitality than the illustrations. Lear remarks that

those who go to Corsica hoping to study antiquities will be disappointed for the manifold charms of classical countries are wanting there; the long lines of Grecian plains, so crowded with spots full of historic and poetic memories, vast and beautiful remains such as those of Sicily, Syria, Egypt do not exist in it; neither the more modern beauties of architecture, the varied forms of tower or a castle, mosque, cathedral or monastery with which Albania or Italy abound. On the other hand, Corsica is full of scenes stamped with original beauty.

Lear finds the island lacking in the romance of costume and brigandry. A traveler may go "in undisturbed monotony of security . . . risk and danger dispersed by the broad daylight of French administration and civilisation. With the old customs and costumes, mystery and murder have alike disappeared from the Corsica of 1868." His Corsican journal strikes a flat and banal note, reminiscent of modern travel brochures that repetitively describe all scenes as unique, memorable, beautiful, and so on. In this journal scenery is all: the people, and even the dogs, are more tail-wagging and less churlish in this journal. Some of the anecdotal charm of Lear's earlier journals is lost. Noakes thinks the subject of this book a poor choice for Lear to have made. She notes the possible trips with better potential, such as Mount Athos, where so few visited, Egypt, or another book on Greece as he once planned. Corsica was his least successful travel book in art, text, and reception, and it was the last journal published in his lifetime.

Discussion of Lear's writing concentrates on him as the nonsense poet and source of limericks. He is compared with Lewis Carroll and William Gilbert, and he certainly had an extraordinary sense of the ridiculous and the musical in his poetry and sketches. In his informal writing he could be just as funny and clever, but he could also be facetious and tiring in his persistence with offbeat spellings, new words or phonetic contortions, emphatic punctuation, and long sentences.

Critics agree that if his absurd poetic images and squiggly drawings can delight children, his poetry can also convey hints of sadness and yearning to adults. He could also summon a flavor of exotic places and unusual circumstances with an absolutely apt construction or a melodious name. Moreover, his places and names were not always as completely imaginary as they might initially seem, so one has to be careful in reading some of Lear's nonsense. Who would not believe that Lear, in India under the British Raj, saw the sellers of Pelican jee, drank a bottle of ring-bo-ree, or met the actual Akond of Swat? When he traveled in south India's Coromandel area, he could have passed by the sublimely unencumbered Yonghy Bonghy Bo with his:

Two old chairs, and half a candle
One old jug without a handle.

Much of his nonsense poetry can be read as a special subset of travel literature – a poetic exotica of strange places, oddly different peoples, foreign and absurd situations. References to traveling, going away and sometimes never returning, occur often in his poems. Consider the Jumblies, who live in "far and few lands," and who sailed away in a sieve to the Western Sea:

And in twenty years they all came back
In twenty years or more

For they've been to the Lakes and the Torrible Zone
And the hills of the Chankly Bore.

How far away, sadly romantic, and like an imagined Arabian fairy tale is the sensuous aura around the maiden who:

sits upon her Bulbul
Through the long, long hours of night
And o'er the dark horizon gleams
The Yashmack's fitful light[.]

Angus Davidson remarks that Lear had an extraordinary mastery of rhythm, "many of his lines – quite irrespective of their content – have a great beauty of sound, which, if Lear were a serious instead of a nonsense poet might have attracted more attention."

Strong rhythms, a mix of joy and sadness, clever wordplay, parody, and imaginary and absurd creations were relegated to his published nonsense and his personal notes and correspondence. His letters describe his visit to Mount Athos in Greece, which he found unpleasant in all respects, except for some of its monastic and mountain scenery. Most of the monks were dirty, vexatious, and unkempt, even if one or two were kind enough. He called them "muttering, miserable, mutton-hating, man-avoiding, misogynic, morose & merriment-marring, monotoning, many-mule-making, mocking, mournful, minced-fish & marmalade masticating Monx." His string of adjectives describe not only the monks with artful alliteration but also his own temperament during his visit. Then, as now, women were forbidden to visit Mount Athos, and Lear, in a letter to an influential friend, wrote that distressed needlewomen in England should be sent out to Athos. The monks would be improved by the presence of women – at least four thousand strong, to subdue the monasteries.

When largely delighted with a place visited, he could spin an incomparable phrase, such as the one in his correspondence about Delhi in India. Initially he disliked the city, which he found too "Britishised," but shortly he began to enjoy himself greatly, "making Delhineations of the Dehlicate architecture as is all impressed on my mind as inDehlibly as the Dehlioterious quality of the water."

Lear put aside his outrageous style in his travel journals, which are factual vignettes filled with much appreciation of visual pleasures. He is said to have written his published journals quickly, making few changes. He gives an impression of speed and ease in writing; his simple style is not labored and is always clear. His journals are unde-

FOREST OF MARMANO

Illustration by Lear for his Journal of a Landscape Painter in Corsica

manding reading to take along on a trip through the Mediterranean area. The journals maintain their interest, not so much for the heavy emphasis on scenery, as for the short stories about people. To read Lear's journals is to recognize both the changed and some of the unchanged aspects of travel and tourism.

Exactly as his titles convey, Lear writes about himself as a traveling landscape artist who gives his impressions (artistic and other) of the places he visits. The substance of his journals is description and anecdote; thus, his books are either picture books or personal accounts, without being guidebooks or sources of systematic information. He gives very little advice and even less information about a country and its peoples as a whole. Although touched on in passing, history and politics, as well as culture and custom, do not deeply interest Lear. Any obligations of this sort are discharged in his introductions, which refer the reader to other books. He often remarks that other writers, such as geographers, antiquarians, classicists, or politicians will have already explained regions, leaving little for a

landscape painter to add. Nevertheless, Lear, with some reason, believes himself to be the only Englishman to have published an account of some places he visited, and, with similar wording in the prefaces to his journals, remarks that "scanty and slight as may be, it is something in these days to be able to add the smallest mite of novelty to the travellers' world of information and interest."

His advice is largely that travel in untrammeled places should, and sometimes must, be as opportunity presents. It is paradoxical that Lear, who often felt unwell, nonetheless must have had a sturdy constitution and could recommend good health as essential for travel. Another necessity was equipment (blanket, cooking pot, a few food staples, quinine for ills). Clothes, carefully wrapped to ensure dryness in inclement weather, included one suit for formal occasions, such as visiting with one's host, and another for actual travel. Perhaps because of his profession, Lear notices the rainy days, and they seem as many as the bad roads. Readers get a true sense of how difficult and uncomfortable travel was in the mid 1800s, when people went with large

216

The Temple of Bassae, *oil painting by Lear (Fitzwilliam Museum, Cambridge)*

encumbrances of baggage to ward off all sorts of exigencies. Naturally, travelers like Lear had a personal servant along to take care of daily routines and problems, but still, he traveled with an intrepidness and simplicity that was unusual for the sightseeing tourist of his time.

As for handling financial matters in the days before traveler's checks, Lear advises that one take as little money as possible, substituting, instead, letters of introduction and credit. Lear himself often mentions money in his writings. He is always pleased to comment on how little it costs to travel and often amazed by how much good – and bad – food can be had for a small expense. Lear, as one learns from his anecdotes, had developed the fine art of moving on, or of being stoic and unresponsive until any demands for additional money dissipated. He must, however, have been worried on more than one occasion. On his visit to the rose-red city of Petra, he encountered various bedouins who demanded payment, and yet more payment, for porterage or tribute. Lear finally had to surrender all his money, because only when the tribesmen were satisfied they had it all did they disappear into the dunes from which they had so threateningly arisen.

On other occasions people stirred by curiosity, superstition, or religious beliefs pestered, ridiculed, or intimidated Lear as he sketched. In what was then the Ottoman Empire, he met conservative rural people who refused to allow themselves to be sketched. People thought him a devil or a spy for the sultan. A shower of stones once followed his retreat. Poor weather, poor accommodations, the badgering of children and dogs were all circumstances he endured as he tried to sketch each day, causing him on more than one occasion to observe, "I was glad enough to leave."

His last extended trip was the one to India in 1873–1875. He went as the guest of Lord Northbrook, viceroy of India, another friend from his days in Rome. He was so delighted with the sights of India that he proclaimed himself ready to divide the world into those who have seen the Taj Mahal and those who have not. He covered a surprising amount of territory in India, produced more than two thousand drawings, and had enough copious notes to do a travel book. Had he done so, it might have been very successful. Picturesque views of India would have been more novel than his additions to the already abundant Mediterranean views. One wonders what he might have written about

India's people and places, and about travel by elephant, after his having made the comment that India was a place of "redundant beauty . . . every foot a picture . . . and altogether a new world."

For all his enthusiasm and experience of wide-ranging travel, his own desire for recognition, his actual reputation, and his financial success through sales of pictures and journals, all centered on the Mediterranean. His home was in Italy, and he died there on 29 January 1888 at his villa in San Remo from a bronchial illness. He had outlived the servant who had portered and traveled with him for more than twenty years, and he had buried his much-loved and aged cat, Foss, for whom he raised a stone not unlike the one that marks his own grave.

His own and later generations did not acclaim him; the prestigious, original set and later supplements of the British *Dictionary of National Biography* have no proper entry for Lear. In the preface to a first 1907 publication of Lear's letters, Constance, Lady Strachey remarked that the English and American public only knew Lear through his books of nonsense. She regretted that only a cultivated few recognized his paintings and fewer yet knew his character or realized "the vein of sadness and other qualities which went to make Lear's humour of the highest order and his pictures of special interest." Several generations later, there is little evidence that the appreciation of Lear is much different from what she had observed.

Some argue and present convincing evidence that Lear is an underappreciated talent among Victorian writers and artists. Others, by their silent neglect or recorded criticism, suggest that his talent was mediocre. Reasons for undervaluations in art and in literature overlap. Neither his painting nor his travel writing are judged to be worth more than a minor place in cultural history. He wrote with humor, but his travel writing is prosaic, containing no great flights of imagination or great insights. Yet, as the occasional art exhibit or new publication demonstrates, there are still some champions of his poetry, his humor, and his art. Lear himself considered that the important parts of his life were not his poetry and his personal travel accounts, but rather the travel itself and the art that he created from it – the one as his interest and inspiration, the other as the focus of his career and ambition. A view of landscape was his enduring pleasure; he once wrote, "When I go to heaven . . . let me have a park and a beautiful view of sea and hill, mountain and river, valley and plain – with no end of tropical foliage."

Letters:

Letters of Edward Lear, edited by Constance, Lady Strachey (London: Unwin, 1907);

Later Letters of Edward Lear, edited by Constance, Lady Strachey (London: Unwin, 1911);

The Corfu Years: A Chronicle Presented Through Letters and Journals, edited by Philip Sherrard (Athens: Harvey, 1988);

Edward Lear: Selected Letters, edited by Vivien Noakes (Oxford: Clarendon Press, 1988).

Bibliography:

William B. Osgood Field, *Edward Lear on My Shelves* (Munich: Bremer, 1933).

Biographies:

Angus Davidson, *Edward Lear: Landscape Painter and Nonsense Poet (1812–1888)* (London: Murray, 1938);

Joanna Richardson, *Edward Lear* (London: Longmans, 1965);

Vivien Noakes, *Edward Lear: The Life of a Wanderer* (Boston: Houghton Mifflin, 1968; revised edition, London: Fontana, 1979; revised edition, London: BBC Publications, 1985);

Susan Chitty, *That Singular Person Called Lear: A Biography of Edward Lear, Artist, Traveller and Prince of Nonsense* (New York: Atheneum, 1989);

Noakes, *The Painter Edward Lear* (London: David & Charles, 1991).

References:

Ina Rae Hark, *Edward Lear* (New York: Twayne, 1982);

Philip Hofer, *Edward Lear* (New York: Oxford Press, 1982);

Hofer, *Edward Lear as a Landscape Draughtsman* (Cambridge, Mass.: Belknap, 1967);

John Lehmann, *Edward Lear and His World* (London: Thames & Hudson, 1977).

Papers:

The largest collection of Edward Lear's manuscripts and papers is in the Houghton Library of Harvard University.

Anna Leonowens

(5 November 1834 – 19 January 1914)

Lorraine Mercer
Portland State University

See also the Leonowens entry in *DLB 99: Canadian Writers Before 1890.*

BOOKS: *The English Governess at the Siamese Court: Being Recollections of Six Years in the Royal Palace at Bangkok* (London: Trübner, 1870; Boston: Fields, Osgood, 1870); republished as *Siam and the Siamese: Six Years' Recollections of an English Governess at the Siamese Court* (Philadelphia: Coates, 1897);

The Romance of the Harem (Philadelphia: Porter & Coates, 1872); republished as *The Romance of Siamese Harem Life* (London: Trübner / Boston: Osgood, 1873); republished as *Siamese Harem Life* (London: Barker, 1952; New York: Dutton, 1953);

Life and Travel in India: Being Recollections of a Journey before the Days of Railroads (Philadelphia: Porter & Coates, 1884);

Our Asiatic Cousins (Boston: Lothrop, 1889).

OTHER: *The Art Movement in America,* edited by Leonowens (New York: Century, 1887).

Anna Leonowens, circa 1862

Anna Harriet Leonowens's life has been surrounded by controversy and myth. From the first publication of her books in the late nineteenth century through the republication of her first two works, *The English Governess at the Siamese Court: Being Recollections of Six Years in the Royal Palace at Bangkok* (1870) and *The Romance of the Harem* (1872), and the more recent and well-known biography by Margaret Landon, *Anna and the King of Siam* (1944), details of her life and literary legacy have been disputed. In spite of the controversies Leonowens remains, except for a few Protestant missionaries, the only European white woman to have been allowed entry to the royal harem of King Mongkut of Siam. Popular Hollywood motion pictures and musicals such as *Anna and the King of Siam* (1946) and *The King and I* (1956) have helped to create popular stereotypes of the English teacher abroad whose concern

for her students, innate wit, and grace find her singing "Getting to Know You" with solid British spunk and good sportsmanship. Such is the stuff that myth and musicals are made of.

According to Leonowens, she was born in Wales on 5 November 1834. In 1840 her father, Capt. Thomas Maxwell Crawford, was transferred to India, and Anna and her older sister, Eliza, were left in Wales. In the following year Captain Crawford was killed in a Sikh uprising, and Mrs. Crawford remarried a British official in the public works department at Poona, India, where Leonowens joined them in 1849. When Anna and her new stepfather disagreed on the husband whom he had selected for her, she left home in 1850, at the age of sixteen, and accompanied the Reverend George Percy Badger and his wife on a tour of Damascus, Jerusalem, and the Nile River. Upon her return to India the following year Anna married Maj. Thomas L. Leonowens in Bombay and settled down to married life.

Although the marriage seemed happy, the first years were marred with difficulty. In 1852 Anna's mother died, and the newlyweds suffered the loss of their first child. Later that year the Leonowenses were shipwrecked off the Cape of Good Hope, and their second baby died in childbirth. The couple then returned to England, where in 1853 their daughter, Avis, was born; a son, Louis, was born the following year. In 1856 the family moved to Singapore, where Major Leonowens had been posted. While in Singapore, Leonowens lost several relatives during the Indian Mutiny of 1857, and the Leonowenses were left financially destitute after the failure of the Indian banks. Two years later Major Leonowens died of sunstroke after a tiger hunt, and Anna was left with few financial resources and two small children to support.

To provide for her family Leonowens opened a small school for officers' children in Singapore. While she was thus employed, Tan Kim Ching, agent to King Mongkut of Siam, recommended her as English teacher to the king's sixty-seven children. Leonowens accepted the position, and in March 1862 she sent Avis to school in England before she and Louis sailed on the steamer *Chao Phya* for Bangkok, where she spent a little more than the next five years working as secretary to the king and as a teacher in the Royal Palace and harem. In 1867 Leonowens left Siam because of ill health. She placed Louis in an Irish boarding school, picked up Avis, and went to America, where she worked as a teacher, lecturer, and writer, living on Staten Island, New York.

Avis Leonowens married Thomas Fyshe, a Scotsman, and in 1876 Anna moved with the couple to Canada; in Halifax, where she first lived, Leonowens was dubbed dean of the Halifax feminists for her interest in women's suffrage in the maritime provinces. At one debate of the Halifax Women's Council, Leonowens said that while she did not mean to stir up a revolution, she believed that "while women are refused the franchise they should refuse to pay taxes." Her later accomplishments include organizing book and reading clubs in Halifax, opening the Berkeley School for Boys in New York, working in Russia as a newspaper correspondent for *Youth's Companion,* and opening the Nova Scotia College of Art, the first art school in Nova Scotia.

Leonowens's version of her life has been shown to be a fiction by W. S. Bristowe in *Louis and the King of Siam* (1976). Bristowe also points out that historians question the accuracy of her narratives after her negative treatment of King Mongkut led them to reexamine those narratives.

In *With Passport and Parasol* (1989) Julia Keay also questions Leonowens's veracity by discussing issues of social respectability and acceptability in Victorian society and pointing out that Leonowens, left penniless with two small children, needed a means of support. The school for officers' children in Singapore could have provided such support, Keay writes, but she argues that Leonowens "knew if such a venture were to succeed she would need more than money and a talented tongue – she would need credentials." According to Keay, the most effective way for a woman to acquire these credentials in the nineteenth century was through the men to whom she was connected. By altering the status of her father or husband, a woman could secure for herself or her family the respectability necessary to be hired as a trusted teacher or governess.

One of the most significant recent discussions of *The Romance of the Harem* is that of Susan Morgan's introduction to the 1991 reprint of the book. Morgan points out that many scholars have felt justified in questioning Leonowens's right to comment on situations in the harem because they not only could assume that she was a religious prude but also, oddly enough, could call her a sex-starved widow who had no business commenting on King Mongkut's royal practices and policies. Many Victorian lady travelers were subjected to such ad hominem attacks. After her painstaking research and discussion of the critics, Morgan concludes that most of the negative comments about Leonowens are based largely on innuendo and surmise, and, along with Keay, Morgan offers some insight into why Leonowens altered parts of her biography.

Leonowens's writing generally addresses three major themes: slavery, women's lives, and the related issues of imperialism and colonialism. Her response to these issues, like that of many nineteenth-century women writers, is ambivalent. This ambivalence in her narratives relates directly to her own marginalized position in British society and to her view of her role as a writer. Leonowens used the genre of travel literature both as a means of support and as a safe and valid platform from which to examine the complexity of the issues that concerned her. By the time she began writing her books she had been influenced by the friendship and the philosophy of American abolitionists such as Harriet

Beecher Stowe and Ralph Waldo Emerson, friendships that provided the lens through which she looked back on the experiences that she was recording in her travel writings.

In 1870, three years after she left Siam, Leonowens published her first book, *The English Governess at the Siamese Court: Being Recollections of Six Years in the Royal Palace at Bangkok.* She was living in the United States with Avis, teaching school, and lecturing about Siam and the Siamese. In this volume Leonowens traces her career in Siam, and her preface includes the frequently quoted letter from King Mongkut offering her the job of English teacher to his children:

> We hope that in doing your education on us and on our children (whom English call inhabitants of benighted land) you will do your best endeavor for knowledge of English language, science, and literature, and not for conversion to Christianity: as the followers of Buddha are mostly aware of the powerfulness of truth and virtue, as well as the followers of Christ, and are desirous to have facility of English language and literature more than new religions.

This is the first of many instances in her book that shows not only the wit, intellect, and determination of her employer, King Mongkut, but also her appreciation of his complex position as ruler of Siam.

Her fascination with the history, religions, customs, and people outside her own background remains constant through all her books. In *The English Governess at the Siamese Court* Leonowens first raises the themes of slavery, the degradation and sorrow of harem life, and the courage of those who live within the confines of these systems. Besides these major concerns Leonowens's text covers many details of Siamese life. After recounting her arrival in Siam with her son, Louis, she begins to examine the royal harem, to which she refers as "his Excellency's own private Utah." Her accounts of life in the Royal Palace are complex and complicated by her own cultural beliefs: she abhors slavery and polygamy as twin evils, but she feels a conflicting loyalty and desire to do the best job she can for King Mongkut, her royal employer. Faced with the impossibility of reconciling these conflicting attitudes, Leonowens produces a narrative unusual in both tone and style: she praises and profanes sometimes in the same sentence. For example, she not only calls King Mongkut a "provoking melange of antiquarian attainments and modern skepticism" but also explains how

in many grave considerations he displayed a soundness of understanding and clearness of judgment – a genuine nobility of mind, established upon universal ethics and philosophic reason, – where his passions were not dominant; but when these broke in between the man and the majesty, they effectually barred his advance in the direction of true greatness; beyond them he could not, or would not, make way.

Her prose becomes somewhat melodramatic in the following paragraph when she says, "Ah, if this man could but have cast off the cramping yoke of his intellectual egotism, and been loyal to the free government of his own true heart, what a demi-god might he not have been among the lower animals of Asiatic royalty!" The book continues with this documentation of Leonowens's conflicting and complex attitudes to the people and culture in which she found herself – and to their enigmatic monarch.

Her description of the king is often harsh. When the book was first published, the Siamese government not only denied Leonowens the legacy of land that her former employer had allegedly left to her but also sent a delegation to the United States to attempt to buy the entire edition in order to keep her negative descriptions of their esteemed, late monarch from the public. Other reactions to the work were mixed. On 9 March 1870 an anonymous review for *The Nation* discussed the failures of the Christian missionaries to Siam in nearly as much space as it discussed Leonowens's book. This mainly favorable review calls the work "one of the most entertaining of recent books of travel" and advises the author to focus exclusively on depictions of life behind the scenes in the palace, scenes to which she is the only westerner to have been privy. Yet the reviewer continues that

> As it is, the book is half-filled up with geographical, historical, and other padding, not very skilfully [*sic*] inserted, and very disorderly in arrangement. Indeed, when the author comes outside the palace gates and away from the immediate care of her pupils, she grows uninteresting.

On 10 December 1870 a more sympathetic reviewer for *The New York Times* wrote that the book is "well written, and abounds with that rich flavor of the East," but an anonymous reviewer in the *Athenaeum* scathingly derogates *The English Governess at the Siamese Court* in accusing Leonowens of multiple inaccuracies that render it "not only valueless but even dangerously misleading."

Contemporary reviewers are still mixed in their opinions of *The English Governess at the Siamese Court.* When Oxford University Press republished

One of Leonowens's pupils in Bangkok, circa 1862

the book in 1990, cover blurbs claimed that the book "remains engaging as a story of adventure, fascinating as a picture of Siam little more than a century ago, and intriguing as an account of King Mongkut's private life." The editor feels compelled, however, to warn readers not to believe Leonowens's account verbatim; it is interesting that this anonymous editorial warning closely echoes the sexist sentiments of many nineteenth-century critics in claiming that "sometimes [Leonowens's] vivid imagination took charge of her pen and, like many Victorian ladies, she was always ready to believe the worst."

Although Leonowens is obviously fascinated by the customs and history of Siam, she is at her best when describing the children and women with whom she worked in the royal harem. Her characters are lovingly drawn, and her anecdotes are compelling. In *The English Governess at the Siamese Court* her focus is on her own life and work in Siam. *The Romance of the Harem,* published in 1872 while she was still teaching and lecturing in the United States, focuses on the lives of the women inside the royal harem. These tales, or "romances," are prefaced with her statement that "Truth is often stranger than fiction." Having received some harsh reviews of her first volume, she attempted to validate a book

that she expected to appear strange and unbelievable to her Western readers. Her preface then stresses that "Most of the stories, incidents, and characters are known to me personally to be real, while of such narratives as I received from others I can say that 'I tell the tale as it was told to me,' and written down by me at the time." This second book is dedicated "To the noble and devoted women whom I learned to know, to esteem, and to love in the city of Nang Harm," and she adds that to them "I dedicate the following pages, containing a record of some of the events connected with their lives and sufferings." This dedication appropriately graces a book filled with stories and accounts of some of the nine thousand women and children who lived in the city of Nang Harm, the royal harem.

It is a perfect companion piece to Leonowens's first book, for it provides detailed accounts of the lives of Siamese women. In this narrative Leonowens grows more eloquent and passionate about her three thematic concerns: imperialism, slavery, and what Victorians called "The Woman Question." These three concerns fuel her narration and provide the complexities inherent in her project. In her description of life inside the harem readers learn that

> this woman's city is as self-supporting as any other in the world: it has its own laws, its judges, police, guards, prisons, and executioners, its markets, merchants, brokers, teachers, and mechanics of every kind and degree; and every function of every nature is exercised by women, and by them only. Into this inmost city no man is permitted to enter, except only the king, and the priests.

One of the most poignant stories is that of Tuptim, the king's temporary favorite, who sickens with sadness over the loss of her childhood love from outside the harem, before she had been made a gift to King Mongkut. So great is her desire to see her young man that one morning she disguises herself as a lesser member of the priest's entourage and follows the procession outside the palace walls. There she flees immediately to the monastery, where her love is living as a monk, but "he did not recognize in the young priest that I seemed to be the Tuptim he had known in his boyhood, and who had once been his betrothed wife." The unfortunate Tuptim is recaptured, brought to trial, and sentenced, alongside the young monk, to death by hanging. Leonowens describes Tuptim's behavior at the trial as that of

> a child of barely sixteen years hurling defiance, at her own risk and peril, at the judges who appeared as giants

beside her. To make such a reply to those executors of Siam's cruel laws was not only to accept death but all the agonies of merciless torture. As her refusal fell like a thunderbolt upon my startled ears, she seemed a very Titan among the giants.

Leonowens's admiration of women such as Tuptim, whose love, generosity, and courage fill her book, is unlimited. She never fails to show the strengths and the beauty of her pupils and friends inside the harem. These women grow in stature throughout the book, and the reader's sympathy, compassion, and admiration for them grows along with that of their tutor, Leonowens.

The reviews of *The Romance of the Harem* were more consistently favorable than those for *The English Governess at the Siamese Court.* Leonowens's style was more vivid and her subjects more immediate than in her first book, and as the critic for *The New York Times* (14 February 1873) says, the work

> disarms criticism. It is so luxuriant, and warmly rich and brilliant and so full of beautiful pictures and strange incidents, that your judgment is charmed to sleep, and you willingly give yourself up to the credulous enjoyment of what the skillful author has provided for you.

In a 15 May 1873 review in *The Nation* the reviewer, while saying that Leonowens is "not a Boccaccio," claims that her tales

> indeed deserve the name of romances, so wild and strange are they in incident and atmosphere . . . revealing the dark places of the earth, full of the habitations of cruelty, but revealing also some of the greatest and brightest qualities of human nature.

The *Atlantic Monthly* (May 1873) lauds *The Romance of the Harem* as a tract teaching "toleration, charity, and modesty, for it teaches that the virtues we call Christian are also Buddhist virtues; and it is in this way not merely a contribution to literature, it is a benefaction to Mankind." As it had been toward *The English Governess at the Siamese Court,* the *Athenaeum* was the harshest in its review of *The Romance of the Harem.* Its review (15 February 1873) grudgingly acknowledges that Leonowens's style "has manifestly improved since the publication of her former work" and adds that "we must at least allow her the merit of having produced a volume of much interest to the general reader" before it closes with this personal criticism of Leonowens:

> On the propriety of the writer's conduct in spending years in the service of the Siamese King, taking his pay, accepting his kindnesses, and afterwards publishing to

the world the incidents that have come to her knowledge while she made her home at his court, it is not for us to pronounce. Mrs. Leonowens, as we believe, has either been crammed by gossiping inventors of marvelous tales, or has, from self-interested motives, put together a sensational work. We prefer the former alternative.

In a 1991 biography, *Anna Leonowens, A Life Beyond the King and I,* Leslie Smith Dow, a Canadian journalist, also speculates on Leonowens's origins. Dow hired a team of professional researchers to gather the basic truths from the confusing accounts about Leonowens. She concludes that Leonowens "may have been among the most accomplished, fearless and adventurous of Victorian ladies, or a complete fake who covered up her ignoble origins by inventing and exaggerating at will, simply to sell copies of her books." Dow does not settle for any definite answers and says that Leonowens "was creative with the truth, to be sure, but not a fake. It is clear that she sought to keep certain elements of her background secret."

Dow claims that Leonowens was born to an Anglo-Indian family in Ahmednugger, India, in the barracks of the East India Company on 6 November 1831. Dow suggests that Anna's father, Thomas Edwards, was a sergeant in the East India Company. He died in late summer 1831, leaving his wife, Mary Anne Glasscott Edwards, with one daughter, Eliza, born in April 1830, and six months pregnant with Anna. Mary Anne remarried on 9 January 1832, to Patrick Donohue, just three months after Anna was born. Mary Anne was born in Bengal, the product of a common-law union.

Dow describes the typical scene of family life in the "fecund confines of an Indian barracks": "Only a screen divided the family's cramped back corner from the raucous noises of upwards of two dozen men, eating, drinking, gambling, undressing and sleeping." She explains that "The stigma attached to being an 'army rat,' as such children were then called, was enormous, particularly for a girl. The chances of escaping a life following the drum were almost nil." Dow elaborates on the options available to girls in Leonowens's situation: "Unless a particularly bright female could get on teaching at the regimental school, or nursing in the infirmary, she would almost certainly be forced, through sheer economic necessity, to marry a much older soldier at some time between her thirteenth and fifteenth birthdays." Dow elaborates on this stigma by explaining that society considered an upbringing in an army barracks to be "fundamentally immoral."

Dow believes that Leonowens "invented an appropriate background for her new life as a proper Victorian lady, much the same as famed explorer-journalist Henry Morton Stanley fabricated his." Dow claims that Leonowens's "forceful personality and resilience helped her make the transition to a new life that would have been impossible for most other young women in her social situation."

Dow adds: "As my research progressed, I wondered why it was so impossible for her critics to praise in a woman the very qualities they applaud in male adventurers." She concludes that "there is no one view of the life, or lives, of this remarkable lady, only degrees of interpretation." Dow's commentary, in addition to her wide research, adds important historical weight and insightful interpretation of Leonowens's life, the fictions she created and the fictions that were created about her.

Despite some outraged critical reactions, the picture of the king that in fact emerges in *The Romance of the Harem* is mainly sympathetic. Leonowens shows the complexities of an enlightened monarch who must carefully plan his course through the minefield of nineteenth-century European imperialism and colonial practices to keep his country a free and sovereign state. Yet Leonowens finds offensive King Mongkut's self-interested definition of freedom, one that can still condone slavery and concubinage, and in *The Romance of the Harem* that emerges as a major topic.

In *Life and Travel in India: Being Recollections of a Journey before the Days of Railroads* (1884) Leonowens returns to the subject of India to examine art, architecture, history, politics, poetry, dance, religion, the military, and family life in India. Everything about India is extraordinary to her. This first-person narrative begins with Leonowens, a fifteen-year-old, sailing to India for the first time. Along with her running commentary on the country she reveals details of her personal life, her friendships, her marriage, and British social life in India, and she relates anecdotes about the native servants of the British. As in her two previous works, her major concerns include the treatment and position of women, servants, and slaves. In one chapter she comments that the rights of the Parsi women were more protected by law than the rights of British women, who, in the time her narrative is set, were as yet unprotected by the Married Women's Property Act of 1870. Although the tone of the work seems one of respectful curiosity about Indian manners, Leonowens still maintains a complicated disposition toward the effects of British colonization.

This stance is illustrated in her prefatory description of the European army barracks:

> It is both pleasing and interesting to see that these [barracks] are well cared for in this foreign land; but the curiosity and charm born in the native parts of the island [Colaba, Bombay], and especially the bazaars, lessen by sure degrees as you see your countrymen quietly and comfortably established in a spot with which they seem so out of harmony in form and color.

This complex treatment of the European presence in India is apparent throughout the volume. Although Leonowens is captivated by and respectful of the native religions and is interested in their origins and practices, she has many harsh and critical things to say of the Catholicism practiced by those of Portuguese descent. Her outrage and intolerance toward the Catholics fuel one of her most vehement tirades. Another telling incident occurs at the dinner party of a wealthy British hostess. Amid the luxury and show of wealth, Leonowens comments on the "dusky-hued attendants" who so quickly and efficiently serve the guests:

> They impressed me very unpleasantly, and that in spite of all the laughter and merriment, the exaltation of British power and British supremacy in India. I had, somehow, a feeling of reserve force pervading those mute, motionless figures around us, and I involuntarily felt, for the first time, that it was a very solemn affair for the Briton to be in India luxuriating on her soil and on her spoils.

Written thirty-five years after Leonowens's first trip to India, *Life and Travel in India* illuminates much of life in India for a young British married couple. Leonowens is always fascinated by present customs and their past origins, and she provides readers with the background and history that she regards as important for a sympathetic understanding of those current practices.

Unlike Leonowens's more personal *Life and Travel in India,* her last work, *Our Asiatic Cousins* (1889), provides mainly historical accounts of various groups – Hindus, Parsis, Egyptians, Phoenicians, and others – inhabiting parts of Asia. Twenty black-and-white illustrations – including one of Kali, the goddess of destruction – as well as drawings of ornate Hindu temples and a Chinese rendition of Confucius are presented. As in her other books, she shows great interest in the origins and practices of social customs and religious beliefs, but the tone in this volume is more patronizing than in her other three books of travel literature. Her first chapter, "The Hindoos," explains that hospitality is a most sacred duty to an Afghan, who is honor bound, at the risk of his own life, to grant any favor to any stranger who happens to enter his home; yet in the same breath she resorts to harsh judgment in generalizing that these same hospitable Afghans, "unlike the English, . . . are fierce, cruel, revengeful, and extremely superstitious. They never forgive."

Of her four works, this final one is the most general, being historical rather than personal. Published in 1889, *Our Asiatic Cousins* has to rely on Leonowens's teenage memories of her first trip to India forty years earlier. Unlike her other books, this work was not based primarily on careful firsthand observations but on research when Leonowens's memory or prior knowledge failed. Although the book is filled with Western biases and judgments, her chief concerns are to show that all cultures are essentially connected, that most religions should be respected, that people are generally kind and cordial, and finally, as her title indicates, that all cultures are ultimately parts of the greater human family.

In the last chapter of *Our Asiatic Cousins* Leonowens returns to familiar ground. She examines the "strange and wonderful land" then known to Westerners as Siam. After providing historical background, including a discussion of religious customs, geographic information and governmental practices, she focuses most of her attention on the role of an unnamed English governess who had been secured for the heir apparent, Prince Chulalonghorn, by his "far-seeing father," King Mongkut, to provide the royal family with the benefits of "a good English education." The remaining pages of the book laud the new King Chulalonghorn for the many liberal reforms for which he has been responsible – reforms such as granting religious freedom, abolishing prostration (the practice of lying prostrate in the presence of royalty), endowing schools for both boys and girls, and finally, abolishing the intricate system of slavery that had kept three-fourths of the inhabitants of Siam enslaved.

Leonowens hints that the lessons of this still-nameless English teacher and governess are chiefly responsible for the new king's actions. She claims that many years before, when the nine-year-old Prince Chulalonghorn had learned of the assassination of President Abraham Lincoln, the young prince "declared that if he ever lived to reign over Siam, he would reign over a free and not enslaved nation." Leonowens was consistent in her dismay at the horrors and unfairness of a political system that exploited lower classes. In *Our Asiatic Cousins* she reproaches not only Siam but also some European and American examples of Siam-like cultural prac-

King Mongkut of Siam with one of his wives, circa 1862

tices in the European feudal system, the former serfdom of Russia, the peonage of Mexico, and the practice of slavery in the United States.

The experiences of which Anna Leonowens writes in her four books of travel are both compelling and perplexing. Although her style seems at times both didactic and weighed down by facts and details, at other times it resonates with emotion, passion, and empathy. While she vividly records her experiences and impressions of various lands, those records of human lives and conditions give her a unique position in English literature. Her examinations of the daily lives of individual women under these cultural conditions significantly contribute to the discussion of race, class, and gender issues during the nineteenth century. Leonowens's ability to create such interest and empathy in her readers was born in her social and political beliefs that no people should be enslaved to a master, an owner, or a religious creed, but instead should be free to seek their own happiness.

In her own day her books were popular reading, referred to and admired by such significant American writers as Henry James, Julia Ward Howe, Henry Wadsworth Longfellow, and Oliver Wendell Holmes. Today her main works, *The English Governess at the Siamese Court* and *The Romance of the Harem,* have been reissued and are enjoying renewed critical attention by academic communities interested in literary, cultural, and women's studies.

Biographies:

Margaret Landon, *Anna and the King of Siam* (Toronto: Longmans, Green, 1944);

Anna Harriet Leonowens Fyshe, "Anna, from the Unpublished Memories of Anna Harriet Leonowens Fyshe," *Chatelaine,* 35 (January 1962): 32–33, 60, 62, 64;

Leslie Smith Dow, *Anna Leonowens, A Life Beyond the King and I* (Lawencteon Beach, Nova Scotia: Pottersfield, 1991).

References:

W. S. Bristowe, *Louis and the King of Siam* (London: Chatto & Windus, 1976);

E. R. Forbes, "Battles in Another War: Edith Archibald and the Halifax Feminist Movement," in his *Challenging the Regional Stereotype* (Fredericton: Acadiensis, 1989), pp. 67–89;

Julia Keay, "Notions of Liberty, Anna Leonowens," in her *With Passport and Parasol* (London: BBC Books, 1989), pp. 31–50;

Susan Morgan, introduction to Leonowens's *The Romance of the Harem* (Charlottesville & London: University of Virginia Press, 1991), pp. ix–xxxix;

Morgan, *Place Matters, Gendered Geography in Victorian Women's Travel Books about Southeast Asia* (New Brunswick, N.J.: Rutgers University Press, 1996);

Freya Stark, introduction to Leonowens's *Siamese Harem Life* (London: Barker, 1952; New York: Dutton, 1953), pp. xi–xiv.

David Livingstone

(19 March 1813 – 1 May 1873)

David Finkelstein
Napier University

BOOKS: *Missionary Travels and Researches in South Africa* (London: Murray, 1857; New York: Harper, 1858); abridged as *A Popular Account of Missionary Travels and Researches in South Africa* (London: Murray, 1861); adapted as *Travels in South Africa, 1840 to 1856,* edited by Alfonzo Gardiner (Leeds & Glasgow: Arnold, [1908]);

Analysis of the Language of the Bechuanas (London: Clowes, 1858);

Dr. Livingstone's Cambridge Lectures, edited by the Reverend William Monk (Cambridge: Deighton, Bell, 1858);

Livingstone's Travels and Researches in South Africa (New Haven, Conn.: Mansfield, 1858);

Travels and Researches in South Africa (Philadelphia: Bradley, 1860; London: Amalgamated Press, 1905) — comprises *Missionary Travels and Researches in South Africa* and *Livingstone's Travels and Researches in South Africa;*

Narrative of an Expedition to the Zambesi and Its Tributaries and of the Discovery of the Lakes Shirwa and Nyassa, 1858–1864, with Charles Livingstone (London: Murray, 1865);

Livingstone and His African Explorations (New York: Adams, Victor, 1872);

Livingstone's Africa: Perilous Adventures and Extensive Discoveries in the Interior of Africa (Philadelphia & Boston: Hubbard, 1872);

The Last Journals of David Livingstone, in Central Africa, from 1865 to His Death, edited by Horace Waller (2 volumes, London: Murray, 1874; 1 volume, Chicago: Jansen, McClurg, 1875); republished as *The Last Journals of David Livingstone, in Central Africa, from Eighteen Hundred and Sixty-five to His Death,* 1 volume (New York: Harper, 1875); abridged edition (Hartford, Conn. & Newark, N.J.: Bliss, 1875);

Life and Explorations of David Livingstone, the Great Missionary Explorer in the Interior of Africa (Saint Louis: Valley, [1874]);

The Story of the Brave Scotchman: Life and Explorations of David Livingstone, the Great Missionary Explorer,

in the Interior of Africa (Philadelphia: Potter, 1874);

The Transvaal Boers (Edinburgh: Constable, 1881);

David Livingstone and Cambridge: A Record of Three Meetings in the Senate House (Westminster: Universities' Mission to Central Africa, 1908);

Autobiography of David Livingstone and Extracts Referring to His Three Journeys, Discoveries and Influence (Hamilton, Scotland: Hamilton Advertiser, 1920s);

Livingstone's Travels, edited by James I. Macnair (London: Dent, 1954) — comprises *Missionary Travels and Researches in South Africa, Narrative of an Expedition to the Zambezi and Its Tributaries,* and *The Last Journals of David Livingstone;*

The Zambesi Expedition of David Livingstone, 1858–1863, 2 volumes, edited by J. P. R. Wallis (London: Chatto & Windus, 1956);

Livingstone's Private Journals, 1851–1853, edited by I. Schapera (London: Chatto & Windus, 1960);

Livingstone's African Journal, 1853–1856, 2 volumes, edited by Schapera (London: Chatto & Windus, 1963);

David Livingstone and the Rovuma: A Notebook, edited by George Shepperson (Edinburgh: University Press, 1965);

David Livingstone: South African Papers, 1849–1853, edited by Schapera (Cape Town: Van Riebeck Society, 1974);

Despatches Addressed by Dr. Livingstone, Her Majesty's Consul, Inner Africa, to Her Majesty's Secretary of State for Foreign Affairs, in 1870, 1871, and 1872 (London: Harrison, n.d.).

SELECTED PERIODICAL PUBLICATIONS – UNCOLLECTED: "John Philip's *Letter to the Directors of the London Missionary Society, on the Present State of Their Institutions in the Colony of the Cape of Good Hope,*" *British Quarterly Review,* 14 (August 1851): 106–113;

"Latest Accounts from Dr. Livingstone, F.R.G.S., of the Central African Expedition," *Papers of the Royal Geographical Society,* 4 (1860): 19–29;

"Paper Prepared for the Royal Geographical Society by Dr. Livingstone," *Journal of the Royal Geographical Society,* 33 (1863): 258–265;

"Exploration of the Niassa Lake," *Papers of the Royal Geographical Society,* 7 (1863): 18–20;

"Missions in Africa and Elsewhere," *Evangelical Christendom,* 6 (2 October 1865): 469–473;

"The Transvaal Boers," *Catholic Presbyterian,* 2 (1879): 412–423.

The life of David Livingstone, nineteenth-century missionary and explorer, has been the subject of numerous biographies and studies since his death in the African subcontinent in 1873. In his time he was revered as the exemplar of the Christian missionary, the lone traveler battling disease and deprivation to bring Christianity to the African interior. The fact that he made only one temporary convert in almost thirty years of travel and residency in Africa did little to detract from this image. Modern reassessments have illustrated that Liv-

ingstone's importance lies in his mapping of the African interior, an endeavor completed under arduous circumstances, and his espousal in his published travel accounts of the twin role of commerce and Christianity in developing and exploiting African resources and society. These accounts were to prove significant in focusing European attention on Africa and its potential value as a colonial region and thereby in paving the way for the European "scramble for Africa" in the 1880s.

David Livingstone was born on 19 March 1813 in Blantyre, Scotland, the second of seven children. His father, Neil Livingstone, was a traveling tea salesman and believed in a strict religious upbringing for his children. His mother, Mary Hunter, came from a family of tailors. After a rudimentary education David Livingstone started work at the age of ten in the Blantyre cotton mills. With tenacious perseverance in his spare time he educated himself, learning to read and write and studying Latin, botany, theology, and mathematics. In 1836 Livingstone was influenced by an appeal from Karl Gutzlaff, a respected Dutch missionary traveler who encouraged people to become trained as medical missionaries and be sent to China; Livingstone enrolled as a medical student at Anderson's College in Glasgow.

In 1838 Livingstone applied and was accepted for missionary training by the London Missionary Society. He moved to the LMS training school in Chipping Ongar, near London, and during the next year studied there as well as in the capital, where he completed his medical studies and graduated as a medical doctor in 1840. Because the Opium Wars had begun in 1839, Livingstone abandoned his original plan to work in China and accepted a post at Kuruman, a South African mission run by Robert Moffat. He set sail for South Africa in December 1840, and following his arrival he traveled around the area — partly to learn the language of the territory, partly to seek sites for further missions. In 1845 he married Mary Moffat, the daughter of Robert, and in 1847 they settled in Kolobeng, near the village of Chief Sechele of the Bakwena. Livingstone made little headway with his missionary work: his only success came in 1848, when he converted the chief, but this proved a short-lived conversion of only three months.

Livingstone found consolation for his evangelizing failures by making several expeditions through what is now Botswana with William Cotton Oswell, a wealthy sportsman retired from the Indian civil service. Between 1849 and 1851 they took trips of several hundred miles, trips on which

Frontispiece to Livingstone's first book, Missionary Travels and Researches in South Africa *(courtesy of the Lilly Library, Indiana University)*

they discovered Lake Ngami in Botswana and reached the upper banks of the Zambezi River. They became the first Europeans to traverse south-central Africa, and Livingstone's reports of the expeditions in 1851 brought him fame, recognition, and awards from the Royal Geographical Society in London.

By 1852 he had become disillusioned with the traditional pattern of missionary work in isolated circumstances, and in particular with his lack of success in converting Africans to Christianity. In the course of his explorations he began to develop a view that a combination of Christianity, commerce and civilization would solve Africa's problems. Livingstone substantially elaborated this argument in later books and speeches. Discovering viable trade routes by which missionaries and traders could more easily implement and impose European views of civilization into the interior became his particular goal.

In Cape Town in 1852 he began planning an extensive expedition to map prospective routes between Angola and Mozambique and to identify potential mission and trading sites along the Zambezi River. Having sent his wife and their four children

to Britain, he embarked on a journey, funded partly by Oswell, to search for sites in the Barotse valley near Linyanti. There he was helped by Sekeletu, chief of the Makololo, who hoped that success would bring material prosperity to his people. Livingstone traveled from Linyanti up the Zambezi River to Luanda, a journey of more than a thousand miles. Not satisfied with this route, he retraced his steps and proceeded downstream along the Zambezi, a route that made him the first European to see what would become known as Victoria Falls. When he reached Quelimane in Mozambique in December 1856, he had completed the first authenticated coast-to-coast crossing of the continent by a European. In his three years of exploration Livingstone had traveled almost six thousand miles.

Livingstone returned to Britain a hero. His exploits had captured the British imagination, and his reports of the possibilities for trade and Christian missions attracted great attention and financial support. Honors were showered on him during his two years in Britain. He was given an honorary degree by Oxford University, and the Royal Geographical Society awarded him a gold medal in recognition of his services in advancing geographical knowledge of Africa.

He spent 1857 writing *Missionary Travels and Researches in South Africa,* for which publisher John Murray offered £2,000 down in advance of two-thirds of the profits. A literary adviser was brought in to help with the work, but Livingstone rejected his advice and completed the book in six months. The book describes Livingstone's travels and African culture, customs, and topography in detail. Often lapsing into lyrical descriptions of great emotional intensity, Livingstone depicts Africa as a paradise on earth:

> How often have I beheld, in still mornings, scenes the very essence of beauty, and all bathed in a quiet air of delicious warmth! yet the occasional soft motion imparted a pleasing sensation of coolness as of a fan. Green grassy meadows, the cattle feeding, the goats browsing, the kids skipping, the group of herdboys with miniature bows, arrows, and spears; the women wending their way to the river with watering-pots poised jauntily on their heads; men sewing under the shady banians; and old grey-headed fathers sitting on the ground, with staff in hand, listening to the morning gossip, while others carry trees or branches to repair their hedges; and all this flooded with the bright African sunshine, and the birds singing among the branches before the heat of the day has become intense, form pictures which can never be forgotten.

Such descriptions were complemented by more pragmatic but equally enthusiastic notes on the limitless possibilities for farming and cotton growing:

> To one who has observed the hard toil of the poor in the old civilized countries, the state in which the inhabitants here live is one of glorious ease. The country is full of little villages. Food abounds, and very little labour is required for its cultivation; the soil is so rich that no manure is required; when a garden becomes too poor for good crops of maize, millet, &c., the owner removes a little farther into the forest, applies fire round the roots of larger trees to kill them, cuts down the smaller, and a new rich garden is ready for the seed.

With such rich land available, Livingstone implied that there was little to stop missionaries and settlers from successfully surviving in Africa. Glossing over his own failure in converting Africans to Christianity, he also suggested that indigenous people were willing to receive and accept Christianity. But such missionary work was best accomplished in conjunction with commercial development. "Sending the Gospel to the heathen," wrote Livingstone,

must, if this view be correct, include much more than is implied in the usual picture of a missionary, namely, a man going about with a Bible under his arm. The promotion of commerce ought to be specially attended to, as this, more specifically than anything else, demolishes that sense of isolation which heathenism engenders, and makes the tribes feel themselves mutually dependent on, and mutually beneficial to, each other. . . . [N]either civilization nor Christianity can be promoted alone. In fact, they are inseparable.

Selling more than seventy thousand copies and providing Livingstone with profits of more than £10,000, the book proved a phenomenal success at its publication in November 1857. Livingstone also toured widely, promoting his work and urging further British activity in Africa — especially along the Zambezi River, which he called "God's Highway." As a result of his encouragement three missionary ventures were launched with public and private funding. These were to end in tragedy, however, because Livingstone had misjudged the navigability of the Zambezi River and the generally inhospitable nature of the sites chosen along its course.

Having secured an appointment (and a higher salary) as a roving ambassador for the British government, Livingstone resigned from the London Missionary Society in 1858. With the backing of the government and the Royal Geographical Society, he led an expedition that included his brother Charles up the Zambezi to establish a research station in Batoka, near the Kafue River. The expedition ran into trouble on discovering the Zambezi to be impassable because of the Cabora Bassa gorge and cataracts above Tete. Quarrels among expedition members, disease, and death from malaria and fever also diminished morale among the members of the expedition. Among those to perish was Livingstone's wife, Mary, who died in late April 1862, four months after joining the expedition. Nevertheless, Livingstone persisted in his search for river routes into the African interior. In six years the expedition explored the Zambezi, Rovuma, and Shire Rivers; Lake Shirwa; and the western shore of Lake Malawi. Its surveys revealed for the first time the prevalence of Portuguese slave trading in areas previously thought to have remained untouched by this scourge. Livingstone also mapped previously unknown sections of central Africa and provided information on natural and agricultural resources. Such information proved significant in subsequent colonization of central Africa.

After much travail the remainder of the party returned to the mouth of the Zambezi in early 1864.

Frontispiece to Livingstone's Narrative of an Expedition to the Zambesi and Its Tributaries

By July Livingstone was back in Britain, where he settled down to write an account and defense of his recent travels by incorporating entries from Charles Livingstone's journals. These inclusions proved so extensive that in the end he named his brother as co-author. Livingstone also drew on help from his friend Oswell to shape the work into the six-hundred-page finished work. *Narrative of an Expedition to the Zambesi and Its Tributaries and of the Discovery of the Lakes Shirwa and Nyassa, 1858–1864* was published by Murray in November 1865. The work sold ten thousand copies within a few months of publication, but it was not reprinted.

Written in the third person, the book gives a brief historical overview of previous explorations of central Africa and follows this with a detailed chronology of the expeditions that Livingstone had led up the Zambezi. He criticizes Portuguese activity in central Africa, and he suggests that it had harmed and hindered his expedition. The work presented a very poor defense against criticism of his failure to negotiate the Zambezi successfully and of the failure of previous missions sent to Africa on Livingstone's

advice. The work proved detrimental to Livingstone because it antagonized the Portuguese authorities with whom Livingstone had enjoyed good relations in previous expeditions, and this antagonism caused problems for him later.

In August 1865 Livingstone set sail for Africa on his third and final expedition. He received funding from the Royal Geographical Society and his friend James Young, and once more he secured a roving, honorary consulship from the British government. His official objective this time was to explore the central African watershed and to establish, if possible, where the source of the Nile lay – a problem left unresolved by the controversy over John Hanning Speke's claim that Lake Victoria was the source. Livingstone's personal objective was not geographical in nature: he hoped to search for ideal sites to establish trading missions.

In March 1866 he sailed from Zanzibar to the mouth of the Rovuma River with more than seventy porters, Indian soldiers, and recruits from the Comoro Islands. His initial plan was to explore the north of Lake Malawi for connections to Lake Tan-

Livingstone's sketch of a fish in Lake Nyasa (from Oliver Ransford, David Livingstone: The Dark Interior, *1978)*

ganyika. Slave trading, however, made this difficult, and the expedition headed south of the lake. Livingstone was to spend the next seven years exploring various lakes and rivers in central Africa – sometimes in the company of slave and ivory traders, more often on his own. He was frequently ill and plagued with deficiencies in supplies. Problems with the Indian soldiers and Comoran recruits arose, and many left or deserted the expedition.

Lack of contact with the Western world, the loss of post and reports sent to British contacts, and rumors spread by some of the deserters that Livingstone had been killed by marauders prompted the Royal Geographical Society to send a rescue expedition in 1872 to search for him. This intention of the society had been anticipated by the editor of the *New York Herald,* who in 1871 commissioned the American-Welsh reporter Henry M. Stanley to find Livingstone. Armed with supplies, Stanley traced Livingstone to Ujiji, on the south side of Lake Tanganyika, and in late October 1871 greeted the explorer with the famous line "Dr. Livingstone, I presume." During the next four months Stanley and Livingstone made several journeys around Lake Tanganyika, during which they disproved Richard F. Burton's claim that it was the source of the Nile.

In March 1872 Stanley left for the coast, where he arranged for fresh supplies to be sent to Livingstone at Tabora. With these resources Livingstone in August 1872 embarked on a final expedition around Lake Tanganyika and crossed into northern Zambia. Lack of communication with Livingstone again prompted two more search parties to be sent from England. After an arduous and difficult struggle through the swamps surrounding Lake Bangweulu, Livingstone arrived, ill and exhausted, at the village of Chitambo. Shortly after his sixtieth birthday he died there on 1 May 1873.

Stanley's enthusiastic reports on Livingstone's travels and Stanley's book, *How I Found Livingstone* (1872), raised Livingstone's reputation worldwide. Livingstone's enshrinement as an icon of his time, an exemplar of the Christian missionary explorer martyred in his quest to open Africa, was complete when news reached England of the extraordinary journey undertaken by his porters to deliver Livingstone's body into European hands. Embalmed and sealed in a watertight cloth and bark wrapping, the body had been carried with Livingstone's books and papers almost a thousand miles to Bagamoyo, opposite Zanzibar. The journey had taken eight months, during which eight members of the group had died. The only reward for the porters at the end of their journey was payment of their regular

wages and a summary dismissal. The body was then shipped to Britain, and on 18 April 1874 Livingstone was given a state funeral in London and buried in Westminster Abbey.

Livingstone's aims and thinking were largely products of his time. Like many who went to Africa during the nineteenth century, he believed that the inhabitants of the subcontinent needed spiritual and moral elevation, an elevation that ultimately meant the destruction and replacement of indigenous cultures and beliefs. His travels throughout central and East Africa were originally intended as part of his evangelizing mission. His failures in converting Africans, however, turned him into an explorer. The result was the development of ideas that profoundly influenced British and European attention directed to Africa.

Livingstone's view was that colonization, or what he saw as Christianity allied with commercial development, was the key to effecting sweeping social change in Africa. This ideology anticipated the rhetoric through which European powers justified later expansion into Africa. His exploration and mapping of unexplored territory were crucial to increasing knowledge of the geographical and mineral resources available for development and exploitation.

At the same time, Livingstone – with his careful, detailed, and sympathetic descriptions of African customs and people – changed Victorian stereotypes of the African. As Tim Jeal concludes in *Livingstone* (1973), Livingstone's Africans were not the grateful, humble slaves portrayed by the abolitionist movement, nor the wild savages of contemporary travel and missionary accounts. Instead, Livingstone presented unadorned, unjudgmental views of those whom he had encountered on his travels. Ironically these images encouraged more missionary and political activity in Africa than there had been, a consequence thus anticipating the precipitous changes and colonization of African states that were to occur by the early twentieth century.

Letters:

Some Letters from Livingstone, 1840–1872, edited by David Chamberlin (London: Oxford University Press, 1940);

The Matabele Mission: A Selection from the Correspondence of John and Emily Moffat, David Livingstone and Others, 1858–1878, edited by J. P. R. Wallis (London: Chatto & Windus, 1945);

David Livingstone: Family Letters 1841–1856, 2 volumes, edited by I. Schapera (London: Chatto & Windus, 1959);

Livingstone's Missionary Correspondence, 1841–1856, edited by Schapera (London: Chatto & Windus, 1961);

The Zambezi Doctors: David Livingstone's Letters to John Kirk, 1858–1872, edited by R. Foskett (Edinburgh: University Press, 1964);

Norman R. Bennett, "Livingstone's Letters to William F. Stearns," *African Historical Studies,* 1, no. 2 (1968): 243–254;

"David Livingstone on the Zambezi: Letters to John Washington, 1861–1863," edited by Gary W. Clendennen, *Munger Africana Library Notes,* 6 (January 1976);

David Livingstone: Letters & Documents, 1841–1872, edited by Timothy Holmes (London: Currey, 1990; Bloomington: Indiana University Press, 1990).

Bibliography:

Gary W. Clendennen and Ian C. Cunningham, *David Livingstone: A Catalogue of Documents* (Edinburgh: National Library of Scotland, 1979); *Supplement* (Edinburgh: National Library of Scotland, 1985).

Biographies:

William Garden Blaikie, *The Personal Life of David Livingstone* (London: Murray, 1880);

Thomas Hughes, *David Livingstone* (London & New York: Macmillan, 1889);

A. Z. Fraser, *Livingstone and Newstead* (London: Murray, 1913);

Reginal Coupland, *Livingstone's Last Journey* (London: Collins, 1945);

Michael Gelfand, *Livingstone the Doctor: His Life and Travels: A Study in Medical History* (Oxford: Blackwell, 1957);

David Seaver, *David Livingstone: His Life and Letters* (London: Lutterworth, 1957);

Tim Jeal, *Livingstone* (London: Heinemann, 1973);

Judith Listowel, *The Other Livingstone* (Lewes, Sussex: Friedmann, 1974);

Timothy Holmes, *Journey to Livingstone* (Edinburgh: Canongate, 1993).

References:

Norman Robert Bennett, "David Livingstone: Explorations for Christianity," in *Africa and its Explorers,* edited by Robert I. Rotberg (Cambridge, Mass.: Harvard University Press, 1970): 95–137;

B. W. Lloyd, ed., *Livingstone, 1873–1973* (Cape Town: Struik, 1973);

George Martelli, *Livingstone's River: A History of the Zambezi Expedition, 1858–1864* (London: Chatto & Windus, 1970);

Bridglal Pachai, ed., *Livingstone: Man of Africa, Memorial Essays 1873–1973* (London: Longman, 1973);

Jack Simmons, *Livingstone and Africa* (London: English Universities Press, 1955);

Henry M. Stanley, *How I Found Livingstone* (London: Sampson Low, Marston, Searle & Rivington, 1872).

Papers:

David Livingstone's papers and journals are held in the National Library of Scotland; the Livingstone Museum, Zambia; the Bodleian Library, Oxford; the British Museum, London; the London Missionary Society; the National Archives of Zambia, Lusaka; and the Public Record Office, Kew, England. Further details on repositories of papers are listed in *David Livingstone: A Catalogue of Documents* and its *Supplement,* by Gary W. Clendennen and Ian C. Cunningham, as listed in the Bibliographies section above.

Emmeline Lott

(Dates unknown)

Michael Wojcik
Miami University

BOOKS: *The Governess in Egypt: Harem Life in Egypt and Constantinople,* 2 volumes (London: Bentley, 1865); republished as *Harem Life in Egypt and Constantinople* (Philadelphia, 1865); republished as *Harem Life in Egypt and Constantinople: The English Governess in Egypt* (2 volumes, London: Bentley, 1866; 1 volume, Philadelphia: Peterson, [1867?]);

The Mohaddetyn in the Palace: Nights in the Harem; or, The Mohaddetyn in the Palace of Ghezire, 2 volumes (London: Chapman & Hall, 1867);

The Grand Pacha's Cruise on the Nile in the Viceroy of Egypt's Yacht, 2 volumes (London: Newby, 1869).

In April 1864 Emmeline Lott arrived in Egypt to assume her position as governess for the grand pacha Ibrahim, son of Ismael Pacha, the Turkish viceroy of Egypt. In August of the same year she departed Constantinople for England, her employment by one of the wealthiest families of the nineteenth century finished. During the next few years she published three highly (some might say excruciatingly) detailed accounts of her observations about the Ottoman harems. Though contemporary reviewers complained about her minute observations of food, clothing, daily activities, and living conditions, her insights may provide the best available account of life in the viceregal household.

Like her brief sojourn, Lott's books brought her little profit or recognition. The most recently published edition of one of her books seems to have been an 1893 volume of her first work, *The Governess in Egypt: Harem Life in Egypt and Constantinople* (1865), which was retitled *Harem Life in Egypt and Constantinople* for its American publication. Bentley, however, the publisher of Lott's first edition of this volume, did produce a microfilm edition of the book as recently as 1985 as part of the African Documents on Microfilm series.

Obscurity is a common though generally undeserved fate of Victorian women travel writers, and Lott is no exception. Her books specify the dates of her travel; publishers' archives supply their dates of publication. Those are the only dates readily available, however. Though the basic biographical facts of her life are quite likely in British records (in the lists of the registrar-general at Somerset House, if nowhere else), her moment in the public eye was too brief to be recorded in the usual public sources. She was not graced with an obituary in the standard periodicals, such as the (London) *Times, The New York Times,* or *The Annual Register.* Most biographical dictionaries omit Lott entirely; *A Supplement to Allibone's Critical Dictionary of English Literature and British and American Authors* (1891) does include a brief entry, but it only lists her publications. No biographical information appears.

Some biographical facts may be ascertained from evidence in her books. Lott provides some idea of the dates of her employment, as she notes in the opening sentence of *The Governess in Egypt* that she arrived in Egypt "in the month of April, 186–." The year is later revealed as 1864 in a description of the "grand state ball on the 8th of June." She recounts how, a few months later, she was forced to resign when she asked for a sick leave of three months. Lott writes that she had been warned against romantic entanglements involving the viceroy. The viceregal agent in England had told her not "to please the Viceroy," and she recounts rumors that arose following her brief visit to the viceregal bedchambers with her charge, the grand pacha. Such details suggest that she was young or middle-aged when she went to Egypt. If so, she most likely had been born in the 1830s or 1840s. She refers casually to her travels in Paris and notes that she had lived for a time "in the *Cours d'Albert,* at that birthplace of our unfortunate sovereign, Richard II" – that is, at Bordeaux.

From her works one can similarly infer Lott's sense of social class and position in the three harems she visited during her employment – at Ghezire, one of Ismael Pacha's private palaces near Cairo; at the summer palace in Alexandria; and finally at the old imperial palace outside Constantinople. Clearly she felt that her position placed her close to, if not among, the ranks of Ismael's wives and the other women of importance in the harem. Another recurrent concern is that of having to dine or share a room with the German launderer and cook. "I could not possibly imagine for a moment that the English governess," she writes in *The Governess in Egypt,* "ought to submit to such an indignity." While the specifics of her own social class background remain uncertain, she drops intriguing hints about having been raised in the presence of "persons of exalted rank in my own country." Again, in discussing her etiquette when she meets the Validè Princess, the viceroy's mother, she relates the following story:

> I had often, when a child, been found by Her Most Gracious Majesty the Queen and the late Prince Consort playing about in the private grounds at Frogmore and Windsor; and when I had encountered the royal pair, who took flowers from my basket which I had gathered in the grounds and smiled, I had stepped aside, stood still, and curtsied – no more.

Not all English children of the era were habitually found in the "private grounds" of the royal estates.

On 10 July 1865, about a year after returning to England, Lott signed a contract with Richard Bentley for the publication of *The Governess in Egypt.* At the time Lott was living at 16 Upper North Landing in the seaside resort of Brighton, the only definite address that has been recorded for her. Displaying the business acumen that occasionally appears in her travel writings, she asked for and received an advance of thirty pounds on the royalties. From 1865 to 1867 sales of the Bentley edition of *The Governess in Egypt* were sufficient to net Lott slightly more than £140 but she was not satisfied with the returns, as her correspondence with Bentley indicates. Sales seem to have dropped quickly.

Even before its publication *The Governess in Egypt* was not well received. Geraldine Jewsbury, a prominent novelist of the day and one of Bentley's most trusted manuscript readers, had found it too occupied with Lott's personal tastes. In a letter of 8 December 1865 Jewsbury had written to Bentley that "the book is full of the author's own talk and has little substance of facts; it has not the freshness of interest that the Harem life possesses." Jewsbury's terse addendum scrawled at the top of the letter stated simply, "I think you may let it go without loss to yourself or the public." But the book had been contracted for and the advance paid; Bentley disregarded his reader's advice and proceeded with publication.

The Governess in Egypt found an American publisher (as *Harem Life in Egypt and Constantinople: The English Governess in Egypt*) in T. B. Peterson in 1867. A review in *The New York Times* on 11 November 1867 was decidedly unenthusiastic; the reviewer found the book contained "much that is utterly worthless, and a great deal that is particularly nasty," and complained that it "is so badly arranged, and so full of repetitious and contradictory statements that it is far from easy to find any coherent description of any of the salient features in harem life." The reviewer extracted several points of potential interest to illustrate the "offensive" and "indelicate" nature of the book and concluded,

> We take leave of Mrs. LOTT without any very great regret. She seems to us to have recklessly undertaken a mission in which success and comfort were alike impossible, and to have made very little use of the opportunities which her position gave her for observation. She was ill advised in going to Egypt, and injudicious in publishing a record of her failure, and in obtruding on the public a catalogue of the annoyances which were incidental to her anomalous position.

While it is impossible to say just what effect this review had on American sales of *The Governess in Egypt,* it cannot have helped, and the book apparently did not remain in print long, either in the Peterson edition or in the Allison edition near the end of the century.

It is easy to see what displeased these reviewers. *The Governess in Egypt* is rife with Lott's complaints and unflattering descriptions of her companions and surroundings. Her account of a rail journey is typical: "The Princesses," she begins, "were most disgusting in their habits, and so totally devoid of decency, that they did not hesitate to empty the contents of their '*vases*' out of the window, as the train was passing along. I thought their manners bad enough in all conscience at *home;* but now I have seen them *abroad,* and I

Emmeline Lott dressed for her role as governess in a royal harem
(frontispiece to Lott's The Governess in Egypt)

never wished to have the honor of travelling with them again."

The viceregal menu and table manners similarly failed to meet Lott's expectations, as she makes clear in her lengthy descriptions of meals such as one in which a particular course "consisted of a small tureen containing a pigeon served up swimming in soup thickened with rice and flour: each one of the family party helped themselves to a spoonful of it. Then the head-nurse took the pigeon in her fingers, tore it to pieces, and then commenced a regular battle, as each of the children desired to have a leg, which ended on the morning in question, as was generally the case, in the separated bird making its exit without being touched." Her accommodations are described as "a small wretchedly furnished dormitory, such a chamber as the lady's-maid of any of the wives of our wealthy commoners would not have slept in two nights." In view of the "disgust and disappointment" she felt, it seems surprising that Lott stayed as long as she did.

On the other hand, a lengthy review attributed to J. G. Maline in the *Catholic World* praised the book in 1868 – ironically, for the same complaints about harem living conditions that Jewsbury and the *Times* reviewer had found objectionable. Maline approved in part because he believed that Lott accurately depicted biblical as well as present-day Egypt, a place he characterized as one where "[p]rogress is a term never heard of near the habitation of the Sphinx." But most crucially for him, the book comprised a tale of Christian virtue opposing heathen degradation, and the review found *The Governess in Egypt* to be a trenchant illustration of the uncivilized nature of non-Christian countries.

More than a century after Lott made her journey and wrote her accounts of it, however, the domestic details and personal tastes she records in the book acquire a value they were unlikely to have for her contemporaries. While historical accounts of nineteenth-century Egypt often discuss the pacha's political and financial dealings, they seldom do more than mention his domestic life. As Billie Melman notes in *Women's Orients* (1992), Lott and Ellen Chennels, another viceregal governess, provide the best information available on the domestic lives of the Ottoman rulers. The incongruous visit paid by Lady Paramount, the pacha's first wife, to the royal laundry, is a striking example: "Her hair, hanging loosely about, was tucked under the handkerchief bound round her head;" as Lott records the scene, "and the sleeves of her dirty cotton wrapper were turned up to the shoulders, and there tied. And thus behold Her Highness, the first wife of Ismael Pacha, the richest Prince in the universe, save his Imperial Majesty the Emperor of All the Russias, in her domestic circles."

These depictions of the daily life in the harem are omitted from standard histories, but learning from them can tell readers about the attitudes toward class, gender, and work in elite Ottoman society. As Lott was well aware, the harems made the viceregal palaces inaccessible to visitors; only an insider such as Lott could provide such information.

Lott's work is also valuable for students of Victorian England. The complex power relations of race, ethnicity, sex, ancestry, wealth, position, and social class that Lott attempts to understand and negotiate can illuminate not only the daily workings of the Ottoman viceregal palace but of Victorian society as well. In *The Governess in Egypt* Lott always depicts her Egyptian experiences negatively, against the "proper" standard provided by her English background. She compares the dress and language of the princesses to those of "Billingsgate fishwomen," for example, and comments ironically on "the European innovation of a dozen common English cane-bottomed chairs" in the Hall of Audience at the palace.

Furthermore, Lott was not ignorant of the commercial and legal matters she witnessed during her stay; she occasionally quotes from legal documents such as the Firman of Investiture of 22 May 1841, which had established the order of succession for the viceroyalty, and discusses many important political figures around her. Her knowledge of Egyptian history is clear in the lessons that she gives the prince (and quotes for the reader's benefit), as she demonstrates in *The Grand Pacha's Cruise on the Nile in the Viceroy of Egypt's Yacht* (1869) when she recounts a lesson on the construction of the Mahmoodeeh Canal. "I informed the Prince," she begins, "that the late Mr. Briggs, an English merchant at Alexandria, with whom his illustrious great-grandfather Mahomed Ali had intimate commercial relations, pointed out to that ruler how desirable it would be for him to construct the canal along which we were then steaming, and which was seventy miles long, ninety feet wide, and eighteen feet deep, with only one lock, and that at Atfeh."

Her conjunction of domestic details and political and financial commentary blurs a distinction between public and private spheres. She transfers the authority traditionally ascribed to Victorian women over children and domestic management into the public realms of politics and economics. At the end of *The Governess in Egypt,* when Lott advocates educating future viceroys in Europe, she does so because she believes that it will improve their abilities to govern effectively.

Lott made two more attempts to profit from accounts of her experience. She sold *The Mohaddetyn in the Palace: Nights in the Harem; or, The Mohaddetyn in the Palace of Ghezire* to Chapman and Hall in 1867 and *The Grand Pacha's Cruise on the Nile* to T. C. Newby in 1869. Neither book seems to have sold very well, as the switch in publisher and the lack of American editions suggest, and they were not republished. Both books are now all but unavailable, which is unfortunate.

Contrary to the scathing review of *The Mohaddetyn in the Palace* that appeared in the *Saturday Review* of 16 March 1867, the book has some value. It illuminates a period covered briefly in *The Governess in Egypt,* when Lott was staying in the viceregal palace at Ghezire, but its tone is much friendlier than that of the earlier book. In *The Mohaddetyn in the Palace* Lott represents both Ottoman Egypt and herself in a kinder light. Rather than providing reports of daily life as in *The Governess in Egypt,* the book recounts stories that Lott claims to have heard from an "amateur Mohaddetyn," or storyteller, who entertained the grand pacha's party each evening. The stories, with the addition of Lott's commentary, describe life as Lott saw it in an Ottoman city.

The Grand Pacha's Cruise also expands on an incident mentioned in *The Governess in Egypt,* one that occurred during her stay in Egypt. For the first time Lott sounds truly pleased with her surroundings; she is certainly impressed by the yacht: "On our return to the yacht we descended into the saloon, which was elegantly fitted up. On its gilded edge panels were painted several of the most interesting landscapes in the vicinity of Alexandria, among which were the villas on the Mahmoodeeh Canal, Kom-el-Dyk, and its suburbs." Egypt in general now seems extraordinarily pleasant:

The azure blue sky was cloudless, and flights of pigeons and here and there a few ibises were hurrying to their nests. The air was elastic, and cast a tranquil halo round my mind. It was like a lovely day in May, and yet it was the month of August. Such was the appearance of beautiful Egypt, whose climate is so delightful that words are wanting to describe its balminess.

While the two later books largely lack the details of harem affairs that the first provides, they are certainly significant representatives of the genre of Victorian travel literature. Both afford many descriptions of urban and rural life in Egypt — as in this sketch of the crowd at the Cairo rail terminal, which Lott presents in *The Grand Pacha's Cruise on the Nile:* "There stood Fellahs, with their plain blue haft gowns; Bedouins, attired in their "abas"; Egyptians, in wide inexpressibles, and short, richly embroidered vests; Indian officers, in most nondescript costumes; European ladies, in toilettes two or three years behind the fashion." Her later books vividly demonstrate many similarities and differences between these two nineteenth-century empires.

Upstaged by more-appealing travel writers such as Anna Leonowens, Emmeline Lott vanished even more thoroughly than most of her lesser-known contemporary authors. The view Lott offers of her particular experience of Turkish-Egyptian-English cultural relations, however, is irreplaceable, and her three books provide much to interest scholars. Though *The Governess in Egypt* is often repetitious and filled with uninspiring detail, *The Mohaddetyn in the Palace* and *The Grand Pacha's Cruise on the Nile* are quite readable, even entertaining.

References:

The Archives of Richard Bentley & Son, 1829–1898, microfilm (Teaneck, N.J.: Somerset House, 1975);

[J. G. Maline], "*Harem Life in Egypt and Constantinople,*" *Catholic World,* 7 (April–September 1868): 407–413;

Billie Melman, *Women's Orients: English Women and the Middle East, 1718–1918: Sexuality, Religion, and Work* (Ann Arbor: University of Michigan Press, 1992);

"Nights in the Harem," *Saturday Review* (16 March 1867): 340–341;

"Oriental Life and Manners," *New York Times,* 11 November 1867, p. 2.

John MacGregor

(24 January 1825 – 16 July 1892)

Laura Nilges-Matias
Loyola University, Chicago

BOOKS: *Three Days in the East* (London: Thomas Dilton, 1851);

Eastern Music: Twenty Melodies from the Egyptian, Greek, Jewish, Syrian, Turkish, and Arabic, for the Voice, Dulcimer, and Drum, with Pianoforte Accompaniments and Illustrations (London: Novello, 1851);

"The Madiai Case," as Developed in the Letters of Viscount Palmerston, the Earl of Aberdeen, the Earl of Carlisle . . . and the Official Documents of the Protestant Deputation to Florence (London, 1852);

Popery in A.D. 1900, as J. M. of the Temple (London: Seeleys, 1852);

Shoe-Blacks and Broomers (London, 1852);

The Nunnery Question; or, Cases Mentioned in the Late Debate on the Inspection of Nunneries, with Authorities and an Outline of the Bill (London, 1853);

Ragged Schools: Their Rise, Progress, and Results (London: Church of England Young Men's Society for Aiding Missions at Home and Abroad, 1853);

The Ascent of Mont Blanc: A Series of Four Views, Printed in Oil Colours by George Baxter, the Original Sketches, and the Description, by J. MacGregor (London, 1855?);

"Go Out Quickly." Luke XIV:21, as A Barrister (London: Seeleys, [1855]);

The Language of Specifications of Letters Patent for Inventions: With the Authorities and Decisions in All the Important and Latest Cases (London: Benning, 1856);

The Law of Reformatories . . . with Information as to the Principal Institutions, the Grants from the Committee of Privy Council, and the Special Provisions under the Poor Laws (London: Benning, 1856);

Supplement to the Law of Reformatories . . . Containing the Acts of Parliament . . . and Other Official Documents . . . Issued Since April, 1856 (London: Benning, 1857);

Our Brothers and Cousins: A Summer Tour in Canada and the States (London: Seeley, Jackson & Halliday, 1859);

The Tail of the Beagle, Ship! Ahoy! Wagged in the Dogwatch by Rob Roy: With Sol's Pictures of the Pack and Seven Shavings from the Log. Chucked to the Kennel by the Whipperin (N.p., 1865);

Description of the New Rob Roy Canoe, Built for a Voyage through Norway, Sweden and the Baltic (London, 1866);

A Thousand Miles in the Rob Roy Canoe on Rivers and Lakes of Europe (London: Sampson, Low & Marston, 1866; Boston: Roberts, 1867);

The Rob Roy on the Baltic: A Canoe Cruise through Norway, Sweden, Denmark, Sleswig, Holstein, the

240

North Sea, and the Baltic (London: Sampson, Low, Marston, Searle & Rivington, 1867; Boston: Roberts, 1867);

The Voyage Alone in the Yawl Rob Roy, from London to Paris and Back by Havre, the Isle of Wight, South Coast, &c. (London: Sampson, Low, Marston, Searle & Rivington, 1867) republished as *The Voyage Alone in the Yawl "Rob Roy," from London to Paris and Back by Havre, the Isle of Wight, South Coast, &c.* (London: Sampson, Low, Marston, Searle & Rivington / Boston: Roberts, 1880);

The Rob Roy on the Jordan, Nile, Red Sea, and Gennesareth, &c.: A Canoe Cruise in Palestine and Egypt, and the Waters of Damascus (London: Murray, 1869; New York: Harper, 1870);

Ten Thousand Street Folk and What to Do with Them, as Rob Roy (London: Reformatory & Refuge Union, 1872);

Quiet Words with Fellow Sunday School Teachers (London: Sunday School Union, [1878]);

Toil and Travel: Being a True Story of Roving and Ranging When on a Voyage Homeward Bound Round the World (London: Unwin, 1892);

Through the Buffer State: A Record of Recent Travels through Borneo, Siam, and Cambodia (London: White, 1896);

Luinneagen Luaineach (Random Lyrics) (London: Nutt, 1897).

OTHER: Noé Antoine François Puaux, *The Voice of a Huguenot; or, A French Pastor's Address to His British Brethren,* edited by MacGregor (London, 1852);

Godfrey Holden Pike, *Beneath the Blue Sky: Preaching in the Open Air, with Contributions by J. MacGregor and G. Kirkham* (London: Hodder & Stoughton, 1888).

"I am in extreme enjoyment." So begins a letter from John MacGregor, recording another successful end to one of his many marine voyages in words that neatly summarize the spirit of his life and travel works. In his four well-known books, which were first published during the 1860s and appeared in many editions, MacGregor recorded his adventures on the rivers and lakes of England, the Continent, and the Middle East in small craft always dubbed with his own nickname, "Rob Roy." Drawing on all his gifts for athleticism, writing, illustration, design, and (most of all) navigation, he virtually created and tirelessly promoted the European sport of canoeing.

He was a happy, generous man who devoted his life to philanthropy, especially for the benefit of "ragged boys" and many Protestant organizations. All the proceeds from his books and lectures were donated to charitable causes. He is remembered as the inspiration for the Royal Canoe Club, as a member of the Ragged School Union, and as a founder of the Shoeblack Brigade, an organization intended to provide employment for poor boys.

Above all else MacGregor was a man in love with water, a man who had been born near it and was nearly killed by it during his infancy. His father was Gen. Sir Duncan MacGregor; his mother, a daughter of Sir William Dick of Prestonfield, near Edinburgh. Awaiting his departure for duty in India, MacGregor, then a major, brought his wife to Gravesend on the Thames River. In these lodgings from which they could see the harbor, their first child, John, was born; a few weeks later Mrs. MacGregor boarded the *Kent* with her baby and husband. On 1 March 1825 the ship caught fire in the Bay of Biscay, and of the 641 people on board, more than 90 died.

After serving two years in the West Indies, unaccompanied by his family, Duncan MacGregor returned in 1828. Henceforth the family traveled with MacGregor's father, and MacGregor attended eight different schools. In 1838 Duncan MacGregor became inspector general of the Irish constabulary at Drumcondra, near Dublin, and in 1839 or 1840 young MacGregor, who had never been at a public school, entered Trinity College in Dublin. After attending several years there, he entered Trinity College, Cambridge, in 1844, where he received his B.A. in 1847 and his M.A. in 1850. He was admitted to the bar in 1851 but, because of his financial resources, he later found it unnecessary to practice his specialty as a patent attorney.

Many of the journeys MacGregor was to make were never recorded in his books. Between 1848 and 1873 he traveled to Paris, Russia, North Africa, the United States, Holland, the Shetlands, and the Azores. He establishes his authority as a travel writer in the opening pages of his first canoeing book, *A Thousand Miles in the Rob Roy Canoe on Rivers and Lakes of Europe* (1866), where he rhetorically adopts the stance of a reader in asking whether the author has "climbed glaciers and volcanoes, dived into caves and catacombs, trotted in the Norway carriole, and galloped on the Russian steppes? Does he know the charms of a Nile boat . . . or has he ever swung on a camel, or glided on a sleigh, or trundled along in a Rantoone?" Indeed, he then replies, having sampled perhaps most of the world's "modes of locomotion," he can vouch that "the pleasure in the canoe was far better than all."

MacGregor dressed for his lecturing appearances

When he wrote *Our Brothers and Cousins: A Summer Tour in Canada and the States* (1859), he was established in life as a philanthropist and adventurer but had not yet conceived his canoeing idea. The book recounts his journey, mainly by rail, through much of North America and is intended to be a rough sketch of a dazzlingly complex subject. Describing America, he writes, is like being "tossed on the wide Atlantic for a fortnight in a steamer" and then being asked on landing "to give a rational account of the best articles in the book." He wishes to allow the reader "to draw his own conclusions," but he adds that this summer tour did provide him enough time to form reliable opinions on some subjects. And he does: this early work is laden with value judgments and nationalistic bombast that obscure his descriptions. He finds his American "cousins" interesting, but he clearly favors his Canadian "brothers." He notes the lack of a significant culture in America, but he acknowledges the unfairness of comparisons between the new nation and "an ancient islet gifted above all in natural advantages, and laboured, for a thousand years, by the noblest race that ever trod the earth."

Landing in Halifax, Nova Scotia, he finds concrete evidence of his brotherhood with Canadians. "Britain," he writes, "never seems so wide as when some thousand miles of sea bring you to yet another England." Yet Halifax is "different enough from England to make you feel abroad," with its Norwegian-looking wooden houses, its mixture of Scotch and Irish cultures, and its sparse Church of England religious orientation. He notes the oddness of hearing people speak in English "of an utterly unknown subject, with new names for people and places. 'We have got the ships at Richibuctoo and Miramici.'" MacGregor's observations of Halifax acquaint readers with some of his characteristic interests – the evangelical promotion of literacy, Bible reading, and the welfare of children – observations on which are scattered throughout all his works. He notes the vigor of the local Young Men's Christian Association, with its "cheerful reading-room" and "lectures well-attended." During a conversation with some "little black children," MacGregor remarks that only one could read, but "they seemed to comprehend very readily the simplest truths of the Bible."

The reader is also introduced to MacGregor's strongest prejudice, his anti-Catholicism, and his pages on Halifax voice some of his strongest disapproval: "The Roman Catholic Archbishop, with numerous priests, works hard to keep the Bible from all children. Romish influence is powerful here." He urges the local Protestant Alliance to "take some vigorous and decided step to enlighten, and then direct, public opinion in relation to popish proceedings. A nunnery forms a prominent object in the environs of the town; and the Romish Cathedral, with the Archbishop's house, asserts a position that cannot be ignored."

Passing by train and steamboat from Nova Scotia to Quebec, Montreal, and Ottawa, he records his first view of America at Saratoga, "the well-known fashionable watering-place with American society in its most startling form." It is "a buzz" of men "and ladies, with alarming circumferences, but without any bonnets" – ladies who "move about as if the whole town were the grounds of a private house. Even in Spain . . . I defy you to find such an upturning of all our conventional notions of woman's outdoor life." Americans, he finds, lack not only taste but civility; he notes the "impressive silence" of meals in the Saratoga dining halls, a silence broken only by the scrape of chairs as each guest rises to leave. Yet MacGregor is impressed with New York City, which he believes rivals "in color, bustle, *luxe,* business, and cheerful variety combined, . . . any single street in the Old World."

Visiting America on the brink of the Civil War, he implies in much of the book that slavery is an indelible blot on the nation's claim that it values freedom; slavery seems to be the root of much of MacGregor's distaste for American culture. Addressing Canadians in his introduction, he writes:

> Doubt not the love of England, or its power or will to help you. Fear not your cousins in America, or their power or will to hurt you. Your federated provinces will yet become a glorious country, allied to Britain by long years of sympathy, where the slave is free and the freeman serves his God.

He notes his meeting in Kentucky with a "real lady, a slave-holding lady – a Sunday-school teacher" – who responds to MacGregor's antipathy toward American slavery by protesting, "Would you have us give up our property? Why I have a slave worth at least twenty-five hundred dollars."

In *A Thousand Miles in the Rob Roy Canoe on Rivers and Lakes of Europe,* MacGregor introduces the kind of travel with which he would make his mark. The book, which was his most popular one, appeared in fifteen editions by 1880. Canoeing, he explains in it, provides "healthy exercise" and "an interest ever varied with excitement," which "keeps fully alert the energies of the mind." His canoe, the *Rob Roy,* was built of oak and cedar, fifteen feet long, twenty-eight inches wide, and nine inches deep, and was propelled by a seven-foot paddle, a lug sail, and a jib. Managing this craft alone, he navigated at least thirteen European rivers, including the Thames, Rhine, Danube, Marne, and Seine; several lakes, including Zurich and Lucerne; and six canals in Belgium and France. In pursuing all these adventures he crossed the English Channel twice by canoe, as well.

River expeditions by canoe encounter such obstacles as shallow depths, rapids, and waterfalls, and canoeists have difficulty approaching scenery. Yet, MacGregor claims, such difficulties "become interesting features to the voyager in a covered canoe." Its low seating and backrest and the readiness of the paddle make canoeing safe and comfortable. The canoeist can turn easily, steer through narrow passages and reeds, hoist and lower a sail without leaving his seat, and carry the craft by hand or stow it on a train or "in a cart drawn by a horse, a bullock, or a cow."

MacGregor found that the inaccuracy of French and German maps necessarily made this a "voyage of discovery," one that enabled him to critique the tameness of alternative modes of travel that he contrasted to his own canoeing innovations.

He intended not to compose a handbook, for he found those tedious; they were "useful for some travellers as a ruled copy-book is of some use to some writers." Yet, MacGregor insists, only the inexperienced traveler needs "to have all made easy, to be carried . . . like a parcel, to stop at hotels Anglified by the crowd of English guests." After following such handbook routines, the adventurous tourist in a canoe can discover "rivers and streams of the Continent . . . scarcely known to the English tourist." One of the main advantages of the canoe is in the new perspective that it provides the canoeist:

> The river-banks one would call tame if seen from the shore are altogether new when you open up the vista from the middle of the stream. The picture that is rolled sideways to the common traveller now pours out before you, ever enlarging from a centre, and in the gentle sway of the stream the landscape seems to swell on this side and that with new things ever advancing to meet you in succession.

The adventurer, MacGregor implies, is one who leaves the comforts and restrictions of civilization. Having readied himself "when the country had caught the election fever, and M.P.'s had run off to scramble for seats, and the lawyers had run after them to thicken the bustle," MacGregor set off from Westminster Bridge, spent the night in a Purfleet hotel, "shoved off into the tide, and lit a cigar. . . . Then there began a strange feeling of *freedom* and *novelty* which lasted to the end of the tour." By this time his feats had been recorded in newspapers. Cheered by crowds on the decks of passing ships, MacGregor set off to cross the English Channel, took a train to Brussels, and reached the Meuse River.

The work richly describes natural wonders, such as his encounters with a school of porpoises and a herd of swimming cattle, and recounts his discovery of what he believed to be the source of the Danube River – a spring in the garden of a prince's estate. Most interesting of all, he writes of the curiosities to be found by a man meandering down a secluded stream and suddenly encountering people who have spent their lives undisturbed by foreigners. Alighting near Bremgarten in Switzerland at a picturesque mill, he walks into the open door of a house, and is treated to "excessive courtesy" by the inhabitants:

> This was a picture of rural life not soon to be forgotten. . . . [T]he old oak furniture was lightened by a hundred little trifles worked by the woman, or collected by the tasteful diligence of their brother; and the sun

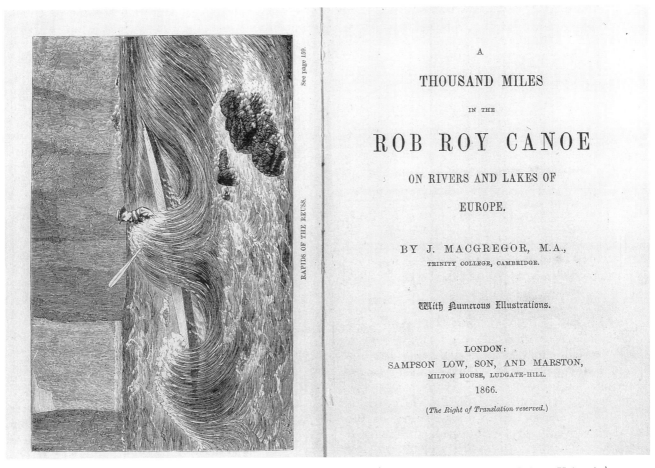

Frontispiece and title page for MacGregor's most popular travel book (courtesy of the Lilly Library, Indiana University)

shone, and the mill went round, and the river rolled by, and all was kindness, "because you are an Englishman."

In the preface of his next book, *The Rob Roy on the Baltic: A Canoe Cruise through Norway, Sweden, Denmark, Sleswig, Holstein, the North Sea, and the Baltic* (1867), MacGregor notes the success of his first canoe voyage and book, the formation of the Canoe Club that had followed, and the organization of canoe trips by several Englishmen. He mentions that reviews of the book had been "very kind," and the "private laudations of the volume, which were no less flattering," had included "the *mot* of an eccentric man, who was asked if he had read the 'Canoe Book,' and replied with animation, 'Of course; it's not *half* so good as 'Ecce Homo.'"

In this canoe, an improved version of MacGregor's original design, he traveled hundreds of miles without seeing a human being, and his descriptions at times lapse into dreamy meditations. Passing into Sweden, he finds a line of cleared timber marking the frontier line, and writes,

Perhaps it was this long ruled mark on the world that suggested to a philosophical dreamer that we of Earth might endeavor to speak to the people of the moon by planting on the snows of Siberia a triangle of trees, and the *pons asinorum* of Euclid done in fir forests, so that any schoolboy in our pale satellite could see plainly that we worldlings are at least geometers.

He is affected by the Scandinavians' education, cleanliness, love of natural beauty, and warm hospitality. Indeed, his travels seem to have broadened his sympathies. "Desperate sticklers we may be for Old England and everything English," he acknowledges, but his "repeated lessons abroad" force him in this book "to confess, that, in comparison with most of these 'outlandish folks,' we English are often very boorish," a realization that may "make us behave in foreign lands with the modesty of those who feel their countrymen have much to learn."

Soon after this voyage he devised still another new type of craft, one which, he hoped, would make "the pleasure of a voyage complete" and would solve some problems of canoeing – the physical effort and the need to go ashore to get provisions and to sleep. To these ends he designed a yawl, also named the *Rob Roy,* which positioned the sailor between the sails and was "double-skinned" for dryness below, with a full deck "to keep out the sea above." It was specially designed to allow cooking, reading, writing, and, when anchored, sleeping on board, and to allow storing enough provisions for three months. On this craft he sailed from Dover across the English Channel to Boulogne.

Although by this time his travel experiences had dampened his sense of cultural superiority, he was not less patriotic. The yawl voyage was in part a display of pride in British efficiency, cleanliness, and fitness of design. He displayed the yawl at the French Exhibition, and, as was his habit when traveling, he distributed many tracts among common folk and children to promote the gospel and "creat[e] goodwill."

In *The Rob Roy on the Jordan, Nile, Red Sea, and Gennesareth, &c.: A Canoe Cruise in Palestine and Egypt, and the Waters of Damascus* (1869), MacGregor recounts his most remarkable voyage. Having brought a new *Rob Roy* canoe from England, he admires its polished cedar deck gleaming in the African sun and embarks lighthearted. After the relative peace and ease of a canoe trip on the Nile, he travels "the Syrian lakes and the rivers and seas of Palestine," and comes upon "scenes never opened before to the traveller's gaze . . . which were entirely inaccessible except in a canoe."

Traveling from the Suez to the Red Sea, he speculates about what site might have been the exact location of the passage of the Israelites. At Cairo he notices "puny children, herded in flocks by cruel task-masters who flog them with long sticks" and is interested in the efforts of "one brave British woman" to establish a school for poor children. When he reaches the Lake of Gennesareth, he looks for the most likely place at which the miracle recounted in the Book of Matthew – the legion of demons entering the swine herd – might have occurred. He scales the inland heights of Mount Carmel to see "the place where Elijah met the priests of Baal." Deep in the sand near this spot "there is buried, no doubt, the golden dust of idols calcined and stamped to pieces by him who was zealous for Jehovah." In the Kishon River he encounters

"within a foot of my paddle . . . and just by my hand . . . the nose and mouth of – a crocodile!" His may have been the first report of the discovery of such creatures in the Kishon.

While standing on the deck of a steamship bound for the Azores in 1873, MacGregor decided to marry, and at age forty-eight, after some years of traveling and writing his early travel books, he married Annie Caffin, daughter of Adm. Sir Richard Caffin, K.C.B. Following his marriage MacGregor settled in Blackheath for a time and ended his feats of navigation, but he continued to lecture on those adventures for the benefit of deserving institutions. He died at his residence in Bournemouth on 16 July 1892, at the age of sixty-seven. Eulogizing him in a letter published in the London *Times* the day after his funeral, a friend called him an "unselfish and noble man."

MacGregor was conscious of his own tendency toward egotism, as in a footnote to *Rob Roy on the Jordan,* in which he wrote, "when a man has to tell by the pencil and pen what he has done with the paddle, it is impossible to be otherwise than individual and personal in the narration, or even egotistical in style." Yet he was always careful to use his genius for publicity and showmanship in the service of good causes.

At the end of his last recorded voyage he writes of launching the *Rob Roy* to meet the *Delta,* the ship that was to carry him and his boat home to England. Amid "angry and boisterous" waves and seas full of sharks he performed a neat turn atop a wave for the benefit of the crew members who were cheering him from the decks of the ship. After a frightening moment his boat "flew along the foam, and carried safe through all her little flag, and a heart that beat high with grateful praise to Him who had vouchsafed to me thus to enjoy the happiest days of a very happy life."

Biography:
Edwin Hodder, *John MacGregor ("Rob Roy")* (London: Hodder, 1894).

Reference:
Arthur Ransome, ed., introduction to MacGregor's *The Voyage Alone in the Yawl Rob Roy* (London: Hart-Davis, 1954; New York: British Book Centre, 1954).

Harriet Martineau

(12 June 1802 – 27 June 1876)

Lila M. Harper
Central Washington University

See also the Martineau entries in *DLB 21: Victorian Novelists Before 1885; DLB 55: Victorian Prose Writers Before 1867; DLB 159: British Short-Fiction Writers, 1800–1880;* and *DLB 163: British Children's Writers, 1800–1880.*

BOOKS: *Devotional Exercises for the Use of Young Persons* (London: Hunter, 1823; Boston: Bowles, 1833);

Addresses with Prayers and Original Hymns for the Use of Families and Schools (London: Hunter, 1826);

Principle and Practice; or, The Orphan Family (Wellington: Houlston, 1827; New York: Gilley, 1828);

The Rioters; or, A Tale of Bad Times (London: Houlston, 1827);

Mary Campbell; or, The Affectionate Granddaughter (Wellington: Houlston, 1828);

The Turn Out; or, Patience the Best Policy (London: Houlston, 1829);

Traditions of Palestine (London: Longman, Rees, Orme, Brown & Green, 1830); republished as *The Times of the Saviour* (Boston: Bowles, 1831);

The Essential Faith of the Universal Church Deduced from the Sacred Records (London: Unitarian Association, 1831; Boston: Bowles, 1833);

Five Years of Youth; or, Sense and Sentiment (London: Harvey & Darton, 1831; Boston: Bowles & Greene, 1832);

Sequel to Principle and Practice (London: Houlston, 1831);

Illustrations of Political Economy (25 monthly parts, London: Fox, 1832–1834; 8 volumes, Boston: Bowles, 1832–1835);

The Faith as Unfolded by Many Prophets: An Essay Addressed to the Disciples of Mohammed (London:

Harriet Martineau in 1849 (portrait by George Richmond; National Portrait Gallery, London)

Unitarian Association, 1832; Boston: Bowles, 1833);

Prize Essays (London: British & Foreign Unitarian Association, 1832);

Providence as Manifested through Israel (London: Unitarian Association, 1832; Boston: Bowles, 1833);

Poor Laws and Paupers, Illustrated (4 volumes, London: Fox, 1833–1834; 1 volume, Boston: Bowles, 1833);

Christmas-Day; or, The Friends (London: Houlston, 1834);

Illustrations of Taxation, 5 volumes (London: Fox, 1834);

The Tendency of Strikes and Sticks to Produce Low Wages, and of Union between Masters and Men to Ensure Good Wages (Durham: Veitch, 1834);

The Children Who Lived by the Jordan: A Story (Salem, Mass.: Landmark, 1835; London: Green, 1842);

The Hamlets (Boston: Munroe, 1836);

Miscellanies, 2 volumes (Boston: Hilliard, Gray, 1836);

Society in America, 3 volumes (London: Saunders & Otley, 1837);

Deerbrook: A Novel, 3 volumes (London: Moxon, 1838; New York: Harper, 1839);

The Guide to Service (London: Knight, 1838);

How to Observe Morals and Manners (London: Knight, 1838; New York: Harper, 1838);

My Servant Rachel, A Tale (London: Houlston, 1838);

A Retrospect of Western Travel (3 volumes, London: Saunders & Otley, 1838; 2 volumes, New York: Lohman, 1838);

The Martyr Age of the United States (Boston: Weeks, Jordan/Otis/Broaders / New York: Taylor, 1839; Newcastle upon Tyne: Emancipation and Aborigines Protection Society, 1840);

The Hour and the Man: A Historical Romance (3 volumes, London: Moxon, 1841; 2 volumes, New York: Harper, 1841);

The Playfellow: A Series of Tales (4 volumes, London: Knight, 1841–1843; 1 volume, London & New York: Routledge, 1883);

Life in the Sick-Room: Essays, by an Invalid (London: Moxon, 1844; Boston: Bowles & Crosby, 1844);

Dawn Island: A Tale (Manchester: Gadsby, 1845);

Letters on Mesmerism (London: Moxon, 1845); republished as *Miss Martineau's Letters on Mesmerism* (New York: Harper, 1845);

Forest and Game-Law Tales, 3 volumes (London: Moxon, 1845–1846);

The Billow and the Rock (London: Knight, 1846);

The Land We Live In, 4 volumes, by Martineau and Charles Knight (London: Knight, 1847);

Eastern Life, Present and Past (3 volumes, London: Moxon, 1848; 1 volume, Philadelphia: Lea & Blanchard, 1848);

Household Education (London: Moxon, 1849; Philadelphia: Lea & Blanchard, 1849);

History of England during the Thirty Years' Peace 1816–46 (2 volumes, London: Knight, 1849; 4 volumes, Philadelphia: Porter & Coates, 1864);

Two Letters on Cow-Keeping, by Harriet Martineau, Addressed to the Governor of the Guiltcross Union Workhouse (London: Gilpin / Edinburgh: Black / Dublin: Gilpin, 1850);

Half a Century of the British Empire: A History of the Kingdom and the People from 1800 to 1850, part 1 (London, 1851);

Introduction to the History of the Peace from 1800 to 1815 (London: Knight, 1851);

Letters on the Laws of Man's Nature and Development, by Martineau and Henry George Atkinson (London: Chapman, 1851; Boston: Mendum, 1851);

Merdhen, The Manor and The Eyrie, Old Landmarks and Old Laws (London: Routledge, 1852);

Letters from Ireland (London: Chapman, 1852);

Charles and Antoine Lucyon, A Tale of the French Revolution (Cincinnati, Ohio: James, 1853);

Guide to Windermere, with Tours to the Neighbouring Lakes and Other Interesting Places (Windermere: Garnett / London: Whittaker, 1854);

A Complete Guide to the English Lakes (Windermere: Garnett / London: Whittaker, 1855);

The Factory Controversy: A Warning Against Meddling Legislation (Manchester: National Association of Factory Occupiers, 1855);

A History of the American Compromises (London: Chapman, 1856);

Sketches from Life (London: Whittaker / Windermere: Garnett, 1856);

British Rule in India: A Historical Sketch (London: Smith, Elder, 1857);

Corporate Tradition and National Rights: Local Dues on Shipping (London: Routledge / Manchester: Dinham, 1857);

Guide to Keswick and its Environs (Windermere: Garnett / London: Whittaker, 1857);

The "Manifest Destiny" of the American Union (New York: American Anti-Slavery Society, 1857);

Suggestions towards the Future Government of India (London: Smith, Elder, 1858);

Endowed Schools of Ireland (London: Smith, Elder, 1859);

England and Her Soldiers (London: Smith, Elder, 1859);

Health, Husbandry and Handicraft (London: Bradbury & Evans, 1861); republished in part as *Our Farm of Two Acres* (New York: Bunce & Huntingdon, 1865);

The History of England from the Commencement of the XIXth Century to the Crimean War (Philadelphia: Porter & Coates, 1864);

Biographical Sketches (London: Macmillan, 1869; New York: Leypoldt & Holt, 1869);

Chicago in 1836: Strange Early Days (Chicago, 1876);

Harriet Martineau's Autobiography, with Memorials by Maria Weston Chapman (3 volumes, London: Smith, Elder, 1877; 2 volumes, Boston: Osgood, 1877);

The Hampdens: An Historiette (London: Routledge, 1880).

OTHER: *Traditions of Palestine,* edited by Martineau (London: Longman, Rees, Orme, Brown & Green, 1830); republished as *The Times of the Saviour* (Boston: Bowles, 1831);

The Positive Philosophy of Auguste Comte, Freely Translated and Condensed, 2 volumes (London: Chapman, 1853; New York: Appleton, 1854).

SELECTED PERIODICAL PUBLICATIONS – UNCOLLECTED: "Female Writers of Practical Divinity," *Monthly Repository,* 17 (October 1822): 593–596;

"Letter to the Deaf," *Tait's Edinburgh Magazine,* new series 1 (April 1834): 174–179.

A woman of keen intellect and prodigious energy, Harriet Martineau transformed the nature of travel writing, making it into an investigative tool of the social sciences, a branch of study in which the provinces of sociology, anthropology, and political science overlap. By extending the boundaries of the genre, she also incorporated women's issues and a pointed concern for the domestic sphere into studies that were intended for a general, presumably largely male audience. In her travel books she presented the domestic sphere as an essential part of society and made the study of household matters a requirement for sociological study. Martineau traveled not as a dilettante tourist nor as a colonizer, but as a professional workingwoman who was the sole director and organizer of her own journeys. Her travel writing helped establish a definition of the ideal traveler as one sympathetic and sensitive to the culture being observed, a role she saw as being particularly suited to women.

In her *Autobiography* (1877) Martineau confessed, "My pleasure in Voyages and Travels is almost an insanity," and this interest, first in armchair travel and then in personal travel, both informed her writing and also bolstered her self-confidence in expressing her views publicly, in an age when such outspokenness by women was rarely condoned. A prolific writer in the Victorian tradition of continuous, steady work, Martineau, despite ill health, turned out a wide range of writing that included journalism, early sociology, explanations of political issues, novels, children's books,

household and farming instruction, and travel writing. Although not well known to modern readers, Martineau's name during her lifetime was a household word to a wide spectrum of the Victorian reading public.

Martineau was born in Norwich, England, in 1802. A descendant of French Huguenot refugees who immigrated to England after the revocation of the Edict of Nantes in 1688, she inherited a strong belief in tolerance and free speech. By the time of her birth, her father, a successful wine importer and bombazine manufacturer, had begun to experience setbacks and was concerned about the long-term success of his business. Thus, although the family was initially well-to-do, Martineau and the other children were taught to care for themselves and to see their education as their only dependable inheritance.

The sixth of eight children and the third daughter, Martineau originally showed musical promise and was educated as a governess. Besides musical training, she received an unusually good education in language, the classics, rhetoric, and philosophy, a curriculum usually reserved for boys. At age eleven Martineau attended a small school run by the Reverend Isaac Perry, where she enjoyed "delectable schooling" for two years and obtained further instruction in Latin, French, composition, and arithmetic.

Initial plans for Martineau's future changed drastically when her deafness became apparent at age twelve. Her already intense childhood fears were greatly compounded by her growing deafness and her fear that she would lose her other senses. She later reported that she never had much sense of taste or smell, and as she gradually lost her hearing she became acutely aware of her "deficiency of three senses out of five." Martineau's family at first did not believe her reports that she could not hear, but they eventually realized she was being truthful and that she would not be able to support herself as a governess. As a woman, her physical disabilities seemed to leave needlework as her only means of livelihood, and she was strongly encouraged to pursue this role, especially by her mother. Martineau, however, was considering other vocations.

In her *Autobiography* she attributed the development of her interest in writing to her younger brother, James, her closest companion. When leaving home for college in 1821, he suggested that his sister try writing something for the *Monthly Repository,* a Unitarian periodical. Construing this suggestion as a command, Martineau submitted a paper

to wondering eyes in studious hours, & believed in from the sole evidence of its surviving grandeur & beauty. While I stood in the wet whirlwind, with the crystal roof above me, the thundering floor beneath, & the foaming whirlpool & eddy flood before me, I saw those quiet, studious hours of the future world when this cataract shall have become a tradition, & the spot on wh. I stood shall be the centre of a wide sea, ~~the inhabitants~~ a new region of life. This was seeing world-making. So it was on the Mississ.t, when a lost if [?] on the waters betokened the birth place of new land. All things help in this creation. The cliffs of the upper Missouri detach their soil, & lend it ~~tens~~ thousands of miles down the stream. The river brings it, & deposits it in continual increase, till a barrier is raised ag.t the rushing waters themselves. The air brings seeds, & drops them where they sprout, & [crossed out] downwards, so that their roots bind the soft soil, & enable it to bear the weight of new accretions. The infant forest, floating, as it appeared, on the ~~[crossed out]~~ surface of the turbid & rapid waters, may reveal no beauty to the painter; but to the eye of one who loves to watch the process of world-making, it is full of delight. These islands are seen in every stage of growth. The cotton wood trees, from being like cresses in a pool, rise breast-high; then they are like thickets, to whose shade the alligator may retreat; then, like groves that bid the sun good-night ~~[crossed out]~~ while he is still lighting up the forest; then like the forest itself, with the wood-cutters house within its screen, & flowers spring up about its stems, & the wild-vine climbing to meet the night breezes on its lofty canopy. This was seeing world-making. Here was strong instigation to the exercise of analysis. I ~~[crossed out]~~ watched also the progress of conventional life. I saw it in every stage of ~~advancement~~, from the clearing in the woods,

Page from the manuscript for Martineau's Society in America, *which she wrote circa 1836–1837 (MA 873, Pierpont Morgan Library)*

on "Female Writers of Practical Divinity," signing it with the initial "V." The paper was published and, by chance, read aloud and admired by her eldest brother, Thomas. When she admitted to authorship, Thomas told her, "Now, dear, leave it to other women to make shirts and darn stockings; and do you devote yourself to this." She took these words as a mandate and started seriously pursuing a writing vocation.

Despite this encouragement, Martineau's writing was still not considered appropriate behavior for a woman of her social class. This situation changed when, in the space of a few years, Martineau saw the death of her brother Thomas and her father, followed by the downfall of the family business after the bank and stock crises of 1825–1826. Although she mourned the passing of family members, the financial setback was almost a relief to Martineau because it allowed her more freedom to pursue her writing. In 1829 she declared that "we had lost our gentility," and as a result she was now able to write openly rather than secretly in the early morning hours. The fall in social status allowed her family, in Martineau's estimation, to live truly instead of vegetating. She continued writing for the *Monthly Repository,* becoming its only paid contributor, writing some fiction but mostly book reviews for fifteen pounds a year. While modern book reviews are generally short, objective productions, nineteenth-century book reviews such as Martineau's used the issues raised in the review as a platform for an extended discussion of the reviewer's own beliefs. By her own estimation in 1830, a particularly productive year, Martineau produced fifty-two separate items for the *Monthly Repository.*

Although she was writing professionally, Martineau still could not convince her family that she had any future as a writer. Hoping to establish more literary connections, she moved to London in 1829 and stayed with an aunt and uncle, continuing to earn her livelihood by sewing during daylight hours and writing into the night. Her mother, however, ordered her back to Norwich after her influential aunt declared that Martineau should focus on her needlework. Such was her insecurity that she obeyed her mother, although she was twenty-seven years old.

Back in Norwich she learned of an essay contest "by which Unitarianism was to be presented to the notice of Catholics, Jews and Mohammedans." Martineau entered three separate essays for each of the three categories and won all of them. Her success finally convinced her mother "to spare" Martineau "for three months in the spring of every year" to go to London.

A turning point in Martineau's literary career came when she established her immensely popular Illustrations of Political Economy series (1832–1834). The idea for the project germinated in 1831 when she used her prize money to travel to Dublin to visit her brother James, now a rising Unitarian minister. Here she wrote out her plan for a political economy series, twenty-five novella-length stories that would illustrate a current economic problem. She had been inspired by Jane Marcet's *Conversations on Political Economy* (1816), a book oriented to a young adult audience. It had struck Martineau at that time "that the principles of the whole science [of political economy] might be advantageously conveyed . . . not by being smothered up in a story, but by being exhibited in their natural workings in selected passages of social life." The project was an overwhelming, massive, long-term commitment, but, devoted as she was to popular education, she had a "thorough, well-considered, steady conviction that the work was wanted – was even craved by the popular mind." No publishers were interested, however, and she finally was reduced to going to Charles Fox, a bookseller, who required her to obtain five hundred subscriptions before publication and the sale of a thousand copies of the first two numbers. In desperation Martineau sent a copy of the prospectus for the series to members of Parliament. The series quickly became a success, selling by subscription and then through workingmen's institutions. Martineau's sense of what the reading public wanted was validated, and her literary fame was assured. By 1834 the series sold an average of ten thousand copies per month.

Martineau firmly established herself as a popularizer of contemporary economics and political issues by making them into human issues. Her series showed how individuals were affected by a problem and then followed with a short lecture on the concept that the story enacted. Martineau met her demanding deadlines by training herself to write in single drafts that did not need recopying. Such was the popularity of Illustrations of Political Economy that Martineau's approval of a motion could be transformed into public support. Her influence over current political issues was, as she pointed out, ironic since, as a woman, she could not vote.

While most of these illustrations were concerned with British issues, Martineau also wrote on France, Siberia, Holland, the West Indies, South Africa, and the United States, gleaning much of her material from the travel accounts of others, since up until this time she had done little traveling outside Britain. It was her reading and studying of travel accounts that led Martineau to consider the possibility of undertaking her own travels.

After the completion of twenty-five parts for the Illustrations series, Martineau escaped with much relief from both work and family obligations to sail to America, where she traveled for two years (1834–1836). She initially resisted the encouragement to write a book on her travels, partly because of her sensitivity to the American resentment of patronizing British accounts of the United States and partly because her tale "Demerara" (1832) in the Illustrations series had established her abolitionist views, which would make her proposed travel in the southern states difficult if it were apparent that she was collecting material for a book.

Eventually, however, she published three books from her American travels. Having made her literary reputation in *Illustrations,* Martineau was moving toward expanding her writing ambitions from the popularization of topical economic issues to independent political and sociological studies; her travels to America gave her the personal experience that validated a more authoritative voice in her writing. In *Society in America* (1837) she presented a sociological study of American institutions; *A Retrospect of Western Travel* (1838) is a more personal and popular account of her travels; and *How to Observe Morals and Manners* (1838) outlines her methodology for sociological study. Additional details of her travel experience that she considered too sensitive for publication during her lifetime were included in her *Autobiography.*

In her accounts Martineau showed a fascination with the sights of travel, a capacity for discomfort, and a mind open to new experiences. She was thirty-two when she and her traveling companion, Louisa Jeffreys, left Liverpool for New York. They sailed on 9 August 1834 on a packet, a type of sailing ship (the first steam-powered travel to America was still four years in the future). Wind conditions delayed the departure date by a day, and occasional weather problems followed them on the voyage. At times the ship was becalmed, and once they experienced hurricane-force winds. Even in such danger Martineau's delight was unabashed. With high winds roaring on the deck, she was so in awe of the sight that she went back down to the cabins "to implore the other ladies to come and be refreshed." After being ignored, she persuaded the captain to lash her to a post so that she could safely experience the storm.

While at sea, Martineau started work on what became one of the earliest, if not the first, texts on sociological methodology: *How to Observe Morals and*

Manners. In this book she explained how she went about observing American society. She had started this project by writing a chapter for a proposed book by an unnamed friend to be called "How to Observe." This writing, prior to her actual American observations, allowed her systematically and abstractly to consider how to perceive and form general conclusions about another society. It eventually formed the basis for her own volume in an aborted series of books on "How to Observe," a multiple-author series on the topic of observation from the perspective of several scientific fields, in which Martineau's was to be the second and final volume. It was not published until 1838, after the publication of her two other American books. Although this book quickly went out of print, it provides a rare glimpse into the formation of a professional discipline and was notable for its call for travelers to exercise a more disciplined regimen in their travel writings so that their observations could serve the needs of the developing fields of sociology and anthropology. Firmly rejecting the argument that the purpose of travel writing was merely to entertain, Martineau proclaimed that travel writing produced the critical data needed for a global understanding of important social issues.

Martineau traveled to the United States with the resolution that her observations would avoid such fault-finding perceptions as those in Basil Hall's *Travels in North America in 1827 and 1828* (1829) and Frances Trollope's *Domestic Manners of the Americans* (1832). Trollope's book had been published just before Martineau began her travels, and it became for her a cautionary model of what to avoid in her own books. Unlike Trollope, she was prepared to applaud evidences of social equality that she observed in the United States; however, like Trollope, she believed that a woman's access to the domestic sphere gave her important insights into the social fabric of a society. In response to the common assertion that being a woman was a disadvantage for a traveler, Martineau responded in *Society in America* that it was actually an advantage, since she had "seen much more of domestic life than could possibly have been exhibited to any gentleman travelling through the country."

Arriving in New York on 19 September 1834, Martineau planned her itinerary so that she could make observations from as many social perspectives as possible. She traveled as far north as the Great Lakes region and as far south as New Orleans, then went up the Mississippi by riverboat. She ventured through Tennessee, Kentucky, and into Ohio, end-

First page of the manuscript for Martineau's A Retrospect of Western Travel *(courtesy of the Lilly Library, Indiana University)*

ing with a series of trips to New England. Although Martineau was never in robust health, she cheerfully endured the discomfort of long-term travel and visited prisons, hospitals, schools, factories, and farms. Aware of the difficulty involved in trying to make large generalizations about an entire country, she stayed with families and fitted herself into the daily routine, visited with different households, gossiped and sewed with the women, and attended local churches and weddings.

Martineau admitted that her deafness, which was complete in one ear but only partial in the other, did not allow her to hear comments made by people on the streets, and there were cases, as in the House of Representatives, where the acoustics prevented her from hearing discussions. She argued, however, that her hearing trumpet inspired a feeling of intimacy in conversation that made up for her hearing limitations. It is apparent from her *Autobiography* that her deafness also allowed her to control what she had to listen to and "cut" a person by refusing to extend her hearing trumpet to those she considered rude or unmannerly.

In her American travel writings Martineau always showed an awareness that her audience included both American and British readers, and she shaped her narrations accordingly. While disagreeing with American positions on the major issues of slavery, the displacement of Native Americans, and women's rights, Martineau was nevertheless encouraged by the evidence she found of a developing egalitarian society. She noted with great approval the wide availability of a basic education and the existence of talented individuals from varying backgrounds. Although annoyed by the heavy use of chewing tobacco and unsettled by rocking chairs, she spoke, on the whole, highly of American hospitality.

Although Alexis de Tocqueville's famous travels in the United States took place from May 1831 to February 1832 — before Martineau's — his *Democracy in America* was not published until 1835, when Martineau was touring the United States. Both authors were simultaneously engaged in studying the application of democratic theory in the developing American society. De Tocqueville's study made insightful but sweeping generalizations, showing the application of democratic ideals, while Martineau set out to judge how well the actual operation of American democracy fulfilled its initial philosophical goals. Unlike de Tocqueville, she took an investigative approach to the subject, feeling the need to substantiate her conclusions with specific examples.

Martineau collected the results of her observations and research in 1837 in *Society in America,* a book that changed the nature of travel writing by making use of a comparative methodology to analyze American society. The original title, "Theory and Practice of Society in America," rejected by her publishers, was a more accurate indication of this work's purpose. The study's three volumes attempted to compare the state of American society with the principles expressed in the Declaration of Independence and the Constitution. The discussion of American society also gave Martineau a vehicle to support the reform movement in Britain at the time of her travels. In her discussion of the non-representation of women in the political process in the United States, she made the analogy of women's position with that of slaves, generalizing her argument to make it applicable to all women, not just Americans.

While Martineau wished to speak with authority on political theory, what appealed most to her readers were her sketches of contemporary figures of Jacksonian America. Noting this response, she later regretted that she had chosen an abstract framework in this book rather than a focus on more-concrete topics. She reported in her *Autobiography* that Thomas Carlyle wrote to her "that he had rather read of Webster's cavernous eyes and arm under his coat-tail, than all the political speculation that a cut and dried system could suggest."

Of these books, *A Retrospect of Western Travel,* published in 1838 with personal accounts of her travel, was the most popular, largely because of Martineau's portrayal of herself as a levelheaded, intelligent individual, sensitive to the feelings of others but accustomed to making her own decisions, quite in contrast to the traditional declarations of inferiority of many women travel writers at this time. Although usually gentle and sympathetic, Martineau was capable of satiric commentary. She particularly disliked boorish British travelers. At a hotel near Niagara Falls she observed one Englishman who "was so anxious about where he should settle, so incessantly pettish, so resolutely miserable, as to bespeak the compassion of all the guests for the ladies of his family, one of whom told me that she had forgotten all about the [Niagara] falls in her domestic anxieties."

At times *Retrospect* becomes a remembrance, as Martineau reflects on the deaths from cholera and tuberculosis of many Americans she had met. (There had been a cholera epidemic in New York the year she arrived.) Later her depressed spirits rose as she described the beauty of Maine beaches, the infant tourist industry forming around Niagara Falls, and the introduction of the Christmas tree to New England. In such descriptions she gives intriguing glimpses of often-ignored details of nineteenth-century American life.

Martineau had a strong need for repose and reflection in the process of sorting through and analyzing her travel observations. A small waterfall near Niagara Falls that caught her eye in *Retrospect* seems a reflection of herself: "solitary in the midst of the crowd of waters, coming out of its privacy in the wood to take its leap by itself." Having taken her leap, though, she needed to retreat again into her solitude to gain distance from her subject and personal strength before she could publish. She chose the word *retrospect* for her title because of her belief that it "is only after sitting down alone at home that the traveller can separate the universal truth from the partial error with which he has sympathized, and can make some approximation towards assurance as to what he has learned and what he believes." This requirement for contemplation was linked to her deep capacity for sympathy and identification with others. She was concerned that in her travels she might inadvertently hurt the feelings of others through ignorance of their culture. This unavoidable "fear and sorrow of hurting others" made it difficult to evaluate a society, and she felt she could only make an honest report when she had placed some physical distance between herself and the subject of her study.

Her philosophical response to both travel and life is summed up in her conclusion to *Retrospect,* a conclusion she had drawn while visiting an American cemetery. Martineau asks, "What is gained by living and travelling?" She makes the analogy between her posttravel ruminations and the necessity of philosophical acceptance of daily stress, where, amid "the turmoil of life," repose and solitude give an opportunity to gain a measure of balance with the realization of the "transient nature of troubles."

Returning to England in 1836, Martineau worked on her travel books. Her writings at this time also included a three-volume guide for domestic service training commissioned by Poor Law authorities, *The Guide to Service* (1838), and a novel of provincial life, *Deerbrook* (1838).

Martineau's efforts against slavery were strengthened by her visit to the United States, and with the authority gained by personal observation, she wrote articles in support of William Lloyd Garrison's abolitionist and racial integration program at a time when he was an unpopular figure.

She reprinted her *Westminster Review* writings in *The Martyr Age of the United States* (1839), followed by her long-contemplated *The Hour and the Man* (1841), a fictional account of a black hero, the Haitian liberator Toussaint-Louverture. In 1840 her efforts were acknowledged by her election as a delegate from Massachusetts to the London Anti-Slavery Convention; however, she was too ill to attend.

Martineau's taste for travel suffered a setback when, during a European tour, she became seriously ill, apparently from a uterine tumor. She moved to Tynemouth to be under the care of her sister Elizabeth and her sister's physician husband. During the next five years of bed rest, she wrote *Life in the Sick-Room* (1844), exploring the psychological effects of long-term illness, and four short children's novels published under the title *The Playfellow: A Series of Tales* (1841–1843). Of the four stories included, "Feats on the Fiord" was the most frequently reprinted. Based on Martineau's study of travel accounts, it is set in Norway and presents issues of cultural differences, belief, and tolerance in a surprisingly sensitive and understanding manner.

Martineau's poor health slowed her literary production and limited her income. While family members helped out, friends became concerned. In 1843 Erasmus Darwin, brother of Charles Darwin, organized a testimonial to give Martineau more financial independence. Her illness became controversial when her pain was apparently reduced by a series of hypnotic trances. Believing that mesmerism was being unjustly ignored by medical science, Martineau wrote of her experiences in "Six Letters on Mesmerism" for the *Athenaeum* in 1844 and republished it in book form in 1845.

Although she never married, Martineau desired her own household. In 1846 she felt that she had regained enough of her health to establish her own home, and she had a house, The Knoll, built in Ambleside in the Lake District. Here, a neighbor to William Wordsworth and Matthew Arnold, she practiced a rigorous daily routine: rising at six, walking and breakfasting by seven-thirty, then writing until two. At The Knoll she experimented with small, self-sufficient farming, while producing a series of books and essays on various aspects of popular self-help topics — for example, *Health, Husbandry and Handicraft* (1861) — along with such accounts of recent history as *History of England during the Thirty Years' Peace 1816–46* (1849), an important resource for nineteenth-century history. She also continued her journalism, contributing to Charles Dickens's *Household Words* and the *Daily News*.

Despite her satisfaction with her own house and self-sufficiency, she did not hesitate to take another long voyage when the opportunity came, leaving Ambleside on a final trip in 1846–1847 across Egypt, Palestine, Syria, and Lebanon. This time she traveled with a group of other Europeans in a land where she did not know the language, and she was more isolated from the native culture by her fellow tourists. While still prepared to respond emphatically to those she met, her isolation caused her travel account to reflect more typically Eurocentric, colonialist attitudes.

The mid nineteenth century was a period marked by religious questionings initiated by the combined sources of science and higher criticism, and Martineau was not exempt from these concerns. Her philosophical exploration into the roots of religious development shaped her final travel account, *Eastern Life, Present and Past* (1848). In 1846, the year Martineau left for Egypt, George Eliot translated David Friedrich Strauss's *The Life of Jesus* (1835–1836), a highly controversial book that related the Gospel accounts to myth. Working from such influences as Strauss's, Martineau, in *Eastern Life,* interweaves her account of her travel with biblical history, offering an imaginative suggestion of how the historical evolution of religious tradition might have occurred. Although one of the most neglected of Martineau's works, *Eastern Life* presents a vivid portrait of the nineteenth-century Mideast and tourism in the dawning age of imperialism.

Martineau began her eight-month travel in Alexandria, Egypt, on 20 November 1846, traveling with Mr. and Mrs. Richard V. Yates and Joseph C. Ewart. Weather was pleasant in November when they started, but by the time they crossed the Sinai Peninsula conditions were extremely hot and dry. Despite her recent invalidism Martineau coped well with the long, exhausting days, traveling by horseback, donkey, and camel. She traveled up the Nile by steamer to Nubia and then as far south as Wadee Halfa. Returning to Cairo, she explored the Nile Valley.

While Martineau always traveled with an awareness that the present she was recording would one day become history, she also traveled to experience imaginatively another time period. When she journeyed to America, she wrote about the nation in the belief that she was seeing intimations of the future, that the United States was a new and developing society, a laboratory for social experimentation. By contrast, her travel to the Middle East reflected a more typically Eurocentric and imperialistic view of other lands as being trapped in the past. While still displaying an unusual sensitivity to other cultures, Martineau's *Eastern Life, Present and Past* was not written with the same awareness of a dual audience that made her American travel accounts so progressive. She did not consider the natives of the Middle East part of her reading public, and this fact, along with her isolation from daily Arab life, affected her observations.

In the Middle East, Martineau saw that world as frozen in biblical history. In *Eastern Life* she was writing history as informed by travel writing, using her own experiences as a means for retrieving lost history. In a letter to Richard Milnes, a previous traveler to Egypt, she wrote, "I rode, day by day, through the glorious sterile valley which leads one among the population of the dead, feeling the same ideas and emotions *must* have been in the minds of those before whose eyes, as before mine, lay the same contrasting scenery of life and death." She designed the itinerary of the trip to follow the historical development of Judaism and Christianity with the idea of emphasizing the connection between Egyptian mythologies and Christian beliefs. From Cairo, Martineau and her companions retraced the path of the Hebrews across the Sinai Peninsula to Jerusalem, Damascus, and finally Lebanon. She sailed back to England in June 1847.

Eastern Life also allowed Martineau to merge the techniques of historical fiction writing she had used in such works as *The Hour and the Man: A Historical Romance* with her travel writing. Seeking those places she was most familiar with in biblical history, she tried to re-create the feelings of biblical characters. She noted, too, how differently the Pentateuch reads in the environs of Mount Sinai, writing in *Eastern Life,* "The light from Egypt and Arabia shining into it illuminates unthought-of places, and gives a new and most fresh colouring to the whole." In this way, she allows her readers to participate in her historical re-creation and reinterpretation of biblical events.

Aware of the effect the other travelers had on her perceptions, Martineau tried to counteract this influence by riding away from the group or taking long walks alone, increasing the sense of privacy and isolation her deafness generally imposed. In this way she felt she could best recapture the past that was contained in the landscape. She carefully noted the domestic details of an encampment. Dirt, poverty, and flies did not escape her attention, but she also points out that she had seen far more evidence of emaciation in a single walk in England than in her entire Egyptian trip. She was most distressed by the religious intolerance she observed

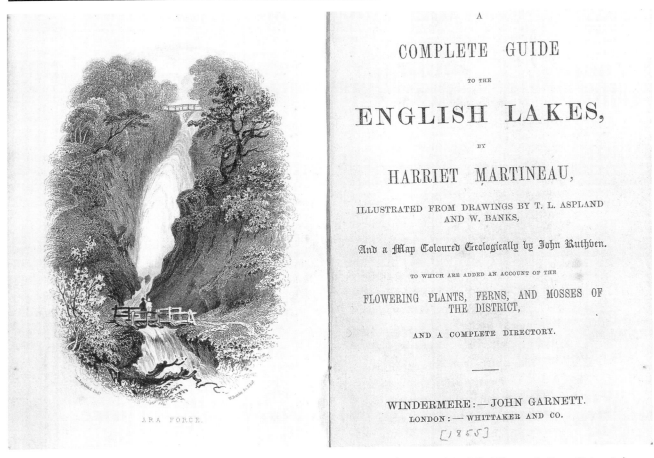

A

COMPLETE GUIDE

TO THE

ENGLISH LAKES,

BY

HARRIET MARTINEAU,

ILLUSTRATED FROM DRAWINGS BY T. L. ASPLAND
AND W. BANKS,

And a Map Coloured Geologically by John Ruthven.

TO WHICH ARE ADDED AN ACCOUNT OF THE

FLOWERING PLANTS, FERNS, AND MOSSES OF
THE DISTRICT,

AND A COMPLETE DIRECTORY.

WINDERMERE: — JOHN GARNETT.
LONDON: — WHITTAKER AND CO.
[1855]

ARA FORCE.

Frontispiece and title page for Martineau's travel guide to the Lake District (courtesy of the Lilly Library, Indiana University)

and the inactivity of the women in the Egyptian harem she visited. Martineau found the women in the harem "the most injured human beings I have ever seen — the most studiously depressed and corrupted women whose condition I have witnessed."

Eastern Life was difficult for Martineau to publish. The publisher John Murray rejected the book because of its atheistic content, but it was eventually published by Edward Moxon. However, even those who accepted her religious investigation objected to the book, believing that a travel book was not an appropriate vehicle for such philosophical discussions and that she had extended the limitations of the genre too far. Despite unfavorable reviews, Martineau remained outwardly aloof and publicly unaffected, but some uncertainty lingered in her mind about the philosophical foundations of her conclusions.

As a result of her travel observations, Martineau's stance became more firmly antireligious. More controversy followed as she explored her antitheological conclusions with Henry George Atkinson, with whom she collaborated on *Letters on the*

Laws of Man's Nature and Development (1851). This publication announced her movement away from Unitarianism to a philosophical position that T. H. Huxley would later call agnosticism; it also finalized a break with her brother James, now a professor at Manchester College and a major spokesman for a transcendentalist "liberal" Christianity.

Martineau's involvement with social reform increased after her return from the Middle East. Starting in 1848, she undertook a series of lectures every winter for the workers of Ambleside on the subject of health, British history, and her travels. She also published *Household Education* (1849), which contained advice on parenting and revealed some of her childhood memories. In the 1850s Martineau started writing editorial material for the *Daily News,* a commitment she continued for the next fifteen years, contributing some sixteen hundred editorials. Furthermore, her conclusions in *Eastern Life* led her to study the positivism of Auguste Comte, whose work was only available in French. Believing in the importance of his writing and noting the increasing interest in Comte in England, she translated and condensed the difficult *Positive Philosophy* from six to two volumes to make it more accessible to general readers, publishing her edition in 1853. Although disagreeing with Comte on many points, she made no attempt to annotate or include her own comments. Comte himself was so impressed by her condensation that he had it retranslated into French for his own students, and it still stands as the standard English translation of his work.

The railways brought increasing interest in and development of the Lake District for vacations, which led Martineau to venture into a new type of travel account, the travel guide. *A Complete Guide to the English Lakes* (1855) is based on her own energetic walks around the countryside. Oriented to the tourist trade, this guide describes routes, scenery, buildings, local history, legends, and noteworthy local inhabitants, along with recommendations for land improvement and sanitation.

In 1853 Martineau took what was, for her time, the unusual step of writing her own autobiography. Victorian women did write about their lives in the form of letters, essays, and fiction, but few wrote autobiographies, and Martineau's is particularly striking for its honesty and directness. It was written when, after ten years of good health, Martineau became convinced that she was suffering from heart disease. She subsequently prepared for her death and even wrote her own obituary. Although she lived, albeit in increasingly worse health, for another twenty-one years, she did not update her *Autobiography* and left it concluded in the year 1855. The two-volume work, with a third *Memorials* volume by Maria Weston Chapman, was published posthumously in 1877. Martineau wrote her *Autobiography* with a strong belief in her own historical importance; her account includes many observations of the literary and political figures of her day and is organized with a running chronology of dates at the top of the pages.

Despite continual illness, Martineau remained in the public eye with her regular editorials for the *Daily News*. After the mutiny in India in 1857, the British colonial administration of India became one of her continual themes. Although she did not question the British presence in India, her criticisms of English colonial policies were consistent with the enlightened respect for native cultures that she exhibited in her travels. In the *Daily News* she was outspoken in her belief that all of Britain's colonies should eventually achieve independence, following her newspaper writing on this issue with *British Rule in India: A Historical Sketch* (1857) and

Suggestions towards the Future Government of India (1858). In *Suggestions* Martineau urged her readers to educate themselves about the religious and cultural differences of Indian society, stating: "We were only strangers in the country, living there first for self-interest, and next for duty; and never from any sympathy for, or real intercourse with the inhabitants."

Martineau was more influential in shaping the British response to American issues than she was in changing British policy in India. She kept the British public informed about political events leading up to the U.S. Civil War, and during the war she kept the issue of slavery at the forefront when Britain was becoming sympathetic to the Southern states. Her final public contribution was her active support, along with Florence Nightingale, for the repeal of the Contagious Diseases Act, an act important in the history of women's rights because the organizing effort formed women into a movement that brought them national attention and increased influence over legislation.

After years of anticipating her own death, Martineau died at The Knoll on 27 June 1876. Her own self-assessment, as expressed in her obituary, was that she was "nothing approaching to genius," but Martineau acquired the power significantly to affect public opinion and was a favorite author for many notable shapers of nineteenth-century intellectual life. Her present-day reputation rests primarily on her fictional work, despite the fact that she focused most of her extraordinary energy on her nonfiction writing. Although she was a significant figure in the early development of the social sciences and a pioneer in the use of direct observation through travel in sociological analysis, her contributions in this area are only recently being recognized. More than anything else, Martineau's life was devoted to writing. Her travels deeply informed her work and helped establish her authoritative voice in a patriarchal society. By writing so persuasively and attentively about other lands and other peoples, she not only enlightened and challenged many of her readers, but she also made it easier for women travelers such as Mary Kingsley and Isabella Bird Bishop to establish their own vocations in travel writing.

Letters:

Harriet Martineau's Letters to Fanny Wedgwood, edited by Elisabeth Sanders Arbuckle (Stanford, Cal.: Stanford University Press, 1983);

Harriet Martineau: Selected Letters, edited by Valerie Sanders (Oxford: Clarendon Press, 1990).

Bibliography:

Joseph B. Rivlin, *Harriet Martineau: A Bibliography of Her Separately Printed Books* (New York: New York Public Library, 1947).

Biographies:

Vera Wheatley, *The Life and Works of Harriet Martineau* (London: Secker & Warburg, 1957);

R. K. Webb, *Harriet Martineau: A Radical Victorian* (London: Heinemann, 1960);

Valerie Kossew Pichanick, *Harriet Martineau: The Woman and Her Work, 1802–1876* (Ann Arbor: University of Michigan Press, 1980).

References:

Deirdre David, *Intellectual Women and Victorian Patriarchy: Harriet Martineau, Elizabeth Barrett Browning, George Eliot* (Ithaca, N.Y.: Cornell University Press, 1987);

Maria H. Frawley, "Desert Places/Gendered Spaces: Victorian Women in the Middle East," *Nineteenth-Century Contexts,* 15, no. 1 (1991): 49–64;

Frawley, "Harriet Martineau in America: Gender and the Discourse of Sociology," *Victorian Newsletter,* 81 (1992): 13–20;

Michael R. Hill, Introduction to Martineau's *How to Observe Morals and Manners* (New Brunswick, N.J.: Transaction, 1989), pp. xv–lii;

Susan Hoecker-Drysdale, *Harriet Martineau: First Woman Sociologist* (Oxford: Berg, 1992);

Linda H. Peterson, "Harriet Martineau: Masculine Discourse, Feminine Sage," in *Victorian Sages and Cultural Discourse: Renegotiating Gender and Power,* edited by E. Thais Morgan (New Brunswick, N.J.: Rutgers University Press, 1990);

Peterson, "Harriet Martineau's Household Education: Revising the Feminine Tradition," *Bucknell Review,* 34, no. 2 (1990): 183–194;

Diana Postlethwaite, "Mothering and Mesmerism in the Life of Harriet Martineau," *Signs: Journal of Women in Culture and Society,* 14 (Spring 1989): 583–609;

Valerie Sanders, *Reason Over Passion: Harriet Martineau and the Victorian Novel* (New York: St. Martin's Press, 1986);

Richard L. Stein, *Victoria's Year: English Literature and Culture 1837–1838* (New York: Oxford University Press, 1987);

Gillian Thomas, *Harriet Martineau* (Boston: G. K. Hall, 1985);

Gayle Graham Yates, ed., *Harriet Martineau on Women* (New Brunswick, N.J.: Rutgers University Press, 1985).

Louisa Anne Meredith

(20 July 1812 – 21 October 1895)

Ann Shillinglaw
Loyola University of Chicago

BOOKS: *Poems,* as Louisa Anne Twamley (London: Tilt, 1835);

The Romance of Nature; or, The Flower-Seasons Illustrated, as Louisa Anne Twamley (London: Tilt, 1836);

Flora's Gems: or, The Treasures of the Parterre (London: Tilt, 1837);

An Autumn Ramble by the Wye, as Louisa Anne Twamley (London: Tilt, 1839); republished as *The Annual of British Landscape Scenery: An Autumn Ramble on the Wye* (London: Orr, 1839);

Our Wild Flowers Familiarly Described and Illustrated (London: Tilt, 1839);

The Parterre; or, Beauties of Flora, by Meredith and James Andrews, with poetical illustrations by Meredith as Louisa Anne Twamley (London: Tilt & Bogue, 1842);

Notes and Sketches of New South Wales, during a Residence in That Colony from 1839 to 1844 (London: Murray, 1844);

My Home in Tasmania, during a Residence of Nine Years, 2 volumes (London: Murray, 1852); republished as *My Home in Tasmania; or, Nine Years in Australia* (New York: Bunce & Brother, 1853);

Loved, and Lost! The True Story of a Short Life (London: Day, 1860);

Some of My Bush Friends in Tasmania: Native Flowers, Berries, and Insects, Drawn from Life, Illustrated in Verse, and Briefly Described (London: Day, 1860);

Over the Straits: A Visit to Victoria (London: Chapman & Hall, 1861); republished as *Travels and Stories in Our Gold Colonies* (London: Griffin, 1862);

The Lacemakers: Sketches of Irish Character, with Some Account of the Effort to Establish Lacemaking in Ireland (London: Jackson, Walford & Hodder, 1865);

Phoebe's Mother: A Novel, 2 volumes (London: Tinsley, 1869);

A Tasmanian Memory of 1834: In Five Scenes (Hobart Town, Tasmania: Walch, 1869);

Grandmamma's Verse Book for Young Australia (Hobart Town, Tasmania: Walch, 1878); republished as *Waratah Rhymes for Young Australia* (London: Vincent Brooks Day, [1891]);

Our Island Home: A Tasmanian Sketch Book (Hobart Town, Tasmania: Walch / London: Ward, 1879);

Tasmanian Friends and Foes, Feathered, Furred, and Finned: A Family Chronicle of Country Life, Natural History, and Veritable Adventure (Hobart Town, Tasmania: Walch / London: Ward, 1880);

Nellie; or, Seeking Goodly Pearls (London: Nisbet, 1882);

Bush Friends in Tasmania: Native Flowers, Fruits and Insects, Drawn from Nature, with Prose Descriptions and Illustrations in Verse (London & New York: Macmillan, [1891]).

Louisa Anne Meredith (née Twamley), also known as Mrs. Charles Meredith, holds an important position in the colonial literature of Australia. As the first Englishwoman to write engagingly for a popular international audience about her travels and life in the new world, Meredith was Australia's first professional female writer. Her firsthand impressions of Australian nature and of colonial family life were disseminated to a sizable public in England and throughout Australia's colonial population. A champion of conservation and animal rights, she also evidences in her work an infectious delight in and respect for animals and plants, as well as an eye for the humorous, practical aspects of domestic life in the harsh colonial landscape. Meredith illustrated her writings with drawings of animals and plants, but she considered herself an author first and an artist second, and as a writer of personal narrative – occasionally transformed into fictional accounts of real experiences – she has had the most impact on literature.

Born on 20 July 1812, Louisa Anne Twamley was the only child of elderly parents. Her father was fifty-five at the time of her birth, and she was

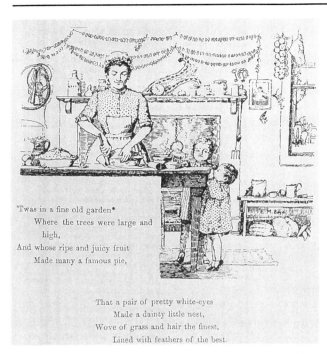

'Twas in a fine old garden*
Where the trees were large and
high,
And whose ripe and juicy fruit
Made many a famous pie,

That a pair of pretty white-eyes
Made a dainty little nest,
Wove of grass and hair the finest,
Lined with feathers of the best.

Page from the first British edition of Meredith's most notable children's book, Waratah Rhymes for Young Australia *(illustration by E. Minnie Boyd)*

later compelled to support herself as a result of her aging father's difficulty in providing for her and her mother. Her ability to handle financial hardships proved useful later when her husband encountered financial difficulties.

Meredith's career divides into two distinct stages. In her native Birmingham, England, her nature writings and artwork were published when she was quite young. The second stage of her career flowered as she took these skills and interests to the exotic world of colonial Australia and became a travel writer, describing the wildlife and challenges that she encountered in the outback, where she gradually came to feel at home.

Meredith showed great early promise as a writer and artist, exhibiting her miniatures while she was still a teenager and publishing her first books before her twenty-sixth birthday. Her first poems and literary critiques were published in the *Birmingham Journal.* In a letter to her uncle, businessman George Meredith, she described herself as having a "restless and enquiring spirit." This maternal uncle had immigrated with his family to Van Diemen's Land (now Tasmania) in 1820, and he invited Louisa to serve as governess to his growing family. She rejected the offer, which would have taken her from where her reputation was growing and where she had the music, art, and stimulation of English society to inspire her.

When her father died in 1834, Meredith supported herself and her aged mother by accepting the job he had held as corn inspector for Birmingham. In the following year her first book, *Poems,* accompanied by her own etchings, was published. Forty of her poems and songs and six plates of flowers and ruins, drawn and etched on copper, comprise the book. Less than a year after *Poems* appeared Meredith published her second book, *The Romance of Nature; or, The Flower-Seasons Illustrated* (1836). In this book she describes flowers blooming as the seasons change and combines poetry and thoughts inspired by flowers with narrative descriptions of her favorite country walks.

Reviewers remarked that a twenty-four-year-old lady publishing her own verses and artwork was an "almost unheard of accomplishment." Her third book, *Flora's Gems; or, The Treasures of the Parterre* (1837), to which she contributed only the poems while artist James Andrews provided the illustrations, was published the following year. Next she published an account of her travel to the Wye Valley in autumn, *An Autumn Ramble by the Wye* (1839), for which various artists provided illustrations. In summary, between 1835 and 1839 she published five books, four of which were primarily floral studies revealing her intense enjoyment of nature's riches.

Meredith again collaborated with artist James Andrews in 1842, publishing *The Parterre; or, Beauties of Flora,* which contained sixteen poems, seven written by Meredith. In addition to her books Meredith was also writing literary critiques, articles, and poems as well as producing miniature portraits. Between 1829 and 1838 she exhibited twenty-six pictures in the galleries of the Royal Birmingham Society of Artists, of which she was a member. Her life was full of potential, and a poem by Leigh Hunt acknowledged her promise. In "Blue Stocking Revels or the Feast of the Violets" Hunt wrote: "Then came young Twamley / Nice sensitive thing / Whose pen and whose pencil give promise like Spring."

Arriving on English soil in 1838 at age twenty-seven, the author's cousin, Charles Meredith, returned to England to pursue a claim on property in Van Diemen's Land. He spent the next year pursuing this claim, seeing England, and renewing his family connections, including that with his cousin Louisa. Their courtship ended with Louisa accepting Charles's proposal. Her marriage would require that she leave Birmingham for a life in the colonies, where Charles was determined to return. She and Charles were married on 18 April 1839 in Birmingham and departed for the colonies in June, leaving behind her elderly mother, other relatives, and friends. The couple planned to return to England within five years.

Meredith's colonial writing commenced with her journey to the new world. Her four-month-long passage to Australia would later be described in her first travel book, *Notes and Sketches of New South Wales, during a Residence in That Colony from 1839 to 1844* (1844), in which Meredith recounted her experiences in a vivid style that captured the imaginations of readers. Published in England, *Notes and Sketches of New South Wales* became one of the most popular books in Murray's Home Colonial Library. The work reveals Meredith's concern for animal welfare and conservation, an increasingly important cause to her, as is evident in her comment on the fate of the kangaroo. "My omitting all allusion to the kangaroo may be deemed an oversight," she writes, "but the reason I do not describe them here is that I did not see one in New South Wales, nor has Mr. Meredith, in all his wandering there, met with more than half a dozen. So effectually is the race being exterminated."

Meredith found herself in untamed rural areas with exotic animals she had never imagined, and her descriptions make her writings vibrant and compelling. Dingoes, for example, flourished around Homebush, the house into which the newlyweds moved, and Meredith listened to their nighttime howling in the surrounding woods. The Merediths had to protect their sheep from the dingoes at night by bringing them into the fold, where they were guarded by a watchman, dogs, and a large fire. To audiences unfamiliar with life in the wild, Meredith's colonial writings provide exciting reading.

Her second colonial book, *My Home in Tasmania, during a Residence of Nine Years* (1852), is also full of observations of colonial life. On an overland trip in 1840 Meredith had enjoyed her first bush barbecue, and in *My Home in Tasmania* she describes in detail how various cuts of kangaroo meat are cooked over a spit. Traveling over sometimes hazardous terrain on the journey, Meredith would leave the carriage and carry her baby, George (born 1 July 1840), over rough spots. On a sandy beach south of Swansea during this trip Meredith and her party rested, using bleached whale vertebrae – relics of the whaling days of the 1820s and 1830s – as seats and footstools.

Cambria, her father-in-law's home, proved a welcome haven in the new world. In *My Home in Tasmania* she lovingly describes its landscape as possessing "native flowering shrubs, mingled with garden flowers half-wild, poppies, stocks, wallflowers,

and bright-eyed marigolds looking merrily up, amidst thickets of the golden wattle and snowy tea-tree; whilst, on the higher ground, huge old gum-trees stand majestically."

Despite Meredith's desire for stability, her husband's pursuit of financial security necessitated regular moves. Yet they did not realize their original plan of returning to England and instead found their lives spent in the colonies, where they gradually came to feel they belonged.

Throughout her life Meredith enjoyed long walks and studied wildlife. She would often take home a new variety of plant, a discovery that she would then sketch and paint. She was aware that her observations held scientific value, and she corresponded with scientists in Europe and Australia in identifying insects, sea plants, and fish. Her brief description of a gum tree in the first volume of *My Home in Tasmania* reveals her eye for detail in observing how this "giant straggling tree that will persist in showing all its twisted elbows, and bare briarean arms, with only tufts of leaves at the fingers' ends, is quite a different affair from a round compact oak or elm, decently apparelled in a proper quantity of foliage."

Meredith had strong opinions about social conditions, and issues regarding the convict population of the colonies found their ways into her writing. In the second volume of *My Home in Tasmania*, for example, she offers her political opinions clearly: "Bad masters and severe dishonest magistrates have devoted more men to live as bushrangers and to die on the scaffold, than any inherent depravity of their victims."

My Home in Tasmania is generally considered her most significant work. An unadorned account of her family's life, the book holds a unique place in Tasmanian colonial history as the first description of life in the colony written by a female permanent resident. Its publication in London in 1852 met with such success that the work was republished a year later in New York as *My Home in Tasmania; or, Nine Years in Australia*. A review of Meredith's literary output raises interesting questions regarding the link between the personal and the literary product. Her preface to *My Home in Tasmania* explains her characteristic use of personal narrative:

> My gossiping *Notes and Sketches of New South Wales* met with a reception so cordial and flattering, and so far beyond my own expectations that a grateful acknowledgment, in the shape of a second series became the natural and inevitable result. . . . I have been induced to adopt a more personal narrative, and to identify ourselves with the simple realities around us . . . because I

Frontispiece by Meredith for her last book

have found from my own feelings in the perusal of works of somewhat similar character that the interest of such unvarnished histories is proportionally enhanced according to the degree of identity preserved by the narrator.

After *My Home in Tasmania* Meredith published *Loved, and Lost! The True Story of a Short Life* (1860), her first book for children. It was written for her son Owen in what Meredith termed "gossip verse" about the life and death of a parakeet that the family had found wounded in the bush and had taken in. In the same year she published *Some of My Bush Friends in Tasmania: Native Flowers, Berries, and Insects, Drawn from Life, Illustrated in Verse, and Briefly Described*. In these she sought to produce meaningful works, not simply lighthearted, humorous narratives of family life or books intended for a child audience. However, she was aware that her works were not regarded with the seriousness she desired. In a 14 February 1892 letter about the reception of *Some of My Bush Friends in Tasmania* she noted retrospectively to Sir Henry Parkes, "I feel very keenly the mischief I have done myself by being an artist. Because my books are illustrated by my own pencil they are reviewed as picture-books chiefly."

In the preface to *Some of My Bush Friends in Tasmania*, her first colonial book to feature colored plates, Meredith notes that her aim is to "supply such illustration and simple description of the most interesting and characteristic of our native flowers as shall, to dwellers in England and other climes, convey a general idea of what we see and gather in our woodland rambles." As a visual artist and writer Meredith sought to integrate her skills in order to communicate as exactly as possible the things she had encountered.

Meredith's position as a pictorial artist was substantial. According to Bernard Smith in *European Visions and the South Pacific 1768–1850* (1960), the four most notable artists in Australia in the early 1840s were George French Angas, Conrad Martens, John Skinner Prout, and Louisa Anne Meredith. In 1862 she won a prize for botanical paintings shown in the Great Exhibition in London, and in 1866 she was the only woman to win a silver medal from the Inter-Colonial Exhibition in Victoria for her work in art and literature.

Her interests extended beyond nature and home life to include technological progress. While she devoted an entire chapter in her next book, *Over the Straits: A Visit to Victoria* (1861), to exposing cruelty to animals, a description of her first view of a telegraph communication reveals her enthusiasm for such technical innovations: "No other of my Melbourne sights so delighted me. Nothing struck me more than the beautiful simplicity of the system altogether. Several messages were sent to Queenscliff, and answered, for our edification." Meredith and her family acquired a small cottage in the township of Swansea, where Meredith had written most of *Over the Straits* in 1855, years before it was published.

By 1862 four editions of *Notes and Sketches of New South Wales;* two editions of *My Home in Tasmania; Some of My Bush Friends in Tasmania; Loved, and Lost!;* and *Over the Straits* had been published in England and received in Tasmania. To this growing oeuvre Meredith added her first novel, *Phoebe's Mother: A Novel* (1869), a melodrama set in Castle Bromwich village, located five miles outside Birmingham. The story of an illegitimate daughter of the miller's wife, it had appeared serially in 1866 under the title *Ebba* in the *Australasian*. Meredith described *Our Island Home: A Tasmanian Sketch Book* (1879) as a companion volume to *Some of My Bush Friends in Tasmania*, with illustrations accompanied by a descriptive text.

Her second and most notable children's book was published in 1878 as *Grandmamma's Verse Book for Young Australia* and later titled *Waratah Rhymes for Young Australia*. Earlier poems and verses available to colonial children featured animals native to England, most of which Australian-born children had never seen. Meredith's book of poems was the first children's book devoted to the animals and birds of the bushland that its young audience knew first-hand. Meredith's desire to provide children with poems about animals that they knew reveals a colonial awareness of the stranglehold that the motherland held in defining what was familiar.

This book was an important example of an Englishwoman's attempt to break free from considering colonial life as second best to living back in England. Meredith acted as her own agent for its publication and went to great lengths to have the book accepted by educational authorities as a literary primer for children in the schools. In 1868 she had named the new house that her family had moved into Malunnah, a Tasmanian aboriginal word for nest, showing her appreciation and support for retaining aboriginal place-names.

Her last major work, a personal narrative loosely turned into fiction, was *Tasmanian Friends and Foes, Feathered, Furred, and Finned: A Family Chronicle of Country Life, Natural History, and Veritable Adventure* (1880). As did her second book for children, it offered text combined with charming depictions of animals and plants. *Tasmanian Friends and Foes* relates the experiences of a fictional family in Tasmania, the Mertons, who are based on members of Meredith's family. Her interest in depicting family life was no doubt inspired by her role not only as a wife but also as a mother to three sons — George, Charles (born 5 April 1844), and Owen (born 6 April 1847).

As with her travel writing, Meredith gives readers of *Tasmanian Friends and Foes* a sense of the challenges that she and her family had faced. For example, her husband, Charles, had tried his hand at farming, but within a few weeks of their arrival at the farm that they had hoped to make into a successful business, days of heavy rain had caused a minor flood. In her narrative Meredith describes the sad aftermath of a major farm flood: swept into a turbulent river, sheep and other farm animals are "rolled onwards to the sea, and the broad sandy beaches near the mouth were strewn for miles with the carcasses washed up in heaps by the tides." Other tests of her protagonists' endurance include encounters with wild outback animals, swarms of insects, dangerous terrain, and intense summer heat.

While living in Port Sorrell, where Charles had taken a post as assistant police magistrate, Mer-

edith gathered experience from real events — such as her husband's participation in searching for four small children who had become lost in the Sassafras Valley — that she would also later incorporate into her fictional narrative of *Tasmanian Friends and Foes*. Similarly, when Meredith had observed Charles's lack of concern for their sons' educations, she added this trait to her husband's fictional alter ego in the book: "Mr. Merton though fond and proud of his boys and heartily desirous of their success did not share his wife's anxious ambition for their mental culture as warmly as she could have desired."

In addition to presenting the fictionalized autobiography of *Tasmanian Friends and Foes,* the novel advocates the protection of animals. In the preface Meredith notes that her purpose for writing is to show "how full of healthy, refining, vivid pleasure is that habit of mind which to ardent, reverent admiration of the Creator's works unites tender care for the comfort and happiness of our dumb friends and companions." Meredith discusses the behavior and traits of various animals, birds, and fish — including the bandicoot; the Tasmanian devil; and "Dumpy," the wombat. The fictional characters discuss cruel, thoughtless people who entertain themselves by feeding coins to emus, an amusement that could kill the animals. One character exclaims, "How horribly wicked!" while another declares, "I'd like to diet such brutes on brass farthings and nothing else for a week."

Meredith's commitment to the humane treatment of animals extended beyond her writings. In 1878 in Hobart she had cofounded the first of the Tasmanian branches of the Society for the Prevention of Cruelty to Animals, and she also once refused to move from the path of a coach until a suffering horse was removed from the carriage team.

In 1882 Meredith published her second novel, *Nellie; or, Seeking Goodly Pearls.* Neither this nor her earlier novel, *Phoebe's Mother,* however, was as successful as her travel writing.

After unsuccessful forays into various careers, Charles Meredith finally achieved some success in politics. While such a career was not financially rewarding, the Merediths valued its power to effect social change. Meredith advanced her environmental interests by urging her husband to introduce protective legislation, and Charles introduced a bill for the protection of the black swan, an animal that had been cruelly treated to obtain its feathers, as Meredith had described in *My Home in Tasmania:*

> The general custom was to take the birds in large quantities in the moulting season, when they are most easily

captured and extremely fat; they were then confined in pens, *without any food,* to linger miserably for a time, till ready to die of starvation, because, whilst they are fat, the down can neither be so well stripped off, nor so effectually prepared.

Charles Meredith died on 2 March 1880 at age sixty-nine, and four years later Louisa Meredith received a government pension for her service to the science, literature, and art of Tasmania that she had rendered through her written and artistic works. Meredith remained indefatigable in old age: at eighty years old, for example, she wrote a critical review of Henrik Ibsen's plays, and she also gave public readings of her work in her later years. Louisa Anne Meredith died on 21 October 1895 in relative poverty.

As a pioneer for female writers in Australia, Meredith demonstrates a changing consciousness of her own identity as a colonial and raises questions about English citizens as they adapt to life in the colonies and come to see themselves not as temporary residents anticipating a return to England but as active participants in the literature and culture of the colonized land. Her oeuvre raises questions about why she has been excluded from most reference works and why it is difficult to locate her works – or even any mention of them.

Her writings document the underrepresented perspective of an Englishwoman, with young children to protect, traveling through hazardous new terrain for which she was not particularly suited or prepared. Meredith's curiosity and delight in the physical world and her appreciation for nature's creations link her to generations of writers who have described travel to new worlds and conveyed to readers the adventures, discouragements, discomforts, and ultimately the thrill of the journies and of what they have found.

Biography:

Vivienne Rae Ellis, *Tigress In Exile: Louisa Anne Meredith* (Sandy Bay, Tasmania: Blubber Head Press, 1979).

References:

Bernard Smith, *European Visions and the South Pacific 1768–1850* (London: Oxford University Press, 1960);

M. Swann, "Mrs. Meredith and Miss Atkinson, Writers and Naturalists," *Royal Australian Historical Society Journal and Proceedings,* 15, part 1 (1929): 1–29;

Karl Rawdon Von Stieglitz, *Six Pioneer Women of Tasmania* (Launceston, Tasmania: Telegraph Printery, 1956).

Florence Nightingale

(12 May 1820 – 13 August 1910)

Bege K. Bowers
Youngstown State University

BOOKS: *The Institution of Kaiserswerth on the Rhine, for the Practical Training of Deaconesses, under the Direction of the Rev. Pastor Fliedner, Embracing the Support and Care of a Hospital, Infant and Industrial Schools, and a Female Penitentiary,* anonymous (London: Inmates of the London Ragged Colonial Training School, 1851);

Letters from Egypt, anonymous (London: Spottiswoode, 1854); abridged as *Letters from Egypt: A Journey on the Nile, 1849–1850,* edited by Anthony Sattin (London: Barrie & Jenkins, 1987; New York: Weidenfeld & Nicolson, 1987);

Female Nurses in Military Hospitals: Presented by Request to the Secretary of State for War (London: Privately printed, 1857); revised and enlarged as *Subsidiary Notes as to the Introduction of Female Nursing into Military Hospitals in Peace and in War: Presented by Request to the Secretary of State for War,* 2 parts, anonymous (London: Harrison, 1858);

Statements Exhibiting the Voluntary Contributions Received by Miss Nightingale for the Use of the British War Hospitals in the East, with the Mode of Their Distribution, in 1854, 1855, 1856 (London: Harrison, 1857);

Notes on Matters Affecting the Health, Efficiency, and Hospital Administration of the British Army, Founded Chiefly on the Experience of the Late War: Presented by Request to the Secretary of State for War (London: Harrison, 1858);

Mortality of the British Army, at Home and Abroad, and during the Russian War, as Compared with the Mortality of the Civil Population in England. Illustrated by Tables and Diagrams, anonymous (London: Harrison, 1858);

Notes on Hospitals: Being Two Papers Read before the National Association for the Promotion of Social Science, Liverpool, in October 1858. With Evidence Given to the Royal Commissioners on the State of the Army in 1857 (London: Parker, 1859; revised and enlarged, London: Longmans, Green, 1863); ap-

Florence Nightingale

pendix revised as *Notes on Different Systems of Nursing* (London: Harrison, 1863);

Notes on Nursing: What It Is and What It Is Not (London: Harrison, [1860]; New York: Appleton, 1860; revised and enlarged, London: Harrison, 1860); abridged and expanded as *Notes on Nursing for the Labouring Classes* (London: Harrison, 1861); abridged and expanded again as *Notes on Nursing* (London: Harrison, 1914);

Suggestions for Thought to the Searchers after Truth among the Artizans of England, anonymous (London: Eyre & Spottiswoode, 1860);

Suggestions for Thought to Searchers after Religious Truth, 2 volumes (numbered 2 and 3), anonymous (London: Eyre & Spottiswoode, 1860);

Notes on Causes of Deterioration of Race, anonymous (N.p.: Privately printed, [1860]);

Sidney Herbert (London: Privately printed, 1861); enlarged as *Army Sanitary Administration, and Its Reform under the Late Lord Herbert* (London: McCorquodale, 1862);

Deaconesses' Work in Syria: Appeal on Behalf of the Kaiserwerth Deaconesses' Orphanage at Beyrout (London: Privately printed, 1862);

Observations on the Evidence Contained in the Stational Reports Submitted to Her by the Royal Commission on the Sanitary State of the Army in India (London: Stanford, 1863);

Proposal for Improved Statistics of Surgical Operations (London: Savill & Edwards, 1863);

Note on the Supposed Protection Afforded against Venereal Disease by Recognizing Prostitution and Putting It under Police Regulation, anonymous (N.p.: Privately printed, [1863]);

Sanitary Statistics of Native Colonial Schools and Hospitals (London: Eyre & Spottiswoode, 1863);

How People May Live and Not Die in India (London: Faithfull, 1863);

Suggestions in Regard to Sanitary Works Required for Improving Indian Stations, Prepared by the Barrack and Hospital Improvement Commission, in Accordance with Letters from the Secretary of State for India in Council, Dated 8th December, 1863 and 20th May, 1864 (London: Eyre & Spottiswoode, 1864);

Death of Pastor Fliedner, of Kaiserswerth (N.p., [1864]);

Suggestions on a System of Nursing for Hospitals in India (London: Eyre & Spottiswoode, 1865);

Note on the Aboriginal Races of Australia (London: Faithfull, 1865);

Suggestions on the Subject of Providing, Training, and Organizing Nurses for the Sick Poor in Workhouse Infirmaries (N.p., [1867]); abridged as *Method of Improving the Nursing Service of Hospitals* (N.p.: Privately printed, [1868]); enlarged as *Suggestions for Improving the Nursing Service of Hospitals and on the Method of Training Nurses for the Sick Poor* (London: Spottiswoode, 1874);

Memorandum on Measures Adopted for Sanitary Improvements in India up to the End of 1867; Together with Abstracts of the Sanitary Reports Hitherto Forwarded from Bengal, Madras, and Bombay (London: Eyre & Spottiswoode, 1868);

Introductory Notes on Lying-in Institutions. Together with a Proposal for Organising an Institution for Training Midwives and Midwifery Nurses (London: Longmans, Green, 1871);

Address from Miss Nightingale to the Probationer-Nurses in the "Nightingale Fund" School, at St. Thomas's Hospital, and the Nurses Who Were Formerly Trained There (London: Privately printed, 1872);

Notes on the New St. Thomas's Hospital ([London, 1873]);

Life or Death in India: A Paper Read at the Meeting of the National Association for the Promotion of Social Science, Norwich, 1873. With an Appendix on Life or Death by Irrigation (London: Spottiswoode, 1874);

Metropolitan and National Nursing Association for Providing Trained Nurses for the Sick Poor: On Trained Nursing for the Sick Poor (London: Cull, 1876); republished as *On Trained Nursing for the Sick Poor* (London: Spottiswoode, 1881);

In Remembrance of John Gerry, Who Fell Asleep in Jesus, at Lea Hurst, July 17, 1877; Aged 22 Years (N.p.: Privately printed, [1877]);

Memorandum for Probationers as to Finger Poisoning (N.p., 1878);

[Letter to] The Joint Secretaries of the Bombay Presidency Association, and to the Joint Secretaries of the Poona Sarvajanik Sabha (London: Privately printed, 1887);

[Letter to] The Joint Secretaries of the Bombay Presidency Association, and to the Joint Secretaries of the Poona Sarvajanik Sabha (London: Privately printed, 1889);

[Letter to] The Joint Secretaries of the Bombay Presidency Association, and to the Joint Secretaries of the Poona Sarvajanik Sabha (London: Spottiswoode, 1891);

Health and Local Government (Aylesbury: Pulton, [1894]);

Health Teaching in Towns and Villages: Rural Hygiene (London: Spottiswoode, 1894);

Village Sanitation in India (London: Spottiswoode, 1894);

A Letter from Florence Nightingale about the Victorian Order of Nurses in Canada (London, 1898).

Collections and Editions: *Florence Nightingale to Her Nurses: A Selection from Miss Nightingale's Addresses to Probationers and Nurses of the Nightingale School at St. Thomas's Hospital,* edited by Rosalind Nash (London: Macmillan, 1914);

Selected Writings of Florence Nightingale, edited by Lucy Ridgely Seymer (New York: Macmillan, 1954);

Florence Nightingale in Rome: Letters Written by Florence Nightingale in Rome in the Winter of 1847–1848, edited by Mary Keele (Philadelphia: American Philosophical Society, 1981).

OTHER: "Hospital Statistics and Plans," in *Transactions of the National Association for the Promotion of Social Science, 1861,* edited by George W. Hastings (London: Parker, 1862), pp. 554–560;

Organization of Nursing: An Account of the Liverpool Nurses' Training School, Its Foundations, Progress, and Operation in Hospital, District, and Private Nursing. By a Member of the Committee of the Home and Training School, introduction by Nightingale (Liverpool: Holden / London: Longman, Green, Reade & Dyer, 1865);

Report on Measures Adopted for Sanitary Improvements in India during the Year 1868 and up to the Month of June 1869; Together with Abstracts of Sanitary Reports for 1867 Forwarded from Bengal, Madras, and Bombay, introductory memorandum by Nightingale (London: Eyre & Spottiswoode, 1869);

[Jane Ellice Hopkins], *Work in Brighton; or, Woman's Mission to Women,* preface by Nightingale (London: Hatchards, 1877);

The Nurse's Shipwreck: From Nurse Wilson's, Nurse Styring's, Nurse Cross's and Nurse Webb's Accounts of the Shipwreck on Their Voyage Home from Canada on Duty, edited by Nightingale (London: Privately printed, 1878);

William Rathbone, *Sketch of the History and Progress of District Nursing, from Its Commencement in 1859 to the Present Date,* introduction by Nightingale (London: Macmillan, 1890);

Dayaram Gidumal, *Behramji M. Malabari: A Biographical Sketch,* introduction by Nightingale (London: Unwin, 1892);

"Sick-Nursing and Health-Nursing," in *Woman's Mission: A Series of Congress Papers on the Philanthropic Work of Women by Eminent Writers,* edited by Baroness Angela Burdett-Coutts (London: Sampson Low, Marston, 1893), pp. 184–205;

"A Few Lines to Workhouse Nurses," in *Agnes Jones; or, She Hath Done What She Could,* by Julia Anne Elizabeth Roundell (London: Bickers, 1896), pp. 53–57;

"Letter to the Lord Provost of Edinburgh," in *Edinburgh and East of Scotland Hospital for South Africa,* edited by A. A. Gordon (Edinburgh: Blackwood, 1900), p. 26;

"Message to the Crimean Veterans," in *The Crimean and Indian Mutiny Veterans' Association, Bristol* (Bristol: Privately printed, 1905), p. 47;

"Curriculum Vitae," in *Florence Nightingale Curriculum Vitae. With Informations* [sic] *about Florence Nightingale and Kaiserswerth,* edited by Anna Sticker (Düsseldorf-Kaiserswerth: Verlag der Diakonissenanstalt, 1957), pp. 5–9.

SELECTED PERIODICAL PUBLICATIONS – UNCOLLECTED: "Sites and Construction of Hospitals," *Builder,* 16 (28 August 1858): 577–578; "Construction of Hospitals: The Ground Plan," *Builder,* 16 (11 September 1858): 609–610; "Hospital Construction – Wards," *Builder,* 16 (25 September 1858): 641–643; "Una and the Lion" *Good Words* (June 1868): 360–366; "A Note on Pauperism," *Fraser's Magazine,* new series 79 (March 1869): 281–290; "On Indian Sanitation," *Transactions of the Bengal Social Science Association,* 4 (1870): 1–9; "A 'Note' of Interrogation," *Fraser's Magazine,* new series 87 (May 1873): 567–577; "A Sub-'Note of Interrogation': What Will Be Our Religion in 1999?," *Fraser's Magazine,* new series 87 (July 1873): 25–36; "Who Is the Savage?," *Social Notes,* 1 (11 May 1878): 145–147; "The United Empire and the Indian Peasant," *Journal of the National Indian Association: In Aid of Social Progress in India,* 90 (June 1878): 232–245; "A Water Arrival in India," *Good Words* (July 1878): 493–496; "The People of India," *Nineteenth Century,* 4 (August 1878): 193–221; "A Missionary Health Officer in India," *Good Words* (July 1879): 492–496; (August 1879): 565–571; (September 1879): 635–640; "Hints and Suggestions on Thrift," *Thrift: A Monthly Journal of Social Progress and Reform,* 1 (January 1882): 4; "The Dumb Shall Speak, and the Deaf Shall Hear; or, the Ryot, the Zemindar, and the Government," *Journal of the East India Association,* 15 (July 1883): 163–238; "Our Indian Stewardship," *Nineteenth Century,* 14 (August 1883): 329–338; "The Bengal Tenancy Bill," *Contemporary Review,* 44 (October 1883): 587–602; "Sanitation in India," *Journal of the Public Health Society [of Calcutta],* 4 (October 1888): 63–65; "The Reform of Sick Nursing and the Late Mrs. Wardroper," *British Medical Journal,* 2 (31 December 1892): 1448; "Health Lectures for Indian Villages," *India,* new series 4, 10 (October 1893): 305–306;

"Health Missioners for Rural India," *India,* new series 7, 12 (December 1896): 359–360.

Florence Nightingale "was not simply the lady with the lamp," wrote A. G. Gardiner in 1914; "she was the lady with the brain and the tyrannic will." The self-effacing figure of popular myth – the "ministering angel" who appeared from nowhere, "moved like a benediction through the horrors of the hospitals of Scutari," and returned home to live the life of an invalid – contrasts sharply with reality. By the time she sailed for Scutari in 1854, Nightingale had made several trips to Europe, traveled up the Nile, established political and literary contacts, and published her first pamphlet. Indeed, she was a prodigious writer who penned more than two hundred books, pamphlets, and reports; hundreds of private "notes"; and some twelve thousand letters, both personal and official, during her lifetime. Although she wrote frequently about faraway places, her days as a traveler ended when her public career began. Jane Robinson's *Wayward Women: A Guide to Women Travellers* (1990) credits Nightingale with just two collections of travel writing: *Letters from Egypt* (1854), composed in 1849–1850 and privately printed the year that Nightingale left for the Crimea, and *Florence Nightingale in Rome: Letters Written by Florence Nightingale in Rome in the Winter of 1847–1848* (1981), a compilation "gleaned from family letters and published over seventy years after their writer's death."

Named for the Italian city that her parents were visiting at the time of her birth, Nightingale was born 12 May 1820 in Florence, the younger daughter of William Edward Nightingale, known as WEN, and Frances Smith Nightingale. (WEN, born William Edward Shore, had assumed the name Nightingale upon inheriting property from a great-uncle in 1815.) The Nightingales customarily spent summers at Lea Hurst, their family estate in Derbyshire, and winters at Embley Park, Hampshire. A wealthy landowner, WEN chose to educate Florence and her sister, Parthenope, at home, where he taught them modern languages, history, philosophy, and the classics and hired a governess to teach them music and art. Florence, the more serious student, prospered under her father's tutelage and begged to study math as well – a plea her parents denied until, at age nineteen, she surreptitiously took up the study with an aunt. Uninspired by what she referred to as drawing-room "trifles" yet driven by a desire to please, young Florence found it increasingly difficult to pursue her personal interests while trying to comply with society's prescriptions for acceptable feminine behavior.

The most significant event in Nightingale's early years, at least by her own account, occurred on 7 February 1837, when the sixteen-year-old who would become the founder of modern nursing experienced the first of at least four "calls" from God. Though she wrote in her personal notes that God had "spoken" and "called [her] to His service," the nature of the service remained unclear until the mid 1840s, and her mission went unrealized for nearly fifteen years – a period during which she made three trips abroad and wrote hundreds of letters, many of which were inspired by her travels.

The first trip, an extended grand tour that completed her formal education, lasted from 8 September 1837 till 6 April 1839. It took Nightingale and her family to France and Italy and provided a respite from some of the discontent that had plagued her at home. Though she produced no published account of the tour, her letters to friends and relatives and her copious notes and diaries convey what she described as the "flavour of [her] life abroad." It is clear from these unpublished materials, writes biographer Edward Cook, "that she entered heartily, and with a wider range of interest than some English travellers show, into the life of foreign society." She prepared a detailed itinerary; showed a keen interest in scenery and art; compiled statistics on the laws, social conditions, and institutions of European cities; developed an "ardent sympathy with the cause of Italian freedom"; and enjoyed the best and most learned society.

Paris, in particular, presented two opportunities that would help shape her life: visits to hospitals and nursing sisterhoods and a growing friendship with the unconventional Mary Clarke, or "Clarkey," in whose circle Nightingale met such distinguished intellectuals as Madame Jeanne-Françoise-Julie-Adélaïde Récamier, François-Auguste-René de Chateaubriand, the medievalist Claude Fauriel, and Julius Mohl, one of the leading orientalists in Europe. According to Cook, the diaries, in which Nightingale mingles politics and social commentary "with artistic and architectural notes," reveal her passion for opera and an assortment of interests unusually broad for a girl of eighteen. In public she exuded charm and exuberance, convincing everyone, including her mother, that the trip had transformed the difficult daughter into a brilliant social success. However, Nightingale's personal notes suggest that while she was drawn to the life she had led in Europe, she continued to wrestle with God's call. The "desire to shine in society," she had written before

First page from the manuscript for Nightingale's "Curriculum Vitae," a summary of her life prior to her arrival in 1851 at the Kaiserswerth Institute for the Training of Protestant Deaconesses (Fliedner archives, Kaiserswerth)

leaving Paris, was a "temptation" that she felt she must endeavor to overcome.

The social transformation that the family had hoped for thus proved illusory and short-lived. After the family returned to England, Nightingale "alternated," as Martha Vicinus and Bea Nergaard report, "between exhilarating social success and burdensome doubts about what she ought to feel, what she ought to do, and where her destiny lay." When her cousin Henry Nicholson proposed marriage in 1843, she turned him down and vowed never to marry. Not until 1844, seven years after her initial call from God, did she decide that her future lay in nursing – a decision that her family adamantly but understandably opposed when she revealed her plans in December 1845. Hospitals in the 1840s were places of squalor. Nurses were too often promiscuous, drunk, and disorderly, and no career was considered proper for a woman of the upper class. The family prevailed, and Nightingale put her plans on hold. But while outwardly she tried to conform to her family's wishes, her despair deepened, and by 1847 she suffered a physical and emotional collapse.

In this context an opportunity for a second trip abroad followed when family friends Charles and Selina Bracebridge asked Nightingale to accompany them to Rome, a journey destined to strengthen her sense of vocation, not to "divert her from it" as her parents and sister had hoped. Instantly the spirits of the twenty-seven-year-old Nightingale revived, as she reimmersed herself in the political, intellectual, and spiritual life of Rome.

The trip, which lasted from 27 October 1847 through early summer 1848, inspired some of Nightingale's most lively letters. Candid, humorous, and even gossipy, they provide an intimate and uncensored account of her life during this period. "The last thing Miss Nightingale had in mind was their publication," writes Mary Keele, editor of *Florence Nightingale in Rome,* the only published edition of the letters. Their content is personal, their style colloquial. But along with hand-drawn sketches and maps, records of personal expenses, details of daily hygiene, irreverent vignettes depicting travel on public conveyances, and "improper" and "impudent" tales that she begs her family not to repeat, the letters reveal, in Selina Bracebridge's words, a "keen perception . . . of every thing that is great and beautiful and her extraordinary power of apprehending what are the conceptions of other minds."

Not a sophisticated art critic, Nightingale acknowledges her "deficiency in art," confesses disappointment in Raphael's *Transformation* because there

is "such a bustle, such a fuz-buz in the picture," and "hate[s] a Museum with a mortal and undying hatred," but she finds personal, spiritual meaning in the art and architecture of Rome. And since her family members, the audience for most of the letters, were familiar with all these things, she wrote in a mode less descriptive than philosophical. In fact, the letters – published ultimately by the American Philosophical Association – express the germs of religious and philosophical thought that Nightingale develops in later works: about the differences between spirit and intellect; the personal nature of faith; the role of historical "accident" in the birth and development of religions; the "unity" of pagan, Jewish, and Christian expression; and the inability of any one church or religion to capture religious truth.

Overall the letters from Rome reflect the hopes and youthful idealism of a woman alive to the glories of Saint Peter's Basilica and the Sistine Chapel, to the religious and political excitement surrounding the election of a new pope, to the fight for political freedom unfolding in the streets around her. With the Bracebridges and other travelers such as Sidney and Elizabeth Herbert, Nightingale enjoyed Italian society – at first reluctantly and then with a "convert's enthusiasm." She picked up souvenirs, including pieces of a child's skeleton in a recently opened tomb; she visited hospitals, convents, and orphanages; and she strengthened her resolve to serve God. She was sorry when the trip ended, curtailed by potential dangers from political revolutions that escalated in Italy and France on the journey home.

After the excitement of life abroad, Nightingale found it difficult to return to daily routine. Society again grew distasteful, and the breach with her family deepened as her mission remained unfulfilled. How could she serve God in luxury, she wondered, "when there is so much misery among the poor"? How could she enjoy society, when she "hated God to hear her laugh"? Such remarks in the letters, diaries, and notebooks from 1848 to 1849 reflect, in Cook's words, the "morbidness . . . of a mind at war with its surroundings." Yet they also reflect the anxiety of a mind at war with itself. The more Nightingale resolved to quit dreaming, the more she dreamed, and when Richard Monckton Milnes, the "man [she] adored," proposed marriage in summer 1849, she agonized before deciding, ultimately, that as tempting as his offer might be to what she characterized as her intellectual and passionate nature, marriage – or living life through another – could never satisfy her more active, moral nature: "voluntarily to put it out of my power . . . to seize the chance of forming for myself a true and rich life would seem to me like suicide."

In the midst of these struggles with self, family, and destiny, Nightingale once again accepted when the Bracebridges offered her an opportunity to travel – and a means to placate her family. Her sister, Parthenope, Cook reports, "was delighted" that Florence would be going away again; the previous "expedition to Rome had not done what was hoped, but here was a second chance." This time Nightingale was to accompany her friends to Egypt, Greece, and Germany, and she wrote "forlornly" after leaving home in autumn 1849, "I hope I shall come back to be more of a comfort to you than I have been." Her account of the Egyptian journey, which lasted from November 1849 through the first week of April 1850, appears in *Letters from Egypt,* the collection of her letters home that Parthenope edited and printed for private circulation in 1854. Florence, though allegedly "not pleased" at the prospect of having her letters printed, as Cook reports, "acquiesced, and corrected the proofs."

Chronologically arranged, *Letters from Egypt* provides an entertaining and sometimes humorous account of midcentury travel along the Nile River, especially if one chose – as Nightingale and the Bracebridges did – to float up and down the river in a large wind-driven *dahabieh* rather than to take the trip in one of the faster (and later more popular) steamers. "I would not go in a steamer on the Nile," Nightingale asserts in one of the letters, "if I were never to see the Nile without it." Though the party traveled in as much luxury as their money and pretty two-cabin "home" could provide, the travelers suffered mishaps and hardships, many of which Nightingale recounts with mock-epic humor. "With regard to beasts," she notes at one point, "you must renounce all expeditions, all intercourse with your fellow creatures, if you have set it down as a first principle to keep free from them; it is impossible." Nevertheless, the indomitable Nightingale manages to "slay" an army of mosquitoes "in a single combat" and to rid the boat of rats "so fierce and bold, that I am obliged to get up at night to defend my dear boots."

In addition to comic mishaps the letters recount occasional tales of true danger, including a life-threatening storm that merely soaks Nightingale and her party but wrecks four or five other boats and kills at least twenty people. As a rule, however, Nightingale (or perhaps at times Parthenope, her editor) takes pains to reassure readers that most Egyptian dangers are only perceived, not real. Pro-

tected by mounted men and a janissary, or running footman, when they are off the boat, the party members seldom have much to fear, and Nightingale – affectionately dubbed the "wild ass of the wilderness" because she longs to be wandering about the desert by herself – generally finds depending on an escort "tiresome beyond what a European can conceive."

Yet these letters, which Robinson describes as among the "most refreshing travel accounts of the period," also possess a dark side that says as much about nineteenth-century prejudices – and about Nightingale's mood at these times – as about the sights and people of Egypt. Doing her best to enter into the spirit of the journey, Nightingale had consulted travel guides before she set out for Egypt "laden with learned books" such as John Gardner Wilkinson's *Modern Egypt and Thebes* (1843) and Harriet Martineau's *Eastern Life, Present and Past* (1848). But none of these books, she argues in one letter, prepares a traveler for the "debasement and misery" of African life: the plunder, indecorum, and lack of respect for the relics of an ancient civilization; the "base and dirty" cities; and the people living in huts, "dirty beyond description."

Unlike Martineau, whom Lucie Duff Gordon criticized for treating people as "part of the scenery," and unlike Gordon, who in her own *Letters from Egypt, 1863–65* (1865) would later attempt to present sympathetic accounts of indigenous people as individuals, Nightingale dwells on what she considers the evils of a savage and inferior race. Throughout the letters she denigrates one group after another, referring to the Arabs as "an intermediate race . . . between the monkey and the man"; characterizing half-clothed, hut-dwelling villagers as evil, degraded creatures; and worse. The letters of late December and early January strike a particularly low tone, as in the following passage dated 2 January 1850:

> I never before saw any of my fellow creatures degraded . . . , but I longed to have intercourse with them, to stay with them, and make plans for them; but here, one gathered one's clothes about one, and felt as if one had trodden in a nest of reptiles. . . . The thieves in London, the ragged scholars in Edinburgh, are still human beings; but the horror which the misery of Egypt excites cannot be expressed, for these are beasts.

To a large extent, of course, such passages illustrate the "distancing" and "othering" techniques that Sara Mills and others find in much colonial discourse. At the same time, however, the pervasively negative tone of Nightingale's *Letters from*

THE SOLDIER'S FRIEND

I have just heard such a pretty account from a soldier, describing the comfort it was to see even Florence pass, she would speak to one and another, and and smile to many more, but she couldn't do it to all, you know, for we lay there by hundreds, but we could kiss her shadow as it fell and lay our heads on the pillow again content!

WRITTEN BY   COMPOSED BY
C. F. RATHURST

*Broadsheet celebrating Nightingale's return to England following
the Crimean War (Wellcome Library)*

Egypt surely reflects the intensity of the personal crisis that tormented her throughout most of the trip. She alludes to the crisis, to her sense of failure and unfulfilled aspirations, in sections of a letter from Memphis dated 18 March 1850: "I do not know any man in all history with whom I sympathise so much as with Moses – his romantic devotion – his disappointments – his aspirations, so much higher than anything he was able to accomplish, always striving to give the Hebrews a religion they could not understand."

Repeatedly, too, she refers to such sights as the great Sphinx, the catacombs, and the Pyramids as "ugly," "repulsive," and "abominable." Then she apologizes for her "stupid" writing and reassures her family that she is grateful for the trip. Though her letters only allude to the crisis, however, what Cecil Woodham-Smith calls her "secret agonies" figure prominently in the private notebook that she kept during the same period, "in writing which wavers and becomes all but indecipherable." Woodham-Smith adds that in a "scribbled" 26 January 1850 entry Nightingale wrote of feeling "Disappointed with *myself* and the effect of Egypt on me" (emphasis added), and she noted that she had "spoiled" the trip with "dreaming"; "Rome was better."

From Egypt the Bracebridges and a still-despondent Nightingale went on to Greece and Germany, but as Cook reports, "She could not find satisfaction in the interests of foreign travel. She was tortured by unsatisfied longings which could find outlet only in a world of dreams." Thoroughly distraught, she wrote in her notebook on 7 July 1850 that these dreams were "rapidly approaching . . . madness." The turning point came in Berlin, where she visited hospitals and other benevolent institutions and "felt how rich" life could be. By the time she reached Kaiserswerth on 31 July, she was able to take advantage of what would prove to be one of the most significant events of the journey: a two-week visit to the Institute for the Training of Protestant Deaconesses, where she observed training in nursing and childcare and the day-to-day operation of the three facilities associated with the institute: a hospital, a penitentiary, and an orphanage. Her spirits restored, she left Kaiserswerth on 13 August, "feeling so brave as if nothing could ever vex me again." Within a week she completed her first pamphlet, *The Institution of Kaiserswerth on the Rhine, for the Practical Training of Deaconesses, under the Direction of the Rev. Pastor Fliedner, Embracing the Support and Care of a Hospital, Infant and Industrial Schools, and a Female Penitentiary* (1851), which she published anonymously soon after her return to England.

Though Nightingale later toured hospitals in Scotland and Ireland and revisited Kaiserswerth, the trip to Egypt, Greece, and Germany was her last extended trip as a private citizen. In May 1854 Charles Dickens, editor of *Household Words,* quoted an unpublished account of religious persecution written by "an English Protestant lady who saw and conversed with the Mother Makrena in February 1848 . . . at Rome." The unidentified lady was Florence Nightingale; the account was one of her letters from Rome. How soon this unknown traveler would lose her anonymity Dickens could not have known, but Nightingale left for the Crimea in October 1854, and as Anthony Sattin remarks in his introduction to *Letters from Egypt: A Journey on the Nile, 1849–1850* (1987), "the rest is history and legend."

Nightingale's published and unpublished travel writings, though interesting in their own right, thus assume special significance as part of the history that preceded the legend. As Nightingale traveled, she made firsthand studies of nursing and hospital administration. She formed attitudes that would shape scores of influential pamphlets, reports, and books, including her most widely known work in the nineteenth century – *Notes on Nursing: What It Is and What It Is Not* (1860) – as well as "Cassandra," a much-reprinted part of the second volume of *Suggestions for Thought to Searchers after Religious Truth* (1860), which is better known today. She also made lifelong friends and political contacts, including fellow travelers Charles and Selina Bracebridge, who would accompany her to Scutari, and Sidney Herbert, who, as secretary at war, would later dispatch her there. No account of this formative period in her personal and professional development would be complete without a look at Nightingale's travel writings, a complex record of the tortured but instrumental years during which the figure who would become the "lady with the lamp" struggled to find and fulfill her vocation.

Letters:

Florence Nightingale's Indian Letters: A Glimpse into the Agitation for Tenancy Reform, Bengal, 1878–82, edited by Priyaranjan Sen (Calcutta: Mihir Kumar Sen, 1937);

"I Have Done My Duty": Florence Nightingale in the Crimean War, 1854–56, edited by Sue M. Goldie (Manchester: Manchester University Press / Iowa City: University of Iowa Press, 1987);

Ever Yours, Florence Nightingale: Selected Letters, edited by Martha Vicinus and Bea Nergaard (Cambridge, Mass.: Harvard University Press, 1990).

Bibliographies:

Edward Cook, "List of Printed Writings, Whether Published or Privately Circulated, by Miss Nightingale, Chronologically Arranged," Appendix A in his *The Life of Florence Nightingale* (New York: Macmillan, 1942), pp. 437–458;

Catalog of the Florence Nightingale Collection (New York: Department of Nursing, Faculty of Medicine, Columbia University/Presbyterian Hospital, School of Nursing, 1956);

W. J. Bishop and Sue Goldie, *A Bio-Bibliography of Florence Nightingale* (London: Dawsons, 1962);

Lois A. Monteiro and Irene S. Palmer, *Letters of Florence Nightingale in the History of Nursing Archive, Special Collections, Boston University Libraries* (Boston: Boston University Mugar Memorial Library, 1974);

Goldie, *A Calendar of the Letters of Florence Nightingale* (Oxford: Oxford Microform Publications, 1983);

Bonnie Bullough, Vern Bullough, and Lilli Sentz, "Nightingale Bibliography," in *Florence Nightingale and Her Era: A Collection of New Scholarship,* edited by Vern Bullough, Bonnie Bullough, and Marietta P. Stanton (New York & London: Garland, 1990), pp. 324–365;

Jane Robinson, *Wayward Women: A Guide to Women Travellers* (New York & Oxford: Oxford University Press, 1990).

Biographies:

Sarah A. Tooley, *The Life of Florence Nightingale* (London: Cassell, 1910);

Edward Cook, *The Life of Florence Nightingale* (2 volumes, London: Macmillan, 1913; New York: Macmillan, 1942);

Annie Matheson, *Florence Nightingale: A Biography* (London & New York: Nelson, [1913]);

Maude E. Seymour Abbott, *Florence Nightingale as Seen in Her Portraits, with a Sketch of Her Life, and an Account of Her Relation to the Origin of the Red Cross Society* (Montreal: McGill University, [1916?]);

Lytton Strachey, *Eminent Victorians: Cardinal Manning, Florence Nightingale, Dr. Arnold, General Gordon* (London: Chatto & Windus / New York: Putnam, 1918);

Mary Raymond Shipman Andrews, *A Lost Commander: Florence Nightingale* (Garden City, N.Y.: Doubleday, 1929);

I. B. O'Malley, *Florence Nightingale: A Study of Her Life down to the End of the Crimean War* (London: Butterworth, 1931);

Dorothy Erskine Sheepshanks Muir, *Florence Nightingale* (London: Blackie, [1946]);

Cecil Woodham-Smith, *Florence Nightingale, 1820–1910* (Edinburgh: Constable, 1950; New York: McGraw-Hill, [1951]);

Elspeth Joscelin Grant Huxley, *Florence Nightingale* (New York: Putnam / London: Weidenfeld & Nicolson, 1975).

References:

Monica Baly, *Florence Nightingale and the Nursing Legacy* (London & Canberra: Croom Helm, 1982);

Nancy Boyd, *Three Victorian Women Who Changed Their World: Josephine Butler, Octavia Hill, Florence Nightingale* (New York: Oxford University Press / London: Macmillan, 1982);

Vern Bullough, Bonnie Bullough, and Marietta P. Stanton, eds., *Florence Nightingale and Her Era: A Collection of New Scholarship* (New York & London: Garland, 1990);

Michael D. Calabria and Janet A. Macrae, introduction to *Suggestions for Thought by Florence Nightingale: Selections and Commentaries,* edited by Calabria and Macrae (Philadelphia: University of Pennsylvania Press, 1994), pp. ix–xl;

Charles Dickens, "The True Story of the Nuns of Minsk," *Household Words,* 216 (13 May 1854): 290–295;

Lucie Duff Gordon, *Letters from Egypt, 1862–1869,* edited by Gordon Waterfield (New York & Washington: Praeger, 1969);

A. G. Gardiner, "Florence Nightingale," in his *Prophets, Priests, & Kings* (London: Dent / New York: Dutton, 1914), pp. 136–172;

Raymond G. Herbert, ed., *Florence Nightingale: Saint, Reformer or Rebel?* (Malabar, Fla.: Krieger, 1981);

Mary Keele, introduction to *Florence Nightingale in Rome: Letters Written by Florence Nightingale in Rome in the Winter of 1847–1848,* edited by Keele (Philadelphia: American Philosophical Society, 1981), pp. xv–xviii;

Harriet Martineau, *England and Her Soldiers* (London: Smith, Elder, 1859);

Sara Mills, *Discourses of Difference: An Analysis of Women's Travel Writing and Colonialism* (London & New York: Routledge, 1991);

George W. Pickering, *Creative Malady: Illness in the Lives and Minds of Charles Darwin, Florence Nightingale, [et al.]* (London: Allen & Unwin / New York: Oxford University Press, 1974);

Mary Poovey, introduction to *"Cassandra" and Other Selections from* Suggestions for Thought, edited by Poovey (New York: New York University Press, 1992), pp. vii–xxix;

Anthony Sattin, introduction to *Letters from Egypt: A Journey on the Nile, 1849–1850,* edited by Sattin (London: Barrie & Jenkins / New York: Weidenfeld & Nicolson, 1987), pp. 11–19;

Elaine Showalter, "Florence Nightingale's Feminist Complaint: Women, Religion, and *Suggestions for Thought,*" *Signs: A Journal of Women in Culture and Society,* 6 (Spring 1981): 395–412;

F. B. Smith, *Florence Nightingale: Reputation and Power* (London & Canberra: Croom Helm, 1982);

Myra Stark, introduction to *"Cassandra": An Essay by Florence Nightingale,* edited by Stark ([New York]: Feminist Press, 1979), pp. 1–23.

Papers:

Nightingale materials are housed in libraries, record offices, hospitals, and private collections throughout the world. The British Library holds the largest collection of letters, diaries, and manuscripts, with additional materials in the Greater London Record Office (originally in the St. Thomas's Hospital Archives). Other repositories include the Boston University Library and the Woodward Biomedical Library, University of British Columbia, among others. The Wellcome Institute for the History of Medicine, London, houses photocopies of letters from private collections.

Laurence Oliphant

(1829 – 23 December 1888)

John C. Hawley
Santa Clara University

See also the Oliphant entry in *DLB 18: Victorian Novelists After 1885.*

BOOKS: *A Journey to Katmandu (the Capital of Nepaul) with the Camp of Jung Bahadoor, Including a Sketch of the Nepaulese Ambassador at Home* (London: Murray, 1852; New York: Appleton, 1852);

The Russian Shores of the Black Sea in the Autumn of 1852, with a Voyage down the Volga, and a Tour through the Country of the Don Cossacks (Edinburgh & London: Blackwood, 1853; revised and enlarged edition, Edinburgh: Blackwood, 1853; New York: Redfield, 1854);

Minnesota and the Far West (Edinburgh & London: Blackwood, 1855);

The Coming Campaign (Edinburgh & London: Blackwood, 1855); republished as *The Trans-Caucasian Provinces the Proper Field of Operation for a Christian Army: Being a Second Edition of "The Coming Campaign"* (Edinburgh & London: Blackwood, 1856);

The Trans-Causasian Campaign of the Turkish Army under Omar Pasha: A Personal Narrative (Edinburgh & London: Blackwood, 1856);

Notes of a Voyage up the Yang-tse-keang, from Wosung to Han-kow (London, 1859);

Narrative of the Earl of Elgin's Mission to China and Japan in the Years 1857, '58, '59 (2 volumes, Edinburgh & London: Blackwood, 1859; 1 volume, New York: Harper, 1860);

Patriots and Filibusters; or, Incidents of Political and Exploratory Travel (Edinburgh & London: Blackwood, 1860);

Universal Suffrage and Napoleon the Third (Edinburgh & London: Blackwood, 1860);

On the Present State of Political Parties in America (Edinburgh & London: Blackwood, 1866);

Piccadilly: A Fragment of Contemporary Biography (Edinburgh & London: Blackwood, 1870; New York: Harper, 1884);

The Tender Recollections of Irene Macgillicuddy (New York: Harper, 1878);

Laurence Oliphant

The Land of Gilead, with Excursions in the Lebanon (Edinburgh & London: Blackwood, 1880; New York, Appleton, 1881);

The Land of Khemi: Up and down the Middle Nile (Edinburgh & London: Blackwood, 1882);

Traits and Travesties, Social and Political (Edinburgh & London: Blackwood, 1882);

Altiora Peto, 2 volumes (Edinburgh: Blackwood, 1883); republished as *Altiora Peto: A Novel* (New York: Harper, 1883);

Sympneumata; or, Evolutionary Forces Now Active in Man (Edinburgh & London: Blackwood, 1885);

Masollam; a Problem of the Period: A Novel, 3 volumes (Edinburgh & London: Blackwood, 1886);

Haifa: or, Life in Modern Palestine (London: Blackwood, 1887; New York: Harper, 1887);

Episodes in a Life of Adventure; or, Moss from a Rolling Stone (Edinburgh & London: Blackwood, 1887; New York: Harper, 1887);

Fashionable Philosophy, and Other Sketches (Edinburgh & London: Blackwood, 1887);

Scientific Religion; or, Higher Possibilities of Life and Practice through the Operation of Natural Forces (Edinburgh & London: Blackwood, 1888; Buffalo, N.Y.: Wenborne, 1889).

OTHER: "A Trip to the North-East of Lake Tiberias, in Jaulan," in *Across the Jordan: Being an Exploration and Survey of Part of Hauran and Jaulan, with Additions by Laurence Oliphant and Guy Le Strange,* by Gottlieb Schumacher, Oliphant, and Guy Le Strange (London: Bentley, 1885; New York: Scribner & Welford, 1886).

SELECTED PERIODICAL PUBLICATIONS –
UNCOLLECTED: "A Sporting Settler in Ceylon," *Blackwood's Magazine,* 75 (February 1854): 226–242;

"The Eastern Shores of the Black Sea," *Blackwood's Magazine,* 78 (November 1855): 521–532;

"Switzerland and French Annexation," *Blackwood's Magazine,* 87 (May 1860): 635–650;

"Campaigning in China," *Cornhill Magazine,* 1 (May 1860): 537–548;

"Captain Speke's Welcome," *Blackwood's Magazine,* 94 (August 1863): 264–266;

"American Diplomacy in the East," *Blackwood's Magazine,* 122 (October 1877): 466–476;

"American Facts and Gladstone Fallacies," *Blackwood's Magazine,* 124 (November 1878): 628–640;

"Turkish Facts and British Fallacies," *Fortnightly Review,* 33 (February 1880): 161–176;

"Backsheesh," *Macmillan's Magazine,* 41 (April 1880): 484–495;

"The Great African Mystery," *Blackwood's Magazine,* 132 (July 1882): 1–17;

"The Jew and the Eastern Question," *Nineteenth Century,* 12 (August 1882): 242–255;

"Our Occupation of Egypt," *Blackwood's Magazine,* 133 (June 1883): 830–838.

Laurence Oliphant fascinated his contemporaries, and with good reason. Whereas most of his readers lived highly domesticated, practical lives peppered with an occasional vacation on the British seashore, Oliphant was sending back colorful, opinionated dispatches from locales that were more than exotic. He found himself in politically sensitive places at the precise time their importance to Britain was becoming clear to readers. Among his diplomatic concerns were the increasing threat in the Crimea and the instability in Turkey, the extension of trade to China and Japan, the mutiny in India in 1857, the rise of a pan-Islamic movement, the relations between Native Americans and their neighbors, and the prospects for a recolonization of Palestine by eastern European Jews. His eye for the telling detail, his patriotic tone, his unabashed willingness to set off for remote lands to engage people with quite unfamiliar customs – all this made him one of the most popular of his generation of travel writers.

Laurence Oliphant, an only child, was born in 1829 in Cape Town, South Africa, where his father, Anthony Oliphant, was attorney general. Anthony and his wife, Maria Campbell, were evangelical Christians from long-established Scottish families. Anthony's father was Ebenezer Oliphant of Condie and Newton, Perthshire, and Maria was the daughter of Colonel Campbell of the Seventy-second Highlanders. For much of her life her health was not good, and Laurence returned to England with her when he was quite young. Anthony was made chief justice of Ceylon in 1839, and Maria and Laurence both rejoined him there in 1841. This was the first of many occasions on which Oliphant's formal education yielded to the family's great interest in travel. During his father's two-year leave in 1846–1848 Oliphant dropped his plans to attend Cambridge and instead accompanied his parents on an extended tour of the Continent. When he returned to Ceylon he was called to the colonial bar and served as his father's private secretary. This skill would later make him quite valuable to James Bruce, Lord Elgin, and others.

Oliphant's first book was *A Journey to Katmandu (the Capital of Nepaul) with the Camp of Jung Bahadoor, Including a Sketch of the Nepaulese Ambassador at Home* (1852). It resulted from his visit to Nepal at the invitation of Jung Bahadoor, who had visited Ceylon at the end of 1851 while returning to his own country from England. Little had been written about Nepal after 1819, and since Bahadoor had aroused great interest during his visit to England, Oliphant dedicated the book to his father in offering it to the English public. He correctly estimated both the interest of the public and his own descriptive skills, for the book was quite successful. Several sites he visited later proved to be of great historical importance – for example, his stop at Cawnpore, which he described as "one of the largest and most disagreeable-looking stations in India," only five years later became an important setting for the Great Mutiny.

Oliphant is a canny observer who generally provides helpful maps of places as well as drawings of significant encounters between principal parties. As a mark of his immaturity and his search for a voice, the persona he adopts in his first book is haughtier than in subsequent works. He once notes that, had he been asked to identify the origin of one group he encounters, he "should have pronounced it to be a mixture of Naples lazzaroni with the scum of an Irish regiment." He notes that the traveler's first principle is to make the best of everything, and he does so, seeing and marveling at so much of the world. An imperial tone provides the backdrop for his observations. On his journey from Segowly to Lucknow he awakes, for example, to a brilliantly sun-drenched view of the Himalaya Mountains after having complained all night that his bearers, in carrying his palanquin through a driving rainstorm, were not keeping him comfortable. Oliphant later admits that his policy was to add a new convenience to his cabinet every day, and he claims that the carriers never seemed to notice: they simply accommodated, "upon the principle of the man who could lift an ox by dint of doing so every morning from the time when it was a calf."

Oliphant definitely has an eye for the exotic and memorable, and his writing unquestionably Orientalizes the world he presents. He notes, for example, beyond the brilliantly attired and bejeweled natives at the court of the king of Oudh, the wiper whose very life is endangered if he fails to cleanse his sovereign's mouth assiduously between spoonfuls. He elsewhere wonders if a sentiment such as gratitude "is known amongst Orientals," and he concludes that "if you do not associate with assassins, you must give up the pleasures of Nepaul society." The *Spectator* in 1888 echoed his patriarchal views: Oliphant "comprehended persons," it recalled, "without experiencing difficulty from the obstacles of race – to many able men an insuperable obstacle – and he exercised over inferiors a charm which, in the case of Orientals, often became an affectionate devotion."

His journey takes him from Ceylon to Calcutta, to Benares, to Ghazipore and the Terai, across the Cheriagotty Hills, through the Cheesapany pass to Katmandu (where he meets Gurkhas and worshipers from Tibet), on to Lucknow, Delhi, Agra, and Bombay. He fills the pages with imaginative detail. His abilities to accommodate to the customs of various countries apparently encourage his hosts to include him in many activities from which foreigners might have been excluded – but he has his queasy moments, as when he is called on to de-

capitate a buffalo. He uses the occasion to remark that Jung Bahadoor's position is much the same as the buffalo's: he is safe only if he keeps moving.

The young writer shows no hesitation in expressing his opinions, favorable or otherwise. He notes the prime minister's despotic tone of voice; he speaks of his own "mingled disgust and horror" at some of the food; he ridicules the Nepali soldiers for their attempts to "persuade themselves they were British grenadiers," and he remarks that "the whole thing was so eminently ridiculous and looked so very like a farce, that it was difficult to maintain that dignified and sedate appearance which was expected from the spectators of a scene so imposing." He does his best, though, to assuage the discomfort of his host, who has just returned from seeing such sights as the inspection of fifteen thousand French soldiers at Versailles. Oliphant admits that Jung Bahadoor (who had apparently assassinated his uncle) was doubtless guilty, in the early years of his yet "uncivilised" life, of great barbarities and crimes, but Oliphant is happy to report that Bahadoor's "late generous and humane conduct might well read a useful lesson to many in the civilised societies in which he learnt to be what he now is."

Oliphant's future interest in international politics clearly informs much of his response to the Nepalese. He criticizes their policy of protecting the country from invaders by keeping roads that lead into it impassable. Oliphant suggests that "neither bad roads, troops, nor any other obstacle that [they] could oppose to our advance, would avail in case of our invading Nepaul," but they have little to fear, since "it would never be worth our while." Then he is on to India. When he departs from Bombay he predicts that these various independent states and their princes will soon be "absorbed into one vast empire."

Following his trip to Nepal, Oliphant returned briefly to Ceylon and then moved to London, where he studied law and became interested in Lord Shaftesbury's work among the poor. He also began studying Scottish law in Edinburgh, but in August 1852 wanderlust struck. His second book, *The Russian Shores of the Black Sea in the Autumn of 1852, with a Voyage down the Volga, and a Tour through the Country of the Don Cossacks* (1853), is a partial account of the trip he took with Oswald Smith to Saint Petersburg, on to Nijni Novgorod, and then to the Crimea. The Crimean War was on the horizon, and to the second edition of the book Oliphant added a chapter specifically dealing with the importance of the Eastern Question to Britain. The book was immensely popular. As the *Westminster Review* recalled

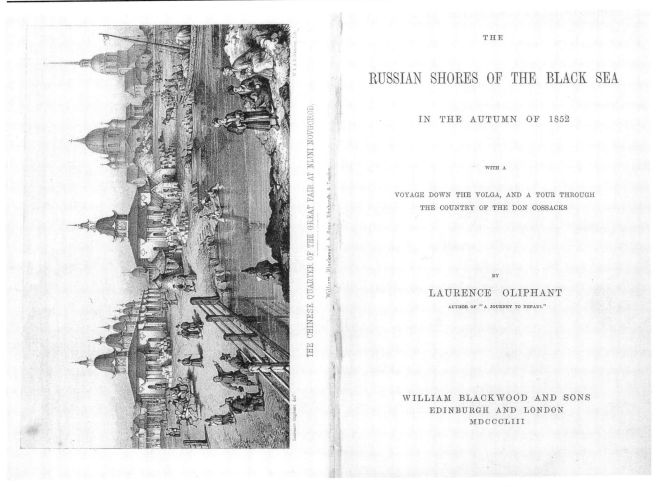

THE

RUSSIAN SHORES OF THE BLACK SEA

IN THE AUTUMN OF 1852

WITH A

VOYAGE DOWN THE VOLGA, AND A TOUR THROUGH
THE COUNTRY OF THE DON COSSACKS

BY

LAURENCE OLIPHANT
AUTHOR OF "A JOURNEY TO NEPAUL"

WILLIAM BLACKWOOD AND SONS
EDINBURGH AND LONDON
MDCCCLIII

Frontispiece and title page for Oliphant's second travel book, including his adventures in prewar Crimea (courtesy of the Lilly Library, Indiana University)

in 1892, "when *Russian Shores of the Black Sea* was published, it was almost the only source of information on the subject. Within a year the fourth edition was issued."

In his preface to the first edition Oliphant argues that there is no country in Europe about which so little has been written as the empire of Russia, probably because its rulers are such annoying autocrats, but also because accommodations for travelers there are "execrable" and transportation is "barbarous." He argues that there is a special need for someone to offer information on the internal economy of this empire, but he admits that he is not the one to do it. Yet he hopes that his description of "the once celebrated kingdom of Crim Tartary" will please his readers and perk their interests in further study.

He then begins his account with a mixed review of Saint Petersburg – which, he finds, has much to offer the visitor and almost enough to

make it worth one's while to endure the pompous and nosy officials. He is definitely not impressed by Izak's church, which he compares to the pyramids in its heft, and he concludes that its "barbaric tinge" is in keeping with the religion to which it is consecrated. On the other hand he finds the martial grandeur of a field day at Krasna Selo, involving a hundred thousand men under review by the emperor, to be truly splendid, full of Circassian glitter. His description of the city's functionaries and their mode of operations – their insistence on multiple documentation, their intransigence in the face of new problems, their awe of military garb – seem strikingly similar to the gloom associated with the Communist regime in the mid twentieth century.

Without regret he boards a train for Moscow. The 450-mile trip takes him twenty-two hours, and he finds the countryside tame and uninteresting. Oliphant estimates that the whole urban population of the empire is no more than five million, only about double that of London. The fact that the country relies so heavily on intermittent trade fairs rather than on good roads and steady commerce suggests to him that the empire is far less interested in the commercial prosperity of the country than in extending its political influence. Thus, he concludes, Russian railroads are constructed not for transporting the public, but for conveying soldiers.

Upon arriving in Moscow he finds the Kremlin striking, even though its architecture is a strange combination of the modern and the barbaric, its buildings "seeming to bear as much affinity to one another as the Taj and the Tuileries." He is especially impressed by Saint Basil's, particularly because of its quaint irregularity. He finds the staterooms of the palace, only completed within the past year, the handsomest in Europe. With British disdain he avoids purchasing the "huge gaudy pictures of hard-favored saints" and moves on to wonderful teashops. In sum, while he finds the streets less beautiful than those of Saint Petersburg ("the modern metropolis"), he concludes that Moscow is far more interesting.

From Moscow he makes the two-and-a-half-day trip to the grand fair of Nijni Novgorod over a macadam road of which he approves. If, as some have suggested, Oliphant sometimes served as a spy for the British government, clearly one of his missions was to assess the prospects for British trade in the various countries he visited. Here he notes that the governmental policy of putting heavy duties on foreign goods while maintaining the great expense of manufacturing and selling home produce effectively defeats foreign-trade prospects. Oliphant's descriptions are also shaped by Victorian stereotypes, as in that he gives of "a dirty little Frankfort Jew" who is "driving his bargain as keenly as if he had one of his own persuasion to haggle with" (a surprising observation in light of Oliphant's later work in Palestine) in the back shop of a "dignified aristocratic-looking Armenian."

The next leg of his journey takes him to the once famous Tatar kingdom of Kazan. Oliphant finds this town of fifty thousand inhabitants the most imposing aspect in Russia, but he discovers that, as in most Russian towns, there are few lights and no one to be seen on the streets after the sun has gone down. At daybreak he wanders the streets and learns that the interior of the city, despite its exterior splendor, is desolate indeed. From this he concludes that "nothing bears looking into in Russia, from a metropolis to a police-officer.... An anxious desire is always visible to produce an im-

pression totally at variance with the real state of the case."

As he continues his trip Oliphant surmises that the poverty of the villages and the spiritually destitute state of the serfs are perhaps the reasons for this secrecy. The Cossacks on every street corner mercilessly beat any offending muzhik, or peasant. He seems to note drunken men on the streets wherever he goes in Russia, and he remarks that "the Russian peasant is so degraded that it amounts to much the same thing whether he be in a state of cultivated intoxication or natural incapacity." He discourses on Baron August von Haxthausen's theories on the necessity of maintaining such peasant labor to ensure agricultural success with the large tracts of land owned by the aristocracy, and he vigorously disputes the theory. The outlines of von Haxthausen's position on the dispute that Oliphant describes closely resemble contemporary nineteenth-century justifications for slavery in the United States. In retrospect, Oliphant's argument against the system of serfdom affords an interesting prelude to the ultimately violent overthrow of the Russian aristocracy.

He wends his way down the Volga to Novo Tcherkask, the capital of the country of the Don Cossacks, and then into Armenia, where he notes that colonies established by Catherine II and filled with commercially astute foreigners are industrious, whereas the Russians themselves are indolent. Musing over the wheat growers' difficulties in regulating prices, Oliphant hopes that Britain will someday be released from its dependence upon foreign grain from America and Russia; soon, he hopes, Britain can turn instead to its "own" land in India to supply grain via a canal through the Isthmus of Suez.

The next stop is Kertch, the ancient capital of the Bosphorus, where British ships have succeeded those of Greeks and Italians as being the principal traders. On his entry into Simpheropol, the new Russian capital of the Crimea, Oliphant reminds his readers that the Crimea was ceded to Russia in 1781 and that previously this city (known before as Ak Mechet) had been the residence of the vice khan. In earlier days it had been adorned with palaces, mosques, and public baths, but it is now reconstructed in the Russian manner, with broad streets and tall white houses decorated with green paint. Despite these facades, there are enough descendants of the former inhabitants to give the city a spark of life.

Seeing so much decline under Russian influence, Oliphant draws an interesting comparison between Americans and Russians. He argues that the two peoples are diametrically opposed to one another in habits and feelings but identical in their indiscriminate patriotism. While the American's patriotism reveals "the genuine outburst of a mind which lacks not honesty, but refinement," that of the Russian reveals the prompting of "a restless consciousness of his own innate barbarism." The Russian hopes that "by continually impressing upon you the high state of civilization of his country and its inhabitants, you may gradually come to doubt the evidence of your own senses, and believe him instead."

Of greatest importance to his later dealings with the British government was Oliphant's decision to visit Sebastopol, "the most celebrated naval station in Russia," without permission (foreigners were admitted there only on the rarest occasions). He describes the town as a vast garrison of forty thousand people, but, seeing so many ships in disrepair, he concludes that, like all great Russian institutions, the navy and its threat to the rest of Europe is "artificial." He notes that few members of the naval fleet seem to be kept on board and passes along the rumor that most get seasick on the few occasions when they do put to sea. His advice soon influenced British policy: from the sea Sebastopol seemed impregnable, but if approached by land from the south, it looked quite weak.

In Bagtchè Serai he discourses on the war in the Caucasus and praises the Circassian leader Schamyl Bey. But in locating a competent military leader his thoughts turn again to India, and he warns his readers that Russian imperialist expansion may soon look in that direction. This was a fear that an increasing number of government officials shared. At length Oliphant arrives at Odessa, which many described as the "Russian Florence" in combining the charms of all the capitals of Europe. Yet Oliphant concludes that its cosmopolitan charms are not sufficient to justify the apparently universal Russian contempt for the merits of other places. He travels up the Danube to Orsova, which he characterizes as "the present limit of Russian aggression," and he offers a closing estimation of the present dangers presented by the sprawling country he has visited.

He argues that the emperor must know that great masses of his empire are united in a common hatred of Russia. One half of the land has been annexed in the past sixty years; his Muslim subjects alone number two and a half million. Should it become necessary to blockade the Baltic coast, his Lutheran and Roman Catholic subjects will rebel and align themselves with the Poles. The rest of Europe should therefore not be frightened, Oliphant concludes, by hollow boasting from such a leader. At the same time the Russian government, because of its instability and false sense of importance, is innately aggressive and unpredictable. He concludes that Russia is a country that bears watching, one that must become better known by the British.

The *London Quarterly Review,* adhering to the Conservative position, loudly agreed with Oliphant's negative impression of the Russian bear. "If such facts as these were disclosed respecting Japan or Chinese Tartary," it opined in 1854,

> we should be divided between indignation and contempt for such barbarians. Yet this is the power which has been lauded at the expense of its intended victim. The chief arguments for breaking up the Ottoman Empire are based on its inefficient social institutions, the gross corruption of all public functionaries, the vicious mode of raising the revenue, general commercial restrictions, religious intolerance, and discordant races whose interests clash. It may be safely affirmed, that, on every one of these vital questions, Turkey will bear a most favourable comparison with its deadly adversary.

Oliphant's observations thus made him an apologist for the British (and French, Turkish, and Sardinian) cause against the Russians, whom they were to defeat in the Crimean War (1853–1856). The details of Oliphant's narrative shaped an image of southeastern Europe, a region over which Britain sought domination, and made the political issues of that area seem less foreign and more obviously pertinent to the lives of his readers.

Oliphant's mother introduced him to James Bruce, the eighth earl of Elgin and governor-general of Canada, an introduction that thus helped him to see the West. Oliphant dedicated his subsequent book, *Minnesota and the Far West* (1855), to Lord Elgin, "to whose administrative talent is due the present prosperity of Canada, and by whose able diplomacy the commercial relations of Great Britain and the United States have been placed upon a basis alike honourable and advantageous to both nations." Oliphant should know, for he was to serve as Lord Elgin's secretary in Washington, D.C., during negotiations for a reciprocity treaty. After the treaty signing, Oliphant accompanied Lord Elgin to Quebec and was made superintendent of Indian affairs. In that capacity he made a journey to Maine, Lake Superior, Dubuque, and Chicago, and his book recounts this trip. This area could offer Oliphant's readers neither the exotic appeal of Nepal nor the current interest in Russian history, so he sought to discuss what he saw to be the truly interesting distinction of Canada and the United States: their unabashed embrace of progress.

Oliphant urges upon readers the "rapid advance of civilisation" in the western United States: "Instead of moralising over magnificence in a process of decay, [the traveler] must here watch resources in a process of development." Oliphant is infected with pragmatism rather than the picturesque; he immediately acquires the "go-ahead" ideas that are producing great wealth and "mushroom" cities along the Mississippi River. All is commerce and acquisition. Travel by train is so rapid that one hardly notices the landscape through the dirty glass; the meals taken on the conveyance are, likewise, rapid – dinner, he notes, lasts seven and a half minutes. The point is to get there.

As he travels, Oliphant muses on topics such as Canadian politics. Arriving in one town on polling day, he observes that the inhabitants clearly vote strictly on personal bases and do not believe in such things as political principles. This, he predicts, will change as the population grows and as the influence of the central government impinges on the lives of those on the frontier. He notes that the British typically know next to nothing (and care less) about the colonies, but he finds the Canadian House of Assembly "thoroughly loyal" to Britain – except for a few idealists in the Rouge party. He finds more Canadians to be interested in retaining their colonial connection to Great Britain than many in the British Parliament seem to be in retaining connections to Canada. Oliphant shares his government's view that Canada offers a welcome buffer to expansionist ambitions of the United States, and he therefore seeks to acquaint his British readers with their Canadian cousins. He finds the people to be a most pleasant combination of work and play, as reflected in their cities: Toronto is a serious town dedicated to business, and Quebec offers "the strongest possible temptations to be sociable."

Native North Americans, on the other hand (and these were people at least nominally under his authority), he describes as indolent and "utterly devoid of enterprise." He specifically rejects the "romantic credulity" that Washington Irving and James Fenimore Cooper attached to these natives. In Oliphant's view, the proximity of such natives to a white population usually provides the stimulus they need as encouragement to exert themselves.

Oliphant gives the plain speakers of the United States their due, as he admits that they both condemn the British as hypocritical imperialists and turn their harshest criticism on themselves. He fears that this bluntness will soon exacerbate racial prob-

lems, and he recognizes that British influence will be unwelcome in resolving the resulting conflict. The *London Quarterly Review* was well pleased with the book and in 1856 pronounced its author "a shrewd observer, a graphic writer, and a lively companion."

Lord Elgin retired in 1854 and Oliphant did not wish to serve under his successor. He took the opportunity to follow up plans that had occurred to him during his Russian trip, plans that he published in a pamphlet titled *The Coming Campaign* (1855). He received a recommendation from Lord Clarendon to Lord Stratford de Redcliffe to go as an envoy to Schamyl Bey, whom Oliphant had praised in the earlier account of his trip to the Crimea, and to see about a diversion against the Russians. The result of his trip is recounted in the articles he sent to the *Times* (London) as an official correspondent, an account elaborated upon in *The Trans-Caucasian Campaign of the Turkish Army under Omar Pasha: A Personal Narrative* (1856).

The opening of the book reveals the comforting, engaging style that typifies so much of Oliphant's writing, a style that reminds the reader that these exotic and often painful experiences are at a safe distance from one's study:

> He only who knows what it is, night after night, to court sleep in defiance of the thundering of a hundred cannon – to be ever conscious, in his dreams of home, of the incessant whistle of shot and shell – and to be generally roused from a rickety stretcher by the explosion of a mine, can fully appreciate the comfort of a quiet cabin far removed from these disturbing influences, where the shrill pipe of the boatswain, or the morning sun gleaming in at the port-hole, remind him that another day of *dolce far niente* has dawned.

Oliphant had a knack for being in the right place at the right time, and this journey, on which his father accompanied him as far as Constantinople, began just one week before the fall of Sebastopol. Oliphant journeyed on with Lord Stratford to the Crimea, where three years before, as described in his Russian book, he had enjoyed a wonderful time in Kertch. Now, however, in place of the fashionable promenaders were a couple of regiments of slouching Turks, some Frenchmen, and British sentinels: "Every house was unroofed, every window encircled by a frame of charred wood." The Turks, he notes, were unsparing in their work of demolition, but he remarked on the devastation wrought by the Russians as well.

Oliphant was not overly impressed on this trip by the various military leaders he encountered.

Woodcut from Oliphant's first book on his North American travels, Minnesota and the Far West *(courtesy of the Lilly Library, Indiana University)*

When he met Sefer Pasha, Oliphant concluded that this Circassian had worked for the Turks long enough to have been corrupted by them. Until Sefer Pasha's followers become more sophisticated, Oliphant remarked, they would continue to fall under the sway of the Ottomans. At Souchoum Kaleh on the eastern coast of the Black Sea he met Prince Michael and discussed Abkhasian politics. Prince Michael's Christian partisans far outnumbered those of Behchit Pasha, the Muslim leader, but the sentiments of both were unclear, and Oliphant was glad that their assistance was not necessary "to demolish the Russian army in Georgia."

In Redoute Kaleh (the "most miserable hole" in which he had been) he looked with skepticism on the soldiers of the Turkish generalissimo Omer Pasha, who was about to attempt an invasion of Georgia. Oliphant concluded that soldiers in the Turkish army paid little attention to their officers, partly because so many of the troops were not Turks at all, but conscripts. The Circassians, who were accompanying Omer Pasha's troops in order to keep them informed of the Russians' proceedings, terrorized the local inhabitants of Mingrelia and became liabilities to Omer Pasha. The resulting disarray came as no surprise to Oliphant. After they

learned of the fall of Kars to the Russians, their own retreat was muddy, confused, and aimless. Oliphant spent four days with Omer Pasha in Choloni and described them as four of the most miserable days of his life. When he got to Redoute Kaleh, though, things were worse. After a few isolated skirmishes the Transcaucasian campaign of the Turkish army under Omer Pasha ended, and Oliphant closes the book by questioning the ignorance in Britain, France, and elsewhere that had allowed Russia so successfully to attack Turkey where it was most exposed. Undaunted, however, he added an appendix, advocating a second campaign in the Transcaucasian provinces, to his account.

It was typical of Oliphant to hold to his opinions, whether they were popular or not. Looking back on Oliphant's advice in 1887, the *Athenaeum* concluded that "many people will agree with the opinion that if the Transcaucasian provinces had been taken from Russia as a result of the war, the Russian advance towards India, which has given rise to so much anxiety in this country, would never have taken place."

When Oliphant returned to London from these adventures, the editor of the *Times* invited Oliphant to accompany him on a brief trip to the southern United States. Oliphant's adventures there and his first trip to the Circassia are described in *Patriots and Filibusters; or, Incidents of Political and Exploratory Travel* (1860), which presented a revised version of articles he had published in *Blackwood's Magazine*.

Lord Elgin asked Oliphant to serve as his personal secretary for his 1857 visit to China and Japan, and a fascinating account in two volumes resulted: *Narrative of the Earl of Elgin's Mission to China and Japan in the Years 1857, '58, '59* (1859). The *Edinburgh Review* in 1860 enthusiastically welcomed the account and noted that "few men of our time have seen more of the globe than Mr. Oliphant, or have described what they have seen with more *apropos*." Oliphant begins by describing in some detail the context of Elgin's mission. Elgin had been designated ambassador to the court of Peking, and France, Russia, and the United States were also dispatching plenipotentiaries extraordinary to China.

After a little more than a week in Singapore, Elgin began his journey up the Canton (Pearl) River. When he reached Hong Kong, he learned from Lord Canning, the governor-general of India, that the rebellion in Delhi had spread to Bengal. Chinese commissioner Yeh had erected triumphal arches in his name in Hong Kong, and Elgin's staying there without sufficient troops would reflect badly on the British government. So Elgin, who heard of the massacre of Cawnpore, returned to Singapore in order to put his troops at the service of Canning in India; within three weeks he reached the Sandheads with seventeen hundred men. Elgin, Oliphant, and company spent August 1857 in Calcutta, during a fearsome time for the British at Delhi, Agra, and Dinapore. Every regiment but two in the Bengal army had mutinied or been disarmed or disbanded, and no more troops were expected to arrive for two months.

Yet the calm in Calcutta was much like that Oliphant had witnessed there seven years previously. The maidan was as crowded by beauty and fashion, and *burra-cannas* were everywhere. Apparent apathy in the face of crisis was not indifference but "deliberate courage and steady determination." Sir Colin Campbell arrived to assume command of the army in India. Clearly none of the forces diverted to India from China could be returned to Elgin, and on 3 September he returned to Hong Kong to await the arrival of fifteen hundred marines to help capture the city before he could proceed to Peking for negotiations.

Meanwhile Oliphant found Hong Kong to be "like a beautiful woman with a bad temper," one who claimed his admiration while repelling his advances. The early characterization of the Chinese in his narrative seems most favorable. They are "the most active, industrious, and enterprising race in the Eastern world" — but, like the good imperialist, Oliphant adds that they have been "mismanaged." In his view Singapore, the most prosperous settlement in the East, owes most of its success to these industrious Chinese. On 28 October the marines arrived.

Oliphant took this occasion to visit Manila, which he describes as entirely different from any other town he had visited in the East: it was Roman Catholic and apparently quite happy. The people were every shade imaginable — Chinese and English, pure Spaniards and mestizos, Malays and Tagalog natives — and their costumes were similarly varied. He was totally charmed by the Philippines. Yet, while the natives were quite productive, the Chinese among them were even more industrious. For this reason Oliphant recommends that Britain encourage Chinese immigration to as many settlements as possible.

Yet after Elgin and Oliphant returned to Hong Kong, Oliphant's portrait of the Chinese generally (and of their rulers certainly) became colored by the deviousness he depicted in Commissioner Yeh. After Yeh had been captured with his papers, Oliphant included those documents in which the hapless commissioner had noted that "Elgin passes day after day at Hong Kong, stamping his foot and sighing." Given Oliphant's negative view of Elgin's foes among the Chinese leadership, it is little wonder that he concludes that British occupation would free the Chinese of their suspicion of Europeans.

Yet Oliphant himself had grown leery. Entering Soochow, they were met by officials with the greatest courtesy, but, Oliphant's book warns, a Chinaman "generally looks most pleased when he has least reason to be so, and maintains an expression of imperturbable politeness and amiability, when he is secretly regretting devoutly that he cannot bastinado you to death." They returned to Shanghai, where Oliphant stayed for ten days, and then departed for Ningpo, a town "celebrated for having produced some of the ablest scholars in China." Here he attended a "sing-song joss," with men assuming the female roles, in one of the temples, and his only regret was the proximity of "very odoriferous Chinamen." The *Edinburgh Review* later agreed with Oliphant in all his main points (and his prejudices, as well). It noted that "the Chinese are a crafty and sagacious people, on whom a more lasting impression may be made by their interests than by their fears."

As in the Philippines, the influence of Roman Catholicism fascinated Oliphant, although he did not completely admire it. Among Yeh's documents had been an assessment that "the doctrine of the Lord of Heaven" (Christianity) was nonthreatening to the Chinese empire, except in cases where exceptional preachers might inflame the populace. After Oliphant's return to Ningpo the party departed for Chusan, where they visited a Roman Catholic mission. Oliphant observes that the Roman Catholic system aims to breed converts rather than make them; this is possible since there are, he estimates, half a million Roman Catholics in the empire. Later Oliphant visited the Jesuit seminary in Siccaway, where he noted that the missionary policies of this Roman Catholic religious order were too ecumenical for his tastes: rather than imbuing their students with Christian dogma, the missionaries educated them in the literature of China to such a point that the students competed successfully with their fellows for the highest honors of the empire. Some would convert, but even those were allowed to blend their Christianity with much Confucianism, and Oliphant wondered how sincere such a conversion as this would be.

Elgin and Oliphant next visited the sacred island of Pootoo, where, he concluded, the bonzes "infested the place like a description of vermin peculiar to it." Between five hundred and two thousand monks and sixty temples, shrines, and monasteries were on the tiny island, and, as in his experience in Ningpo, Oliphant found that "the odour of their sanctity became altogether unbearable." They seemed quite devoted to their religious activities, though Oliphant recorded that many were criminals who had sought asylum there to atone for their past lives by a life of "idleness and filth, superstition and celibacy."

After many delays Elgin's party proceeded north to force direct negotiations upon the imperial government. The emperor was represented by the elderly and much-respected mandarin Kweiliang and the younger Hwashana; these two were soon joined by Keying, who had signed the treaty of Nankin exactly fifteen years before and had become famous throughout Europe. Oliphant portrays Keying's private mission here as deceptive. Elgin humiliates Keying before the assembled company by reading aloud a personal document in which Keying explained how to manipulate the "blindly unintelligent" barbarians. Keying mocked the Europeans, who "make much of their women." As a star-

tling denouement, Oliphant notes that Keying was so disgraced by this exposé that he returned to Peking, where he was ordered to commit suicide.

Turning his attention to the inhabitants of Tientsin and to their city, Oliphant is less dramatic but no less devastating. He records that they had been very respectful of foreigners at first, but as soon as Keying arrived they had become quite insolent. Their pride, he explains, was based on past glories. Much of the wealth of the empire used to pass through Tientsin, but other routes had been found and the city was now full of the poor: "Certainly if the imagination of the Chinaman who named this city Tientsin, 'heavenly spot,' could form no higher idea of an abode of bliss, it is difficult to conceive what must have been his notion of the opposite extreme." Elgin's occupation of the river had greatly raised the price of rice in the town, and that was part of his object. "In no part of the world," Oliphant writes,

> have I ever witnessed a more squalid, diseased population than that which seemed rather to infest than inhabit the suburbs of the city. . . . There was an eddy just in front of our yamun, in which dead cats, &c., used to gyrate, and into which stark naked figures were constantly plunging, in search of some delicate morsel.

The hauteur suggests how uncomfortable Oliphant had become with the Chinese and, perhaps, with his own powerlessness. Following a locust infestation at the end of June – fortunately after the harvest – Oliphant notes that children hunt and fry them – "I had the curiosity to eat one, and thought it not unlike a periwinkle," a sea snail. Again, the tone ignores the need that would make such food necessary.

The Treaty of Tientsin was signed on 26 June 1858, and in retrospect it can be seen as one piece of a larger historical pattern whereby Britain gradually surrendered informal control of most of the tropics for formal control of one quarter of it. The treaty allowed for the vast extension of British trade to the interior of the empire and for a resident minister in Peking. The British also demanded £1.3 million in compensation for their troubles in Canton. During all these belligerencies, Oliphant notes, commerce between the two nations continued without much disturbance. In commending his employer, Lord Elgin, Oliphant records that the treaty had been gained at the cost of twenty British lives; happily, he notes, this was a far more extensive treaty than that signed fifteen years before, following a bloody and expensive war that had been protracted for more than two years.

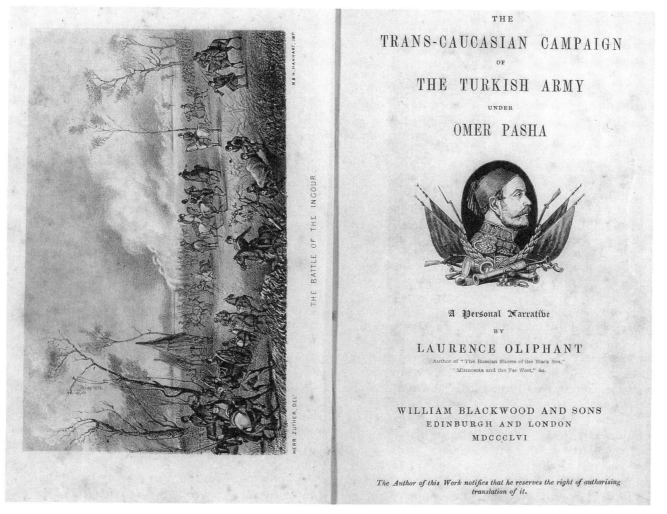

THE

TRANS-CAUCASIAN CAMPAIGN

OF

THE TURKISH ARMY

UNDER

OMER PASHA

A Personal Narrative

BY

LAURENCE OLIPHANT

Author of " The Russian Shores of the Black Sea,"
" Minnesota and the Far West," &c.

WILLIAM BLACKWOOD AND SONS

EDINBURGH AND LONDON

MDCCCLVI

*The Author of this Work notifies that he reserves the right of authorising
translation of it.*

THE BATTLE OF THE INGOUR.

MESSR ZUTHER, DEL.   M & N. HANHART, IMP.

Frontispiece and title page for Oliphant's narrative of his second trip to the Crimea (courtesy of the Lilly Library, Indiana University)

On the last day of July Oliphant sailed for Japan, in anticipation of visiting scenes "veiled in the mystery of a jealous and rigid seclusion." As readers begin his second volume Oliphant's organizing principle becomes clear: he intends to offer a contrast between the two countries, and he finds the differences stark. He writes that "all comparisons made with that Empire were in favour of Japan. . . . There exists not a single disagreeable association to cloud our reminiscences of that delightful country." Whereas the Chinese were resistant, the Japanese were welcoming: "It was like being compelled to eat a whole *paté de foie gras* at a sitting." He finds the people polite, friendly, efficient, and intelligent. The *Edinburgh Review,* as one would expect, finds that this "second volume is in every respect more entertaining and more curious than the first."

Since Nagasaki, the site of the earliest successes for Christian missionaries, was designated by the Japanese as the port of entry for foreigners, Oliphant uses this link to introduce his readers to the similarities and greater dissimilarities between British and Japanese cultures. Throughout the volume he takes pains to portray as nobility what others might brand an excessive formality in the Japanese. It is true, he notes, that Christians were thrown to their deaths at the entrance to Nagasaki, but he suggests that this was a consequence of the negative experiences that the Japanese had suffered with the Portuguese and the Dutch. He notes that Saint Francis Xavier in the sixteenth century had amazing success, and Oliphant attributes this partly to the high level of civilization of the Japanese: "There can be no doubt that the imaginative Japanese, hearing of Christianity for the first time, would receive it in a very different spirit from an untamed New Zealander, or a calmly-sceptical Chinaman." Their conversions were sincere and led to great courage in the face of persecution.

Oliphant's increasingly frequent theological discussions in his travel books hint at the depth of his own spiritual exploration, which was to dominate his later years. He offers an appreciative account of the history of the Jesuits in Japan and their negotiations with the various levels of society, but he suggests that

> it is to be regretted that the inordinate love of political power which characterises the disciples of Loyola, should have led the successors of the first missionaries into intrigues which terminated so disastrously for themselves and their creed, for thereby they have closed Japan to those Protestant missionary efforts which the government of that Empire are now firmly resolved on resisting.

Especially unfortunate, in Oliphant's opinion, is the lack of opportunity to explain that Protestants have far less certitude about eternal punishment than do the Catholics; the Japanese especially disliked this doctrine, since it condemned their ancestors to eternal suffering.

On 5 August he sailed from Nagasaki to Simoda and described the volcanic coastline. In such a country of "fire and brimstone," he notes, it is not unusual that the people should speculate learnedly on the infernal regions. He observes that "in Japan, religion is not used as in some countries to conceal immorality, but rather to give it countenance and support, so that practically there is very little difference here between a temple and a teahouse."

Turning his attention to native Japanese religion, Oliphant visits a graveyard and finds in its tranquil beauty suggestions that the Japanese have sentiments about death that are similar to the Westerners'. He describes the role of the mikado, the "Spiritual Emperor of Japan," whom he compares to the Pope, and he briefly describes the simplicity of Shinto worship and the characteristics that distinguish it from Buddhism. He suggests that the elevated and mystic tenets of Buddhism appeal to the refined classes of society, but "the humbler portion of the population take refuge in the idolatry of that gross material form which can alone satisfy their coarse, sensuous requirements." These are much the same feelings as those that he had expressed toward Roman Catholicism in the Philippines. He notes that Buddhism is the religion of 315 million people throughout the world, people "who

are all morally and intellectually inferior to the Japanese." From this he concludes that Shintoism, and not Buddhism, must have had the greater impact on the Japanese.

When real negotiations get under way, Oliphant's account begins to sound reminiscent of his experiences in China – though it is a bit less blunt. His appreciation of foreign cultures has its limits, and it shows whenever a question of British authority arises. Five miles from Yedo, capital of the empire, the British negotiators met the translator, Moriyama, whom Oliphant compares to Talleyrand, "always silky and smiling, anxious to impress upon you that he was a mere humble interpreter, while through his bland diffidence it was easy to distinguish a latent ambition to have everything his own way, and a perfect confidence in his own powers."

When Elgin and company finally proceed through Tokyo the populace goes wild with excitement. In the crowd Oliphant notes the women, whom he describes as naturally beautiful but self-disfiguring through their plucking of eyebrows and blackening of teeth. This preserves their virtue for their husbands, but the husbands, meanwhile, are notoriously licentious. Nonetheless, "there is probably no Eastern country in which the women have so much liberty or such great social enjoyment," and in any case adultery in Japan is punished by death for both parties.

Oliphant seems more taken by Japan than by any other country, and this is reflected in his detailed observation of Japanese customs. He describes customs involving their quarters at some length. At first Oliphant's party respected Japanese custom by removing their shoes before entering the house, but they soon decided simply to ignore the dirt they were grinding into the floor matting. The emperor sent them a typical Japanese meal, which delighted the party. Oliphant brags that he tried everything, but he recommends that future visitors show more discretion. The next day the party traveled throughout the town, and he concludes that "the charm of everything we saw at Yedo [Tokyo] lay in the fact of its being purely for Japanese use. Every article was illustrative of the customs of the country." Somewhat intimidating, however, are the large street dogs, which are protected by the state.

Oliphant offers an introductory description of the Japanese government. The mikado is actually a puppet. The tycoon, ostensibly the administrator of the empire, is enclosed in his citadel and effectively stripped of his power. The real government consists of a council of eight of the titular princes, influenced by the public opinion of the aristocracy. Should the tycoon and this council disagree on a weighty matter, it is referred to a council of three "princes of the blood." Should they agree with the tycoon, the entire council of eight is allowed to save its honor by committing suicide. As Oliphant notes, in England this would be "an exceedingly unpopular way of solving a constitutional difficulty."

Every individual in the society is "a slave to conventional rules of the most precise and rigid description," with several results. First, Oliphant finds it curious that "in Japan, where the individual is sacrificed to the community, he should seem perfectly happy and contented; while in America, where exactly the opposite result takes place, and the community is sacrificed to the individual, the latter is in a perpetual state of uproarious clamour for his rights." Second, a custom of *nayboen* – that is, a "recognised incognito" – exists, whereby people of the highest office may mingle with the lower classes and pursue activities in which their dignity might otherwise forbid them to indulge. The whole system is held in place by means of an elaborate system of spies: every member of society, from top to bottom, is secretly observed and called to task by another. This results in a government that is, as far as Oliphant can judge, incorruptible. "In this respect Japan affords a brilliant contrast to China, and even to some European countries," he writes.

Oliphant also denigrates Chinese education, as he claims that he never met a Chinaman who could read, speak, and write English correctly, but in Japan "there is a rage for the acquisition of every description of knowledge." This he attributes to the Japanese educational system, more widely diffused throughout that society than the British educational system is in England. He goes on to discuss Japanese lacquer design, clever uses of paper, the Japanese funeral system, modes of dressing ladies' hair, the excellence of Japanese steel, the use of tattoos ("it must be dreadful to feel that one can never undress again"), Japanese religious festivals, taxation, the variety of Japanese musical instruments, and the effect of strict laws ("though we left the most tempting English curiosities constantly displayed, yet we never had to complain of a single article missing, even of the most trifling value"). He claims never to have heard a scolding woman, or a disturbance on the streets, crowded though they were.

Despite all this adulation, Oliphant adds that the Japanese nonetheless strike him as "notoriously vindictive, superstitious, haughty, exceedingly tenacious of their honour, and often cruel." They are also "a somewhat frivolous and pleasure-loving race," but he prefers this to "the apathetic indifference of a Chinese mandarin, who thinks gaiety undignified."

On 26 August 1858, just two months after the signing of the Treaty of Tientsin, Elgin signed a treaty with Japan. Not until two months later did they learn that the tycoon had died near the time of their arrival in Tokyo; this had been kept secret during the negotiations, in another example of nayboen.

Oliphant's reaction to the British diplomatic success shows his blend of superciliousness and anthropological objectivity. The *Nation* warned its readers in 1891 that Oliphant "is a pretty strong Jingo, and can feel a sympathy with arbitrary and sanguinary violence." As it noted, he was among those who had defended Gov. Edward Eyre in his brutal handling of a famous incident of native rebellion in Jamaica. Yet Oliphant here predicts that the Japanese may cool a bit toward the English as they experience the "overbearing and insolent" behavior many Englishmen show toward "semi-civilised races." The English, unfortunately, "rarely make allowances for different moral standards" and forget that "*truth* is a virtue unknown except to a mere fraction of the human family, . . . a fact which in no way militates against Asiatics being in some respect superior to Europeans."

After a brief return to China for the signing of addenda to the treaty, Elgin's party left for home. "On the 4th of March," Oliphant writes, "we watched with inexpressible delight the rugged coast of China sink behind the horizon." Oliphant concludes by noting with sadness the current events in China and with hopes that all the work involved in obtaining the Treaty of Tientsin would not be for naught. The two volumes provide fascinating reading. The *Edinburgh Review* wrote that "these transactions will be read with the strongest interest now, and deserve to retain a permanent place in the literary and historical annals of our time." There is some accuracy in this estimation: a new edition of the book appeared in 1970, but in reviewing it, the *Journal of the American Oriental Society* noted that "the narrative contains a large and unwieldy mass of material, presented in a somewhat discursive and sometimes journalistic manner."

When he returned to England Oliphant was without a job and soon became involved in a series of intrigues. It was not long before he was traveling again – this time to Italy, where he plotted with Giuseppe Garibaldi to avoid the annexation of Nice by France. As with many such prolific writers, all events in Oliphant's life became grist for the mill. In this case the advantages and dangers of the plebiscite are discussed in his pamphlet *Universal Suffrage and Napoleon the Third* (1860). In 1861, because of his experiences with Elgin, he was appointed first secretary of the legation in Japan, and his admiration for the country was sorely tested. On 5 July 1861 he was attacked in the embassy by a Japanese; the sword wound was severe, and he had to return to England to recover. On the way home, however, he stopped in Korea, discovered a covert Russian naval force, and negotiated their withdrawal. He subsequently visited Corfu in 1862 with the Prince of Wales, and in 1863 he visited Poland and Moldavia.

In the next few years Oliphant published several books dealing with politics, and one novel written in the mode of William Makepeace Thackeray, *Piccadilly: A Fragment of Contemporary Biography* (1870). His next travel book, *The Land of Gilead, with Excursions in the Lebanon,* appeared in 1880. Its subject reflects the political decisions taken by the British government after the defeat of the Ottoman Empire in the Russo-Turkish War of 1877–1878 and Britain's increasingly direct involvement in the Levant. Of more importance to Oliphant's career, the book launched a final phase, a period of confused and disruptive searching for religious meaning and community.

Much had happened in Oliphant's life in the intervening years. He had been elected to Parliament in 1865 for the Stirling burghs but had quickly grown disillusioned. As *Blackwood's Magazine* noted in 1889, "Mr. Oliphant had come into Parliament as a Liberal, and follower of Mr. Gladstone. After Mr. Disraeli had intimated his intention of reviving Mr. Gladstone's Reform Bill," Oliphant concluded that both parties simply sought party advantage.

The most tumultuous events centered on his involvement with the religious leader Thomas Lake Harris. Oliphant resigned from Parliament in 1867 and joined Harris's religious community in Brocton, New York, where his mother also joined him. Harris's creed demanded celibacy in most marriages, since one's true spiritual counterpart was seldom one's marital partner. Harris was a severe taskmaster who exercised an amazing control over his disciples. Oliphant had to seek special permission from Harris before accepting a position as correspondent for the London *Times* during the Franco-Prussian War and as a writer for a newspaper in Paris in 1871.

In this latter assignment he was fortunate to meet Alice le Strange, a twenty-six-year-old woman to whom he became engaged in 1872, and they were married in June of that year. She also joined Harris's cult. Oliphant brought Alice to Brocton, and for the next several years he was engaged in raising money for the religious community. In 1878 Harris moved to the San Francisco Bay area and brought Alice Oliphant with him. Laurence visited, but he was forbidden to see her. Oliphant remained under Harris's influence until about 1882. Despite his voluminous travel writing, this eccentric religious and psychological turn in his career has garnered the most critical attention.

In 1879 Oliphant visited Palestine and again turned his travel to good account. The *Spectator* of 29 January 1881 complained that the resulting book, *The Land of Gilead, with Excursions in the Lebanon,* "reads somewhat like an auctioneer's advertisement" and shows "a frequent want of accuracy," but the reviewer nonetheless welcomed Oliphant's creative proposals. The book offers diverting descriptions of the Holy Land, but the real importance of *The Land of Gilead* is in its presentation of Oliphant's scheme for the resettlement of Jews in Palestine.

He suggests that maintaining the integrity of the Ottoman Empire in Asia is not only in the interests of England (this was generally the government's position, though it became increasingly untenable), but of European peace as well. Oliphant argues that his project, the development of a single province, would increase the revenue of the empire, add to its population and resources, secure and protect life and property, and enlist the sympathy of Europe — all without affecting in any way the sovereign rights of the sultan.

Oliphant found European Jews to be the perfect colonists for many reasons. Impoverished Muslim refugees from Bulgaria would not elicit sufficient sympathy from European Christians to encourage the latter to contribute adequate funding. On the other hand, from the sultan's point of view Christians came in such a variety of sects and were so constantly at each others' throats that a peaceful colony composed of their adherents seemed unlikely. Jews, though, generally had enough personal finances that they would not need exorbitant subvention from Christians, and Oliphant reasoned that they "had never alarmed the Turkish Government by national aspirations" and had proven to be excellent citizens wherever they lived. They had historical connections with Asiatic Turkey and would, therefore, be likely to accept Turkish conditions for colonization. Finally, the toleration that the sultan would accord them would be far preferable to the persecution that they endured in various

Oliphant (bearded and nearest to the mast) on the quarterdeck of H.M.S. Furious *during his 1858 travels*

Christian capitals. Oliphant noted that even the Jews attested that "Christian fanaticism in Eastern Europe is far more bitter than Moslem." By demonstrating his clemency in contrast to such Christian intolerance, the sultan would gain great sympathy among those Christians who favored the Jewish cause. Furthermore, in recent years the Jews had acquired "an almost commanding influence in the finance and press of many civilized countries," and any nation wishing to enlist their power in its cause would find it advantageous to support a Jewish colony. Palestine seemed the ideal corner of the Turkish empire for such a project. The claims of others to the land apparently did not much concern Oliphant.

Oliphant estimated that there were between six and seven million of "the Hebrew race" in the world. Five million of these lived in Europe, and half of these five million lived in Russia. There were about twenty-five thousand in Palestine, of a "men-

dicant" class, but Oliphant proposed to colonize the area with Eastern European and Russian Jews who had enough funds to establish themselves as "desirable" colonists. He admitted that some had objected that the Jews to which he referred were not agriculturalists, but he argued that, once given the opportunity to own land in Palestine, they would quickly pick up the skills needed and could, in any case, hire local labor if it were needed. He quoted from the *Jewish Chronicle* to show Jewish enthusiasm for his scheme.

The region he proposed to colonize, in the first instance, was the entire district of the Belka, and in the middle of February 1880 he set out. By this time in his life Oliphant could not have been considered an orthodox Christian. When he arrived in Wady Ajlun, of which three-fourths of the people were Christian, he remarked, "Although I generally prefer lodging with a Mohammedan to being cheated by a Christian in the more civilized parts of Turkey, in these remote regions, where the cupidities of the latter have not been stimulated by their contact with Western civilization, one finds them almost as hospitable as Mussulmans." When he reached the Belka region he admitted that both the Christians and the Arabs shared a dislike for the Turkish government, but he suspected that they would feel this way about any government that would try to keep them in order.

His disaffection colors his observations as he reached the center of Jerusalem. There he witnessed Passover and Holy Week observances and was far from edified: "The crowds of pilgrims and devotees calling themselves Christian, who were only kept from flying at each other's throats over the tomb of the founder of their religion by a strong guard of Muslim soldiers, evidently inspired the latter with a contempt and disgust which one felt compelled to share." Oliphant condemns both the Christians' prejudice against the local Jews and the unjust taxation of the Muslim peasantry by the representatives of the Turkish government: "It is for the poor down-trodden Muslim peasantry, devout according to their lights, whether Arab or Turk, than whom a race braver and more enduring in war, or more patient and well-conducted in time of peace, does not exist, that I would plead." This was not the first time in his travels that Oliphant had protested on behalf of the poor and voiceless in a country that he was visiting.

Having shaken the dust from his feet, Oliphant set out for Damascus. Oliphant's plans for the future took shape as he briefly visited a German colony in Haifa. He was greatly impressed with its efficiency and productivity, and he later used it as a model when he returned to establish his own colony. When he arrived in Damascus, the "queen of Oriental cities," with a sigh of relief, he reverted to simple tourism. He attended a meal where dervishes skewered their cheeks with no apparent pain, pulled snakes in two, and calmly ate live scorpions. (Oliphant describes one such dervish: "His countenance as he went on munching was so impassive that I could not judge whether live scorpion is nice or not: Probably it is an acquired taste.") But he admitted that he did not succeed in his principal purpose – that of convincing the Turkish government that a Jewish province would be mutually beneficial. As one commentator later noted, Oliphant was born ahead of his time.

In the summer of 1882 he and Alice traveled to Constantinople, and he wrote his final travel book – *Haifa: or, Life in Modern Palestine* (1887). This is an account of his three years of residence in the country and comprises the edited letters that he originally published in the *New York Sun*. Much of the book elucidates archaeological subjects having to do with biblical sites and popularizes the Palestine Exploration Fund of London. The findings that he called to the attention of his British audience have been generally supplanted, for twentieth-century readers, by other accounts.

The nonhistorical musings of this well-traveled man are frequently diverting elaborations of his earlier *Land of Gilead,* as they are seen through the eyes of one who has combined the concerns of that earlier book with his interest in forming an alternative religious community, somewhat reminiscent of Harris's failed attempt in New York. Combining his interest in returning Jews to Palestine with that of founding a community based on his own spiritual beliefs, the book reflects eschatological concerns of the day as the end of the century approached, and it reemphasizes Oliphant's evangelical upbringing. He and his wife had moved to Haifa near the end of 1882, and many sympathizers, some from the Brocton community and some Jewish immigrants, came to live near them. The Oliphants gave symposia on their religious ideas but gradually scared away some of their followers with fanciful views such as those detailed in *Sympneumata; or, Evolutionary Forces Now Active in Man* (1885).

Haifa is written in the style of Oliphant's earlier travel books, engaging and not notably metaphysical. In one letter he visits a settlement just begun by the Central Jewish Colonization Society of Roumania and witnesses negotiations between the Romanian Jews and Muslim fellahin. He finds these Jews haughty and effeminate, unlike both the "stalwart" fellahin and the "stout, handsome" Arabic Jew who serves as interpreter. But he remains convinced that time will teach the colonists to learn from the locals. In a later letter on "the Jewish question in Palestine," in which he laments Turkish governmental restrictions on Jewish immigration, he remarks that the Russian government appears disposed to "espouse in Turkey the cause of the race which it oppresses so unmercifully at home." Yet he also laments the relative apathy of most European Jews toward the struggle of Eastern European and Russian Jews now living in Palestine. Oliphant had an enduring interest in this cause and no doubt helped shape future policy, at least, by keeping the issue alive for the public.

What quickly becomes clear, though, is that so much of Oliphant's life is not apparent in his writings. When he travels and recounts his diverting experiences, he is living as an individual; when he gravitates toward the orbit of Thomas Lake Harris, he seems to be living as someone else. This dichotomy is so striking that readers today might well wonder how he could have accomplished so much in the public realm, though never as much as his contemporaries had apparently anticipated. In the winter of 1880, for example, Harris had allowed Alice to reunite with her husband, and together the two traveled to Egypt. Oliphant's timing again coincided with governmental interests: Britain was occupying Egypt by the autumn of 1882.

Oliphant's book that recounts this experience, *The Land of Khemi: Up and down the Middle Nile* (1882), met with generally favorable reviews, but it was not a significant effort. The *Westminster Review* in 1892 admitted that the book was "not written in [Oliphant's] usual fascinating style." It seems, in fact, a willful effort to take his mind off the pressing problems and confusions of his daily life. The book is a compilation of reports that Oliphant had written for *Blackwood's Magazine*. Oliphant notes that he had first visited Egypt forty years before and had subsequently traveled through it seven or eight times. As in the later *Haifa,* this book gave Oliphant a chance to perform a little amateur (and now outdated) archaeology and to encourage the British government to continue such work.

The most imposing scene that he describes is the pyramid of Howara, which prompts his suggestive image of the grinding of grain by buffalo "blindfolded in order that they may be spared a consciousness of the monotonous nature of their occupation." It seems an unspoken reference to the poor whom he has encountered wherever he has turned throughout his wandering life. His state of mind is suggested in his description of a Coptic marriage ceremony: "I had seen enough to satisfy me that there are more kinds of Christianity in the world than are dreamt of in our philosophy." Standing amid the ruins of a temple to Isis, he speculates on the influence that Egyptian theology had on Greek philosophy, Judaism, and Christianity. His decision to establish a religious colony separate from any such established church was on the horizon.

During this period Oliphant, his mother, and his wife distanced themselves from Harris, and Oliphant took legal action to recover his stake in the Brocton property. Harris responded by trying unsuccessfully to enlist Alice in a plan to institutionalize Oliphant. As if to escape not only the Western world but also facticity, Oliphant turned to fiction. He wrote two novels in the years that follow: *Altiora Peto* (1883) and *Masollam; a Problem of the Period: A Novel* (1886). The *Spectator* of 15 September 1883

found the first enjoyable, but its heroine "is a bore, and would be a bore of the first magnitude, were it not that the portentous prig who marries her is a bigger bore still." The *Nation* on 20 September 1883 was less generous, finding "very little that is original or new," and ridiculing the heroine's "purity of heart which, in Mr. Oliphant's view of the world, the absence of conventionality tends to produce." This seems a thinly veiled allusion to the growing public obsession with Oliphant's religious tutelage under Thomas Harris. Perfectly aware of how odd he had come to be seen by the public, Oliphant offers, in *Masollam,* his fictionalized account of his disaffection from Harris.

But he also wrote several books of theology that indicate Harris's continuing philosophical influence and satirically attack British society. This befuddling combination of religious mysticism and cynical social commentary drove many readers increasingly to conclude that Oliphant had, in effect, concocted a life that would fascinate future readers no less than it confused his contemporaries. Thus, when Margaret Oliphant wrote her memoir of him, the *Nation* on 9 July 1891 offered the following estimation, one that has set in stone the profile by which Oliphant is recognized today:

A specimen more curious than this biography sets before us is probably not to be found in the whole psychological museum. . . . [H]ere we have the history of a man who lived two lives not only distinct, but so strangely contrasted with each other that, if we did not know it was impossible, we might think we had a veritable case of Dr. Jekyll and Mr. Hyde, only that neither of Laurence Oliphant's personalities is wicked.

One century later, in fact, Laurence Oliphant appears as the protagonist in *The Difference Machine* (1991), William Gibson and Bruce Sterling's science fiction reimagining of the late-Victorian era, and Oliphant seems perfectly suited to the bizarre fictional world in which he appears. Reviewing his life in 1891, *Macmillan's Magazine* sadly judged that Oliphant's life had revealed "some deep defect in his composition," but *Temple Bar* in that same year offered a more sympathetic assessment. "Laurence Oliphant," its reviewer wrote,

was born out of due time. He ought to have entered the world when Puritanism was struggling into being. He would have joined the Puritans who left Europe in which they were persecuted, and settled in America where they thought to serve God by persecuting others. His name would have been as conspicuous in the history of New England as that of Roger Williams. He would not have tamely submitted to tyranny from the rulers of Massachusetts; and he, like Williams, might have founded a colony in which his principles would have had free scope. He was too original for the age in which he lived; too great a mystic for the society in which he moved.

When Alice Oliphant died from a fever on 2 January 1887, Oliphant nonetheless undertook the lecture tour in England that they had planned together. He also published an account of his early adventures, *Episodes in a Life of Adventure; or, Moss from a Rolling Stone* (1887), and a collection of stories, *Fashionable Philosophy, and Other Sketches* (1887). He returned briefly to Haifa but moved to England in 1888. There inspired, he said, by a kind of possession by the spirit of his wife, he wrote *Scientific Religion; or, Higher Possibilities of Life and Practice through the Operation of Natural Forces* (1888). In 1889 the *London Quarterly Review* seemed bewildered with the book:

> We write with all the respect due to the sincere conviction which evidently possesses Mr. Oliphant, and which has certainly moved him to a life of remarkable self-denial for many years past, but it is difficult for us seriously to review the extraordinary mixture of unscientific science and crude mysticism which he has put forth under the name of "Scientific Religion."

Its early reviews of Oliphant's travel writings had been extremely favorable, and the perplexity of its reviewer before the unexpected turn in Oliphant's interests was widespread in society.

With the publication of this speculative book Oliphant became something of a guru in London, and as such he traveled to the United States. He returned to London with a new fiancée, Rosamond Dale Owen, the rather angular granddaughter of social reformer Robert Owen. The two married on 16 August 1888. Oliphant's plan was for Rosamond to be the conduit for both healing powers and a message to the world from his first wife, a spiritual presence that Laurence had experienced from beyond the grave. But on 23 December 1888 he died of lung cancer.

Throughout his varied life Laurence Oliphant rather unself-consciously presented himself as an adventuresome member of the British Empire, one who brought to the far corners of the globe a common sense that could make his British contemporaries proud. He was blatant in his discussion of both those cultural mores that he finds praiseworthy and the chinks in the armor of various political establishments he encountered. He remarked on the allure of the material resources from which a properly prepared Great Britain could and should profit. In being far more than a simple entertainer, he struck the proper Victorian tone by alerting readers to their responsibilities for managing a complex and sometimes disturbing world.

In his early career he was eminently successful in these roles. As the *London Quarterly Review* noted in its 1854 review of *The Russian Shores of the Black Sea,* he appeared to be "a good sample of the English character, — shrewd, observant, straightforward, and practical; disposed to see for himself, rather than take things on hearsay evidence; and willing to brave a little danger, and much inconvenience, for the sake of procuring authentic information."

Yet as his career advanced he wrote also as a *late* Victorian, aware of the political instability in much of the empire, the increasing harshness of political realities back home, and his unanswered personal questions. Twentieth-century readers cannot help but recognize — in his truncated parliamentary career, his fascinating but bizarre religious life, and his equally mysterious sexual life — a perfect arbiter for an empire supremely self-confident in its diplomacy and increasingly curious about its own internal workings.

That one could see so much of the world, reputably serve as a British agent in events he later memorably describes, and nonetheless break off his flourishing public career to serve a questionable leader such as Harris suggests that Oliphant's life was an odyssey in search of something more than simple knowledge, social esteem, and worldly success. In some ways his later religious writings such as *Sympneumata* and *Scientific Religion* might almost be considered part of his travel journals, though the worlds into which he gazed in these books transcend that which his earlier works had recorded with such verve. The *Spectator* in 1888 recognized that many individuals had been at ease in the world of diplomacy and practical management and yet had given this up when they discerned a higher calling. "It was," wrote the *Spectator,*

> generally known that this man, who had "lived everywhere, gone everywhere, and done everything"; who knew Khatmandoo as well as London, and Jerusalem better than either; who had unknown Oriental Princes for intimate friends, and half the statesmen of Europe for correspondents, firmly believed that the veil between the visible and the invisible worlds was a thin one, that it could be rent, that it had been rent, and that he had evidence sufficient for himself, at all events, of its liability to rending.

Following his death some argument arose over the possibility that Oliphant may have suffered from syphilis for much of his life. Another implication was that shortly before his death charges of homosexuality were to have been brought against him, but his recent biographer has disputed this latter speculation. In Oliphant's last years his work to put individuals in touch with what he called the "sympneuma" and Rosamond's work for the cause after his death invited much public suspicion.

Yet obituaries in the London *Times* and elsewhere offer a more balanced and appreciative view of his long public life, with some comparing him with Gen. Charles Gordon. Some mystery remains around Laurence Oliphant, but certainly his many engaging books are great achievements – it seems reasonable to conclude, as did the *Nation* in 1891, that "his character belongs to a period of transition which, though fruitful of eccentricities, has hardly produced a greater or more notable eccentricity than Laurence Oliphant."

Biographies:

Margaret Oliphant, *Memoir of the Life of Laurence Oliphant and of Alice Oliphant, His Wife,* 2 volumes (Edinburgh & London: Blackwood, 1891; New York: Harper, 1891);

Anne Taylor, *Laurence Oliphant, 1829–1888* (New York: Oxford University Press, 1982).

References:

Alexander Kinglake, *The Invasion of the Crimea* (Edinburgh: Blackwood, 1863);

Louis Liesching, *Personal Reminiscences of Laurence Oliphant* (London: Marshall, 1891);

Rosamond Dale Owen, *My Perilous Life in Palestine* (London: Allen & Unwin, 1928);

Herbert Wallace Schneider, *A Prophet and a Pilgrim: Being the Incredible History of Thomas Lake Harris and Laurence Oliphant* (New York: Columbia University Press, 1942);

John Hanning Speke, *Journal of the Discovery of the Source of the Nile* (Edinburgh: Blackwood, 1863).

Julia Pardoe

(1804 – 26 November 1862)

Anita G. Gorman
Slippery Rock University

BOOKS: *Lord Morcar of Hereward: A Romance of the Times of William the Conqueror,* 4 volumes (London: Newman, 1829);

Traits and Traditions of Portugal Collected During a Residence in That Country, 2 volumes (London: Saunders & Otley, 1833; Philadelphia: Carey, Lea & Blanchard, 1834);

Speculation: A Novel. By the Author of Traits and Traditions of Portugal, 3 volumes (London: Saunders & Otley, 1834; New York: Harper, 1834);

The Mardens and the Daventrys: Tales, by the author of Traits and Traditions of Portugal, 3 volumes (London: Saunders & Otley, 1835; Philadelphia: Carey, Lea & Blanchard, 1835);

The City of the Sultan, and Domestic Manners of the Turks in 1836, 2 volumes (London: Colburn, 1837; Philadelphia: Carey, Lea & Blanchard, 1837);

The River and the Desart, or Recollections of the Rhone and the Chartreuse, 2 volumes (London: Colburn, 1838; Philadelphia: Carey & Hart, 1838);

The Beauties of the Bosphorus (London: Virtue, 1838);

The Romance of the Harem (3 volumes, London: Colburn, 1839; 2 volumes, Philadelphia: Carey & Hart, 1839);

The City of the Magyar, or, Hungary and Her Institutions in 1839–40, 3 volumes (London: Virtue, 1840);

The Hungarian Castle (London: Boone, 1842); republished as *Hungarian Tales and Legends* (New York: Wilson, 1842);

The Confessions of a Pretty Woman, 3 volumes (London: Colburn, 1846; New York: Harper, 1846);

Louis the Fourteenth, and the Court of France in the Seventeenth Century, 3 volumes (London: Bentley, 1846; New York: Harper, 1847);

The Rival Beauties: A Novel, 3 volumes (London: Bentley, 1848; Philadelphia: Peterson, n.d.);

The Court and Reign of Francis the First, King of France, 2 volumes (London: Bentley, 1849; New York: Scribner & Welford, 1887);

Flies in Amber, 3 volumes (London: Shorberl, 1850);

Julia Pardoe

The Life of Marie de Medicis, Queen of France, Consort of Henry IV, and Regent of the Kingdom Under Louis XIII, 3 volumes (London: Colburn, 1852; New York: Scribner & Welford, 1890);

Reginald Lyle, 3 volumes (London: Hurst & Blackett, 1854; New York: Burgess & Day, 1854); republished as *The Adopted Heir* (Philadelphia: Peterson, n.d.); republished as *The Rich Relation* (London: Clarke, 1862);

The Jealous Wife, 3 volumes (London: Chapman & Hall, 1855; New York: Fetridge, 1855);

The Wife's Trials: A Novel (New York: Fetridge, 1855);

Lady Arabella; or, The Adventures of a Doll (London: Kerby & Son, 1856);

Abroad and At Home: Tales Here and There (London, 1857);

Pilgrimages in Paris (London: Lay, 1857);

The Poor Relation: A Novel, 3 volumes (London: Hurst & Blackett, 1858);

Episodes of French History During the Consulate and the First Empire, 2 volumes (London: Hurst & Blackett, 1859; New York: Harper, 1859);

A Life-Struggle, 2 volumes (London: Booth, 1859; New York: Pooley, 1860); republished as *The Earl's Secret* (Philadelphia: Peterson, 1865).

OTHER: Guido Sorelli, *La Peste, Poema di Guido Sorelli,* translated by Pardoe (London: Dulau, 1834);

"The Will," in *Seven Tales by Seven Authors,* edited by F. E. Smedley (London: Hoby, 1849);

Anita George, *Memoirs of the Queens of Spain,* edited by Pardoe (London: Bentley, 1850); republished as *Annals of the Queens of Spain* (New York: Baker & Scribner, 1850);

Prosper Denaux and Ernest Legouvé, *Louise de Lignerolles: A Tragic Drama in Five Parts,* adapted by Pardoe (London: Lacy, 1854);

The Thousand and One Days: A Companion to the "Arabian Nights," introduction by Pardoe (London: Lay, 1857; Baltimore: Murphy, 1858); republished as *Hassan Abdallah: Or, The Enchanted Keys, and Other Tales; a Companion to the "Arabian Nights"* (Baltimore: Kelly, Hedian & Piet, 1860);

Alone! A Ballad, poetry by Pardoe, music composed by Sir Jules Benedict (London: Cramer, n.d.).

SELECTED PERIODICAL PUBLICATIONS –
UNCOLLECTED: "On the Rise and Progress of Magyar Literature," *Foreign and Colonial Quarterly Review,* 29 (April 1842): 204–227;

"A Scene in the Life of Torquato Tasso," *Dublin University Magazine,* 21 (April 1843): 482–485;

"Hayti, Its Past and Present State," *Foreign and Colonial Quarterly Review,* 3 (1844): 553–591.

A prolific travel writer, novelist, and collector of tales, Julia Pardoe ranks with Lady Mary Wortley Montagu as one of the most knowledgeable and influential English interpreters of Turkish life; she is also credited with shaping the generally positive view of Hungary held by nineteenth-century English readers. Although twentieth-century readers know little about her work, Pardoe's narrative gift and grace of style secured a wide popularity for her writings in her own day.

Julia Sophia H. Pardoe was the second daughter of Maj. Thomas Pardoe, an English officer who served at the Battle of Waterloo, and his wife Elizabeth. Although 1806 is commonly thought to have been the year of her birth, baptismal records from Saint John parish in Beverley, Yorkshire, her birthplace, confirm that Pardoe was baptized on 4 December 1804. Pardoe did not write an autobiography, but an unsigned memoir attached to the 1887 edition of her book *The Court and Reign of Francis the First, King of France* (1849) is an important supplement to other sources about her life. She began to write in childhood, publishing in her early teens a volume of poetry dedicated to her uncle Capt. William Pardoe; the book was successful enough to merit a second edition. One of her contemporaries, Samuel Carter Hall, in his *Book of Memories of Great Men and Women of the Age* described Pardoe in 1826 as a "fairy-footed, fair-haired, laughing, sunny girl," adding that Pardoe tried even in her later years "to be as vivacious as she was at eighteen." In 1829 she published *Lord Morcar of Hereward: A Romance of the Times of William the Conqueror.* Because the family worried that their daughter's "consumptive symptoms" (alluded to in the 1887 memoir) would result in tuberculosis, Pardoe, like many English people of the time, traveled to a warmer climate on the Continent, where she found material both for her novels and her travel literature. Her first book to draw interest was *Traits and Traditions of Portugal Collected During a Residence in That Country* (1833), reflections on a fifteen-month stay on the Continent and dedicated to the Princess Augusta, who had encouraged her efforts. The work illustrates Pardoe's faults as well as her talents. The author of the unsigned biography of Pardoe in *The Court and Reign of Francis the First* described Pardoe's Portuguese memoir thus: "Written in early youth and amidst the brilliant scenes it described, it had the charm of freshness and enthusiasm, and it is not surprising that a second edition was quickly called for." A twentieth-century reader may find the book dated in its style: "How often do my thoughts revert to the sunny hours which I passed on your mountains and in your valleys; among your kind-hearted and friendly peasantry, and amid the lordly halls and cloisters of your palaces and convents!" Nevertheless, the book ably satisfied the Victorian thirst for travelogue and for tales of romance, violence, and intrigue. Both chatty and rambling, *Traits and Traditions of Portugal* moves from eyewitness descriptions of various locales to anecdotes or legends told to the author. Although Pardoe speaks of "PLEASANT Portugal!" and her "many delightful memories" of the country,

Frontispiece and title page for Pardoe's book about her travels to southern France (courtesy of the Lilly Library, Indiana University)

she frequently reveals a condescending as well as an anti-Catholic attitude. On the other hand, Pardoe often conveys the reality of a beautiful place, even if she errs on the side of Victorian richness:

> Let the imagination revel amid groves of orange trees, laden at once with fruit, flower, and perfume – amid tracts of the dark olive and stately pine, relieved by the fragrant and lively foliage of the myrtle and geranium – clumps of the delicate gumcistus, carpeting the earth with the leaves of its own frail and fairy-like flowers – groups of graceful almond trees, shedding at once their soft perfume and their sweet flowers on the summer wind – alleys of lemon and citron, bowers of roses and springs and rills of the coolest and clearest water, yielding nature's own mirror to the clinging tufts of violets and wild lilies which blossom spontaneously on their margin – let it do all this, and yet it will scarcely trace on its mental table the luxuriant landscape.

In 1835 Pardoe traveled with her father to Constantinople, another site of literary inspiration for her, even if her visit was fraught with some danger because of an outbreak of cholera. The *Dictionary of National Biography*, echoing the

1887 memoir, states that Pardoe and Montagu, who wrote in the previous century, knew more about Turkey than any other women writers. Pardoe's *The City of the Sultan, and Domestic Manners of the Turks in 1836*, published in 1837, was favorably reviewed in the *London Atlas* and reprinted as a three-volume work in 1838, 1845, and 1854. Her appreciation for the Islamic culture of Turkey surpasses her earlier, lukewarm appreciation of Catholic Portugal; and her descriptions of dervishes, harems, baths, mental hospitals, and slaves still command interest. *The Beauties of the Bosphorus* (1838), another work inspired by her trip to Turkey and reprinted under the title *Picturesque Europe* (1854), begins with a particularly eloquent appreciation of experience:

> Every enjoyment of life has three distinct stages – anticipation – reality – and reminiscence; and it is more difficult than it at first appears to be, to decide on the comparative extent and value of each. Hope is the most extravagant and imaginative; action, the most engrossing and tangible; and memory, the most calm, and durable, and sober.

In the book, handsomely illustrated by W. H. Bartlett and characterized by Pardoe as a "purely descriptive work," she writes that the "true charm of the Bosphorus . . . lies in its endless variety of perspective; it is like a garland, woven by the hand of beauty, of which each blossom is brighter than the last; not a rock, not a tree, not a tower, could be displaced without injury to the whole." Throughout her book Pardoe extols the beauty, variety, and exotic appeal of the places she and her illustrator visit, in the "hope that our pictorial and literary pictures may induce the traveller on his summer trip to Palmyra, Balbek, or Jerusalem, not to overlook in his haste the fair city of Byzantium."

A trip to the south of France resulted in *The River and the Desart, or Recollections of the Rhone and the Chartreuse* (1838), a book criticized by the *Athenaeum* but commended by both the *Court Journal* and the *London Atlas*. Consisting of affectionate letters written by Pardoe to a friend, the book is dedicated to Mrs. John Hearne, probably the original recipient of the letters. In the preface Pardoe calls attention to the book's spontaneity, writing that she kept the "irrelevant matter." Acknowledging that "the heaviest blame which has hitherto been visited on my works, has been their 'ornate and ambitious style,' " she writes that, because these are personal letters, "in the present instance this defect cannot be supposed to exist." She adds that if the defect does indeed exist, she offers her tongue-in-cheek apology by quoting Mascarille's remark in Molière's comedy *Les Precieuses Ridicules:* "Tout ce que je fais me vient naturellement, c'est sans tude" (Everything that I do comes to me naturally, it is without study).

The effusive letters in *The River and the Desart* include an account of a liturgy at the Cathedral of Notre Dame in Paris, a visit to that other well-known English travel writer Frances Trollope (about whom Pardoe reveals little), references to seasickness, nostalgia for home, and philosophical discussions concerning such matters as the effect of circumstances on "human character" and the contrast between memory and hope. Pardoe alludes to female dependency, citing "a beauty in the helplessness of woman," admitting that "such dependence of woman in the common affairs of life is, nevertheless, rather the effect of custom than necessity: we have many and brilliant proofs that, where need is, she can be sufficient to herself, and play her part in the great drama of existence with credit, if not with comfort." An outbreak of cholera in Marseilles evokes the drama and fear of an eyewitness to death: "Another day of terror! The sun is broad and scorching; the sea lies rippleless like a sheet of lead, for there is not a breath of air to break its mirror-like surface." With her view of Catholic culture apparently broadened since her sojourn in Portugal, Pardoe writes lyrically of the landscape of southern France, of religious processions, of the "Carthusian Desart" and the impressive monastery of La Grande Chartreuse. "Let the Atheist come here, and tremble!" she writes. "He may approach with scoffing upon his lip; but, ere he turn away, he will have raised a shrine within his heart to the God of Nature and of Love!" Like other of her books, *The River and the Desart* combines travel literature and tales — in this case, "The Boatman's Story" in letter 23.

In *The City of the Magyar, or, Hungary and Her Institutions in 1839–40* (1840) Pardoe mixes her travelogue with comments on Hungarian politics and society. The essays in the book are structured thematically around such topics as agriculture, the press, education, food, government, and churches and are intertwined with excursions from Pest, the "city of the Magyar." Later scholars have credited Pardoe with being one of the originators of the positive view of Hungary held by many English people in the nineteenth century.

During this period Pardoe translated Guido Sorelli's poem *La Peste* (1834) and also produced novels and collections of tales, including *Speculation* (1834), *The Mardens and the Daventrys* (1835), *The Romance of the Harem* (1839), and *The Hungarian Castle* (1842).

Pardoe left London about 1842 to live with her parents on Perry Street, near Gravesend, and later at Northfleet in Kent. Other works of fiction followed, including *The Confessions of a Pretty Woman* (1846), *The Rival Beauties* (1848), *Flies in Amber* (1850), *Reginald Lyle* (1854), *The Jealous Wife* (1855), *Lady Arabella* (1856), *A Life-Struggle* (1859), and *The Rich Relation* (1862). More nonfiction works also appeared during this period, among which were *The Court and Reign of Francis the First* and *Louis the Fourteenth, and the Court of France in the Seventeenth Century* (1846). *Pilgrimages in Paris* (1857) is a collection of tales that includes some description of the French capital. In 1857 Pardoe wrote the introduction to *The Thousand and One Days; a Companion to the "Arabian Nights,"* a book described in the British Museum catalogue as "a Collection of Oriental tales . . . principally derived from the works of different Oriental Scholars on the Continent." The book was republished in the United States in 1860 as *Hassan Abdallah: or, The Enchanted Keys, and Other Tales: A Companion to the "Arabian Nights."* Many of Pardoe's works were originally serialized for British and American periodicals, including the *Foreign and Colonial Quarterly Review*, which in 1844 published her lengthy and thoughtful analysis of the Haitian Revolution, "Hayti, its Past and Present State."

In January 1860 the British government granted Pardoe a civil list pension "in consideration of thirty years' toil in the field of literature, by which she has contributed both to cultivate the public taste and to support a number of helpless relations." Pardoe died at Upper Montagu Street, London, on 26 November 1862.

J. Cody Jeaffreson, in *Novels and Novelists, from Elizabeth to Victoria* (1858), said about the writing of his contemporary that "Miss Pardoe has shown herself capable of constructing ingenious plots, of charming by lively, and at times, gorgeously coloured narrative, and of giving an attractive and novel exposition of history." S. Austin Allibone, in his *Critical Dictionary* (1871), gives an extensive list of her publications and quotes Henry Theodore Tuckerman's judgment that "Miss Pardoe's pictures of French history are as charming as a novel" (probably not the sort of judgment a historian would relish). The *Dictionary of National Biography* calls Julia Pardoe "a warm-hearted woman, singularly bright and animated; a capital raconteuse, and, notwithstanding her literary talents, learned in the domestic arts." Her portrait, drawn by J. Lilley in 1849 and engraved by Samuel Freeman, appears with the memoir that accompanies the second edition of *The Court and Reign of Francis the First.* Although "all" her books were published in the United States, according to Sarah Josepha Hale, the American compiler of *Woman's Record: or, Sketches of all Distinguished Women from the Creation to A.D. 1868* (1873), "she has never been a favourite in our reading republic. There seems to us something wanting in her writings; her works of fact want historic truth in details, those of fiction want impassioned truth in sentiment." Whereas Hale asserts that British reviewers generally admired Pardoe's work, Pardoe herself was sensitive to negative criticisms of her books, remarking in a letter to Sir John Philippart in 1855 concerning her novel *The Jealous Wife:* "All reviews have hitherto been most favorable, except the *Athenaeum* that has its usual snarl at me as a matter of course." But it was the *Athenaeum* that had the last word in its assessment of Pardoe's work a few weeks after her death:

> The list of her works is very long, and as most of her works appeared in three volumes, a collection of them would fill a shelf. *The City of the Sultan* had in its day a certain share of success, but neither that nor any of its fellows had the strong quality which keeps a book alive. The writer's reputation was of the kind which belongs to a day like a fashion in dress or a caprice in music.

Still, a caprice in music is worth hearing again, and fashions return in another age; similarly, Julia Pardoe's travel literature, especially her work on Turkey, Hungary, and France, deserves to be re-read and studied.

References:

William Morris Coles, *Literature and the Pension List* (London: Society of Authors, 1889);

Sarah Josepha Hale, *Woman's Record: or, Sketches of all Distinguished Women from the Creation to A.D. 1868* (New York: Harper, 1873);

Samuel Carter Hall, *Book of Memories of Great Men and Women of the Age, from Personal Acquaintances,* third edition (London: Virtue, n.d.);

J. Cody Jeaffreson, *Novels and Novelists, from Elizabeth to Victoria,* 2 volumes (London: Hurst & Blackett, 1858);

Judit Kadar, "Two English Authoresses on Hungary in the Early Victorian Age," *Neohelicon: Acta Comparationis Litterarum Universarum,* 17, no. 2 (1990): 213–228;

Lola L. Szladits, "A Victorian Literary Correspondence: Letters from Julia Pardoe to Sir John Philippart, 1841–1860," *Bulletin of the New York Public Library,* 59 (1955): 367–377.

Papers:

Letters written by Julia Pardoe to Sir John Philippart (1841–1860) are in the Berg Collection, New York Public Library. The British Library houses some plays of Julia Pardoe, as well as publishing agreements with Bentley and a biographical notice. Letters from Pardoe to Francis and Margaret Bennoch and to Samuel Carter and Anna Maria (Fielding) Hall are housed in the University of Iowa Libraries, Iowa City. An untitled poem which begins "Joy be to you! Oh, Joy! Whom lengthening years . . . " and inscribed "To my dear friends Mr. and Mrs. Hearne on the 19th Anniversary of their Wedding-Day" (30 May 1840) forms part of the Ruby T. Scott Collection, University of Toledo (Ohio). A letter to Leigh Hunt (19 December 1842) from Pardoe is in the Leigh Hunt Collection, Indiana University, Bloomington. Some letters of Julia Pardoe are included in the Abrahams Autograph Collection, Knox College Archives, Galesburg, Illinois.

Sophia Poole

(16 January 1804 – 6 May 1891)

Sandra W. Stephan
Youngstown State University

BOOKS: *The Englishwoman in Egypt: Letters from Cairo, Written During a Residence There in 1842, 3, and 4, with E. W. Lane Esq.* (2 volumes, London: Knight, 1844; 1 volume, Philadelphia: Zieber, 1845);

The Englishwoman in Egypt: Letters from Cairo, Written During a Residence There in 1845–46, with E. W. Lane Esq., by his sister, second series (London: Knight, 1846).

OTHER: Francis Frith, *Egypt, Sinai, and Jerusalem: A Series of Twenty Photographic Views,* with descriptions by Poole and Reginald Stuart Poole (London: MacKenzie, [1860]);

Frith, *Cairo, Sinai, Jerusalem, and the Pyramids of Egypt: A Series of Sixty Photographic Views,* with descriptions by Poole and Reginald Stuart Poole (London: Virtue, [1860–1861]).

Sophia Poole was uniquely qualified to provide an account of Egyptian life, manners, and customs. No mere traveler, Poole actually made Cairo her home for more than seven years. As sister of the eminent Arabic scholar Edward William Lane, with whom she resided, she enjoyed access to the homes, harems, and conversations of some of that city's most prominent citizens. The popularity of Lane's work, *An Account of the Manners and Customs of Modern Egyptians* (1836), assured an eager audience for Poole's personal accounts of Egyptian life from a woman's point of view, *The Englishwoman in Egypt* (1844), and her work forms a lively companion piece to her brother's. Her experiences in Egypt and her scholarly interests in the East prepared her well to write the texts that accompanied Francis Frith's powerful photographs published in the early 1860s.

Little is recorded about Poole's early life and education, but it is certain that she was nurtured by influences both creative and scholarly. Born in Hereford, England, on 16 January 1804, she was the youngest child and only daughter of the Reverend Theophilus Lane, prebendary of Hereford, and Sophia Gardiner Lane, a niece of the artist Thomas Gainsborough. In addition to Edward she had two other brothers, Theophilus and Richard, the latter of whom became a renowned London lithographer. Her father died when she was only ten years old. Her mother was a woman of strong intellect and great strength and influence, deeply admired by her children, particularly Sophia and Edward, her two youngest, and indeed by all who met her. In 1829 Sophia married Edward Richard Poole, a Cambridge barrister who had recently taken holy orders. Like her brother, Poole's husband was a scholar; he gained a modest reputation as a bibliographer and book collector and anonymously published a work on the best editions of Greek and Roman classics, *The Classical Collectors' "Vade Mecum"* (1822). In 1830 Sophia bore her first son, Edward Stanley Poole; her second son, Reginald Stuart Poole, was born in 1832.

Although the date of Edward Poole's death is uncertain, by 1842 Poole and her two children were living with her elderly mother in Hastings. Her mother's death that same year precipitated the remarkable circumstances that removed Poole from her quiet English country life and thrust her into the exotic society of Cairo. Poole's brother Edward, whose reputation as an orientalist was by now firmly established, was preparing to return to Egypt for his third visit and convinced her to accompany him. She needed little persuasion, having developed an "eager curiosity" about the land in which her brother had spent so many years and about which he had written so authoritatively. On 1 July 1842 Poole, her two young sons, Lane, and his wife set sail for Egypt, where they were destined to stay until October 1849 – an experience that shaped the lives and careers not only of Poole but of her children, and subsequently of two of her grandsons.

Even before her departure from England, Poole, at the urging of her brother, had proposed to record her observations of Egyptian society for the purpose of publication. Not only could she provide a woman's perspective on the culture Lane had so definitively described, but as a woman Poole would have access to the intimate aspects of Egyptian women's lives, from which Lane would always be barred. Her plan was to write of her experiences, especially as they related to her "insight into the mode of life of the higher classes of the ladies in this country." The work would take the form of a series of familiar letters, which her brother would edit or approve before sending on to England. In addition to Poole's personal observations, the letters would include some of Lane's own descriptions and observations, gleaned by Poole from manuscript notes he provided her. She also knew that her brother's reputation would pave the way for the public reception of her own work. The readers in whom Lane's work had aroused such widespread interest would certainly be more than eager to learn of an English-woman's responses to the Eastern world, and particularly to discover that aspect of Egyptian life that could only be experienced by a female – life behind the harem curtain.

Poole depended heavily on Lane's reputation, as well as on his writings. She saw her own work almost as an appendix to his more scholarly editions, referring her reader to his works on many occasions and quoting him extensively. Whether it was Lane's idea, as Poole suggests in her preface, or her own, the letter format was fortunate. The letters, addressed to "My Dear Friend," are, for the most part, lively, informative, and splendidly descriptive. Poole's genial, interesting, almost chatty letters contrast sharply with the lengthy and sometimes excruciatingly detailed historical and geographical descriptions by Lane that she occasionally chose to include. Poole was obviously comfortable with the format, and the personality that emerges as she relates her experiences is that of an enthusiastic, curious, adventurous – yet still quite proper – woman, eager to engage as fully as possible in Eastern life. Her brother had adopted the language, dress, and manners of the Egyptians from his first visit, and there was no question that Poole would do the same.

Poole faced her first long voyage – and her new life – with both anticipation and trepidation, and she suffered both seasickness and homesickness on the voyage out. "The sea-sickness was welcome to me," she writes, "for it confined me to my bed, and spared me the pain of seeing my own dear country, which holds so many and so much we love, fade from my sight." The party arrived in Alexandria on 19 July 1842 and a few days later set out for Cairo, where they would spend the duration of their stay, with the single exception of a short excursion to the pyramids. The trip to Cairo was not without difficulties; for the first leg of the journey they traveled in a horse-drawn, iron-track boat, during which Poole learned a hard lesson on the necessity of mosquito netting in such a climate. Reaching the Nile River, they found that the boat they had hired had been sent on another mission, and they were forced to wait two more days in oppressive heat before beginning their three-day sail to Cairo; here the whole party fell quite ill, Poole's boys particularly, and return to England was contemplated. But the illness passed, and they proceeded, reaching port on 27 July. As soon as they arrived, Poole experienced for the first time the Eastern costume: "Imagine the face covered closely by a muslin veil, double at the upper part, the eyes only uncovered, and over a dress of coloured silk an overwhelming covering of black silk, extending, in my idea, in every direction; so that, having nothing free but my eyes, I looked with dismay at the high bank I must climb, and the donkey I must mount." Before long she was quite comfortable in the native clothing; she was also quite aware that without it, she would not gain access to the harems that she hoped to visit.

Poole's quest to be invited to enter the harems of Cairo was soon successful. In February 1843 she was introduced to the harem of Habeeb Effendi, the former governor of Cairo, by the wife of the resident English missionary, Poole's mentor and guide. To call on the high harem Poole was obliged to ride the "high ass," a rather precariously perched saddle, rather than the prayer carpet and ordinary donkey saddle to which she had become accustomed. She found it, to her surprise, "infinitely more agreeable," although it did require her constant vigilance for the overhanging bay windows of the city. Within the harem Poole was received as a welcomed and honored guest, first having her riding dress ceremoniously removed by the elder daughter, rather than by a slave, and then being seated next to the place of honor reserved for the "Chief Lady." On these occasions Poole chose to wear her English dress under the Muslim riding outfit, "thus avoiding the necessity of subjecting myself to any humiliation." In the Turkish indoor costume, she

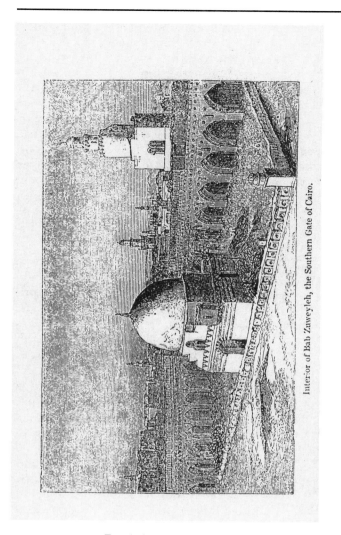

THE

ENGLISHWOMAN IN EGYPT:

LETTERS FROM CAIRO,

WRITTEN DURING A RESIDENCE THERE IN 1842, 3, & 4,

WITH

E. W. LANE, Esq.

AUTHOR OF 'THE MODERN EGYPTIANS.'

BY HIS SISTER.

IN TWO VOLUMES—VOL. I.

LONDON:

CHARLES KNIGHT AND CO.,

LUDGATE-STREET.

1845.

Frontispiece and title page to Poole's first book, her observations on Egyptian society and harem life

explained, "the manner of my salutations must have been more submissive than I should have liked."

During her stay in Egypt, Poole revisited this harem several times and was once given the seat of honor. She also visited the harem of an unfortunate Turkish grandee who had been imprisoned, leaving his family sadly distraught. Ultimately she gained entrance to the harem of the pasha himself, where she participated in a nine-day wedding festival for the pasha's daughter, during which she stayed the night in the harem apartments. In a visit to a less exalted harem, that of the keeper of the tombs of the southern cemetery, she was distressed to find their play with the children encouraging domestic violence – a facet of Arab life that Poole encountered on several occasions. She also participated in the harem activities associated with funeral rites, observing the washing, dressing, wrapping, and entombment of the body. At the funeral observance

for one of the wives of Mohammed Ali, in 1846, she attended the ritual breaking of dishes and glasses as a symbol of mourning.

The habit of the Lane-Poole household of eating according to local practice served her well when she was entertained by the pasha's women, who, as is their custom, use no utensils and serve their honored guests using their fingers. "And here I must digress," she writes, "to beg you not to say 'How very disgusting!' but read *how* we do it." Poole enjoyed the sweetmeats, sherbets, stews, and coffees, delicious and elegantly served, and was quite comfortable seated on elegant carpets at the low serving tables. She even grew used to the scent of the tobacco that the women of the harem smoked in jeweled pipes. In fact, she saw much to recommend harem life, "a little world of women," with a clear hierarchy and set of rules, much like a convent. She saw the women of the harem as having a great deal of autonomy and was interested to hear them engage in discussions of politics and international affairs, although she bemoaned the fact that they were, for the most part, illiterate. Poole was especially intrigued by the fact that a pair of slippers placed outside the harem curtain served as a signal to the husband that a female guest was visiting and therefore he must not enter.

Poole also availed herself of the public bath, which she found to be "extremely agreeable," although she was astonished to see so many naked women and girls. Poole participated in the entire process of the bath (with a few exceptions), including the steam room, the massage, the joint cracking (here Poole declined to partake), the body rubbing (she did not approve of the rasps but preferred the coarse woolen mitts), the repeated lathering and rinsing of face and head, and the final and most agreeable general lathering and rubbing. Poole found "the very foreign scenes" and the "deafening and incessant" noise of the children to be the only drawbacks of the public bath.

In addition to her formal and public experiences, observing wedding rituals and funeral processions, participating in holiday festivals, taking part in harem ceremonies, and her brief excursion to the pyramids in February 1844, Poole's stay in Cairo was punctuated by personal experiences that she willingly and engagingly related. For example, within a month of their arrival and after much difficulty, she and her brother were able to engage, at an exceptionally reasonable rate, a remarkably lovely house located in the outskirts of the city. When the servants complained that the bath was haunted, Poole dismissed their concerns as Muslim superstition. The disturbances continued, however, until Poole was almost convinced that a spirit did indeed reside in the house. Ultimately forced to vacate the place, Poole reported that six families after theirs had moved in and out in as many weeks; "I have said much upon it, but I must be held excusable, as 'tis passing strange.' "

Shortly after arriving in Cairo, Poole described her communication difficulty with a young servant girl who ran away every time Poole beckoned her. After several of these odd flights, Poole discovered that the European signal to come forward was the same as the Arab signal to go away. On another occasion she discovered a huge brown snake in her apartments. When the servant was sent to find a snake charmer, he returned with a man who was nearly blind and mistook a towel for the serpent. Amid the confusion the snake escaped into the house, leaving her with only the snake charmer's assurance that it was merely a harmless house snake – better, she concluded, than the dreaded scorpion. When they visited the pyramids, Poole's party was met by a group of young Arabs who had sought them out in hopes of seeing the faces of European women. Although they were quite disappointed to find Poole and her companions in Muslim dress, the men related that they had been able to see an American lady a few weeks before. Although her letters cease in 1846, Poole stayed in Egypt for three more years. Little is known about her experiences during that time, except that for awhile she fell dangerously ill with cholera and typhus. She and her entourage left Egypt on 16 October 1849 and set sail for England.

The Englishwoman in Egypt appeared in 1844 in two volumes, beginning with a letter dated July 1842 and ending abruptly with a letter of April 1844. An editor's note explains that "through some accidental circumstances, the communication has been interrupted," and the volume is filled out with appendixes taken from Lane's *Modern Egyptians*. In 1846 a third volume appeared, containing letters dated from January 1845 to March 1846, and this was followed by appendixes drawn from Lane's notes to *The Thousand and One Nights*. Poole's letters were published in the Knight's Weekly Volume series, the same one in which Lane's translation of *The Thousand and One Nights* had been published in monthly installments through 1838–1840, and his *Modern Egyptians* appeared in a fourth edition in 1847. That Lane's name was intended to serve as a draw for Poole's work is evidenced by the fact that his name alone, and not Poole's, appears on the title page; the author is identified only as "his sister," although her full name follows the preface.

In fact, Poole's work was lauded on the strength of her own writing, as the reviewer for *Blackwood's Magazine* noted in March 1845: "The authoress can very well afford to rest her claim to popularity on her own merits; and we prefer to follow her, in her own peculiar sphere, into those mysterious recesses of an Oriental establishment, wither [*sic*] no male footstep can ever penetrate." As the only Englishwoman to gain access to the scenes of Egyptian domestic life, which she so admirably described, Poole was able to provide her readers with full, enlightening, and engaging pictures of the life of Egyptian women. She reports her observations with a receptive eye, exhibiting, for the most part, respect for Muslims' beliefs and admiration for their moral behavior, only occasionally expressing the inevitable Christian concerns regarding questions of salvation. If she seems at times to relate more than a representative number of episodes in which Egyptians are depicted as swindlers or cheats, she also spends a good deal of time discussing the favorable aspects of the harem system.

Poole's two 1844 volumes were published in one volume in America in 1845 and reprinted in England in 1851–1853, and their popularity is evidenced by the fact that in his revision of *Modern Egyptians* in 1846 Lane refers his readers to Poole's work, "which has been too well received to need my recommendation."

After her return to England from Egypt in 1849, Poole and her family settled with her brother, first in Hastings, then in Worthing. It was here that, in collaboration with her younger son, Reginald Stuart, she wrote the text to accompany Francis Frith's photographs of Egypt, Jerusalem, Sinai, and the pyramids. When the volumes were published in 1860 and 1861, Poole's literary reputation was sufficiently established that the title pages bear her name, "Mrs. Poole," with no reference to her brother. Although there had been abundant illustrations in her earlier work, there they served to illuminate the text. In these luxurious volumes the photographs became the central focus that the text served to explain. The writing here is necessarily more formal and less personal than that of *The Englishwoman in Egypt*, and, indeed, circumstances were quite different for travelers by that time as well. Egypt and the Holy Lands were no longer quite so exotic and unreachable as they had been nearly twenty years earlier when Poole first set out on her travels, and the advent of photography altered the needs of the reader for descriptions. The success of these texts, then, rests not in relation of the experiences of the travel writer, but in the ability of the writer to breathe life into the images the camera has captured. Poole's descriptions are relatively brief, providing historical, geographical, and cultural information to accompany each photograph, occasionally quoting the Arabian poets but more frequently citing the Bible — no doubt more appropriate for her Victorian audience. There is little room for anecdote in these works, the form in which Poole had excelled in her earlier work, and the descriptions, with only one or two exceptions, are of landscape or landmarks or ruins; there is no room at all for the intimate descriptions of the daily course of women's lives. Nevertheless, Poole's descriptions created for the reader a mood of the scenes pictured. In a description of the desert, for example, she writes

The desert is vast as the sea, more silent, and as unmarked by the ever-passing, but never-resting, sons of men. Its air is purer, its heaven clearer, and its stars more bright, than where the rivers and watered plains send up their thick vapours. With a prospect so grandly harmonious, and with so perfect a climate, life is more enjoyable than in any other condition. The body feels no weariness, and the spirits never flag. In the hottest season the fierce sun often oppresses and almost strikes down the wanderer; but if he take shelter in his tent, the evening will bring the freshest and purest of breezes to restore his strength, and he will set forth with new vigour for a march in the cool of the early morning.

The Frith photographs with Poole's text were immensely well received.

Poole lived with her brother in Worthing for the rest of his life. Both her sons became prominent scholars — Edward, an Arabic scholar and editor of his uncle's works; and Reginald, a noted archaeologist and orientalist. After the death of her elder son, Edward, in 1867, her three young grandchildren joined the household. Two of these grandsons were to become distinguished in their own right: Reginald Lane Poole as an Oxford historian and curator of the Bodleian, and Stanley Lane Poole as an orientalist and Arabic scholar. Following Lane's death in 1876, Poole moved to the home of her son Reginald in the British Museum, where he was keeper of coins and medals. There she died on 6 May 1891 at the age of eighty-seven.

Poole's travel volumes, though slender, provide a lively and detailed record of experiences in a culture on the brink of immense and irrevocable change, change that she herself lamented as early as July 1843, when the pasha ordered renovations in the city that essentially eliminated the Arab architectural features of the city. The opening of the East to Europeans through the development of steam travel by rail and sea altered forever the society that Poole had described. Her writings preserve for readers a taste of the exotic East that was fast disappearing.

References:

[Frederick Holme], "Mrs. Poole's 'Englishwoman in Egypt,'" *Blackwood's Magazine*, 57 (March 1845): 286–297;

Edward William Lane, *The Manners and Customs of the Modern Egyptians*, edited by Edward Stanley Poole (London: Dent, 1908);

Billie Melman, *Women's Orients: English Women and the Middle East, 1718–1918* (Ann Arbor: University of Michigan Press, 1992);

Stanley Lane Poole, *The Life of Edward William Lane* (London: Williams & Norgate, 1877).

Marianne Postans

(circa 1810 - 1865)

Edward A. Malone
University of Missouri – Rolla

BOOKS: *Cutch; or, Random Sketches, Taken During a Residence in One of the Northern Provinces of Western India; Interspersed with Legends and Traditions,* as Mrs. Postans (London: Smith, Elder, 1839);

Western India in 1838, 2 volumes, as Mrs. Postans (London: Saunders & Otley, 1839);

Facts and Fictions, Illustrative of Oriental Character, 3 volumes, as Mrs. Postans (London: W. H. Allen, 1844);

Persecution in Tuscany: A Call for the Protection of Religious Liberty Throughout the World. A Letter to the Right Hon. W. E. Gladstone, M.P., Chancellor of the Exchequer, as "An English Traveller" (London: Seeleys, 1853);

Our Camp in Turkey, and the Way to It, as Mrs. Young (London: Bentley, 1854);

Aldershot, and All about It, with Gossip, Literary, Military, and Pictorial, as Mrs. Young (London: Routledge, 1857);

The Moslem Noble: His Land and People, with Some Notices of the Parsees, or Ancient Persians, as Mrs. Young (London: Saunders & Otley, 1857).

In *Victorian Women Travel Writers in Africa* (1982) Catherine Barnes Stevenson classifies her subjects as wives, missionaries, and vacationers. Her classifications, of course, apply not only to women travel writers in Africa. Victorian women who chronicled their travels in foreign countries, whether in Africa, America, or Asia, were almost always military wives, missionaries, or amateur travelers. Marianne Postans was no exception. As a military wife in India, she began her eighteen-year literary career (from 1839 to 1857) writing about the province of Cutch. After she had remarried, she became a vacationer and traveled in search of other, more exotic locations for her books. By the end of her career she had returned to England, where she wrote about her native country but also continued to write about India from memory. Her body of work, rich in variety and occasionally innovative in form, not only reflects her transformation from a lit-

erate military wife to a literary vacationer and eventually a retired traveler, but also documents her evolution from a patriotic, religious chauvinist to a compassionate, if not always accepting, student of diverse cultures.

Not much has been written about Postans's life. She is not included in the *Dictionary of National Biography,* nor is she mentioned in any recent reference works on Victorian writers, travel writers, or women authors. In the *Cyclopedia of English Literature* (1853) she is described as a writer who "resided some years in the province of Cutch." In *A Critical Dictionary of English Literature and British and American Authors* (1859), Samuel Austin Allibone identifies Postans as the wife of Thomas Postans — captain in the Bombay army, former assistant to the political agent in Sindh, and the author of two books, *Hints to Cadets* (1842) and *Personal Observations on Sindh* (1843). Noting that she had remarried, Allibone lists Marianne Postans as Mrs. M. Young, in the supplement to his dictionary (1896).

Between 1839 and 1857 Postans published six travel books, which can be divided into three sets. Her first two books, *Cutch; or, Random Sketches . . . of Western India* (1839) and *Western India in 1838* (1839), belong to her early period, when she was writing about India as a military wife. Her middle period, in which she published *Facts and Fictions, Illustrative of Oriental Character* (1844) and *Our Camp in Turkey, and the Way to It* (1854), spans approximately fifteen years, during which she became a vacationer, remarried, and changed her name from Postans to Young. The term *vacationer* suggests that Young traveled to foreign lands, rather than lived in them, for the purpose of writing books. Young's late period includes two books, *Aldershot, and All about It, with Gossip, Literary, Military, and Pictorial* (1857) and *The Moslem Noble: His Land and People* (1857), both written after the author had retired to England.

In the introduction to *Cutch; or, Random Sketches . . . of Western India,* Postans promises to give "a few slight sketches" of India's "more striking characteristics." The term *sketches* is doubly significant because Postans was an amateur artist as well as an aspiring writer and drew the sixteen illustrations for her book. The book opens with a narrative of her journey to the outpost where her husband has been stationed. She travels from Bombay to the British camp near Bhooj, stopping briefly at the palace of the local rao. In a chapter titled "The Harem" Postans describes her visit to the rao's harem, laments the secluded and degraded condition of his five ranis, or wives, and naively asserts that "[t]he Rao most sensibly regrets the existence of this characteristic custom of his country." After this chapter the narrative structure disintegrates, and the book becomes a series of discursive essays. The last chapter constitutes a summary or an overview of Cutch.

The randomness of the volume seems to confirm Mary Wollstonecraft's contention that "[a] man when he undertakes a journey, has in general, the end in view; a woman thinks more of the incidental occurrences, the strange things that may possibly occur on the road." *Cutch* consists mainly of "incidental occurrences" and "strange things," such as a discussion of female infanticide among the Rajput Jharrejah tribe and a chapter titled "Juggling, Snake-Charming, and Magic." Although she rails against tourist writers and painters who "bathe a favourite spot in all the light of graceful beauty, and the bright hues their own glowing and poetic imaginations suggest," Postans offers little of "the simple and vivid delineation of truth" that she extols as "the real triumph of literature and the fine arts" – a statement that simultaneously dismisses the fashionable Romanticism of her age and seems to anticipate the realism of the succeeding age. Her religious prejudice and sincere belief in her own superiority cause her to characterize the native population as indolent, ignorant, and dishonest. She ignores many of their virtues and tends to focus not on the ordinary features of their lives but on more sensational customs, such as the self-cremation (or suttee) of a Hindu woman at her husband's funeral.

Whereas the one-volume *Cutch* is discursive in content and random in organization, the two-volume *Western India in 1838* has a clear purpose and discernible structure. After thanking the public for the warm reception of her first book, Postans states her intention to sketch changes in the native gentry and represent western India as accurately as possible "through the medium of a lady's pen." To welcome the reader, she assumes the point of view of a long-term resident, who comes from the interior of India to greet a newcomer from England.

The book begins at the harbor in Bombay and fans out gradually to encompass most of western India. The first volume specifically deals with the presidency of Bombay and with its people. Its chapters cover the nonnative settlers, such as the Parsis and the Armenians; the European soldiers and their wives, who drink excessively and deport themselves immorally; the Indian peasants, mostly Hindus; and the "Flowers of the Prophet," Postans's favorite epithet for the Muslims. The style of volume one is dominated by the rhetorical figure *distributio,* which takes the form of myriad catalogues, such as an inventory of goods available at the bazaars in Bombay and a tedious list of birds to be found near the ancient city of Bassein.

Volume two, which focuses mainly on the area outside of the Bombay presidency, begins with a narration of Postans's trip in May 1838 to the holy hill of Girnar, "one of the five mounts sacred to the Jain sect." There she spends more than a week enjoying the serenity and sketching the landscape. On the way back from Girnar, Postans visits Muslim and Brahman harems, and her description of the secluded women allows her to use "a lady's pen" to its fullest advantage. The principal wife of the Muslim nuwaub questions Postans about England's female sovereign, desiring "to know whether our queen's power was great," and Postans takes great pleasure in edifying her. Having "never crossed the threshold of their father's house," the women in the Brahman harem are uncommonly ignorant in Postans's eyes. Consequently, rather than talk to them about customs and politics, Postans teaches them how to make tea in the English style. The remaining chapters include sketches of various religious festivals, a discussion of "Fortune Hunting in India," and an exhortation on "the Condition of Western India."

In the introduction to the book Postans promises to provide data about India's problems and its conditions so that others may analyze the information, which in turn may serve as the impetus for action and improvement. She structures each chapter rhetorically, first providing detailed information about a subject, then suggesting a means for improvement, and finally apologizing for being presumptuous enough to offer an opinion. In one of the early chapters of volume one, for example, she discusses the educational system of India, recounting her visit to a model school in Bombay, where the Parsi boys impress her by displaying their considerable knowledge of English history and literature. She laments the fact that they refuse to abandon their false religion, concedes that improvement

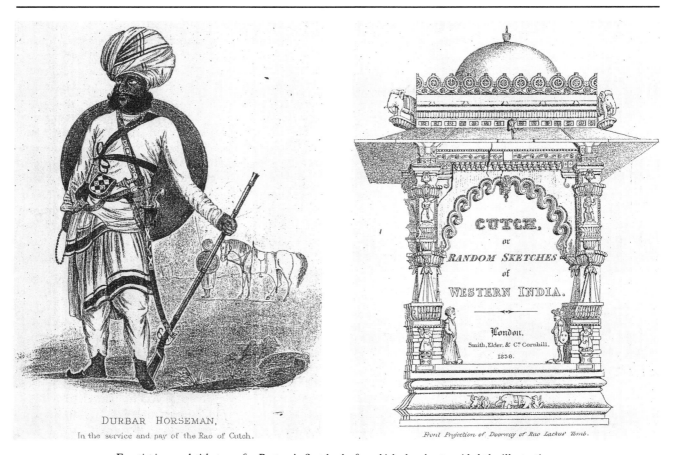

DURBAR HORSEMAN,
In the service and pay of the Rao of Cutch.

CUTCH,
or
RANDOM SKETCHES
of
WESTERN INDIA.

London.
Smith, Elder, & C? Cornhill.
1838.

Front Projection of Doorway of Rao Lackas' Tomb.

Frontispiece and title page for Postans's first book, for which she also provided the illustrations

must be effected in stages, and then says, "The aim of education must be to civilize, and through the medium of civilization, to *Christianize* the natives of India." She also maintains that military power cannot control India forever and that the British army must leave more than animosity in its wake. After offering these opinions, however, Postans apologizes: "It was not . . . my intention to dilate upon a subject which might be so much better treated by others, but simply to describe such scenes as have most particularly excited my attention."

Postans censures the Muslims harshly for invading India, butchering the natives, and ransacking the Hindu temples. She offers them as a negative example to the British, who must govern more wisely and humanely in India. In Postans's opinion the Muslims follow the Koran blindly and "believe anything, if told 'in the name of the prophet.' " She depicts her domestic servant, Abdool Kureem, as a figure of ridicule, grossly comic, with a "defective" memory. It is obvious that Postans prefers the Hindus, whom she describes as "a more docile race, more kindly in their natures,

more grateful, more capable of respect and attachment to their superiors." Beneath her condescension and prejudice lies a genuine sympathy for their poverty, filthy living conditions, and long history of persecution. Her even greater respect for the Buddhists is evident when she laments their persecution by the Brahmans and acknowledges "the high moral tone, and metaphysical subtilties [*sic*] of Buddism [*sic*]."

Apparently *Western India in 1838* was not well received by the English reading public. In the "Advertisement" to her third book, *Facts and Fictions, Illustrative of Oriental Character,* Postans writes:

Having passed many years in India, been charmed with its scenery, informed by its general characteristics, an expectation naturally arose, that my European friends would be gratified by a faithful transcript of that, which had afforded me so much pleasure.

Facts, however, disabused me of this opinion. The reading public I discovered to be totally uninterested in India, and all that concerned it, while I observed generally that a very ill-concealed lack of sympathy evidently existed towards the people of the East.

To create sympathy for native Indians and an interest in her subject, Postans decided to dip her pen "in the colours of romance" and tried nevertheless to be truthful. The result was a series of articles published in the *Asiatic Journal* between 1839 and 1844. Later she compiled these articles and added several more to form *Facts and Fictions,* a three-volume work that suggests her growing tolerance of and even fondness for Hindus and Muslims, of whom she is far less critical.

Early in volume one Postans narrates her visit to the Hospice of the Great St. Bernard in the Swiss Alps. Although seemingly out of place in a book about the "Oriental Character," the chapter serves as an invocation or prayer to the patron saint of travelers. The rest of the book consists, in alternating chapters, of a narrative of Postans's trip through Egypt, sketches of various characters and places, essays on India, and tales of forbidden love. To the narration of her Egyptian trip Postans devotes eight chapters, in which she discusses her visit to a Turkish harem in Cairo, her voyage up the Nile to the site of ancient Thebes, and her exploration of the pyramids and mummy tombs. In one memorable scene Postans inquires about buying a mummy and is shown a warehouse of partially decomposed bodies. She apparently visited Egypt in the aftermath of the wanton destruction of tombs and the pillaging of artifacts by European "explorers." Entering one tomb, she sees "Belzoni" written on the wall and berates the Italian explorer, Giovanni Battista Belzoni, for defacing the ancient glory of Egypt.

The sketches focus mainly on exotic places and characters, such as a famous Sindhian outlaw, whom she visited in a British prison, while the essays resemble the chapters in her previous books on India. In one essay she discusses her memories of Sind, where she and her first husband were stationed; in another she expounds upon the virtues of "Outstation Life," which she characterizes as solitary and difficult but also credits as the source of her fondness for "the country of [her] adoption." The tales, which constitute the "fictions" of the book's title, are romantic adventures in which a young woman of a wealthy family typically elopes with a man of the wrong religion. In one tale a daring outlaw rescues a young widow from a forced suttee. Together they flee to the hills, where they live long, happy lives together. Although shamelessly romantic and formulaic, these tales illustrate the customs and beliefs of the diverse Indian people more amiably than the expository essays do and probably appealed to Postans's English readers, who had a greedy appetite for romance.

In the summer of 1854, having already remarried, Young traveled to the British military camp in Turkey and bivouacked with the army near Varna as it waited for orders to move against the Russians. This trip formed the basis of *Our Camp in Turkey, and the Way to It,* which reached the English public at the height of the fighting in the Crimea. The narrative begins on 9 May 1854 in Malta, where Young is frantically searching for a ship to take her to Turkey. She finally locates a willing captain with a small but seaworthy craft and embarks on her voyage in the company of a Swiss governess, a young military man, a trio of Turks, and a goat. Arriving two days later in Constantinople, she encounters rain and overcrowded hotels and almost immediately sets out for the British camp. For several weeks she lives in a tent, first on the Gallipoli Peninsula, then near Varna, enduring the summer heat and ministering to the sick British forces. When the army is finally ordered to the Crimea, Young eagerly returns to Constantinople, which she again finds disappointing and leaves abruptly. Her adventure ends anticlimactically on 11 August 1854 in Malta.

Our Camp in Turkey is interesting for several reasons. First, it shows the author's increasing tendency to criticize the British military. Throughout the book Young praises the organization and discipline of the French army in their nearby camp and criticizes the idleness and lack of preparation of the English soldiers, who seem ill-equipped for the impending battle. She also bewails the treatment of military wives, who are allowed to accompany their husbands to the front and exposed to harsh conditions that erode their morality and dampen their spirits. Second, the book shows her burgeoning, though begrudging, acceptance of religious diversity. Whereas in previous works she had expressed her sincere hope that non-Christian people in India and elsewhere would be converted someday, in this book she questions the possibility of ever converting the Turks, and she rebukes recent authors for promulgating the rumor that Turks have been converting to Christianity in droves. Third, the book reaffirms her antipathy for romanticized travel literature. Armed with John Murray's *A Handbook for Travellers* (1840), Young tours the mosques and markets of Constantinople in disappointment and writes, "I am afraid I shall be considered a very unromantic chronicler of experiences in Turkey, because it seems necessary always to represent Constantinople and the Bosphorus as a species of fairyland, that can never be wet, gloomy, or disagreeable, like other places." The chronicle of her trip to

Turkey is anything but romantic. Rain and sickness abound, and the British camp is more like a hell than a fairyland.

In *Aldershot, and All about It, with Gossip, Literary, Military, and Pictorial,* Young again criticizes the British military, this time focusing on its famous training camp, which in her opinion fails to prepare soldiers for self-sufficiency and foreign duty. *Aldershot* is Young's only book about England. Although tedious and trite, it offers an interesting contrast to her previous works. Not only does she write about her native land, but she also uses her experiences in India, Egypt, and Turkey to illuminate and clarify her discussion. The inappropriateness of this technique causes one to question her purpose. Is she being intentionally satiric by calling attention to her residence and travels in foreign countries? Or does she really believe that she is offering a unique and valuable perspective on her subject? The early chapters of the book are interesting for the information they provide about the living conditions in the camp. Young provides a sketch of an officer's quarters, which apparently afforded the occupants greater luxury than those of an enlisted man. Wives and children live at the camp, and as many as six or seven people have to share a single room, forgoing the convenience of privacy and any pretensions of modesty.

As interesting as these facts are, they cannot compensate for the inanity of subsequent chapters. Young argues that amateur theatricals should be a mandatory part of a soldier's training, describes her unsuccessful attempt to enter the Queen's Pavilion at the camp, and relates several practical jokes played on the men by their fellow trainees. By the end of chapter 6 she has exhausted her subject and must venture into the countryside for people and places to write about. She describes the "hopping" celebration in nearby Farnham; she gives a history of Moor Park, Jonathan Swift's home, and of the Abbey of Waverly; and she recounts her visit to the towns of Selbourne and Guildford. Recognizing the dullness of these chapters, Young writes:

> [W]e shall not complain of dulness, but, on the contrary, discover how much enjoyment lies in well-employed power of observation. So that in fact when people travel from Dan to Beersheba, and complain that all is barren, it is fair to suppose that much of the barrenness is in their own spirit, which, wanting in internal resource, has no flowers wherewith to make life's path more gay.

This rhetorical ploy, while clever, probably did not convince readers of the merit of the book.

In her final book, *The Moslem Noble: His Land and People,* Young returns to her favorite subject — India. This one-volume book consists of a series of recollections addressed to an unnamed English reader. To unify the work Young employs the figure of the meer Jafur Alee, in whose house she stays while she is visiting Bombay. In the course of her narrative she attends the wedding of the meer's daughter, greets her friends at his palace, and makes an excursion to a nearby town. But the book contains more exposition than narration. Some of the chapters are character sketches representing the professions of India. For example, in one chapter Young introduces the reader to a washerwoman in the service of the meer and discusses the habits of washerwomen in general, eventually launching into an encomium on Asian wells. This kind of enthusiasm prompted one reviewer to write that "Mrs. Young's admiration of everything oriental is so fervent that her praise, like the rain, falls everywhere." In another chapter Young discusses and classifies Indian peddlers; in yet another, she examines the profession of cotton cleaning.

The rhetorical purpose of *The Moslem Noble,* like that of *Facts and Fictions,* is to create sympathy among the English for the people of India. Her own conversion is conspicuous in her frequent praise of the Hindus, the Parsis, and even the Muslims, whom in previous books she had censured harshly. She tacitly — and sometimes overtly — criticizes the British for lacking sympathy and respect for India's people, who are treated very differently when they travel to England and visit the drawing rooms of the rich and influential. Throughout the book Young works hard to keep the attention and interest of her audience, whom she believes to be bored with the topic of India and intolerant of serious discussions of its culture, geography, and politics. Conscious of women's issues, she repeatedly calls attention to changes in the habits and lifestyles of Indian women, for example, commending the meer's daughter for marrying a man not the age of her father and not a tyrant bent on degrading women. Just as she uses India as a touchstone for explaining the culture of Egypt in *Facts and Fictions,* in this book she uses Egypt to explain the culture and people of India.

Chapter 8, titled "The Old Fort," constitutes a sophisticated satire on the amateur traveler, who emphasizes itinerary and speed over appreciation and learning on his tour through the "show places" of India. Ever in search of familiar cuisine and "capital accommodation," he is seldom willing to experience the "travails" of Indian life. Using plural first-person pronouns (*we, us, our*), Young escorts the reader, a "supposed companion," on a tour through the tombs of Aurangabad and the old fort at Deogurh (formerly Dowlutabad), not stopping long enough to absorb the sights and sounds of the environment. She wryly contrasts her previous visit to the same location, when she lingered long and leisurely to make sketches and feed "the tame carp with bread." Young makes clear that, as the reader hastens from place to place, he is also hastening toward his grave. In fact, she compels him to spend the night in a dilapidated tomb, which she knows cannot possibly suit a fussy English traveler. The chapter closes with the two travelers, Young and her imaginary companion, standing on the battlements of the old fort, viewing the tombs from which they have just come.

Panned harshly by a reviewer for the *Athenaeum* (18 July 1857) and ignored by readers, *The Moslem Noble* marked the inauspicious end of Young's literary career. She had evolved from a religious, patriotic chauvinist to an enthusiastic multiculturalist. In her final work she was effectively (if not intentionally) revising her earlier depictions of India, supplying the reader with fresh recollections of her foster country and its diverse population, whom she had grown to love and appreciate. Although seldom read today, her works are worthy of study because they document the mind and sympathies of a Victorian woman who was able to overcome the ethnocentrism of her native people.

References:

Billie Melman, *Women's Orients: English Women and the Middle East, 1718–1918* (Ann Arbor: University of Michigan Press, 1992);

Catherine Barnes Stevenson, *Victorian Women Travel Writers in Africa* (Boston: Twayne, 1982).

Mary Jane Grant Seacole

(May 1805 – 14 May 1881)

James J. Schramer
Youngstown State University

BOOK: *Wonderful Adventures of Mrs. Seacole in Many Lands* (London: Blackwood, 1857; New York: Oxford University Press, 1988).

A freeborn Jamaican of Creole descent, Mary Jane Grant Seacole enjoyed a remarkable life in traveling to the Bahamas, Haiti, Cuba, England, and the Isthmus of Panama. She is best known, however, for her travels in the Crimea during the Crimean War. After several of her applications for nursing positions were rejected, Seacole used her own funds to open a convalescent hospital for wounded British officers in the Crimea. After the war, in an attempt to recover some of her expenses, she wrote about her experiences in *Wonderful Adventures of Mrs. Seacole in Many Lands* (1857).

Although Seacole wrote only one book, she is an important figure among British travel writers because her work challenged many Victorian stereotypes about the proper role of women of color. Among the works by nineteenth-century African American women writers published by Oxford University Press, *Wonderful Adventures of Mrs. Seacole in Many Lands* represents a daring incursion into male-dominated genres. Although women travel writers were not as scarce in the nineteenth century as traditional literary historians would suggest, a small number of Afro-Caribbean women travel writers were published during the nineteenth century. Like many travel books, Seacole's work is a literary hybrid: part travel narrative, part pensioner's appeal, and part military campaign narrative.

William L. Andrews notes in his introduction to the Oxford edition that Seacole's book is also "a special kind of success story in which a woman tries to reconcile her desire for economic independence and worldly recognition with a more socially acceptable role of being properly selfless and useful to men." Andrews observes that her book differs from other accounts of black life in Jamaica because it is a secular rather than a spiritual autobiography. For comparison he cites Nancy Gardner Prince's *A Nar-*

rative of the Life and Travels of Mrs. Nancy Prince (1850), in which Prince claims that complete dependence on divine providence is the only assurance of safe passage through a world concerned more with money than with salvation. Although Seacole is religious, she does not give God sole credit for the good that comes to her; she credits herself for making the most of opportunities available to an independent woman in Jamaica and Panama.

In another introductory essay, that to *Caribbean Women Writers: Essays from the First International Conference* (1990), Selwyn R. Cudjoe describes Seacole's narrative as "a counterdiscourse to the nineteenth-century bourgeois ideology of what a woman's place and behavior ought to have been in her society." In their introduction to a 1984 edition of Seacole's *Wonderful Adventures* Ziggi Alexander and Audrey Dewjee provide useful details about early-nineteenth-century Jamaica and Seacole's place, as a mulatto, in a society in which most of the estimated three hundred thousand Africans were slaves.

Born in May 1805 in Kingston, Jamaica, Mary Jane Grant grew up in a household that was comparatively well off by Jamaican standards. Her Scottish father, about whom little else is known, was an army officer. Her mother, a freeborn black woman, kept a boardinghouse that catered to army and navy officers, and she enjoyed considerable local fame as an herbalist and nurse. In the mid 1830s Mary Jane Grant married Edwin Horatio Seacole (godson of Viscount Horatio Nelson), who died within a few months of the marriage. There is no official record of any children from the marriage, although Alexander and Dewjee note that in *Soyer's Culinary Campaign* (1857) Alexis Soyer mentions an "Egyptian beauty, Mrs. Seacole's daughter Sarah." The young woman was probably a maid whom Seacole had hired to assist her in running what she called her "British Hotel."

In her book Seacole carefully distinguishes herself from the stereotypical "lazy Creole" by

310

claiming that her "Scotch blood" might have accounted for her "energy and activity." She traces her medical talents to her mother, who was "an admirable doctress." It was natural, she writes, that she should inherit her mother's tastes. From her early years she straddled two worlds: the white culture, which she emulated in dress, decorum, and business acumen; and the black culture, which she admired for its fortitude, strength, and knowledge of the natural world. A trip she took to London as a young woman taught her how difficult life would be for one who saw herself as partly white when others saw her as mostly black:

> Strangely enough, some of the most vivid of my recollections are the efforts of the London street-boys to poke fun at my and my companion's complexion. I am only a little brown — a few shades duskier than the brunettes whom you all admire so much; but my companion was very dark, and a fair (if I can apply the term to her) subject for their rude wit.

In this incident Seacole's desire to be accepted as an equal by white society accounts for her apparent acceptance of color-based discrimination. Her desire to please the powerful men who ruled that society accounts for the conventional aim of her work, that of showing that her independence does not diminish her ability to nurture. Her conventionality is, however, a politic means to an economic end: it shapes a receptive audience to a petition for financial recompense, a petition that frames a story characterized by unconventional relations between men and women, blacks and whites.

Despite its conventionality, its acceptance of racial and social snobbery, and its often uncritical promotion of Victorian middle-class values, *Wonderful Adventures of Mrs. Seacole in Many Lands* is a complex study of ways in which nineteenth-century women of color negotiated places for themselves in a world dominated by white males. The lines between white and black cultures are both sharply drawn and seriously challenged in New Granada (present-day Panama), to which Seacole traveled in the early 1850s.

The overland transit site for North Americans traveling to the California goldfields, New Granada was what Mary Louise Pratt has called a "contact zone," where Seacole witnessed the best and the worst of American manners and customs. The worst customs included the attitudes of Americans toward blacks. Compared with the slaves held by American Southerners or the blacks shunned by American Northerners, the blacks of New Granada epitomize dignity and decency. In them Seacole sees

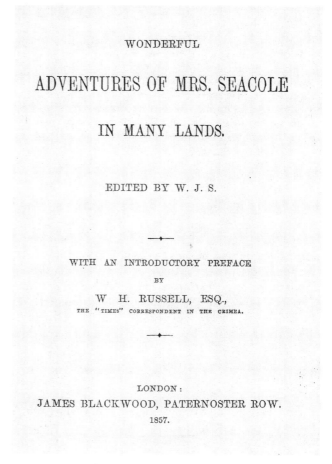

WONDERFUL

ADVENTURES OF MRS. SEACOLE

IN MANY LANDS.

EDITED BY W. J. S.

WITH AN INTRODUCTORY PREFACE
BY
W H. RUSSELL, ESQ.,
THE "TIMES" CORRESPONDENT IN THE CRIMEA.

LONDON:
JAMES BLACKWOOD, PATERNOSTER ROW.
1857.

Title page for Seacole's only book

a version of herself that she realizes whites, no matter how much they admire her, will never see.

She describes Americans as coming from a society so blinded by racism that they refuse to see blacks as people: "my experience of travel has not failed to teach me that Americans (even from the Northern States) are always uncomfortable in the company of coloured people." She recounts how Americans refused to acknowledge that New Granadans had their own rule of law and rights to apply those laws equally to blacks and whites. When an American is brought before a black New Granadan judge on a charge of robbery, an angry crowd of fellow Americans — "abusing and threatening the authorities in no measured terms, all of them indignant that a nigger should presume to judge one of their countrymen" — surrounds the soldiers as they guard the prisoner.

Even when giving what they consider a compliment, Americans cannot disregard race. At a Fourth of July party a tobacco-chewing American orator praises Seacole for her work in combating cholera in New Granada:

> Well, gentlemen, I expect there are only tu things we're vexed for; and the first is, that she ain't one of us, a citizen of the great United States; and the other thing is, gentlemen, that Providence made her a yaller woman. I calculate, gentlemen, you're all as vexed as I am that she's not wholly white, but I du reckon on your rejoicing that she's so many shades removed from being entirely black; and I guess, if we could bleach her by any means we would, and thus make her as acceptable in any company as she deserves to be.

Seacole tells the Americans that she does not "altogether appreciate" the speaker's "kind wishes with respect to my complexion" and adds that if she were darker, she would be "just as happy and useful." As to their offer to bleach her so that she could gain admission to American society, she declines the "honor" and caustically observes that "judging from the specimens I have met with here and elsewhere, I don't think I shall lose much by being excluded from it."

The American women whom Seacole meets fare little better than American men. Seacole finds them crude and totally lacking any sense of decorum in matters of dress or deportment. Assuming the tone and socially superior position of a genteel Victorian lady, she scorns women who flaunt their unconventionality:

> Many were clothed as the men were, in flannel shirt and boots; rode their mules in unfeminine fashion, but with much ease and courage; and in their conversation successfully rivalled the coarseness of their lords. I think, on the whole, that those French lady writers who desire to enjoy the privileges of man, with the irresponsibility of the other sex, would have been delighted with the disciples who were carrying their principles into practice on the streets of Cruces.

A loyal British subject who has nothing but disdain for the sad remains of Spanish colonialism, Seacole also distinguishes herself and other blacks in New Granada from the degraded "Spanish Indians" whom she finds there:

> I found something to admire in the people of New Granada, but not much; and I found much more to condemn unequivocally. Whatever was of any worth in their institutions, such as their comparative freedom, religious toleration, etc., was owing to the negroes who had sought the protection of the republic. I found the Spanish Indians treacherous, passionate, and indolent, with no higher aim or object but simply to enjoy the present after their own torpid, useless fashion.

Seacole's responses to these groups (American men and women and the blacks and Indians of New Granada) illustrate the complexity of the Creole view of a multiracial society. As a person of color she repudiates attempts by North Americans to install a color-biased social heirarchy in New Granada. But when she thinks and acts as a British citizen, she views the Indians and mestizos of New Granada from a perspective just as racially biased as that of the Americans whom she justly takes to task. As a woman of color she carefully protects those social graces that she feels distinguish her from the less inhibited American women. Shifting her position from being part of the spectacle (a person of color in a world where color matters) to being a spectator (an observer from a class outside the world in which she finds herself), Seacole preserves her hard-won identity.

When Seacole returned to Jamaica in 1853, she soon learned of war in the Crimea and decided that she could be useful as a nurse to wounded British soldiers. Desiring to help her "old friends" who had served in Jamaica and were among the British regiments in the Crimea, Seacole sailed to England in 1854. After her applications to the War Office for a post as a hospital nurse were rejected, Seacole offered her services as a nursing recruit to one of Florence Nightingale's companions. When this plan also failed, she applied to the Crimea Fund but was again rejected. Initially philosophical about her rejection from the War Office, she had reasoned that British authorities might not value the service of a "motherly yellow woman" as readily as Jamaican officials would. Yet after being rejected by Nightingale's organization and the Crimea Fund, she asked, "Was it possible that American prejudices against color had some root here?" Despite these setbacks Seacole sailed to the Crimea at her own expense and in hopes that her friends in the regiments would help her set up a "British Hotel" for convalescing officers.

As she had done in New Granada, Seacole rates the polyglot nationalities of the Crimea according to their degrees of civility and trustworthiness. The English receive her highest accolades. Among the English allies, the Sardinians are the most praiseworthy; the French Zouaves are likable scamps; Greeks and Maltese are lowest on the scale. The Turks are pushed around by everyone: "Very often an injured Turk would run up to where I sat, and stand there, wildly telegraphing his complaints against some villainous-looking Greek, or Italian, whom a stout English lad would have shaken out of his dirty skin in five minutes."

Mary Seacole (standing, second from right) speaking to Alexis Soyer at a Crimean hotel (from Seacole's Wonderful Adventures of Mrs. Seacole in Many Lands, *1857)*

Like Panama, the Crimean battlefield is an indeterminate space where Seacole can be herself without worrying about race or gender. Within this space are the more particularized settings of the hostelry and hospital ward, where rules of hospitality and caregiving supersede rigid racial and social divisions. Seacole quickly becomes "Mother Seacole" to her favorites among the British regiments. She helps perpetuate this role by using familial metaphors to describe her anxiety as she waits to learn what has happened to her "sons" in the siege trenches: "I used to think it was like having a large family of children ill with fever, and dreading to hear which one had passed away in the night."

Andrews astutely comments on the irony of "Mother Seacole" creating an identity for herself that depends upon the upheaval of war:

In the Crimea she became "Mother" Seacole, not the sentimentalized black "Aunty" of condescending white American imagination, but an independent and highly respected maternal figure, the acme of female achievement in Victorian culture, the symbol of all that "home" signified to British soldiers alienated by war. Was Seacole aware of the pathetic irony of her situation, namely, that she found home only when war had sundered the homes of her beloved "sons"?

Her narrative suggests that she was indeed aware of the irony that war, with all its horrors, offered her the opportunity to prove her worth and usefulness, for "That battle-field was a fearful sight for a woman to witness, and if I do not pray God that I may never see its like again, it is because I wish to be useful all my life, and it is in such scenes of horror and distress that a woman can do so much." Her recognition of this irony did not, however, make it any easier for her to accept the transitory nature of her role as "Mother" and nurse and the loss of the privilege and intimacy that would follow when the drama ended.

When an armistice was signed in 1856, she had mixed feelings about returning to England. Although genuinely happy that her "sons" would no longer be taken ill, wounded, or killed, she knew she would miss the camaraderie of the field and the esteem she had won in the hearts of the officers and men she had treated. She recognized that a special time in her life was ending: "all this going home seemed strange and somewhat sad," she wrote, "and sometimes I felt I could not sympathise with the glad faces and happy hearts of those who were looking forward to the delights of home." She compared herself to a professional soldier contemplating the emptiness and unemployment of peace:

> He had no home, no loved friends; the peace would bring no particular pleasure to him, whereas war and action were necessary to his existence, gave him excitement, occupation, the chance of promotion. . . . Was it not so with me? Had I not been happy through the months of toil and danger, never knowing what fear or depression was, finding every moment of the day mortgaged hours in advance, and earning sound sleep and contentment by sheer hard work?

As a woman of color Seacole experienced freedom in the chaotic society of the battlefield, where she was defined not by cultural limitations of gender and race but rather by her abilities. As a woman she was aware that her domestic talents – her cooking, her caregiving – would be devalued in a peacetime society that took them for granted and deemed them unworthy of notice or reward. In the social disorientation of war, however, what was devalued or taken for granted by men in peacetime and at home was valued precisely because it reminded them of home.

When Seacole returned from the Crimea, she undertook the daunting task of trying to pry recompense for her services from a government more willing to praise than to pay its Crimean heroines and heroes. After friends in the military tried to recover her expenses through a series of fund-raising campaigns that yielded little, she took her case to the public by writing her book in hopes of capitalizing on her fame. The *Illustrated London Times* on 25 July 1857 gave the book a glowing review and reported that a "Grand Military Festival" would be held in her honor on four successive evenings, 27 July through 30 July, at Surrey Gardens. Although more than ten thousand people attended the festival each evening and wildly cheered Seacole, the entertainment netted less than £300. Not until 1867 did a committee of her military and governmental friends, having drawn Queen Victoria's attention to the case, succeed in putting Seacole "beyond the reach of want," as Alexander and Dewjee report. She spent the remaining years of her life traveling frequently between England and Jamaica. When she died on 14 May 1881, her estate reportedly amounted to £2,615 11s. 7d., a considerable sum by the standards of the day.

Although she finally received the public adulation and compensation that she justly merited, Seacole's greatest rewards came from the friendships she had formed on the Crimean battlefields. In the dislocations of travel and war Seacole found peace and purpose. Like travelers before and after her, she discovered that many people travel and have adventures not so much to explore new places as to escape the restrictions of day-to-day life – to escape limitations both self-imposed and imposed by others.

References:

Ziggi Alexander and Audrey Dewjee, Introduction to *Wonderful Adventures of Mrs. Seacole in Many Lands* (Bristol, U.K.: Falling Wall, 1984);

Selwyn R. Cudjoe, Introduction to *Caribbean Women Writers: Essays from the First International Conference,* edited by Cudjoe (Wellesley, Mass.: Caloux Publications, 1990);

Mary Louise Pratt, *Imperial Eyes: Travel Writing and Transculturation* (London: Routledge, 1992).

John Hanning Speke

(4 May 1827 – 16 September 1864)

David Finkelstein
Napier University

BOOKS: *My Second Expedition to Eastern Inter-tropical Africa* (Cape Town: Solomon, 1860);
Journal of the Discovery of the Source of the Nile (Edinburgh & London: Blackwood, 1863; New York: Harper, 1864);
Capts. Speke's and Grant's Travels and Adventures in Africa: A Thrilling Narrative of the Perils and Hardships Experienced by Captains Speke and Grant, the Celebrated African Explorers (Philadelphia: Barclay, [1864]);
What Led to the Discovery of the Source of the Nile (Edinburgh & London: Blackwood, 1864);
Considerations for Opening Africa (London: Privately printed, 1864);
Scheme for Opening Africa (London: Privately printed, 1864);
Lake Victoria: A Narrative of Explorations in Search of the Source of the Nile, Compiled from the Memoirs of Captains Speke and Grant, edited by G. C. Swayne (Edinburgh & London: Blackwood, 1868).

OTHER: Sir Richard Francis Burton, *First Footsteps in East Africa* (London: Longman, Brown, Green, & Longman, 1856); includes a revised and edited portion of Speke's 1854–1855 journal.

SELECTED PERIODICAL PUBLICATIONS –
UNCOLLECTED: "Captain J. H. Speke's Discovery of the Victoria Nyanza Lake, the Supposed Source of the Nile," *Blackwood's Magazine,* 86 (October 1859): 391–419;
"Journal of a Cruise on the Tanganyika Lake, Central Africa," *Blackwood's Magazine,* 86 (October 1859): 339–357;
"Return from Nyanza," *Blackwood's Magazine,* 86 (November 1859): 565–582;
"Captain Speke's Discoveries in Central Africa," *Cape Monthly,* 7 (1860): 159–167;
"Captain Speke's Adventure in Somali Land," *Blackwood's Magazine,* 87 (May 1860): 561–580;

John Hanning Speke

87 (June 1860): 674–693; 88 (July 1860): 22–36;
"The Upper Basin of the Nile," *Journal of the Royal Geographic Society,* 7 (1863): 322–346.

John Hanning Speke's African travel writing appeared just prior to the great scramble for Africa, when European expeditions, financed privately or by political and scientific institutions, began systematically probing and mapping the interior of a subcontinent that had, until then, remained a cipher for Europeans. Speke's achievement was that of being the first to identify Lake Victoria as the source of the Nile River, a geographical mystery that had puzzled commentators and explorers for several centuries. The particular position Speke occupies in the history of travel writing derives not only from the

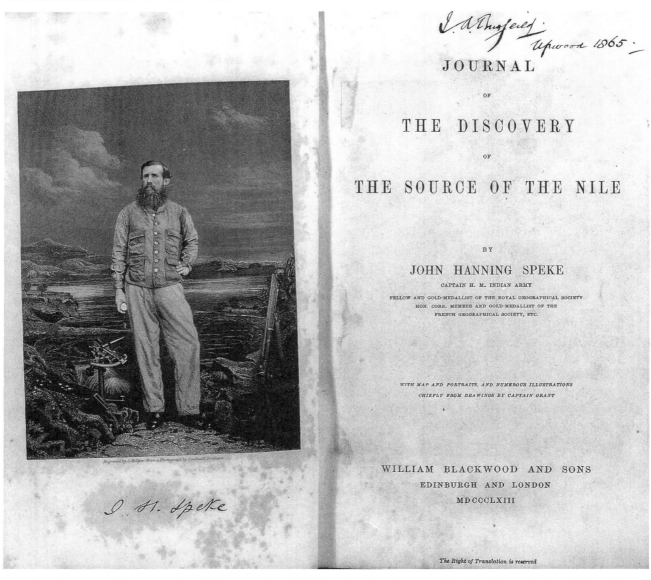

JOURNAL

OF

THE DISCOVERY

OF

THE SOURCE OF THE NILE

BY

JOHN HANNING SPEKE

CAPTAIN H. M. INDIAN ARMY

FELLOW AND GOLD-MEDALLIST OF THE ROYAL GEOGRAPHICAL SOCIETY
HON. CORR. MEMBER AND GOLD-MEDALLIST OF THE
FRENCH GEOGRAPHICAL SOCIETY, ETC.

WITH MAP AND PORTRAITS, AND NUMEROUS ILLUSTRATIONS
CHIEFLY FROM DRAWINGS BY CAPTAIN GRANT

WILLIAM BLACKWOOD AND SONS
EDINBURGH AND LONDON
MDCCCLXIII

The Right of Translation is reserved

Frontispiece and title page for Speke's first narrative of his Nile explorations (courtesy of the Lilly Library, Indiana University)

controversy that surrounded his discovery and from the peculiar circumstances under which his work was produced and received, but also from the way in which his work reflects nineteenth-century British perceptions of Africa and the role of the imperial explorer and adventurer.

John Hanning Speke was born at Orleigh Court, near Bideford in Devon, on 4 May 1827, the second son of William Speke and Georgina Elizabeth Hanning. His father, a retired army captain, farmed a large estate in the area, and the family seat was at Jordans, near Ilminster. After a desultory education Speke in 1844 joined the Indian army as a cadet officer. During the next decade he saw action in the Punjab, and while on leave he indulged

his passions for hunting and for traveling extensively throughout the Himalayas and elsewhere in India.

In 1854 Speke left the Indian army on extended leave and set about fulfilling his most cherished ambitions — to explore Africa and gather wildlife specimens to build a natural history collection at home in Britain. He traveled to Aden with almost £400 in barter goods, with which he hoped to enlist guides and porters for his travels. In Aden he met Richard F. Burton, who had just returned from an expedition through Abyssinia. Encountering difficulties in gaining official approval for his plans, Speke joined Burton's party to travel to Zanzibar via Somalia.

The expedition was an unqualified disaster for Speke. He accomplished little, and he failed to satisfy his desire to explore the African interior. In addition, Speke was captured and severely wounded during a raid on the British camp by Somali tribesmen. In spite of horrible injuries, he managed to escape and rejoin Burton and another officer aboard an Arab vessel. Burton and Speke returned to England in mid 1855 and volunteered to serve as officers in the final stages of the Crimean War. Burton subsequently published an official account of the Somalian journey, an account that included a substantially revised and unacknowledged portion of Speke's personal journal as part of the final chapter. This angered Speke, who felt aggrieved that his contribution to the expedition had not been adequately recognized.

In 1856 Burton proposed a major expedition to explore the Nile basin and seek to establish an accurate location for the source of the Nile River. He invited Speke to join him on the trip, and Speke, seeing no other means of fulfilling his ambitions to reach Africa, accepted. With financing from the British Foreign Office and official patronage from the Royal Geographical Society, the two set off for Zanzibar in late 1856. From there they left on a journey that would subsequently cause bitter controversy and divide the two friends.

The debate that followed this expedition had much to do not only with Speke's claims to have sighted the Nile River, but also with the controversial manner in which he had made and announced his discovery. The special fascination that the mysterious source of the Nile had exercised over European explorers, cartographers, and historians for several centuries also intensified the acrimony. As the last major area in the world left unexplored and relatively untouched by nineteenth-century European intrusions, the unmapped surfaces of the African continent posed a particularly enticing challenge to Victorian explorers and adventurers, and finding the source of the Nile River was the ultimate challenge.

Speke's initial sighting of Lake Victoria occurred near the end of the two-year expedition. Traveling through difficult terrain and battling disease and misfortune most of the way, Burton and Speke had discovered the site of Lake Tanganyika. Burton, ill with an ulcerated jaw by late June 1858, paused to recuperate at Tabora, in what is now Tanzania; this allowed Speke to continue and investigate reports of a large lake to the north. Speke returned six weeks later, excitedly claiming to have found the lake – which he believed to be the true source of the Nile. Basing his contention only on a partial sighting of the lake and having few accurate or substantive measurements to back up his claim, Speke found his surmise not taken seriously by Burton. When both travelers reached the Aden coast several months later, Burton chose to remain behind to recuperate while Speke took passage in the first boat to Britain. As Burton discovered when he finally reached Southampton in late May 1859, twelve days after Speke, Speke had taken this opportunity not only to announce his discovery to the Royal Geographical Society but also to diminish Burton's role in the expedition. No doubt one motive for this lay in Speke's wishing to ensure that his role in the expedition would not be downplayed, as it had been at the conclusion of their first expedition.

In spite of bitter opposition from Burton, Speke began preparations for a second expedition to Lake Victoria, one undertaken this time without his former traveling companion. Burton and his supporters launched several attacks on Speke's findings, and Speke responded through an avenue of his own.

He had first approached publisher John Blackwood in late June 1859. On the urging of Laurence Oliphant, one of Blackwood's favorite and most prolific writers, whom Speke had met on his voyage home from Africa, Speke wrote to Blackwood to solicit interest in the possible publication of his account of those recent travels. In subsequent correspondence and personal meetings Blackwood encouraged Speke to use the *Blackwood's Magazine* as a medium for airing his views about the source of the Nile. Speke did so, using the journal also to attack Burton and other opponents as well as to justify his actions and claims.

The magazine featured four major pieces by Speke between September 1859 and July 1860. Because Speke was not a particularly gifted stylist, however, substantial editorial revision of his articles prior to their publication had been necessary, and this had been done by Speke's friends Robert Lambert Playfair, later British consul at Zanzibar in 1862, and Laurence Oliphant. As Blackwood confessed in a 22 July 1863 letter to his nephew and colleague William Blackwood III, Speke "writes in such an abominable, childish, unintelligible way" that it seemed "impossible to say what any body could make of [his remarks], and yet he is full of matter, & when he talks and explains all is right."

In late April 1860 the Royal Geographical Society had raised £2,500 for another expedition, and Speke set sail for Africa with a new traveling com-

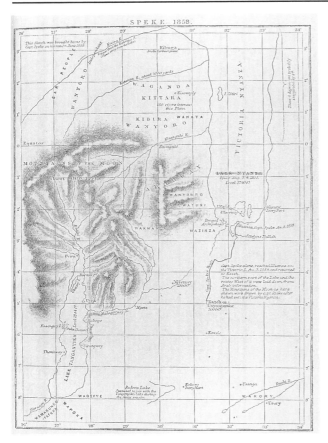

Speke's map of his African explorations, which he brought to England in 1859 (Royal Geographical Society, London)

panion – James Augustus Grant, a former Indian army officer who was a skilled draftsman and botanist and who had become a good friend of Speke during their days in India. Grant was to become one of Speke's staunchest supporters in subsequent battles over Speke's claims regarding the source of the Nile. With Grant's help Speke hoped to establish conclusively that Lake Victoria was indeed the source of the Nile River and to trace the course of the river to Egypt.

Their search was to last three years, and the success of the two explorers was celebrated with their triumphant return to Britain on 17 June 1863. However, doubts about their claims soon followed – doubts based on information Speke provided not only in speeches to the Royal Geographical Society but also in his published journal account. The fact that Speke had again left behind his temporarily incapacitated companion, James Grant, at a crucial moment in their expedition made Speke's contemporaries uneasy about his findings. The action smacked too much of ungentlemanly behavior, and Speke's reputation as a heroic figure suffered.

Speke set about getting his account of the trip published soon after he arrived in Britain. John Blackwood fought off stiff competition from publisher John Murray, a specialist in travel literature, to gain the rights to publish Speke's *Journal of the Discovery of the Source of the Nile* (1863). Despite Speke's weaknesses as a writer, Blackwood offered him £2,000 for publication rights; as he subsequently explained to William Blackwood on 20 December 1863, "It was too much considering what I knew of his literary powers, but when others offer so keenly I could not possibly let the fair fellow get less from us than he could have got elsewhere."

Speke traveled to Scotland to complete his writing of the book, but the quality of his writing soon prompted the publisher to bring in a ghostwriter, the Scottish historian and bibliophile John Hill Burton, to rewrite the work entirely. In doing so Blackwood set about creating a work that would answer Speke's critics and prove to be of wider interest to the general public. Speke's spelling, grammar, and punctuation were changed, and passages that might prove potentially damaging to the image that Blackwood envisioned for Speke were rewritten or suppressed. The result, as John Blackwood noted in writing to John Delane, editor of the London *Times* on 7 December 1863, was a work that "realises savages and savage life in a way that nothing else ever did."

It was an account that emphasized Speke's struggle in an inhospitable and primitive land and the eventual triumph of the ideal, imperial explorer over nature and inferior races. Speke, not the Nile River, was the protagonist in this epic drama, which presented him battling against a naked, dark Africa disconnected from, and untouched by, European impulses and civilization. African society was depicted as dominated by superstitious beliefs, and its people as lacking moral values, being nomadic in nature, and lacking strong, effective governments to control tribal rivalries and create structured, agricultural economies. Such rhetoric, much of it imposed on Speke's text by its ghostwriter and editors, reflected common nineteenth-century British views of Africa. It also foreshadowed the increasing use of religious and political generalizations to justify later colonial activity in the African subcontinent. Thus, the depiction of Speke's triumph over "savages" and "savage life" in his *Journal of the Discovery of the Source of the Nile* adhered wholly to standard nineteenth-century protocols invoking Christian discipline and vigorous, centralized government to manage the subcontinent's population and resources.

THE AUTHOR'S ESCAPE FROM THE SOMALI

WHAT LED TO THE DISCOVERY

OF THE

SOURCE OF THE NILE

BY

JOHN HANNING SPEKE

CAPTAIN H.M. INDIAN ARMY

AUTHOR OF 'JOURNAL OF THE DISCOVERY OF THE
SOURCE OF THE NILE'

WILLIAM BLACKWOOD AND SONS
EDINBURGH AND LONDON
MDCCCLXIV

The Right of Translation is reserved.

Frontispiece and title page for Speke's second version of his explorations (courtesy of the Lilly Library, Indiana University)

Such themes were key features of reviews appearing after the publication of the work in December 1863. As Blackwood had hoped would happen, although most reviewers criticized Speke for lacking literary sophistication, they focused on his heroism and on the struggles he had faced in his search for the source of the Nile. They also suggested that the work was of interest not only for its account of the source of the Nile River, but also for its accurate record of "savage" life in Africa. The anonymous reviewer for the *Athenaeum* of 19 December 1863, for example, found the book a "tale left in its naked form, naked as one of Captain Speke's equatorial kings," and added that "the picture we proceed to draw from Capt. Speke's narrative, shall be such as will best display those passions and relations which interest human beings always and everywhere."

Likewise, the reviewer for the *Quarterly Review* early in 1864 wrote that "If it does not possess literary merit, to which its author probably never aspired, it abounds with very extraordinary incidents; and this graphic narrative affords probably a clearer insight into savage life than any more artistic production could have given." The *Quarterly Review* concluded that such accounts as Speke's highlighted previously unknown regions of the world and stimulated commercial and religious interest in these areas: "By bringing to light the resources of vast and hitherto unknown countries, he tempts commerce – the sure harbinger of civilization – into regions which would otherwise remain permanently shrouded in darkness." To this were added religious conviction and activity, communicating "an impulse never to be arrested until it has accomplished the work to which it is unconsciously set, and thus becomes the secondary instrument for imparting the blessings of purer morals and a purer faith to millions of the human race."

On the basis of such intense interest in what Speke had to say about Africa and its people and in the wake of the heated controversy over his claims about the source of the Nile River, the work proved extremely popular. Within a year of publication, it had gone through three editions and sold more than seventy-five hundred copies. Foreign rights to the work were also negotiated in France, Germany, and the United States — proof that the interest Speke's publishers had envisioned in the formula of heroic adventure in foreign lands was not confined to British shores.

The heroic vision of Speke as the ideal, vigorous imperial explorer, the image created by John Hill Burton's editorial efforts, required that a firm eye be kept on Speke following publication of the work. On 29 December 1863 John Blackwood warned Speke not to respond to any periodical or newspaper attacks without first consulting him, for, as Blackwood disingenuously told Speke, "your composition generally does require supervision before it is presented to the public." Likewise William Blackwood was told before he visited Speke to keep a careful eye on him and anything he wrote: "Warn him against writing letters to the papers," John wrote to his brother on 20 December 1863, "if you see the slightest symptoms."

Such warnings became even more necessary as criticism mounted during the eight months following publication of the work. Further fuel was added to the fire by the September 1864 republication (under the title *What Led to the Discovery of the Source of the Nile*) of Speke's controversial articles from *Blackwood's Magazine*. The pressure to answer Speke's critics led to the scheduling of a debate on 16 September 1864 between Speke and his old antagonist Richard F. Burton. But this never took place: Speke died that day in a shooting accident at his cousin's estate. Controversy over whether Speke's death was accidental or suicidal has never been satisfactorily resolved.

The issues raised by Speke's claims about his discovery were not settled until 1875, when a circumnavigation of Lake Victoria by Henry Morgan Stanley conclusively proved it to be the source of the Nile River. Speke's achievement as the first Eu-

ropean to discover the source of the Nile, however, had been overshadowed by bitter contemporary debate over the issue and by the feuding between him and Burton. Speke's writing, however, deserves serious assessment as an important reflection of contemporary views regarding Africa and as a foreshadowing of the official rhetoric and manner by which European powers subsequently colonized the subcontinent.

Bibliography:
James A. Casada, "British Exploration in East Africa: A Bibliography with Commentary," *Africana Journal*, 5 (Fall 1974): 195–239.

Biography:
Alexander Maitland, *Speke and the Discovery of the Source of the Nile* (London: Constable, 1971).

References:
Roy C. Bridges, "John Hanning Speke: Negotiating a Way to the Nile," in *Africa and Its Explorers*, edited by Robert I. Rotberg (Cambridge, Mass.: Harvard University Press, 1970), pp. 95–137;
Bridges, "John Speke and the Royal Geographical Society," *Uganda Journal*, 26 (1962): 23–43;
John Hill Burton, "Captain Speke's Journal," *Blackwood's Magazine*, 45 (January 1864): 1–24;
Kenneth Ingham, "John Hanning Speke: A Victorian and His Inspiration," *Tanzanya Notes and Queries*, 49 (1957): 247–255;
Alexander Maitland, "Speke's First Footsteps," *Blackwood's Magazine*, 309 (March 1971): 265–272;
Maitland, "Speke's Nile Diary," *Blackwood's Magazine*, 321 (May 1977): 371–385;
Matilda Pine-Coffin, *The Speke Family* (Exeter: Godfrey & Bartlett, 1914).

Papers:
Speke's Nile journals and corrected proofs of the published versions, as well as letters between Speke, James A. Grant, and publisher William Blackwood and Sons, are located in the National Library of Scotland in Edinburgh. Further material can also be found in the archives of the Royal Geographical Society in Bridson, England.

Frances Trollope

(10 March 1779 – 6 October 1863)

Helen Heineman
Framingham State College

See also the Trollope entry in *DLB 21: Victorian Novelists Before 1885.*

BOOKS: *Domestic Manners of the Americans,* 2 volumes (London & New York: Whittaker, Treacher, 1832);

The Refugee in America: A Novel (3 volumes, London: Whittaker, Treacher, 1832; 2 volumes, London & New York: Whittaker, Treacher, 1833);

The Mother's Manual; or, Illustrations of Matrimonial Economy: An Essay in Verse (London: Treutel & Wurtz & Richter, 1833);

The Abbess: A Romance, 3 volumes (London: Whittaker, Treacher, 1833);

Tremordyn Cliff, 3 volumes (London: Bentley, 1835);

Belgium and Western Germany in 1833; Including Visits to Baden-Baden, Wiesbaden, Cassel, Hanover, the Harz Mountains, etc., 2 volumes (London: Bentley, 1836);

Paris and the Parisians in 1835 (2 volumes, London: Bentley, 1836; 1 volume, New York: Harper, 1836);

The Life and Adventures of Jonathan Jefferson Whitlaw; or, Scenes on the Mississippi, 3 volumes (London: Bentley, 1836); republished as *Lynch Law; or, The Life and Adventures of Jonathan Jefferson Whitlaw* (London: Bentley, 1857);

The Vicar of Wrexhill, 3 volumes (London: Bentley, 1837); revised edition (London: Bentley, 1840);

Vienna and the Austrians; with Some Account of a Journey through Swabia, Bavaria, the Tyrol, and the Salzbourg, 2 volumes (London: Bentley, 1838);

A Romance of Vienna (3 volumes, London: Bentley, 1838; 2 volumes, Philadelphia: Carey & Hart, 1838);

The Widow Barnaby, 3 volumes (London: Bentley, 1839);

The Life and Adventures of Michael Armstrong, the Factory Boy (3 volumes, London: Colburn, 1839; 2 volumes, New York: Harper, 1840);

Frances Trollope (National Portrait Gallery, London)

The Widow Married: A Sequel to "The Widow Barnaby," 3 volumes (London: Colburn, 1840);

One Fault: A Novel, 3 volumes (London: Bentley, 1840);

Charles Chesterfield; or, The Adventures of a Youth of Genius, 3 volumes (London: Colburn, 1841);

The Ward of Thorpe Combe, 3 volumes (London: Bentley, 1841); republished as *The Ward* (London: Bentley, 1842);

The Blue Belles of England, 3 volumes (London: Saunders & Otley, 1842);

A Visit to Italy, 2 volumes (London: Bentley, 1842);

The Barnabys in America; or, Adventures of the Widow Wedded, 3 volumes (London: Colburn, 1843);

republished as *Adventures of the Barnabys in America: A Sequel to The Widow Barnaby* (London: Ward & Lock, [1859]);

Hargrave; or, The Adventures of a Man of Fashion, 3 volumes (London: Colburn, 1843);

Jessie Phillips: A Tale of the Present Day, 3 volumes (London: Colburn, 1843);

The Laurringtons; or, Superior People, 3 volumes (London: Longman, Brown, Green & Longmans, 1844);

Young Love: A Novel, 3 volumes (London: Colburn, 1844);

The Attractive Man: A Novel, 3 volumes (London: Colburn, 1846);

The Robertses on Their Travels, 3 volumes (London: Colburn, 1846);

Travels and Travellers: A Series of Sketches, 2 volumes (London: Colburn, 1846);

Father Eustance: A Tale of the Jesuits, 3 volumes (London: Colburn, 1847);

The Three Cousins: A Novel, 3 volumes (London: Colburn, 1847);

Town and Country: A Novel, 3 volumes (London: Colburn, 1848); republished as *The Days of the Regency (George the Fourth); or, Town and Country* (London: Colburn, 1857);

The Young Countess; or, Love of Jealousy, 3 volumes (London: Colburn, 1848);

The Lottery of Marriage: A Novel, 3 volumes (London: Colburn, 1849);

The Old World and the New: A Novel, 3 volumes (London: Colburn, 1849);

Petticoat Government: A Novel, 3 volumes (London: Colburn, 1850; New York: Harper, 1850);

Mrs. Mathews; or, Family Mysteries: A Novel, 3 volumes (London: Colburn, 1851);

Second Love; or, Beauty and Intellect: A Novel, 3 volumes (London: Colburn, 1851);

Uncle Walter: A Novel, 3 volumes (London: Colburn, 1852);

The Young Heiress: A Novel, 3 volumes (London: Hurst & Blackett, 1853);

The Life and Adventures of a Clever Woman, 3 volumes (London: Hurst & Blackett, 1854);

Gertrude; or, Family Pride, 3 volumes (London: Hurst & Blackett, 1854);

Fashionable Life; or, Paris and London, 3 volumes (London: Hurst & Blackett, 1856).

OTHER: Thomas Adolphus Trollope, *A Summer in Brittany,* 2 volumes, edited by Frances Trollope (London, 1840);

Thomas Adolphus Trollope, *A Summer in Western France,* 2 volumes, edited by Frances Trollope (London, 1841).

Frances Trollope began life as a clergyman's daughter in March 1779 in the small Hampshire village of Heckfield. She shared this modest background with other women writers such as Jane Austen and Charlotte, Emily, and Anne Brontë. Loss of their mothers, a solid if unfocused education directed by their fathers, and an uncertainty about marital prospects seemed conducive to the development of women writers of fiction. Frances Trollope, however, added to her accomplishments as a writer the role of traveler, an unusual one for women of her time. To be a lady traveler in the early years of the nineteenth century required a special combination of qualities — tough independence, innate curiosity about the world, and radical personal needs: in Trollope's case, desperate economic need was the immediate stimulus. But clearly she enjoyed being on the road, and in the first ten years of her developing career as a writer, she made six major tours and produced travel accounts of these in five books: *Domestic Manners of the Americans* (1832); *Belgium and Western Germany in 1833; Including Visits to Baden-Baden, Wiesbaden, Cassel, Hanover, the Harz Mountains, etc.* (1836); *Paris and the Parisians in 1835* (1836); *Vienna and the Austrians; with Some Account of a Journey through Swabia, Bavaria, the Tyrol, and the Salzbourg* (1838); and *A Visit to Italy* (1842). In the same ten years she also wrote thirteen novels; the experience of travel obviously stimulated her creative energies. Indeed, it unlocked her artistic talent and made her a professional writer.

Her tours were made without her husband but always in the company of some of her children. Thus, she preserved the requisite commitment to domestic matters while shaping her identity through the kind of adventurous experience usually reserved for men. Beginning with her trip to the United States, where she learned quickly that the only commodity that she had to sell was what she saw with "the lynx-like eye of the female," traveling also made her a close observer. Her subjects were unconventional — American slavery, or the situation of women — and her approach was original. She eschewed the traditional travel narrative — with its focus on cities, buildings, and natural wonders like Niagara Falls — and concentrated instead on people. The titles of many of her travel books underline this emphasis: "Domestic Manners" in America; "Parisians" and "Austrians," not Paris or Austria.

Trollope used the genre of the travel book as a vehicle to advance both physically and psychologically the frontiers of women's emancipation in the nineteenth century. Informal, experimental, and daring in their ways, Trollope's travel volumes initiated an extensive literary career, the dimensions of which she never suspected when she left England in 1827 with three of her children and their French artist tutor to reside in the utopian colony of her friend Frances Wright in the United States.

What Charles Dickens later said of *The Posthumous Papers of the Pickwick Club* (1837) could also be said of *Domestic Manners of the Americans* – that it was a favorite because it had made its own way. Similar to young Charles Dickens, Trollope made her fame and fortune with *Domestic Manners of the Americans,* a work conceived out of necessity, born of scattered notes made on the blank pages and under the covers of her children's writing pads, composed while she sat without shoes and wrote far into the night so that she and her children could survive – even while "starving," as she put it, "in that land of plenty." Appearing as it did amid the controversy surrounding the Reform Bill of 1832 in England, the book sparked controversy from the start. Those disputes, engaged in by liberals and conservatives on both continents, made the book an instant bestseller. With publication of this book Trollope began, at the age of fifty-three, the long literary career in which she was to produce more than thirty novels and six travel books.

Domestic Manners of the Americans is a chronological narrative of her travels and experiences in America, a record of her transformation from intrepid adventurer on the Mississippi, to beleaguered resident in the bustling city of Cincinnati (then the "Athens of the West"), to note-taking tourist in Niagara Falls, and, finally, to author. The book was solidly original, rich with dramatic anecdotes and refreshing dialogue. It also featured new kinds of illustration, recalling those people-centered scenes found in novels rather than those scenes of city views and maps that then prevailed in travel books. In addition, the book developed many unifying themes, often charged with controversy and emotion. Trollope spoke out on political, social, and domestic subjects. She compared the amenities of American life to those of Britain and found the inhabitants of this new country brash and lacking respect for others, objectionable qualities all made visible in their rude postures and repulsive customs such as spitting. She had much to say about religion in American life and, most important of all, about the position of women in the United States.

The technique of the book was also original. Mixing a kind of oral history with her own general commentary kept to a minimum, Trollope let her subjects speak for themselves. In one chapter she details the activities of a Philadelphia lady, re-creates overheard conversations on steamboats and in museums, and relates comments by neighbors and servants. Recorded with verve and accuracy, these slices of American life still ring true, albeit with some alterations through the years.

The narrative of *Domestic Manners of the Americans* falls into three parts, each with a distinctive subject matter and style. The first section, the shortest, is Trollope's adventure narrative, in which she appears as intrepid female traveler in wild and exotic territory. The second, the most famous and vital part of the book, concerns her domestic trials in Cincinnati, where she appears as heroic resident in a settled but rude land. The last part, starring a narrator who is an expert observer of American places, recounts her journey through the mid-Atlantic states in rendering her impressions of America's tourist attractions.

The adventure narrative of *Domestic Manners of the Americans* (chapters 1–3) describes the landscape of Mississippi mudbanks, bulrushes, crocodiles, Spanish moss, and oranges growing outside, even at Christmastime. She watches the Kentucky flatboat men, the rude and taciturn Americans she meets on steamboats, and begins to draw strong conclusions about American social life, which permitted crude eating habits and excluded women from positions of influence. She briefly describes the Nashoba project, the utopian community to which she had originally come, and then, ending the adventure narrative, she begins the central and most important section of her book, an account of her thirty-month residence in Cincinnati, in the heartland of the United States.

These chapters are devastating snapshots of a nineteenth-century midwestern river town, where hogs clear the streets of refuse, spitting is an acceptable social amenity, and the liveliest show in town is the Owen-Campbell debate on the evidence of Christianity. Trollope found the city architecturally undistinguished, although amazing in terms of its size and importance, given "that thirty years ago the aboriginal forest occupied the ground where it stands."

In this section Trollope adopts the approach of the documentary and turns her camera on Americans by letting them speak and act. In a series of brief scenes the thematic logic of the Cincinnati section emerges. The narrative line of the arrival and settlement of the Trollopes provides a further structure, as the family awaits the arrival of Mr. Trollope and the eldest son, Tom, who is to bring funds necessary for building their bazaar, an event mentioned only in the barest outlines. Within this overall framework Mrs. Trollope is free to discuss the domestic manners of American life.

Foremost for Trollope was the unattractiveness of American social life. In her view an egalitarian political system and philosophy had given birth to a "total and universal want of manners." In a clever sketch of an evening in company she describes a dismal scene: "The gentlemen spit, talk of elections and the price of produce, and spit again. The ladies look at each other's dresses till they know every pin by heart." After a massive meal the participants "remained together as long as they could bear it."

She found that the American character tended to turn in upon itself. When she visits a farmer's wife, the woman professes being unused to company and sociability: "I expect the sun may rise and set a hundred times," she tells Mrs. Trollope, "before I shall see another human that does not belong to the family." She also finds Americans to be a "money-grubbing" people: "Every bee in the hive is actively employed in search of that honey of Hybla, vulgarly called money; neither art, science, learning, nor pleasure, can seduce them from its pursuit." She pays little attention to the role of leisure in American life; to be sure, Americans would finally develop a concept of leisure only when it could become a marketable commodity.

She also found America deficient in the realm of art. She overhears one conversation in which, defensive and insular, a "literary gentleman" claims that Shakespeare is obscene and Chaucer has had his day. Such evidence was of course anecdotal, but it had the power of observed experience.

Like many travelers Trollope examined in closer detail those subjects that were most important to her. Thus, the role of women became a motif of *Domestic Manners of the Americans,* and the Cincinnati section, with its domestic orientation, presented the best opportunity to evaluate the quality of the lives of American women. Indeed, hardly a chapter of this section passes without some reference to women, whose social situations she assessed in a harsh, pithy phrase: "lamentable insignificance." While these references and scenes are distributed throughout the whole narrative, a presentation of the American woman's characteristic life from youth to marriage does emerge from her pages.

Spinsterhood was short; American women married young and had little time for education or intellectual development. As Trollope observes, "in no rank of life do you meet with young women in that delightful period of existence between childhood and marriage wherein, if only tolerably well spent, so much useful information is gained." Even for those with the means and opportunity to receive some training before marriage, educational institutions for the American female were inadequate – merely "a 'quarter's' mathematics, or 'two quarter's' political economy, moral philosophy, algebra, and quadratic equations." Such training was scarcely enough to stand "the wear and tear of half a score of children and one help."

Once married, the opportunities for development dwindled further for American women. Most, Trollope observed, became domestic slaves or "teeming wives," and she blamed this submersion in household affairs on the lack of dependable servants. Her frequent depictions of unruly servants, so often derided by her egalitarian critics, arose from her view that domestic help was necessary for the full development of women.

Even in leisure hours women encountered entrapment. At evening parties they talked mainly to one another. *Domestic Manners of the Americans* is full of scenes in which women "herd together at one part of the room, and the men at the other." Given the radical differentiation of their spheres of action, conversation between the sexes was awkward. Thus, the separation of the sexes, obvious during business hours, spilled into social life. Women, as Trollope noted, were "guarded by a seven-fold shield of habitual insignificance." Yet, "should the women of America ever discover what their power might be, and compare it with what it is, much improvement might be hoped for." In her opinion the moral and social tone of the new republic would be improved by greater participation of women in forming the domestic manners of Americans.

Only in religion did American women find "that degree of influential importance which, in the countries of Europe, is allowed them throughout all orders and ranks of society." Trollope was amazed to see the women bedecked in their best ribbons and bonnets, crowding into chapels, churches, meetinghouses and outdoor camps, participating not in an established liturgical religion but rather in a rough-and-tumble emotionalism that in her view only demeaned and excited its participants. Her many descriptions of women at revivals – women dominated by their ministers, nervous about sexual matters, and yet aroused by the evangelical atmosphere – afforded a dramatic background for Trollope's conclusion: "I never saw or read, of any

The dog wood is another
the splendid white blossoms that
the adorn the woods of America
Its lateral branches are flat like
a fan, and dotted all over with
white flowers about the size and
shape of the blossoms of the horn chestnut
Another shrub of smaller size
but greatly superior in elegance
is the Poison Alder. It is well
that its noxious quality is very
generally known, for it is most
tempting to the eye, by its delicate
fringe-like branches of white flowers
The white colour of these flowers
is the purest white I ever saw
in vegetation; the lily herself not
green leaves, to shew off the white blossoms
excepted. Even the touch of
this shrub is poisonous, and
produces violent swelling.
The Arbor Judas it is unnecessary
to describe as it is well known in
the gardens of England, and its
here it is very common in the woods
bright and delicate pink is the
earliest harbinger of the American
Spring.

Page of notes that Trollope made during her American travels and used in writing Domestic Manners of the Americans *(courtesy of the Lilly Library, Indiana University)*

country where religion had so strong a hold upon the women, or a slighter hold upon the men." Obviously religion had become the American woman's means to gaining self-importance.

In the Cincinnati section Trollope describes several indoor revival meetings and a vividly drawn outdoor camp meeting. In the latter she dramatically describes the preacher's "shrill voice of horror" and "impressive eloquence." "No image that fire, flame, brimstone, molten lead, or red hot pincers could supply, with flesh, nerves, and sinews quivering under them, was omitted." With perspiration streaming down his face, "his eyes rolled, his lips covered with foam and every feature had the deep expression of horror." Repeatedly he invited the female audience to

> come then . . . and we will make you see Jesus, the dear gentle Jesus. . . . But you must come to him! You must not be ashamed of him; we will make way for you; we will clear the bench for anxious sinners to sit upon. Come, then! Come to the anxious bench, and we will show you Jesus! Come! Come! Come!

At this incantation and amid violent cries and shrieks and "convulsive accents," calling out, " 'Oh Lord, Oh Lord Jesus! Help me Jesus,' while the ministers comforted them with from time to time a mystic caress," young girls, trembling, sighing, sobbing, groaning, seated themselves. Trollope insists that these events were representative, and she concludes with a provocative question: "Did the men of America value their women as men ought to value their wives and daughters, would such scenes be permitted among them?"

Framed by pointed rhetorical questions and sharp generalizations, these vignettes made the Cincinnati section of *Domestic Manners of the Americans* unforgettable and controversial. These pictures of life in an egalitarian city on America's frontier accurately reproduced actions and speech idioms for an English public curious about the Yankees across the water. She drew from such details powerful generalizations about American life, some as true today as when she wrote them. As a perceptive observation of the ordinary domestic life of a people, the Cincinnati chapters of *Domestic Manners of the Americans* have not often been surpassed.

In March 1830 Trollope departed from Cincinnati and began a slow journey eastward. She intended to return to England but could not yet afford the fare. On these travels she continued to compile notes for her projected volumes on the United States, now no longer as a resident but as a tourist. As she wrote about the states east of Cincin-

nati, she continued her unsparing accounts of the inconveniences and irritations of American life, but she focused on those associated with travel: bad accommodations and food, unsuitable inns, uncongenial company. In the third section of *Domestic Manners of the Americans* many of her old themes remain, especially her preoccupation with religion and with the role of women, and some new ones emerge, particularly in her tendency to compare whatever she saw in the United States with things English. Also in this third phase of the narrative Trollope raises aesthetic and political issues and more amply describes scenery and landscape.

Her descriptions of place in this section are unremarkable. Moving quickly through an area, she captured essentials as an average tourist would. Wheeling (West Virginia), she reports, is a flourishing town but rather black with coal mining and not beautiful, except for the Ohio River. Baltimore is a beautiful city with a handsome approach, full of stately monuments, cathedrals, and museums. The highlight of her description is in a visit to an infant school there, which she finds impressive. Mount Vernon presents fine river scenery and associations with Gen. George Washington, that "truly great man." Albany merits one sentence: "the state capital of New York, which has some very handsome public buildings, also contains some curious relics of the old Dutch inhabitants." Like many other nineteenth-century travelers she records the variety of trees (cedars, tulip, plane, sumac, juniper, and oak) and describes the picturesque Mohawk Valley; the Hudson Valley, with the perpendicular Palisades; Manhattan Island's "leafy coronet gemmed with villas"; the New York Highlands; and Washington Irving's Sleepy Hollow. Repeatedly she focuses on picturesque combinations of rocks, trees, and water. In this section her writing lacks the strong emotions and deeply felt experiences evident in the Cincinnati section. Only when she has stayed longer than a few days in a place, had opportunities to talk to people, and had some adventures do her passages reveal the life of earlier sections.

Trollope's lengthiest portrait is of the greatest American natural wonder, Niagara Falls, which she believed her book must include in order to be successful. Actively seeking sublime subject matter, she approached the falls in "wonder, terror, delight" and adopted a florid style for her description. Niagara Falls is thus a "mighty cauldron," a "stupendous cataract," which presents "an idea of irresistible power. . . . [A] shadowy mystery hangs about it." Her language relies repeatedly on hyperbole: the "awful beauty," the "wondrous crescent," the "hundred silvery torrents," the "liquid emerald" water, the "fantastic wreaths," and, finally, the "shadowy mist that veils the horrors of its crash below, constitute a scene almost too enormous in its features for man to look upon." She resorts to quotation ("Angels might tremble as they gazed") and to classical allusions ("What was that cavern of the winds of which we heard of old, compared to this? A mightier spirit than Aeolus reigns here"). Such worked-up scenic descriptions contrast unfavorably with others written in her more characteristic, critical voice.

Having left the Falls, she stayed a few days in "queerer-looking" Buffalo, whose buildings had

> the appearance of having been run up in a hurry, though everything has an air of great pretension; there are porticos, columns, domes, and colonnades, but all in wood. Everybody tells you there, as in all their other new-born towns, and everybody believes, that their improvement, and their progression, are more rapid, more wonderful, than the earth ever before witnessed; while to me, the only wonder is how so many thousand, nay millions of persons, can be found, in the nineteenth-century, who can be content so to live. Surely this country may be said to spread rather than to rise.

In this offhand comment Trollope uncovered some hard truths of American life. In the interests of haste Americans had begun to spread out, burn forests to clear the land, erect buildings they knew would not last, and move west when they tired of what they had created. These fundamental carelessnesses about landscape and building would remain American problems in the twentieth century.

Other problems appear in the final section of *Domestic Manners of the Americans,* which contains criticisms of American social and political flaws. While she does not engage in lengthy philosophical examinations of democracy and egalitarian principles, Trollope describes American treatment of three underprivileged groups – Native Americans, black slaves, and women. In their situations she locates keys to the fundamental flaws of the nation. For these groups American principles of equality had failed, and the consequences had included debased human relations, perverted religious and cultural norms, and a daily life that was ungraceful and often ugly.

On negotiations between Native Americans and the federal government Trollope remarked pointedly of members of that government, "If the American character may be judged by their conduct in this matter, they are most lamentably deficient in every feeling of honour and integrity." American treachery toward "the unhappy Indians" was evi-

dent in "the contradictions in [the] principles and practice" of American government officials. When she visited Lake Canandaigua in upstate New York, she noticed, next to the ubiquitous American hotel, "the white man's mushroom palace," a shed housing two Indians, whom she depicted sympathetically. "There they stood, the native rightful lords of the fair land, looking out upon the lovely lake which yet bore the name their fathers had given it, watching the threatening storm that brooded there; a more fearful one had already burst over them."

When the Trollopes traveled, the Native Americans received them with smiles, whereas the white Americans were rude and aggressive. Once when a "lady," helped by some rowdy whiskey drinkers, shoved her way into their carriage places, Trollope wondered "whether the invading white man, in chasing the poor Indians from their forests have [*sic*] done much towards civilizing the land." She answered her own question: "For myself, I almost prefer the indigenous manner to the exotic." Certainly, Native American culture had provided material for the land's most authentic artistic expression. In Washington the architectural detail on the pillars of the Capitol – arrangements of ears and leaves of Indian corn – "was the only instance . . . in which America has ventured to attempt national originality; the success is perfect."

Her sympathy for Native Americans matched that which she held for American slaves, a subject she would treat extensively in her novel *The Life and Adventures of Jonathan Jefferson Whitlaw; or, Scenes on the Mississippi* (1836), in which she also portrayed Native Americans favorably. Her experiences in America persuaded Trollope that slavery constituted the great central flaw at the heart of American government and society:

> The same man who beards his wealthier and more educated neighbor with the bullying boast, "I'm as good as you," turns to his slave, and knocks him down, if the furrow he has ploughed, or the log he has felled, please not this stickler for equality. There is a glaring falsehood on the very surface of such a man's principles that is revolting.

To teach a slave to read was illegal in Virginia, and "this law speaks volumes," she remarked. While domestic slaves generally were well cared for, "they may be sent to the South and sold," and the southern plantations were "the terror of American negroes." One man who heard that such was to be his fate, Trollope reported, "sharpened the hatchet with which he had been felling timber, and with his right hand severed his left from the wrist."

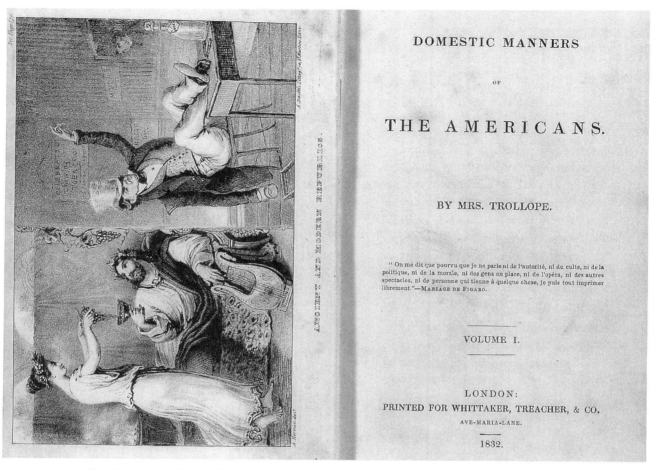

Frontispiece and title page for Trollope's first book (courtesy of the Lilly Library, Indiana University)

Her stories unforgettably illustrate the ways in which "the greatest and best feelings of the human heart were paralyzed by the relative positions of slave and owner." In one, a young female slave about eight years old had eaten a biscuit "temptingly buttered" but "copiously sprinkled with arsenic for the destruction of rats." When Trollope saw this, she prepared and administered an emetic. A young white girl, astonished and repelled by this action, exclaimed, "My! If Mrs. Trollope has not taken her in her lap, and wiped her nasty mouth! Why I would not have touched her mouth for 200 dollars."

For Trollope the incident epitomized the way in which white Americans refused to regard the black as a fellow human being. As in the Cincinnati section, such scenes as these reveal the truth of the American character in memorable tableaux. Trollope was not complimentary in her final evaluation of American society, and her negative assessment was based on three objections. First, she confesses about the people, "I do not like them. I do not

like their principles, I do not like their manners, I do not like their opinions." Second, she does not like their system of government. In a fanciful depiction of its formation she writes,

Their elders drew together, and said, "Let us make a government that shall suit us all; let it be rude, and rough, and noisy; let it not affect either dignity, glory, or splendour; let it interfere with no man's will, nor meddle with any man's business. . . . [L]et every man have a hand in making the laws, and no man be troubled about keeping them."

Trollope's third offense is taken at the tyranny and insularity that Americans display toward strangers. Americans will not accept criticism, for they believe that "they are the first and best of the human race, that nothing is to be learnt, but what they are able to teach, and that nothing is worth having which they do not possess."

Although she had identified some serious problems, Trollope believed that remedies could be found. Greater tolerance for diversity and a reform of domestic manners (brought about through the agency of women) could, she suggested, smooth the rough edges and help remove the hypocrisies that flawed this democratic republic. Should Americans ever learn the graces, refinements, "the chivalry of life," they would become "one of the finest countries on the earth," she felt. Yet her own experience in the heartland of this new country had not made her optimistic about the likelihood that such remedies would be adopted.

With earnings from *Domestic Manners of the Americans, The Refugee in America: A Novel* (1832), and her experimental gothic potboiler, *The Abbess: A Romance* (1833), Trollope began to plan another trip – this time to Germany. She told her friend Julia Garnett Pertz, who lived in Hanover, that she was ready to "start for some watering place on the Rhine with the commission to make a book." She could not indulge in a lengthy visit with her friend, for, as she explained, "I must be ready with my book by November and as yet I have merely notes."

Trollope was hoping to capitalize on her own recent successes and on the current vogue in travel books. Indeed, in *Belgium and Western Germany in 1833* one of her first big scenes recounts a visit to the battlefield at Waterloo, where the setting recalls the adventures of that encounter, "the battered walls, the dismantled and fire-stained chapel . . . the traces of attack upon attack, still renewed and still resisted," which "bring the whole scene before one with tremendous force." Trollope dramatically brings imagined scenes to life. "I fancied I saw [the victorious generals] surrounded by their staff, waiting with trembling eagerness to learn who among their brave companions still lived to share their triumph," she writes. The field seems so awful that "no great stretch of imagination seemed necessary to people it," although "a poet might easily have fancied that the air has darkened by the waving banners of a specter host careening over it." She was, however, equally aware of how contemporaries were exploiting the interest held by such places to make tourist traps of them:

A mile before we reached the ground, we were addressed on each side of the carriage by men who offered to be our guides over it: women, too, with baskets on their arms containing relics of the battle, came offering imperial eagles, bullets, and brass buttons for sale.

She was not alone in her interest in travel or in Germany. In the same year that *Belgium and Western Germany in 1833* appeared, the *Westminster Review* described eight other travel books about this area. The world had become an easier place in which to travel. The number of tourists and tours was increasing; the number of travel books was also growing, and specific features of these books had established themselves. Some – designated "light sketches," "airy nothings" – indicated the aims of their authors in providing pleasure tours. Others were books about remote parts of the earth, and strangeness was the main basis of their appeal. Some were guidebooks for the increasingly peripatetic Englishman. Others were more serious works giving views of political and religious topics, works more often directed at reforming English institutions than at describing foreign places.

As the number of such books grew, prospective readers began to look more closely at the abilities of the travel writer and at his or her personality, and attention in the writing and reading of travel books subtly shifted from a focus on subject matter to style and personality. Rather than the description of landscape, the genius and peculiarities of authors, their habits of mind and manners of presentation, became the central focus. In this increasingly crowded genre Trollope's distinctive voice and growing abilities as a novelist made her books successful.

Indeed, because she was always writing a novel at the same time that she was compiling travel notes, the travel-book genre merged with that of the novel. Narrating events at hand and of the evolving journey became her "plots." The people she saw became mouthpieces of the ideas and social situations they represented, and she heightened them in almost Dickensian fashion. She made character prominent in a genre where landscape and exposition usually had dominated, and she treated opinions, ideas, and culture dramatically. Fictional techniques enliven her travel books: digressions, catalogues, dialogues, and set scenes appear throughout. Her books had narrative structures; vivid characters; settings rich with the sights, sounds, and smells of everyday; and above all, a world view. Her style was a mixture of satire and the familiar personal essay. To her magpie instinct to collect facts, she added a growing artistic ability to shape such facts into scenes vibrant with life. With such credentials, and her natural courage and physical stamina, she was well qualified to embark upon the writing of travel books.

In her second travel account, *Belgium and Western Germany in 1833,* she continued to develop more techniques as well as her fundamentally conservative bias. Her interest in the geographical area arose from political considerations. In the summer of

1830 revolt had broken out in the United Nether-lands. Rebels had proclaimed the independence of Belgium and had drafted the most liberal constitu-tion in Europe. Later it would serve as a model dur-ing the upheavals of 1848. Trollope's book criti-cized the result of that 1830 revolution and praised the authoritarian style of monarchy, and at least in part her aim was to attack the liberal reforms then being implemented in England. She noted point-edly,

> At home, I had of late been accustomed to hear every voice from the class, emphatically styled **the people,** whether heard through the medium of the press, or in listening to their conversation, expressive of contempt and dislike for their own country, its institutions, and its laws.... Far different is the state of public feeling in Germany. Ask a Prussian . . . his opinion of his country . . . and you will be answered by such a hymn of love and praise, as might teach those who have ears to hear, that passing a reform bill is not the most successful manner of securing the affection and applause of **the multitude.**

Repeatedly she used her observations of the German system to lecture the English public. "Where everyone knows his place, and keeps it," she wrote, "there can be no danger of jostling." Aware of the criticism that such remarks were sure to receive, she nevertheless defended the accuracy and seriousness of her conclusions:

> It may be objected, to any opinion I may give as to the political feeling of Germany, that it is not in the course of a summer's tour, any important information on such a subject can be obtained.... Truth, however, is not the less true, because it is obvious.

Her political message was clear throughout: the Germanies should stand as lessons and models for England in their orderliness and political and social stability.

Still sensitive to the concerns for women that she had developed in *Domestic Manners of the Ameri-cans,* her new book contained many vignettes of the lives of women. She included a journal of a Belgian lady given to her by a friend, and she visited a con-vent of Belgian sisters who could be absolved from their vows, if they were to choose to do so. Trollope noted that few took advantage of this privilege, a fact that she was quick to analyze. These women lived in comfort and freedom and had "quite a little town within their walls." Each had her own house with her name over its door, and they "altogether seem . . . to be of more consequence, each in her own circle, than they would have been had they re-tained their situations as individual single women,

instead of becoming members of a large commu-nity." She had nothing but praise for these self-sufficient, comfortable young women.

Much of what she saw in Germany, however, she idealized – as when she watched the female vine dressers "perched 300 feet above the river . . . with-out a thought of danger, or the peasant girl cultivat-ing her rich flower-bed, and singing the delicious strains of her country with taste and feeling . . . as refined a picture of rural life as we can hope to find anywhere, beyond the bounds of Arcadia." Lacking the intimate knowledge of the Germans that she had gained of the Americans, she resorted to romanti-cized portraits – to a provincial sketch of a Belgian lady or to external details of dress, as when she is struck in Antwerp by "the Spanish air of the women," with "mantillas and concealment of face." And while her observations were surely careful (she once coaxed the lady of the house where she was staying to "exhibit the stays she wore on great occa-sions. They were unquestionably of many pounds weight; and were furnished on both sides with iron bars, which . . . must enter, if not into her soul, at least into her heart, every time she stooped"), she could not analyze society based on the condition of its females as she had done in her more com-prehensive presentation of the position of women in America.

While her conservative politics and interest in women remained, Trollope's angle of vision had radically altered. She who had lacked letters of in-troduction in America and had lived as an outcast from polite society now hobnobbed with the great. She called upon the landgravine of Hesse-Homburg, a princess of England, and was shown through her palace near Frankfurt. Yet Trollope's inability to speak German, as well as this social dis-tancing from the domestic manners of the people, put her at a disadvantage in writing this second travel book. Although she did not provide a broad compendium of information about life in Belgium and western Germany, she made the most of the more limited scenes she presented.

With the novelist's instinct she again let peo-ple reveal themselves in skillfully managed speech and action, and she pointed her dramatic stories to-ward general truths. Her book abounds in vivid sketches of representative people. Some are brief: smoking gentlemen "with the stupefying pipe continually in their hands," Jews at synagogue in Frankfurt, and the rabbi who "twisted a white blan-ket, edged with blue, around him, and chanted from a large volume, in a most inconceivable variety of tones; bowing his head, as he did so, almost incessantly." The radical students, their hair "long and exquisitely dishevelled; throats bare, with collars turned back almost to the shoulders," present foreheads bared "a la Byron" and wild eyes "rolling a la Juan." Longer descriptions of the gamblers at Baden and other pleasure spots reveal more about the contemporary madness for gambling than the more-objective, statistical accounts of some other travel books.

Description of scenery is also important, and Trollope depicts Charlemagne's Aix-la-Chapelle, the ruins of Heidelberg, the "wildly picturesque" streams that descend from the Black Forest to the Rhine River. She sketches the rich fields of Flanders and the gardens of Schwetzingen, full of "terraces, fountains, aviaries, temples, waterfalls, grottos, groves, parterres, lawns, lakes, statues, mosques, baths, boats, and bridges." The book abounds with descriptions of castles, ruins, terraces, forests, and gardens on the Rhine and the "pellucid" Neckar Rivers. As she remarked in approaching Neckarsteinach, a lovely town surrounded by towering rocks, the ruins of two stately castles, bright green meadows around the river, boats, houses, and hanging gardens, "it was just such scenery as one longed to revel in."

Scenery and people merged as Trollope developed a new source of material: the modern tourist. In an age just discovering the delights and drawbacks of tours for middle-class travelers, Trollope also turned a sharp eye on her fellow passengers who sought rapid "grand tour" experiences. She thought Cologne needed two months, rather than two days, to appreciate, "but as long as steamboats keep running up the Rhine, the giddy throng . . . will never spare time to examine this interesting old city, with one tenth part of the attention it deserves." On land, too, travel had accelerated. A lady in a diligence told Trollope, "I and my nephews make a point of never stopping to look at things."

Whenever she was forced to travel this way, Trollope resented the need to keep up the pace: "The more beautiful the objects on every side, the more discontented I grow at being whisked past them." The book became a plea for a leisurely kind of travel, as she showed her readers what tourism lacked in its group arrangements, its cheap souvenirs, and its rapid, impersonal transportation. At Marburg she failed to indulge a desire to explore the castle because "there stood the diligence, with the horses all ready, and the horn of the conductor at his mouth! and there stood I, inwardly vowing that I would never again chain myself in the same manner." At the Protestant Church of St. Thomas

she found the Count of Nassau and his daughter's remains "kept in glass cases and clothed in trumpery garments," exhibited "for a penny a-piece to all comers," and in all that she found something "revoltingly indecent." Speed was her most constant complaint, as she frequently wrote of "the vexation of being whirled past objects that you are longing to gaze upon."

As the book approaches its conclusion Trollope, in contrast to her hapless fellow tourists, emerges firmly as an ideal traveler. She has taken time, looked long, and explored the land. She has even had herself locked inside a dungeon for half an hour, just to experience imprisonment in a medieval castle. Her readers relished this touch of the Gothic, as did Trollope, who while stepping into "this region of blackest night" recorded that "I did not shrink from the undertaking."

When she reached the Brocken, highest of the Harz Mountains and rich in associations with witches and devils, she saw the potential for more "sublime" scenery, as Niagara Falls had provided. Yet she resisted static presentations of landscape ("It is always dangerous to dwell in description upon any scene, the effect of which is greatly to excite the imagination") and cast herself, instead, as the adventuring traveler with place as a mere backdrop. She ascended the Brocken on a mule, over rocks, through gigantic pines, amid rain and storm, across noisy torrents, and spent the night in a small cabin. She noted pointedly, "I was lost in admiration at my own undaunted courage." The next day, in the middle of a raging storm, she made the descent strapped to the donkey. Despite breathlessness and even some fear, she felt that "exaltation of spirits" that travel always aroused in her.

The book was fresh and genuine, and critics praised her initiative and daring. The *Spectator* wrote, "She was not satisfied to tread in the footsteps of the common tourist and to yield herself implicitly up to the guidance of an innkeeper, a valet de place, or a coachman. She sought out objects for herself, pursued the picturesque where it was likely to be found." Soon she was writing her publisher with plans for yet another travel account: "Did circumstances permit, I should greatly like to scribble a little gossip on the present queer state of society in Paris."

She regarded herself as a professional travel writer. She was troubled by the delays in publishing her most recent novel only because it represented an important source of traveling funds. In a letter of 24 June 1835 to her publisher, Richard Bentley, she

An American caricature of Trollope in 1833, showing the anger and resentment aroused by Domestic Manners of the Americans *(from D. C. Johnston,* Trollopiana: Scraps for the Year 1833 *[1833])*

set forth the relationship between these two parts of her writing life:

> Since I have felt it my duty to write, I have devoted such a portion of each day to the occupation, as would enable me to keep my place before the public. . . . Though my novels are read, my reputation must chiefly be sustained by traveling, and I love the occupation well enough to look forward with hope and pleasure to future excursions. I have been often told that I ought to visit Italy (Venice particularly) and Sicily – and I hope to be able to do so – but the truth is, that however well the public may like my traveling memoranda, the expenses incurred in collecting them are much too heavy to render the employment profitable, or even prudent. The publishing [of] some work of imagination, written in the retirement of my quiet home, in the interval between my costly ramblings, is the only method by which I can enable myself to undertake them.

As Trollope tried to maintain a balance between her traveling accounts and novels, the two genres influenced each other. While fictional techniques permeated the travelogues, her novels also benefited from this cross-fertilization of types – from *Jonathan Jefferson Whitlaw* through *A Romance of Vienna* (1838), *The Barnabys in America; or, Adventures of the Widow Wedded* (1843), and *The Robertses on Their Travels*

(1846) to the work that concluded her writing career, *Fashionable Life; or, Paris and London* (1856). Such artistic interaction stimulated Trollope to produce works of increasing originality.

Whereas America and Germany had been new milieus for Trollope, Paris was more familiar and had always been a favorite place, the home of friends such as the Garnetts, whom she had visited in 1823 when she produced one of her first writing efforts, a journal of a visit to La Grange, home of the much admired Gen. Marie-Joseph-Paul-Yves-Roch-Gilbert du Motier Lafayette. By now she was so accomplished a writer of travels that an 1836 *Spectator* review suggested that *Paris and the Parisians in 1835* might be used to "deduce the laws of the craft" for writing travel books. Indeed, as the reviewer concluded, "to anybody who would wish to acquire the trade of book-making, *Paris and the Parisians* should be read, studied, and analyzed."

For this book Trollope again employed fictional techniques; rather than writing pure exposition, she used the device of writing letters home to a friend and cast much of her material as dialogues in which characters debate the relative merits of French and English social habits, modern French literature, the process of trial by jury, or the government of King Louis Phillipe. Profuse catalogues of her observations, descriptive scenes, and light essays on current subjects were mingled with those dialogues. As one critic noted of the book, "All she writes is amusing, partly because of the originality of her own ideas, and partly because she has a curious way of illustrating the ideas of others."

The most original part of the book is its structure, which reflected her judgment that Paris was a city of contradictions. Its surface provided an air of "ceaseless jubilee" and "eternal holiday" that she described copiously. Parisians loved to bask in the open air and show the world their joie de vivre: "The bright, clear atmosphere seems made on purpose for them," she wrote, "and whoever laid out the boulevards, the quays, the gardens of Paris" knew how the citizens loved to assemble for shared pleasure. Sorrow and suffering seemed banished.

> Everywhere else you see people looking anxious and busy at least . . . but here the glance of every eye is a gay one; and even though this may perhaps be only worn in the sunshine, and put on just as other people put on their hats and bonnets, the effect is delightfully cheering to the spirits of a wandering stranger.

Repeatedly she noted

> that indescribable air of gayety which makes every sunshiny day look like a fete: the light hilarity of spirit . . . the cheerful tone of voice, the sparkling glances of the numberless bright eyes; the gardens, the flowers, the statues of Paris[, which,] taken together, produced an effect very like enchantment.

But her book also showed a grim side of urban Paris through a series of interpolated narratives about murders and suicides and through a visit to the crowded Paris morgue. In addition, she summarizes the action of two violent Victor Hugo dramas then playing to crowded audiences. By such imaginative and diverse means she projected the brutalities hidden behind the "delightful spectacle" that Paris presented to the merely casual visitor.

Heightening the representative traits of people enabled her to draw people in strong outlines, and one critic emphasized the pictorial qualities of her art: "There is a brightness about her portraits . . . that at once fixes upon our memory." Her subjects ranged from the famous (Madame Jeanne-Françoise-Julie-Adélaïde Récamier, Victor Hugo, George Sand) to prisoners and revolutionaries, some in conical crowned hats with "long matted locks that hang in heavy, ominous dirtiness." Using talk and gestures, she animated brief sketches of people, from street orators and ragamuffin rioters to impoverished duchesses. She told readers who were expecting descriptions of scenes rather than of people, "I am more earnestly bent . . . upon availing myself of all my opportunities for listening to the conversation within the houses, than on contemplating all the marvels that may be seen without." Sometimes she participated in debates, many of which provided opportunities for her to air her strong views.

In many of these dialogues her familiar concerns about women returned. What was woman's role in France? She records a lengthy discourse with a Frenchman on the fate of the many single women in England. Other letters record conversations discussing the differences between the lives of women in England and in France. In England young unmarried ladies are the center of society; in France wives are more important than young ladies. Indeed, she noted, it is "as if the heart and soul of a French girl were asleep, or at least dozing, till the ceremony of marriage awakened them."

After observing the "character, position, and influence" of Parisian women, Trollope concludes that women generally enjoy more social influence than the women of England. French politeness to women "is very far from superficial," for they are shown real "domestic respect." Even more important, French ladies do not share that worst terror of young Englishwomen – that "of being called learned." In France no "blue badge" is attached to female possessors of talent and information. Lecturing her British countrymen, Trollope recalls with sorrow how "the dread of imputed blueism weighs down many a bright spirit." In France, however, "the higher efforts of the female mind" are honored.

Her political conservatism, as always, emerges clearly. She opposes "any further trial of a republican form of government," as well as freedom of the press, "the most awful engine that Providence has permitted the hand of man to wield." These strong opinions color her reporting of the new literature of Honoré de Balzac and George Sand, of the Exhibition of Living Artists at the Louvre. Yet her biases did not detract from her insights. Even while disapproving of Sand's morality, Trollope could appreciate the gracefulness of her style. While she castigated the "corrupt creations" of Victor Hugo, her descriptions projected the power of those creations. Her method and distinctive voice gave the book originality, but beyond her clever handling of materials lay the astute observations of an eye on which little was lost. Her recording of the surface of French life and letters in 1835 make the book a rich resource of scenes, characters, and conversations, a resource that brings the life of the period closer to the grasp of the social and intellectual historian.

In April 1836 Trollope concluded an agreement with Bentley for two novels and two more travel books, one to be a "work describing Mrs. Trollope's Travels in Austria and more particularly her residence in Vienna, to be treated in a similar manner to her recent book called 'Paris and the Parisians,'" and "a similar account of her Travels and Residence in Various parts of Italy." It was an ambitious contract for a fifty-seven-year-old woman. That summer she left for Italy by way of Vienna with her children Tom and Cecilia, now grown and treasured traveling companions. After a stop in Paris to see the Garnetts, they arrived in Vienna to begin the touring and socializing that was necessary to gather materials. Because her daughter's health had declined, by December she proposed a return to England before continuing to Italy. In a letter of 27 February 1837 to Bentley she cited professional reasons: "I would much rather that my book on Austria be published before my journey to Italy began. They must be quite distinct, and if possible, unconnected even in feeling." Her publisher agreed, and by 4 July 1837, with her characteristically in-

"*Soiree,*" *engraving from Trollope's* Paris and the Parisians in 1835 *(courtesy of the Lilly Library, Indiana University)*

difficulty of her voyages, about the "stout heart" needed to become "an avant-couriere" who describes things "as they are."

In the second volume her inspiration flags under the spell of her delight in Vienna's high society. She fails to use dramatic anecdotes and becomes lost in endlessly describing festivities and dropping aristocratic names of the veritable litany of kings, queens, nobles, and other elites who cross her path. Her place descriptions are conventional and uninteresting. She tours the principal churches and records her views of "noble landscapes," and she apologizes frequently for the tedium of such descriptions. Following her journey from Stuttgart, through the Tyrol and Vienna to her residence and activities in Viennese society, the book lacks the sharp commentary of her previous works.

Her politics remain conservative. In a lengthy passage with which Prince Metternich helped her, she praises the Austrian system of government and outlines its intricacies. This bias enraged many English reviewers, in particular a critic in the *Athenaeum,* who wrote that

> Mrs. Trollope is just the person to trumpet for the virtues of a self-styled paternal government, to illustrate the animal satisfactions and material comforts of the pampered tradesmen of an aristocratic capital, and to mistake these for national prosperity; to rejoice in the gorgeous pageantry of doting feudality, and to calumniate (as far as such a writer's censure can prevail) whatever tends to enlarge the mind of man and to enoble [*sic*] his nature.

The reviewer concluded, "She is more bigoted, more slavish, more intolerant, more common-place and unintellectual than usual; and of all her publications, this is the one we have read with most disgust and with less pleasure." In addition to her usual penchant for offending liberal critics, Trollope had succeeded in creating a dull book in her Vienna volumes.

A Visit to Italy completed her decline as a travel writer. She was now pouring her major creative energy into works of fiction, the most recent of which was reformist and satiric. This approach had once accounted for her successes in the travel genre, as her first book had attacked a country and a culture that she had found incompatible. Her last travel book, however, became a panegyric rhapsody on a country and a culture that she had long loved.

The problem with *A Visit to Italy* was not, however, solely one of manner and familiarity of material. In this book people recede to the background in favor of art, architecture, and the literature of the

credible energy, Trollope had her work on Austria ready for the press.

Although she brought to this book her usual talents for observations and dramatization, *Vienna and the Austrians* represented a decline. Her greatest gift had always been for sharp satiric caricature, but in Vienna she found only gorgeous scenery and a man who quickly became her hero, Prince Clemens von Metternich, chancellor of Austria, whom she called "one of the most admirable characters that I have ever known." Flattered by his attentions and those of his family, Trollope settled into a dangerous contentment with all she saw. She did not discard all the successful devices of her earlier works, for in this book she cast herself as the daring picaresque heroine. In one adventure she, Tom, and Auguste Hervieu, an artist friend, outwit a landlord who wants more money and even threatens to kill them. As a traveler par excellence, she again ascends mountains, visits the remote waterfalls, and makes a dangerous descent to an underground salt mine. She pointedly reminds her readers about the past. She who had been a pioneer in writing travel books that emphasized people rather than landscapes now shifted her focus. Throughout the book she preferred to describe antiquities of Italy, its heritage of culture and art, rather than its present appearance. After a perfunctory description of Naples ("The people eat great quantities of maccaroni . . . make coral trinkets and cheap gloves" and have a theater that "is the largest in the world"), she admitted being surprised at her own concentration on antiquity: "I would not beforehand have believed it possible that I could have ever learned to care so much more about things that are not, than about things that are." Yet such was the prevailing pattern of her book.

In one passage she candidly noted, "I know I shall be involved in a sort of labyrinth of astonishment and admiration, which will make it exceedingly difficult to be intelligible." She repeatedly apologized to her readers: "I am almost afraid to ask you to go with me to the Pitti again lest you should fancy that I intend to turn myself into a catalogue, and then insist upon your reading me. But I will do no such thing." Despite such resolutions, however, Trollope expatiated frequently on her favorite artists – Paolo Veronese, Giotto di Bondone, Donato de Betto di Bardi Donatello, Raphael, Andrea del Verrochio, Michelangelo, Andrea del Sarto, Peter Paul Rubens, Bartolomé Murillo, and Titian. She weakly concluded, "And now if I can help it, I will talk to you no more about the pictures of the Pitti Palace." Yet page after page of descriptions of architectural monuments followed.

The book predictably contained comprehensive descriptions of Rome and Saint Peter's Basilica during a papal mass, of Venice and the Armenian convent of George Gordon, Lord Byron, and even of recently discovered Pompeii. She made the requisite stop at the house of Petrarch, where she picked a passion flower to serve as a relic of the visit. While some scenes were competently drawn, readers were inundated by an endless succession of churches, processions, palaces, the Leaning Tower, Filippo Brunelleschi's dome, and countless royal villas.

Uncritical awe suffused her accounts. She had approached Florence in a "fever of anticipation. . . . I almost felt as if I were going to enter bodily into the presence of Dante, Petrarch, and Boccaccio." Having visited the library of St. Lawrence, she asked, "Who can see the oldest manuscript of Virgil extant, and not feel that exciting species of curiosity, which is a sort of glory to feel and to indulge?" By its end Trollope was aware of the book's shortcomings: "Why should I recite the names of endless palaces and of temples sufficient to turn my pages into a Pantheon?" she asked. Yet a pantheon it was, enshrining her love of Italy's past and providing no insights into the contemporary lives of its people. The book was a failure. As the reviewer for the *Athenaeum* complained, "the last thing one should have expected from Mrs. Trollope is a work whose pages are characterless."

Some have said that travelers are always searching for themselves. They travel to test against a wide and changing reality that essential inner self about which they are still uncertain. If such had been, at least in part, Trollope's motives for her peripatetic life, in Italy the self and the environment had quickly become one and, like most such loving encounters with what seemed to be perfection to her, the experience had left her voice silenced in uncritical awe. For Frances Trollope, a visit to Italy was an introduction to a permanent home and the end of her traveling and travel accounts.

Starting with *Domestic Manners of the Americans,* Trollope had written five travel books, all of which were reprinted in subsequent editions. Each had a strong authorial voice. In *Domestic Manners of the Americans* the disappointed liberal had been disgusted with utopian or democratic experiments. In *Belgium and Western Germany in 1833* the conservative traveler had admired the authoritarian king of Prussia and lectured English readers on the errors of their Reform Bill. In *Paris and the Parisians in 1835* the Tory Englishwoman had deplored the disruptions of revolutions and supported King Louis Phillipe, no rightful monarch, but at any rate a king. In *Vienna and the Austrians* a bedazzled Trollope had hobnobbed with Prince Metternich and the social elite and praised Austrian absolutism. In *A Visit to Italy* she had become a Virgilian guide to art treasures and the past. Whatever her subject had been, readers could never forget the presence of Frances Trollope or her strong views about what she had seen.

Biographies:

Thomas Adolphus Trollope, *What I Remember* (New York: Harper, 1888);

Frances Eleanor Trollope, *Frances Trollope: Her Life and Literary Work from George III to Victoria,* 2 volumes (London: Bentley, 1895);

Eileen Bigland, *The Indomitable Mrs. Trollope* (New York: Lippincott, 1954);

Johanna Johnston, *The Life, Manners, and Travels of Fanny Trollope: A Biography* (New York: Hawthorn, 1978);

Helen Heineman, *Mrs. Trollope: The Triumphant Feminine in the 19th Century* (Athens: Ohio University Press, 1979);

Heineman, *Restless Angels: The Friendship of Six Victorian Women* (Athens: Ohio University Press, 1983).

References:

Carl Abbott, "The Location and External Appearance of Mrs. Trollope's Bazaar," *Journal of the Society of Architectural Historians,* 29 (October 1970): 256–260;

Timothy Flint, "Travelers in America, etc." *Knickerbocker, or New York Monthly Magazine,* 2 (1833): 283–302;

Russell A. Griffin, "Mrs. Trollope and the Queen City," *Mississippi Valley Historical Review,* 37 (September 1950): 289–302;

Helen Heineman, *Frances Trollope* (Boston: G. K. Hall, 1984);

Heineman, "Frances Trollope in the New World: *Domestic Manners of the Americans,*" *American Quarterly,* 21 (Fall 1969): 544–559;

Heineman, "Starving in that Land of Plenty: New Backgrounds to *Domestic Manners of the Americans,*" *American Quarterly,* 24 (December 1972): 643–660;

Clay Lancaster, "The Egyptian Hall and Mrs. Trollope's Bazaar," *Magazine of Art,* 43 (March 1950): 94–99;

Ada B. Nisbet, "Mrs. Trollope's 'Domestic Manners,' " *Nineteenth Century Fiction,* 4 (March 1950): 319–324;

Louis Leonard Tucker, "Cincinnati: Athens of the West, 1830–1831," *Ohio History,* 75 (Winter 1966): 10–25;

Henry T. Tuckerman, *America and Her Commentators, with a Critical Sketch of Travel in the United States* (New York: Scribner, 1864).

Mary Louisa Whately

(31 August 1824 – 9 March 1889)

Pam J. Lieske
University of Massachusetts – Amherst

BOOKS: *Ragged Life in Egypt* (London: Seeley, Jackson & Halliday, 1862);

More about Ragged Life in Egypt (London, 1863);

Child-Life in Egypt (Philadelphia: American Sunday-school Union, [1866]); republished as *Ragged Life in Egypt, and More about Ragged Life in Egypt* (London: Seeley, Jackson & Halliday, 1870);

The Story of a Diamond: Illustrative of Egyptian Manners and Customs (London: Religious Tract Society, [1867]; Philadelphia, 1868);

Among the Huts in Egypt: Scenes from Real Life (London: Seeley, Jackson & Halliday, 1871; New York, 187?–);

A Memoir of Mansoor Shakoor, of Lebanon (London, 1873);

The Prism. Unequally Yoked . . . Life in a Swiss Chalet . . . From Darkness to Light . . . , by Whately, H. W[ale], and E. M. M[oore]; edited, with a preface, by Elizabeth Jane Whately (London: Religious Tract Society, 1878);

Letters from Egypt to Plain Folks at Home (London: Seeley, Jackson & Halliday, 1879); republished as *Letters from Egypt* (New York: Dodd, Mead, 1879?);

Lost in Egypt (London: Religious Tract Society, 1881);

Scenes from Life in Cairo: A Glimpse behind the Curtain (London: Seeley, Jackson & Halliday, 1883);

Stories of Peasant Life on the Nile (London: Religious Tract Society, 1888).

Mary Louisa Whately (engraving by Whymper)

Critics assume that Mary Louisa Whately's writing is strictly religious, because she was first and foremost an Anglican missionary who worked in Egypt for nearly thirty years and promoted a Christian agenda throughout her life. Without funding or assistance from any church she opened a school for Muslim girls in one of the poorest sections of Cairo, and eventually she opened a school for boys when she acquired such assistance. She later added to these achievements the founding of a medical mission and a school for children from various religious and ethnic groups. Her limited fame has thus been as a missionary and a religious writer.

Nevertheless, her travel writing is noteworthy. Unlike many nineteenth-century writers who wrote about Egypt by describing monuments, museums, or quaint trips on the Nile, Whately lived and worked among the poor of Cairo, and her perspective on the daily lives and habits of people is unusual. Moreover, while some British travel writers romanticize or infantilize the people they write about, Whately describes Egyptians sensitively yet realistically, and in this way she helped to dismantle myths and stereotypes about them. Finally, as Whately's missionary career developed, her writing also expanded, from its initial focus on Muslim girls in Cairo to a more inclusive focus on such diverse groups as the Circassians, blacks, Turks, Copts, and Bedouins. Though Whately was a devout Christian, in writing about such diverse people she exhibited a remarkable sensitivity and tolerance for cultural, ethnic, and religious differences. At the same time, however, she maintained a belief that Egyptian women were unfairly oppressed by social customs and by the Muslim religion.

As the third child and second daughter of Richard Whately, later the archbishop of Dublin, and Elizabeth Pope, of Hillingdon Hall, Uxbridge, Mary Louisa Whately was born at Halesworth, in Suffolk. Her father was a noteworthy and controversial figure who edited works of Francis Bacon and William Paley in addition to writing many religious, political, and educational works. He also tutored and subsequently worked with John Henry (later Cardinal) Newman. His opinions have been described as narrow and intractable, but as a national education commissioner he favored mass education for the Irish people.

In 1827 the family moved to Oxford, and in 1831, after Richard Whately was named archbishop of Dublin, they moved to Dublin. Except for occasional trips to England and the Continent Whately lived in Ireland until her first trip to Egypt in 1856. Exactly how many siblings she had is unknown, but these included at least one brother and three sisters — one of whom, Elizabeth Jane Whately, wrote a biography of her. Another sister died in 1860.

Elizabeth Jane Whately describes young Mary as an energetic and intelligent child who liked to learn and to make up stories. Her parents directed her education, and the entire family was deeply committed to various religious and philanthropic activities. The children helped the neighboring poor, and Mary and Elizabeth Jane helped teach other children and prepare texts for those who attended a school founded by their father on the grounds of the family estate. In addition, the family did religious and charitable work with Roman Catholics, Italians, and the charity schools and orphanages connected with the Irish Church Mission. According to Elizabeth Jane Whately, work with the Irish Church Mission was the turning point in Mary Whately's spiritual life.

In the winter of 1849–1850 Whately accompanied her brother on a trip to Nice, Florence, and other parts of Italy. Besides having the opportunity to paint and to improve her Italian, Whately was exposed to Continental evangelical work through the pastor J. P. Meille of La Tour. Because of poor health, in 1856 she took her first trip to Egypt and spent time in Cairo. Before returning home she visited the Holy Land, where she was impressed with missionary work among the Jews.

According to Elizabeth Jane Whately, records of Mary Whately's early trips abroad were lost. This claim has not been verified, and there have often been more questions than answers about the extent of Whately's writing. Passages attributed to work written late in her life are included in the biography, *The Life and Work of Mary Louisa Whately* (1890), yet many of these closely resemble passages in her first published work, *Ragged Life in Egypt* (1862). Other lengthy quotations that Elizabeth Jane claims are from Mary Whately's work also appear in this same biography, but the original sources for these quotations and the events on which they are based are often unclear. This authorial fuzziness is typical of both Whately sisters, as both omit or gloss over exact details concerning Mary Whately's writing. In all probability scholars have yet to discover all of Whately's published and unpublished writing, particularly her work for periodicals.

In the winter of 1860 Whately and a cousin returned to Cairo to live and work. Whately's first published work, *Ragged Life in Egypt*, soon followed. According to Elizabeth Jane, only because of their father was the book published at all. She reports that after a friend had read some of Mary's letters to her brother, Richard told his daughter, " 'Mary, you ought to publish these papers.' Her first answer was, 'Oh, people are tired of Egypt! they have had so many books of travels there, and so many details!' 'Yes,' he rejoined; 'but yours will be new; you have reached a stratum lower than any foreign visitor has yet done.' "

This belief that readers would want to know about the lower classes was correct. *Ragged Life in Egypt* underwent four editions and was eventually republished with its sequel, *More about Ragged Life in Egypt* (1863) in an American edition titled *Child-Life in Egypt* (1866) before making its final British appearance as *Ragged Life in Egypt, and More about Ragged Life in Egypt* in 1870. In the introduction to the 1870 edition Whately echoes her father's assessment of her writing. She claims that this edition is important because it occupies a middle ground between conventional missionary books and travel books: it fills a void between "the general reports of missionaries in regular stations, and the vague and hasty sketches of rapid travellers, who can only see the surface as they hurry along through various countries." This concern with knowing the details of people's lives — especially the lives of poor women — is evident in all of Whately's published work.

The Ragged Life books relate Whately's efforts to open a school for poor, mainly Muslim girls in Cairo during the winter of 1860 and her subsequent attempts to educate her scholars in a Christian way of life. Additions to front- and end-matter in the various works bring the story up to date: the 1862 edition, for instance, ends with a report about Whately's return to England in the spring of 1861. Changes in the 1870 edition include an introduction, details on how the school and its pupils have expanded over the years, and sections on the Shakoor brothers and their involvement with Whately's missionary effort.

The changes that Whately chronicles in her Ragged Life books are best exemplified by the transformation in the girls' school initially located in Whately's house. On her first day as a teacher in 1860, Whately went out into the streets to recruit her first scholars, nine little Muslim girls, and brought them back to her house, where classes were held. Eight years later, as mentioned in the appendix to *Ragged Life in Egypt, and More about Ragged Life in Egypt,* 70 girls and 170 boys attended schools in two separate buildings that Whately had built outside Cairo. Another indication of how expansive and expensive Whately's missionary venture became is an entry in the appendix to the 1863 third edition of *Ragged Life in Egypt,* which lists a London address to which donations for the newly opened boys' school could be sent.

In the 1870 edition of *Ragged Life* Whately claims that her narrative results from direct observation and that she has not altered or embellished the truth: she thus writes a kind of social history. Living in a native house "in a quarter where all the poorer residents were Moslims," Whately was able to observe the everyday life and customs of those around her, especially since much daily life occurred outdoors. The book states that she feels that the poor usually "come before passing travellers most frequently in a disagreeable manner" – as "beggars" or as "dirty and ragged" creatures. However, as soon as such travelers know particulars about the lives of these poor, surface differences dissipate and similarities between the poor and other groups emerge. To illustrate this point the 1870 *Ragged Life* describes local customs of diet, dress, sexual segregation, and local economic practices, as well as brief individualized portraits of Whately's scholars and their families.

At times she places herself within the narrative, as when she discusses her attempts at house hunting, her visit to Suez, and her trips to the desert communities outside Cairo. This participation in the narrative is never intrusive or overbearing and often provides a window into the lives of the local people and into their feelings about foreigners. Her recollection of the difficult time she had in first finding suitable lodging and then negotiating with the disinterested workmen is particularly telling.

Such glimpses into how Whately adjusted to living in Egypt have little in common with the writing of other British women who lived in Africa during this time. Harriet Ward's *Five Years in Kaffirland* (1848), Elizabeth Melville's *A Residence at Sierra Leone* (1849), and Lady Mary Anne Barker's *A Year's Housekeeping in South Africa* (1877) are domestic narratives about women and their families struggling to adapt to a strange land. In contrast, Whately's focus is always on the people around her. References to herself always concern her identity as a missionary doing public work, never as a woman adapting to a foreign land. Her cultural objectivity and her clear, unadorned writing style have more in common with eighteenth-century travel narratives than with the more personal, author-centered travel works of her own time.

Only a few months after establishing her school for girls, Whately returned to Ireland in the spring of 1861, as unspecified family matters needed her attention. That winter and the following spring she traveled to Pau, in southwestern France, both for relaxation and for her health.

Especially during the 1860s Whately's life was busy, and it is remarkable that her literary production continued. While she was in Ireland her school in Cairo had closed, and upon returning to Egypt in 1862 Whately had to start her missionary efforts from scratch – by rehiring teachers, relocating her pupils, and resuming school operations. She also resumed her own Arabic lessons. Until this time she had financed her missionary work entirely with her own money – first with an allowance from her father and after his death with income from the property he had left her. The school, however, was growing so rapidly that Whately was forced to turn to others for financial support.

The Prince of Wales was one source of aid. He visited Egypt in the 1860s, and through his intervention with Ismail Pasha, Whately was granted land outside Cairo for a permanent school, the only stipulation being that the buildings had to be attractive, because they would be seen from the road. Another source of assistance was through the Syrian missionary, Mansoor Shakoor. In the early 1860s he became a valuable associate to Whately, as did his brother, Joseph, later. The elder Shakoor brother in 1864 married a young Lebanese woman who became an intimate friend and companion of Whately.

In 1867 *The Story of a Diamond: Illustrative of Egyptian Manners and Customs* was published in London, and an American edition followed a year later. As its title suggests, the work is a study of the Egyptian people and their lives. This book was followed in 1871 by *Among the Huts in Egypt: Scenes from Real Life.* Unlike *The Story of a Diamond,* which was published in only one edition, *Among the Huts in Egypt* was more successful: it was republished in three British editions and one American edition.

In the introduction to *Among the Huts in Egypt* Whately states that she decided to write the book because friends who had read the Ragged Life books requested "further details concerning the people among whom I dwell, and the schools established for their children." She adds that *Among the Huts in Egypt* is based on extracts from diaries and letters that she had previously written. Sounding like eighteenth-century British women writers who emphasize the truthfulness of their work and apologize for their meager skills, Whately says that her text re-creates "almost word for word" the people of whom she writes, "in the hope that the simplicity and truthfulness of the sketches may atone for the homeliness of some, and the want of striking incidents in almost all."

Despite this rhetorical posturing, *Among the Huts in Egypt* is not as naive or reductive as one might assume. In fact, later in the introduction Whately reproaches writers who romanticize Egypt and says that she will tell the truth about the ignorance and bad habits of the Egyptian. Notwithstanding such claims to be objective, Whately never leaves any doubt about where her sympathies lie. In one especially moving passage she explains that the Egyptian's "dark side is not presented solely to the reader, nor are the descriptions exaggerated by dislike, for I love Egypt and her people sincerely, and appreciate all that is to be admired in both."

Among the Huts in Egypt is a hybrid of literary genres. Its opening chapter discusses the weather patterns, trees, plants, and other vegetation of Egypt in a voice that is both dry and detached. Reminiscent of a textbook on botany or horticulture, the tone and content of this chapter are similar to those found in the opening chapter of Whately's later work, *Letters from Egypt to Plain Folks at Home* (1879). Unfamiliar terms are defined and word origins are traced as if Whately conceives her work as a dictionary or a scientific treatise and her audience as uninformed students hungry for information.

The forced didacticism of this chapter disappears as Whately resorts to what she does best: describing people, their habits, and her encounters with them. Subsequent chapters focus on daily lives of the Egyptian people, on Whately's missionary efforts, or on some combination of the two. Excerpts of the diary or letters, from which the text is said to originate, are absent. The chronology of related events is also unclear, although Whately occasionally mentions specific years, such as 1863 and 1870. The text discusses her experiences with Bedouins in the desert, pilgrims on the way to Mecca, and poor Muslim families in Cairo.

The chapter on a bazaar is especially effective. In it Whately relates humorously, yet informatively, her experiences buying such items as red clay pottery, bulk rice, and petroleum for lamp oil. In another chapter entitled "The Fellah." Whately describes her encounter with an old woman whom she visits in a fishing village during one of her yearly missionary trips on the Nile River. As Whately sits reading the Bible to a group of old women, one of them (apparently knowing that Whately sometimes distributes simple remedies) asks Whately for some medicine. The woman wants henna to dye her hair and is greatly disappointed that Whately cannot give her any. Whately comments wryly that the encounter illustrates "the devotion of our sex to personal appearance."

Whately's interest in the material conditions of women's lives is evident in *Among the Huts in Egypt.* With characteristic honesty and frankness she discusses her visit to a harem and gives three reasons that she prefers visiting poor Coptic and Muslim women rather than women who are wealthy. She says that, first of all, most wealthy people speak Turkish, and she does not have time to learn another language. Wealthy women are also difficult to meet, because as a rule they are kept more secluded than women from lower classes. And finally she simply finds poorer women more interesting: they are more active than wealthy women who spend their days in seclusion, and they have more to say. While wealthy women generally come from other lands, poorer women are usually born in Egypt and are its true people.

Whately, however, does not group all poor Egyptians together. One of the strengths of her work is in the careful, thoughtful way she delineates various ethnic and religious groups. In *Among the Huts in Egypt* she describes a trip to the desert, where she meets people probably of mixed Bedouin races because their appearances and habits differ from those of conventional Bedouins. This attention to detail of race and class sets Whately apart from other writers on Egypt who tend to place its people into reductive categories.

Among the Huts in Egypt is also notable because certain of its stories reappear in Whately's later work. One chapter on Egyptian marriages recounts the story of a young Coptic couple, newly married, who share a love of Scriptures. The bride is granted an unusual amount of freedom for a woman of her position, and the couple's relationship is egalitarian and mutually beneficial. This woman reappears in a later chapter when Whately describes how the wife, with her husband's permission, visits Whately before the traditional six months of seclusion for new brides has concluded. This couple also serves as the model for the central couple of Whately's later fictional effort, *Scenes from Life in Cairo: A Glimpse behind the Curtain* (1883).

The story of a Greek slave woman in *Among the Huts in Egypt* is likewise almost certainly retold in *Scenes from Life in Cairo*. In both stories refined, dignified, young women are taken from their homes and forced to live and work as slaves among Muslim peasants. Both women are healers with extraordinary powers and are befriended either by Whately or, in the fictional *Scenes from Life in Cairo*, a figure closely resembling her. With Whately's aid the slaves rediscover their Christian heritage and find a sense of peace. Describing the slave in *Among the Huts in Egypt,* Whately finds "an undefined something in her manner and voice that struck me as unusual – a degree of refinement, and a quiet sad expression of countenance."

In *Among the Huts in Egypt* and *Scenes from Life in Cairo* Whately speculates on the previous life of the slave woman – when she had lived among her people as a Christian and had held a position of some influence – and on her present feeling as she lives among Muslim peasants. This speculation begets no romanticism, however; Whately remains a realist. In both works descriptions of the characters and their lives are virtually the same, and even the narrative persona and tone are similar.

In 1872 Mansoor Shakoor died, and the following year Whately published a memoir of him. She maintained close ties with many members of the Shakoor family, with whom she lived and worked from the early 1860s until her death in 1889. At the request of Mansoor Shakoor in the early 1860s Whately had lived with and educated his prospective bride, then a thirteen- or fourteen-year-old girl. One wonders what Whately's feelings about this arrangement had been. Generally tolerant of cultural differences in her writing, she was

quick to condemn the early ages at which Egyptian women married, as she pointed out that once they became wives they almost always lost any chance of continuing their educations. Her own objections to early marriage, though, did not prevent Whately from helping to rear the two daughters from Shakoor's marriage.

A younger sister of this Mrs. Shakoor married a doctor in 1879 – more than likely a Dr. Azoury – and Whately engaged his services as a medical missionary. He accompanied her on yearly medical and missionary trips on the Nile, and with his and Mrs. Shakoor's assistance Whately opened medical clinics near the school buildings and a European branch school for Jewish and Syrian girls of mixed parentage. Whately remained close to her own family in Ireland – a sister visited her in Egypt at least once – but the Shakoors were important parts of her personal and professional life.

Little is known about *The Prism. Unequally Yoked . . . Life in a Swiss Chalet . . . From Darkness to Light . . .* (1878), a collection of miscellaneous verse and tales written by Whately and two members of her family. The following year, however, *Letters from Egypt to Plain Folks at Home* was published. Whether or not Whately knew that both Florence Nightingale (in 1854) and Lucie Duff Gordon (in 1865) had already written travel books using a shorter version of this title (*Letters from Egypt*) is unclear. Nevertheless, when Whately's work was republished for an American audience, its title was abbreviated to *Letters from Egypt*.

Whately's *Letters from Egypt* is unlike both Nightingale's and Duff Gordon's. Nightingale's is largely a descriptive guide to Egypt's monuments and buildings, while Duff Gordon's combines political critique and humorous personal narrative. In contrast, even Whately's title is a misnomer: rather than being a collection of letters, her book is a collection of essays on various topics such as superstitions, slavery, and life in towns and villages. In its introduction Whately states that her aim is to "write some simple familiar accounts of the land of Egypt where I dwell, which might be useful and pleasant."

Despite the simplicity of this statement, Whately's concept of herself as a writer has changed from previous volumes. In *Ragged Life in Egypt, and More about Ragged Life in Egypt* she had claimed that her work filled a void between travel writing and missionary reports. In *Letters from Egypt* Whately sees herself as a specific kind of travel writer. She states that most travel writers are ignorant of the language of the country they visit and that they stay for only a short time in the countries about which they write. The result is that their works "are apt to be full of mistakes and incorrect notions." Whately, on the other hand, claims that

> I have lived a great many years here, and my business has been among the people, especially the poor, and the children. I began to study the language as soon as I arrived, and am accustomed to converse in it with different classes of the people, and also to visit them and receive them in my turn, so that I can tell you a good deal about their ways and habits.

Her implication, then, is that she will correct "the mistakes and incorrect notions" that other travel writers are wont to propound.

Such correction does not occur, however, until late in the work. Whately begins *Letters from Egypt* with three chapters discomfortingly like those of other travel writers. Through her detached, third-person voice she lists the people and places of biblical Egypt, describes how the countryside is cultivated by the Nile, and identifies what plants, flowers, and trees are found in typical Egyptian gardens.

After these initial chapters Whately abandons her attempt to write a scientific study of Egypt, and her voice is more relaxed and less overbearing. The resulting work is more engaging. Unlike earlier travel works, subjects are discussed in depth, and Whately appears frequently as a character in the narrative, although she generally remains an unobtrusive, interested observer. In discussing topics such as slavery or Muslim weddings, she remains unafraid to speak her mind. Remembering how she and her companions had seen a slave boat of young boys on its way to Cairo, she remarks: "it made our blood boil to think of the amount of cruelty that must have been used for this one boat-load of human beings to be dragged from their home and penned up like cattle to be sold as if they had no souls." As for a young Muslim newlywed, Whately claims that the lavish dress, downcast eyes, and emotionless behavior of a Muslim bride receiving visitors make her look "more like an idiot than a rational being."

In one of the more fascinating sections of *Letters from Egypt* Whately discusses unusual childcare practices that result from Egyptian fears of infant mortality. Many Egyptians, especially Muslims, keep their children dirty and unattractive, place charms around their necks, and mark their faces with soot to ward off the evil eye – a force believed to be responsible for high infant mortality rates. Cultural belief and not ignorance about personal hygiene is clearly responsible for these practices,

which continue until the children reach a certain age and parental fears of their deaths diminish.

Letters from Egypt is both intimate and charming, yet at times Whately uses direct argument rather than quiet example to advance her argument that Egypt and its people are more complex than most Europeans realize. In a section on the variety of skin colors that Egyptians have, Whately asserts that "some persons in England have a vague sort of idea that every real African must be black or nearly so, and this is a great mistake." In a discussion of the harem and slavery systems, she explains that, except for the very poor, all people employ slaves, and all slaves are not black; some are white. Moreover, in regard to the common notion that a man has many wives in a harem, Whately explains that Muslim men rarely have more than two or three.

In addition to its revisionist aim, what distinguishes *Letters from Egypt* from Whately's earlier work is the limited time that she spends discussing her role as a missionary. In the Ragged Life books and even in *Among the Huts in Egypt* Whately's role as a missionary was prominent. In this volume, however, Whately's missionary work is separated from the larger narrative by being placed in a chapter near the conclusion. She claims that she has purposefully done this in order to provide some cultural background about the Egyptian people before she presents details about the schools, for missionary work can be "very dry reading." In effect this final chapter, "About the School," functions as Whately's condensed autobiography. In it she summarizes her life in Egypt and provides chronological information about her schools, starting with her first efforts to open the girls' school and ending with recent efforts to open a branch school for boys in the city of Damietta. In a brief conclusion she directly appeals to God for assistance in continuing her work.

One of Whately's last published works, a rare attempt at fiction, is *Scenes from Life in Cairo: A Glimpse behind the Curtain*. Set in a Cairo harem, the story opens in spring, with a fair Circassian lady patiently writing while the rest of the ladies are sleeping. Though the plot is melodramatic and hard to follow at times, the story centers upon this lady, Sitt Ain el Hayat; her husband, Zohrab Bey (the son of the powerful widow, Fatmeh Sidd); and their conversion to Christianity by Mrs. Irene Hillyard. With her Christian zeal and European dress, Hillyard is clearly patterned after Whately, although the fictional character is unlike Whately in having been born of mixed parentage in Egypt and in being now a widow. Two subplots involve various malicious attempts to discredit the bey and Hillyard's kindness to the old servant Zobeide, who had been captured during the Turkish war and whose Christianity and humanity are revived through the efforts of Hillyard. The work ends with the bey and his wife openly declaring their Christian faith and preparing to go into exile.

While it is a work of fiction, *Scenes from Life in Cairo,* like Whately's travel literature, depicts everyday life – but in this case through the quotidian lives of various women (from Negro slaves to wives and mothers-in-law) within an upper-class harem. It also provides information on Cairo's legal system, its social and political economy, and the lives of desert nomads or Bedouins. Whately's propensity for direct observation makes it likely that the bey, his wife, and Zobeide are fashioned after her real-life acquaintances. In fact, her introduction claims that the narrative "is in great measure taken from real life, and though the story itself and many of the characters are fictitious, not a few of the conversations are literally true."

Though Whately's love and concern for the Egyptian people are evident, not much is known about her political views, including those on British colonialism in Egypt. The nationalist rising of Arabi Pasha in 1881 prompted Whately's temporary exile to Naples and England; in 1882 she returned to Egypt and her mission work. Her writing gives little indication of how she felt about the British occupation, although Elizabeth Jane Whately reports that her sister "pleaded for Egypt and Islam at meetings" during her rare trips to England.

In 1888 Whately made her last visit to England, and with a sister and a niece she spent some time in Switzerland. She returned to Egypt in the autumn, and the following spring she planned her annual trip on the Nile. Dr. Azoury, Mrs. Shakoor, and others were on holiday, but Whately, ever eager to continue her mission work, decided to take the trip without them. She hired a boat and undertook the journey with her sister and two other companions, and on this trip she contracted the respiratory ailment that eventually killed her. Surrounded by family and friends, she died in Cairo on 9 March 1889.

With her devotion to mission work and a Christian way of life, Mary Louisa Whately was an important figure in the British evangelical movement in Africa during the nineteenth century. She is also an important British travel writer. In its sensitivity and insight her writing provides an unusual perspective on the daily lives of the Egyptian people and on their attitudes toward women and the poor. Generally tolerant of cultural, ethnic, and religious differences, Whately provides a refreshing counterbalance to the stridency of nineteenth-century British nationalism. A minor figure during her lifetime and largely forgotten today, Whately wrote works that deserve attention.

Biography:

Elizabeth Jane Whately, *The Life and Work of Mary Louisa Whately* (London: Religious Tract Society, 1890).

References:

Patricia S. Cale, "A British Missionary in Egypt: Mary Louisa Whately," *Vitae Scholasticae,* 3 (Spring 1984): 131–143;

Mrs. Emma Raymond Pitman, "Mary Louisa Whately: The Story of Her Mission Life and Work in Egypt," in *Missionary Heroines in Eastern Lands: Woman's Work in Mission Fields* (New York: Revell, 1884?), pp. 128–160;

Lyle L. Vander Werff, *Christian Mission to Muslims: The Record* (South Pasadena, Cal.: William Carey Library, 1977);

Charles R. Watson, *In the Valley of the Nile: A Survey of the Missionary Movement in Egypt* (New York: Revell, 1908).

Christopher Wordsworth

(30 October 1807 – 21 March 1885)

James Barszcz
William Paterson College

BOOKS: *The Druids: A Poem, Which Obtained the Chancellor's Medal at the Cambridge Commencement, July 1827* (Cantabrigiae: Smith, 1827);

Delos, as Christophorus Wordsworth (Cantabrigiae, 1827);

The Invasion of Russia by Napoleon Buonaparte: A Poem, Which Obtained the Chancellor's Medal at the Cambridge Commencement, M.DCCC.XXVIII (Cambridge, 1828);

On the Admission of Dissenters to Graduate in the University of Cambridge: A Letter to the Right Hon. Viscount Althorp (Cambridge: Pitt, 1834);

Ode Performed in the Senate-House, Cambridge, on the Seventh of July, M.DCCC.XXXV, at the Installation, and in the Presence, of the Most Noble John Jeffreys, Marquess Camden . . . Chancellor of the University (Cambridge: Pitt, 1835);

Athens and Attica: Journal of a Residence There (London: Murray, 1836); revised as *Athens and Attica: Notes of a Tour* (London: Murray, 1855);

Inscriptiones Pompeianae; or Specimens and Facsimiles of Ancient Inscriptions Discovered on the Walls of Buildings at Pompeii (London: Murray, 1837);

Greece: Pictorial, Descriptive, and Historical (London: Orr, 1839); republished with *A History of the Characteristics of Greek Art,* by George Scharf (London: Murray, 1852; revised edition, London: Orr, 1853); enlarged, with notices of recent discoveries by H. F. Tozer (London: Murray, 1882);

Sermons Preached at Harrow School (London, 1841);

Theophilus Anglicanus; or, Instruction for the Young Student Concerning the Church and Our Own Branch of It (London: Rivington, 1843); republished as *Theophilus Anglicanus; or, Instruction for the Young Student Concerning the Church and the Anglican Branch of It* (London: Rivington, 1847); republished as *Theophilus Anglicanus; or, Instruction Concerning the Church, and the Anglican Branch of It. For the Use of Schools, Colleges, and Candidates for Holy Orders* (London: Rivington, 1850); republished as *Theophilus Anglicanus; or, Manual of*

Instruction on the Church, and the Anglican Branch of It (London: Rivingtons, 1873);

Discourses on Public Education (London: Rivington, 1844);

Diary in France, Mainly on Topics Concerning Education and the Church (London: Rivington, 1845);

Letters to M. Gondon, Author of "Mouvement religieux en Angleterre," "Conversion de Soixante ministres Anglicans," etc., on the Destructive Character of the Church of Rome, Both in Religion and Policy (London, 1847);

Sequel to Letters to M. Gondon on the Destructive Character of the Church of Rome, Both in Religion and Polity (London: Rivington, 1848);

National Warnings on National Education: A Sermon (London, 1848);

On the Canon of the Scriptures of the Old and New Testament, and on the Apocrypha: Eleven Discourses, Preached before the University of Cambridge; Being the Hulsean Lectures for the Year 1847 (London: Rivington, 1848);

Lectures on the Apocalypse: Critical, Expository and Practical (Philadelphia, 1848); republished as *Lectures on the Apocalypse; Critical, Expository, and Practical: Delivered before the University of Cambridge; Being the Hulsean Lectures for the Year 1848* (London: Rivington, 1849);

Elements of Instruction Concerning the Church, and the Anglican Branch of It (London, 1849); republished as *Elements of Instruction on the Church* (London: Rivingtons, 1868);

Occasional Sermons Preached in Westminster Abbey, 7 series (London: Rivington, 1850–1857);

On the Inspiration of Holy Scripture; or, On the Canon of the Old and New Testament, and on the Apocrypha: Twelve Lectures, Delivered before the University of Cambridge (London: Rivington, 1851; Philadelphia: Hooker, 1854);

Memoirs of William Wordsworth, Poet-Laureate, D.C.L., 2 volumes (London: Moxon, 1851); edited by Henry Reed (Boston: Ticknor, Reed & Fields, 1851);

Theophilus Americanus; or, Instruction for the Young Student, Concerning the Church, and the American Branch of It, edited by Hugh Davey Evans (Philadelphia: Hooker, 1851; revised edition, Philadelphia: Hooker, 1852);

A Sermon Preached in the Abbey Church, Bath, on Tuesday, Jan. 27, 1852, on the Occasion of the Third Jubilee of the Society for the Propagation of the Gospel in Foreign Parts (London, 1852);

St. Hippolytus and the Church of Rome in the Earlier Part of the Third Century: From the Newly-Discovered Philosophumena (London: Rivington, 1853); enlarged as *St. Hippolytus and the Church of Rome, in the Earlier Part of the Third Century, from the Newly-Discovered "Refutation of All Heresies"* (London: Rivingtons, 1880);

St. Patrick, the Apostle of Ireland: His Life and Times (London, 1853);

Notes at Paris, Particularly on the State and Prospects of Religion (London: Rivingtons, 1854);

On Religious Restoration in England: A Series of Sermons Preached in Westminster Abbey (London: Rivingtons, 1854);

Remarks on M. Bunsen's Work on St. Hippolytus, Particularly on the Preface of His New Edition (London: Rivingtons, 1855);

On Divorce (London, 1857);

On a Proposed Subdivision of Dioceses: A Letter to Viscount Dungannon (London, 1860);

The Inspiration of the Bible: Five Lectures, Delivered in Westminster Abbey (London: Rivingtons, 1861); republished as *On the Inspiration of the Bible: Five Lectures* (London, 1863); republished as *On the Inspiration of the Bible: Five Lectures Delivered in Westminster Abbey* (London: Rivingtons, 1870);

The Interpretation of the Bible: Five Lectures, Delivered in Westminster Abbey (London, 1861);

The Holy Year; or, Hymns for Sundays and Holydays, and for Other Occasions (London: Rivingtons, 1862); republished as *The Holy Year; or, Hymns for Sundays and Holy Days, and for Other Occasions* (London: Rivingtons, 1864); republished as *The Holy Year; or, Hymns for Sundays, Holydays, and Daily Use* (London: Rivingtons, 1868);

A Bicentenary Sermon on the Book of Common Prayer (London, 1862);

Remarks on the Proposed Admission of the Rev. Dr. Stanley to the Place of Dean in the Collegiate Church of St. Peter, Westminster (London: Rivingtons, 1863);

Journal of a Tour in Italy, with Reflections on the Present Condition and Prospects of Religion in That Country, 2 volumes (London: Rivingtons, 1863);

The Church of Ireland, Her History and Claims: Four Sermons Preached before the University of Cambridge (London: Rivingtons, 1866);

Union with Rome. "Is Not the Church of Rome the Babylon of the Apocalypse?": An Essay (London: Rivingtons, 1866);

State of the Soul between Death and the Resurrection: A Sermon (London, 1866); republished as *The Intermediate State of the Soul between Death and the Resurrection: A Sermon* (London, 1875);

Mormonism and England: A Sermon, Preached in Westminster Abbey, on Sunday Evening, July 28, 1867 (London: Rivingtons, 1867);

On the Punishment of Death for Wilful Murder: A Sermon Preached in Westminster Abbey, on Sunday, Nov. 24, 1867 (London: Rivingtons, 1867);

The Law of the Church on Ritual: A Letter to the Archbishop of Canterbury (London, 1868);

Sacred Music: A Sermon, Preached at the Anniversary of the Choral Association of the Diocese of Llandaff, Sept. 2, 1868 (London: Rivingtons, 1868);

The History of the Church of Ireland, in Eight Sermons Preached in Westminster Abbey (London: Rivingtons, 1869);

Clerical Non-Residence: An Earnest Appeal from the Bishop of Lincoln to the Clergymen of the Diocese Who Are Not Resident in Their Parishes (London: Rivingtons, [1870]);

A Charge Delivered to the Clergy and Churchwardens of the Diocese of Lincoln at His Primary Visitation (London, 1870);

The Maccabees and the Church; or, The History of the Maccabees Considered with Reference to the Present Condition and Prospects of the Church: Two Sermons Preached before the University of Cambridge (London: Rivingtons, 1871);

On the Athanasian Creed: A Speech to the Upper House of Convocation, Feb. 8, 1872 (London, 1872);

College Statutes, College Fellowships and College Legislation: A Letter to the Principal of Brasenose College, Oxford (London: Rivingtons, 1872);

The Danger of Altering Our Ordinal: A Letter to the Lord Bishop of Derry (Dublin: Hodges, Foster, 1872);

The Old Catholics and the Cologne Congress of 1872 (Lincoln, 1872);

Old Catholic Congress: A Letter from the Bishop of Lincoln on His Return from the Congress at Cologne (London: Rivingtons, 1872);

On the Procession of the Holy Spirit with a Proposal for a Synodical Declaration Thereupon: Sermon Preached in Lincoln Cathedral on Whitsunday, 1872 (London: Rivingtons, 1872);

Twelve Addresses Delivered at His Visitation of the Cathedral and Diocese of Lincoln in the Year MDCCCLXXIII (London: Rivingtons, 1873);

On Temperance Societies (Lincoln: Williamson, 1873);

A Pastoral to the Wesleyan Methodists in the Diocese of Lincoln (Lincoln: Williamson, 1873);

A Plea for Toleration by Law, in Certain Ritual Matters; with Reference to the Public Worship Regulation Bill (Lincoln: Williamson, 1874);

On the Sale of Church Patronage, and Simony: A Pastoral (Lincoln: Williamson, 1874);

On Burning of the Body; and on Burial: A Sermon Preached in Westminster Abbey, on Sunday, July 5, 1874 (Lincoln: Williamson, 1874);

On Confession and Absolution: A Pastoral Letter to the Clergy and Laity of the Diocese of Lincoln (Lincoln: Williamson, 1874);

Results of an Inquiry on Ritual, with Remarks (Lincoln: Wiliamson, 1875);

Irenicum Wesleyanum; or, Proposals for Union with Wesleyan Methodists (Lincoln: Williamson, 1876);

Diocesan Addresses Delivered at His Third Triennial Visitation, in the Year 1876 (Lincoln: Williamson, 1876);

The Newtonian System: Its Analogy to Christianity. A Sermon (London, 1877);

Letter from the Bishop of Lincoln to the Rev. Canon Hole on Lord Penzance's Decisions (London, 1877);

On the Duration and Degrees of Future Rewards and Punishments: Two Sermons Preached at Nottingham, in St. Thomas' Church on Advent Sunday, 1877 (New York: Protestant Episcopal Tract Society, 1877; London, 1878);

The New Lectionary Examined, with Reasons for Its Amendment at the Present Time, by Wordsworth, Edward Meyrick Goulburn, and John William Burgon (London: Rivingtons, 1877);

On Sisterhoods and Vows: A Letter to the Ven. Sir George Prevost, Bart. (London: Rivingtons, 1878);

Miscellanies, Literary and Religious, 3 volumes (London: Rivingtons, 1879);

A Letter to the University of Oxford Commissioners on the Announcement of Their Intention to Make Statutes for Brasenose and Lincoln Colleges (Lincoln: Williamson, 1879);

Ten Addresses at the Triennial Visitation of the Cathedral Church and Diocese of Lincoln in October, 1879 (Lincoln: Williamson / London: Rivingtons, 1879);

A Letter to the Members of Lincoln College, Oxford, on Certain Proposed Changes in Their College (Lincoln: Williamson, 1880);

A.D. 1640–1660: Thoughts on the Times; an Address in Southwell Minster, on May 30th, 1880 (London: Williamson, 1880);

On the Revised Version of the New Testament: An Address (Lincoln: Williamson, 1881; New York, 1881);

On the Present Disquietude in the Church: A Letter to the Clergy and Laity of the Diocese of Lincoln (London: Rivingtons, 1881);

A Church History, 4 volumes (London: Rivingtons, 1881–1883; New York: Pott, 1881–?);

On the Controversy with Rome: A Paper Read at the Church Congress, Derby, 1882 (Lincoln: Williamson, 1882);

The Hope of Glory and the Future of Our Universities: Two Sermons Preached before the University of Cambridge in Ascension-tide, 1882 (London: Rivingtons, 1882);

Conjectural Emendations of Passages in Ancient Authors, with Other Papers (London: Rivingtons, 1883);

An Address on Marriage with a Deceased Wife's Sister (London: Williamson, 1883);

John Wiclif, His Doctrine and Work: An Address at the Lincoln Diocesan Conference, on Thursday, October 16th, 1884 (Lincoln: Williamson, [1884]);

The Pontifical Offices Used by David de Bernham, Bishop of S. Andrews (Edinburgh: Pitaligo, 1885);

How to Read the Old Testament: A Letter to His Grandchildren (London: Society for Promoting Christian Knowledge / New York: Young, 1887);

On the Millennium: Two Lectures (London: Stock, 1896).

OTHER: Richard Bentley, *The Correspondence of Richard Bentley, D.D., Master of Trinity College, Cambridge,* edited by Wordsworth (London: Murray, 1842);

Theocritus, *Codicum manuscriptorum ope,* edited by Wordsworth (Cantabrigiae: Parker, 1844);

The Apocalypse; or, Book of Revelation: the Original Greek Text with MSS. Collations. An English Translation and Harmony, with Notes; and an Appendix to the Hulsean Lectures for 1848 on the Apocalypse, 2 parts, edited and translated by Wordsworth (London: Rivington, 1849);

The New Testament . . . in the Original Greek, edited, with introductions, by Wordsworth (London: Rivingtons, 1856);

The Epistles of St. Paul in the Original Greek, edited by Wordsworth (London: Rivingtons, 1859);

The Holy Bible, 6 volumes, edited, with introductions, by Wordsworth (London: Rivingtons, 1864–1871);

The Book of Daniel, edited, with an introduction, by Wordsworth (London: Rivingtons, 1871);

Richard Sanderson, *Bishop Sanderson's Lectures on Conscience and Human Law; Delivered in the Divinity School at Oxford,* edited, with a preface, by Wordsworth (Lincoln: Williamson, 1877);

Genesis and Exodus in the Authorized Version, edited by Wordsworth (London: Rivingtons, 1879);

Church of England, *The Manner of the Coronation of King Charles the First of England, at Westminster, 2 Feb., 1626,* edited by Wordsworth (London: Henry Bradshaw Liturgical Text Society, 1892);

Ceremonies and Processions of the Cathedral Church of Salisbury, edited by Wordsworth (Cambridge: Cambridge University Press, 1901);

The Fifteenth Century Cartulary of St. Nicholas' Hospital, Salisbury, with Other Records, edited by Wordsworth (Salisbury: Brown, 1902);

Oxford Historical Society, *The Ancient Kalendar of the University of Oxford, from Documents of the Fourteenth to the Seventeenth Century* (Oxford: Oxford Historical Society, 1904).

A prominent clergyman, educator, and religious polemicist, Christopher Wordsworth was a writer of prodigious energy and learning. In published accounts of his travels, which make up only a small part of his complete works, he brought to Victorian readers a sense of the geography and architecture of ancient Greece as well as an under-

standing of the religious and educational institutions of Italy and France.

He was the youngest son of Christopher Wordsworth, younger brother of William Wordsworth, and of Priscilla Lloyd Wordsworth, who came from a prominent family in Birmingham. Trained early to construe accurately and fluently in both Greek and Latin, he won prizes for both English and Latin composition at Winchester College and, having distinguished himself athletically as well, earned the nickname "The Great Christopher." Wordsworth and his two older brothers, John and Charles, developed a close and lasting relationship with their Uncle William's household at Rydal Mount. William Wordsworth took pride in Christopher's academic and literary accomplishments, and in the 1840s, when his own eyes were weak, asked Christopher to oversee the publication of a new edition of *The Excursion* (1814).

Having graduated from Trinity College, Cambridge, in 1830 after remarkable success as a scholar and an athlete, Wordsworth was elected a fellow at the school and soon became an assistant college tutor. He entered his career in the Anglican clergy at this time, being ordained a deacon in 1833 and a priest in 1835.

Self-disciplined and devout, Wordsworth found his next position, as headmaster at the Harrow school from 1838 to 1844, to be particularly trying because of the irreligious and unruly nature of public-school life at the time. Nevertheless, he was an active headmaster, closely overseeing the instruction of the students. While at Harrow he began the travels abroad that would afford the bases of his first publications. In 1838 he married Susanna Hatley Frere, a quiet, even-tempered woman who was a perfect complement to her animated, sometimes acerbic husband.

Wordsworth made his first trip to Greece in 1832–1833, three years after the Greek war of independence had ended. He kept a journal during this trip, and a segment of this was published with the title *Athens and Attica: Journal of a Residence There* (1836). Its style may discourage modern readers partly because it reads like a journal, written to remind the author of his experiences rather than to inform others about them. Like many travel books it begins abruptly, offering no discussion of who the author is, how he has arrived in Greece, or why he has come there. Moreover, the experiences he memorializes seem, especially today, highly rarefied. They comprise almost exclusively a kind of literary archaeology, in which the author identifies the remains of sites mentioned in the works of classical

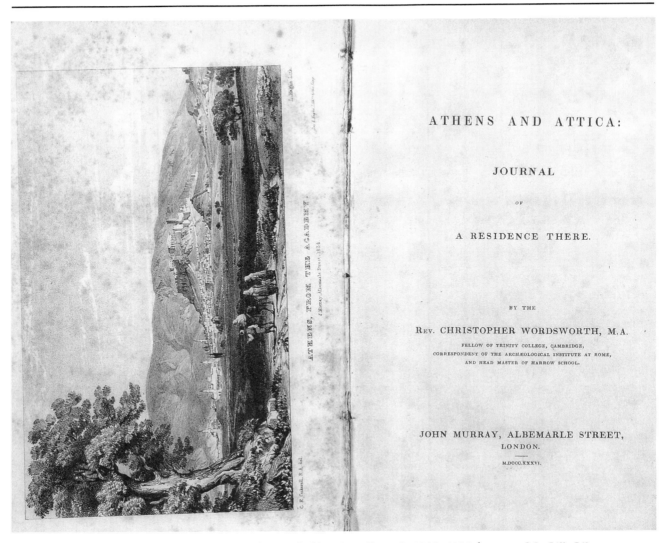

Frontispiece and title page for Wordsworth's journal of his trip to Greece in 1832–1833 (courtesy of the Lilly Library, Indiana University)

writers. Such a project requires not only a thorough knowledge of those works but also an ability to organize and recall pertinent passages relative to such topics as geography, place-names, and architecture. This is a project perfectly suited to someone of Wordsworth's education and industry, but to appreciate it fully a reader must possess a similar level of sophistication.

When Wordsworth made his trip to Greece, the country was, in a sense, unknown: many of the ruined sites could not be identified, and many of the places and buildings mentioned by ancient authors could not be found. The site of one of the most important oracles, Dodona, for example, could not be located, as George Gordon, Lord Byron, laments in *Childe Harold's Pilgrimage* (1812–1818). In addition, travelers were preyed upon not only by bandits but also by the military forces responsible for protecting civilians from the bandits. Im-

poverished economically and culturally, the country was effectively cut off from western Europe by the Ottoman Turks, who had occupied the Balkan Peninsula from the fifteenth century until the end of the war of independence in 1829.

Some modern readers may see Wordsworth's book as part of an imperialist campaign by western Europe to dominate weaker cultures, as epitomized in the expropriation of the Elgin marbles from Athens by Thomas Bruce, Lord Elgin, in 1806, and indeed his book does exhibit some qualities now characterized as literary imperialism. He aestheticizes the landscape, for example, by choosing a vantage point and simplifying its features, by erasing its modern inhabitants or dismissing them as uncultured. As Mary Louise Pratt has argued in *Imperial Eyes,* this is the verbal equivalent of the typical travel-book illustration: a site of geographic or historic importance appears in the middle distance and, in the foreground, contemporary shepherds, bandits, or natives are passing by, unmindful of that importance. Three such illustrations – which demonstrate the exquisite effects of aerial perspective achievable by steel engraving – are inserted as plates in the first edition of the book.

Yet one hesitates to label Wordsworth as a mere tool of an imperial culture. He expresses a notable respect for the modern Greeks he encounters, and he has esteem for their forebears and sympathy for their impoverishment under Ottoman rule. He also displays none of the misgivings common among other Victorian philhellenes who express guilt about their attraction to "heathen" Greek or Roman cultures. Wordsworth simply admits that he is, in spirit, largely a Greek himself, dominated there and at home by those past cultures.

To get a sense of Wordsworth's concentration on literary-historical themes in this book, it is instructive to consider the personally significant details that he leaves out. He fails to mention, for example, that he was the first Englishman officially to meet the new king, Otho (or Otto) I, the ruler chosen for Greece by the European powers at the close of the Greek war of independence. On another occasion his traveling party was attacked by bandits in the mountains north of Attica, and his journal entry describing the event is reprinted in Wordsworth's official biography by John Henry Overton and Elizabeth Wordsworth. But in *Athens and Attica* the attack is mentioned only as part of a discussion of the harsh climate of northern Greece.

The treatment of Greece is more extensive in Wordsworth's second travel book, and its comprehensive title signals the differences: *Greece: Pictorial, Descriptive, and Historical* (1839). Prepared at the request of a publisher, the book, nearly five hundred pages long, took less than a year to complete. Known informally as "Wordsworth's *Greece*," it went through six editions, was translated into French, and was reprinted as late as 1882. Although the quality of the editions varied, Wordsworth's *Greece* is a splendid example of Victorian book arts. Its table of contents lists twenty-one steel engravings and about four hundred engravings on wood.

This work is directed to the armchair traveler – certainly one familiar with Greek history and literature but not necessarily possessed of the philological expertise that *Athens and Attica* expects of its readers. The first chapter surveys the topography of the entire country by describing the view from various vantage points. Thirteen chapters then focus on particular regions or cities, beginning in the southeast

with Attica, Aegina, and Athens; moving northeasterly through Boeotia and Thessaly to the Ionian Islands; and then south again to the Peloponnesian peninsula, Sparta, and Corinth.

Wordsworth speculates – perhaps too freely for modern readers – about the influence of geography on national character. He lists the landscape features that isolated Sparta, for example, and then attempts to relate them to the Spartan ethos: "all these her natural properties spoke of restraint and control, of abstinence and self-denial." The Spartan "trod the path of duty, and that led him to glory. Here was the same spirit that afterwards produced the Conqueror at Waterloo." On the other hand, the ports and open spaces of Athens "led to the adoption of a system of Education, which produced the greatest possible development and exercise of individual energy and personal enterprise in quest of glory." Though one may feel that these generalizations on regional character go uncomfortably far, they may betoken an understandable urge to find human significance in the potentially barren endeavor of topographical description.

Closing the book with a description of Corinth, Wordsworth alludes to Saint Paul's epistle to the Corinthians, and through its references to the Corinthian stadium, theater, and amphitheater, he leaves no doubt about his own esteem for Greek culture:

> The traveller in Greece feels a lively pleasure in reading ancient historical descriptions of sieges, of battles, of civil assemblies, of harangues, and of social conversations, upon the spots and amid the scenes where they took place; but the delight will be more exquisite which he will enjoy in tracing, at Corinth, the reference to the objects before him which he finds in the language of Inspiration.

In helping Wordsworth to establish a perspective for his admiration of the ancient world, religion is an intermittent, though important, presence in Wordsworth's two books on Greece. In two other books based on his travels religion is a central subject. His *Diary in France, Mainly on Topics Concerning Education and the Church* (1845) and *Journal of a Tour in Italy, with Reflections on the Present Condition and Prospects of Religion in That Country* (1863) explicitly set out to show the debilitating influence of the Roman Catholic religion in Europe.

Wordsworth published these two later books in the era of the Oxford Movement in England, the campaign by John Henry Newman, John Keble, and others to revive early forms of Christian worship in the Church of England. Several prominent members of the movement, including Newman and Wordsworth's childhood friend Henry Manning, eventually con-

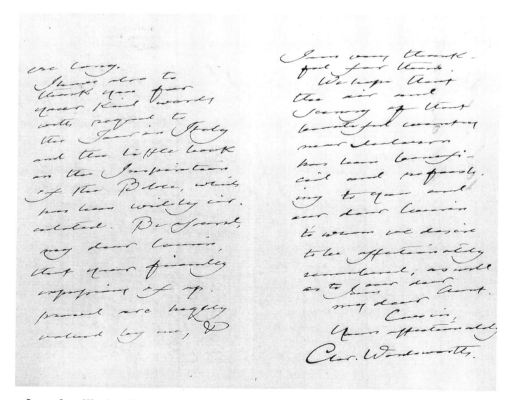

*Letter from Wordsworth to his cousins thanking them for a copy of a book about the prophet Daniel
(courtesy of the Lilly Library, Indiana University)*

verted to Roman Catholicism. Wordsworth, like many traditionalists of the Church of England, detested the Catholic Church, and he responded to this drift toward Rome by publishing anti-Catholic polemics in various forms – sermons, letters, textbooks, hymnals, as well as these two books of travel.

The *Diary in France* appeared after Wordsworth had traveled to France to conduct literary research. Possessing what one of his successors at Trinity College called a genius for scholarship, Wordsworth undertook a critical edition of the poems of Theocritus, a study that required him to travel to Paris to collate earlier editions held at the Bibliothèque du Roi in Paris. As he describes the project in his preface to the *Diary,* he composed a series of letters to an unnamed female friend on the subject of French religious and educational institutions, and he was later induced to publish these letters as a book.

As Wordsworth sees it, French society is approaching a climactic moment that results from the weakening of religious institutions and might be safely overcome by a reform of the French church. The church, with its ultra-Montane clergy, has become disconnected from the government, and Wordsworth argues for a revivification of a "Gallican" church in France. Gallicanism differs from ultra-Montanism in recognizing the primacy of a council of French bishops over the dictates of the Vatican. It is thus a national church, much as is the Church of England. Wordsworth foresees that, without returning to a constitutionally established religion of this kind, French society will continue to slide into political chaos:

> The crown has been jealous of the Church, and has kept the doors of the colleges of the state closed against her; but it now finds that in so doing it has excluded Christianity; and that it has to deal at present with a generation which has been educated without any sense of religious obligation, or of moral and civil duty, and which has no more regard for the Throne, or for the Sovereign upon it, than it has for Christianity and the Church.

Principled and learned as Wordsworth is in this book, he is not especially likable. The enthusiasms expressed in his earlier writings on Greece have earned him a place among British travelers who abandon the phlegmatic manner of their countrymen when they come to the Mediterranean and exhibit an "insular faculty to gush," as John Pemble quotes Henry James's characterization of them in *Italian Hours* (1909). But Wordsworth's writings on France, like his subsequent ones on Italy, are grudging. He shows contempt or pity for almost everyone and everything he sees in France, and in every debate he records, he gets the better of his antagonist.

Published almost twenty years after *Diary in France,* the *Journal of a Tour in Italy* was occasioned by Wordsworth's excursion to Rome to observe the canonization of Jesuit missionaries martyred in Japan in the seventeenth century. Like *Diary in France,* the *Journal of a Tour in Italy* is concerned with the reform of the Roman Catholic Church, although Wordsworth in this later work sees not simply one country at risk, but all of European culture.

This was the era of the risorgimento in Italy, when nationalist leaders were attempting to unify in a single modern state the various autonomous regions of Italy. Some of the regions – the so-called papal states that the Pope of that era, Pope Pius IX, resisted giving up – were directly controlled by the Roman Catholic Church. The Pope's obstruction of the nationalist efforts, coupled with his recent proclamations of the Immaculate Conception of Mary and of papal infallibility, elicited a bitter anti-Catholicism in Wordsworth.

Wordsworth held that, whatever the spiritual or eternal consequences might be, the Church of Rome must be reformed for the sake of European liberty, a liberty best protected in every country by a separate national church such as the Anglican and Gallican churches. A transnational church, like that of Rome, aggravated the potential for revolution, disorder, and decay within a country. He saw one way to prevent such a cataclysm: "the maintenance of constitutional Monarchy on the foundation of genuine Christianity." This would not only rid Italy of "papal corruptions" and restore the purity of its forms of worship but also "harmonize" the church of France with the nation of France by neutralizing the ultra-Montane tendencies of the French clergy.

Some have suggested that Wordsworth's appreciation for northern climate and lands reflects his suspicion of southern European cultures, in which he saw sources of weakness and decadence. Noting that the northern city of Turin now dominates other more glorious Italian cities, Wordsworth asks,

> [H]ow has this been effected? By the hardy valour and military prowess of the House of Savoy, one of those vigorous races which has not been enfeebled by the enervating influences of Southern Italy, and seems to have been nerved and braced to deeds of heroic valour by the bleak winds which blow upon it from the Alps.

Embodying ideas popularized by Friedrich Schlegel, this discussion of northern and southern racial identities takes up barely one page in a work of more than seven hundred pages and, at least for readers of his other travel books, Wordsworth's preferences for Athens over Boeotia and for Greeks over Albanians make dubious his commitment to such simple dichotomies.

Near the time of the publication of *Diary in France* Wordsworth left the headmastership of Harrow for a series of clerical posts associated with the chapter (the group of canons presided over by a dean) of Westminster Cathedral. He eventually assumed the archdeaconship of the chapter in 1865, and in 1868 he accepted his final promotion when Benjamin Disraeli nominated him to be bishop of Lincoln. As always, he took his duties seriously. He became involved in various ecclesiastical controversies, most of which are obscure today, though many were viciously contested.

Wordsworth died on 21 March 1885, a few weeks after resigning his see. Susanna Wordsworth had died the previous autumn, and some said that Wordsworth had never smiled during the five months he survived her. They had seven children, two sons and five daughters. One son, John, became bishop of Salisbury; the other son, Christopher, wrote on the history of Oxford University as well as on religious subjects. The eldest daughter, Elizabeth, who contributed to the biography of her father by John Overton, was the first principal of Lady Margaret Hall, a college for women at Oxford.

Christopher Wordsworth's contemporaries knew him well, as we can infer from the variety and number of his publications and many editions of some of those publications that appeared. Yet apart from his association with his Uncle William, the poet laureate, Christopher Wordsworth is rarely mentioned either by his contemporaries or by modern scholars of Victorian culture. Nonetheless, the representative nature of his insights into modern and ancient cultures as well as his impressive erudition and industry continue to make him worthy of attention.

Biography:

John Henry Overton and Elizabeth Wordsworth, *Christopher Wordsworth, Bishop of Lincoln* (London: Rivingtons, 1888).

References:

Richard Jenkyns, *The Victorians and Ancient Greece* (Cambridge, Mass.: Harvard University Press, 1980);

John Pemble, *The Mediterranean Passion: Victorians and Edwardians in the South* (Oxford: Clarendon Press, 1987);

Mary Louise Pratt, *Imperial Eyes: Travel Writing and Transculturation* (London: Routledge, 1992).

Travel Writing, 1837–1875

This checklist of selected travel writing is arranged chronologically, because the names of many travel writers are unfamiliar. It serves as a chronicle of events in the history of travel, because many titles identify the destinations and sometimes even the motives for the journeys taken by the authors.

Campbell, Thomas. *Letters from the South*. London: Colburn, 1837.

Earl, George Windsor. *The Eastern Seas of Voyages and Adventures in the Indian Archipelago, in 1832–33–34, Comprising a Tour of the Island of Java – Visits to Borneo, the Malay Peninsula, Siam, & Co.; Also an Account of the Present State of Singapore with Observations on the Commercial Resources of the Archipelago*. London: W. H. Allen, 1837.

Slade, Adolphus. *Turkey, Greece, and Malta*. London: Saunders, 1837.

Addison, C. G. *Damascus and Palmyra: A Journey to the East*. London: Bentley, 1838.

Bell, Andrew. *Men and Things in America*. London: Smith, 1838.

Felton, Mrs. *Life in America*. London: Hull, 1838.

Wellsted, J. R. *Travels in Arabia*. London: Murray, 1838.

Beattie, William. *Polynesia; or, Missionary Trails and Triumphs in the South Seas*. London: Snow, 1839.

Broughton, Elizabeth. *Six Years Residence in Algiers*. London: Saunders & Otley, 1839.

Murray, Charles Augustus. *Travels in North America*. London: Bentley, 1839.

Nugent, Lady Maria. *A Journal from the Year 1811 Till the Year 1815, Including a Voyage to and Residence in India, with a Tour to the North Western Parts of the British Possessions in That Country, under the Bengal Government*. London: Private circulation only, 1839.

Nugent, Lady Maria. *A Journal of a Voyage to, and Residence in the Island of Jamaica, from 1801 to 1805, and of Subsequent Events in England from 1805–1811*. London: Boone, 1839.

Roberts, Emma. *The East-India Voyager; or, Ten Minutes Advice to the Outward Bound*. London: Madden, 1839.

Beckford, William. *Italy, Spain, and Portugal*. London: Bentley, 1840.

Slade, Adolphus. *Travels in Germany and Russia: Including a Steam Voyage by the Danube and the Euxine from Vienna to Constantinople, in 1838, 39*. London: Longman, Orme, Brown, Green & Longmans, 1840.

Taylor, Catherine. *Letters from Italy to a Younger Sister*. London: Murray, 1840–1841.

[Anley, Charlotte]. *The Prisoners of Australia*. London: Hatchard, 1841.

Damer, Georgina Emma Seymour Dawson. *Diary of a Tour in Greece, Turkey, Egypt, and the Holy Land*. London: Colburn, 1841.

Davies, Catherine. *Eleven Years' Residence in the Family of Murat, King of Naples*. London: How & Parsons, 1841.

[Eastlake, Lady Elizabeth (Rigby)]. *A Residence on the Shores of the Baltic, Described in a Series of Letters*. London: Murray, 1841.

Egerton, Lady Francis (Harriet Catherine, Countess of Ellesmere). *A Journal of a Tour in the Holy Land, in May and June 1840*. London: Harrison, 1841.

Granville, A. B. *The Spas of England*. London: Colburn, 1841.

Roberts, Emma. *Notes of an Overland Journey through France and Egypt to Bombay*. London: W. H. Allen, 1841.

Burnes, Sir Alexander. *Cabool: Being a Personal Narrative of a Journey to and Residence in That City, in the Years 1836, 1837, and 1838*. London: Murray, 1842.

Holmes, Dalkeith (E. Augusta). *A Ride on Horseback to Florence through France and Switzerland, Described in a Series of Letters*. London: Murray, 1842.

Strutt, Elizabeth. *Domestic Residence in Switzerland*. London: Newby, 1842.

[Westminster, Elizabeth Grosvenor, Marchioness of]. *Narrative of a Yacht Voyage in the Mediterranean, during 1840–1841*. London: Murray, 1842.

Calderon De La Barca, Frances Erskine. *Life in Mexico, during a Residence of Two Years in That Country*. London: Chapman & Hall, 1843.

Maitland, Julia Charlotte. *Letters from Madras, during the Years 1836–1839*. London: Murray, 1843.

Romer, Isabella Frances. *The Rhone, the Darro, and the Guadalquivir; a Summer Ramble in 1842*. London: Bentley, 1843.

Sale, Lady Florentia. *A Journal of the Disasters in Afghanistan, 1841–2*. London: Murray, 1843.

Thackeray, William Makepeace [M. A. Titmarsh, pseud.]. *The Irish Sketch Book*. London: Chapman & Hall, 1843.

Wilkinson, Sir John Gardner. *Modern Egypt and Thebes: Being a Description of Egypt, Including the Information Required for Travellers in That Country*. London: Murray, 1843.

Eden, Emily. *Portraits of the People and Princes of India*. London: Dickinson, 1844.

Londonderry, Frances Anne Emily, Marchioness of. *Narrative of a Visit to the Courts of Vienna, Constantinople, Athens, Naples, Etc*. London: Colburn, 1844.

[Montiefiore, Lady Judith]. *From the Private Journal of a Visit to Egypt and Palestine by Way of Italy and the Mediterranean*. London: Rickerby, 1844.

Shelley, Mary Wollstonecraft. *Rambles in Germany and Italy, in 1840, 1842, and 1843*. London: Moxon, 1844.

Costello, Dudley. *A Tour through the Valley of the Meuse, with the Legends of the Walloon Country and the Ardennes*. London: Chapman & Hall, 1845(?).

Griffith, Lucinda. *A Journey across the Desert, from Ceylon to Marseilles: Comprising Sketches of Aden, the Red Sea, Lower Egypt, Malta, Sicily, and Italy.* London: Colburn, 1845.

Stanhope, Lady Hester Lucy. *Memoirs of the Lady Hester Stanhope, as Related by Herself in Conversations with Her Physician: Comprising Her Opinions and Anecdotes of Some of the Most Remarkable Persons of Her Time.* London: Colburn, 1845.

Thomson, Mrs. *Life in the Bush.* London: Chamber's Miscellany of Useful and Entertaining Tracts, 1845.

Wolff, Joseph. *Narrative of a Mission to Bukhara, in the Years 1843–1845, to Ascertain the Fate of Colonel Stoddart and Captain Conolly.* London: Parker, 1845.

Yates, Mrs. Ashton. *A Winter in Italy.* London: Colburn, 1845.

Romer, Isabella Frances. *A Pilgrimage to the Temples and Tombs of Egypt, Nubia, and Palestine, in 1845–6.* London: Bentley, 1846.

Stanhope, Lady Hester Lucy. *Travels of Lady Hester Stanhope; Forming the Completion of Her Memoirs, Narrated by Her Physician.* London: Colburn, 1846.

Thackery, William Makepeace [M. A. Titmarsh, pseud.]. *Notes of a Journey from Cornhill to Grand Cairo, by Way of Lisbon, Athens, Constantinople, and Jerusalem, Performed in the Steamers of the Peninsular and Oriental Company.* London: Chapman & Hall, 1846.

Maury, Sarah. *An Englishwoman in America.* London: Richardson, 1848.

Ward, Harriet. *Five Years in Kaffirland; with Sketches of the Late War in That Country, to the Conclusion of Peace. Written on the Spot.* London: Colburn, 1848.

Wilkinson, Sir John Gardner. *Dalmatia and Montenegro: With a Journey to Mostar in Herzegovina, and Remarks on the Slavonic Nations; the History of Dalmatia and Ragusa, the Uscocs, Etc.* London: Murray, 1848.

Chisholm, Caroline. *The A. B. C. of Colonization.* London: Olliver, 1849.

Bartlett, W. H. *The Nile Boat; or, Glimpses of the Land of Egypt.* London: Hall, Virtue, 1849.

Melville, Elizabeth. *A Residence in Sierra Leone, Described from a Journal Kept on the Spot, and from Letters Written to Friends at Home,* edited by Mrs. Norton. London: Murray, 1849.

Sturt, Charles. *Narrative of an Expedition into Central Australia, Performed under the Authority of Her Majesty's Government, during the Years 1844, 1845, and 1846.* London: Boone, 1849.

Houston, Mrs. C. J. *Hesperos: Or, Travels in the West.* London: Parker, 1850.

[Parlby, Fanny Parks]. *Wanderings of a Pilgrim, in Search of the Picturesque, during Four-and-Twenty Years in the East; with Revelations of Life in the Zenana.* London: Pelham Richardson, 1850.

Robertson, Janet. *Lights and Shades on a Traveller's Path: Or, Scenes in Foreign Lands.* London: Hope, 1851.

Wortley, Lady Emmeline Stuart. *Travels in the United States, Etc., during 1849 and 1850.* London: Bentley, 1851.

Egerton, Francis. *Journal of a Winter's Tour in India: With a Visit to the Court of Nepaul.* London: Chapman & Hall, 1852.

Kemble, Frances Ann. *Journal . . . 1838–1839*. London: Longman, Brown, Green & Longmans, 1852.

Moodie, Susanna. *Roughing It in the Bush; or, Life in Canada*. London: Bentley, 1852.

[Sewell, Elizabeth Missing]. *A Journal Kept during a Summer Tour, for the Children of a Village School*. London: Longman, Brown, Green & Longmans, 1852.

[Wortley, Victoria Stuart]. *A Young Traveller's Journal of a Tour in North and South America*. London: Bosworth, 1852.

Clacy, Ellen. *A Lady's Visit to the Gold Diggings of Australia in 1852–53: Written on the Spot*. London: Hurst & Blackett, 1853.

Eaton, Charlotte. *The Days of Battle; or, Quatre Bras Waterloo*. London: Bohn, 1853.

Mackenzie, Helen Douglas. *Life in the Mission, the Camp, and the Zenana; or, Six Years in India*. London: Bentley, 1853.

Moodie, Susanna. *Life in the Clearings Versus the Bush*. London: Bentley, 1853.

Parkyns, Mansfield. *Life in Abyssinia*. London: Murray, 1853.

Wortley, Lady Emmeline. *Sketches of Travel in America: North America, Caribbean and Peru*. London: Bosworth, 1853.

Bartrum, Katherine Mary. *Lights and Shadows of Australian Life*. London: Hurst & Blackett, 1854.

McDougall, Harriette. *Letters from Sarawak: Addressed to a Child*. London: Grant & Griffith, 1854.

Wortley, Lady Emmeline. *A Visit to Portugal and Madeira*. London: Chapman & Hall, 1854.

Duberly, Frances Isabella. *Journal Kept during the Russian War: From the Departure of the Army from England in April 1854, to the Fall of Sebastopol*. London: Longman, Brown, Green & Longmans, 1855.

Galton, Sir Francis. *The Art of Travel; or, Shifts and Contrivances Available in Wild Countries*. London: Murray, 1855.

Hooker, Sir Joseph Dalton. *Himalayan Journals: Notes of a Naturalist in Bengal, the Sikkim and Nepal Himalayas, the Khasia Mountains, &c.* London: Murray, 1855.

Porter, J. L. *Five Years in Damascus*. London: Murray, 1855.

Baikie, William Balfour. *Narrative of an Exploring Voyage up the Rivers Kwora and Binue in 1854*. London: Murray, 1856.

Murray, Amelia Matilda. *Letters from the United States, Cuba and Canada*. London: Parker, 1856.

Nicol, Martha. *Ismeer, or Smyrna and Its British Hospital in 1855*. London: Madden, 1856.

Robertson, Janet. *Castles near Kreuznach*. London: Williams & Norgate, 1856.

Sheil, Lady Mary Leonora. *Glimpses of Life and Manners in Persia*. London: Murray, 1856.

Wills, Alfred. *Wanderings among the High Alps*. London: Bentley, 1856.

Wortley, Lady Emmeline. *The Sweet South*. London: Barclay, 1856.

Cary, Amelia (Viscountess Falkland). *Chow Chow: Being Selections from a Journal Kept in India, Egypt and Syria*. London: Hurst & Blackett, 1857.

Davis, Elizabeth. *The Autobiography of Elizabeth Davis, a Balaclava Nurse, Daughter of Dafydd Cadwaladyr*, edited by Jane Williams. London: Hurst & Blackett, 1857.

[Lowe, Emily]. *Unprotected Females in Norway; or, the Pleasantest Way of Travelling There, Passing through Denmark and Sweden: With Scandinavian Sketches from Nature*. London: Routledge, 1857.

[Bartrum, Katherine Mary]. *A Widow's Reminiscences of the Siege of Lucknow*. London: Nisbet, 1858.

[Eastlake, Elizabeth]. "Lady Travellers," *Quarterly Review*, 76 (June 1858): 98–136.

[Harris, G.]. *A Lady's Diary of the Siege of Lucknow: Written for the Perusal of Friends at Home*. London: Murray, 1858.

Hornby, Lady Emilia (Bithynia). *In and around Stamboul*. London: Bentley, 1858.

Inglis, Lady Julia Selina. *Letter Containing Extracts from a Journal Kept by Lady Inglis during the Siege of Lucknow*. London: Private circulation only, 1858.

Ball, John. *Peaks, Passes and Glaciers*. London: Green, Longmans & Roberts, 1859.

Cole, Mrs. Henry Warwick. *A Lady's Tour round Monte Rosa: With Visits to the Italian Valleys . . . in a Series of Excursions in the Years 1850–56–58*. London: Longman, Brown, Green, Longmans & Roberts, 1859.

Coopland, Ruth M. *A Day's Escape from Gwalior and Life in the Fort of Agra during the Mutinies of 1857*. London: Smith, Elder, 1859.

Crawford, Mabel Sharman. *Life in Tuscany*. London: Smith, Elder, 1859.

Duberly, Frances Isabella. *Campaigning Experiences in Rajpootana and Central India, during the Suppression of the Mutiny, 1857–1858*. London: Smith, Elder, 1859.

Lowe, Emily. *Unprotected Females in Sicily, Calabria, and on the Top of Mount Aetna*. London: Routledge, Warnes & Routledge, 1859.

M'Clintock, Sir Francis Leopold. *Voyage of the Fox in the Arctic Seas: A Narrative of the Discovery of the Fate of Sir John Franklin and His Companions*. London: Murray, 1859.

Murray, Elizabeth. *Sixteen Years of an Artist's Life in Morocco, Spain, and the Canary Islands*. London: Hurst & Blackett, 1859.

Trollope, Anthony. *The West Indies and the Spanish Main*. London: Chapman & Hall, 1859.

Trotter, Isabella Strange. *First Impressions of the New World on Two Travelers from the Old, in Autumn of 1856*. London: Longman, Brown, Green, Longmans & Roberts, 1859.

Wolff, Joseph. *Travels and Adventures*. London: Saunders & Otley, 1860.

Park, Mungo. *Travels in the Interior of Africa*. Edinburgh: Black, 1860.

Cubley, Lucy Mathilda. *The Hills and Plains of Palestine*. London: Day, 1860.

Lady, A. *My Experiences in Australia: Being Recollections of a Visit to the Australian Colonies in 1856–7*. London: Hope, 1860.

Beaufort, Emily A. (Viscountess Strangford). *Egyptian Sepulchres and Syrian Shrines Including Some Stay in the Lebanon, at Palmyra, and in Western Turkey*. London: Longman, Green, Longman & Roberts, 1861.

Bromley, Clara Fitzroy. *A Woman's Wanderings in the Western World: A Series of Letters Addressed to Sir Fitzroy Kelly, M.P.* London: Saunders & Otley, 1861.

Catlow, Agnes, and Maria E. Catlow. *Sketching Rambles; or, Nature in the Alps and Apennines*. London: Hogg, 1861.

Crichton, Kate. *Six Years in Italy*. London: Skeet, 1861.

Freshfield, Mrs. Henry. *Alpine Byways; or, Light Leaves Gathered in 1859 and 1860*. London: Longman, Green, Longman & Roberts, 1861.

Harvey, Anne Jane. *Our Cruise in the Claymore, with a Visit to Damascus and the Lebanon*. London: Chapman & Hall, 1861.

Charles, Elizabeth Rundel. *Wanderings over Bible Lands and Seas*. London: Nelson, 1862.

Freshfield, Mrs. Henry. *A Summer Tour in the Grisons and Italian Valleys of the Bernina*. London: Longman, Green, Longman & Roberts, 1862.

Mackenzie, Georgina, and Adeline Irby. *Across the Carpathians*. London: Macmillan, 1862.

[Sewell, Elizabeth Missing]. *Impressions of Rome, Florence, and Turin*. London: Longman, Green, Longman & Roberts, 1862.

Trollope, Anthony. *North America*. London: Chapman & Hall, 1862.

Atkinson, Lucy. *Recollections of Tartar Steppes and Their Inhabitants*. London: Murray, 1863.

Staley, Mrs. *Autumn Rambles; or, Fireside Recollections of Belgium, the Rhine, the Moselle, German Spas, Switzerland, the Italian Lakes, Mont Blanc, and Paris*. Rochdale: Wrigley, 1863.

Bates, Henry Walter. *The Naturalist on the River Amazons: A Record of Adventures, Habits of Animals, Sketches of Brazilian and Indian Life, and Aspects of Nature under the Equator during Eleven Years of Travel*. London: Murray, 1863.

Crawford, Mabel Sharman. *Through Algeria*. London: Bentley, 1863.

D'[Almeida], Anna. *A Lady's Visit to Manilla and Japan*. London: Hurst & Blackett, 1863.

Dufferin, Lady Helen Selina Sheridan [the Hon. Impulsia Gushington, pseud.]. *Lispings from Low Latitudes; or, Extracts from the Journal of the Hon. Impulsia Gushington*. London: Murray, 1863.

Kemble, Frances Anne (Butler). *Journal of a Residence on a Georgia Plantation in 1838–1839*. London: Longman, Green, Longman, Roberts & Green, 1863.

Rogers, Mary Eliza. *Domestic Life in Palestine*. London: Bell & Daldy, 1863.

Beaufort, Emily A. *The Eastern Shores of the Adriatic in 1863: With a Visit to Montenegro*. London: Bentley, 1864.

Madden, Thomas More. *On Change of Climate: A Guide for Travellers in Pursuit of Health*. London: Newby, 1864.

Muter, Elizabeth. *Travels and Adventures of an Officer's Wife in India, China, and New Zealand*. London: Hurst & Blackett, 1864.

Resident, A. Lady. *The Englishwoman in India: Containing Information for the Use of Ladies Proceeding to, or Residing in, the East Indies, on . . . Outfit, Furniture, Housekeeping, the Rearing of Children, Duties and Wages of Servants . . . and Arrangements for Travelling, to Which Are Added Receipts for Indian Cookery*. London: Smith, Elder, 1864.

[Tuckett, Elizabeth]. *How We Spent the Summer; or, A "Voyage en Zigzag" in Switzerland and Tyrol, with Some Members of the Alpine Club: From the Sketch Book of One of the Party*. London: Longman, Green, Longmans, 1864.

Walker, Mary Adelaide. *Through Macedonia to the Albanian Lakes*. London: Chapman & Hall, 1864.

Beke, Emily Alston. *Jacob's Flight; or, A Pilgrimage to Harran, and Thence in the Patriarch's Footsteps into the Promised Land*. London: Longman, Green, Longmans, 1865.

Eyre, Mary. *A Lady's Walks in the South of France in 1863*. London: Bentley, 1865.

Eyre, Mary. *Over the Pyrenees into Spain*. London: Bentley, 1865.

Mott, Augusta. *Stones of Palestine: Notes of a Ramble through the Holy Land*. London: Seeley, Jackson & Halliday, 1865.

Paget, Georgiana Theodosia. *Camp and Cantonment: A Journal of Life in India in 1857–1859, with Some Account of the Way Thither*. London: Longman, Green, Longmans, 1865.

Wyse, Sir Thomas. *An Excursion in the Peloponnesus in the Year 1858*, edited by W. M. Wyse. London: Day, 1865.

Eden, Emily. *"Up the Country": Letters Written to Her Sister from the Upper Provinces of India*. London: Bentley, 1866.

Thackery, William Makepeace [M. A. Titmarsh, pseud.]. *The Kickleburys on the Rhine*. London: Smith, Elder, 1866.

Trollope, Anthony. *Travelling Sketches*. London: Chapman & Hall, 1866.

[Tuckett, Elizabeth]. *Beaten Tracks; or, Pen and Pencil Sketches in Italy*. London: Longmans, Green, 1866.

Madden, Thomas More. *The Spas of Belgium, Germany, Switzerland, France, and Italy, a Hand-book of the Principal Watering Places of the Continent, Etc.* London: Newby, 1867.

Herbert, Mary Elizabeth (Baroness Herbert of Lea). *Impressions of Spain in 1866*. London: Bentley, 1867.

Herbert, Mary Elizabeth (Baroness Herbert of Lea). *Cradle Lands*. London: Bentley, 1867.

Moore, A. W. *The Alps in 1864: A Private Journal*. London: Vickers & Harrington, 1867.

Tuckett, Elizabeth. *Pictures in Tyrol and Elsewhere: From A Family Sketchbook*. London: Longmans, Green, 1867.

Hotten, John Camden, ed. *Abyssinia and Its People; or, Life in the Land of Prester John*. London: Hotten, 1868.

Leitner, G. W. *Results of a Tour in Dardistan*. London & Lahore: Indian Public Opinion Press & Trubner, 1868.

Palgrave, William Gifford. *Personal Narrative of a Year's Journey through Central and Eastern Arabia*. London: Macmillan, 1868.

Marryat, Florence. *"Gup": Sketches of Anglo-Indian Life and Character*. London: Bentley, 1868.

Wingfield, Lewis Strange. *Under the Palms in Algeria and Tunis*. London: Hurst & Blackett, 1868.

Bates, Henry Walter, ed. *Illustrated Travels: A Record of Discovery, Geography, and Adventure*. 6 volumes. London & New York: Cassell, Petter & Galpin, 1869–1875.

Fotte, Mrs. Henry Grant. *Recollections of Central America and the West Coast of Africa*. London: Newby, 1869.

Murray, Amelia Matilda. *Pictorial and Descriptive Sketches of the Odenwald; or, Forest of Odin*. London: Robert & Dickinson, 1869.

Petherick, John, and Mrs. John Petherick. *Travels in Central Africa and Explorations of the Western Nile Tributaries*. London: Tinsley, 1869.

Clerk, Alice. *The Antipodes and round the World*. London: Hatchard, 1870.

Ely, Jane (Marchioness Loftus). *Mafeesh, or Nothing New: The Journal of a Tour in Greece, Turkey, Egypt, the Sinai Desert, Petra, Palestine, Syria, and Russia*. London: Clowes, 1870.

Grey, Theresa. *Journal of a Visit to Egypt, Constantinople, the Crimea, Greece, &c. in the Suite of the Prince and Princess of Wales*. New York: Harper, 1870.

Sketchley, Arthur. *Out for a Holiday with Cook's Excursion through Switzerland and Italy*. London: Routledge, 1870.

Harvey, Anne Jane. *Turkish Harems and Circassian Homes*. London: Hurst & Blackett, 1871.

Kingsley, Charles. *At Last: A Christmas in the West Indies*. London: Macmillan, 1871.

Miller, Ellen Clare Pearson. *Eastern Sketches: Notes of Scenery, Schools and Tent Life in Syria and Palestine*. Edinburgh: Oliphant, 1871.

Sketchley, Arthur. *Mrs. Brown on the Grand Tour*. London: Routledge, 1871.

Sketchley, Arthur. *Mrs. Brown up on the Nile*. London: Routledge, 1871.

[Tuckett, Elizabeth]. *Zigzagging amongst Dolomites*. London: Longmans, Green, 1871.

Tyndall, John. *Hours of Exercise in the Alps*. Longmans, Green, 1871.

Whymper, Edward. *Scrambles amongst the Alps in the Years 1860–1869*. London: Murray, 1871.

Wyse, Sir Thomas. *Impressions of Greece*. London: Hurst & Blackett, 1871.

Herbert, Mary Elizabeth (Baroness Herbert of Lea). *A Search after Sunshine; or, Algeria in 1871*. London: Bentley, 1872.

Hinderer, Anna. *Seventeen Years in the Yoruba Country.* London: Seeley, Jackson & Halliday, 1872.

Lever, Charles. *The Dodd Family Abroad.* London: Chapman & Hall, 1872.

Lever, Charles. *Upon Men, Women, and Things in General.* London: Chapman & Hall, 1872.

Stanley, Henry Morton. *How I Found Livingstone: Travels, Adventures and Discoveries in Central Africa.* London: Sampson Low, Marston, Low & Searle, 1872.

Baillie, E. C. L. *A Sail to Smyrna; or, An Englishwoman's Journal: Including Impressions of Constantinople, a Visit to a Turkish Harem, and a Railway Journey to Ephesus.* London: Longmans, Green, 1873.

Trollope, Anthony. *Australia and New Zealand.* London: Chapman & Hall, 1873.

Symonds, J. A. *Sketches and Studies in Italy and Greece.* London: Smith, Elder, 1874.

Gaskell, George. *Algeria as It Is.* London: Smith, Elder, 1875.

Hill, Rosamond, and Florence Davenport. *What We Saw in Australia.* London: Macmillan, 1875.

Plunkett, Frederica (Louisa Edith). *Here and There among the Alps.* London: Longmans, Green, 1875.

Warburton, P. E. *Journey across the Western Interior of Australia,* edited by H. W. Bates. London: Sampson Low, Marston, Low & Searle, 1875.

Checklist of Further Readings

Adams, Percy G. *Travelers and Travel Liars, 1600–1800.* Berkeley: University of California Press, 1962.

Adams. *Travel Literature and the Evolution of the Novel.* Lexington: University of Kentucky Press, 1983.

Adams, ed. *Travel Literature through the Ages: An Anthology.* New York & London: Garland, 1988.

Adams, William H. Davenport. *Celebrated Women Travellers of the Nineteenth Century.* London: Swan Sonnen-schein, 1883.

Aitken, Maria. *A Girdle round the Earth.* London: Constable, 1987.

Allen, Alexandra. *Travelling Ladies.* London: Jupiter, 1980.

Anderson, Patrick. *Over the Alps: Reflections on Travel and Travel Writing with Special Reference to the Grand Tours of Boswell, Beckford, and Byron.* London: Hart-Davis, 1969.

Andrews, Malcolm. *The Search for the Picturesque: Landscape Aesthetics and Tourism in Britain, 1760–1800.* Stanford: Stanford University Press, 1989.

Barr, Pat. *The Memsahibs: The Women of Victorian India.* London: Secker & Warburg, 1976.

Bathe, Basil W. *Seven Centuries of Sea Travel.* London: Barrie & Jenkins, 1972.

Batten, Charles L., Jr. *Pleasurable Instruction: Form and Convention in Eighteenth-Century Travel Literature.* Berkeley: University of California Press, 1978.

Behdad, Ali. *Belated Travelers: Orientalism in the Age of Colonial Dissolution.* Durham, N.C.: Duke University Press, 1994.

Berger, Max. *The British Traveller in America, 1836–1860.* New York: Columbia University Press, 1943.

Birkett, Dea. *Spinsters Abroad: Victorian Lady Explorers.* Oxford: Blackwell, 1989.

Bishop, Peter. *The Myth of Shangri-La: Tibet, Travel Writing and the Western Creation of Sacred Landscape.* Berkeley: University of California Press, 1989.

Brent, Peter. *Far Arabia: Explorers of the Myth.* London: Weidenfeld, 1977.

Brinnin, John Malcolm. *The Sway of the Grand Saloon.* London: Macmillan, 1972.

Burgess, Anthony, and Francis Haskell. *The Age of the Grand Tour.* London: Elek, 1967.

Burkhardt, A. J., and S. A. Medlik. *Tourism Past, Present, and Future.* London: Heinemann, 1974.

Buzard, James. *The Beaten Track: European Tourism, Literature, and the Ways to "Culture" 1800–1918.* Oxford: Clarendon Press/Oxford University Press, 1993.

Callaway, Helen. *Gender, Culture and Empire: European Women in Colonial Nigeria.* Urbana: University of Illinois Press, 1987.

Casada, James A. "British Exploration in East Africa: A Bibliography with Commentary," *Africana Journal,* 5, no. 3 (1974): 195–239.

Clark, Ronald W. *Men, Myths and Mountains.* London: Weidenfeld, 1975.

Clark. *The Victorian Mountaineers.* London: Batsford, 1953.

Clark, William R. [Ronald W. Clark]. *Explorers of the World.* London: Aldus Books, 1964.

Cocker, Mark. *Loneliness and Time: The Story of British Travel Writing.* New York: Pantheon, 1992.

Cole, Garold. *Travels in America from the Voyages of Discovery to the Present.* Norman: University of Oklahoma Press, 1984.

Croall, Thomas. *A Book about Travelling.* London & Edinburgh: Nimmo, 1877.

Crossley-Holland, Kevin, ed. *The Oxford Book of Travel Verse.* New York: Oxford University Press, 1987.

Damiani, Anita. *Enlightened Observers: British Travellers to the Near East, 1715–1850.* Beirut, Lebanon: American University of Beirut, 1979.

de Beer, Gavin Rylands. *Travellers in Switzerland.* London & New York: Oxford University Press, 1949.

Dodd, Philip, ed. *The Art of Travel: Essays on Travel Writing.* London: Cass, 1982.

Dowie, Ménie Muriel, ed. *Women Adventurers.* London: Unwin, 1893.

Edwardes, Michael. *Glorious Sahibs: The Romantic as Empire-Builder, 1799–1838.* London: Eyre & Spottiswoode, 1968.

Eisner, Robert. *Travelers to an Antique Land: The History and Literature of Travel to Greece.* Ann Arbor: University of Michigan Press, 1991.

Feifer, Maxine. *Tourism in History: From Imperial Rome to the Present.* New York: Stein & Day, 1986.

Forbes, Vernon S. *Pioneer Travellers of South Africa: A Geographical Commentary upon Routes, Records, Observations and Opinions of Travellers at the Cape, 1750–1800.* Cape Town: Balkema, 1965.

Foster, Shirley. *Across New Worlds: Nineteenth-Century Women Travellers and Their Writings.* New York: Wheatsheaf Harvester, 1990.

Fowler, Marian. *Below the Peacock Fan: First Ladies of the Raj.* New York: Viking, 1987.

Fraser, Keath, ed. *Bad Trips.* New York: Vintage Departures, 1991.

Frawley, Maria H. *A Wider Range: Travel Writing by Women in Victorian England.* Rutherford, N.J.: Farleigh Dickinson University Press, 1994.

Freeth, Zahra, and Victor Winstone. *Explorers of Arabia: From the Renaissance to the Victorian Era.* London: Allen & Unwin, 1978.

Fussell, Paul, ed. *The Norton Book of Travel.* New York: Norton, 1987.

Galton, Sir Francis. *The Art of Travel; or, Shifts and Contrivances Available in Wild Countries.* London: Murray, 1855.

Graham-Brown, Sarah. *Images of Women: The Portrayal of Women in Photography of the Middle East, 1860–1950.* New York: Columbia University Press, 1988.

Greenhill, B., and A. Gifford. *Women under Sail.* London: David & Charles, 1970.

Hamalian, Leo, ed. *Ladies on the Loose: Women Travellers of the 18th and 19th Centuries.* New York: Dodd, Mead, 1981.

Headrick, Daniel R. *The Tools of Empire: Technology and European Imperialism in the Nineteenth Century.* New York: Oxford University Press, 1981.

Hibbert, Christopher. *The Grand Tour.* London: Spring Books, 1974.

Holmes, Winifred. *Seven Adventurous Women.* London: Bell, 1953.

Hopkirk, Peter. *Foreign Devils on the Silk Road: The Search for the Lost Cities and Treasures of Chinese Central Asia.* London: Murray, 1980.

Hopkirk. *Trespassers on the Roof of the World: The Race for Lhasa.* London: Murray, 1982.

Hutchins, Francis. *The Illusion of Permanence: British Imperialism in India.* Princeton: Princeton University Press, 1967.

Hyam, Ronald. *Empire and Sexuality: The British Experience.* Manchester: Manchester University Press, 1990.

Jameson, Fredric. *The Political Unconscious: Narrative as a Socially Symbolic Act.* Ithaca, N.Y.: Cornell University Press, 1981.

Kabbani, Rana. *Europe's Myths of Orient: Devise and Rule.* London: Macmillan, 1986.

Keay, John. *Eccentric Travellers: Excursions with Seven Extraordinary Figures from the Eighteenth and Nineteenth Centuries.* London: Murray, 1982.

Keay. *The Gilgit Game: The Explorers of the Western Himalayas, 1865–95.* London: Murray, 1979.

Keay. *When Men and Mountains Meet: The Explorers of the Western Himalayas, 1820–75.* London: Murray, 1977.

Keay, ed. *The Royal Geographical Society History of World Exploration.* London: Hamlyn, 1991.

Keay, Julia. *With Passport and Parasol: The Adventures of Seven Victorian Ladies.* London: BBC Books, 1989.

Kiernan, V. G. *The Lords of Human Kind: Black Man, Yellow Man, and White Man in an Age of Empire.* Boston: Little, Brown, 1969.

Lane, Edward William. *Manners and Customs of the Modern Egyptians.* 1836; reprinted, London: Dent, 1936.

Lawrence, Karen R. *Penelope Voyages: Women and Travel in British Literary Tradition.* Ithaca, N.Y.: Cornell University Press, 1994.

Leed, Eric J. *The Mind of the Traveler: From Gilgamesh to Global Tourism.* New York: Basic Books, 1991.

Lochsberg, Winifred. *History of Travel.* Liepzig: Edition Leipzig, 1979.

MacCannell, Earle Dean. *The Tourist, a New Theory of the Leisure Class.* London: Macmillan, 1976.

MacGregor, John. *Tibet: A Chronicle of Exploration.* London: Routledge & Kegan Paul, 1970.

MacKenzie, John. *Imperialism and Popular Culture.* Manchester: Manchester University Press, 1986.

Macmillan, Margaret. *Women of the Raj.* London: Thames & Hudson, 1988.

Mahood, Molly. *The Colonial Encounter: A Reading of Six Novels.* London: Collins, 1977.

Marsden-Smedley, Philip, and Jeffrey Klinke, eds. *Views from Abroad: The "Spectator" Book of Travel Writing.* London: Grafton, 1988.

Massingham, Hugh, and Pauline Massingham, eds. *The Englishman Abroad.* London: Phoenix House, 1962.

Melman, Billie. *Women's Orients: English Women and the Middle East, 1718–1918.* Ann Arbor: University of Michigan Press, 1992.

Michael, Maurice Albert, ed. *Traveller's Quest: Original Contributions towards a Philosophy of Travel.* Freeport, N.Y.: Books for Libraries, 1950.

Middleton, Dorothy. *Victorian Lady Travellers.* New York: Dutton, 1965.

Miller, Luree. *On Top of the World: Five Women Explorers in Tibet.* New York & London: Paddington, 1976.

Mills, Sara. *Discourses of Difference: An Analysis of Women's Travel Writing and Colonialism.* New York & London: Routledge, 1991.

Mitchell, Timothy. *Colonising Egypt.* Cambridge: Cambridge University Press, 1988.

Moorehead, Alan. *The White Nile.* London: Hamish Hamilton, 1960.

Morgen, Susan. *Place Matters: Gendered Geography in Victorian Women's Travel Books about Southeast Asia.* New Brunswick, N.J.: Rutgers University Press, 1996.

Morris, Mary, ed. *Maiden Voyages: Writing of Women Travellers.* New York: Vintage, 1993.

Mulvey, Christopher. *Anglo-American Landscapes: A Study of Nineteenth-Century Anglo-American Travel Literature.* London: Cambridge University Press, 1983.

Mulvey. *Transatlantic Manners: Social Patterns in Nineteenth-Century Anglo-American Travel Literature.* London: Cambridge University Press, 1990.

Nevins, Allan. *America through British Eyes.* New York: Oxford University Press, 1948.

Newby, Eric, ed. *A Book of Travellers' Tales.* New York: Penguin, 1985.

Oliver, Caroline. *Western Women in Colonial Africa.* Westport, Conn.: Greenwood Press, 1982.

Oswell, W. Edward. *William Cotton Oswell: Hunter and Explorer,* 2 volumes. New York: Doubleday, Page, 1900.

Ousby, Ian. *The Englishman's England: Taste, Travel, and the Rise of Tourism.* New York: Cambridge University Press, 1991.

Owen, Charles. *The Grand Days of Travel.* Exeter: Webb & Bower, 1979.

Pemble, John. *The Mediterranean Passion: Victorians and Edwardians in the South.* London: Clarendon Press / New York: Oxford University Press, 1987.

Pimlott, J. A. R. *The Englishman's Holiday: A Social History.* London: Faber & Faber, 1947.

Porter, Dennis. *Haunted Journeys: Desire and Transgression in European Travel Writing.* Princeton: Princeton University Press, 1991.

Pratt, Mary Louise. *Imperial Eyes: Studies in Travel Writing and Transculturation.* New York: Routledge, 1992.

Raskin, Jonah. *The Mythology of Imperialism.* New York: Random House, 1971.

Rice, Warner G., ed. *Literature as a Mode of Travel.* New York: New York Public Library, 1963.

Ridley, Hugh. *Images of Imperial Rule.* London: Croom Helm, 1983.

Robinson, Jane. *Wayward Women: A Guide to Women Travellers.* Oxford: Oxford University Press, 1990.

Robinson, ed. *Unsuitable for Ladies: An Anthology of Women Travellers.* Oxford: Oxford University Press, 1994.

Robinson, Jeffrey C. *The Walk: Notes on a Romantic Image.* Norman: University of Oklahoma Press, 1989.

Robinson, Ronald, and John Gallagher. *Africa and the Victorians: The Official Mind of Imperialism.* London & New York: St. Martin's Press, 1961.

Russell, Mary. *The Blessings of a Good Thick Skirt: Women Travellers and Their World.* London: Collins, 1986.

Said, Edward. *Culture and Imperialism.* New York: Knopf, 1993.

Said. *Orientalism.* New York: Pantheon, 1978.

Schivelbusch, Wolfgang. *The Railway Journey: The Industrialization of Time and Space in the Nineteenth Century.* Berkeley: University of California Press, 1986.

Severin, Timothy. *The Oriental Adventure: Explorers of the East.* London: Angus & Robertson, 1976.

Sigaux, Gilbert. *History of Tourism,* translated by Joan White. London: Leisure Arts, 1966.

Spurr, David. *The Rhetoric of Empire: Colonial Discourse in Journalism, Travel Writing, and Imperial Administration.* Durham, N.C.: Duke University Press, 1993.

Stefoff, Rebecca. *Women of the World: Women Travelers and Explorers.* New York: Oxford University Press, 1991.

Stephen, Sir Leslie. *The Playground of Europe.* London: Longmans, Green, 1871.

Stevenson, Catherine Barnes. *Victorian Women Travel Writers in Africa.* Boston: Twayne, 1982.

Swinglehurst, Edmund. *Cook's Tours: The Story of Popular Travel*. Poole, Dorset: Blandford, 1982.

Swinglehurst. *The Romantic Journey: The Story of Thomas Cook and Victorian Travel*. New York & London: Harper, 1974.

Sykes, Christopher. *Four Studies in Loyalty*. London: Collins, 1946.

Tidrick, Kathryn. *Empire and the English Character*. London: Tauris, 1981.

Tidrick. *Heart-Beguiling Araby*. New York: Cambridge University Press, 1981.

Tinling, Marion. *Women into the Unknown: A Sourcebook on Women Explorers and Travelers*. New York: Greenwood Press, 1989.

Trease, Robert G. *The Grand Tour*. London: Heinemann, 1967.

Tregaskis, Hugh. *Beyond the Grand Tour: The Levant Lunatics*. London: Ascent Books, 1979.

Van Martels, Zwerder. *Travel Fact and Travel Fiction: Studies on Fiction, Literary Tradition, Scholarly Discovery and Observation in Travel Writing*. New York: Brill, 1951.

Van Thal, Herbert. *Victoria's Subjects Travelled*. London: Barker, 1951.

Vaughan, John. *The English Guide Book, c. 1780–1870: An Illustrated History*. Newton Abbot, Devon: David & Charles, 1974.

West, Herbert Faulkner. *The Mind on the Wing: A Book for Readers and Collectors*. New York: Coward-McCann, 1947.

Williams, Cicely. *Women on the Rope: The Feminine Share in Mountain Adventure*. London: Allen & Unwin, 1973.

Woodcock, George. *Into Tibet: The Early British Explorers*. London: Faber & Faber, 1971.

Contributors

Dana E. Aspinall..*University of Montevallo*
James Barszcz ....*William Paterson College*
Margaret Boe Birns..*New York University*
Bege K. Bowers...*Youngstown State University*
Barbara Brothers ....*Youngstown State University*
Timothy M. Clark...*Ohio State University*
Joan Corwin ....*Evanston, Illinois*
Claire England ....*University of Toronto*
David Finkelstein..*Napier University*
Julia M. Gergits..*Youngstown State University*
Anita G. Gorman..*Slippery Rock University*
Lila M. Harper ....*Central Washington University*
John C. Hawley ....*Santa Clara University*
Helen Heineman..*Framingham State College*
David C. Judkins ....*University of Houston*
Scott A. Leonard...*Youngstown State University*
Pam J. Lieske...*University of Massachusetts – Amherst*
Teresa A. Lyle ....*Miami University*
Edward A. Malone ....*University of Missouri – Rolla*
Lorraine Mercer..*Portland State University*
J. Lawrence Mitchell ....*Texas A&M University*
Laura Nilges-Matias ....*Loyola University of Chicago*
Patricia O'Neill ....*Hamilton College*
John R. Pfeiffer ....*Central Michigan University*
Deborah L. Phelps..*Sam Houston State University*
Carol Huebscher Rhoades...*Austin, Texas*
Samuel J. Rogal..*Illinois Valley Community College*
Mike Rubingh ....*Miami University*
James J. Schramer..*Youngstown State University*
F. S. Schwarzbach..*Kent State University*
Faiza Shereen...*University of Dayton*
Ann Shillinglaw..*Loyola University of Chicago*
Sandra W. Stephan ....*Youngstown State University*
Michael Wojcik...*Miami University*
D. C. Woodcox ....*Truman State University*

368

Cumulative Index

Dictionary of Literary Biography, Volumes 1-166
Dictionary of Literary Biography Yearbook, 1980-1995
Dictionary of Literary Biography Documentary Series, Volumes 1-13

Cumulative Index

DLB before number: *Dictionary of Literary Biography,* Volumes 1-166
Y before number: *Dictionary of Literary Biography Yearbook,* 1980-1995
DS before number: *Dictionary of Literary Biography Documentary Series,* Volumes 1-13

H

L

N

S

ISBN 0-8103-9361-1